A.W.

Research Methods in Physical Activity

Second Edition

Jerry R. Thomas, EdD
Arizona State University

Jack K. Nelson, EdD
University of Idaho

Human Kinetics Books
Champaign, Illinois

Library of Congress Cataloging-in-Publication Data

Thomas, Jerry R.
   Research methods in physical activity / Jerry R. Thomas, Jack K.
Nelson. -- 2nd ed.
      p. cm.
   Rev. ed. of: Introduction to research in health, physical
education, recreation, and dance. c1985.
   Includes bibliographical references.
   ISBN: 0-87322-291-1
   1. Physical education and training--Research. 2. Health-
-Research. 3. Recreation--Research. 4. Dancing--Research.
I. Nelson, Jack K. II. Thomas, Jerry R. Introduction to research
in health, physical education, recreation, and dance. III. Title.
GV361.T47   1990
613.7'1'072--dc20   90-31414
                                                        CIP

ISBN: 0-87322-291-1

Copyright © 1990, 1985 by Jerry R. Thomas and Jack K. Nelson

Excerpts on pp. 30 and 74 adapted from *Conducting Educational Research*, Second Edition by B.W. Tuckman, copyright © 1978 by Harcourt Brace Jovanovich, Inc., reprinted by permission of the publisher.

Developmental Editor: Holly Gilly
Assistant Editor: Timothy Ryan
Copyeditor: Bruce Owens
Proofreader: Peter Nelson
Production Director: Ernie Noa
Typesetters: Sandra Meier and Angela Snyder
Text Design: Keith Blomberg
Text Layout: Denise Lowry and Tara Welsch
Cover Design: Hunter Graphics

Cover Photos: Wilmer Zehr
Models: Faith McElwee, Keith Blomberg,
   Robert King, Rosalva Torres, and
   Marianeeta Brent
Text Illustrations: Judi Connelly, David Gregory,
   and William Pardy
Printer: Versa Press
Binder: Dekker & Sons

Printed in the United States of America

10 9 8 7 6 5 4

Human Kinetics Publishers
Box 5076, Champaign, IL 61825-5076
1-800-747-4457

Canada Office:
Human Kinetics Publishers
P.O. Box 2503, Windsor, ON N8Y 4S2
1-800-465-7301 (in Canada only)

Europe Office:
Human Kinetics Publishers (Europe) Ltd.
P.O. Box IW14
Leeds LS16 6TR
England
0532-781708

Australia Office:
Human Kinetics Publishers
P.O. Box 80
Kingswood 5062
South Australia
374-0433

Contents

Preface

The first edition of this book, *Introduction to Research Methods in Health, Physical Education, Recreation, and Dance* (1985), was well received by the graduate students and faculty at over 100 institutions, mostly in the United States but also in several other countries. As we had anticipated (and noted in the preface to the first edition), use of the book was mainly for the first graduate research methods course, which frequently is required of master's students. However, there was little use across the sometimes allied areas of health, recreation, and dance. Thus the second edition focuses directly on research methods associated with the study of physical activity. We intend the term "physical activity" to encompass exercise science, sport science, and physical education to be certain that the discipline dealing with the study of human movement and the profession frequently associated with it are reflected. Some would prefer other terms, such as "kinesiology." We intend the contents of this book to apply conceptually to any aspect of the study of physical activity, whether in the context of exercise, sports, physical education instruction, industry, and so on.

The book remains organized as in the first edition. Part I provides a complete overview of the research process, with particular attention given to using the library for the literature review. Part II covers statistical concepts in research: descriptive, correlational, differences among groups, multivariate, and nonparametric. Part III presents various types of research: historical, philosophic, meta-analysis, descriptive, experimental, and qualitative. Part IV focuses on measurement, the concepts of validity and reliability, movement measures, and written responses. Finally, Part V provides information on preparing the research report: proposals, results and discussion, and ways of presenting the research. The appendices include statistical tables, statistical computer programs and examples for SPSSx on micro- and mainframe computers, and descriptions of mainframe packages.

We have made a number of revisions to this new edition, all of which are improvements, we hope. Several individuals provided helpful reviews of the first edition in various journals; we carefully read and evaluated these, noting the positive and muttering under our breath about the negative. We can commiserate with Day (1983, p. xi), who had a reviewer describe his book "as 'both good and original.' Unfortunately, he went on to add that 'the part that is good is not original and the part that is original is not good.'" Many of you told us directly what you liked as well as things you would like to see changed, added, deleted, and so on. (Note we have avoided the word "disliked," as we know none of you disliked the first edition, although a few of you did remark disparagingly about our sense of humor or lack thereof.) Thus, in this edition we include some new jokes, funny figures and tables, and humorous sayings, as well as retaining the old ones that scored above 7 (scale 1-10) on the applause meter.

A new section, Alternate Models for Research, was added to the first chapter to broaden the approaches to and views of research, especially as considerably more qualitative research is being done in physical education, exercise science, and sport science. We also added a chapter (chapter 15) on qualitative approaches to research. Chapter 8 (Understanding Multivariate Techniques) is new. It reflects the removal of the multivariate techniques from chapters 6 and 7 and incorporates these and additional ones in a single chapter. Chapter 8 focuses on conceptually understanding the use of the various multivariate techniques (with examples provided) but not on the mathematics that underlie them. Chapter 9 is new and covers some of the basic nonparametric techniques that are frequently used.

Historical research (chapter 10) has been completely rewritten. Dr. Nancy Struna, a noted sport historian from the University of Maryland, is the author. A new chapter on philosophic research (chapter 11) written by Kathy Pearson from Western Illinois University has also been added. The excellent contributions of these two writers should serve to encourage more students with research interests in sport history and sport philosophy.

Much has been revised and added to the other chapters that were in the first edition and that remain in the new edition. The chapter on using the literature (chapter 2) has undergone a major revision, especially with regard to library work. We have provided greater detail and better samples of materials dealing with the use and protection of human subjects in research and added a section on the use of animals in research. The chapter on meta-analysis (chapter 12) has been expanded to provide greater detail and a complete example of meta-analytic procedures. The chapter on descriptive research (chapter 13) has been expanded considerably. We have devoted more attention to alternative ways of preparing the thesis and dissertation

(chapter 21), as that section was rather sketchy in the first edition. Increasingly, colleges and universities are going to a journal format for the body of the thesis and dissertation.

Our approach to the use of statistics on the microcomputer has changed. In the first edition we supplied you with listings of statements for statistical microcomputer programs in the appendix as well as sample runs on problems in the book. Now, mainframe statistical packages (e.g., SPSSx, SAS, BIOMED) have developed versions for micros. In this edition the problems from the statistical chapters have been set up and run on SPSSx for the micro and the mainframe. Included in Appendix B are the statements to run the programs and printouts of the problems. These programs are much more flexible and useful, and running them on the mainframe and the micro should help your understanding of statistics and computers and increase your computer literacy. We thank Dr. Katherine T. Thomas of Arizona State University for doing the statistical computer work that appears in that appendix.

We are also grateful to the Literary Executor of the late Sir Ronald A. Fisher, F.R.S., to Dr. Frank Yates, F.R.S., and to Longman Group Ltd., London for permissions to reprint Tables A.3 and A.5 from their book *Statistical Tables for Biological, Agricultural and Medical Research* (6th Edition, 1974).

This new edition is still designed for the beginning master's student enrolled in the first research methods course. Of course we hope it is useful for everyone with an interest in conducting and understanding research on physical activity. Do not hesitate to buy a copy or two for your own use or as a gift for a friend (we need the money—our children are in college, and retirement can be seen jogging toward us from the far distance; some say retirement is, or should be, running up our backs). What a wonderful birthday, Christmas, or anniversary gift a copy of this book would make. (*Disclaimer:* We take no responsibility for any divorce that results from using this book as an anniversary present.)

As we indicated in the first edition, we have had a little help from our friends. As often as possible, we give credit through citation to the published literature.

> But how about the many ideas and procedures that one has picked up from discussions with colleagues? After the passage of time, one can no longer remember who originated what idea. After the passage of even more time, it seems to me that all of the really good ideas originated with me, a proposition which I know is indefensible. (Day, 1983, p. xv)

We believe this book provides the necessary information for both the consumer and the producer of research. Although no amount of knowledge about the tools of research can replace expertise in the content area, it is unlikely that good scholars in physical education, exercise science, and sport science can function apart from the effective use of research tools. Researchers, teachers,

technicians, counselors, and coaches need to understand the research process. If they do not, they are forced to accept information on face value or the recommendation of others. Although neither is necessarily bad, the ability to carefully evaluate and reach a valid conclusion is the mark of a professional.

We firmly believe that the topic of research need not be presented in a dry, pompous manner. As in any human enterprise, there are humorous occurrences. In fact, attempts at being overly dignified and scholarly lead to amusing and sometimes ludicrous results. Therefore, we have interjected a few anecdotes and sketches as well as some "laws" and "corollaries" that emphasize various points we hope you will find as enjoyable as we have in preparing them and this second edition. Our attempts at humor are designed to enliven the reading but not distract from the content. Research processes are not mysterious events that graduate students should fear. To the contrary, research processes are useful tools to which every professional should have access; they are, in fact, the very basis by which professionals make competent decisions.

Jerry R. Thomas
Jack K. Nelson

□

Acknowledgments

As we indicated in the preface, a few of our friends and loved ones have helped us (or tolerated us, or both) during the revision of this book. Some of them have suggested ideas to include, have done specific parts (or provided us with needed materials and organization to do these parts), or have suggested alterations. We thank them for this assistance. We thank the following people for their specific contributions: Dr. Karyn Nelson, assistant professor at the University of Idaho, for ideas and suggestions on chapter 15 (Qualitative Research) and for continuing to live with Jack during this revision; Dr. Nancy Struna, University of Maryland, for writing chapter 10 (Historical Research); Dr. Kathy Pearson, retired from Western Illinois University, for writing chapter 11 (Methods of Philosophic Inquiry in Physical Activity); and Dr. Katherine Thomas, visiting assistant professor at Arizona State University, for doing the SPSSx computer programs and sample runs included in Appendix B and for continuing to live with Jerry during this revision. Finally, we acknowledge considerable assistance from Holly Gilly, our developmental editor at Human Kinetics—especially since she likes our jokes.

PART I

Overview
of the Research Process

This part provides you with an overall perspective of the research process. The introductory chapter defines and reviews the various types of research done in exercise and sport science and physical education and gives you some examples. *Science* is defined as systematic inquiry, and the steps in the scientific method are discussed. This logical method answers the following four questions (Day, 1983, p. 4), which constitute the parts of a typical thesis report:

1. What was the problem? Your answer is the Introduction.
2. How did you study the problem? Your answer is the Materials and Methods.

3. What did you find? Your answer is the Results.
4. What do these findings mean? Your answer is the Discussion.

Alternative approaches for doing research are also presented relative to a more philosophical discussion of science and ways of knowing. In particular, qualitative research, the use of field studies, and methods of introspection are discussed as alternate strategies in answering research questions instead of relying on the traditional scientific paradigm as the only approach to research problems. In addition, chapter 1 includes a brief history of research in exercise and sport science and physical education in the United States and concludes with ways of locating and identifying research problems.

Chapter 2 suggests ways of using the literature to identify the research problem, specify hypotheses, and develop the methodology. In particular, a system for searching, reading, analyzing, synthesizing, organizing, and writing the review of literature is proposed.

Presented in the final two chapters in Part I is the format of the research proposal with examples. This information is typically required of the master's or doctoral student before collecting data for the thesis or dissertation. Chapter 3 defines and delimits the research problem, including the introduction, statement of the problem, research hypothe-

ses, operational definitions, assumptions and limitations, and significance. Chapter 4 covers methodology, or how to do the research. Included are the topics of subject selection, instrumentation or apparatus, procedures, and design and analysis. The emphasis is on the value of pilot work conducted before the research and on the protection of human subjects.

Once you have completed Part I, you should better understand the research process. Then comes the tricky part—learning all the details. These details are presented in Part II (Statistical Concepts in Research), Part III (Types of Research), Part IV (Measurement), and Part V (Writing the Research Report).

Chapter 1

☐

Introduction to Research in Physical Activity

Mention the word "research" to several different people and, depending on their backgrounds, each will conjure up a different picture in his or her mind. One might think of going to the nearest encyclopedia; another might visualize a lab filled with test tubes, vials, and Bunsen burners. It is important, then, when beginning a text on the subject, to establish a common understanding of research. In this chapter we introduce you to the nature of research. We do this by discussing methods of problem solving and types of research. We give an overview of the history of research then explain the research process and relate it to the parts of a thesis. By the time you reach the end of chapter 1, you should have a good understanding of what research really means.

THE NATURE OF RESEARCH

Research implies a careful and systematic means of solving problems and has five characteristics (Tuckman, 1978):

- *Systematic.* Problem solving is accomplished through the identification and labeling of variables and is followed by the design of research that tests the relationships among these variables. Data are then collected that, when related to the variables, allow for the evaluation of the problem and hypotheses.

- *Logical.* Examination of the procedures used in the research process allows researchers to evaluate the conclusions that are drawn.
- *Empirical.* The researcher collects data on which to base decisions.
- *Reductive.* Research takes many individual events (data) and uses them to establish more general relationships.
- *Replicable.* The research process is recorded, enabling others to test the findings by repeating the research or to build future research on previous results.

Problems to be solved come from many sources and can entail resolving controversial issues, testing theories, and trying to improve present practice. For example, a popular topic of concern is fatness and methods of losing weight. Suppose we want to investigate this by comparing two exercise programs as to their effectiveness in reducing fat. Of course, we know that caloric expenditure will result in the loss of fat, so we will try to find out which program will do this better under specified conditions. (Note: Our approach here is to give a very brief and simple overview of a research study. It is not intended to be a model of originality or sophistication.)

This study is definitely an example of applied research (more on this in the next section). Rather than try to measure the calories expended and so on, we approach it strictly

3

from a programmatic standpoint. Say that we are operating a health club and that we offer aerobic dance and jogging classes for people who desire to lose weight. Our research question is, Which program is more effective in reducing fat?

Suppose that we have a pool of subjects to draw from and that we can randomly assign two thirds of the subjects to the two exercise programs and one third of the subjects to a control group. We have their scout's honor that none is on a drastic diet or engaging in any other strenuous activities while the study is in progress. Both the aerobic dance and the jogging classes are 1 hour long and are held five times a week for 10 weeks. The same enthusiastic and immensely qualified instructor teaches both classes.

Our measure of fatness is the sum of skinfold measurements taken at eight body sites. Of course, we could use alternative measures such as percent fat estimated from hydrostatic weighing (or total body water or some other such estimate of fatness). However, our measures can be defended as being a valid and reliable indicator of fatness, and skinfolds are functional field measures. We will measure all the subjects, including the control subjects, at the beginning and the end of the 10-week period. During the course of the study we would try to ensure that the two programs were similar in procedural aspects such as motivational techniques and the aesthetics of the surroundings. In other words, we would not favor one group by cheering them on and not saying anything encouraging to the other; nor would we have one group exercising in an air-conditioned, cheerful, and healthful facility while the other had to sweat it out in some dingy room or parking lot. It is very important that we try to make the programs as similar as possible in every respect except for the experimental treatments. The control group would not engage in any regular exercise.

So, after we have measured all the subjects on our criterion of fatness at the end of the study, we are ready to analyze our data. We want to see how much change in skinfold thickness had occurred and whether there were differences between the two types of exercise. Because we are dealing with samples of people (from a whole universe of similar people), we need to use some type of statistics to establish how confident we can be in our results. In other words, we need to determine the *significance* of our results. Suppose the mean scores for the groups were as follows:

- Aerobic dance = −21 mm
- Jogging = −25 mm
- Control = +8 mm

These values (which we made up) represent the average change in the combined skinfold thicknesses of the eight body sites. The two experimental groups lost fat, but the control group actually showed increased skinfold thicknesses over the 10-week period.

We decide to use the statistical technique of analysis of variance with repeated measures. We find that there is a significant F ratio, indicating that there are significant differences among the three groups. We then use a follow-up test procedure and discover that both exercise groups are significantly different from the control group but that there is no significant difference between the aerobic dance and the jogging groups.

Many of you may not have the foggiest idea what we are talking about with the statistical terms "F ratio" and "significance," but do not worry about it. All this is ex-

Many of you may not have the foggiest idea what we are talking about with the statistical terms, but do not worry about it. All this is explained later. This book is about these kinds of things.

plained later. This book is about these kinds of things.

Our conclusion from this study is that both aerobic dance and jogging are effective (apparently equally so) in bringing about a loss in fatness of overweight subjects (like the ones in our study) over the course of 10 weeks. Although these results are reasonable, please remember that this is only an example. We can also pretend that this study was published in a prestigious journal and that we won the Nobel Prize.

Research Continuum

Research in our field can be placed on a continuum with *applied research* at one extreme and *basic research* at the opposite extreme. The research extremes have certain characteristics generally associated with them (see Figure 1.1). Applied research tends to address immediate problems, to use so-called real-world settings, to use human subjects, and to have limited control over the research setting but to give results that are of direct value to practitioners. At the other extreme, basic research usually deals with theoretical problems, has the laboratory as the setting, may frequently use animals as subjects, has carefully controlled conditions, and produces results that have limited direct application.

The strengths of applied research are the weaknesses of basic research and vice versa.

Considerable controversy exists in the literature on psychology, education, and physical education (for examples from physical education, see Martens, 1979, 1987; Siedentop, 1980; Thomas, 1980) about whether research should be more basic or more applied. This issue, labeled *ecological validity*, deals with two concerns:

- Is the research setting perceived by the subject in the way intended by the experimenter?
- Does the setting have enough of the real-world characteristics to allow for generalizing to reality?

Of course, most research is neither purely applied nor purely basic but rather incorporates some degree of both. We believe that systematic efforts are needed to produce research from sound theoretical frameworks in carefully controlled settings that are followed by studies with more of the characteristics of applied research. An example of this type of effort can be found in the research of Smoll, Smith, and colleagues (Thomas, 1984) on the effects of coaching behaviors on youth-league baseball players. Smoll and Smith went from developing and testing a theoretical base for assessing and influencing coach-player interactions to developing and evaluating a training program for coaches. More efforts of this type are needed in physical education, exercise science, and sport science. Although the

------Applied Research-----------------Basic Research------→

Answers immediate problems	Deals with theoretical issues
Human subjects	Animal subjects
Real-world settings	Laboratories
Lacks control	Carefully controlled
Results directly useful	Results lack application

Figure 1.1 Characteristics of studies at the extremes of the research continuum. From Hoenes and Chissom (1975). Reprinted by permission.

research base has grown tremendously in our field over the past 20 years, much remains to be done.

There is a great need to prepare proficient consumers and producers of research. To be proficient at either or both requires a thorough understanding of the appropriate knowledge base (e.g., exercise physiology, motor behavior, pedagogy, and the social and biological sciences) as well as the necessary tools of research methods. In this book we attempt to provide an understanding of the tools necessary to consume and produce research. Many of the same methods are used in the various areas of physical education, exercise science, and sport science (as well as other areas such as psychology, sociology, education, and physiology). Quality research efforts always involve some or all of the following components:

- Identification and delimitation of a problem
- Searching, reviewing, and effectively writing about relevant literature
- Specifying and defining testable hypotheses
- Designing the research to test the hypotheses
- Selecting, describing, testing, and treating the subjects
- Analyzing and reporting the results
- Discussing the meaning and implications of the findings

Research for the Consumer

We recognize that not everyone will be a researcher. Many people in our profession have little interest in research per se. In fact, some have a decided aversion to it. Researchers are sometimes viewed as kind of strange people who deal with insignificant problems and who are out of touch with the real world (we know that none of you feel that way). In a very informative yet entertaining book on writing scientific papers, Day (1983) related the story about two men who took a ride in a hot-air balloon and who encountered some cloud coverage that eventually led to their becoming lost. When they finally descended, they did not recognize the terrain and had not the faintest idea where they were. It so happened that they were drifting over the grounds of one of our more famous scientific research institutes. When the balloonists saw a man walking alongside a road, one of them called out, ''Hey, mister, where are we?'' The man looked up, took in the situation, and, after a few moments of reflection, said, ''You're in a hot-air balloon.'' One balloonist turned to the other and said, ''I'll bet that man is a researcher.'' The other balloonist said, ''What makes you think so?'' The first replied, ''His answer is perfectly accurate—and totally useless'' (p. 152).

Practicality and Accessibility

All kidding aside, the need for research in any profession just cannot be argued. After all, one of the primary distinctions between a profession and a trade is that the trade deals only with *how* to do something, whereas the profession concerns itself not only with ''how'' but also with ''why'' something should be done in a certain manner (and why it should even be done). However, even though most people in a profession recognize the need for research, most of those people do not read research results. This situation is not unique only to our field. It has been reported that only 1% of chemists read research publications, less than 7% of psychologists read psychological research journals, and so on. The big question is *why*. We would guess that most professionals who do not read research believe it is not necessary to do so. The research is not practical enough or does not directly pertain to one's work. Another reason given by practitioners for not reading research publications is that they cannot understand them. The language is too technical and the terminology unfamiliar and confusing. This is a valid complaint; however, it could be argued that if the professional preparation programs were more subject oriented, this would not be such a problem. Nevertheless, under the present circumstances, the research literature is extremely difficult for the nonresearcher to understand.

Someone once said that a scientific paper was not meant to be read but rather that it was meant to be published. Unfortunately, there is considerable truth to that observation. We, as writers, are often guilty of trying to use language to dazzle the reader and perhaps to give the impression that our subject matter is more esoteric than it really is. We tend to write for the benefit of a rather small number of readers, that is, other researchers in our particular field. We have the problem of jargon, of course. In any field—whether it is physics, football, or cake baking—there is a jargon that confounds the outsider. The use of jargon serves as a kind of shorthand. It provides meaning to the people within the field because everyone uses those words in the same context. Research literature is famous for using a three-dollar word when a nickel one would do. As Day (1983, p. 147) asked, what self-respecting writer would use a three-letter word like "now" when one can use the elegant expression "at this point in time"? Researchers never "do" anything, they "perform" it; they never "start," they "initiate"; and they "terminate" instead of "end." Day further remarked that an occasional author will slip and use the word "drug," but most will salivate like Pavlov's dogs in anticipation of using "chemotherapeutic agent."

Reading Research

For years there has been a recognized need to try to bridge the gap between the researcher and the practitioner. The American Alliance for Health, Physical Education, Recreation and Dance (AAHPERD) launched a series of publications titled *What Research Tells the Coach* [of a particular sport]. The *Journal of Physical Education, Recreation and Dance* has a feature called "Research Works" that is designed to disseminate applied research information to teachers, coaches, and fitness and recreation leaders. Yet despite these and other attempts to bridge the gap, the gap is still an imposing one.

It goes without saying that if one is not knowledgeable about the subject matter, one cannot read the research literature. Conversely, if you know the subject matter, you can probably wade through the researcher's jargon more effectively. For example, if you know baseball and the researcher is recommending that by shortening the radius one can increase the angular velocity, you can figure out that the researcher means to choke up on the bat.

One of the big stumbling blocks is the statistical analysis part of research reports. Even the most ardent seeker of knowledge can be turned off by descriptions such as "The tetrachoric correlations among the test variables were subjected to a centroid factor analysis, and orthogonal rotations of the primary axes were accomplished by Zimmerman's graphical method until simple structure and positive manifold were closely approximated." Please note that we are not criticizing the authors for such descriptions, as the reviewers and editors require them. We are just acknowledging the fact that it is frightening to someone who is trying to read a research article and who does not know a factor analysis from a volleyball. The widespread use of computers and the computer language probably compound the mystique associated with statistics. Many people believe anything that comes out of a computer. Others are more old-fashioned and check the computer's accuracy with their calculators. A classic case of a computer mistake was in a high school in which the computer printed the students' locker numbers in the space where their IQs were supposed to go. It is classic because no one noticed the error at the time, but at the end of the year the students with the highest locker numbers got the best grades.

Despite all the hurdles that loom in the path of the practitioner with regard to reading research, we contend that one can read and profit (not materially, unfortunately) from the research literature even if he or she is not well grounded in research techniques and statistical analysis. We would like to contend that after you read this book you can read any journal in any field, but the publisher would not let us. Thus, we offer the following suggestions to the practitioner on reading the research literature.

How to Read Research

• *Become familiar with a few publications that contain pertinent research in your field.* You might get some help on this from a professor or librarian.

• *Read only studies that are of interest to you.* That may sound too trite to mention, but some people feel obligated to wade through every article.

• *Read it as a practitioner would.* Don't look for eternal truths. Look for ideas and indications. No study is proof of anything. Only when it has been verified time and again does it constitute knowledge.

• *Read the abstract first.* This will save time by helping you determine whether you wish

to read the whole thing. If you are still interested, then you can read the study to better understand the methodology and the interpretations, but do not get bogged down with details.

• *Do not be too concerned about statistical significance.* It certainly helps to know the meaning of the concept of significance, but a little common sense will serve you about as well as knowing the difference between the .02 and the .01 levels, or a one-tailed test versus a two-tailed test. Think in terms of meaningfulness. For example, if two methods of teaching bowling result in an average difference of 0.5 pins, what difference does it make whether it is significant? On the other hand, if there is a big difference that is not significant, it could mean that further investigation is warranted, especially if the study involved a small number of subjects. It is certainly helpful to know the concepts of the different types of statistical analysis, but it is not crucial to being able to read a study. Just skip that part.

• *Be critical but objective.* You can usually assume that a national research journal selects studies for publication by the jury method. Two or three supposedly qualified individuals read and judge the relevance of the problem, the validity and reliability of the procedures, the efficacy of the experimental design, and the appropriateness of the statistical analysis. It is true that some studies are published that should not be, yet if you are not an expert in research, you do not need to be overly suspicious about the scientific worth of a study that is published in a recognized journal. If it is too far removed from any practical application to your situation, do not read it.

You will find that the more you read, the easier it becomes to understand, simply because you become more familiar with the language and the methodology. It is like the man who was thrilled to learn he had been speaking prose all his life.

An Example of Practical Research

To illustrate our research consumer suggestions, consider the lighthearted account of a young physical education teacher and coach named Sonjia Roundball (Nelson, 1988). In a moment of weakness, Sonjia glances through the table of contents of the *Research Quarterly for Exercise and Sport* that was left in her car by a graduate student friend of hers (they had used it to keep their tacos from dripping on the upholstery). She experiences a spark of interest when she notices an article entitled ''The Effects of a Season of Basketball on the Cardiorespiratory Responses of High School Girls.'' With lukewarm curiosity, she turns to the article and begins to read. The first part of the article consisted of an introduction that maintained that relatively little specific information was available on the physiological changes in girls due to sport participation. A short review of literature cited a few studies on swimmers and other sport participants, and generally the upshot was that women athletes possess higher levels of cardiorespiratory fitness than do nonathletes. It was emphasized that no studies had tried to detect changes in fitness of girls as a result of a season of basketball.

The next section of the study dealt with methods. Details were given about the length of the season, the number of games, the number of practices and their length, and the breakdown in terms of the amount of time devoted to drills, scrimmaging, and individual practice. The subjects were 12 girls on the high school basketball team (the participants) and 14 girls in the nonparticipant group who were from physical education classes and who had similar academic and activity schedules as the participants. All sub-

jects were tested at the beginning (and end) of the season on maximal oxygen consumption and various other physiological measurements dealing with ventilation, heart rate, and blood pressure. Sonjia remembered those things from her exercise physiology course a number of years ago and was willing to accept these as being good indicators of cardiorespiratory fitness.

The results were then presented and tables shown. She did not understand these things but was willing to trust the authors as to their appropriateness. A stated finding was that there were no significant increases in any of the cardiorespiratory measures from the preseason test to the postseason test for either group. This jolted Sonjia to the quick! Surely, a strenuous sport such as basketball should produce improvements in fitness. Something must be wrong here, she thought. She further read (with small consolation) that the basketball players had higher values of maximal oxygen consumption than the nonparticipants at both the beginning and the end of the season. Sonjia then proceeded to read the discussion, which mentioned things like the values being higher than similar values in other studies (So what, Sonjia thought). She read with more interest the observations by the authors that boys' basketball programs were more strenuous in terms of length and number of workouts. Sonjia began to think about this. The authors admitted that the number of subjects was small and maybe that some changes could not be detected, and there were some other speculations. The conclusion was, however, that the training program used in this study was not strenuous enough to induce significant improvement in cardiorespiratory fitness.

Sonjia was sophisticated enough to realize the limitations of one study. Nevertheless, it was very similar to her schedule and general practice routines. She noticed in the references for the article three studies from a journal called *Medicine and Science in Sports and Exercise*. She had never read this journal but decided to drive over to the university the next weekend to look up this publication in the library. When she located the journal, the latest issue happened to have an article on conditioning effects of swimming on college women. Although this was a different sport and a different age-group, she reasoned that the review of literature might prove fruitful. She was right. There was reference to a recent study on aerobic capacity, heart rate, and energy cost during a season of girls' basketball. Sonjia quickly located this study and now read with the excitement that comes from the personal discovery of ideas. She also was pleasantly surprised to find that it was easier reading than the first study because she was now more familiar with the terminology and the general organization of the article.

This study also reported no improvement in aerobic capacity during the season. A part of the study involved monitoring heart rates during games by telemetry, and it was found that heart rates of over 170 beats per minute (bpm) were frequently observed. The study concluded that the practice sessions were apparently too moderate in intensity and that the training should be structured to meet both the skill and the fitness demands of the sport.

Sonjia returned to her school determined to take a more scientific approach to her basketball program. To start with, she had one of her managers chart the number of minutes that players were actually engaged in movement in the practice sessions. Sonjia also had the players take their pulses at various intervals during the sessions. She was surprised to find that the heart rates rarely surpassed 130 bpm. As an outgowth of her recent literature search, she remembered that there is an intensity threshold necessary to bring about improvement in cardiorespiratory fitness. She knew that for this age-group a heart rate of about 160 bpm was needed to provide a significant training effect. Consequently, she initiated some changes in her practice sessions (including more conditioning drills) and made the scrimmages more intensive and gamelike. To end this saga of Sonjia, you will be happy to know that Coach Roundball's team went on to win all its games, the district and the state championships, and the world games.

Summarizing the Nature of Research

Thomas Huxley wrote that science is simply common sense at its best. Research should be viewed more as a method of problem solving than as some dark and mysterious realm inhabited by impractical people who speak and write in baffling terms. We think practitioners can read research literature, and we are dedicated in this text to try to facilitate the process of becoming a research consumer.

UNSCIENTIFIC AND SCIENTIFIC METHODS OF PROBLEM SOLVING

Although there are many definitions of research, nearly all of them characterize research activity as some sort of structured problem solving. The word "structured" refers to the fact that a number of research techniques can be used as long as the techniques are considered acceptable by scholars in the field. Thus, research is concerned with problem solving, which then may lead to new knowledge.

The problem-solving process involves several steps whereby the problem is developed, defined, and delimited; hypotheses are formulated; data are gathered and analyzed; and the results are interpreted with regard to the acceptance or rejection of the hypotheses. These steps are often referred to as the *scientific method of problem solving*. The steps also basically constitute the chapters, or sections, of the research paper, thesis, and dissertation. Consequently, much of this text is devoted to the specific ways these steps of obtaining knowledge are accomplished.

Some Unscientific Methods of Problem Solving

Before we go into more detail concerning the scientific method of problem solving, it is important to recognize some other ways by which humankind has acquired knowledge. All of us have used these methods, so they are recognizable. Helmstadter (1970) labeled the methods as tenacity, intuition, authority, the rationalistic method, and the empirical method.

Tenacity

People sometimes cling to certain beliefs regardless of the lack of supporting evidence. Our superstitions are good examples of this method called *tenacity*. Coaches and athletes are notoriously superstitious. A coach may wear a particular sport coat, hat, tie, or shoes because the team won the last time he wore it. Athletes frequently have a set pattern that they consider lucky for dressing, warming up, or entering the stadium. Even though they acknowledge no logical relationship between the game's outcome and the particular routine, they are afraid to break the pattern.

Take, for example, the man who believed that black cats brought bad luck. One night when he was returning to his ranch, a black cat started to cross the road. The man swerved off onto the prairie to keep the cat from crossing in front of him and hit a hard

bump that caused the headlights to go off. Unable to see the black cat in the dark night, he sped frantically over rocks, mounds, and holes until he came to a sudden stop in a ravine, wrecking his car and sustaining moderate injuries. Of course, this just confirmed his staunch belief that black cats do indeed bring bad luck. Obviously, tenacity has no place in science. It is the least reliable source of knowledge.

Intuition

Intuitive knowledge is sometimes considered to be common sense or self-evident. However, a number of self-evident truths are subsequently found to be false. That the earth is flat is a classic example of the intuitively obvious; that the sun is farther away in winter than in summer was once self-evident; that no one could run a mile in less than 4 minutes once was self-evident. Furthermore, for anyone to shot-put over 70 feet or pole-vault over 18 feet or for a woman to run distances over a half-mile was impossible. One of the fundamental tenets of science is that we must be ever cognizant of the importance of substantiating our convictions with factual evidence.

Authority

Reference to some authority has long been used as a source of knowledge. Although this is not necessarily invalid, it does depend on the authority and on the rigidity of adherence. However, the appeal to authority has been carried to absurd lengths. Even personal observation and experience have been deemed unacceptable when they disputed authority. Supposedly, people refused to look in Galileo's telescope when he disputed Ptolemy's explanation of the world and of the heavens. Consequently, he was later jailed and forced to recant his beliefs. Bruno also rejected Ptolemy's theory and was burned at the stake. (Ptolemy's book on astrology and astronomy was read and believed for 1,200 years after his death!) In 1543, Vesalius wrote a book on anatomy, much of which is still correct today. However, because his work clashed with Galen's theories, he met with such scorn and ridicule that he gave up his study of anatomy.

Perhaps the most crucial aspect of the appeal to authority as a means of obtaining knowledge is the right to question and to accept or reject the information. Furthermore, the qualifications of the authority and the methods by which the authority acquired the knowledge also determine the validity of this source of information.

Rationalistic Method

In this method, knowledge is derived through reasoning. A good example is the following classical syllogism:

All men are mortal. (major premise)
The emperor is a man. (minor premise)

Therefore, the emperor is mortal. (conclusion)

Although you probably would not argue with this reasoning, the key to this method is the truth of the premises and their relationship to each other. For example,

All basketball players are tall.
Tom Thumb is a basketball player.
Therefore, Tom Thumb is tall.

In this case, however, Tom Thumb is a dwarf. The conclusion is trustworthy only if derived from premises (assumptions) that are true. Also, the premises may not in fact be premises but rather descriptions of events or statements of fact. The statements are not connected in a cause-and-effect manner. For example,

All elementary school children with big feet are good in mathematics.
Herman is an elementary school child and has big feet.
Therefore, Herman is good in mathematics.

Of course, in the first statement the factor common to both mathematics achievement and shoe size is age. Older children tend to be bigger and thus have bigger feet than younger children. Older children also have higher achievement scores in mathematics, but there is no cause-and-effect relationship. You must always be cognizant of this when dealing with correlation. Reasoning is fundamental in the scientific method of problem solving but cannot be used by itself to arrive at knowledge.

The Empirical Method

The word *empirical* denotes experience and the gathering of data. Certainly, data gathering is part of the scientific method of solving problems. However, there can be pitfalls in relying too much on your own experience (or data). First, your own experience is very limited. Furthermore, your retention depends substantially on how the events agree with your past experience and beliefs, on whether things "make sense," and on your state of motivation to remember. Nevertheless, the use of data (and the empirical method) is high on the continuum of methods of obtaining knowledge as long as you are aware of the limitations of relying too heavily on this method.

The Scientific Method of Problem Solving

The methods of acquiring knowledge previously discussed lack the objectivity and control that characterize the scientific approach to problem solving. Several basic steps are involved in the scientific method. Some authors list seven or eight steps, and others condense these steps into three or four. Nevertheless, all the authors are in general agreement as to the sequence and processes that are involved. The steps are briefly described next. Greater detail concerning the basic processes are covered in other chapters.

Step 1: Developing the Problem (Defining and Delimiting It)

This step may sound a bit contradictory, for how could the development of the problem be a part of solving it? Actually, the discussion here is not about finding a problem to study (ways of locating a problem are discussed later in this chapter); the assumption is that the researcher has already selected a topic. However, to design and execute a sound investigation, the researcher must be very specific about what is to be studied and to what extent it will be studied.

Many ramifications constitute this step, an important one being the identification of the independent and the dependent variables.

The *independent variable* is what the researcher is manipulating. If, for example, two methods of teaching a motor skill are being compared, then the teaching method is the independent variable; this is sometimes called the *experimental*, or *treatment*, *variable*.

The *dependent variable* is the effect of the independent variable. In the comparison of teaching methods, the measure of skill is the dependent variable. If you think of an experiment as a cause-and-effect proposition, the cause is the independent variable and the effect the dependent variable. The latter is sometimes referred to as the *yield*. Thus, the researcher must define exactly what will be studied and what will be the measured effect. When this is resolved, the experimental design can be determined.

Step 2: Formulating the Hypothesis

A *hypothesis* is an expected result. When a person sets out to conduct a study, he or she generally has an idea as to what the outcome will be. This anticipated solution to the problem may be based on some theoretical construct, on the results of previous studies, or perhaps on the experimenter's past experience and observations. The last source is probably least likely or defensible because of the weaknesses of the unscientific methods of acquiring knowledge discussed previously. Regardless, the researcher should have some experimental hypothesis about each of the subproblems in the study.

> The hypothesis cannot be a type of value judgment or an abstract phenomenon that cannot be observed.

One of the essential features about a hypothesis is that it be "testable." The study must be designed in such a way that the hypothesis can be either supported or refuted.

It should be obvious to you, then, that the hypothesis cannot be a type of value judgment or an abstract phenomenon that cannot be observed.

For example, you might hypothesize that success in athletics is dependent solely on fate. In other words, if a team wins, it is because it was meant to be; similarly, if a team loses, it was just not meant to be. There is no way to refute this hypothesis because there is no evidence that could be obtained to test it.

Step 3: Gathering the Data

Of course, before step 2 can be accomplished, the researcher must decide on the proper methods of acquiring the necessary data to be used in testing the research hypotheses. The reliability of the measuring instruments, the controls that are employed, and the overall objectivity and precision of the datagathering process are crucial to the solution of the problem.

In terms of difficulty, gathering data may be the easiest of the steps because in many cases it is routine. However, planning the method is one of the most difficult steps. Good methods attempt to maximize both the internal and the external validity of the study.

Internal validity and external validity relate to the research design and controls that are used. *Internal validity* refers to the extent to which the results can be attributed to the treatments used in the study. In other words, the researcher must try to control all other variables that could influence the results. For example, Jim Nasium wants to scientifically assess the effectiveness of his physical education program in developing physical fitness. He tests his students at the beginning and then at the end of the year and concludes that the program brought about significant improvement in fitness. What is wrong with Jim's conclusion? His study contains several flaws. The first is that Jim gave no consider-

ation to maturity. Nine months of maturation produced significant changes in size and in accompanying strength and endurance. Also, what else were the students doing during this time? How do we know that their other activities were not responsible, or partly so, for the changes in their fitness levels? Chapters 4 and 14 deal with these threats to internal validity.

External validity pertains to the generalizability of the results. To what extent can the results apply to the real world? This often produces a paradox for research in the behavioral sciences because of the controls required for internal validity. In motor learning studies, for example, the task is usually something novel so as to control for past experience. Furthermore, it is desirable to be able to measure the performance objectively and reliably. Consequently, the learning task is frequently a maze, a rotary pursuitmeter, or a linear positioning task, all of which may meet the demands for control with regard to internal validity. But then you are faced with the question of external validity: How does performance in a laboratory setting with a novel, irrelevant task apply to learning gymnastics or basketball? These questions are important and sometimes vexing, but they are not insurmountable (they are discussed later).

Step 4: Analyzing and Interpreting Results

The novice researcher finds this step to be the most formidable for several reasons. First, this step usually involves some statistical analysis, and the novice researcher (particularly the master's student) has a rather limited background and a fear of statistics. Second, analysis and interpretation requires considerable knowledge, experience, and insight, which the novice may lack.

That analysis and interpretation of results is the most challenging step is without question. It is here that the researcher must provide evidence for the support or the rejection of the research hypothesis. In doing this, the researcher also compares the results with those of others and perhaps attempts to relate and integrate the results into some theoretical model. Inductive reasoning is employed in this step (whereas deductive reasoning is primarily used in the statement of the problem). The researcher attempts to synthesize the data from his or her study along with the results of other studies to contribute to the development or substantiation of a theory.

ALTERNATE MODELS FOR RESEARCH

In the preceding section we summarized the basic steps in the scientific method of problem solving. *Science* is a way of knowing and is often defined as structured inquiry. One of the basic goals of science is to explain things, or to be able to generalize and build a theory. When a scientist develops a useful model to explain behavior, scholars often test predictions from this model using the steps of the scientific method. The model and the approaches used to test the model are called a *paradigm*.

Normal Science

For centuries, the scientific approaches used in studying problems in both the natural and the social sciences have been what Thomas Kuhn (1970), a noted historian of science, has termed *normal science*. Normal science is characterized by the elements we listed at the beginning of this chapter (i.e., systematic, logical, empirical, reductive, and replicable). Its basic doctrine is objectivity. Normal science is grounded in the natural sciences, which have long adhered to the idea of the orderliness and reality of matter, that nature's laws are absolute and discoverable by

objective, systematic observations and investigations that are not influenced by (in other words, independent of) humans. The experiments are theory driven and have testable hypotheses.

Normal science received a terrific jolt with Einstein's theory of relativity and the quantum theory, which indicated that nature's laws could be influenced by humans; that is, that reality depends to a great extent on how one perceives it. Moreover, some things, such as the decay of a radioactive nucleus, happen for no reason at all. The fundamental laws that were believed to be absolute were now considered to be statistical rather than deterministic. Phenomena could be predicted statistically but not explained deterministically (Jones, 1988).

Challenges to Normal Science

Relatively recently (since about 1960), there have been serious challenges regarding normal science's concept of objectivity (i.e., that the researcher can be detached from the instruments and conduct of the experiment). Two of the most powerful challengers to the ideal of objective knowledge have been Kuhn and Michael Polanyi (1958). They contend that objectivity is a myth. From the first inception of the idea for the hypothesis through the selection of apparatus to the analysis of the results, the observer is involved. The conduct of the experiment and the results can be considered expressions of the researcher's point of view. Polanyi has been especially opposed to the adoption of normal science for the study of human behavior.

Kuhn (1970) maintains that normal science does not really evolve in systematic steps the way scientific writers describe it. Kuhn discusses the *paradigm crisis phenomenon*, in which researchers who have been following a particular paradigm begin to find dir epancies in it. The findings no longer agree with the predictions, and a new paradigm is advanced. Interestingly, the old paradigm does not die completely but only develops varicose veins and fades away. Many researchers with a great deal of time and effort invested in the old paradigm are reluctant to change, so it is usually a new group of researchers who propose the new paradigm. Thus, normal science progresses by revolution, with a new group of scientists breaking away and replacing the old. Kuhn and Polanyi concur that the doctrine of objectivity is simply not a reality. Nevertheless, normal science has been and will continue to be successful in the natural sciences and in certain aspects of the study of humans. However, Martens (1987) contends that it has failed miserably in the study of human behavior, especially in the more complex functions.

Martens, as a sport psychologist, has asserted that laboratory experiments have limited use in answering questions about complex human behavior in sport. He considers his role as a practicing sport psychologist to have been far more productive in gaining knowledge about athletes and coaches and the solutions to their problems. Other workers in the so-called helping professions have made similar observations about both the limitations of normal science and the importance of alternate sources of knowledge in forming and shaping professional beliefs. Schein (1987), a noted scholar of social psychology, related an interesting (some might call it shocking) revelation concerning the relative impact of published research results versus practical experience. At a conference, he and a number of his colleagues were discussing what they relied on most for their classroom teaching. There seemed to be widespread agreement among these professors polled that the data they really believed in and used in the classroom came from personal experience and information learned in the field. Schein was making the point that

different categories of knowledge can be obtained by different methods. In effect, some people are more influenced by sociological and anthropological research models than by the normal science approach.

For some time many scholars in education, psychology, sociology, anthropology, sport psychology, physical education, and other disciplines have proposed methods of studying human behavior other than those of conventional normal science. Anthropologists, sociologists, and clinical psychologists have used in-depth observation, description, and analysis of human behavior for nearly three quarters of a century. For about 30 years, researchers in education have used participant and nonparticipant observation to obtain comprehensive, firsthand accounts of teacher and student behaviors as they occur in real-world settings. More recently, physical educators and sport psychologists have been engaged in this type of field research. A number of names given to this general form of research are ethnographic, qualitative, grounded, naturalistic, and participant observational research. Regardless of the names and the commitments and the beliefs of the researchers, this type of research has not been well received by the adherents of normal science. In fact, this form of research (we will include all forms of it under the name of qualitative research) has often been labeled by normal scientists as superficial, lacking in rigor, and just plain unscientific. It has been criticized as being essentially subjective, which is the antithesis of objectivity, the underpinning of normal science.

Martens (1987) has referred to such adherents of normal science as the gatekeepers of knowledge because they are the editors and reviewers of the research journals who decide who will get published, who will serve on the editorial boards, and whose papers will be presented at conferences. Studies without internal validity do not get published, yet studies without external validity lack practical significance. Martens (p. 42) charges that normal science (in psychology) prefers publishability to practical significance.

The debates between qualitative and normal (often classified as quantitative) research have been heated and prolonged. The qualitative proponents have gained confidence and momentum in recent years, and there is no question that this point of view will need to be reckoned with and recognized as a viable method of addressing problems in the behavioral sciences. Credibility is established by systematically categorizing and analyzing causal and consequential factors. The naturalistic setting of qualitative research both facilitates analysis and precludes precise control of so-called extraneous factors. The holistic interrelationship among observations and the complexity and dynamic processes of human interaction make it impossible to limit the study of human behavior to the sterile, reductionistic approach of normal science. The term "reductionistic" refers to normal science's characteristic of *reductionism*, which assumes that complex behavior can be reduced, analyzed, and explained as parts that can then be put back together as a whole and understood. Critics of the conventional approach to research believe the central issue is the unjustified belief that normal science is the only source of true knowledge.

Implications of This Discussion

There are many implications. For example, when we study simple movements, such as linear positioning in a laboratory to reflect cognitive processing of information, do we learn anything about movements in real-world settings such as the performance of sport skills? When we evaluate EMG activity in specific muscle groups during a simple movement, does it really tell us anything about the way the nervous system controls movements in natural settings such as athletics? Can we study the association of psychological processes related to movement in laboratory settings and expect the results to apply in sport and exercise situations? When we conduct these types of experiments, are we studying nature's phenomena or laboratory phenomena?

Do not misinterpret the intent of these questions. They do not mean that nothing important can be discovered about movement behavior from laboratory research. What they suggest is that these findings do not necessarily model accurately the way humans plan, control, and execute movements in natural settings associated with exercise and sport.

Kuhn's (1970) descriptions about how science advances and the limitations of applying normal science to natural settings point out that scientists need to consider the various ways of knowing and that the strict application of the normal scientific method of problem solving may sometimes hinder rather than advance science. If the reductionistic approach of the scientific method has not served well the natural scientists who developed it, then certainly researchers in human behavior need to carefully assess the relative strengths and weaknesses of conventional and alternate research paradigms for their particular research questions.

Alternate Forms of Scientific Inquiry

Martens (1987, p. 52) has suggested that we view knowledge not as being either scientific or unscientific or reliable or unreliable but rather as existing on a continuum, such as illustrated in Figure 1.2. This continuum, labeled "DK," ranges from "Don't Know" to "Damn Konfident." Considered in this way, varying approaches to disciplined inquiry are useful in accumulating knowledge. As examples, Martens (1979, 1987) has urged sport psychologists to consider the idio-graphic approach, introspective methods, and field studies instead of relying on the paradigm of normal science as the only answer to research questions in sport psy-chology. Thomas, French, and Humphries (1986) detailed how to study children's sport knowledge and skills in games and sports. Costill (1985) discussed the study of physio-logical responses in practical exercise and sport settings. Locke (1989) presented a tutorial on the use of qualitative research in physical education and sport. In later chap-ters we give greater detail about some of these alternative strategies for research.

What we hope you gain from this section is that science is disciplined inquiry, not a set of specific procedures. Although advocates

DK Theory

Damn
Konfident

Scientific method
(Using the heuristic paradigm)

Systematic observation

Single case study

Shared (public) experience

Introspection

Intuition

Don't
Know

Figure 1.2 The Degrees of Knowledge theory with examples of different types of methods varying in degree of reliability. From Martens (1987). Reprinted by permission.

of alternative methods of research are often very persuasive, we certainly do not want you to conclude that the study of physical education, exercise science, and sport science should abandon the traditional methods of normal science. We have learned much from these techniques and will continue to do so. Furthermore, we certainly do not want you to toss away this book as being pointless. We have not even begun to tell you all the fas-cinating things we have learned over the years (it is hard to tell whether these things should be classified as normal or abnormal science). In addition, we have many funny stories yet to tell (abnormal humor). Aside from these compelling reasons for continu-ing with the book, we want you to realize and appreciate that even though so-called normal science may not be the solution to all ques-tions raised in our field, it is the recognized model for research, and it is often taught as the only approach in graduate study. Fur-thermore, none of the alternative methods of research denounce the scientific method of problem solving. The main bones of conten-tion are with the methods, the setting, the controls, the types of data, and the analysis.

The bottom line is that different problems require different solutions. As we said before, science is disciplined inquiry, not a set of specific procedures. We need to embrace all systematic forms of inquiry. Rather than argue about the differences, we should capitalize on the strengths of both methods to provide useful knowledge about human movement.

TYPES OF RESEARCH

Research is a structured way of solving prob-lems. There are different kinds of problems in the fields of physical education, exercise science, and sport science; thus, different types of research are used to solve these problems. This text concentrates on these four types of research:

- Analytical
- Descriptive
- Experimental
- Qualitative

A brief description of each follows (see also Table 1.1).

Table 1.1 Types of Research in Physical Activity

Category	Example
Analytical	Historical
	Philosophic
	Literature review
	Meta-analysis
Descriptive	Survey
	Questionnaire
	Interview
	Normative survey
	Case study
	Job analysis
	Documentary analysis
	Developmental
	Correlational
Experimental	Predesigns
	True designs
	Quasi designs
Qualitative	Interpretive
	Ethnographic
	Participant observer
	Case study

Analytical Research

As the name implies, *analytical research* involves in-depth study and evaluation of available information in an attempt to explain complex phenomena. The different types of analytical research are historical, philosophic, reviews, and meta-analysis.

Historical Research

Obviously, *historical research* deals with events that have already occurred. The researcher tries to locate as many pertinent sources of information as possible concerning the specific problem and then analyzes the information as to its authenticity and accuracy. Sources are collected and classified as *primary* (e.g, the person was at the scene) or *secondary* (e.g, a report from someone else, or a history book), and the material is scrutinized for internal and external validity; that is, the source is evaluated to determine whether it is genuine, and the information is criticized as to whether it is accurate and reliable.

Historical research focuses on events, organizations, institutions, and people. In some studies, the researcher is interested mostly in preserving the record of events and accomplishments of the past. In other investigations, the writer attempts to discover facts that will provide more meaning and understanding of past events to explain the present state of affairs. Some historians have even attempted to use information from the past to predict the future. The research procedures associated with historical studies are addressed in considerable detail in chapter 10.

Philosophic Research

Critical inquiry characterizes *philosophic research*. The researcher establishes hypotheses, examines and analyzes existing facts, and synthesizes the evidence into a workable theoretical model. Many of the most important problem areas must be dealt with by the philosophic method. Problems dealing with objectives, curricula, course content, requirements, and methodology are but a few of the important issues that can be resolved only through the philosophic method of problem solving.

Although some authors emphasize the differences between science and philosophy, the philosophic method of research follows essentially the same steps as other methods of scientific problem solving. The philosophic approach uses scientific facts as the bases for formulating and testing research hypotheses.

The philosophic approach to the solution of problems is greatly influenced by the cultural confines in which the problem is studied and by the time and the facts available. Consequently, principles developed through philosophic research can be expected to change as the culture and the available facts change. There have been several philosophic research studies in the field of physical education. An excellent example is the dissertation of Arthur A. Esslinger (1938), in which he established principles on which the selection of the content of the physical education program could be based. Esslinger used the facts related to growth and development, child interests, and capacities from the fields of anatomy, physiology, education, and psychology. He also examined the social trends at the time. Through analysis and synthesis, Esslinger developed principles concerning the selection of activities and the formulation of the overall curriculum. Practical implications were then proposed for the physical education program on the basis of the principles that had been established.

In philosophic research, the breadth of experience and education are essential because, as in any type of research, the formulation of hypotheses and the suggested solutions to problems are a function of experience, imagination, and intelligence. The logical thinking, the scrupulous regard for the limitations and scope of the data, and the recognition of personal biases are implicit factors in the philosophic method.

Having an opinion is not the same as having a philosophy. In philosophic research, beliefs must be subjected to rigorous criticism in light of the basic, underlying assumptions. Academic preparation in philosophy and a solid background in the fields from which the facts are derived are necessary.

Another example of sound philosophic research in physical education was Morland's 1958 study, in which he analyzed the educational views held by leaders in American physical education and categorized them into educational philosophies of reconstructionism, progressivism, essentialism, and perennialism. Other examples and a more detailed explanation of philosophic research are given in chapter 11.

Reviews

A *review* paper is a critical evaluation of recent research on a particular topic. The author must be very knowledgeable about the available literature as well as the research topic and procedures. A review paper involves analysis, evaluation, and integration of the published literature, often leading to important conclusions concerning the research findings up to that time.

Certain publications consist entirely of review papers, such as the *Psychological Review*, the *Annual Review of Physiology*, and the *Review of Educational Research*. A number of journals publish reviews periodically, and some occasionally devote entire issues to reviews. For example, the 50th-anniversary issue of the *Research Quarterly for Exercise and Sport* (Safrit, 1980) contains some excellent review papers on various topics.

Meta-Analysis

Reviews of literature are difficult to write because they require that a large number of studies be synthesized to determine common underlying findings, agreements, or disagreements. To some extent this is like trying to make sense of data collected on a large number of subjects by simply looking at the data. Glass (1977) and Glass, McGaw, and

Smith (1981) proposed a quantitative means of analyzing the findings from numerous studies; this is called *meta-analysis*. Findings between studies are compared by changing results within studies to a common metric called *effect size*. Glass et al. (1981) provided numerous formulas for transforming means, standard deviations, and other statistics to effect size, which may then be treated with standard statistical techniques for summarizing and analyzing the data points (findings from various studies). A few cases of meta-analyses have been reported in the physical education literature (Feltz & Landers, 1983; Sparling, 1980). This technique is discussed in more detail in chapter 12.

Descriptive Research

Descriptive research studies are concerned with status. Of the several descriptive research techniques, the most prevalent is the questionnaire. Other forms of descriptive research include the interview, the normative survey, the case study, the job analysis, the documentary analysis, developmental studies, and correlational studies.

Chapter 13 provides detailed coverage of descriptive research procedures. The following paragraphs give a brief identification of the different types of descriptive research techniques.

The Questionnaire

The main justification for using a questionnaire is the need to obtain responses from persons from a wide geographical area. The questionnaire usually strives to secure information about present practices, conditions, and demographic data. Occasionally, a questionnaire asks for opinions or knowledge.

The researcher must take great care in preparing the questionnaire to obtain valid and reliable responses (the importance of the cover letter, pilot study, and follow-up is discussed in chapter 13). However, the questionnaire has acquired an unfavorable reputation as a research tool in some fields. This has been the result mainly of poorly designed and overused questionnaires.

The Interview

The interview and the questionnaire are essentially the same technique insofar as their planning and procedures are concerned. Obviously, the interview has certain advantages over the questionnaire in that the researcher can rephrase questions and ask additional ones to clarify responses and secure more valid results. Becoming a skilled interviewer requires training and experience. Telephone interviewing has become increasingly more common in recent years, mainly because of cost. Telephone interviewing costs about half as much as face-to-face interviews and has the additional advantage of being able to cover a wide geographical area, which is generally a limitation in personal interviews. Some other advantages of the telephone interview technique are discussed in chapter 13.

The Normative Survey

There have been a number of notable surveys in the fields of physical education and health education. The normative survey generally seeks to gather performance or knowledge data on a large sample from a population and to present the results in the form of comparative standards, or norms.

The development of the norms for the *AAHPERD Youth Fitness Test Manual* (AAHPERD, 1958) is an outstanding example of a normative survey. Thousands of boys and girls ages 10 to 18 throughout the United States were tested on a battery of motor fitness items. Percentiles were then established to provide information for students, teachers, administrators, and parents as to comparative performances. Actually, the Youth Fitness Test was developed in response to another survey, the Kraus-Weber test, which revealed that American children scored dramatically lower on a test battery of minimum muscular fitness when compared with European children.

The Case Study

The case study is used to provide detailed information about an individual (or institution, community, etc.). The case study aims to determine unique characteristics about the subject or condition. This descriptive research technique is used widely in fields such as medicine, psychology, counseling, and sociology. The case study is also a technique used in qualitative research.

The researcher attempts to gather and analyze as much information about the case as possible. Sometimes, subjects who are high achievers are studied, and often the lower performer serves as the subject. For example, Popp (1959) compared case studies of boys with the 20 lowest and the 20 highest physical fitness scores as to medical records, nutritional status, living habits, and personal problems.

The Job Analysis

The objective of the job analysis is to describe in detail the various duties, procedures, responsibilities, preparation, advantages, and disadvantages of a particular job. Used widely in vocational training and counseling, the job analysis research procedures require time, attention to details, and a variety of data-gathering techniques. The job analysis has not been used to a great extent in health, physical education, recreation, and dance, but some studies dealing with the duties of the athletic director, intramural director, and physical education teacher have been conducted.

The Documentary Analysis

In some respects, the *documentary analysis* could be classified under analytical research because it is used in literature reviews, historical studies, and other areas. However, the form of documentary analysis included in descriptive research is directed primarily at establishing the status of certain practices; areas of interest; and the prevalence of certain errors, usage of terms, and space counts. For example, newspapers or magazines might be studied to determine the extent of coverage (and thus public interest) devoted to certain sports or recreational activities. A study to ascertain the frequency of use of various statistical procedures in a research journal also falls under the category of documentary analysis.

Developmental Studies

In developmental research, the investigator is usually concerned with the interaction of learning or performance with maturation. For example, a researcher may wish to assess the extent to which the ability to process information can be attributed to maturation as opposed to strategy, or the researcher may desire to determine the effects of growth on a physical parameter such as aerobic capacity.

Developmental research can be undertaken by what is called the *longitudinal* method, whereby the same subjects are studied over a period of years. Obvious logistical problems are associated with longitudinal studies, so an alternative is to select samples of subjects from different age-groups to assess the effects of maturation. This is called the *cross-sectional* approach.

Correlational Studies

The purpose of the correlational study is to examine the relationship between certain performance variables, such as heart rate and ratings of perceived exertion; the relationship between traits such as anxiety and pain tolerance; or the correlation between attitudes and behavior, as in the attitude toward fitness and the amount of participation in fitness activities.

Sometimes, correlation is employed to predict performance. For example, a researcher may wish to predict percent body fat from skinfold measurements. First, the correlation between percent body fat (as measured by a method such as underwater weighing) and skinfold measurements is established with a sample of subjects. Percent fat can then be predicted for other subjects on the basis of this relationship simply by using skinfold measurements. Correlational research is descriptive in that you cannot presume a cause-and-effect relationship. All that can be established is that there is an association between two or more traits or performances.

Experimental Research

Experimental research is usually acknowledged as being the most scientific of all the types of research because the researcher can manipulate treatments to cause things to happen (i.e., a cause-and-effect situation can be established). This is in contrast to other types of research in which already existing phenomena or data from the past are observed and analyzed.

For an example of an experimental study, assume that Virginia Reel, a dance teacher, hypothesizes that students would learn more effectively through the use of a videotape. First, she randomly assigns students to two sections. One section is taught by the so-called traditional method (explanation, demonstration, practice, and critique). The other section is taught in a similar manner, except the students are filmed while practicing and can thus observe themselves at the same time the teacher critiques their performances. After 9 weeks, a panel of dance teachers evaluates both sections. In this study, method of teaching is the independent variable and dance performance (skill) the dependent variable. After the groups' scores are compared statistically, Virginia can conclude whether her hypothesis can be supported or refuted.

In experimental research, the researcher attempts to control all factors except the experimental (or treatment) variable. If the extraneous factors can be successfully controlled, then the researcher can presume that the changes in the dependent variable are due to the independent variable.

Experimental research is usually acknowledged as being the most scientific of all the types of research because the researcher can manipulate treatments to cause things to happen.

Several research designs are used in experimental research. Not all designs are truly experimental in that the independent variable cannot always be manipulated. In a study of learning strategies of brain-damaged and normal children, the researcher certainly would not take a sample of children and cause half of them to become brain damaged; instead, children with brain damage would be chosen for the study. Similarly, a researcher wishing to compare training responses of men and women would select subjects from each sex and then compare their responses. Thus, when there are preexisting differences such as sex, race, age, and personality traits, the independent variable is not truly independent but categorical. Such a design is an example of a quasi-experimental design. Experimental research procedures and the different types of designs are discussed in detail in chapter 14.

Qualitative Research

In physical education, exercise science, and sport science, *qualitative research* is the so-called new kid on the block. Actually, qualitative research has been used for many years in other fields, such as anthropology and sociology. Researchers in education have been engaged in qualitative methods longer than researchers in our field. As previously mentioned, several names are given to this type of research (ethnographic, naturalistic, interpretive, grounded, phenomenological, subjective, and participant observational). Some of these are simply name differences, whereas some have different approaches and points of focus. We have arbitrarily lumped them all under the heading of qualitative research as that seems to be the most common term used in our field.

It is important to note that the term "qualitative" infers interpretive, as opposed to simple, description. Description is a technique and as such does not constitute a research method (Erickson, 1986). The term "ethnography" has been closely associated with anthropology, although it has been adapted by educational researchers. The term refers to the process of re-creating for the reader the shared beliefs, practices, and behaviors of some group of people (Goetz & LeCompte, 1984). Participant observation refers to the extent to which the researcher is actually involved in the group that is being studied. Thus, the role of the observer can range from an observer who has almost no involvement in the activity to a complete participant who is totally involved in the activity

(Goc Karp, 1989). The degree of involvement is determined by the type of information desired and sometimes by how much involvement is permitted. The case study was mentioned in the section on descriptive research. It is also an important technique in qualitative research. It is used for diagnosing problems; for evaluating programs, practices, and policies; and for developing insights into the behavior of individuals and groups.

The basic characteristics of qualitative research include the following:

- Intensive, longtime observation and participation in a natural setting
- Precise and detailed recording of what happens in the setting through the use of field notes, audiotapes, videotapes, and other kinds of documentary evidence
- Interpretation and analysis of the data through the use of rich description, interpretive narratives, direct quotes, charts and tables, and sometimes statistics (usually descriptive)

Unlike quantitative research, the nature of the data and analysis sometimes leads to questions different than those formulated at the beginning of the study if they more accurately capture the participants' perspectives than the original focus questions (Griffin & Templin, 1989).

Qualitative research is different from other research methods. It is a systematic method of inquiry, and it follows the scientific method of problem solving to a considerable degree; however, it deviates in certain dimensions. Qualitative research rarely establishes hypotheses at the beginning of the study. It proceeds in an inductive process in developing hypotheses and theory as the data unfold. Theory is grounded in the data (Glaser & Strauss, 1976). The researcher is the primary instrument in the data collection and analysis. Qualitative research is characterized by intensive firsthand presence. The tools of data collection are observation, interviews, and researcher-designed instruments (Goetz & LeCompte, 1984).

The *narrative vignette* is a fundamental component of the qualitative research report. Detailed descriptions of an event, a class, a game, a workout, or a physical setting are presented, including what people say, do, think, and feel in that setting. The goal is to richly and accurately portray the experiences and perceptions of the participants (Griffin & Templin, 1989). The vignette captures the reader's attention and helps give the reader a sense of being there. The participants' own words are used as much as possible. The data are primarily verbal as opposed to the numerical data in quantitative types of research.

The qualitative researcher is interested more with the process than the product. The basic question, What is going on here? guides

the researcher's efforts (Locke, 1989). The research is done in the natural setting. The term *fieldwork*, borrowed from anthropology, is used in describing methodology. Data analysis is begun as soon as the data collection is begun rather than at the end, as in quantitative research. The researcher sorts and categorizes the data, formulates hypotheses to explain the data, and makes interpretive connections between narrative vignettes and other forms of description. The interpretations of the analysis of data are confirmed through triangulation, which means cross-checking through other sources of data, other methodologies, other researchers, and other theories (Fielding & Fielding, 1986).

Qualitative research is becoming increasingly popular and will undoubtedly continue to do so. It is not an easy type of research, as it takes a great deal of time, effort, and

analytical skill. Qualitative research offers an interesting and valuable alternative approach to solving problems in our field.

A BRIEF HISTORICAL OVERVIEW OF RESEARCH IN PHYSICAL ACTIVITY IN THE UNITED STATES

All of the types of research we have been talking about didn't just happen randomly or by chance. Research has systematically evolved in the United States since the mid-1800s. We present here a chronicle of that evolutionary process. Our information came from several secondary sources (Hackensmith, 1966; Lee, 1983; Leonard & Affleck, 1947; Van Dalen & Bennet, 1971). Particularly helpful were Lee's summaries of research (see Lee, 1983, chaps. 6, 9, 13, and 16).

Early Physical Education Research

The beginnings of systematic research in physical education in the United States closely followed the establishment in 1854 of the first department of hygiene and physical education at Amherst College. Although John Hooker was the first director of this department, the appointment of Edward Hitchcock (MD, Harvard Medical School, 1853) as director in 1861 represents the beginnings of research efforts in physical education. Dr. Hitchcock frequently made anthropometric measurements and used chin-ups to assess arm strength. Over the next 20 years, the list of measurements taken was extended considerably. The tabulation of these measurements was first published in the *Anthropometric Manual* (1887; revised editions in 1889, 1893, and 1900), which represents one of the first data-based research publications of physical education in the United States.

Then, Dudley Sargent, who received his MD from Yale Medical School in 1878, estab-lished a private gymnasium in New York, where he began applying a series of bodily measurements to participants. Two years later, he was appointed assistant professor at Harvard and made director of the new Hemenway Gymnasium. All entering freshmen were given an examination, including both strength tests and anthropometric measures. Dr. Sargent collected more than 50,000 anthropometric measures on individuals during his career. In fact, lifelike statues of typical American youths were constructed on the basis of his measurements and displayed at the 1893 Chicago World's Fair. This might be listed as the first formal research presentation in physical education in the United States. Sargent was also a leader in the development of strength testing, and he used these tests to determine membership of Harvard's athletic teams. Following the lead of Sargent, several women's colleges (Bryn Mawr, Mount Holyoke, Radcliffe, Rockford, Vassar, and Wellesley) in the 1880s established programs of anthropometric measurements and strength tests of students.

When a new gymnasium was constructed at Johns Hopkins in 1883, Edward Hartwell (PhD, Johns Hopkins; MD, Medical College of Ohio) was appointed its director. There, in 1897, he began the use of survey research in physical education through his evaluations of gymnastics in the United States.

To measure throwing, running speed, and distance jumped, Dr. Luther Gulick devised the very first achievement test in 1890. This test, called the Pentathlon Test, was initially created for the Athletic League of the YMCAs of America but was further developed in the early 1900s for the Public School Athletic League in New York.

In the late 1800s and early 1900s, several books were published that either reported, summarized, or influenced early research in physical education. Among those were Blaikie's *How to Get Strong and How to Stay So* (1879), which reported Sargent's early work and influenced Harvard (Blaikie was a Harvard alumnus) to employ Sargent. In Berlin in 1885, DuBois-Reymond published *Physiology of Exercise*, which was translated into English in *Popular Science Monthly*. Following Sargent's lead in anthropometric measurement, Seaver published *Anthropometric and Physical Examinations* in 1896.

The beginning of the 20th century saw a continuing interest in research in physical education. In particular, an interest arose in tests of physical achievement and cardiovascular efficiency. Physicians (both within and outside the profession of physical education) showed increased interest in classifying people for exercise intensity based on cardiovascular function. At Springfield College (Massachusetts), James McCurdy (1895-1935) began studying changes occurring over the adolescent years in heart function and blood pressure. The first of the widely used cardiovascular efficiency tests was developed in 1917 by Schneider at Connecticut Wesleyan College and was used in World War I for evaluating the fitness of aviators.

Physical achievement testing advanced considerably in the early 1900s, and in 1922 the American Physical Education Association set up a committee under McCurdy's direction to develop motor ability tests. The two most recognized tests of the 1920s were Sargent's Physical Test of Man and Roger's Physical Fitness Index. By the 1930s many schools and colleges were administering physical achievement tests. In fact, this increase in motor performance and fitness testing probably led to the establishment in 1930 of *Research Quarterly* by the American Physical Education Association (for a review of the history of *RQ*, see Park, 1980). This was the first journal established specifically to report research in physical education.

Beginning in the 1930s, tests and measurements became the most active research area in physical education. Many physical fitness and motor ability tests were developed and widely used in both public schools and colleges and universities. Names of particular importance in test development were David Brace and C.H. McCloy.

The progressive education movement (1930s), frequently characterized as "teach what the child wants to learn," had a significant impact on both academic education and physical education. Physical educators began to concentrate on making the curriculum fun. This resulted in questionnaire research that was designed to discover what children liked to do. However, a statement by McCloy (1960) seemed to put everything into perspective: "I hope the next fifty years will cause physical education to . . . seek for facts, proved objectively; to question principles based on average opinions of people who don't know but are all anxious to contribute their average ignorance to form a consensus of uninformed dogma" (p. 91).

As testing became more popular in the schools during the 1930s, the use of true-false knowledge tests for physical education activities increased considerably. With the advent of new statistical techniques, both physical and knowledge tests were provided with increased scientific rigor and standards for physical education. However, sometimes the emphasis on numbers got out of hand: "We lived in one long orgy of tabulation. . . . Mountains of fact were piled up, condensed, summarized and interpreted by the new quantitative technique. The air was full of normal curves, standard deviations, coefficients of correlation, regressive equations" (Rugg, 1941, p. 182).

Postwar Research

The outbreak of World War II brought renewed interest in physical fitness as large numbers of the men drafted did not meet the minimum standards for physical fitness. In fact, one third of the men examined were found unfit for service, and even those accepted generally lacked adequate levels of physical fitness. Many physical education leaders were placed in roles in which they were responsible for the testing and conditioning of servicemen. Thus, a considerable number of advances were made in both testing and training in exercise physiology.

World War II also led to the development of the area known today as motor learning and control. Many psychologists were involved in the development of training programs for pilots. The motor coordination involved in learning to control an airplane is considerable, and this led to many studies of motor skill performance and learning being conducted. Unfortunately, when the war ended, most of the interest in motor skill acquisition was lost as experimental psychologists returned to their interest in cognitive performance.

The 1950s brought a renewed interest in physical fitness. The 1953 publication of the Kraus-Weber test results revealed the poor record of American children when compared to European children. Although the test does not assess many of the factors considered important in fitness today (e.g., cardiovascular endurance and strength), the fact that nearly 60% of the American children failed compared to less than 9% of the European children attracted national attention. As a result, President Eisenhower called a special White House conference in 1956. This conference and several subsequent ones led to the establishment of the President's Council on Youth Fitness and the development of the AAHPERD Fitness Test. This emphasis gave a considerable boost to research in exercise physiology and to tests and measurements.

Beginning in the 1960s, research in physical education began to expand rapidly. Franklin Henry's historic memory drum theory (Henry & Rogers, 1960) launched a renewed interest in motor learning and control. Henry (1964) contributed still further to the promotion of research with his paper

about physical education being a discipline. This led to the identification of a knowledge base for physical education that was frequently called "human movement." Research expanded dramatically as exercise physiology, biomechanics, motor learning and control, motor development, sport psychology, and sport sociology began to produce knowledge about movement. The *Research Quarterly* was expanded, and new journals such as *Medicine and Science in Sport* and the *Journal of Motor Behavior* began publication.

The 1970s saw a continued interest in research in the discipline of human movement, but renewed interest evolved in research within the professional base of physical education. Observational techniques were developed and refined that allowed accurate assessment of teaching behavior and student-teacher interaction. The area of classroom observation called "research on teaching" in education was developed for use in the gymnasium and playing fields in physical education. Research on curriculum theory in physical education, measurement and evaluation, and the history of sport and physical education received renewed attention.

Many researchers from the discipline of human movement began to establish specific professional groups outside the traditional affiliations these researchers had held in AAHPERD. Such groups as the American College of Sports Medicine, the North American Society for Sport History, the North American Society for the Psychology of Sport and Physical Activity, and several others became major contributors to the research base. Responding to these inroads into membership and activities, AAHPERD created various academies, elevated the Research Consortium to the research arm of the alliance, and changed the name of *Research Quarterly* to *Research Quarterly for Exercise and Sport*. The first issue under the new name was the 50th-anniversary issue (Safrit, 1980), in which the editor and the advisory committee had solicited papers from the various subdisciplines in physical education: biomechanics, exercise physiology, psychology of sport, measurement and research design, sociology of sport, motor development, and motor behavior.

This increased emphasis on research in both the discipline of human movement and the professional base of physical education can lead only to increased knowledge and higher scholarly standards. While the discipline based on the study of human movement continues to undergo growing pains and an identity crisis (e.g., What shall we call ourselves—kinesiology, exercise and sport science, movement science?), quality graduate programs, research, and scholarship are evident. For example, a special issue of *Quest* was published in the fall of 1987 devoted completely to graduate education. New scholarly journals have evolved, particularly associated with specialized subareas of the discipline (e.g., *Journal of Exercise and Sport Psychology, Journal of Sport Sociology*).

School- and community-based exercise and sport skill programs are now refining their unique goals (developing physical fitness and motor skills) based on a solid knowledge of human movement and on increased sophistication in planning and teaching physical education to children and adults. New scholarly journals have evolved in these areas as well, such as the *Journal of Teaching in Physical Education*, to accommodate the growth in knowledge produced. Each of these factors should result in a more knowledgeable, physically fit, and skillful population during the next 20 to 30 years.

BEGINNING THE RESEARCH PROCESS

Getting started is the hardest part of almost any new venture, and research is no excep-

tion. You can't do any significant research until you have identified the area you want to investigate and until you know how to conduct the investigation.

Identifying the Research Problem

Of the many major issues facing the graduate student, a primary one is the identification of a research problem. Problems may arise from real-world settings or be generated from theoretical frameworks. Regardless, a basic requirement for proposing a good research problem is in-depth knowledge about the area of interest. To some extent, this seems ironic because the research methods course is typically taken in the first semester (or quarter) of graduate school before the student has had the opportunity to acquire the necessary in-depth knowledge. The usual result is that selected research problems are trivial, lack a theoretical base, and frequently only replicate earlier research. Although this is a considerable shortcoming, the advantages of taking the research methods course early in the program are substantial in terms of success in other graduate courses. This is because the student learns

- to approach and solve problems in a scientific way,
- to search the literature,
- to write in a clear scientific fashion,
- to understand basic measurement and statistical issues,
- to use an appropriate writing style,
- to be an intelligent consumer of research, and
- to appreciate the wide variety of research strategies and techniques used in physical education, exercise science, and sport science.

How, then, does a student without much background select a problem? It seems that the harder you try to think of a topic, the more you are inclined to think that all the problems in the field have already been solved. Adding to this frustration is the pressure of time.

To help alleviate the topic-finding problem, we offer the following suggestions. First, be aware of the research being done at your institution, for research spawns other research ideas. Often, a researcher will have a series of studies planned. Another suggestion is to be alert for any controversial issues in some area of interest. Lively controversy prompts research in efforts to resolve the issue. In any case, be sure to talk to professors and advanced graduate students in your area of interest and to use their suggestions to focus on a topic. Then locate and read a review paper (possibly in a review journal, research journal, or recent textbook). From there, read several of the research studies in the reference lists and locate other, more current research papers on the topic. Using all this information, list either research questions that appear unanswered or logical extensions of the material you have read. Then, apply the criteria for choosing a problem (see Table 1.2). Of course, no single problem will necessarily meet all the criteria perfectly. For example, some theoretical problems may have limited direct application; however, theoretical problems should be directed toward issues that may ultimately prove useful to practitioners. By honestly answering the questions in this table, a practical evaluation of the selected problem is possible.

Inductive and Deductive Reasoning

The means for identifying specific research problems comes from two methods of reasoning: inductive and deductive. Figure 1.3 provides a schema of the *inductive-reasoning* process. Individual observations are tied together into specific hypotheses, which are grouped into more general explanations that

Table 1.2 Criteria in Selecting a Research Problem

Workability. Is the contemplated study within the limits and range of your resource and time constraints? Will you have access to the necessary sample in the numbers required? Is there reason to believe you can come up with an "answer to the problem"? Is the required methodology manageable and understandable?

Critical mass. Is the problem of sufficient magnitude and scope to fulfill the requirement that has motivated the study in the first place? Are there enough variables? enough potential results? enough to write about?

Interest. Are you interested in the problem area, specific problem, and potential solution? Does it relate to your background? to your career interest? Does it "turn you on"? Will you learn useful skills from pursuing it?

Theoretical value. Does the problem fill a gap in the literature? Will others recognize its importance? Will it contribute to advancement in your field? Does it improve the "state of the art"? Is it publishable?

Practical value. Will the solution to the problem improve educational practice? Are practitioners likely to be interested in the results? Will education be changed by the outcome? Will your own educational practices be likely to change as a result?

Note. From Tuckman (1978, pp. 24-25). Copyright 1978 by Harcourt Brace Jovanovich. Reprinted by permission.

are united into theory. To move from the level of observations to that of theory requires many individual studies that test specific hypotheses. But even beyond the individual studies, someone must see how all the findings relate and then offer a theoretical explanation that encompasses all the individual findings.

An example of this process can be found in the motor learning and control area. Adams (1971) proposed a *closed loop theory* of motor skill learning. Basically, a closed loop theory is one in which information received as feedback from a movement is compared to some internal reference of correctness (assumed to be stored in memory). Then the discrepancies between the movement and the intended movement are noted. Finally, the next attempt at the movement is adjusted to more nearly approximate the movement goal. Adams's theory was developed to tie together many previous observations about movement response. The theory was tightly reasoned but limited to slow-positioning responses. This limitation really makes it a "more general explanation," according to Figure 1.3. Schmidt (1975) proposed a *schema theory*, which extended Adams's reasoning to include more rapid types of movements, frequently called ballistic tasks. (Schema theory also deals with several other limitations of Adams's theory that are not important to this discussion.) The point is that schema theory proposed to unify two general explanations, one about slow movements and the other about ballistic (rapid) movements, under one theoretical explanation—clearly an example of inductive reasoning.

However, reasoning must be careful, logical, and causal; otherwise one of our examples of inappropriate induction may result (Thomas, 1980):

A researcher spent several weeks training a cockroach to jump. The bug became well trained and would leap high in the air on the command "Jump." The researcher then began to manipulate his independent variable which was to remove the bug's legs one at a time. Upon removing the first leg, the researcher said "Jump," and the bug did. He then removed the second, third, fourth, and fifth leg and said "Jump" after each leg was removed, and the bug jumped every time. Upon removing the sixth leg and giving the "Jump" command, the bug just lay there. The researcher's conclusion from this research was: "When all the legs are removed from a cockroach, the bug becomes deaf." (p. 267)

A model of *deductive reasoning* is presented in Figure 1.4. Deductive reasoning moves from a theoretical explanation of events to specific hypotheses that are tested against (or compared to) reality to evaluate whether the hypotheses are correct. Using the previously presented notions from his schema theory (to avoid explaining another theory), Schmidt advanced a hypothesis frequently called *variability of practice*. Essentially, this hypothesis (reasoned or deduced from the theory) says

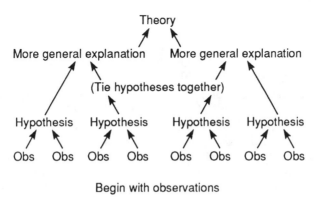

Figure 1.3 Inductive reasoning. From Hoenes and Chissom (1975, p. 22). Copyright 1975 by Vog Press. Reprinted by permission.

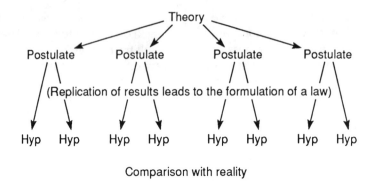

Comparison with reality

Figure 1.4 Deductive reasoning. From Hoenes and Chissom (1975, p. 23). Copyright 1975 by Vog Press. Reprinted by permission.

that practice of a variety of movement experiences (within a movement class), when compared to practicing a single movement, facilitates transfer to a new movement (but still within the same class). This hypothesis, identified by deductive reasoning, has since been tested by a number of studies and found viable. In fact, within any given study, both inductive and deductive reasoning are useful. The total research spectrum is presented in Figure 1.5. Notice how the deductive and inductive processes operate; that is, at the beginning of a study, the researcher deduces hypotheses from relevant theories and concepts and induces hypotheses from relevant findings in other research.

Process Overview

A nice overview of the research methods course, as well as an introduction to this book, is provided in Figure 1.5. This flowchart provides a linear way to think about planning a research study. Once the problem area is identified, reading and thinking about relevant theories and concepts, as well as a careful search of the literature for relevant findings, leads to the specification of hypotheses. Operational definitions are needed in a research study so that the reader knows exactly what the researcher means by certain

terms. *Operational definitions* are observable phenomena that enable the researcher to test empirically whether the predicted outcomes (hypotheses) can be supported. The study is designed, and the measuring devices are selected and made operational. The data are then collected and analyzed and the findings identified. Finally, the results are related back to the original hypotheses and discussed in relation to theories, concepts, and previous research findings.

THE PARTS OF A THESIS: A REFLECTION OF THE STEPS IN THE RESEARCH PROCESS

In this chapter, you have been introduced to the research process. The theme of the chapter has been the scientific method of problem solving. Generally speaking, a thesis or research article has a rather standard format. This is for the purpose of expedience in that the reader knows where to find the different information, such as purpose, methods, and results. The format also reflects the steps in the scientific method of problem solving. We now look at a typical thesis format and see how the chapters account for the steps in the scientific method.

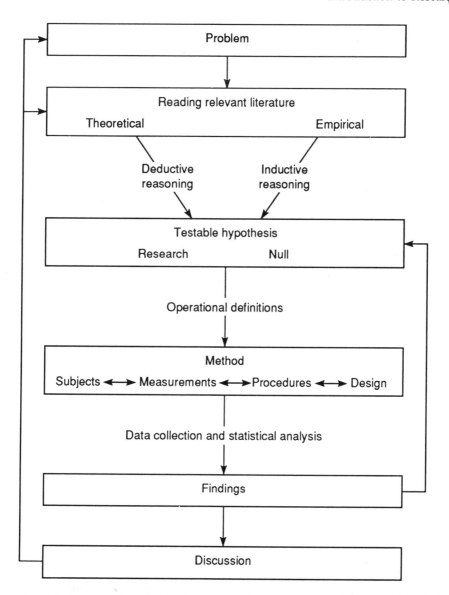

Figure 1.5 The total research setting.

Chapter 1: Introduction

Here the problem is defined and delimited. The researcher specifically identifies the problem and states the research hypotheses. Certain terms critical to the study are opera-

tionally defined for the reader, and limitations and perhaps some basic assumptions are acknowledged.

The literature review may be in the first chapter, or it may warrant a separate chapter. When it is in the first chapter, it more closely adheres to the steps in the scientific method of problem solving; that is, the literature review is instrumental in the formulation of hypotheses and the deductive reasoning leading to the statement of the problem.

Chapter 2: Method

Often, this chapter is the review of literature as, for example, in this text. However, because the purpose here is to make the thesis format parallel to the data-gathering steps, this chapter relates to the scientific method. First, the researcher explains how the data were gathered. The subjects are identified, the measuring instruments are described, the measurement and treatment procedures are presented, the experimental design is explained, and the methods of analyzing the data are summarized. The major purpose of the method chapter is to describe the study in such detail and with such clarity that you could duplicate it.

The first two chapters often comprise the research proposal and are presented to the student's thesis committee prior to the research being undertaken. When this occurs, these two chapters should be written in future tense, then changed to past tense when the final version of the thesis is completed.

Chapter 3: Results

The results chapter presents the pertinent findings from the analysis of the data. It corresponds to the step in the scientific method in which the results are scrutinized as to their meaningfulness and reliability.

Chapter 4: Discussion and Conclusions

In this last step in the scientific method, the researcher employs inductive reasoning in an effort to analyze the findings, to compare these findings with previous studies, and to integrate them into a theoretical model. In this chapter, the research hypotheses are judged as to their acceptability. Then, on the basis of the analysis and discussion, conclusions are usually made. The conclusions should address the purpose and subpurposes that were specified in the first chapter.

SUMMARY

Research is simply a way of solving problems. Questions are raised, and methods are devised to try to answer them. There are different ways of approaching problems (research methods). Sometimes the nature of the problem dictates the method of research. For example, if one wants to discover the origins of a sport, the historical method of research is used. Sometimes one wishes to look at a problem from a particular angle and selects a research method that can best answer the question.

Research on the topic of teaching effectiveness, for example, can be approached in several different ways. An experimental study could be conducted in which different teaching methods are compared as to their effectiveness in bringing about measurable achievement. Or a survey study could be designed in which teachers are observed and their behaviors coded and evaluated using some observational instrument. Or another form of descriptive research could be used that employs the questionnaire or the interview technique to examine teachers' responses to questions concerning their beliefs or practices. Or perhaps a qualitative study could be undertaken to systematically observe and interview one teacher in one school over an extended period to portray the experiences and perceptions of the teacher in the natural setting.

The point is that there isn't a single way to do research. It is true that some people do just one type of research, and, being human, some people are critical of the methods used by others. However, anyone who believes his or her type of research is the only "scientific" way to solve problems is narrow and downright foolish. Science is disciplined inquiry, not a set of specific procedures.

Some research is called basic research in that it deals primarily with theoretical problems, and the results are not intended to have immediate application. Applied research, on the other hand, strives to answer questions that have direct value to the practitioner.

There is a need to prepare proficient consumers of research as well as researchers. Thus, one purpose of a book on research methods is to help the reader understand the tools necessary both to consume and to produce research.

We have presented here an overview of the nature of research. The scientific method of problem solving was contrasted with "unscientific" methods by which people acquire information. Multiple research models were discussed to emphasize that there isn't just one way to approach problems in our profession.

We identified the four major types of research used in physical education, exercise science, and sport science: analytical, descriptive, experimental, and qualitative. These basic categories and the different techniques that they encompass will be covered in detail in later chapters.

A brief history of the beginning of research in our field was given to provide perspective with regard to early leaders, directions, and the evolution of specialized fields of inquiry. We concluded with a discussion of the importance of inductive and deductive reasoning in identifying research problems, formulating hypotheses, and guiding the overall research process. Finally, the parts of a typical thesis format were shown to reflect the general steps in the research process.

Chapter 2

□

Using the Literature in Developing the Problem

Browsing in a library confirms that information—and lots of it—exists. The dilemma lies in knowing how to locate the information you want and, ultimately, how to use the information once you've found it. This chapter focuses on how the literature review can be used to develop research questions in physical education and exercise and sport science. It explains how to search for literature and finally gives instruction on how to write a literature review.

PURPOSES OF THE LITERATURE REVIEW

Reviews of literature serve many purposes. Frequently, they are used as a basis for inductive reasoning. A scholar may seek to locate and synthesize all the relevant literature on a particular topic to develop a more general explanation or a theory to explain certain phenomena. An alternate way of analyzing the literature, mentioned in chapter 1, is meta-analysis (Glass et al., 1981), which will be discussed in detail in chapter 12.

The major problem of literature reviews is how all those studies can be related to one another in an effective way. Most frequently, authors attempt to relate studies by similarities and differences in theoretical frameworks, problem statements, methodologies (subjects, instruments, treatments, designs, and statistical analyses), and findings. Results are then determined by vote counting.

For example, you would write, "From the eight studies with similar characteristics, five found no significant difference between the treatments; thus, this treatment has no consistent effect."

This procedure is most easily accomplished through use of a summary sheet (see Table 2.1). This table could be used to relate the frequency and intensity of exercise to the percentage of change in body fat. The conclusion from looking at these studies might be that exercising 20 minutes per day for 3 days per week for 10-14 weeks at 70% of the maximum heart rate produces moderate losses of body fat (4%-5%). However, more frequent exercise bouts produce minimal increases, but less frequent or intense exercise decreases fat loss substantially. Techniques of this type lend themselves to the development of the literature review around central themes or topics. Not only does this approach allow synthesis of the relevant findings, but it also makes the literature review interesting to read.

Identifying the Problem

As discussed in chapter 1, the literature review is useful in identifying the specific problem. Of course the first task, after locating a series of studies, is to decide which studies are related to the topic area. This can frequently be accomplished by reading the abstract and, if necessary, some specific parts

Table 2.1 Sample Form for Synthesizing Studies (Hypothetical Example)

Study	Problem statement	Characteristics of studies			Finding
		Subject description	Instrument	Procedure and design	
Smith (1985)	Effects of exercise on body fat	30 college-age males	Underwater weighing	Exercise 3 d/wk at 70% of (220 − age) for 12 wk	4% reduction in body fat
Johnson (1978)	Effects of exercise on body fat	45 college-age males	Underwater weighing	Jog 3 d/wk at 70% or 50% of (220 − age) for 10 wk	5% for 70% gp 2% for 50% gp
Andrews (1989)	Effects of frequent and intense exercise on body fat	36 college-age males	Skinfold calipers	Jog 2, 4, 6 d/wk at 75% of (220 − age) for 12 wk	1% for 2 d 4% for 4 d 5% for 6 d
Mitchell (1980)	Effects of work load on body fat	24 high school males	Skinfold calipers	Pedaled at 30, 45, 60 rpm with 2 kp resistance for 20 min, 3 d/wk for 14 wk	1% at 30 rpm 3% at 45 rpm 4% at 60 rpm

of the paper. Once a few key studies are identified, a careful reading will usually produce several ideas and unresolved questions. You will find it useful to discuss these questions with a professor or advanced graduate student in his or her area of specialization. Doing so can eliminate unproductive approaches or dead ends. After the problem is specified, an intensive library search begins.

Developing Hypotheses

Hypotheses are deduced from theory or induced from other empirical studies and real-world observations. These hypotheses are based on logical reasoning and, when predictive of the outcome of the study, are labeled *research hypotheses*. For example, after spending a good deal of time at registration as undergraduates, graduate students, and fac-

ulty members, we are able to put forth the following hypothesis for you to test:

The shortest line at registration will always be the slowest. If you change lines, the one you left will speed up, and the one you enter will suddenly stop.

Developing the Method

Although considerable work is involved in identifying the problem and specifying hypotheses, one of the more creative parts of research is developing the method to test the hypotheses. If the method is planned and pilot tested appropriately, the outcome of the study will allow the hypotheses to be evaluated. We believe that the researcher fails when the results of a study are blamed on methodological problems. Post hoc methodological blame results from lack of (or poor) planning and pilot work before undertaking the research.

> If the method is planned and pilot tested appropriately, the outcome of the study will allow the hypotheses to be evaluated.

The review of literature can be extremely helpful in identifying methods that have been successfully used to solve particular types of problems. Valuable elements from other studies may include the characteristics of the subjects, data collection instruments and testing procedures, treatments, designs, and statistical analyses. All or parts or combinations of the previously used methods are quite helpful as the researcher plans the study, but these should not limit the researcher in designing the study. Creative methodology is a key to good hypothesis testing. But neither other scholars' research nor creativity ever replaces the need to conduct careful and thorough pilot work before the study.

THE LITERATURE SEARCH

The prospect of beginning a literature search can sometimes be frightening or depressing to some people. How and where do you begin? What kind of sequence or strategy should you use in locating relevant literature? What services does the library offer in your search?

Search Strategies

Authors of research texts have advanced various strategies for finding pertinent information on a topic. There is no single "right" way of doing it. The search process depends

considerably on your initial familiarity with the topic. In other words, if you have virtually no knowledge about a particular topic, your starting point and sequence would be different from that of someone already quite familiar with the literature.

Haag (1979) has presented a logical, comprehensive strategy for literature searching in physical education, exercise science, and sport science that is applicable to any subject area. This system deserves merit because it provides a search strategy for the person totally unfamiliar with the information on a subject. Furthermore, those with more knowledge about the subject can enter the structure at different points along the continuum. In this strategy, you proceed from sources that provide an overview of information about the subject to sources that are mostly location devices. Figure 2.1 illustrates

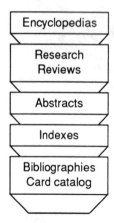

Figure 2.1 The continuum for a literature search strategy.

the continuum. Because topics differ and each search has unique characteristics, you do not always proceed in the same step-by-step manner. Instead, you will often move back and forth along the continuum.

Library Resources

You are undoubtedly familiar with many of the library's resources. As technology advances, however, more and more resources are becoming available. This section presents an overview of the kinds of resources available at most university libraries.

Encyclopedias

Encyclopedias provide an overview of information on research topics and summarize knowledge about subject areas. General encyclopedias provide broad information about an entire field. Specialized encyclopedias pertain to much narrower topics. Examples are *Encyclopedia of Sport Sciences and Medicine, Encyclopedia of Physical Fitness,* and the *Encyclopedia of Physical Education, Fitness, and Sports.*

Because a rather lengthy period (years) often passes from the time the authors sub-

mit their contributions until the publication date, you should be aware that the information in an encyclopedia is dated. Still, you can get important background information about a subject, become familiar with basic terms, and note references to some of the pertinent research journals.

Reviews of Research

Reviews of research are an excellent source of information for three reasons:

- Some knowledgeable person has spent a great deal of time and effort in compiling the latest literature on the topic.
- The author has not only located the relevant literature but also critically reviewed and synthesized it into an integrated summarization of what is known about the area.
- The reviewer often suggests areas of needed research, which the graduate student greatly appreciates.

Some actual review publications are the *Annual Reviews of Medicine,* the *Annual Review of Psychology,* the *Review of Educational Research, Physiological Reviews,* the *Psychological Review,* and *Exercise and Sport Science Reviews.*

A number of reviews are published by AAHPERD. One is a series called *What Research Tells the Coach,* which is about different sports such as baseball, football, sprinting, distance running, swimming, tennis, and wrestling. Another AAHPERD series includes *Kinesiology Reviews I, II,* and *III.* Many other research journals regularly publish reviews, to which some occasionally devote entire issues.

Abstracts

Concise summaries of research studies are valuable sources of information in the literature search on a topic. Abstracts of papers presented at research meetings are available at national, district, and most state conventions. *Abstracts of Research Papers* is also sold through AAHPERD Publications. *Completed Research in Health, Physical Education, Recreation and Dance*, a publication sponsored by the Research Consortium of AAHPERD, publishes hundreds of thesis and dissertation abstracts each year. It also contains a bibliographical section of titles of research articles from over 160 periodicals. *Medicine and Science in Sports and Exercise* publishes a special supplement of abstracts each year for papers to be presented at the annual meeting of the American College of Sports Medicine.

Other abstract sources are *Dissertation Abstracts International*, which contains abstracts of dissertations from most colleges and universities in the United States; the *Index and Abstracts of Foreign Physical Education Literature* provides abstracts from journals outside the United States. Sources of abstracts in related fields include *Biological Abstracts, Psychological Abstracts, Sociological Abstracts*, and *Resources in Education*, which is a part of the ERIC system (ERIC will be discussed in a later section).

Microform Publications

This project, conducted by the College of Human Development and Performance at the University of Oregon, provides a special type of resource to researchers in physical education, exercise science, and sport science. The emphasis is placed on producing unpublished research materials on microfiche (particularly dissertations and theses) as well as out-of-print scholarly books and journals.

Indexes

Several indexes provide references to magazine and journal articles concerning specific topics. Some of the indexes commonly used in physical education, exercise science, and

sport science are the *Current Index to Journals in Education* (which is part of ERIC), the *Education Index*, the *Reader's Guide to Periodical Literature, Current Contents*, the *New York Times Index*, and the *Physical Education Index*. Despite the title, this last source provides a comprehensive subject index to domestic and foreign periodicals in the fields of dance, health education, recreation, sports, physical therapy, and sports medicine.

Index Medicus. This is widely used in the area of exercise science. The index provides access to over 2,500 biomedical journals around the world. It is published monthly, and each issue has subject and author sections and a bibliography of medical reviews. *Index Medicus* can also be computer searched.

PsycINFO. This is a computer search of much of the behavioral science literature. Just like other computer searches, key words are selected and appropriate titles with journal and authors identified.

Current Contents. This is a useful service published by the Institute for Scientific Information. The small magazine is mailed weekly to subscribers and contains the table of contents of journals published recently within a general content area (e.g., social and behavioral sciences) and divides journals by subarea (e.g., psychology, education rehabilitation, and special education). The journal titles are indexed by topic and author. Addresses are provided for the author of each paper, thus helping you obtain reprints. *Current Contents* also publishes a section on current books in each issue as well as weekly editions for life sciences; physical, chemical, and earth sciences; social and behavioral sciences; agriculture, biology, and environmental sciences; clinical medicine; engineering, technology, and applied sciences; and arts and humanities.

ERIC. We have mentioned ERIC with regard to abstracts, *Resources in Education (RIE)*, and the *Current Index to Journals in Education* (*CIJE*). The acronym ERIC stands for Educational Resources Information Center. It is an information system that collects, sorts, classifies, and stores thousands of documents on various topics concerning education and related fields.

The basic indexes of ERIC are *RIE* and *CIJE*. Besides containing the abstracts, *RIE* provides information on how you can obtain an article: whether you can purchase it on microfilm, order an ERIC copy, or request the original copy from the publisher. Both *RIE* and *CIJE* provide valuable assistance in the search for information on specific topics. In addition, ERIC produces a thesaurus containing thousands of index terms that can be used in locating references and in conducting a computer search for information.

Bibliographies

Bibliographies list books and articles relevant to specific topics. They come in many different forms, depending on how the information is listed. Basically, all contain the authors, titles of books or articles, journal names, and publishing information. Some bibliographies are *annotated*, meaning that a brief description of the nature and scope of the article or book is included with each reference.

The bibliography of a recent study on the topic in question is an invaluable aid to the researcher. Some authors have made the statement that one of the most valuable (if not the most valuable) contributions of a dissertation is the review of literature and bibliography. However, you cannot simply lift the literature review from a previous study. Just because someone else has reviewed pertinent sources does not relieve you from the responsibility of reading each of the sources and making an evaluation yourself. Keep in mind the following two things: (a) The previous author may have been careless and cited the source or sources incorrectly, and (b) the previous author may have taken the results of a study out of context or from a point of view different from the original author's or your own. We have found incorrect bibliographic entries on numerous occasions. A good search strategy is to look for the most recent sources of information and then work backward. You will save much time by consulting the most recent studies, and you will profit from the searches of others.

Some examples of bibliographies are the *Annotated Bibliography on Movement Education*; *Completed Research in Health, Physical Education, Recreation and Dance*; the *Bibliography of Research Involving Female Subjects*; the *Bibliography on Perceptual Motor Development*; the *Bibliography of Medical Reviews in Index Medicus*; the *Annotated Bibliography in Physical Education, Recreation and Psychomotor Function of Mentally Retarded Persons*; and *Social Sciences of Sports*.

Card Catalog

Use the card catalog when you are looking for a specific title or author. The traditional card catalog with little trays of cards containing bibliographic information by author and subject is rapidly being phased out. Most university libraries have gone to a computerized catalog system, and it seems inevitable that all libraries will adopt this method as finances permit.

There are different types of computerized catalogs. In general, the searcher first selects the type of search from a menu, such as by author, title, or key word. The computer has function keys that perform various operations for different options as the screen lists authors, titles, or subjects. The final full display for a particular reference includes author, title, publication information, all the index terms, and the call number. Many colleges and universities also have computer dial-up systems for the card catalog and other services that allow faculty and students to use their personal computers to dial up the library and use many of the services.

Some people who have used the older system for years are nostalgically reluctant to see it disappear. They maintain that while browsing through the cards they often experienced serendipity, which is where one finds something of value when searching for something else. Nevertheless, as one becomes familiar with the computer operations, the search process becomes much faster and more productive. Remember, if you have questions about any of the operations of a library, ask a librarian. They tend to be remarkably helpful and courteous.

Some Periodicals in Physical Education, Exercise Science, and Sport Science

Within the last 20 years, the number of periodicals available in our fields has increased tremendously. More specialization is one reason for this increase as the so-called generalist is giving way to the specialist.

Consequently, the vast amount of research and development of new knowledge about the special areas of interest has led to new audiences with common interests. Following is a compilation of many journals that publish research in physical education, exercise science, and sport science.

Journals Publishing Research in Physical Education, Exercise Science, and Sport Science

Acta Physiologica Scandinavica
Adapted Physical Activity Quarterly
American Corrective Therapy Journal
American Educational Research Journal
American Journal of Physical Anthropology
American Journal of Physical Medicine
American Journal of Physiology
American Journal of Sports Medicine
Athletic Administration
Athletic Training
Australian Journal of Sports Medicine
British Journal of Physical Education
British Journal of Sports Medicine
Canadian Journal of the History of Sport and Physical Education
Child Development
Clinical Kinesiology
Educational and Psychological Measurement
European Journal of Applied Physiology and Occupational Physiology
Human Factors
Human Performance
International Journal of Biomechanics
International Journal of Sport Biomechanics
International Journal of Sport Psychology
International Journal of Sport Sociology
International Journal of Sports Medicine
Journal of Applied Physiology
Journal of Applied Sport Psychology
Journal of Biomechanics
Journal of Comparative and Physiological Psychology
Journal of Educational Psychology
Journal of Experimental Child Psychology
Journal of Experimental Psychology
Journal of Learning Disabilities
Journal of Motor Behavior
Journal of the Philosophy of Sport
Journal of Physical Education
Journal of Physical Education, Recreation and Dance
Journal of Physiology
Journal of Sport Behavior
Journal of Sport History
Journal of Sport Management
Journal of Sport and Exercise Psychology
Journal of Sports Medicine and Physical Fitness
Journal of Teaching in Physical Education
Medicine and Science in Sport and Exercise
The Olympian
Pediatric Exercise Science
Perceptual and Motor Skills
Physical Educator
Physical Therapy
Physician and Sportsmedicine
Physiological Reviews
Psychological Bulletin
Psychological Reviews
Psychology in the Schools
Quest
Research Quarterly for Exercise and Sport
Sociological Abstracts
Sociology of Sport Journal
The Sport Psychologist

Computer Searching

Computer service facilities can greatly expedite the literature search. Automated searching provides more effective and efficient access to indexes and information than does manual searching. The computer search covers many abstracting and indexing services in the sciences, humanities, and social sciences. There is a fee for a computer search, and the more extensive the search, the more costly. However, the fee usually is not prohibitive, especially if the searcher is careful in selecting pertinent descriptors and limiting the number of most recent and relevant documents.

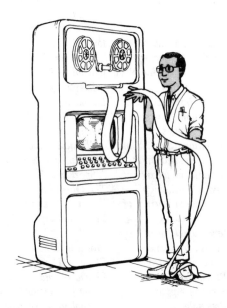

ERIC provides a computer search. The Thesaurus of ERIC Descriptors contains all descriptors that ERIC uses. A listing of all titles in the file classified according to a given set of descriptors can be provided by the computer search. The vast coverage of *Index Medicus* can be accessed through MEDLINE. A listing of approved subject headings is published annually and should be consulted before you begin a subject search. Many abstracting and indexing services in relevant fields are available, including *PsycINFO*, *Sociological Abstracts*, *Exceptional Child Education Resources*, and *Dissertation Abstracts*. Remember, a computer search cannot judge or screen as to quality, which again relates to the selection of a number of descriptors for simultaneous searching.

Today, more colleges and universities have access to some sort of computer retrieval systems. Data bases are predominantly in the sciences and social sciences. Numerous data bases are available, the most common being the Lockheed Information Systems, the System Development Corporation, Bibliographic Retrieval Services, and the National Library of Medicine.

Most data bases are machine-readable indexes that provide comprehensive bibliographies. Remember, the key to a successful literature search is careful planning. Therefore, write down your statement of the problem succinctly and then formulate cogent descriptors and key indexing terms. Printed indexes and abstracts are helpful in this regard. It is also beneficial to find one or more journal articles pertaining to your topic to assist you in the search strategy.

Searches are scheduled through your library. You will complete a form on which to specify the research statement and key words. The library personnel will be extremely helpful in the literature search process, which usually takes about a week. Search results can also be typed on-line and downloaded onto your diskette so that you can print it at your convenience. In most cases, the resulting bibliography is well worth the expense, especially in light of the comprehensiveness and the short amount of time and energy you expend.

Other Library Services

The library services available depend mostly on the size of the institution, as larger schools generally provide more financial support for the library. However, some relatively small institutions have excellent library resources that provide outstanding support for the institutional and research aspects of the school.

Besides the usual services of card catalogs, reference and circulation departments, and bibliographic collections and stack areas, libraries also offer resources and services such as copy services, newspaper rooms, government document sections, telephone directories, college catalogs, and many other special features and services. One such valuable service is the interlibrary loan, which enables you to get books, theses and dissertations (occasionally), and photocopies of articles in journals that your library does not carry. An interlibrary loan usually takes 2-4 weeks from the date you request it until it is received. Most libraries will lend material for 2 weeks from the date it is received.

Universities typically have extensive collections of resources available on *microform*, which is a general term embracing microfilm, microfiche, microcard, and microprint. Microforms are simply miniaturized photographic reproductions of the contents of a printed page. You must use special machines called *readers* to enlarge the information so it can be read.

An obvious advantage of microforms is economy of space. In addition, they are useful for acquiring material that would otherwise not be available. Rare books and manuscripts and deteriorating materials can be preserved on microform. Some journals are on microform because it represents an economical means for the library to obtain them. Collections of government documents are often contained on microform, as are ERIC publications. The library will have a reader/printer that can make paper copies of microform material. Microform holdings are normally listed in the library's card catalog system and periodical listings.

Many libraries offer guided tours, short courses for orientation to the library, and self-guided tour information. Get acquainted with your library. It will be the wisest investment of time spent as a graduate student.

Use of the Microcomputer for Literature Storage and Retrieval

You should also be aware of the capabilities of microcomputers for storing bibliographic entries, abstracts, and even reprints of studies. A number of commercial programs are available for this purpose. The information can be retrieved by the use of pertinent key words, author names, or journal names. Additions, changes, and deletions are easily accomplished, and hundreds of items can be stored on a single disk. Each new entry is automatically stored in alphabetical order, and the complete bibliography is always instantly accessible. Often laboratories (e.g., exercise science and physical education) will keep files of reprints and use a software library program for a microcomputer to catalog these materials.

READING AND RECORDING THE LITERATURE

Collecting all the related literature is a major undertaking, but the next step is even more time consuming—you must read, understand, and record the relevant information from the literature, keeping in mind one of the many (anonymous) Murphy's Laws: "No matter how many years you save an item, you will never need it until after you have thrown it away."

It is likely that the person originating this quote was a researcher working on a literature review. You may count on the fact that if you throw away one note from your literature search, that paper will be cited incorrectly in your text or reference list; or, if you throw away your notes on an article because you do not believe it is relevant to your research, your major professor, a committee member, or the journal to which you submit the paper will request inclusion of the article. Then, when you go back to locate the article in the library, either it will be ripped out of the journal, the whole journal will be missing, or a professor will have checked it out and never returned it (and the librarian will not reveal the professor's name). Therefore, when you find a particular paper, take careful and complete notes, including exact citation information.

> You may count on the fact that if you throw away one note from your literature search, that paper will be cited incorrectly in your text; or, if you throw away your notes on an article because you do not believe it is relevant, your major professor will request inclusion of the article.

To help you understand the literature you read, Table 2.2 lists each scientific phase. Once you understand what each phase really means, you should have little difficulty understanding the literature you read. In particular, you, as researcher, should note the following information from your research:

- Statement of the problem (and maybe hypotheses)
- Characteristics of the subjects
- Instruments and tests used (including reliability and validity information if provided)
- Testing procedures
- Independent and dependent variables
- Treatments applied to subjects (if an experimental study)
- Design and statistical analyses
- Findings
- Questions raised for further study
- Citations to other relevant studies not located

Furthermore, when studies are particularly relevant to the proposed research, make a photocopy. Include the complete citation on the title page (if the journal does not provide this, write in the citation yourself). Also, indicate on a note card the studies that are photocopied.

Another of the more useful ways to learn to read and understand related literature is to critique a few studies. Table 2.3 includes a series of questions to use when critiquing a study. Table 2.4 is a sample form that we use and includes suggestions for reporting critiques. A few critiquing attempts should aid you in focusing on the important information contained in research studies.

To summarize, the best system for recording relevant literature is probably a combination of note taking and photocopying. By using index cards (4-by-6-inch cards are usually large enough), the important information about most studies can be recorded and indexed by topic. Always be sure to record the complete and correct citation on the card with the appropriate citation style used by your institution (e.g., American Psychological Association [APA], *Index Medicus*).

WRITING THE LITERATURE REVIEW

After you have located and read the necessary information and have recorded the appropriate bibliographic data, you are ready to begin to write the literature review. The literature review has three basic parts:

- Introduction
- Body
- Summary and conclusions

The introduction should explain the purpose of the review and the how and why of its organization. The body of the review should be

Table 2.2 A Key to Understanding Scientific Research Literature

What the researcher said	What the researcher meant
It has long been known that . . .	I haven't bothered to look up the original reference but . . .
Of great theoretical and practical importance	Interesting to me
While it has not been possible to provide definite answers to those questions . . .	The experiment didn't work out, but I figured I could at least get a publication out of it.
The W-PO system was chosen as especially suitable to show the predicted behavior.	The researcher in the next lab had some already made up.
Three of the samples were chosen for detailed study.	The results on the others didn't make sense.
Accidentally strained during mounting	Dropped on the floor
Handled with extreme care throughout the experiment	Not dropped on the floor
Typical results are shown.	The best results are shown.

Agreement with the predicted curve is:
    excellent
    good
    satisfactory
    fair
	
	fair
	poor
	doubtful
	imaginary

It is suggested that . . . It is believed that . . . It may be that . . .	I think . . .
It is generally believed that . . .	A couple of other researchers think so, too.
It is clear that much additional work will be required before a complete understanding . . .	I don't understand it.
Unfortunately, a quantitative theory to account for these results has not been formulated.	Neither does anybody else
Correct with an order of magnitude . . .	Wrong
Thanks are due to Joe Glotz for assistance with the experiments and to John Doe for valuable discussion.	Glotz did the work and Doe explained what it meant.

organized around important topics. Finally, the review should conclude with a summary, important implications, and directions for future research. The purpose of the review is to demonstrate that your problem needs investigation and that you have considered the value of relevant past research in developing your hypotheses and methods; that is,

you know and understand what other people have done and how that relates to and supports what you plan to do.

The introduction to the review (or to topical areas within the review) is very important. If these paragraphs are not well done and interesting, the reader may skip the entire section. Attempt to attract the reader's

Table 2.3 Criteria for Critiquing a Research Paper

I. Overall impression (most important): Is the paper a significant contribution to knowledge about the area?

II. Introduction and review of literature
    A. Is the research plan developed within a reasonable theoretical framework?
    B. Is current and relevant research cited and properly interpreted?
    C. Is the statement of the problem clear, concise, testable, and derived from the theory and research reviewed?

III. Method
    A. Are relevant subject characteristics described, and are the subjects appropriate for the research?
    B. Is the instrumentation appropriate?
    C. Are testing or treatment procedures described in sufficient detail?
    D. Are the statistical analyses and research design sufficient?

IV. Results
    A. Do the results evaluate the stated problem?
    B. Is the presentation of results complete?
    C. Are the tables and figures appropriate?

V. Discussion
    A. Are the results discussed?
    B. Are the results related back to the problem, theory, and previous findings?
    C. Is there excessive speculation?

VI. References
    A. Are all references in the correct format, and are they complete?
    B. Are all references cited in the text?
    C. Are all dates in the references correct, and do they match the text citations?

VII. Abstract
    A. Does it include a statement of the purpose; description of subjects, instrumentation, and procedures; and a report of meaningful findings?
    B. Is the abstract the proper length?

VIII. General
    A. Are key words provided?
    B. Are running heads provided?
    C. Does the paper provide for use of nonsexist language, protection of human subjects, and appropriate labeling of human subjects?

The purpose of the review is to demonstrate that your problem needs investigation and that you have considered the value of relevant past research in developing your hypotheses and methods.

attention by identifying in a provocative way the important points to be covered.

The body of the literature review requires considerable attention. Relevant research must be organized, synthesized, and written in a clear, concise, and interesting way. There is no unwritten law dictating that reviews of the literature must be boring and poorly written, although we suspect that some graduate students work from that assumption. Part of the problem stems from graduate students' perceptions that they must find a way to make their scientific writing complex and wonderful as opposed to simple and straightforward. Apparently the rule is, Never use a short and simple word when a longer, more complex one can be substituted.

Although Table 2.5 is humorous, Day (1983) has provided a useful aid to potential research writers. In fact, we strongly recommend Day's book, which can easily be read in 4-6 hours. It provides many excellent and humorous examples that are valuable in

Table 2.4 Form for a Critique

I. Basic information
  A. Name of journal
  B. Publisher of journal
  C. How many articles in this issue?
  D. Are there publication guidelines for authors? Which issue?
  E. Who is editor?
  F. Is there a yearly index? Which issue?
  G. What writing style is used (APA, *Index Medicus*, etc.)?
  H. Complete reference in APA style for article you will review

II. Summary of the article

III. Critique of the article
  A. Introduction and review

  B. Method
  C. Results
  D. Discussion
  E. References
  F. Overall

IV. Attach one photocopy of the article.

V. Information about critique
  A. It must be typed (double-spaced) in APA style.
  B. Do not put it in any type of folder; just staple the pages in upper left-hand corner.
  C. Use a cover page identifying course, purpose, and yourself.
  D. Critique may not exceed five typewritten pages exclusive of cover page.

Table 2.5 Words and Expressions to Avoid

Jargon	Preferred usage	Jargon	Preferred usage
a considerable amount of	much	as of this date	today
		as to	about (or leave out)
a majority of	most	at an earlier date	previously
a number of	many	at the present time	now
absolutely essential	essential	at this point in time	now
accounted for by the fact	because	based on the fact that	because
		by means of	by, with
along the lines of	like	completely full	full
an order of magnitude faster	10 times faster	consensus of opinion	consensus
		definitely proved	proved
are of the same opinion	agree	despite the fact that	although
as a consequence of	because	due to the fact that	because
as a matter of fact	in fact (or leave out)	during the course of	during, while
as is the case	as happens	elucidate	explain

(Cont.)

Table 2.5 (Continued)

Jargon	Preferred usage	Jargon	Preferred usage
end result	result	it is clear that much additional work will be required before a complete understanding	I don't understand it
entirely eliminate	eliminate		
fabricate	make		
fewer in number	fewer		
finalize	end		
first of all	first	it is doubtful that	possibly
for the purpose of	for	it is evident that *a* produced *b*	*a* produced *b*
for the reason that	since, because		
from the point of view of	for	it is of interest to note that	(leave out)
give rise to	cause	it is often the case that	often
has the capability of	can	it is suggested that	I think
having regard to	about	it is worth pointing out in this context that	note that
in a number of cases	some		
in a position to	can, may	it may be that	I think
in a satisfactory manner	satisfactorily	it may, however, be noted that	but
in a very real sense	in a sense (or leave out)		
in case	if	it should be noted that	note that (or leave out)
in close proximity	close, near	it was observed in the course of the experiments that	we observed
in connection with	about, concerning		
in many cases	often		
in my opinion it is not an unjustifiable assumption that	I think	lacked the ability to	couldn't
		large in size	large
in order to	to	let me make one thing perfectly clear	(a snow job is coming)
in relation to	toward, to	militate against	prohibit
in respect to	about	needless to say	(leave out, and consider leaving out whatever follows it)
in some cases	sometimes		
in terms of	about		
in the event that	if	of great theoretical and practical importance	useful
in the possession of	has, have		
in view of the fact that	because, since	on a daily basis	daily
inasmuch as	for, as	on account of	because
initiate	begin, start	on behalf of	for
is defined as	is	on the basis of	by
it has been reported by Smith	Smith reported	on the grounds that	since, because
		on the part of	by, among, for
it has long been known that	I haven't bothered to look up the reference	our attention has been called to the fact that	we belatedly discovered
it is apparent that	apparently	owing to the fact that	since, because
it is believed that	I think	perform	do
it is clear that	clearly	pooled together	pooled

Jargon	Preferred usage	Jargon	Preferred usage
prior to	before	there is reason to believe	I think
protein determinations were performed	proteins were determined	this result would seem to indicate	this result indicates
quite unique	unique	through the use of	by, with
rather interesting	interesting	ultimate	last
red in color	red	utilize	use
referred to as	called	was of the opinion that	believed
relative to	about	ways and means	ways, means (not both)
resultant effect	result	we have insufficient knowledge	we don't know
smaller in size	smaller		
subsequent to	after	we wish to thank	we thank
sufficient	enough	with a view to	to
take into consideration	consider	with reference to	about (or leave out)
terminate	end	with regard to	concerning, about (or leave out)
the great majority of	most		
the opinion is advanced that	I think	with respect to	about
the question as to whether	whether	with the possible exception of	except
the reason is because	because	with the result that	so that

Note. From Day (1983, pp. 166-169). Copyright 1983 by ISI Press. Reprinted by permission.

writing for publication and for theses and dissertations.

In addition to removing as much jargon as possible (using Day's suggestions), your scientific writing should be clear and to the point. We advocate use of the KISS Principle (Keep It Simple, Stupid) as a basic tenet for writing. Many grammatical errors can be avoided by use of simple declarative sentences. Proper syntax (the way words and phrases are put together) is the secret of successful writing. We always enjoy receiving a questionnaire that includes one or more items such as the following:

Indicate your degree of success in placing your graduate students, broken down by sex.

In questioning our graduate students, none will admit that they are, although we have observed a few professors who appear to be. The following is another excerpt of improper syntax from a thesis draft:

. . . responses pertaining to suicide and death by means of a questionnaire.

We are aware that some questionnaires can be ambiguous, irrelevant, and trivial, but we had no idea they were fatal.

In Table 2.6, Day (1983) rephrases a list from a 1968 *Council of Biology Editors Newsletter.* The first 10 items are Day's, but we have included a few of our own comments as well.

As mentioned previously, the literature

Table 2.6 The Ten Commandments of Good Writing—Plus a Few Others

1. Each pronoun should agree with their antecedent.
2. Just between you and I, case is important.
3. A preposition is a poor word to end a sentence with. (Incidentally, did you hear about the streetwalker who violated a grammatical rule? She unwittingly approached a plainclothesman, and her proposition ended with a sentence.)
4. Verbs has to agree with their subjects.
5. Don't use no double negatives.
6. A writer mustn't shift your point of view.
7. When dangling, don't use participles.
8. Join clauses good, like a conjunction should.
9. Don't write a run-on sentence it is difficult when you got to punctuate it so it makes sense when the reader reads what you wrote.
10. About sentence fragments.
11. Don't use commas, which aren't necessary.
12. Its' important to use apostrophe's right.
13. Check to see if you any words out.
14. As far as incomplete constructions, they are wrong.
15. "Last but not least, lay off cliches."

review should be organized around important topics. These topics serve as subheadings in the paper to direct the reader's attention. The best way to organize the topics and the information within topics is to develop an outline. The more carefully the outline is planned, the easier the writing will be. A good task is to select a review paper from a journal or from a thesis or dissertation review of literature and reconstruct the outline the author must have used. In looking at older theses and dissertations, we find that the literature review tends to be a historical account, often presented in chronological order. We suggest that you not select one of these older studies, as this style is cumbersome and usually poorly synthesized.

To write a literature review effectively, you should write as you like to read. No one wants to read abstracts of study after study presented in chronological order. A more interesting and readable approach is to present a concept and then discuss the various findings about that concept, documenting findings by the various research reports related to it. In this way, consensus and controversy can be identified and discussed in the literature review. More relevant and important studies can be presented in greater detail and several studies with the same outcome covered in one sentence.

In a thesis or dissertation, the two important aspects of the literature review are criticism and completeness. The various studies should not simply be presented relative to a topic, but the theoretical, methodological, and interpretative aspects of the research should be criticized—not necessarily on a study-by-study basis but rather across studies. This criticism not only demonstrates the writer's grasp of the issues but also identifies problems that should be overcome in the study you are planning. Frequently, the problems identified by criticism of the literature may provide justification for your research.

Completeness (not in the sense of the length of the review but rather of reference completeness) is the other important aspect of the literature review. You should demonstrate to your committee that you have located, read, and understood all the related literature. Many studies may be redundant and only need appropriate citing, but they must be cited. The thesis or dissertation is your passport to graduation because it demonstrates your competence; therefore, never fail to be thorough. This, however, applies only to the thesis or dissertation. Writing for publication or the use of alternate thesis or dissertation formats does not require emphasizing the completeness of the literature cited (note "cited," not "read"). Journals do not have the necessary space and usually want the introduction and literature review integrated and relatively short.

SUMMARY

There are no shortcuts to locating, reading, and indexing the literature and then writing the literature review. If you follow our suggestions, however, you can do it effectively, but much hard work is still required. A good scholar is careful and thorough. Do not depend on what others report, as they are often incorrect. Look it up yourself.

No one can just sit down and write a good literature review. A carefully thought-out plan is necessary. First, outline what you propose to write, write it, and then write it again. When you are convinced that the review represents your best effort, have a knowledgeable graduate student or faculty member read it, then welcome their suggestions. Next, have a friend who is not as knowledgeable read it. If your friend can understand it, then your review is probably in good shape. Of course, your research methods professor will find something wrong, or at least something he or she thinks should be different. Just remember that professors feel obligated to find errors in graduate students' work. This obligation comes from years of reading examples of unclear writing (see Table 2.7).

Table 2.7 Examples of Unclear Writing

Sentences taken from letters received by government agencies:

- I am forwarding my marriage certificate and six children. I had seven but one died which was baptized on a half sheet of paper.
- I am writing to say that my baby was born two years old. When do I get my money?
- Mrs. Jones has not had any clothes for a year and has been visited regularly by the clergy.
- I am glad to report that my husband who is missing is dead.
- This is my eighth child. What are you going to do about it?
- Please find for certain if my husband is dead. The man I am living with can't eat or do anything until he knows.
- I am very much annoyed to find that you have branded my son illiterate. This is a dirty lie as I was married a week before he was born.
- I am forwarding my marriage certificate and my three children; one of which is a mistake as you can see.
- In accordance with your instructions, I have given birth to twins in the enclosed envelope.
- I want my money as quick as I can get it. I have been in bed with a doctor for two weeks and he doesn't do me any good. If things don't improve, I will have to send for another doctor.

Sentences taken from job recommendations that are *not quite* clear:

- In my opinion you will be very fortunate to get this person to work for you.
- All in all, I cannot say enough good things about this candidate or recommend him too highly.
- I am pleased to say this candidate is a former colleague of mine.
- I can assure you that no person would be better for this job.

Unclear excuses for missing school:

- Please excuse Mary for being absent. She was sick and I had her shot.
- Please excuse Fred from being absent yesterday. He had diarrhea and his boots leak.
- Please excuse Mary from Jim [Gym?] yesterday. She is administrating.

(Cont.)

Table 2.7 (Continued)

A couple of others:
- This horse is an eight-year-old gelding trained by the owner who races him with his wife.
- She rode 106 miles on a bicycle with 1400 other people.

Table 2.8 Library Assignment

Choose a topic in which you are interested. The topic should be fairly general. In the sources listed below find the required information concerning your topic. Limit your selections to the past 3 years if possible. Use APA style for references (or the style required by your professor).

Source	Information
1. *Current Index to Journals in Education*	One article: author, date, title, periodical, volume, page numbers
2. *Reader's Guide to Periodical Literature*	One article: author, date, title, periodical, page numbers
3. *Completed Research in Health, Physical Education, Recreation and Dance*	One article in bibliography section: author, date, title, source; one study in thesis section: author, date, title, university
4. *Index Medicus*	One article: author, date, title, periodical, volume, page numbers
5. Card catalog system	One book: author, date, title, city, publisher, call number
6. A thesis from your university	One study: author, date, title
7. A dissertation from your university	One study: author, date, title
8. *Health, Physical Education and Recreation Microform Publications Bulletin*	One study: author, date, title, university
9. *Current Contents in Social and Behavioral Sciences*	One study: author, date, title, location
10. *Dissertation Abstracts International*	One study: author, date, title, university
11. *Research Quarterly for Exercise and Sport*	One study: author, date, title, volume, page numbers
12. Look up call numbers and library location (floor level) for each of 10 references listed in this chapter.	
13. Get information (author, date, title, journal, volume number, page numbers) from the most recent issues of three journals. Try to avoid using journals that have already been cited.	

Problems

Throughout this chapter we have made several suggestions for exercises that will help you locate, synthesize, organize, critique, and write the literature review. These suggestions are summarized below. You will need to return to various points in the chapter to read about these exercises and to refer to the necessary tables.

1. Do the library assignment in Table 2.8.
2. Critique a research study in your area of interest. Use the questions in Table

2.3 as the basis for the critique. Report the critique in the form suggested by Table 2.4.

3. Select a review paper from a journal or the literature review from a thesis or dissertation. Construct the outline the author probably used to write this paper.

Chapter 3

□

Chapter 1 of the Thesis or Dissertation: Presenting the Problem

In a thesis or dissertation, the first chapter is titled "Introduction." Its purpose is to do just that: to inform the reader about the problem being studied. Several sections in the first chapter serve to convey the significance of the problem and set forth the dimensions of the particular study. This chapter discusses each of the following sections of the first chapter of a thesis or dissertation:

- Title
- Introduction
- Problem statement
- Hypothesis
- Definitions
- Assumptions and limitations
- Significance

Not all thesis advisors subscribe to the same thesis format, for there is no universally accepted one. Moreover, because of the nature of the research problem, there will be differences in format. For example, a historical study would not adhere to the same format as that used in an experimental study. We are merely presenting sections, each with a purpose and specific characteristics, typically found in a first chapter.

TITLE

Although it may seem logical to discuss the title first, it might surprise you to learn that the choice of the title is often not determined until after the study is written. However, at the time of the proposal meeting, you must have a title (even though it may be provisional), so we will discuss it first.

In recent times, the length of titles has changed, generally becoming shorter. Years ago the title was, in essence, the statement of the problem (in fact, some even included the methods section). Here is an example of a too lengthy title (*Note:* The examples we use as representing poor practices are fictional. Frequently, they have been suggested by actual studies, but any similarity to a real study is purely coincidental.):

> An Investigation of a Survey and Analysis of the Influence of PL 94-142 on the Attitudes, Teaching Methodology, and Evaluative Techniques of Randomly Selected Male and Female Physical Education Teachers in Public High Schools in Cornfield County, State of Confusion.

Simply too much information is in such a title. Day (1983) humorously responded to this problem by reporting a conversation between two students. When one asked whether the other had read a certain paper, the reply was, "Yes, I read the paper, but I haven't finished the title yet" (p. 10). A better title for the study mentioned previously would be "PL 94-142's Influence on Physical Education Teachers' Attitudes, Methodology, and Evaluations."

The purpose of the title is to convey the content, but this should be done as succinctly as possible. For example, "The Twelve

Minute Swim as a Test for Aerobic Endurance in Swimming'' (Jackson, 1978) is a good title because it tells the reader exactly what the study is about. It defines the specific purpose, which is the validation of the 12-minute swim, and it delimits the study to the assessment of aerobic endurance for swimmers.

However, do not go to the other extreme in striving for a short title. A title such as ''Professional Preparation'' is not very helpful. It does not include the field or the aspects of professional preparation that were studied. The key to the effectiveness of a short title is whether it reflects the content of the study. A title that is specific is more easily indexed and more meaningful for a potential reader who is searching for literature on a certain topic.

Avoid wasted phrases such as ''An Investigation of,'' ''An Analysis of,'' and ''A Study of,'' for they simply increase the length of the title and contribute nothing to the description of the content. Consider this title: ''A Study of Three Teaching Methods.'' Half the title consists of wasted words: ''A Study of.'' The rest of the title is not specific enough to be indexed effectively: Teaching what? What methods?

Furthermore, always be aware of your audience. You can assume that your audience is reasonably familiar with the field, the accepted terminology, and the viable problem areas. An outsider can question the relevance and importance of studies in any field. Some titles of supposedly scholarly works are downright humorous. For a rousing good time, peruse the titles of theses and dissertations completed at a university in any given year; for example, ''The Phospholipid Distribution in the Testes of the House Cricket.'' How weird can you get? We are joking of course. The point is that there is a tendency to criticize studies done in other disciplines simply because the critic is ignorant about the discipline. An example of this in our own

field could be a recent scholarly article by Grabe and Widule (1988) entitled ''Comparative Biomechanics of the Jerk in Olympic Weightlifting.'' To someone totally unfamiliar with the sport, this might seem to be a case study about some unpopular weightlifter in the Olympic Games.

INTRODUCTION

The introductory portion of a thesis or research article is designed to create interest as to the significance of the problem. The introduction is used to acquaint the reader with the problem, provide some background and necessary information, bring out areas of needed research, and then skillfully and logically lead to the specific purpose of the study.

A good introduction requires literary skill because it should flow smoothly yet be reasonably brief. Be careful not to overwhelm the reader with technical jargon, for the reader must be able to understand the problem to gain an interest in the solution. Therefore, an important rule is, Do not be too technical. A forceful, simple, and direct vocabulary is more effective for purposes of communication than scientific jargon and worship of polysyllables. Day (1983) related a classic story of the pitfalls of scientific jargon:

This reminds me of the plumber who wrote the Bureau of Standards saying he had found hydrochloric acid good for cleaning out clogged drains. The Bureau wrote back ''The efficacy of hydrochloric acid is indisputable, but the corrosive residue is incompatible with metallic permanence.'' The plumber replied that he was glad the Bureau agreed. The Bureau tried again, writing ''We cannot assume responsibility for the production of toxic and noxious residues with hydrochloric acid and suggest that you use an alternative procedure." The plumber again said that he was glad the Bureau agreed with him. Finally, the Bureau wrote to the plumber "Don't use hydrochloric acid. It eats hell out of pipes." (pp. 147-148)

> Do not be too technical. A forceful, simple, and direct vocabulary is more effective than scientific jargon.

Audience awareness is very important. Again, you can assume that the reader is reasonably informed about the topic (or he or she probably would not be reading it in the first place). However, even an informed reader needs some refresher background information to understand the nature of the problem, to be sufficiently interested, and to fully appreciate the author's rationale for studying the problem. You must remember that your audience has not been as completely and recently immersed in this particular area of research as you have been.

The introductory paragraphs must create interest in the study; thus, your writing skill and knowledge of the topic are especially valuable in the introduction. The narrative should introduce the necessary background information quickly and explain the rationale behind the study. A smooth, unified, well-written introduction should lead to the statement of the problem with such clarity that the reader could state the purpose of the study before specifically reading it.

> A smooth, unified, well-written introduction should lead to the statement of the problem with such clarity that the reader could state the purpose of the study before specifically reading it.

The following introductions were selected from a research journal for their brevity of presentation as well as for their effectiveness. This is not to say that brevity in itself is a criterion, for some topics require more comprehensive introductions than others. For example, studies developing or validating a theoretical model usually necessitate longer introductions than does an applied research topic. Furthermore, theses and dissertations almost always have longer introductions than journal articles simply because of the page-cost considerations in the latter.

The following examples specify some of the desirable features in an introduction, including a general introduction, background information, a mention of gaps in the literature and areas of needed research, and a logical progression leading to the statement of the problem.

Examples of Good Introductions

Example #1 (From Blattner & Noble, 1979). Reprinted by permission from *Research Quarterly for Exercise and Sport*, **50**, pp. 583-588. *RQ* is a publication of the American Alliance for Health, Physical Education, Recreation and Dance, 1900 Association Dr., Reston, VA 22091.

[General Introduction]

Vertical jumping ability is of considerable importance in numerous athletic events, and coaches and physical educators have used various training methods to improve this ability. Two of the most recent training methods are isokinetic and plyometric exercises. The purported advantage of isokinetic exercises is that they allow the muscles to work at maximal force throughout the entire range of motion for each and every repetition, thereby providing a greater training stimulus. The effectiveness of such exercises in improving vertical jumping performance has been demonstrated in several studies during the past decade (Hunter, 1976; Knight & George,

1972; Tanner, 1971; Testone, 1972; Van Oteghan, 1975).

[*Background Information*]

Plyometric exercise is a relatively new concept of training that applies the specificity principle regarding the preset stretch condition of the muscle prior to explosive contraction (Wilt, 1975). The effects of plyometric exercises in increasing vertical jumping performance have been studied experimentally (Herman, 1976; Parcells, 1976; Scoles, 1978),

[*Lead-In*]

but no attempt has been made to determine if they are more effective than isokinetic exercises.

Example #2 (From Byrd & Thomas, 1983). Reprinted by permission from *Research Quarterly for Exercise and Sport*, **54**, pp. 296-298. *RQ* is a publication of the American Alliance for Health, Physical Education, Recreation and Dance, 1900 Association Dr., Reston, VA 22091.

[*General Introduction*]

Interest in the determination of body composition in athletes and in the general population has increased in the last 10 years. The two most widely used methods are anthropometric techniques and hydrostatic weighing (HW), with the latter considered the more accurate (Behnke, 1961; Buskirk, 1961). Body weight, underwater weight, and lung volume are variables which are measured to compute HW body density. Investigators have observed that a significant change in body weight alone, due to varying hydration levels, does affect the determination of body density (Girandola, Wiswell, & Romero, 1977; Thomas & Etheridge, 1979).

[*Background Information*]

Previous research indicates that body weight increases due to fluid retention may occur during the normal menstrual cycle. For example, Keates and Fitzgerald (1976) reported that a rise in leg volume

occurred at midcycle in 30 females due to peripheral blood flow and venous distensibility. Weekly changes in leg volume were found in all of the cycles, the changes varying between 30 and 100 ml of water in different individuals. Bruce and Russel (1962) reported a premenstrual body weight increase which seldom exceeded 0.5 kg in 10 subjects on a fixed intake of food, water, and sodium, as well as a controlled amount of exercise. Thorn, Nelson, and Thorn (1938) noted an average weight gain of 1.0 kg during the ovulation stage of the menstrual cycle in 38 women.

[*Lead-In*]

Therefore, the HW method of determining body density may have varying reliability depending on the time during the menstrual cycle when the woman is measured.

See if you can write the purpose for each study. It should be possible to state the purposes at this point.

STATEMENT OF THE PROBLEM

The statement of the problem follows the introduction. We should point out that the review of literature is often included in the introductory section and thus precedes the statement of the problem. If this is the case, then a brief statement of the purpose should appear fairly soon in the introductory section before the review of literature.

The statement of the problem in example #1 from Blattner and Noble is "To compare the effects of isokinetic and plyometric training on the vertical jumping performance of college males." The statement of the problem in the Byrd and Thomas study is also obvious from the introduction. The purpose was stated as "To determine if weight fluctuations during the menstrual cycle are great enough to affect body density and percent fat as assessed by hydrostatic weighing."

Identifying the Variables

The statement of the problem should be rather brief and to the point. However, when the study has a number of subpurposes, this is not always easily accomplished. The statement of the problem should identify the different variables in the study, including the independent variable, the dependent variable, and the categorical variable (if any). Usually, some control variables can also be identified in the statement of the problem.

The independent and dependent variables have already been mentioned in chapter 1. The independent variable is the experimental, or treatment, variable; it is the "cause." The dependent variable is what is measured to assess the effects of the independent variable; it is the "effect."

A *categorical variable* is sometimes referred to as a *moderator variable* (Tuckman, 1978). This variable is a kind of independent variable, except that it cannot be manipulated because it is categorized by, for example, age, race, and sex. It is studied to determine whether the cause-and-effect relationship of the independent and dependent variables is different in the presence of the categorical variable or variables.

The following is an actual study in which the independent, dependent, and categorical variables can be identified. Anshel and Marisi (1978) studied the effect of synchronized and asynchronized movement to music on endurance performance. One group performed an exercise in synchronization to background music; one group exercised with background music that was not synchronized to the pace of the exercise; and a third group exercised with no background music.

The independent variable was the background music condition. There were three levels of this variable: synchronized music, asynchronized music, and no music. The dependent variable was endurance performance, which was reflected by the amount of time the subject could exercise on a bicycle ergometer until exhaustion.

In this study, the endurance performances of men and women under the synchronized, asynchronized, and absence-of-music conditions were compared. The authors thus sought to determine whether men responded differently than women to the exercise conditions. Sex, then, represented a categorical variable. Not all studies have categorical variables, however. In the isokinetic-plyometric study (Blattner & Noble, 1979) referred to in the introduction, there was no categorical variable. The independent variable was type of training (one group used isokinetic exercises, one group used plyometric exercises, and the control group did not train). The dependent variable was vertical jumping performance. If, for example, the authors thought it important to compare training effects of athletes and nonathletes, then this would be a categorical variable.

Control variables are factors that might influence the results and are kept out of the study. The researcher chooses not to assess a variable's possible effect on the relationship between the independent and dependent variables, so this variable is controlled. For example, suppose a researcher is comparing stress-reduction methods on the competitive state anxiety of gymnasts before dual meets. The years of competitive experience of the subjects might have a bearing on their anxiety scores, so the researcher could control the variable of experience by having subjects all of similar experience.

A control variable could become a categorical variable if the researcher wishes to study it. In the previous example, if half the subjects were experienced (e.g., 5 years of experience) and half inexperienced (1 year), then experience would be a categorical variable. Of course, amounts of experience other than these two levels would be controlled by not being included.

In the study of the effects of synchronized music on endurance (Anshel & Marisi, 1978), the factor of fitness level was controlled by giving all the subjects a physical working capacity test. Then, on the basis of this test, each subject exercised at a work load that would bring about a heart rate of 170 bpm. Thus, even though the ergometer resistance settings would be different from subject to subject, all subjects would be exercising at approximately the same relative work load; the differences in fitness were controlled in this manner. Another way of controlling fitness as a variable would be to test subjects on a fitness test and just select those subjects of a certain level of fitness.

Extraneous variables refer to those factors that could affect the relationship between the independent and dependent variables but that are not included or controlled. The possible influence of an extraneous variable is usually brought out in the discussion section. Anshel and Marisi (1978) speculated that some of the differences in the performances of men and women might be due to the reluctance of the females to exhibit maximum effort in the presence of a male experimenter. Consequently, this would be an extraneous variable (all the variables are discussed in more detail in chapter 14).

Rarely are the variables labeled as such in the actual statement of the problem. Occasionally, the researcher will identify the independent and dependent variables, but mostly these variables are just implied. Often, only one or two sentences are necessary to state the problem. In the previous Blattner and Noble example, the statement of the problem following the introduction was "To compare the effects of isokinetic and plyometric training on the vertical jumping performance of college males." We have already identified the independent and dependent variables and have observed that there were no categorical variables. Can you identify any control variables? If you answered age and sex, you are correct. Age was controlled by using only college-age subjects and sex by using only males.

In summary, an effectively constructed introduction leads smoothly to the purpose of the study. This purpose is expressed as the statement of the problem and should be as clear and concise as the subpurposes, or variables, allow it to be.

Structuring the Problem Statement

To achieve clarity in the statement of the problem, a final but important aspect you must consider is sentence structure, or syntax. For example, suppose a researcher conducted a study whose purpose was "To compare sprinters and distance runners on anaerobic power, as measured by velocity in running up a flight of stairs." Observe the difference in meaning if the researcher had worded the purpose as "To compare the anaerobic power of sprinters and distance runners while running up a flight of stairs." It sounds as though the researcher would have to be in good shape to make those comparisons while running up stairs. Another example of faulty syntax was the case in which the purpose of the study was "To assess gains in quadriceps strength in albino mice using electrical stimulation.'' Those mice had to be awfully clever to use electrical instruments.

RESEARCH HYPOTHESIS

After you have stated the research problem you must present the hypothesis. The formulation of hypotheses was discussed in chapter 1. The discussion here is on the statement of the hypotheses and the distinction between research hypotheses and the null hypothesis. Remember that research hypotheses are the expected results. In the study by Anshel and Marisi (1978), a research hypothesis might be that endurance performance would be enhanced by exercising to synchronized music. The introduction produces a rationale for that hypothesis. Another hypothesis might be that exercise to asynchronized music would be more effective than exercising with no background music (because of the pleasurable sensory stimuli blocking the unpleasant stimuli associated with the fatiguing exercise). As a further example, a researcher in cardiac rehabilitation might hypothesize that distance from the exercise center is more influential as a factor in exercise adherence of patients than the type of activities offered in the cardiac rehabilitation program. In the example given in chapter 1, a dance teacher hypothesized that the use of videotape in the instructional program would enhance the learning of dance skills.

In contrast, the *null hypothesis* is primarily used in the statistical test for the reliability of the results and says that there are no differences between treatments (or no relationship between variables). For example, any observed difference or relationship is due simply to chance (see chapter 7). The null hypothesis is usually not the research hypothesis. Generally, the researcher expects one method to be better than others or antici-

pates a relationship between two variables. In other words, a person does not embark on a study if nothing is expected to happen. On the other hand, a researcher sometimes hypothesizes that one method is just as good as another. For example, in the multitude of studies done in the 1950s and 1960s on isometric versus isotonic exercises, it was often hypothesized that the ''upstart'' isometric exercise was just as effective as the traditional isotonic exercise, provided there was regular specific knowledge of results. In a study on the choice of recreational activities of mentally retarded children, Matthews (1979) showed that most research in this area, which reported differences between retarded and nonretarded children, failed to consider socioeconomic status. Consequently, he hypothesized that there were no differences in frequency of participation in recreational activities between mildly mentally retarded and nonretarded children when socioeconomic status was held constant.

Furthermore, sometimes the researcher does not expect differences in some aspects of the study but does expect a difference in others. For example, a researcher might hypothesize that children of high aptitude in learning would do better with one style of teaching, whereas children of low aptitude would fare better with another style. In a study of age differences in the strategy for recall of movement (Thomas, Thomas, Lee, Testerman, & Ashy, 1983), the authors hypothesized that because location is automatically encoded in memory, there would be no real difference between younger and older children in remembering location (where an event happened during a run). However, they hypothesized that there would be a difference in remembering distance because the older child spontaneously uses a strategy for remembering and the younger child does not. The formulation of hypotheses is a very important aspect of defining and delimiting the research problem.

OPERATIONAL DEFINITIONS

Another task in the preparation of the first chapter of a thesis or dissertation is operationally defining certain terms so that the researcher and the reader can adequately evaluate the results. It is imperative that the dependent variable be operationally defined.

So what is an operational definition? It is an observable phenomenon, as opposed to a synonym definition or dictionary definition. To illustrate, a study such as Anshel and Marisi's (1978), which investigated the effects of music on forestalling fatigue, must operationally define "fatigue." The author cannot use a synonym, such as "exhaustion," because that is not concrete enough. We all might have our own concepts of what fatigue is, but if we are going to say that some independent variable has an effect on fatigue, we must supply some observable evidence of changes in fatigue. Therefore, "fatigue" must be operationally defined. In Anshel and Marisi's study, the term "fatigue" was not actually used, but from their description of procedures we can infer its operational definition as being when the subject was unable to maintain the pedaling rate of 50 revolutions per minute for 10 consecutive seconds.

Another researcher might define "fatigue" as the point when maximal heart rate was achieved; still another might define "fatigue" as the point of maximal oxygen consumption. In all cases, though, it must be an observable criterion.

A study dealing with dehydration must provide an operational definition such as a loss of 5% of body weight. The term "obesity" could be defined as having 25% body fat (for males). A study of different teaching methods on learning must operationally define "learning." To use the old definition "a change in behavior" is meaningless in providing evidence of learning. Learning might be demonstrated by five successful maze traversals or some other observable performance criterion.

You may not always agree with the investigator's definitions, but at least you know how a particular term is being used. A common mistaken notion with novice researchers is to think that every term needs to be defined. (We have seen master's students define terms not even used in their studies!) An example of an unnecessary definition would be in a study dealing with the effects of strength training on changes in self-concept. "Self-concept" would need to be defined (probably as represented by some scale), but the term "strength" would not. The strength-training program used would be described in the methods section. Basically, operational definitions are directly related to the research hypotheses because, if you predict that some treatment will produce some effect, you must define how that effectiveness will be manifested.

BASIC ASSUMPTIONS AND LIMITATIONS

Besides writing the introduction, stating the research problem and hypothesis, and operationally defining your terms, you must outline the basic assumptions and limitations under which you performed your research.

Assumptions

Every study has certain fundamental premises without which it could not proceed. In other words, you must assume that certain conditions will exist and that the particular behaviors in question can be observed and measured (along with various other basic suppositions). A study in pedagogy that compares teaching methods must assume that the teachers involved are capable of promoting learning; if this assumption is not made, the whole study is worthless. Furthermore, in a learning study the researcher must assume that the sample selection (e.g., random selection) results in a normal distribution with regard to learning capacity.

A study designed to assess an attitude toward exercise is based on the assumption that this attitude can be reliably demonstrated and measured. Furthermore, you can assume that the subjects will respond truthfully, at least for the most part. If you cannot assume those things, you might as well not waste your time conducting the study.

Of course, the experimenter does everything possible to increase the credibility of the premises. The researcher takes great care in selecting measuring instruments, in sampling, and in gathering data with regard to such things as standardized instructions and motivating techniques. Nevertheless, the researcher still must rely on certain basic assumptions.

Consider the following studies. Johnson (1979) investigated the effects of different levels of fatigue on visual recognition of previously learned material. Among his basic assumptions were that (a) the mental capacities of the subjects were within the normal range for university students, (b) the subjects understood the directions, (c) the mental task was representative of the types of mental tasks encountered in athletics, and (d) the physical task demands were representative of the levels of exertion commonly experienced in athletics.

Lane (1983) compared skinfold profiles of black and white girls and boys and tried to determine which skinfold sites best indicated total body fatness with regard to race, sex, and age. Among her assumptions were that (a) the skinfold caliper is a valid and reliable instrument for measuring subcutaneous fat, (b) skinfold measurements taken at the body sites are indicative of the subcutaneous fat stores in the limbs and trunk, and (c) the sum of all skinfolds represents a valid indication of body fatness.

In some physiological studies, the subjects are instructed (and agree) to fast or to refrain from smoking or drinking liquids for a specified period of time before testing. Obviously, unless the study is conducted in some type of prison environment, the experimenter cannot physically monitor the subjects' activities. Consequently, a basic assumption is that the subjects will follow instructions.

Limitations

Every study also has limitations. Some refer to the scope of the study, which is usually imposed by the researcher. These are sometimes called *delimitations*. Kroll (1971) has described delimitations as choices the experimenter makes to effect a workable research problem, such as the use of one particular personality test in the assessment of personality characteristics. Moreover, in a study dealing with individual-sport athletes, the researcher may choose to restrict the selection of subjects to just two or three sports, simply because all individual sports could not be included in one study. Thus the researcher delimits the study. You probably notice that these delimitations are very similar to operational definitions. Although they are similar, they are not alike. For example, the size of the sample is a delimitation but would not be included under operational definitions.

You can also see that basic assumptions are entwined with delimitations as well as with operational definitions. The researcher must proceed on the assumption that the restrictions imposed on the study will not be so confining as to destroy the external validity (generalizability) of results.

Remember, theses or dissertations do not have one "correct" format. An examination of studies will show numerous variations in organization. You will see some studies that have delimitations and limitations described in separate sections. Some will use a combination heading, some will list only one heading but include both in the description, and so on. As with all aspects of format, much depends on how the advisor was taught. Graduate schools often allow great latitude in format as long as the study is internally consistent. You will even find considerable differences in format within the same department.

Limitations are possible shortcomings or influences that either cannot be controlled or are the results of the delimitations imposed by the investigator. In the example Kroll (1971) used of delimiting the scope of the study to just two sports to represent individual-sport athletes, there is an automatic limitation with respect to how well these represent all individual sports. Moreover, if the researcher is studying personality traits of these athletes and delimits the measurement of personality to just one test, this results in a limitation. Furthermore, there is one (or more) limitation in all instruments as to the truthfulness of the responses in which the subject responds to questions about his or her behavior, likes, or interests.

Thus, you can see that limitations also accompany the basic assumptions to the extent that the assumptions fail to be justified; and, as with assumptions, the investigator tries as much as possible to reduce limitations that might stem from faulty procedures. In Johnson's 1979 study of fatigue effects on visual recognition of previously learned material, he had to have the subjects first learn the material. He established criteria for learning (operational definition) and tried to control for overlearning (i.e., differences in the level of learning). However, he recognized that despite his efforts a limitation was that there may have been differences in the degree of learning that could certainly influence recognition.

In the study of skinfold profiles by Lane (1983), she had to delimit the study to a certain number of subjects in one part of Baton Rouge, Louisiana. Consequently, a limitation was that the children were from only one geographical location. She also recognized that there are changes in body fatness associated with the onset of puberty, but she was unable to obtain data on puberty or other indices of maturation, and this therefore posed a limitation. Still another limitation was the inability to control possible influences on skinfold measurement, such as dehydration and other diurnal variations. Finally, because there are no internationally recognized standard body sites for skinfold measurement, generalizability may have been limited to the body sites used in this study.

You should not be overzealous in searching for limitations, or you can apologize away the worth of the study. For example, one of our advisees who was planning to meet with his proposal committee was overapologetic with these anticipated limitations:

- The sample size may be too small.
- The tests may not represent the parameter in question.
- The training sessions may be too short.
- The investigator lacks adequate measurement experience.

As a result, there was a major revision in the proposal and a reassessment of the method.

Remember, there is no perfect study. You must carefully analyze the delimitations to determine whether the resulting limitations outweigh the delimitations. In addition, careful planning and painstaking methodology will increase the validity of the results, thus greatly reducing possible deficiencies in a study.

SIGNIFICANCE OF THE STUDY

The inevitable question you face at both the proposal meeting and the final oral exams deals with the worth, or significance, of the study, which may be asked in different ways, such as, So what? or, What good is it? or, How is this of any importance to your profession? Regardless of the manner in which the question is asked, it can be unsettling and must be dealt with. Perhaps because of the inevitability of the question being asked, most students are required to include a section in the first chapter titled "Significance of the Study," or sometimes, "The Need for the Study."

Basic and Applied Research Revisited

To a large extent, the worth of the research study is judged by whether it is basic or applied research. In chapter 1, we explained that basic research does not have immediate social significance; it usually deals with theoretical problems and is conducted in a very controlled laboratory setting. Applied research addresses immediate problems for improving practice. There is less control but ideally more real-world application. Consequently, basic and applied research cannot be evaluated by the same criteria.

The significance of a basic research study obviously depends on the specific purpose of the study, but usually the criteria focus on the extent to which the study contributes to the formulation or validation of some theory. The worth of applied research must be evaluated on the basis of its contribution to the solution of some immediate problem.

Writing the Significance-of-the-Study Section: Continuity with the Introduction

The significance section is often a difficult one to write, probably because the student thinks only in terms of the practicality of the study, for example, how the results can be immediately used to improve some aspect of the profession. One of our students, frantic to find some application from a rather theoretical study, suggested that the results could possibly be used in the space program. (Talk about far out!)

Kroll (1971) emphasized the importance of maintaining continuity of the significance section with the introduction. Too often the sections are written with different frames of reference instead of a continuous flow of thought. The significance section should focus on such things as contradictory findings of previous research and gaps in knowledge in particular areas. Difficulties in measuring aspects of the phenomenon in question are sometimes emphasized. Rationale for the need to verify existing theories may be the focus of the section in some studies, whereas in others the practical application is the main concern.

> In being asked the inevitable question in the final orals about the significance of the study, do not reply with "It was necessary to get my degree."

Just as the length of the introduction varies, the length of the significance section varies considerably from study to study. A sample of a significance section in a study referred to previously (Lane, 1983) may serve to illustrate an approach that focuses on some conflicts between previous research findings and present practice.

Since the measurement of body composition has become an important aspect of physical fitness testing, the validity, reliability and administrative feasibility of the measurements are of paramount concern. Adult formulas for estimating percent fat are not considered valid for children, thus skinfolds are in themselves used as measures of body composition.

The AAHPERD Health Related Physical Fitness Test Manual (1980) contains two skinfold measurements: the triceps and subscapula. Norms for the total of these two measures are provided for boys and girls ages 6 to 17 years. Abbreviated norms are also given for the triceps skinfold only. Norms were taken from HES data (Johnston et al., 1974). There is minimal evidence as to why these two body sites were selected, especially when one, the subscapula, poses some problem with regard to modesty. If the triceps and subscapula were selected as representing one from the limbs and one from the trunk, are they the most predictive of total fatness as indicated by the sum of several skinfolds from the limbs and trunk? Furthermore, if some sites are equally predictive, the ease of administration needs to be considered.

Of major significance in this study is whether the skinfolds which best represent body fatness in white children are equally suitable for black children. Authors (Cronk & Roche, 1982; Harsha et al., 1974; Johnston et al., 1974) have reported that there are differences in skinfold thicknesses between black and white children, yet the AAHPERD norms make no distinction. If norms are to be of value they must be representative of the population for which they are intended. Moreover, there may be greater differences in fatness between blacks and whites at different ages.

Similarly, it may be that a different combination of skinfolds would be more valid for girls than boys. It does not seem to be of any great administrative advantage to use the same sites for both sexes if other sites are equally valid indicators of total fatness. (pp. 14-15) Reprinted by permission.

A final word of warning: In being asked the inevitable question in the final orals about the significance of the study, do not reply with ''It was necessary to get my degree.''

The stony silence will serve only to unnerve you.

THE DIFFERENCE IN THESIS FORMAT AND THE RESEARCH ARTICLE

A mere glance at research articles in journals reveals that a number of the sections found in the traditional thesis or dissertation described in this chapter are missing. At least two reasons account for this. The first is financial; periodicals are concerned about publishing costs, so brevity is emphasized. Second, a kind of novice-master ritual seems to be in operation. The novice is required to explicitly state the hypotheses, define terms, state assumptions, recognize limitations, and justify the worth of the study in writing. Certainly these steps are all part of defining and delimiting the research problem, and it is undoubtedly a worthwhile experience to address each step formally.

The research journal author, on the other hand, need not explain the step-by-step procedure he or she used in developing the problem. Typically, a research journal has an introduction that includes a short review of literature. The length varies considerably, and some journals insist on very brief introductions.

The purpose of the study is nearly always given but is usually not designated by a heading; rather, it is often the last sentence or so in the introduction. For example, in 30 articles in the *Research Quarterly for Exercise and Sport*, 24 had sentences at the end of the introduction that began with the words "The purpose of the study was . . ."; 1 had a section titled "Purpose of the Study"; 4 indicated the purpose with sentences such as "This study was designed to . . ." or "The intent of the study was . . ."; and 1 study did not state the purpose at all. In these cases, the authors and editors felt that the purpose was evident from the title and introduction.

Research hypotheses are sometimes given but with little uniformity. Of course, journals may vary, but we would estimate that the hypotheses are stated in less than 30% of the articles. Operational definitions, assumptions, limitations, and significance of the study are virtually never stated in research articles. Apparently, for the "master" researcher these steps were accomplished in the development of the problem and are understood, obvious, or both and need not be stated. If the article is well written, you should be able to discern the operational definitions, the assumptions and limitations, and the independent, dependent, categorical, and control variables even though they are not specifically stated. Moreover, the significance of the study should be implicitly obvious if the author has written a good introduction.

SUMMARY

This chapter discussed the information that is typically presented in the first chapter of a thesis or dissertation (excluding the review of literature). First, the length and substance of the study title were considered. The importance of a good, short, descriptive title with respect to indexing and searching the literature is sometimes overlooked.

The introduction of a research study is often difficult to write. It requires a great deal of thought, effort, and skill to convey to the reader the importance and potential worth of the study. If it is poorly done, the reader may not bother to read the rest of the study.

The statement of the problem and the research hypotheses are common features of most research studies, whether they are theses or dissertations, journal articles, or research grants. Operational definitions, assumptions, limitations and delimitations, and the significance of the study are primarily included only in theses and dissertations. The purpose of these sections is basically to help (or force) the researcher to succinctly define and delimit the research problem.

Operational definitions provide specific descriptions of how certain terms (especially the dependent variables) are being used in a particular study. Assumptions identify the basic conditions that must be assumed to exist for the results of the study to have credibility. Delimitations relate to the scope of the study imposed by the researcher, such as the number and characteristics of the subjects, the treatment conditions, and the specific dependent variables that are used. Limitations are possible influences on the results that are consequences of the delimitations or that cannot be completely controlled.

The significance of the study section forces the researcher to address the inevitable question of the worth of the study. It should be a continuation of the introduction in terms of the contextual flow. It usually calls attention to the relationship (and differences) between this study and previous ones, controversies and gaps in the literature, and the contribution that this study might make to the practitioner, existing theoretical models, or both.

Problems

1. For each of the following brief descriptions of studies, write a title, the purpose or purposes, and three research hypotheses.

   The researchers assessed the following:

   a. Skill acquisition of three groups of fourth-grade boys and girls who had been taught by different teaching styles (A, B, and C)

   b. Self-concept of two groups of boys (a low-strength group and a high-strength group) before and after a strength-training program

   c. Body composition (estimated percent fat) using the electrical impedance analysis method on subjects at normal hydration and again after they had dehydrated

   d. Grade point averages of male and female athletes of major and minor (club) sports from large universities and small, private colleges

2. Locate five articles from research journals, and for each try to determine (a) the hypotheses, if not stated; (b) the operational definitions; (c) the limitations; and (d) the assumptions.

Chapter 4

☐

Chapter 2 of the Thesis or Dissertation: Formulating the Method

The previous chapter provided an overview of the introduction chapter in the proposal for a thesis or dissertation. As already indicated, some formats include the literature review (see chapter 2 in this book) in the first chapter, whereas others have the literature review as a separate chapter. Regardless, once the introduction has been completed, the researcher must describe the methodology for the research. Typically, this chapter is labeled ''Method,'' and we overview it here. For our purposes, let's assume that the literature review was included in the first chapter of your thesis or dissertation and that the methods chapter is chapter 2.

Much of the remainder of this book is focused on the method: who the subjects are (this chapter), how to analyze the results (Part II), how to design the study (Part III), and how to measure the variables and associated procedures (Part IV). The purpose of the method chapter is to explain how to conduct the study. The standard rule is, The description should be thorough enough for a competent researcher to reproduce the study. Science as we know it today grew out of the murky lore of the Middle Ages (e.g., sorcery and religious ritual).

But while witches, priests, and chiefs were developing taller and taller hats, scientists worked out a method for determining the validity of their experimental results: they learned to ask, ''are they reproducible?''—that is, would anyone using the same materials and methods arrive at the same results? For example, it is very important to scientists that two iron balls of unequal mass dropped together from the leaning tower of Pisa hit the ground simultaneously whether dropped by Galileo in 1590 or Mr. T today. (Scherr, 1983, p. ix)

> The purpose of the method chapter is to explain how to conduct the study. The standard rule is, The description should be thorough enough for a competent researcher to reproduce the study.

Dissertations and theses differ considerably from published articles in the methodological details provided. Journals try to conserve space, but space is no issue in a dissertation or thesis. Thus, where standard techniques in a journal article are referenced only to another published study (in an easily obtainable journal), a thesis or dissertation should provide considerably greater detail. Note that we indicated a technique could be referenced to an easily obtainable journal. When writing for publication, use common sense in this regard. Consider, for example, this citation:

Farke, F.R., Frankenstein, C., & Frickenfrack, F. (1921). Flexion of the feet by footfetish feet feelers. *Research Abnormal: Perception of Feet*, **22**, 1-26.

By most standards, this citation would not be considered easily obtainable. Therefore, if you are in doubt, give the details of the study or technique.

Furthermore, because theses and dissertations have appendices, much of the detail that would clutter and extend the method chapter may be placed there. Examples include exact instructions to subjects, samples of tests and answer sheets, diagrams and pictures of equipment, sample data-recording sheets, and informed-consent agreements.

The method chapter has four sections:

• Subjects
• Instruments or apparatus
• Procedures
• Design and analysis

The purpose of this planning is to eliminate any alternate or rival hypotheses. This really means that when you design the study correctly and the results are as predicted, the only explanation is what you did in the research. Using a previous example to illustrate, our hypothesis is that "Shoe size and mathematics performance are positively related during elementary school." To test this hypothesis, we go to an elementary school, measure shoe sizes, and obtain standardized mathematics performance scores of the children in Grades 1-5. When we plot these

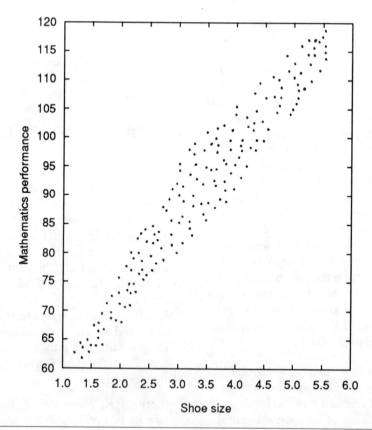

Figure 4.1 Relationship of academic performance and shoe size of children Grades 1-5.

scores, they appear as in Figure 4.1, each dot representing a single child. If you move from the dot to the *y*-axis, you can read their mathematics performance scores. By referring to the *x*-axis, you can see their shoe sizes. Look! we say, we are correct. As shoe size gets larger, the children's mathematics performance increases. Eureka! All we need to do is buy the children bigger shoes and their mathematics performance will improve. But wait a minute! The authors have overlooked two things. The obvious one is that there is a rival explanation: Both shoe size and mathematics performance are related to age. That really explains the relationship. As the kids get older, their feet get bigger and they perform better on mathematics tests. In addition, we made another error, which we will discuss in a later chapter; namely, because two things are related does not mean that one causes the other. Correlation does not imply causation. Obviously, we cannot improve children's math performance by stretching their feet.

In research we want to use the *MAXICON principle*: MAXimize true variance, or increase the odds that the real relationship or explanation will be discovered; minImize error variance, or reduce all the mistakes that could creep into the study to disguise the true relationship; and CONtrol extraneous variance, or make sure that rival hypotheses are not the real explanations of the relationship.

SUBJECTS

This section of the second chapter of a thesis or dissertation describes how and why the subjects were selected and what characteristics they have that are pertinent to the study.

Describing Subjects

The exact number of subjects should be given, as should any loss of subjects during

the time of study. In the proposal for the study, some of this information may not be exact. For example, the following might describe the potential subjects:

Subjects. For this study 48 males, ranging in age from 21 to 34 years, will be randomly selected from a group ($N = 147$) of well-trained distance runners ($\dot{V}O_2max = 60$ ml $\cdot$ kg $\cdot$ min^{-1} or higher) who have been competitive runners for at least 2 years. Subjects will be randomly assigned to one of four groups ($n = 12$).

Once the study is completed, details would be available on the subjects, so now this section might read as follows:

Subjects. In this study 48 males, ranging in age from 21 to 34 years, were randomly selected from a group ($N = 147$) of well-trained runners ($\dot{V}O_2max = 60$ ml $\cdot$ kg $\cdot$ min^{-1} or higher) who had been competitive runners for at least 2 years. The subjects had the following characteristics (standard deviations in parentheses): age, $M = 26$ years (3.3); height, $M = 172.5$ cm (7.5); weight, $M = 66.9$ kg (8.7); and $\dot{V}O_2max$, $M = 65$ ml $\cdot$ kg $\cdot$ min^{-1} (4.2). Subjects were randomly assigned to one of four groups ($n = 12$).

The subjects' characteristics listed are extremely pertinent in an exercise physiology study but not at all, for example, in a study of equipment use by children on the playground. The nature of the research dictates the subject characteristics of interest to the researcher. Carefully think through the important characteristics you will report in your research. Look at related studies for ideas of important characteristics to report.

The characteristics about subjects you identify and report must be clearly specified. Note in the example that "well-trained runners" were exactly defined; that is, their

$\dot{V}O_2$max must be equal to 60 ml • kg • min^{-1} or higher. Where subjects of different ages are to be used is another good example. Just to say 7-, 9-, and 11-year-old children will be the subjects is not sufficient. How wide an age range is 7 years old: $\pm$ 1 month, $\pm$ 6 months, or what? In the proposal, you may say that 7-, 9-, and 11-year-old children will be included in the study. At the time of testing, each age will be limited to a $\pm$ 6-month age range. Then, when the thesis or dissertation is actually written, it may read as follows:

At each age level 15 children were selected for this study. The mean ages are as follows (standard deviations in parentheses): the youngest group, 7.1 years (4.4 months); 9-year-olds, 9.2 years (3.9 months); and the oldest group, 11.2 years (4.1 months).

In the proposal the age range is delimited, whereas in the thesis or dissertation the actual means (group averages) and standard deviations (group variability) for each age-group are reported.

Ethics in Research: Protecting Subjects

Most of the research in physical education, exercise science, and sport science deals with humans, oftentimes children. Therefore, the researcher must be concerned about any circumstances in the research setting or activity that could harm the participants. Harm should be interpreted to mean to frighten, embarrass, or negatively affect the lives of subjects (Tuckman, 1978). Of course, researchers always run the risk of creating a problem. What must be balanced is the degree of risk and the rights of the subjects. The important issue is the potential value of research in contributing to knowledge, to the development of technology, and to the improvement of people's lives. Tuckman (1978) has summarized the subjects' rights that experimenters must consider:

Research Subjects' Rights*

- *The right to privacy or nonparticipation.* This includes the fact that researchers should not ask for unnecessary information and should obtain direct consent from adults and consent from parents for children (as well as the consent of the children themselves where appropriate).

- *The right to remain anonymous.* The researcher should explain that the study focuses on group data and that an I.D. number (rather than the subject's name) will be used to record data.

- *The right to confidentiality.* Subjects should be told who (keep this to as few people as possible) will actually have access to original data by which the subject might be identified.

- *The right to expect experimenter responsibility.* In particular that the experimenter is well meaning and that he or she will be sensitive to human dignity. If the subject is not told the purpose of the study (or is misled), the subject must be debriefed immediately after the completion of testing.

Qualitative research (discussed in detail in chapter 15) lends itself to some potential ethical problems because of the close, personal interaction with subjects. The researcher often spends a great deal of time in contact with the subjects, getting to know them and having them share their thoughts and per-

---

*For the guidelines on which these ethical considerations are based, see "Ethical Principles of Psychologists" (American Psychological Association, 1981).

ceptions. Griffin and Templin (1989) raised questions concerning potential ethical dilemmas regarding whether to share field notes, how to protect a participant's self-esteem without compromising accuracy in the research report when the two are in conflict, and what to do if you are told about (or observe) something illegal or immoral in the collection of data.

There are no easy answers to situational ethics in fieldwork. Qualitative research sometimes deals with so-called deviants, such as drug addicts and unlawful motorcycle gangs. Informed consent is impossible in some circumstances. Punch (1986, p. 36) made this point when he described his research with police when the patrol car in which he was riding was directed to a fight. The policemen jumped out and started wrestling with the combatants. Punch wondered whether he was supposed to yell ''freeze,'' thrust his head between the entangled limbs, and, Miranda-like, chant out the rights of the participants. Or, when Powermaker (cited by Punch) came face to face with a lynch mob, should she have flashed her academic identity card and explained to the crowd about the nature of her presence?

By these two examples we are not implying that qualitative researchers are exempt from considerations such as informed consent and deception. We are simply pointing out that certain types of qualitative research situations face special problems dealing with ethics. We invite you to read the discussion by Punch (1986) and consult some of the sources he cites about this issue.

Persons with disabilities are a special issue as research subjects. The fact that the subject has a disability is protected under the Right to Privacy Act. Thus, institutions are prohibited from releasing the names of persons with disabilities as potential research subjects. The researcher must contact the institution about possible subjects. The institution then requests permission from the parents to release the child's name and nature of the disability to the researcher. If the parents approve, the institution allows the researcher to contact the parents to seek approval for the particular research to be undertaken. Although this procedure is rather cumbersome and varies from state to state, individuals clearly have the right not to be cited in studies and labeled as ''handicapped'' unless they so choose.

Protection of Human Subjects and Informed Consent

Consideration must be given to the protection of human subjects. The researcher is required to protect the rights and well-being of subjects in his or her study. The regulations detailing the procedures are published by the U.S. Department of Health and Human Services (45 CFR 46.101). Most institutions regulate this protection in two ways. First, researchers are required to complete some type of form describing their research. Sample Form D.1 in Appendix D is a sample of the form used for conducting research with human subjects at Arizona State University.

Typically, institutions require that you include your informed-consent form with your application to conduct human-subject research. Sample Form D.2 is the model for the form used for adults at Arizona State University. If the subjects are minors, then you must obtain their parents' permission (Sample Form D.3) and the children's permission (Sample Form D.4) if they are old enough to understand. It may be useful to put this form on a microcomputer disk so that graduate students or faculty can answer the questions and print out the completed form. The researcher completes this form, attaches an abstract, and has it approved before beginning any work, including pilot work. The source of approval may vary; for example, some institutions may require that all forms be approved by a central committee, whereas others may delegate approval for so-called standard types of research to a lower level (e.g., a college committee).

Following are the basic elements of informed consent as specified by the advisory committee of the *Research Quarterly for Exercise and Sport* (Thomas, 1983, p. 221):

- A fair explanation of the procedures to be followed, including an identification of those which are experimental.
- A description of the attendant discomforts and risks.
- A description of the benefits to be expected.
- A disclosure of appropriate alternative procedures that would be advantageous for the subject.
- An offer to answer any inquiries concerning the procedures.
- An instruction that the subject is free to withdraw consent and to discontinue participation in the project or activity at any time. In addition, the agreement should contain no exculpatory language through which the subject is made to waive, or appear to waive, any legal right, or to release the institution or its agents from liability or negligence.

The researcher is required to comply with any institutional guidelines both for protection of human subjects and for informed consent. A description of this compliance should be included under the subject section in the method chapter of the thesis or dissertation. Most journals also require a statement with regard to this issue. The form used for informed consent is normally placed in an appendix of the thesis/dissertation.

Protection of Animal Subjects

If animals are used as subjects for research studies in exercise science, institutions require adherence to the *Guide for the Care and Use of Laboratory Animals*, published by the U.S. Department of Health and Human Services, as detailed in the Animal Welfare Act (PL 89-544, PL 91-979, and PL 94-279). Most institutions also support the rules and procedures for recommended care of laboratory animals as outlined by the American Association for Accreditation of Laboratory Animal Care.

Basically, all these documents recognize that for advancements to be made in human and animal research, animals must be used. These animals must be well cared for, and if their use results in the animals being incapacitated or sacrificed, this must be done humanely. Sample Form D.5 is the form used at Arizona State University to assure compliance with all regulations involving the use of animals in research.

INSTRUMENTS

The instruments, apparatus, or tests used to collect the data are described in this section. This information is used to generate the dependent variables in the study. For example, in a sport psychology study, you are interested in the influence that a unit on knowledge about and attitudes toward steriod use has on a group of university football players. In addition, you suspect that the players' attitudes might be modified by certain personality traits, so you select three tests—a steriod knowledge test, an attitude inventory about responsible drug use, and a trait personality measure—and administer these three tests to all subjects. The knowledge and attitude tests will probably be given before and after the unit and the trait personality test only before the unit (traits should not change, and this test is being used to stratify subjects in some way). In the instrument section, you describe the three tests and probably put complete copies of each in the appendix. You also describe the reliability (consistency) and validity (what the test measures) information that is available on each test with appropriate citations. You then explain the scoring sheets (place a sample in the appendix) and also the scoring methods.

Another example might be a motor behavior study in which subjects' reaction and movement times are measured under various conditions. In this section a description of the testing apparatus would be provided along with a diagram or picture. If the apparatus were interfaced with a microcomputer to control the testing situation and data collection, you should describe the microcomputer (brand name and model) and how the interface was made. At least a description of how the computer program operates should be included in the appendix (if not a complete copy of the program). The dependent variables generated for reaction and movement time should be explained and reliability estimates given for these characteristics. All the necessary information can be presented by the appropriate use of both the instrument (or apparatus) part of the method chapter and the appendix, thus allowing the method section to flow smoothly.

PROCEDURES

This section should describe how the data are obtained. All testing procedures for obtaining scores on the variables of interest should be explained. How tests are given and who gives them are important features. The setup of the testing situation and instructions given to the subjects are detailed (although some of this information may be placed in the appendix). If the study is experimental, then the treatments applied to the different groups of subjects are described. One of our favorite summaries of the problems encountered and solutions proposed is presented in Table 4.1. These statements are extracted from an article by Martens (1973) titled ''People Errors in People Experiments.''

The procedures section contains most of the detail that allows another researcher to replicate the study. Tuckman (1978) outlined these details, which generally include

- the specific order in which steps were undertaken;
- the timing of the study (e.g., time for different procedures and time between different procedures);
- instructions given to subjects; and
- briefings, debriefings, and safeguards.

Table 4.2 provides a humorous view of all the things that go wrong in the procedures.

Table 4.1 Errors in Experiments

Sources of errors in experiments:
Martens's method
(for eliminating people errors
in people experiments)

Martens's method derives from the basic premise that:

In people experiments people errors increase in disproportionate ratio to the contact people have with people.

It is obvious that the most logical deduction from this premise is:

To reduce people errors in people experiments, reduce the number of people.

Although this solution might be preferred for its elegant simplicity, its feasibility can be questioned. Therefore, the following alternative formulation warrants consideration:

The contact between people testers and people subjects in people experiments should be minimized, standardized, and randomized.

Note. From Martens (1973, pp. 331-332). Copyright 1973 by Human Kinetics. Adapted by permission.

Unless you carefully pilot all your procedures, "quirk theory" will apply to your research. No single item in this book is more important than our advice to pilot all your procedures. Physical education, exercise science, and sport science have produced thousands of studies in which the discussions centered on methodological faults that caused the research to lack validity. We are aware that we are repeating ourselves, but placing post hoc blame on the methodology for inadequate results is unacceptable. Every thesis or dissertation proposal should present pilot work that verifies that all instruments and procedures will function as specified on the type of subjects for which the research is intended. In addition, you must demon-

**Table 4.2 "Quirk Theory,"
or the Universal Perversity of Matter**

Law of experiment

First Law: In any field of scientific endeavor, anything that can go wrong will go wrong.
 Corollary 1: Everything goes wrong at one time.
 Corollary 2: If there is a possibility of several things going wrong, the one that will go wrong is the one that will do the most damage.
 Corollary 3: Left to themselves, things always go from bad to worse.
 Corollary 4: Experiments must be reproducible; they should fail in the same way.
 Corollary 5: Nature always sides with the hidden flaw.
 Corollary 6: If everything seems to be going well, you have overlooked something.

Second Law: It is usually impractical to worry beforehand about interference; if you have none, someone will supply some for you.
 Corollary 1: Information necessitating a change in design will be conveyed to the designer after, and only after, the plans are complete.
 Corollary 2: In simple cases presenting one obvious right way versus one obvious wrong way, it is often wiser to choose the wrong way so as to expedite subsequent revisions.
 Corollary 3: The more innocuous a modification appears to be, the further its influence will extend, and the more plans will have to be redrawn.

Third Law: In any collection of data, the figures that are obviously correct, beyond all need of checking, contain the errors.
 Corollary 1: No one whom you ask for help will see the errors.
 Corollary 2: Any nagging intruder who stops by with unsought advice will spot it immediately.

Fourth Law: If in any problem you find yourself doing a transfinite amount of work, the answer can be obtained by inspection.

To assist in the research suggested, the following rules have been formulated for the use of those new to this field.

Rules of experimental procedure

---

1. Build no mechanism simply if a way can be found to make it complex and wonderful.
2. A record of data is useful; it indicates that you have been busy.
3. To study a subject, first understand it thoroughly.
4. Draw your curves; then plot your data.
5. Do not believe in luck; rely on it.
6. Always leave room when writing a report to add an explanation if it doesn't work. (Rule of the way out.)
7. Use the most recent developments in the field of interpretation of experimental data.
   a. Items such as Finagle's constant and the more subtle Bougeurre factor (pronounced "Bugger") are loosely grouped, in mathematics, under constant variables, or, if you prefer, variable constants.
   b. Finagle's constant, a multiplier of the zero-order term, may be characterized as changing the universe to fit the equation.
   c. The Bougeurre factor is characterized as changing the equation to fit the universe. It is also known as the "Soothing" factor; mathematically, somewhat similar to the damping factor, it has the characteristic of dropping the subject under discussion to zero importance.
   d. A combination of the two, the Diddle coefficient, is characterized as changing things so that the universe and the equation appear to fit without requiring any change in either.

Note. From "Quirk theory or the universal perversity of matter" (1968, p. 59). Copyright 1968 by *Illinois Technograph*. Adapted by permission.

strate that you can use these procedures and apparatus accurately and reliably.

During our years as major professors, editors, and researchers, we have seen abstracts of thousands of master's theses and doctoral dissertations. More than 75% of these research efforts are unpublishable and make no contribution to theory or practice because of major methodological flaws that could have been easily corrected with pilot work. Sadly, this reflects negatively not only on the discipline and profession but also on the graduate students who conducted the research and the faculty who directed it. Yet, nearly all the problems could be corrected by increased knowledge about the topic, better research design, and pilot work on the procedures.

> No single item in this book is more important than our advice to pilot all your procedures.

Graduate students frequently seek information about appropriate procedures from related literature (and they should). Procedures for intensity, frequency, and duration of experimental treatments are often readily available, as is information about testing instruments and procedures. However, it is important to remember that procedures in one area do not necessarily work well in another, as the example on the next page illustrates.

DESIGN AND ANALYSIS

Design is the key to controlling the outcomes from experimental and quasi-experimental research. The independent variables are manipulated in an attempt to judge their effects on the dependent variable. A well-designed study is one in which the only explanation for change in the dependent variable is how the subjects were treated (independent variable). The design has enabled the researcher to eliminate all rival or alternate hypotheses. The design requires a section heading in the method chapter for experimental and quasi-experimental research.

The plans for data analysis must also be reported. In most studies some type of

Research Procedures May Not Generalize

Dr. I.M. Funded was a good life scientist who studied the biochemistry of exercise in a private research laboratory. He had also done several studies with a colleague in sport psychology to determine whether some biochemical responses he had found were factors in psychological responses to exercise. Thus, he had a firm grasp of some of the social science techniques as well as those of life science.

Unfortunately, Dr. Funded's funding ran out, and he lost his job. A friend of his was the superintendent of a large school district. Dr. Funded went to his friend, Dr. Elected, and said, "I am a good scientist well trained in problem-solving techniques. Surely, you must need someone like me in your administrative structure. In addition I have an undergraduate degree in physical education, so I am certified to teach, although I never have." Dr. Elected agreed to hire him as his teaching effectiveness supervisor because the school system was having difficulty identifying good teaching. Dr. Elected thought that perhaps a scientist with good problem-solving skills and the ability to make careful measurements could find a solution.

Dr. Funded decided that his first task was to identify some good teachers so he could determine the characteristics they possessed. He would use some of the techniques he had acquired from his colleague in sport psychology to identify good teachers. He had learned that questionnaires were effective in surveying large groups but that interviews were more valid. Dr. Funded drew a random sample of 6 schools from the 40 in the district. Then, he randomly selected 6 teachers in each school and interviewed them. He used a direct interview question: "Are you a good teacher?" All 36 indicated they were. So he went back to Dr. Elected, explained what he had done, and said, "You don't have a teaching problem. All of your teachers are good" (of course he noted there could be some sampling error, but he was certain of his results). Dr. Elected was not very happy with Dr. Funded's procedures and results and suggested that perhaps he needed more sophisticated techniques and strategies to identify good teachers.

Dr. Funded was slightly distraught but thought to himself, I have always questioned the techniques of those psychologists anyway—I will return to my life science techniques to determine the answer. He went back to the previously selected 36 teachers with a plan to draw blood, sample urine, and do muscle biopsies (at four sites) once per week for 4 weeks. Immediately, 34 teachers said no, but 2 who were triathletes agreed to participate. Dr. Funded noted that the subject mortality rate was about normal for biopsy studies, so the data should be generalizable. He collected all the data, did the correct chemical analyses, and reported back to Dr. Elected. He indicated that effective teachers had 84% slow-twitch fiber, higher-than-average amounts of hemoglobin per deciliter of blood, and a specific profile of catecholamines (epinephrine and norepinephrine) in the urine. In addition, good teachers trained for at least 100 miles per week on the bicycle, 50 miles running, and 7,500 meters swimming. Dr. Funded sat back smugly and said, "Techniques for the life sciences can be applied to solve many problems." Dr. Elected said, "You are fired."

statistical analysis is used, but there are exceptions (e.g., historical or qualitative research).

Typically, the researcher will explain the proposed application of the statistics. In nearly all cases, descriptive statistics are provided, such as means and standard deviations for each of the variables. If correlational techniques (relationships among variables) are used, then the variables to be correlated and the techniques are named; for example, ''The degree of relationship between two estimates of percent fat will be established by using Pearson r to correlate the sum of three skinfolds with underwater weighing.'' In experimental and quasi-experimental studies, descriptive statistics are provided for the dependent measures, and the statistics for establishing differences among groups are reported; for example, ''A t test was used to determine whether youth league hockey players watching professional games produced more violent actions during their games than youth league players who did not watch professional hockey games.''

> A well-designed study is one in which the only explanation for change in the dependent variable is how the subjects were treated (independent variable).

The major problem graduate students encounter in the description of statistical techniques is the tendency to feel the need to instruct everyone about their knowledge of statistics. Of course, that is not much of a problem for the new graduate student. But if your program of studies is a research-oriented one in which you take several statistics courses, your attitude may change rapidly.

Hiawatha, who at college majored in applied statistics, consequently felt entitled to instruct his fellow men on any subject whatsoever. (Kendall, 1959, p. 331)

The point of this line of poetry is for you to describe your statistical analyses but not to instruct in their theoretical underpinnings and proper use.

SUMMARY

This chapter has provided an overview of the method for the research study. We have identified the major parts as subjects, instruments or apparatus, procedures, and design and analysis. Table 4.3 shows the four parts of the method chapter and their major purposes: to eliminate alternative or rival hypotheses, or to control any explanation for the results except the hypothesis the researcher intends to evaluate. The MAXICON

Table 4.3 Summary of the Methods Chapter

Total research situation

Considerations for formulating the study:
  Subjects
  Instruments
  Procedures
  Design and analysis

Eliminate alternate or rival hypotheses

MAXICON principle:
  Maximize experimental variance
  Minimize error variance
  Control extraneous variance

Note. From Hoenes and Chissom (1975, p. 72). Copyright 1975 by Vog Press. Adapted by permission.

principle shows the way to accomplish this: (a) maximize the true or planned sources of variation, (b) minimize any error or unplanned sources of variation, and (c) control any extraneous sources of variation. In the following sections, we detail how to do this from the viewpoints of statistics (Part II), design (Part III), and measurement (Part IV). We will explain the final chapters of the thesis or dissertation in Part V.

Problems

1. Locate an experimental study in *Research Quarterly for Exercise and Sport* and critique the method section. Comment on the degree to which the author provided sufficient information concerning the subjects (and informed consent), instruments, procedures, and design and analysis.
2. Locate a survey study and compare and contrast its method description with that in the study in Problem 1.

PART II

Statistical Concepts
in Research

In the following five chapters, some basic statistical techniques are presented that are frequently used in research in physical education, exercise science, and sport science. More attention has been given here to the basic statistical techniques than to the more complex methods. A general understanding of the underlying concepts of the statistical techniques has been emphasized rather than any derivation of formulas or extensive computations. Because an understanding of how the basic statistical techniques work facilitates an intuitive grasp of the more advanced procedures, the computational procedures for most of the basic statistics, as well as examples of their use, have been provided. In addition, Appendix B contains programming statements and sample printouts for the example problems used. We used the SPSSx statistical package for both the micro- and the mainframe computers because programs like this (also SAS and BIOMED) are widely available.

Chapter 5 discusses the need for statistics. Different types of sampling procedures are described, and the basic statistics used in describing data, such as measures of central tendency and measures of variation, are summarized. The emphasis here is that statistics can reveal two things about data: reliability and meaningfulness. The concepts of probability and significance are explained as they relate to inference or to generalizing the results of a study.

Chapter 6 pertains to relationships among variables. Different correlational techniques are reviewed, such as the Pearson r for the relationship between only two variables. Partial correlation is explained as a technique in which one can determine the correlation between two variables while holding the influence of a third (or more) variable constant. The use of correlation for prediction is discussed when using one predictor variable and when using more than one variable to predict a criterion (multiple regression).

Chapter 7 focuses on statistical techniques for comparing treatment effects on groups, such as different training or different samples. The simplest comparison of differences is between two groups: the t test. Next, analysis of variance is described as a means of testing the significance of the differences among more than two groups. Also discussed is the use of factorial analysis of variance, in which two or more independent variables can be compared.

The approach in chapter 8 is different from the previous two. Here we deal with multivariate techniques, for which the mathematics are very complex. However, a conceptual understanding of the multivariate techniques can be gained from extending ideas from univariate procedures and the use of examples. This is what we have done. Discriminant analysis, multivariate analysis of variance, and multivariate analysis of covariance are extensions of simple analysis of variance, factorial analysis of variance, and analysis of covariance. Conceptually, these techniques represent the same idea, except a composite is formed from multiple dependent variables. From the same perspective, canonical correlation, factor analysis, and structural modeling are extensions of Pearson r and multiple R. For each technique, we present a conceptual description of the procedures and an example.

Chapter 9 provides information on nonparametric techniques for data analysis. These are procedures in which the data fail to meet one or more of the basic assumptions of parametric techniques described in chapters 5-7. Nonparametric techniques for comparisons and relationships between categories and ranked scores are discussed. Some statistical comparisons between two samples and among multiple samples are described for both independent and dependent groups. Simple and more complex relationships between variables expressed in nominal and ordinal forms are also presented.

After reading the five chapters in Part II, you will not be a statistician (unless you were one before you started). However, if you read and study these chapters carefully and perhaps explore some of the references further, you should be able to comprehend the statistical analysis sections of most research studies.

Chapter 5

□

Becoming Acquainted
With Statistical Concepts

The concept of statistics frightens many people. If you are one of them, you needn't be. Statistics is one of the few ways data can be reported uniformly to allow relevant, accurate conclusions and comparisons to be made. They are methodical, logical, and necessary, not random, inconsistent, or terrifying. Our approach to statistics in this book is to acquaint you with the basic concepts and give you a working knowledge; it is not our purpose to make you a statistician.

THE NEED FOR STATISTICS

Statistics is simply an objective means of interpreting a collection of observations. Various statistical techniques are necessary to allow the description of the characteristics of data, test relationships between sets of data, and test the differences among sets of data. For example, if height and a standing-long-jump score were measured for each person in a seventh-grade class, you could sum all the heights and then divide the sum by the number of people. The result (statistic to represent the average height) is the mean ($\Sigma X/N$, where Σ = sum, X = each person's height, and N = number of people; read this as "sum all Xs and divide by N"). The mean (M) describes the average height in the class; it is a single characteristic that represents the data.

An example of testing relationships between sets of data would be to measure the degree of association between height and the scores on the standing long jump. You might hypothesize that taller people can jump farther. By plotting the scores (Figure 5.1), you can see that, in general, people who are taller do jump farther. But note that the relationship is not perfect. If it were, the scores would begin in the lower left-hand corner of the figure and proceed diagonally in a straight line toward the upper right-hand corner. One measure of the degree of association between two variables is called *Pearson* r (or simple correlation). When two variables are unrelated, their correlation (r) is approximately zero. In the case of Figure 5.1, the two variables (height and standing-long-jump score) have a moderately positive correlation (r is probably between .40 and .60). Relationships and correlation are discussed in greater detail in the next chapter, but for now you should see that researchers frequently want to investigate the relationship between variables.

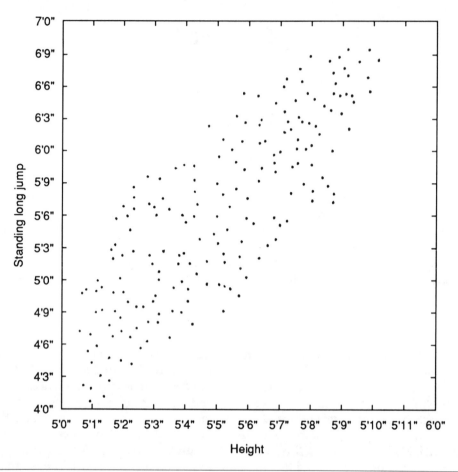

Figure 5.1 Relationship of height and standing long jump.

Besides descriptive and correlational techniques, a third category of statistical techniques is used to measure differences among groups. Suppose you believe that weight training of the legs will increase the distance one can jump. You take a seventh-grade class, divide it into two groups, and have one group participate for 8 weeks in a weight-training program designed to develop leg strength. The other group continues their regular activities. You want to know whether the independent variable (weight training versus regular activity) produces a change in the dependent variable (standing-long-jump score). Therefore, you measure the two groups' standing-long-jump scores at the end of the 8 weeks (treatment period) and compare their average performances. In this case, a statistical technique to assess differences between two independent groups, a t *test*, would be used. By calculating t and comparing it to a value from a t table, you can judge whether the two groups were significantly different on their average long-jump scores. Ways for assessing differences among groups are discussed in chapter 7.

COMPUTERS AND STATISTICS

Computers are very helpful in the calculation of statistics. Computers do not make the mistakes that occur in hand calculations and are many times faster.

Microcomputers

Two types of computers are referred to for statistical analysis in Part II. First, *microcomputers* are frequently used in laboratories, offices, and homes for statistical calculations. Micros are small, desktop computers. The computer and its attachments (disk drives, monitors, printers, hard disks, and modems) are called *hardware*, and the computer programming is called *software*. There are numerous programs (software) written for these computers that will calculate statistics.

We use a widely accepted set of microcomputer programs in this book called the Statistical Package for the Social Sciences, Version X (SPSSx). These programs are versatile and are available both commercially and through most college and university computing facilities. Specific routines in the SPSSx package are referred to for solving the various statistical problems in Part II. Appendix B provides the exact statements needed to run each problem presented in these chapters, and we refer you to this appendix at the appropriate times. Also, a printout is shown that depicts how the output from that program will appear. There are many other computer programs available for microcomputers to make statistical calculations. We selected SPSSx because it is widely available, it is available for both micro- and mainframe computers, and it is easy to use. In addition, SPSSx has a complete set of statistical routines and a well-written reference manual.

There are two limitations of micros for statistical analyses. First, some of the sophisticated statistical routines (e.g., multivariate analysis of variance and canonical correlation) have seldom been adapted to micros. Second, micros cannot handle large data sets.* Both these limitations are due to the limited memory capacity of micros. However, micros are continually increasing in memory capacity. In ancient history, when we were in graduate school, mainframe computers (yes, they had been invented by then) had about the same capacity as the micros we used to prepare this book. The deficit for micros is the major advantage of large mainframe computers.

---

*The exact size of the data set that a microcomputer can handle cannot be specified in terms that the lay reader will understand. It depends on the interaction of the memory capacity of the micro, the size of the statistical program to be used, the number of subjects, the number of scores for each subject, and the size of the numbers. For example, the limit is first set by the memory of the micro, which might range from very small (128K) to fairly large (1,000K). Next, a simple statistical program, such as calculating the mean and standard deviation of a measure, requires fewer programming statements than a more sophisticated program such as a factorial analysis of variance. If the memory is smaller and the program larger, less memory space remains for data, that is, number of subjects, number of scores for each subject, and larger (more digits) versus smaller numbers. These factors are normally not an issue when using mainframe computers.

Mainframes

The second type of computer used for statistical analyses are the large computers (frequently called *mainframes*). Most colleges and universities have these systems. Several well-known computer packages for mainframes are available, including the UCLA Biomedical Series (BIMED), the Statistical Package for the Social Sciences (SPSS), and the Statistical Analysis System (SAS).

A brief overview of these three most widely used mainframe statistical packages is included in Appendix C. Most colleges and universities have one or more of these packages, which can be used from a terminal or through a microcomputer (with proper hardware and software). Your computer center will have information about equipment and services that are available. Most frequently, you will need to acquire a computer number (and other identification information), which can be obtained easily. Many computer centers provide so-called user services or user consultant centers where you can get advice about the hardware and software available and how to use it. Most institutions also teach statistics courses in which these packages are used. Statistics departments may also offer consulting services on the appropriate use of statistics for research projects. You should carefully investigate the services your institution offers. Senior graduate students and faculty can also advise you on available services.

Reference to the packages for mainframes will not be made again; all these packages include the appropriate programs for techniques presented in these chapters (as well as many other techniques; see Appendix C for an overview). The main advantage of mainframes is that the statistical packages are more sophisticated, well documented, and flexible. Also, these packages can handle large data sets.

DESCRIPTION AND INFERENCE

At the beginning of this chapter we stated that statistical techniques allow the description of data characteristics, testing of relationships, and testing of differences. When we discuss description and *inference*, though, we are not discussing statistical techniques, although those two words are sometimes confused with statistical techniques. This confusion is the result of saying that correlations describe relationships and that cause-and-effect is inferred by techniques for testing differences among groups. These statements are not necessarily true. The results of any statistic describe the sample of subjects for which it was calculated. If the sample of subjects represents some larger group, then the findings can be inferred (or generalized) to the larger group. However, the statistic used has nothing to do with inference. The method of selecting the sample is what does or does not allow inference.

SELECTING THE SAMPLE

The *sample* is the group of subjects on which the study is conducted. The key issue is how this group is selected.

Random Selection

The sample might be randomly selected from some larger group, or a *population*. For example, if your college or university has 10,000 students, you could randomly select 200 for a study. You would assign each of the 10,000 students a number-name. The first number-name would be 0000, the second 0001, the third 0002, up through the last (the 10,000th), who would have the number-name 9999. Then a *random number table* (see Table A.1 in Appendix A) would be used. The numbers in this table are arranged in two-digit sets so that any combination of rows or columns is unrelated. In this case (number-names 0000-9999), you need to select 200 four-digit numbers. Because the rows and columns are unrelated, you can choose any type of systematic strategy to go through the table. Enter the table at random (close your eyes and put your finger on the page). Suppose the place of entering the table is the sixth column of a two-digit number on row 8. The number-name here is 9953 (includes column 6 and 7 for a four-digit number). The subject with that number-name (9953) is selected, then 9386 is, and so on until 200 subjects are selected. Continue down this column to the bottom of the page, then begin at the top of column 8 with the number-name 2392 and continue until 200 subjects are selected. Column 7 is not used because it was included with column 6 to yield a four-digit number.

The system used in the random number table is not the only one. You can use any systematic way of going through the table. You could read across rows rather than down columns. Of course, the purpose of all this is to select a sample of subjects randomly so that the sample is representative of the larger population; that is, the findings in the sample can be inferred back to the larger population. From a statistical viewpoint, this says that a characteristic, relationship, or difference found in the sample is likely to also be present in the population from which the sample was selected (inference).

> The purpose of all this is to select a sample of subjects randomly so that the sample is representative of the larger population; that is, the findings in the sample can be inferred back to the larger population.

Computer programs can also be used to generate a set of random numbers. These programs operate much like the procedures just described. You tell the program the population size and how many cases to randomly select.

Stratified Random Sampling

Another type of sampling is *stratified random sampling*. In this case the population is divided (stratified) on some characteristic before random selection of the sample. Returning to the previous example, the selection was of 200 subjects from a population of 10,000. Suppose your college is 30% freshmen, 30% sophomores, 20% juniors, and 20% seniors. You could stratify on class before random selection to make sure the sample was exact in terms of class representation. In this case, you would randomly select 60 subjects from the 3,000 freshmen, 60 from the 3,000 sophomores, 40 from the 2,000 juniors, and 40 from the 2,000 seniors. This still yields a total sample of 200.

Stratified random sampling might be particularly appropriate for survey or interview research. Suppose you suspect that attitudes toward exercise participation change over the college years. You might use a stratified random sampling technique for interviewing 200 college students to test this hypothesis. Another example would be to develop normative data on a physical fitness test for Grades 4-8 in a school district. Because performance would be related to age, you should stratify the population by age before randomly selecting your sample on which to collect normative data.

Systematic Sampling

If the population from which the sample is to be selected is very large, assigning a number-name to each potential subject is time consuming. Suppose you want to sample a town with a population of 50,000 concerning the need for new sport facilities. An approach would be to use systematic sampling from the telephone book. You might decide to call a sample of 500 people. To do so, you would select every 100th name in the phone book. Of course, you are assuming that the telephone book represents the population, or, said another way, that everyone you need to sample has a telephone. This turned out to be a very bad assumption in the 1948 presidential election (Dewey vs. Truman). The pollsters had predicted Dewey to win by a substantial margin. However, the pollsters had sampled from telephone books in key areas. Unfortunately for Dewey, many people without telephones voted for Truman. His victory was called an upset, but it was an upset only because of poor sampling procedures. Systematic sampling will yield a good sample and should be equivalent to random sampling if the sample is fairly large. However, random sampling is generally preferred.

Difficulty of Random Selection

Sometimes random sampling of subjects is nearly impossible to achieve. This is a particular problem in research that is more field oriented (applied). For example, children are placed in classrooms in schools at the beginning of the year. It may be impossible to randomly select children from classes or schools. In this case, the unit that is randomly selected might change. If three school systems are to participate in a study, each class within a school could be given a number-name and

25 classes randomly selected; or classes could be stratified by grade level before random selection. The procedures are the same; only the unit has changed from the individual child to the class. The same idea can be applied to school systems, athletic teams, and physical education activity classes. Although random selection of subjects is preferred, any unit of random selection adds to the ability to generalize the results.

Random Assignment

In experimental research, groups are formed within the sample. The issue here is not how the sample was selected but how the groups are formed within the sample. Chapter 14 discusses experimental research and true experimental designs. All true designs require that the groups within the sample be randomly assigned or randomized. Although this requirement has nothing to do with the selection of the sample, the procedures used for random assignment are the same. Each subject in the sample is given a number-name. If the sample has 30 subjects, the number-names range from 00 to 29. In this case, suppose three equal groups ($ns = 10$) are to be formed. Enter a table of random numbers; the first number-name encountered between 00 and 29 goes in Group 1, the second in Group 2, and so on until each group has 10 subjects. This process allows the researcher to assume that the groups are equivalent at the beginning of the experiment, which is one of several important features of good experimental design in which the purpose of the research is to establish cause-and-effect.

Computer programs are also available to randomize groups. You supply the sample size and the number of groups and decide whether the groups are to have an equal number of subjects. The computer program will then randomly assign subjects.

Post Hoc Explanations

Frequently, the sample for research is not randomly selected; rather, the researcher will attempt a post hoc justification that the sample is representative of some larger group. A typical example might include showing that the sample does not differ in average age, racial balance, or socioeconomic status from some larger group. Of course, the purpose is to allow the findings on the sample to be generalized to the larger group. A post hoc attempt at generalization may be better than nothing, but it is not the equivalent of random selection, which allows the assumption that the sample does not differ from the population on the characteristics measured (as well as any other characteristics). In a post hoc justification, only the characteristics measured can be compared. Whether those are the ones that really matter is open to speculation.

This same justification is used to compare intact groups, or groups within the sample that are not randomly formed. Except in this case, the post hoc justification is that because the groups did not differ on certain measured characteristics before the beginning of study, they can be judged equivalent. Of course, the same point applies: Are the groups different on some unmeasured characteristic that affects the results? This question cannot be answered satisfactorily. But, as before, a good post hoc justification of equivalence does add strength to comparisons of intact groups.

MATHEMATICAL CONCEPTS
AND STATISTICAL SYMBOLS

By now you should have a basic understanding of the concept of statistics—why they are necessary, how computers can be used to calculate them, why description and inference aren't statistical techniques, and why you should randomly select your statistical sample. It is time now to explain the "how to's" of statistics.

But, before we begin a discussion of statistical techniques, a review of basic mathematical concepts may be helpful. The presentation in Table 5.1 is rather basic, so do not hesitate to skip over it if you are proficient in the operations presented.

Statistical formulas frequently use symbols in combination with mathematical functions. Table 5.2 explains the symbols to be used and provides some examples of their use in connection with the mathematical functions used in Table 5.1.

Table 5.1 Mathematical Functions

1. + means add
2. − means subtract
3. × or • means multiply
4. ÷ or / or ⌐ means divide
5. $\sqrt{}$ means take the square root
6. ^{2} superscript or raised number means to multiply the number by itself that many times:
   $2^2 = 2 \times 2 = 4$; $3^3 = 3 \times 3 \times 3 = 27$
7. ( ) means perform mathematical acts inside parentheses first: $3(2 + 3) = 3(5) = 15$
8. Multiply and divide before adding and subtracting unless parentheses indicate otherwise
9. Like signs are always added: $-7 - 4 = -11$

	Useful examples
Addition of signed numbers	$+3 - 2 = 1$, $-3 + 1 = -2$, $-5 + 4 - 3 = (-5 - 3) + 4 = -8 + 4 = -4$
Subtraction of signed numbers	$-4 - 3 = -7$, $+4 - 3 = 1$, $-4 + 3 = -1$, $(-4) - (-3) = -4 + 3 = -1$
Multiplication of signed numbers	$(-3) \times (-4) = +12$, $(-3) \times 4 = -12$, $+5 \bullet -3 = -15$, $(3)(4)(-2) = -24$
Division of signed numbers	$-12/-4 = 3$, $-24/-3 = 8$, $(9/-3)(-2) = 6$, $4/2 + -8/2 = -2$
Complex cases	$(3 - 4)(-5 - 2) = (-1)(-7) = 7$, $(3 + 5)/(-3 + 1) = 8/-2 = -4$

Table 5.2 Statistical Symbols

1. Σ means to sum or add
2. X or Y represents a given number
3. $\bar{X}$ or M represents the mean or average of several numbers
4. x or y is a deviation score: $x = X - M$
5. N is the number of subjects in the sample
6. n is the number of subjects within sample subgroups
7. SD or s represents the standard deviation
8. s^2 represents the variance

Examples

1. $x_1 = 2, x_2 = 4, x_3 = 1, x_4 = 5$
   $\Sigma X = 2 + 4 + 1 + 5 = 12$
2. $Y_1 = 7, Y_2 = 3, Y_3 = 2, Y_4 = 4$
   $\Sigma Y = 7 + 3 + 2 + 4 = 16$
3. $\Sigma X^2 = 2^2 + 4^2 + 1^2 + 5^2 = 4 + 16 + 1 + 25 = 46$
4. $(\Sigma X)^2 = (2 + 4 + 1 + 5)^2 = 12^2 = 144$

MEASURES OF CENTRAL TENDENCY AND VARIABILITY

Some of the more easily understood statistical and mathematical calculations are those that find central tendency and variability of scores. When you have a group of scores, one number may be used to represent the group. That number is generally the mean, median, or mode. These terms are ways of expressing *central tendency*. Within the group of scores, each individual score will differ to a given degree from the central tendency score. The degree of difference is the score's *variability*. Two terms that describe the variability of the scores are standard deviation and variance.

Central Tendency Scores

The statistic for the central tendency score with which most of you are familiar is the *mean* (M), or average:

$$M = \Sigma X / N \tag{5.1}$$

Thus, if you have the numbers 4, -5, 3, 6, -2, -1, 4, -2, 3, and -3, then

$$M = [(4 + 3 + 6 + 4 + 3) + (-5 - 2 - 1 - 2 - 3)]/10$$
$$= (20 - 13)/10$$
$$= 7/10 = 0.7$$

The number 0.7 is the average and represents this series of numbers.

Sometimes the mean may not be the most representative or characteristic score. Suppose you have the numbers 4, 5, 4, 6, 3, 5, 26, 3, 4. The mean is 6.7, a number larger than all but one of the scores. It is not very representative because one score (26) made the average high. In this case, another measure of central tendency, called the *median*, is more useful. The median is defined as the score in the middle. In our example, if you arrange the numbers from lowest to highest—3, 3, 4, 4, 4, 5, 5, 6, 26—the median (middle score) is 4, which is a much more representative score.

Most often you will be interested in the mean of a group of scores. You may occasionally be interested in the median or perhaps in another measure of central tendency, the *mode*, which is defined as the most frequently occurring score. In the previous example, the mode is also 4, as it occurs three times.

Variability Scores

Another characteristic of a group of scores is the variability. An estimate of the variability, or spread, of the scores can be calculated as the *standard deviation (s)*:

$$s = \sqrt{\Sigma(X - M)^2/(N - 1)} \qquad (5.2)$$

This formula translates as the following. Calculate the mean by Formula 5.1, subtract the mean from each subject's score $(X - M)$, square the answer, sum the squared scores, divide by the number of subjects minus one $(N - 1)$, and take the square root of the answer. Table 5.3 provides an example.

The mean and standard deviation together are good descriptors of a set of scores. If the standard deviation is large, the mean may not be a good representation. Roughly 68% of a set of scores fall between $\pm 1\,s$, about 95% of the scores fall between $\pm 2\,s$, and about 99% of the scores fall between $\pm 3\,s$ (this is called a normal distribution and is discussed in the next section).

Table 5.3 Calculation of Mean and Standard Deviation

Subjects	X	X − M	(X − M)²
1	2	−2	4
2	4	0	0
3	3	−1	1
4	5	1	1
5	6	2	4
Σ	20	0	10

$M = \Sigma X/N = 20/5 = 4$

$s = \sqrt{\Sigma(X - M)^2/(N - 1)} = \sqrt{10/4} = \sqrt{2.5} = 1.58$

Formula 5.2 was used to help you understand the meaning of the standard deviation. For use with a hand calculator, Formula 5.3 is simpler:

$$s \equiv \sqrt{[N\Sigma X^2 - (\Sigma X)^2]/[N(N - 1)]} \qquad (5.3)$$

One final point for later consideration is that the square of the standard deviation is called the *variance*, or s^2. Appendix B contains a description of the computer program to compute standard deviation (see the section on descriptive statistics), the program itself, and a sample printout. The data analyzed are those from Table 5.3.

Range of Scores

Sometimes the range of scores may also be reported, particularly when the median rather than the mean is used. The median and the mean may be used in connection with each other. For example, 15 subjects might be given 10 blocks of 10 trials (100 total trials) on a reaction time (RT) task. The experimenter may decide to use the median RT of a subject's 10 trials as the most representative score in each block. Thus, each subject would have 10 median scores, or 1 for each of the 10 trial blocks. In this case, the range of scores from which the median was selected should be reported. Both the mean and the standard deviation would be reported for the 15 subjects' scores at Trial Block 1, Trial Block 2, and so on. Thus, the range is reported for the selection of the median at each trial block, whereas the standard deviation is reported for the group mean at each trial block.

BASIC CONCEPTS OF STATISTICAL TECHNIQUES

Besides measures of central tendency and variability, there are other, slightly more complicated statistical techniques. Before we explain each of them in detail, however, it is important that you understand some general information about statistical techniques.

Statistical Tests

There are two general categories of statistical tests, and the use of the various tests depends on meeting the assumptions for those tests.

The first category, *parametric statistical tests*, has two assumptions about the distribution of the data:

- The population from which the sample is drawn must be normally distributed on the variable of interest.
- The samples drawn from a population must have the same variances on the variable of interest.

In addition, certain parametric techniques have additional assumptions. The second category, *nonparametric statistics*, is so-called distribution free because the two assumptions need not be met.

Whenever the assumptions are met, parametric statistics are preferred because they have more *power*. To have power means to increase the chances of rejecting a false null hypothesis. You frequently assume that the two assumptions for use of parametric statistics are met. The assumptions can be tested by using estimates of skewness and kurtosis. (Only the meaning of these tests is explained here. Any basic statistics textbook provides considerably more detail; for a helpful discussion on skewness and kurtosis, see Newell & Hancock, 1984.)

To understand skewness and kurtosis, first consider the *normal distribution* in Figure 5.2. This is a *normal curve*, which is characterized by the mean, median, and mode being at the same point (center of the distribution). In addition, ± 1 *s* from the mean includes 68% of the scores, ± 2 *s* from the mean includes 95% of the scores, and ± 3 *s* includes 99% of the scores. Thus, data distributed as in Figure 5.2 would meet the two assumptions for use of parametric techniques. *Skewness* of the distribution describes the direction of the hump of the curve (labeled A) and the nature of the tails of the curve (labeled B and C). If the hump (A) is shifted to the left and the long tail (B) to the right (Figure 5.3a), the skewness is positive. If the shift of the hump (A) is to the right and the long tail (C) to the left (Figure 5.3b), the skewness is negative. *Kurtosis* describes the shape of the curve, for example, whether the curve is more peaked or flatter than the normal curve. Figure 5.4a shows a more peaked curve and 5.4b a flatter curve.

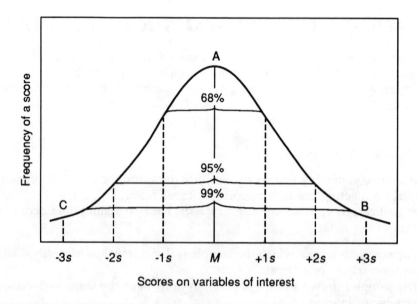

Figure 5.2 The normal curve.

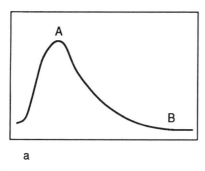
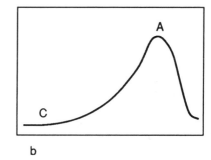

Figure 5.3 Skewed curves: a, positive skewness; b, negative skewness.

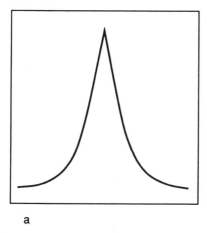
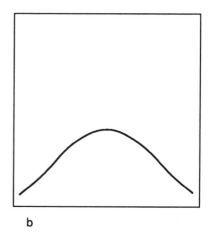

Figure 5.4 Curves with abnormal kurtosis: a, more peaked; b, more flat.

Appendix A contains Table A.2, which is a unit normal distribution (z) for a normal curve. The column z shows the location of the mean. Thus, when the mean is in the center of the distribution, its z is equal to .00; thus, .50 of the distribution is beyond the mean, leaving .50 of the distribution as a remainder. As the mean of the distribution moves to the right in a normal curve (say to a z of $+1$ s), .8413 (84%) of the distribution is to the left of the mean (remainder) and .1587 is to the right of the mean (beyond). This table allows you to determine the percentage of the normal distribution included by the mean plus any fraction of a standard deviation. Suppose you want to know what percentage of the distribution would be included by the mean plus one half (.50) of a standard deviation. Using Table A.2 you can see that it would be .6915 (remainder), or 69%.

For chapters 6-8, consider that the two basic assumptions for parametric statistical tests have been met. This is done for three reasons. First, the assumptions are very *robust* to violations, meaning that the outcome of the statistical test is relatively accurate even with fairly severe violations of the assumptions. Second, most of the research in physical activity uses parametric tests. Finally, nonparametric tests are relatively easy to understand. (For a good presentation on nonparametric tests, see Conover, 1971. In addition, chapter 9 covers basic nonparametric techniques.)

Functions of Statistical Techniques

The statistical techniques presented in the next four chapters answer the following two questions about the data to which they are applied:

- Is the effect or relationship of interest a reliable one? That is, can you count on it? In other words, if the research is repeated, will the effect or relationship be there again (is it significant)?
- How strong (or meaningful) is the effect or relationship of interest? This refers to the magnitude or size of the effect or relationship.

Two facts are important about these two statements. First, Statement 1 always takes precedence over Statement 2, for the strength of the relationship or effect is not of interest until it is known to be reliable (significant). Second, Statement 2 is always of interest if the effect or relationship is significant. Sometimes, in elating over the significance of effects and relationships, one loses sight of the need to look at the strength or meaningfulness of these relationships. This is particularly true in research in which differences among groups are compared. The experimenter frequently forgets that relatively small differences can be significant. That means only that the differences are reliable or that the same answers can be obtained if the research is repeated. The experimenter then needs to look at the size of the differences to interpret whether the findings are meaningful. For each technique presented in the next four chapters, testing emphasizes first whether the relationship or effect is significant (reliable). Then, ways to evaluate the strength (meaningfulness) of the relationship or effect are suggested.

Categories of Statistical Techniques

It is practical to divide statistical techniques into two categories: (a) statistical techniques used to test relationships between or among several variables in one group of subjects (regression or correlation) and (b) techniques used to test differences between or among groups of subjects (t tests and analysis of variance). This division is inaccurate because both sets of techniques are based on the general linear model and only involve different ways of entering data and manipulating variance components. However, an introduction to research methods is the place neither to reform the "world of statistics according to Thomas and Nelson" nor to confuse you. Thus, the techniques as two distinct groups are considered (for a discussion of the relationship between analysis of variance and regression techniques, see Pedhazur, 1982). Chapter 6 discusses relationships between variables (simple and multiple correlation), and chapter 7 discusses differences between and among groups (t tests and analysis of variance). Teaching you the relatively simple calculations underlying the easier techniques and then building on this helps you intuitively understand the more complex ones. Chapter 8 then presents extensions of simple and multiple correlation into canonical correlation, path analysis

> Causation is not determined from any statistic. Cause-and-effect is established by the total experimental situation, of which statistics is a part.

(LISREL), and factor analysis as well as extensions of analysis of variance into discriminant analysis and multivariate analysis of variance. Do not panic because statistics involves manipulating numbers, for you can escape from this section with a reasonable grasp of how, why, and when the various statistical techniques are used in the study of physical activity.

Remember, however, that correlation between two variables does not indicate causation. Causation is not determined from any statistic or correlation. Cause-and-effect is established by the total experimental situation, of which statistics is a part. As summarized by Pedhazur (1982),

> "Correlation is no proof of causation." Nor does any other index prove causation, regardless of whether the index was derived from data collected in experimental or in nonexperimental research. Covariations or correlations among variables may be suggestive of causal linkages. Nevertheless, an explanatory scheme is not arrived at on the basis of the data, but rather on the basis of knowledge, theoretical formulations and assumptions, and logical analyses. It is the explanatory scheme of the researcher that determines the type of analysis to be applied to data, and not the other way around. (p. 579)

For example, Descartes has been credited with the logical statement, "I think, therefore I am." However, the famous philosopher Edsall Murphy "recognized it as a syllogism with an unstated major premise.

Major Premise: A non-existent object cannot think.
Minor Premise: I think.
Conclusion: Therefore, I am." (Morgenstern, 1983, p. 112)

Murphy was not satisfied with this and so tried to search for deeper meaning and a better logical analysis.

Q: How can you be sure that you exist?
A: I think.
Q: How can you be sure you are thinking?
A: I can't, but I do think that I think.
Q: Does that make you sure that you exist?
A: I think so.

This should make it clear that Descartes went too far. He ought to have said:

"I think I think, therefore I am." or possibly "I think I think, therefore I think I am, I think." . . . you do not really exist unless others are aware of your existence. Murphy proclaimed, "I stink, therefore I am." (Morgenstern, 1983, p. 112)

...cept that deals with statistical techniques that you need to understand ...ty. *Probability* asks what are the odds that certain things will happen. ...obability in everyday events. What are the chances that it will rain? You ...a weather report that probability of rain is 90%. You wonder whether that m... s it will rain in 90% of the places or, more likely, that the chances are 90% that it will rain where you are. The terms *subjective*, or *personalistic*, *probability* are used to describe this concept.

A second concept of probability is called *equally likely events*. For example, if you roll a die, the chances of the numbers from 1 to 6 occurring is equally likely (i.e., 1 in 6). The third approach to probability involves *relative frequency*. To illustrate, suppose you toss a coin 100 times. You would expect a head 50 times and a tail 50 times; the probability is one half, or .50. However, when you toss, you may get a head 48 times, or .48. That is the relative frequency. You might do this 10 times and never get .50, but the relative frequency would be distributed closely around .50, and you would still assume the probability as .50.

In a statistical test, you sample from a population of subjects and events. You use probability statements to describe the confidence you place in the statistical findings. Frequently, you will encounter a statistical test followed by a probability statement such as $p < .05$. This interpretation would be that a difference or relationship of this size would be expected less than 5 times in 100 due to chance.

20% CHANCE OF RAIN

Alpha

In research, the test statistic is always compared to a probability table for that statistic that tells you what the chance occurrence is. The experimenter establishes an acceptable level of chance occurrence (called *alpha*, α) before the study. This level of chance occurrence can vary from low to high but can never be eliminated. For any given study, the probability of the findings being due to chance always exists; or, to quote Holten's Homily, "The only time to be positive is when you are positive you are wrong."

In behavioral research, alpha (probability of chance occurrence) is frequently set at .05 or .01 (the odds the findings are due to chance are either 5 in 100 or 1 in 100). There is nothing magic about .05 or .01. They are used to control for a *Type I error*. In a study, the experimenter may make two types of error. A Type I error is to reject the null hypothesis when the null hypothesis is true, whereas a *Type II error* is not to reject the null hypothesis when the null hypothesis is false. Figure 5.5 is called a *truth table*, which demonstrates Type I and II errors. As you can see, to accept a true null hypothesis or reject a false one is the correct decision. You control for Type I errors by setting alpha. For example, if alpha is set at .05, then, if 100 experiments are conducted, a true null hypothesis of no difference or no relationship would be rejected on only 5 occasions. Although the chances for error still exist, the experimenter has specified them exactly by establishing alpha before the study.

	H_0 true	H_0 false
Accept	Correct decision	Type II error (β)
Reject	Type I error (α)	Correct decision

Figure 5.5 Truth table for null hypothesis (H_0).

Although some people disagree, alpha should be specified before the research, and findings reported at the alpha that has been specified. Results are either significant at the specified alpha or they are not (not much is in between). It is like being pregnant—one either is or is not. Alpha works the same way. It is established as a criterion, and results either meet the criterion or they do not. Although experimenters sometimes may report borderline significance (if alpha is .05, the label from .051 to .10 is borderline).

To some extent the issue is, if you had to make an error, which type error are you willing to make? In fact, the level of alpha reflects the type error you are willing to make. In other words, if you had to make an error, would you rather reject a true null hypothesis or not? For example, in a study of the effect of a drug on curing cancer, the experimenter would not want to accept the null hypothesis of no effect if there was any chance the drug worked. Thus, the experimenter might set alpha at .30 even though the odds of making a Type I error would be inflated. The experimenter is making sure that the drug has every opportunity to show its effectiveness. On the other hand, setting alpha at .001 decreases the odds of sending other researchers on a wild goose chase because it reduces the odds of making a Type I error.

We cannot tell you where to set alpha; however, we can say that the levels .05 or .01 are widely accepted in the scientific community. If alpha is to be moved up or down, be sure

> Alpha should be specified before the research, and findings reported at the alpha that has been specified.

to justify the reason: "Surely God loves the .06 nearly as much as the .05" (Rosnow & Rosenthal, 1989). Regardless, set alpha beforehand and compare your values to the established level. If borderline findings are to be reported, clearly label them as borderline.

Even when experimenters set alpha at a specific level (e.g., .05) before the research, they often report alpha for the specific effects of the study at the level it occurred (e.g., .012). Nothing is wrong with this procedure, as they are only demonstrating to what degree alpha exceeded the specified level.

Beta

Although the magnitude of Type I error is specified by alpha, you may also make a Type II error, the magnitude of which is determined by *beta* (β). By looking at Figure 5.6, you can see the overlap of the score distribution on the dependent variable for X (the sampling distribution if the null hypothesis is true) and Y (the sampling distribution if the null hypothesis is false). By specifying alpha, you indicate that the mean of Y (given a certain distribution) must be at a specified distance before the null hypothesis is rejected. However, if the mean of Y falls anywhere between the mean of X and the specified Y, you could be making a Type II error (β); that is, you do not reject the null hypothesis when, in fact, there is a true difference. Although we will not go into the formulas here, beta can be calculated (Kirk, 1968; Winer, 1971). As you can see, there is a relationship between alpha and beta; for example, as alpha is set increasingly smaller, beta becomes larger.

Once beta is determined, then power ($1 - \beta$) can be determined. Remember, power is the probability of rejecting the null hypothesis when the null hypothesis is false (e.g., $1 - \beta$), or the chances of making a correct decision. Having power in the statistical analysis is important because it increases the odds of rejecting a false null hypothesis. Once beta is determined (along with certain other parameters shown in the following list), the necessary sample size needed for any level of power can be calculated. As Kirk (1968, p. 9) has indicated, the following five factors are necessary to estimate the sample size required to test a statistical hypothesis:

- Minimum treatment effects an experimenter is interested in detecting
- Number of treatment levels
- Population error variance

- Probability of making a Type I error
- Probability of making a Type II error

References for Further Information

Of course, all the necessary information may not be available in all experiments. However, the formulas for estimating some of the previously mentioned parameters as well as power and sample size can be found in Kirk (1968) and Winer (1971). This is discussed further in chapter 7, although our approach is more post hoc, as it involves reporting the effect size and variance accounted for in significant findings and interpreting whether this is a meaningful effect. The procedures described previously and calculated a priori are more desirable but not always applicable (for a more detailed discussion of important factors associated with establishing significance levels and determining power, see Franks & Huck, 1986).

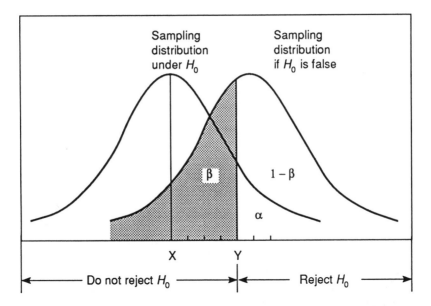

Figure 5.6 Regions under the normal curve corresponding to probabilities of making Type I and Type II errors. From Kirk (1968, p. 30). Copyright 1968 by Brooks/Cole. Adapted by permission.

SUMMARY

Statistics are used to describe data, to determine relationships among variables, and to test for differences among groups. In this chapter we tried to make the point that the type of statistics used does not determine whether findings can be generalized; rather it is sampling that permits (or limits) inference. Whenever possible, random sampling is the method of choice. In some types of research, such as surveys, stratified random sampling is desirable for the study to be representative of certain segments of a population. In experimental research, random assignment of subjects to groups is definitely desirable so that the researcher can assume equivalence at the beginning of the experiment.

We began our coverage of statistical techniques with basic concepts such as measures of central tendency and variability and normal distribution. It is important to remember that statistics can do basically two things: establish significance and assess meaningfulness. Significance means that a relationship or difference is reliable—that you could expect it to happen again if the study were repeated. Meaningfulness refers to the importance of the results—whether they are of any consequence.

Probability is an important component of statistics. Probability statements refer to the confidence you place in the statistical findings. The null hypothesis is used in statistical tests. It basically states that there is no difference (or no relationship in a study), that any observed finding is simply a chance occurrence.

The possibility of committing statistical error always exists. A Type I error is rejecting the null hypothesis when it is true. A Type II error is accepting the null hypothesis when it is false. These two errors work in opposition; as you strive to avoid one, you increase the likelihood of committing the other. The researcher must decide what level of significance (alpha) to accept—in other words, the degree to which one is willing to be wrong. That decision basically depends on the consequences of being wrong in which direction.

Problems

Two groups ($ns = 7$) of 7-year-old children are led on a 35-m jog down a 50-m string placed on the ground. They are then asked to reproduce the distance by jogging 35 m on a second 50-m string placed at a right angle to the first string. The experimental group is told before they begin that the best way to remember the distance jogged is to count steps. The control group is told to remember as best they can. Following is the error (in meters) each subject made when asked to estimate the distance jogged.

Experimental group	Control group
2.55	7.68
3.62	6.80
3.42	5.68
2.86	3.97
2.00	7.23
1.08	5.48
1.16	6.03

1. Use Formula 5.1 to calculate the mean for each group.
2. Use Formula 5.2 to calculate the standard deviation for each group.

3. Use Formula 5.3 to calculate the standard deviations to see whether the answer is the same as that derived from Formula 5.2.

4. Make a list of 50 names. Using the table of random numbers (Table A.1 in Appendix A), randomly select 24 subjects and then randomly assign them to two groups of 12 each.

Chapter 6

□

Relationships Among Variables

In chapter 5 we promised that after we had presented some basic information to help you understand statistical techniques we would begin to explain in detail some of the specific techniques. We begin with correlation.

Correlation is a statistical technique used to determine the relationship between two or more variables. This chapter briefly discusses several types of correlation, the reliability and meaningfulness of correlation coefficients, and the use of correlation for predictions, including partial and semipartial correlations and multiple regression equations.

WHAT CORRELATIONAL RESEARCH INVESTIGATES

Often a researcher is interested in the degree of relationship between, or correlation of, performances, such as the relationship between performances on a distance run and a step test as measures of cardiovascular fitness. Sometimes an investigator wishes to establish the relationship between traits and behavior, such as how personality characteristics relate to participation in high-risk recreational activities. Still other correlational research problems might involve relationships between anthropometric measurements, such as skinfold thicknesses and percent fat as determined by underwater weighing. Here, the researcher may wish to predict percent fat from the skinfold measurements.

Correlation may involve two variables, such as the relationship between height and weight, or more than two variables, as when one investigates the relationship between a criterion (dependent variable) such as cardiovascular fitness and two or more predictor variables (independent variables) such as body weight, percent fat, speed, muscular endurance, and so on. This is multiple correlation. There is also a technique, canonical correlation (discussed in chapter 8), to study the relationships between two or more dependent variables and two or more independent variables.

SOME TYPES OF CORRELATION

The *coefficient of correlation* is a quantitative value of the relationship between two or more variables. The correlation coefficient can range from 0.00 to 1.00 in either a positive or a negative direction. Thus, perfect correlation is 1.00 (either +1.00 or −1.00), and no relationship is 0.00.

Positive Correlation

There is a *positive correlation* when a small amount of one variable is associated with a small amount of another variable or when a large amount of one variable is associated with a large amount of another. Strength and body weight are positively correlated in that heavier persons are generally stronger than lighter persons. (However, some lighter people are stronger than some heavier people and weaker than some who weigh even less.)

Figure 6.1 is a graphic illustration of a perfect positive correlation. Notice that Tom's body weight is 1 s above the mean, for he weighs 110 lb, and the mean is 90. Thus, he is 20 lb heavier than the mean, which is 1 s (s = 20). His strength score is 250 lb, which is 50 lb higher than the mean of 200. Because the standard deviation is 50, he is 1 s above the mean on strength, just as he was on body weight. The second boy, Bill, is 1 s below the mean on weight and 1 s below on strength. The third boy is exactly at the mean on both variables (he weighs 90 lb and has a strength score of 200). Joe is .50 s above and Dick is .50 s below the means for weight and strength.

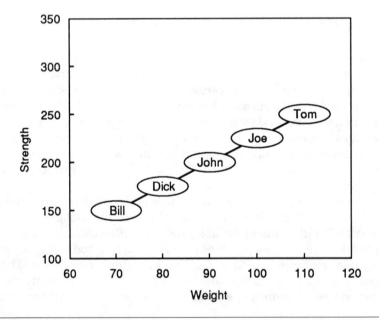

Figure 6.1 Perfect positive correlation.

Thus, when the scores are plotted, they form a perfectly straight diagonal line. This is perfect correlation (r = 1.00). The relative positions of the boys' pairs of scores are identical in the two distributions. In other words, each boy is the same relative distance from the mean of each set of scores. Common sense tells us that perfect correlation does not exist in human traits, abilities, and performances because of so-called people variability and other influences.

Figure 6.2 illustrates a more realistic relationship between body weight and strength ($r = .67$). (Fictional examples have been used for purposes of presentation in this and other chapters. These examples do not represent actual data.)

When these 10 sets of body weights and strength scores are plotted, they no longer constitute a straight line but do form a diagonal plot in the same lower-left-to-upper-right pattern as in the previous example (Figure 6.1).

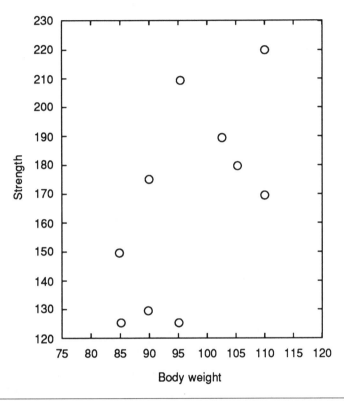

Figure 6.2 A more realistic correlation between body weight and strength ($r = .67$).

Negative Correlation

Next, in Figure 6.3, let us plot the body weights and pull-up scores for the same 10 boys. A pull-up is performed by hoisting one's body weight from a hanging position until the chin is above the bar. For this test, body weight is somewhat of a liability, often indicating that heavier persons tend to do fewer pull-ups than do lighter persons. As a result, a small number of pull-ups is associated with larger body weights and, conversely, a greater number of pull-ups with lesser body weights. This is a *negative correlation*. A perfect negative correlation would be a straight diagonal line in the opposite direction (the upper left corner of the graph to the lower right corner) as that of the perfect positive correlation. Figure 6.3 depicts a negative

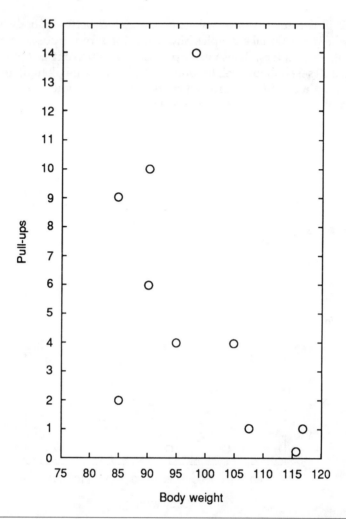

Figure 6.3 Negative correlation between body weight and pull-ups ($r = -.54$).

correlation but of a rather low degree ($r = -.54$). However, an upper-left-to-lower-right pattern is still apparent.

When there is virtually no relationship between variables, the correlation is 0.00. This denotes independence between sets of scores. The plotted scores exhibit no discernible pattern at all. The interpretation of correlations as to their reliability and meaningfulness is explained later.

Pearson Product Moment Correlation

Several times in the preceding discussion we have used the symbol r. This symbol denotes the *Pearson product moment coefficient of correlation*. In this type of correlation, there is one criterion (or dependent) variable and one predictor (or independent) variable. Thus, every subject has two scores, such as body weight and strength.

The computation of the correlation coefficient involves the relative distances of the scores from the two means of the distributions. The computations can be accomplished with a number of different formulas; we will present just one. This formula is sometimes called the computer method because it involves operations similar to those performed by a computer. The formula appears large and imposing but actually consists of only three operations:

1. summing each set of scores,
2. squaring and summing each set of scores, and
3. multiplying each pair of scores and obtaining the cumulative sum of these products.

The formula is

$$r = \frac{N\Sigma XY - (\Sigma X)(\Sigma Y)}{\sqrt{N\Sigma X^2 - (\Sigma X)^2}\sqrt{N\Sigma Y^2 - (\Sigma Y)^2}} \tag{6.1}$$

To illustrate the calculations involved, we use the body weight and pull-up scores from Figure 6.3 and designate body weight as the X variable. In a correlation problem that simply determines the relationship between two variables, it does not matter which one is X and which is Y. If the investigator wants to predict one score from the other, then Y designates the criterion (dependent) variable (that which is being predicted) and X the predictor (independent) variable. In this example, strength performance would be predicted from body weight, as it would not make much sense to predict body weight from strength scores. Prediction equations are discussed later in this section.

The computations for the correlation between body weight and pull-ups are shown in Table 6.1. Note that N refers to the number of paired scores, not the total number of scores.

The ΣX^2 and ΣY^2 columns are the raw scores squared and summed. For the $(\Sigma X)^2$ and the $(\Sigma Y)^2$ values, the sums of the raw scores for X and Y are then squared. Notice that these values are not the same as the ΣX^2 and ΣY^2 values. The ΣXY (the sum of the cross products of the X and Y scores) determines the direction of the correlation as to whether it is positive or negative. In this example, a negative correlation was obtained because the first half of the numerator ($N\Sigma XY$) was smaller than the second half ($\Sigma X)(\Sigma Y)$.

The negative correlation between body weight and pull-ups means that as body weight increased, pull-up performance decreased. Sometimes a negative correlation coefficient results when the relationship is really positive. Confusing? The following examples should clarify the meaning. Suppose we were to correlate scores on the vertical jump and the 40-yd dash. Both performances are heavily loaded with power. Thus, persons who score well on the vertical jump should also do well on the 40-yd dash because the two tests are measuring much the same thing; thus, the relationship between performances is positive. However, the vertical jump is

Table 6.1   Calculating r

X (body wt.)	Y (pull-ups)	X^2	Y^2	XY
104	4	10,816	16	416
86	2	7,396	4	172
92	6	8,464	36	552
112	1	12,544	1	112
96	4	9,216 ·	16	384
98	13	9,604	169	1,274
110	0	12,100	0	0
86	9	7,396	81	774
105	1	11,025	1	105
91	10	8,281	100	910
980	50	96,842	424	4,699

$$r = \frac{N\Sigma XY - (\Sigma X)(\Sigma Y)}{\sqrt{N\Sigma X^2 - (\Sigma X)^2}\sqrt{N\Sigma Y^2 - (\Sigma Y)^2}}$$

$$r = \frac{(10)4,699 - (980)(50)}{\sqrt{10(96,842) - (980)^2}\sqrt{10(424) - (50)^2}}$$

$$r = \frac{46,990 + 49,000}{\sqrt{968,420 - 960,400}\sqrt{4,240 - 2,500}}$$

$$r = \frac{-2,010}{\sqrt{8,020}\sqrt{1,740}}$$

$$r = \frac{-2,010}{(89.6)(41.7)} = \frac{-2,010}{3,736.3} = -.54$$

scored in inches (or centimeters), where a high score is good; and the 40-yd dash is scored in seconds, where a low number (fewer seconds) is good. Therefore, the correlation coefficient would be negative.

The correlation between the distance a person could run in 12 min and heart rate after exercise would also be negative. This is because a greater distance covered is good and because a lower heart rate after exercise is good. A person who has good cardiovascular endurance would have a high score on one test (the run) and a low score on the other.

RELIABILITY AND MEANINGFULNESS OF CORRELATION

So far we have dealt with the nature of correlation as to direction (positive or negative) and the calculation of r. An obvious question that arises is, What does a co-

efficient of correlation mean in terms of being high or low, satisfactory or unsatisfactory? This seemingly simple question is not so simple to answer.

Interpreting Reliability of r

First, there are several ways of interpreting r. One criterion is its *reliability*, or *significance*. Does it represent a real relationship? That is, if the study were repeated, what is the probability of getting a similar relationship? For this statistical criterion of significance, simply consult a table. In using the table, select the desired level of significance, such as the .05 level, and then enter the table in accordance with the appropriate degrees of freedom (*df*) (*df* are based on the number of subjects corrected for sample bias), which is equal to $N - 2$. Table A.3 in Appendix A contains the necessary correlation coefficients for significance at the .05 and .01 levels. Refer to the example of the correlation between body weight and pull-ups ($r = -.54$). The degrees of freedom are $N - 2 = 10 - 2 = 8$ (remember, the variable N in correlation refers to the number of pairs of scores). When entering the table at 8 *df*, we see that a correlation of .632 is necessary for significance of a two-tailed test at the .05 level (and .765 at the .01 level). Therefore, we would have to conclude that our correlation of $-.54$ is not significant. (We will explain how to know whether to find alues under the column for a one-tailed or two-tailed test in the preting *t* in chapter 7.)

e at Table A.3 reveals a couple obvious facts. The correlation needed decreases with increased numbers of subjects (*df*). In our example, subjects (or pairs of scores). However, if 4 more boys had been in = 14), then there would be 12 *df*, and the correlation required for the .05 level for 12 *df* would be .532. Our correlation of − .54 meets that significance. But notice that very low correlation coefficients can be significant if you have a large sample of subjects. At the .05 level, a correlation of .38 is significant with 25 *df*, *r* = .27 is significant with 50 *df*, and .195 is significant with 100 *df*. In fact, with 1,000 *df*, a correlation of .08 is significant at the .01 level.

The second observation noted from the table is that a higher correlation is required for significance at the .01 level than at the .05 level. This should make sense. Remember, chapter 5 stated that the .05 level means that if 100 experiments were conducted, the null hypothesis (that there is no relationship) would be rejected incorrectly, just by chance, on 5 of the 100 occasions. At the .01 level, we would expect a relationship of this magnitude less than 1 time in 100 due to chance. Therefore, the test of significance at the .01 level is more stringent than at the .05 level, and so a higher correlation is required for significance at the .01 level.

Interpreting Meaningfulness of *r*

The interpretation of a correlation for statistical significance is important, but, because of the vast influence of sample size, this criterion is not always meaningful. As chapter 5 explained, statistics can answer two questions about data: Are the effects reliable? Are they meaningful?

The most commonly used criterion for interpreting the correlation coefficient as to meaningfulness is the *coefficient of determination* (*r*²). In this method, the portion of common

> Statistics can answer two questions about data: Are the effects reliable? Are they meaningful?

association of the factors that influence the two variables is determined. In other words, the coefficient of determination indicates the portion of the total variance in one measure that can be explained, or accounted for, by the variance in the other measure.

For example, the standing long jump and the vertical jump are common tests of explosive power. The tests are so commonly used that we tend to think of them as interchangeable, that is, as measuring the same thing. Yet correlations between the two tests usually range between .70 and .80. The coefficients of determination range from .49 (.70²) to .64 (.80²). Usually, the coefficient of determination is multiplied by 100 and then expressed as percent of variation. Thus, .70² = .49 × 100 = 49% and .80² = .64 × 100 = 64%.

For a correlation of .70 between the standing long jump and the vertical jump, only about half (49%) of the variance (or influences) in one test is associated with the other. Both tests involve explosive force of the legs with some flexing and extending of the trunk and swinging of the arms. Both are influenced by body weight in that the subject must propel his or her body through space, both involve the ability to get psychologically and physiologically ready to generate explosive force, both involve relative strength, and so on. These are factors held in common in the two tests. If $r = .80$, then 64% of the performance in one test is associated with, or explained by, the factors involved in the performance of the other test.

But what about the unexplained variance—$(1.0 - r^2)100$? With a correlation of .70, there is 49% common (explained) variance and 51%, $(100 - .70^2)100$, error (unexplained) variance. What are some unique factors to each test? We cannot explain this fully, but some of the factors could be (a) that the standing long jump requires that the body be propelled forward and upward, whereas the vertical jump is only upward; (b) that the scoring of the vertical jump neutralizes one's height because standing reach is subtracted from jumping reach (but in the standing long jump perhaps the taller person has some advantage); and (c) that perhaps more skill (coordination) is involved in the vertical jump because the person must jump and turn and then touch the wall.

The foregoing is not intended to be any sort of mechanical analysis of the two tests. These are simply suggestions of what might be some factors of common association, or explained variance, and some factors that might be unexplained or unique to each test of power.

When we use the coefficient of determination to interpret correlation coefficients, it becomes apparent that a rather substantial relationship is needed to account for a great amount of common variance. It takes a correlation of .71 to account for just half the variance in the other test, and a correlation of .90 accounts for only 81%. In some of the standardized tests used to predict success in college and graduate school, the correlations between the tests and success are generally quite low, usually somewhere around .40. You can see by the coefficient of determination that a correlation of .40 accounts for only 16% of the factors contributing to academic success; therefore, there is a great deal of unexplained variance. Still, these measures are often used very rigorously as the criterion for admission. Of course, the use of multiple predictors can greatly improve the estimate for success. The comparative sizes of correlations by means of the coefficient of determination can also be observed. A correlation of .90 is not simply three times larger than a correlation of .30; it is nine times larger ($.30^2 = .09$, or 9%, and $.90^2 = .81$, or 81%).

Interpreting the correlation coefficient is further complicated by the fact that it depends on the purpose of the correlation with regard to whether correlation is "good" or "inadequate." For example, if we are looking at the reliability (repeatability) of a test, a much higher correlation is needed than if we are determining simply whether there is a relationship between two variables. A correlation of .60 would not be acceptable for the relationship between the odd- and even-numbered questions on an exercise knowledge test, but a correlation of .60 between exercise knowledge and exercise behavior would be quite noteworthy.

Z Transformation of r

Occasionally, a researcher wants to determine the average of two or more correlations. It is statistically unsound to try to average the coefficients themselves because the sampling distribution of coefficients of correlation are not normally distributed. In fact, the higher the correlation, in either a positive or a negative direction, the more skewed the distribution becomes. The most satisfactory method of approximating normality of a sampling distribution of linear relationships is by transforming coefficients of correlation to Z values. This is often referred to as the *Fisher Z transformation*. (This Z should not be confused with the z used to refer to the height of the ordinate in the area of the normal curve.)

The transformation procedure involves the use of natural logarithms. However, we need not use Fisher's formula to calculate the transformations (these conversions have been done for us in Table A.4). We simply consult the table and locate the corresponding Z value for any particular correlation coefficient.

Suppose, for example, that we obtained correlations between maximal oxygen consumption and a distance run (e.g., an 8-min run-walk) on four groups of subjects of different ages. We would like to combine these sample correlations to obtain a valid and reliable estimate of the relationship between these two measures of cardiorespiratory endurance. The data for the following steps are shown in Table 6.2.

Table 6.2 Average of Correlation Coefficients by Use of the Z Transformation

Age-group	N	r	Z	$N - 3$	Weighted Z
13-14	30	.69	.85	27	22.95
15-16	44	.85	1.26	41	51.66
17-18	38	.70	.87	35	30.45
19-20	35	.77	1.02	32	32.64
				135	137.70

1. First, convert each of the correlations to Z values by use of Table A.4. For example, the correlation of .69 for the 13- to 14-year-olds has a corresponding Z value of .85, the next correlation of .85 for the 15- to 16-year-old sample has a Z value of 1.26, and so on.
2. The Z values are then weighted by multiplying them by the degrees of freedom for each sample, which in this process is $N - 3$. So, in the 13- to 14-year-olds, the Z value of .85 is multiplied by 27 for a weighted Z value of 22.95. We do the same for the other three samples.
3. The weighted Z values are summed, and the mean weighted Z value is calculated by dividing by $\Sigma(N - 3)$: $137.7/135 = 1.02$
4. The mean weighted Z value is converted back to a mean correlation by consulting Table A.4 again. We see that the corresponding correlation for a Z value of 1.02 is .77.

Some authors declare that to average correlations by the Z-transformation technique you must first establish that there are no significant differences among the four correlations. A comparison for differences could be made using a chi-square test of the weighted Z values (chi-square is discussed in chapter 9). Other statisticians contend that averaging coefficients of correlation is permissible as long as the average correlation is not interpreted in terms of confidence intervals.

The Z transformation is also used for statistical tests (such as those for the significance of the correlation coefficient) and for determining the significance of the difference between two correlation coefficients. After reading chapter 7, you may wish to consult a statistics text, such as that by Morehouse and Stull (1975), for further discussion on the use of the Z transformation for these procedures.

USING CORRELATION FOR PREDICTION

We have stated several times that one of the purposes of correlation may be prediction. College entrance examinations are used to predict success. Sometimes, we try to predict a criterion such as percent fat by the use of skinfold measurements or maximal oxygen consumption by a distance run. In studies of this type, the predictor variables (skinfold measurements) are less time consuming, less expensive, and more feasible for mass testing than the criterion variable; thus, a *prediction*, or *regression*, *equation* is developed.

Prediction is based on correlation. The higher the relationship between two variables, the more accurately you can predict one from the other. If the correlation were perfect, you could predict with complete accuracy.

Regression Equations

Of course, we do not encounter perfect relationships in the real world, but in introducing the concept of prediction (regression) equations, it is often advantageous to begin with a hypothetical example of a perfect relationship.

Verducci (1980) provided one of the best examples in introducing the regression equation concerning monthly salary and annual income. If there are no other sources of income, we can predict with complete accuracy the annual income of, for example, teachers simply by multiplying their monthly salaries by 12. Figure 6.4 illustrates this perfect relationship. By plotting the monthly salary (the X, or predictor, variable), the annual income (the Y, or criterion, variable) can be obtained. Thus, if we know that another teacher (Ms. Brooks, e.g.) earns a monthly salary of $1,750, we can easily plot this on the graph where $1,750 on the horizontal (x) axis (the *abscissa*) intercepts the vertical (y) axis (the *ordinate*) at $21,000. The equation for prediction ($\tilde{Y}$, predicted annual income) is thus $\tilde{Y} = 12X$. In the previous example, Ms. Brooks's monthly salary (X) is inserted in the formula: $\tilde{Y} = 12(1,750) = 21,000$.

Next, suppose that all teachers got an annual supplement of $1,000 for coaching or supervising cheerleaders or some other extracurricular activity. Now, the formula becomes $\tilde{Y} = 1,000 + 12X$. Ms. Brooks's annual income is predicted as follows: $\tilde{Y} = 1,000 + 12(1,750) = 22,000$. All teachers' annual incomes could be predicted

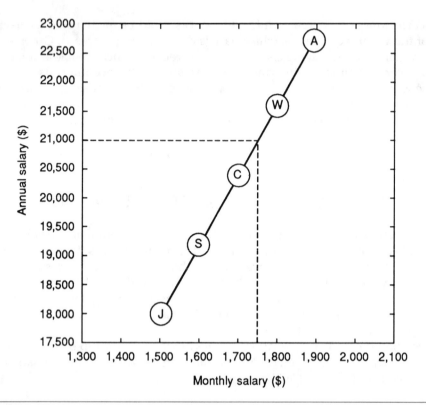

Figure 6.4 Plotting monthly and annual salaries with perfect r. *Note.* Letters refer to teachers' initials.

in the same manner. This formula is the general formula for a straight line and is expressed as follows:

$$\tilde{Y} = a + bX \tag{6.2}$$

where $\tilde{Y}$ = the predicted score, or criterion; a = the intercept; b = the slope of the regression line; and X = the predictor.

In this example, the b factor was ascertained by common sense because we know that there are 12 months in a year. The slope of the line (b) signifies the amount of change in Y that accompanies a change of 1 unit of X. Therefore, any X unit (monthly salary) is multiplied by 12 to obtain the Y value.

In actual regression problems we will not intuitively know what b is, so we must calculate it by this formula:

$$b = r(s_y/s_x) \tag{6.3}$$

where r = the correlation between X and Y, s_y = the standard deviation of Y, and s_x = the standard deviation of X.

In our previous example, application of Formula 6.3 uses these data:

X = (monthly salary) Y = (annual income)
M_x = 1,700 M_y = 21,400 (1,000 added—Figure 6.4)
s_x = 141.42 s_y = 1,697.06

$$r = 1.00$$

Therefore, the computation of b is b = 1.00(1,697.06)/141.42 = 12. The a in the regression formula indicates the intercept of the regression line on the y-axis; or, in other words, a is the value of Y when X is zero. On a graph, if you extend the regression line sufficiently, you can see where the regression line intercepts Y. The a is a constant because it is added to each of the calculated bX values. Once again, in our example we know that this constant is 1,000. In other words, this is the value of Y even if there were no monthly salary (X). But to calculate the a value, you must first calculate b. Then use the following formula:

$$a = M_y - bM_x \qquad (6.4)$$

where a = the constant (or intercept), M_y = the mean of the Y scores, b = the slope of the regression line, and M_x = the mean of the X scores. In our example, a = 21,400 − 12(1,700) = 1,000. Then the final regression equation is $\tilde{Y} = a + bX$, or $\tilde{Y}$ = 1,000 + 12X.

Next, let us use a more practical example in which the correlation is not 1.00. We can use the data used in Figure 6.2, where the correlation between body weight and dynamometer strength was .67. The means and standard deviations are as follows:

X (body weight) Y (strength)
M_x = 98.00 M_y = 167.00
s_x = 9.44 s_y = 33.52

$$r = .67$$

First, we calculate b as follows from Formula 6.3:

$$b = r(\frac{s_y}{s_x}) = .67(\frac{33.52}{9.44}) = 2.38$$

Then, a is calculated as follows from Formula 6.4:

$$a = M_y - b(M_x) = 167 - 2.38(98) = -66.24$$

The regression equation (Formula 6.2) becomes

$$\tilde{Y} = a + bX$$

so

$$\tilde{Y} = -66.24 + (2.38)X$$

For any body weight, we can calculate the predicted strength score. For example, a boy weighing 100 lb (X) would have a predicted strength score ($\tilde{Y}$) of $\tilde{Y} = -66.24 + (2.38)100 = 171.8$ lb.

The main difference between this example and the example of monthly and annual salaries is that there was no error of prediction in the latter because the correlation was 1.00. When we predicted strength from body weight, however, the correlation was less than 1.00, so there is an error of prediction.

Appendix B provides a computer program to calculate Pearson r and to compute the regression equation. In addition, this program provides a predicted $\tilde{Y}$ for any X variable entered. A sample on this program using the data from Figure 6.2 is included.

Line of Best Fit

Before presenting the formula for calculating error of prediction, let us return to the derivation of the prediction formula. Figure 6.2 shows that there was no straight line connecting the weight and strength scores as there was in the hypothetical example in Figure 6.1. Consequently, we calculate a line of *best fit* to predict Y from the X scores. To do this, we take a high score (body weight) such as 110 and a low body weight such as 91 and apply the prediction formula. For a body weight of 110, we predict $\tilde{Y} = -66.24 + (2.38)110 = 195.6$. For a body weight of 91, we predict $\tilde{Y} = -66.24 + (2.38)91 = 150.3$.

Then we plot these two predicted values and connect them with a straight line. This line passes through the intersection of the X and Y means. Figure 6.5 shows this line of best fit. The 10 actual body weight and strength scores are also plotted. You can readily see that the scores do not fall on the straight line as they did with perfect correlation.

In constructing this line of best fit, we selected a high body weight (110) and a low body weight (91) and predicted their Y values. When we examine their actual Y values, we see there is some error in prediction. The predicted strength score for the 110-lb boy was 195.6, yet the boy actually scored only 170 lb, a difference of -25.6 lb. The 91-lb boy was predicted to score 150.3 lb on the dynamometer, yet he scored 175 lb, a difference of $+24.7$ lb. These differences between predicted and actual Y scores represent the errors of prediction and are called *residual scores*. If we computed all the residual scores, the mean would be zero and the standard deviation the *standard error of prediction*, or *standard error of estimate* ($s_{y \cdot x}$).

A simpler way of obtaining the standard error of estimate is to use the formula

$$
\begin{aligned}
s_{y \cdot x} &= s_y \sqrt{1 - r^2} \\
&= 33.5\sqrt{1 - .67^2} \\
&= 24.9
\end{aligned}
\tag{6.5}
$$

The standard error of estimate is interpreted the same way as the standard deviation. In other words, the predicted value (strength) of a boy in our example, plus or minus the standard error of estimate, will occur approximately 68 times out of 100. Thus, we predict that a 104-lb boy will score 181.3 ± 24.9. To express it another

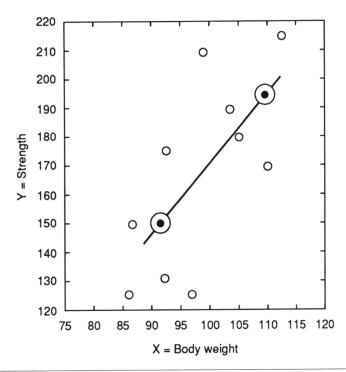

Figure 6.5 Regression line of best fit between body weight and predicted strength scores.

way, the "prediction range" will be 156.4-206.2 lb 68 times out of 100 (or the chances are 2 in 3).

The larger the correlation, the less the error of prediction. Also, the smaller the standard deviation of the criterion, the smaller the error. In the previous problem, if we had a correlation of .85, for example, the standard error of estimate would be only

$$s_{y \cdot x} = 33.5\sqrt{1 - .85^2} = 17.6$$

The line of best fit is sometimes called the least squares method. This means that the calculated regression line is one about which the sum of squares of the vertical distances of every point from the line is minimum. We will not develop this point here. Sum of squares is discussed in the next chapter.

PARTIAL CORRELATION

The correlation between two variables is sometimes misleading and may be difficult to interpret when there is little or no correlation between the variables other than that brought about by their common dependence on a third (or several other) variable.

For example, there are many attributes that increase regularly with age from 6 to 18 years, such as height, weight, strength, mental performance, vocabulary, reading skills, and so on. Over a wide age range, the correlation between any two of these traits will almost certainly be positive and will probably be high because of the common maturity factor with which they are highly correlated. In fact, the correlation may drop to zero if the variability caused by age differences is eliminated. We can control this factor of age in two ways. We can select only children of the same age and we can partial out the effects of age statistically by holding it constant.

The symbol for partial correlation is $r_{12 \cdot 3}$ which means the correlation between variables 1 and 2 with variable 3 held constant (we could partial out any number of variables, e.g., $r_{12 \cdot 345}$).

The calculation of partial correlation among three variables is quite simple. Let us refer back to the correlation of shoe size and achievement in mathematics. This is a good example of *spurious correlation*, which means that the correlation between the two variables is due entirely to the common influence of another variable (age or maturing). When the effect of the third variable (age) is removed, the correlation between shoe size and achievement in mathematics diminishes or vanishes completely. We label the three variables as follows: 1 = math achievement, 2 = shoe size, and 3 = age. Then, $r_{12 \cdot 3}$ is the partial correlation between variables 1 and 2 with 3 held constant. We can make up some correlation coefficients between the three variables: $r_{12} = .80$; $r_{13} = .90$; and $r_{23} = .88$.

The formula for $r_{12 \cdot 3}$ is

$$
\begin{aligned}
r_{12 \cdot 3} &= \frac{r_{12} - r_{13} r_{23}}{\sqrt{1 - r_{13}^2} \sqrt{1 - r_{23}^2}} \\
&= \frac{.80 - (.90 \times .88)}{\sqrt{1 - .90^2} \sqrt{1 - .88^2}} \\
&= \frac{.80 - .792}{\sqrt{1 - .81} \sqrt{1 - .77}} \\
&= .038
\end{aligned}
\tag{6.6}
$$

Thus, we see that the correlation between math achievement and shoe size drops to about zero when age is partialed out.

The primary value of partial correlation is that it is used to develop a multiple regression equation with two or more predictor variables. In the selection process, when a new variable is "stepped in," its correlation with the criterion is determined with the effects of the preceding variable partialed out. The size and the sign of a partial correlation may be different from the zero-order (two-variable) correlation between the same variables.

SEMIPARTIAL CORRELATION

In the previous section on partial correlation, the effects of a third variable on the relationship between two other variables were partialed out. In other words, in $r_{12 \cdot 3}$,

the relationship of variable 3 to the correlation of variables 1 and 2 is partialed out. In some situations, the investigator may wish to partial out a variable from only one of the variables being correlated. This is called *semipartial correlation*. The symbol is $r_{1(2 \cdot 3)}$, which indicates that the relationship between variables 1 and 2 is determined after the influence of variable 3 on variable 2 has been partialed out.

Suppose, for example, that a researcher is studying the relationship between perceived exertion (i.e., one's feelings of how hard he or she is working) and heart rate (HR) and work load (WL). Obviously, WL is going to be correlated with HR. The researcher wants to investigate the relationship between perceived exertion (PE) and HR while controlling for WL. Regular partial correlation will show this relationship. However, regular partial correlation will partial out the effects of WL on the relationship between PE and HR. But the researcher does not want to remove the effects of WL on the relationship of PE and HR; rather, he or she wants only to remove the effects of WL on HR. In other words, the main interest is in the net effect of HR on PE after the influence of WL has been removed. Thus, in semipartial correlation, WL is partialed out from HR but not from PE. The uses of semipartial correlation are discussed further in chapter 8.

MULTIPLE REGRESSION

Multiple regression consists of one dependent variable (usually a criterion of some sort) and two or more predictor variables (independent variables). The use of more than one predictor variable almost always increases the accuracy of prediction. This should be self-evident. If you wished to predict basketball-playing ability, you would expect to get a more accurate prediction by using several basketball skills tests rather than by using only one.

Some years ago, it was rather common practice to construct a motor fitness test by the use of multiple regression. The typical methodology was to define the components of fitness, such as cardiovascular endurance, strength and muscular endurance, power, speed, and so on. Then a number of test items were chosen that purportedly measured each of the components. Thus, there may be 20 or more test items selected and administered to a sample of subjects. The scores (usually standard scores) of all the tests were then added. The resulting total score was used as the criterion of fitness.

The motor fitness test battery was established by a multiple correlation technique called the *Wherry-Doolittle test selection method*. We will not go into the statistical steps. The process involves the calculation of zero-order (two-variable) correlation coefficients among the independent variables and between the independent variables and the criterion. Then the process selects the independent variables in the order of their importance, insofar as they relate highly with the criterion and poorly with the other independent variables (items that relate highly with one another are probably measuring the same thing). The result of the Wherry-Doolittle test selection method is a battery of the fewest items that contribute the most to the criterion. It is based on the premise that when there are a number of predictor variables, there is usually much overlap, which means that the prediction is probably just as good with a few variables as with many.

The Wherry-Doolittle method is a stepwise method in that multiple correlation (R) is calculated, cumulatively, after the selection of each variable until the size of the multiple correlation no longer increases to any extent. When this happens, the battery is established. Believe it or not, the Wherry-Doolittle method used to be performed by hand before the days of the pocket calculator. Now the computer does all of the multiple prediction (regression) calculations in seconds. There are several programs, or approaches, to accomplish the selection of the independent variables that best predict the criterion. Brief descriptions of some of these approaches follow.

> When there are a number of predictor variables, there is usually much overlap, which means that the prediction is probably just as good with a few variables as with many.

Forward Selection Multiple Regression

In the *forward selection* method, a new predictor variable is added at each step. The first variable selected is the one that has the highest correlation with the criterion. Then, at each subsequent step, a variable is added that, with the one or more already chosen, results in the best prediction. (It is difficult to explain these methods without using terms with which you are probably not yet familiar.) The variables selected cumulatively produce the least residual sum of squares, meaning that the residual sum of squares constitutes error. Recall from our discussion of linear regression with two variables that the differences between predicted and actual scores are termed *residuals*.

Sometimes, the researcher will set a probability level for entry, such as .05 or .01. In this way, variables are stepped in until they no longer significantly increase the prediction of the criterion. Recall the concept of *overlap*, in which some predictor variables often are measuring about the same thing; thus, if we have two such variables, the inclusion of both is no better than the use of only one.

Another important concept is that after the first step, the selection of additional variables is determined by the combined effect, not only the additive effect. In other words, the process takes into account the interrelationship among the X variables. If there were no relationships among the X variables, prediction could be made simply in an additive fashion, but, of course, this is never the case. After each X variable is stepped in, the remaining correlations between the criterion and the X variables are recomputed with the selected variables partialed out.

Thus, in forward selection multiple regression, variables are stepped in as to their importance, and the process stops when there is no further significant contribution to the prediction. In essence, this is similar to the Wherry-Doolittle test selection method.

Backward Selection Multiple Regression

In the *backward selection* procedure, the independent variables (Xs) are eliminated in respect to their importance; that is, you begin with all the independent variables and drop out those variables that do not significantly contribute to the prediction of the criterion. Once again, you usually set a significance level, and those variables that do not meet this level, insofar as they are included in the linear composite of predictor variables, are dropped. In most cases (but not always), you end up with the same battery of important predictor variables with the backward selection method as you did with the forward method.

Maximum R-Squared Method

In the *maximum R-squared* (R^2) *method*, the so-called best of all possible one-variable models is selected, as is the best two-variable model, the best three-variable model, and so on. The term "best" relates to the size of the *R*-squared value.

As explained in an earlier discussion of the coefficient of determination (r^2), squaring *r* (in this case, *R*) can estimate the degree of meaningfulness in terms of the amount of common association (or amount of variance held in common) between the dependent and the independent variables.

The maximum *R*-squared method continues until the full model is included. However, the researcher usually sets some criterion as to when to stop. It may be a level of significance or a measure of meaningfulness, such as the amount of variance accounted for (for a discussion of this, see chapter 7). Usually, it is a combination of significance and meaningfulness. The researcher also may incorporate some practical criteria in the selection process, such as amount of time and effort involved in obtaining the measurements for the different-size models (as in test batteries).

Stepwise Regression Procedure

The *stepwise regression method* is a variation of the forward technique except that each time a new predictor variable is stepped in, the new relationship between the criterion and the predictor variables is reevaluated, that is, to see whether the predictor variables already selected still significantly contribute when variables are added later. It is possible, then, that a predictor entered earlier may be dropped out later when new predictors are brought into the equation. In most cases, however, the stepwise method is identical to the forward selection method.

Multiple Regression Prediction Equations

The prediction formula resulting from multiple regression is basically that of the two-variable regression model, $\tilde{Y} = a + bX$. The difference is merely that there is more than one X variable; thus, the equation is

$$\tilde{Y} = a + b_1X_1 + b_2X_2 + \ldots + b_iX_i$$

We will not delve into the formula for the calculation of the a and the bs for the selected variables. As we have indicated before, a researcher will undoubtedly use a computer in a multiple regression problem. An example of what a multiple prediction formula might look like follows. In this equation, a man's lean body weight (LBW) is being predicted from several anthropometric measures, including skinfold thicknesses, circumferences, and diameters. The following formula, developed by Behnke and Wilmore (1974), has a correlation of .958 and a standard error of estimate of 2.358, which is interpreted just the same as in the regression equation with only one predictor variable.

LBW = 10.138 + 0.9259 (wt) − 0.1881 (thigh skinfold) + 0.637 (bi-iliac diameter)
+ 0.4888 (neck circumference) − 0.5951 (abdominal circumference)

Some Problems Associated With Multiple Regression

The basic determiner in multiple regression is the same as it is in regression with only two variables: the size of the correlation. The higher the correlation, the more accurate the prediction. However, some other factors should be mentioned.

One limitation of prediction relates to generalizability. Regression equations that were developed with a particular sample often lose considerable accuracy when applied to others. This is called *population specificity* (this, along with ways of improving generalizability through cross-validation, is discussed more in chapter 16). Recognize that the more accuracy is sought through selection procedures (forward, backward, stepwise, maximum R-squared) that capitalize on specific characteristics of the sample, the more difficult it is to generalize to other populations. Thus, the researcher should select the sample carefully with regard to the population for which the results are to be generalized.

In prediction studies the number of subjects in the sample should be sufficiently large. Usually, the larger the sample, the more likely that the sample will represent the population from which it is drawn. However, another problem with small samples in multiple regression studies is that the correlation may be spuriously high. A direct relationship exists between the correlation and the ratio between the number of subjects and the number of variables. In fact, if there are the same number of variables as subjects, the correlation will be 1.00. A subject-to-variable ratio of at least 10 to 1 or higher is ideal.

SUMMARY

We have explored some statistical techniques for determining relationships among variables. The simplest type of correlation is the zero-order correlation, which establishes the relationship between two variables. We introduced linear regression, which can be used to predict one variable from another. Correlation is interpreted for significance (reliability) and meaningfulness (r^2), which indicates the portion of the total variance in one measure that can be explained or accounted for by the other measure.

Partial correlation is a procedure in which a correlation between two variables is obtained while the influence of one or more other variables is partialed out. Semipartial correlation partials out the influence of a third variable on only one of the two variables being correlated. Partial correlation (or semipartial correlation) is used in multiple correlation and in developing multiple regression formulas.

In multiple regression two or more predictor (independent) variables are used to predict the criterion variable. The most efficient weighted linear composite of predictor variables is determined through such techniques as forward selection, backward selection, stepwise selection, and maximum R-squared.

Problems

1. What is the correlation (r) between fat deposits on two different body sites? Variable X is the triceps skinfold measure and variable Y the suprailiac skinfold measure.

X	Y	X	Y
16	9	13	6
17	12	14	5
17	10	4	1
15	9	7	4
14	8	12	7
11	6	7	1
11	5	10	3
12	5		

2. Using Table A.3, determine whether the correlation obtained in Problem 1 is significant at the .01 level. What size would the correlation need to be for significance at the .01 level if you had 30 subjects? What is the percent of common variance between the two skinfold measurements in Problem 1?
3. Compute the regression equation (Formula 6.2) for predicting maximal oxygen consumption ($\dot{V}O_2$max) from scores on the 12-min run. The information you need follows:

X (12-min run)	Y ($\dot{V}O_2$max)
M_x = 3,120 yd	M_y = 52.6 ml • kg • min^{-1}
s_x = 334 yd	s_y = 6.3 ml • kg • min^{-1}

$$r = .79$$

4. Using the prediction formula developed in Problem 3, what is the predicted $\dot{V}O_2$max for a subject who ran 3,230 yd in 12 min? For a subject who ran 2,940 yd in 12 min?
5. What is the standard error of estimate (Formula 6.5) for the prediction equation in Problem 3? How would you interpret the predicted $\dot{V}O_2$max for the subjects in Problem 4?

SUGGESTED READINGS

Bartz, A.E. (1976). *Basic statistical concepts in education and the behavioral sciences.* Minneapolis: Burgess.

Cohen, J., & Cohen, P. (1983). *Applied multiple regression in behavioral research.* New York: Holt, Rinehart and Winston.

Pedhazur, E.J. (1982). *Multiple regression in behavioral research.* New York: Holt, Rinehart and Winston.

Chapter 7

□

Differences Among (

Besides finding relationships among variables, as we discussed in chapter 6, statistical techniques are also used to determine differences among groups. These techniques are most frequently used for data analysis in experimental and quasi-experimental research. They enable us to evaluate the effects of an independent (cause) or categorical (gender, age, race, etc.) variable on a dependent variable (effect). Remember, however, that the techniques described in this chapter are not used to establish cause-and-effect but only to evaluate the influence of the independent variable. Cause-and-effect is not established by statistics but by the total nature of the research design.

In experimental research, the levels of the independent variable may be established by the experimenter. For example, the experiment might involve the investigation of the effects of intensity of training on cardiorespiratory endurance. Thus, intensity of training is the independent variable (or treatment factor), whereas a measure of cardiorespiratory endurance is the dependent variable. Intensity of training could have any number of levels. If it is evaluated as a percentage of maximal oxygen consumption ($\dot{V}O_2$max), then it could be 30%, 40%, 50%, and so forth. The investigator would choose the number and the intensity of levels. In a simple experiment, the independent variable might be two levels of intensity of training, for example, 40% and 70% of $\dot{V}O_2$max. The length of each session (30 min), frequency (three times per week), and number of weeks of training (12) are controlled (equal for both groups). The dependent variable is the distance a person runs in 12 min.

The purpose of the statistical test is to evaluate the null hypothesis at a specific level of probability ($p < .05$). In other words, do the two levels of treatment differ significantly ($p < .05$) so that these differences would not be attributable to a chance occurrence more than 5 times in 100? The statistical test is always of the null hypothesis. All that statistics can do is reject or fail to reject the null hypothesis. Statistics cannot accept the research hypothesis. Only logical reasoning, good experimental design, and appropriate theorizing can do so. Statistics can determine only whether the groups are different, not why they are different.

In using logical techniques to infer cause-and-effect after finding significant differences, you must be careful to consider all possibilities. For example, we might propose the theorem that all odd numbers are

> Statistics cannot accept the research hypothesis. Statistics can determine only if the groups are different, not why they are different.

primary numbers (this example is from Ronen et al., cited in Scherr, 1983, p. 146). You know that prime numbers are those that can be divided only by 1 and selves. Thus, one is a primary number; three is a primary number; five is a primary number; seven is a primary number. . . . Using the induction technique of reasoning, every odd number is a primary number. In Ronen et al.'s example, a very small number of levels of the independent variable (primary numbers) were sampled, and an error was made in inferring that all levels of the independent variable were the same.

When you use statistics that test differences among groups, you want to establish not only whether the groups are significantly different but also the strength of the association between the independent and dependent variables, or the size of the difference between two groups. The t and the F ratios are used throughout this chapter to determine whether groups are significantly different. Omega squared (ω^2) is used to estimate the degree of association (or percent variance accounted for) between the independent and dependent variables. To some extent, ω^2 is similar to r^2 for the correlations presented in chapter 6; both represent the same idea, which is percent variance accounted for. Another way of considering the meaningfulness of the differences is effect size (ES). Effect size is the standardized difference between two groups and is also used as an estimate of meaningfulness.

The use of the t and the F distributions as presented in this chapter have four assumptions (in addition to the assumptions for parametric statistics presented in chapter 5) (Kirk, 1982, p. 74):

- Observations are drawn from normally distributed populations.
- Observations represent random samples from populations.
- The numerator and denominator are estimates of the same population variance.
- The numerator and denominator of F (or t) ratios are independent.

Although t and F tests are robust (only slightly influenced) to violations of these assumptions, the assumptions still are not trivial. You should be sensitive to their presence and to the fact that violations affect the probability levels that may be obtained in connection with t and F ratios.

TYPES OF t TESTS

The t tests are of three types: t test between a sample and a population mean, t test for independent groups, and t test for dependent groups.

t Test Between a Sample and a Population Mean

First, we may want to know whether a sample of subjects differs from a larger population. For example, suppose that for a standardized knowledge test on physical fitness, the mean is 76 for a large population of college freshmen. When tested, a fitness class ($n = 32$) that you are teaching has a mean of 81 and a standard deviation of 9. Does your class have significantly more knowledge about physical fitness than does the typical college freshman class?

The t test is a test of the null hypothesis, which states that there is no difference between the sample mean (M) and the population mean (μ), or $M - \mu = 0$. Formula 7.1 is the t test between a sample and a population mean:

$$t = \frac{M - \mu}{s_M/\sqrt{n}} \qquad (7.1)$$

Table 7.1 shows this formula applied to the means and standard deviation of the example for the standardized fitness knowledge test. Note that the t value obtained (3.14) is significant. The number in parentheses is the degrees of freedom (df) for the t test. Degrees of freedom are based on the number of subjects with a correction for bias:

$$df = n - 1 \qquad (7.2)$$

Degrees of freedom are used to enter a t table to determine whether the calculated t is as large as or greater than the tabled t value. Refer to Table A.5 in Appendix A. Note that across the top of the table are probability levels. Read across to the .05 level. Now read down the left side (df) to the number in the t test from Table 7.1 ($df = 31$). Read where the df row and the .05 column intersect. Is the calculated value ($t = 3.14$) larger than this value (2.04)? Yes, it is; so t is significant at $p < .05$. Thus, our sample class is reliably (significantly) different from the population average on the fitness test.

Table 7.1 Using a t Test Between a Sample and a Population Mean

Population ($N = 10,000$)	Sample fitness class ($n = 32$)
$\mu = 76$	$M = 81$
$\alpha = 7$	$s = 9$

$$t = \frac{M - \mu}{s_M/\sqrt{n}}$$

$$t = \frac{81 - 76}{9/\sqrt{32}} = \frac{5}{1.59} = 3.14$$

$$df = n - 1 = 32 - 1 = 31$$

$$t(31) = 3.14, \ p < .05$$

Independent t Test

The previous t test, applied to determine whether a sample differs from a population, is not used very frequently. The most frequently used t test determines whether two sample means differ reliably from each other and is called an *independent t test*.

Using the Independent t Test

Suppose we return to our example at the beginning of this chapter: Do two groups, training at different levels of intensity (40% or 70% of $\dot{V}O_2$max, 30 min per day, 3 days per week for 12 weeks), differ from each other on a measure of cardiorespiratory endurance (12-min run)? Let us further assume that there were 30 subjects who were randomly assigned to form the two groups of 15 each.

Formula 7.3 is the t-test formula for two independent samples:

$$t = \frac{M_1 - M_2}{\sqrt{s_1^2/n_1 + s_2^2/n_2}} \tag{7.3}$$

where M_1 = the mean for the 70% group, M_2 = the mean for the 40% group, s_1^2 = the variance (standard deviation squared) for the 70% group, s_2^2 = the variance for the 40% group, n_1 = the number of subjects in the 70% group, and n_2 = the number of subjects in the 40% group. The degrees of freedom for an independent t test are calculated as follows:

$$df = (n_1 + n_2) - 2 \tag{7.4}$$

Formula 7.5 is the version of the t-test formula most easily performed with a calculator:

$$t = \frac{M_1 - M_2}{\sqrt{\frac{[\Sigma X_1^2 - (\Sigma X_1)^2/n_1 + \Sigma X_2^2 - (\Sigma X_2)^2/n_2] \times (1/n_1 + 1/n_2)}{(n_1 + n_2) - 2}}} \tag{7.5}$$

Table 7.2 shows how these formulas would be applied to the intensity-of-training experiment. Thus, you can see that the 70% intensity of training allowed subjects to run reliably farther (M = 3,004 m) than did the 40% intensity of training (M = 2,456 m). If the 12-min run is a valid measure of cardiorespiratory endurance and if all other conditions were controlled, we can say that the cause of this increased level of cardiorespiratory endurance was the fact that the 70% group's training was more intense than the 40% group's.

Homogeneity of Variance

All of the comparison-between-groups techniques assume that the variances (standard deviation squared) between the groups are equivalent. While mild violations of this assumption do not present major problems, serious violations are more likely if group sizes are not approximately equal. Formulas given here and used in most computer programs allow unequal group sizes. However, the homogeneity assumption should be checked if group sizes are very different, or even when variances are very different (these techniques are not presented here but are covered in basic statistical texts).

Table 7.2 An Independent t Test

Characteristics	70% $\dot{V}O_2$max	40% $\dot{V}O_2$max
M	3,004 m	2,456 m
s	114 m	103 m
n	15	15

$$t = \frac{M_1 - M_2}{\sqrt{\dfrac{s_1^2}{n_1} + \dfrac{s_2^2}{n_2}}}$$

$$t = \frac{3,004 - 2,456}{\sqrt{\dfrac{(114)^2}{15} + \dfrac{(103)^2}{15}}} = \frac{548}{39.67} = 13.81$$

$df = (n_1 + n_2) - 2 = (15 + 15) - 2 = 28$

$t(28) = 13.81, p < .05$

$$\omega^2 = \frac{t^2 - 1}{t^2 + n_2 + n_2 - 1} = \frac{190.72 - 1}{190.72 + 15 + 15 - 1} = \frac{189.72}{219.72} = .86$$

Note. Appendix B provides an example of an independent t test using the data from Table 7.4.

Estimating Meaningfulness of Treatments

The question now is, How meaningful is this effect? Or, stated more simply, Is the increase in cardiorespiratory endurance of running an additional 548 m (3,004 − 2,456) worth the additional work of training at 70% of $\dot{V}O_2$max as compared to 40% of $\dot{V}O_2$max? What we really want to know, given the total variation in running performance of the two groups, is how much of this variation is accounted for by (associated with) the difference in the two levels of the independent variable (70% vs. 40%).

Omega Squared (ω^2). One way to estimate this variation is to use the following formula (Tolson, 1980) to calculate *omega squared (ω^2)*:

$$\omega^2 = \frac{t^2 - 1}{t^2 + n_1 + n_2 - 1} \tag{7.6}$$

The bottom of Table 7.2 shows the application of this formula to our example. We can conclude that $\omega^2 = .86$ means 86% of the variance in the distance run can be accounted for by the difference in the two groups' levels of training. The remaining variance, 14% (100% − 86% = 14%), is accounted for by other factors. The question now becomes, Is this a meaningful percentage of variance? No one can answer that but you. Are you willing to increase the intensity of training 30% to produce this effect? There is no statistical answer—only the person involved can answer that. The research has told you only what will happen if you increase the intensity of training from 40% to 70% of $\dot{V}O_2$max.

Effect Size. Another way to estimate the degree that the treatment influenced the outcome is by effect size (ES), the standardized difference between the means (this concept is also used in meta-analysis, discussed in chapter 12). Formula 7.7 provides an effect size formula:

$$ES = \frac{M_1 - M_2}{s} \tag{7.7}$$

where M_1 = the mean of one level of treatment, M_2 = the mean of a second level of treatment, and s = the standard deviation. The question is what standard deviation should be used. Considerable controversy exists over the answer to this question. Some statisticians think that if there is a control group, then its standard deviation should be used. If there is no control group, then the pooled standard deviation (Formula 7.8) should be used. Some advocate the use of the pooled standard deviation on all occasions. Either can be defended; however, when there is no clear control group (as in the example used here), we recommend you use the pooled standard deviation:

$$s_P = \sqrt{\frac{s_1^2(n_1 - 1) + s_2^2(n_2 - 1)}{n_1 + n_2 - 2}} \tag{7.8}$$

where s_P = the pooled standard deviation, s_1^2 = the variance of Group 1, s_2^2 = the variance of Group 2, n_1 = the number of subjects in Group 1, and n_2 = the number of subjects in Group 2.

Effect size can be interpreted as follows: an ES greater than .8 is large, an ES around .5 is moderate, and an ES less than .2 is small. Thus, in the example used in Table 7.2, ES is calculated as follows:

$$ES = \frac{3,004 - 2,456}{\sqrt{\frac{(114)^2(15 - 1) + (103)^2(15 - 1)}{15 + 15 - 2}}} = 5.0$$

An ES of 5.0 is a large value and would typically be judged as a meaningful treatment effect.

Dependent t Test (correlated)

We have now considered use of the t test to evaluate whether a sample differs from a population and whether two independent samples differ from each other. A third application is called a *dependent t test*. This means that the two groups of scores are related in some manner. Usually, the relationship takes one of two forms:

- two groups of subjects are matched on one or more characteristics and thus are no longer independent, or

Dependent t revised

- one group of subjects is tested twice on the same variable, and the experimenter is interested in the change between the two tests.

For example, 10 dancers are given a jump-and-reach test (difference between height they can reach and touch a wall and how high they can jump and touch), then 10 weeks of dance activity that involves leaps and jumps 3 days per week. The dancers are again given the jump-and-reach test after the 10 weeks. (This is not proposed to be a real experiment, just a simple example illustrating the statistical technique.) Our research hypothesis is that the 10 weeks of dance experience will improve jumping skills as reflected by the change in jump-and-reach scores. The null hypothesis (H_0) is that the difference between the pre- and the posttest of jumping is not significantly different from zero, $H_0 = M_{pre} - M_{post} = 0$. The formula for a dependent t test is as follows:

$$t = \frac{M_{pre} - M_{post}}{-\sqrt{s_{pre}^2/n_{pre} + s_{post}^2/n_{post} - 2r_{pp} \cdot s_{pre} \cdot s_{post}}} \tag{7.9}$$

Notice that the top part of this formula is the same as the independent t-test formula (7.3). In addition, the bottom (under the square-root symbol) is also the same on the left side. However, an amount is subtracted from the bottom (error term) of the t test $(-2r_{pp} \cdot s_{pre} \cdot s_{post})$. This series of numbers and letters is read as "two times the correlation (r) between the pre- and posttest times the standard deviation for the pretest times the standard deviation for the posttest." The independent t test (7.3) assumes that the two groups of subjects are independent. In this case, the subjects are the same people tested twice (pre and post). Thus, we adjust downward (make smaller) the error term of the t test by taking into account the relationship (r) between the pre- and posttests adjusted to their standard deviations. The degrees of freedom for the dependent t test is

$$df = N - 1 \tag{7.10}$$

where N = the number of paired observations. Formula 7.9 is rather cumbersome to compute because the correlation (r) between the pre- and posttest must be calculated. Thus, the raw-score formula is much easier to use:

$$t = \frac{\Sigma D}{-\sqrt{[N\Sigma D^2 - (\Sigma D)^2]/(N - 1)}} \tag{7.11}$$

where D = the pretest minus the posttest for each subject and N = the number of paired observations. Table 7.3 provides an example of Formula 7.11 applied to the dance study reported previously. The results indicate that the posttest mean (19.7 cm) was significantly better than the pretest mean (16.5 cm), $t(9) = 4.83$, $p < .05$. The null hypothesis can be rejected, and, if everything else has been properly controlled in the experiment, we can conclude that the dance training produced a reliable increase in the height of jumping performance of 3.2 cm.

A computer program for calculating t tests is included in Appendix B. The first example following this program is for a dependent, or correlated, t test. The example uses the data from Table 7.3, and the results are the same. Compare the sample printout to Table 7.3.

A standard formula is not available for calculating ω^2 for a dependent t test. But we could estimate the magnitude of the effect by dividing the average gain by the pretest mean and multiplying by 100 as in the bottom of Table 7.3. The gain is 19.4% of the pretest and represents nearly a 20% improvement. Although this is a rather crude way of estimating the effect, it does suffice. Or, we could estimate ES for the pretest to posttest change by subtracting the pretest M from the posttest M and dividing by the pooled s_p (pool pre- and posttest s^2) as in formulas 7.7 and 7.8.

Table 7.3 A Dependent t Test

Subject	Jump-and-reach test		D	D^2
	Pre	Post		
1	12 cm	16 cm	4	16
2	15 cm	21 cm	6	36
3	13 cm	15 cm	2	4
4	20 cm	22 cm	2	4
5	21 cm	21 cm	0	0
6	19 cm	23 cm	4	16
7	14 cm	16 cm	2	4
8	17 cm	18 cm	1	1
9	16 cm	22 cm	6	36
10	18 cm	23 cm	5	25
Σ	165	197	32	142
M	16.5	19.7	3.2	

$$t = \frac{\Sigma D}{\sqrt{[N\Sigma D^2 - (\Sigma D)^2]/(N - 1)}} = \frac{32}{\sqrt{[10(142) - (32)^2]/(10 - 1)}}$$

$$= \frac{32}{\sqrt{(1{,}420 - 1{,}024)/9}} = \frac{32}{6.63} = 4.83$$

$df = 10 - 1 = 9$

$t(9) = 4.83,\ p < .05$

$$\text{Magnitude of increase} = \frac{M_D}{M_{\text{pre}}} \times 100 = \frac{3.2}{16.5} \times 100 = 19.4\%$$

INTERPRETING t

You have now learned to perform the calculations that determine differences among groups. What do the results mean? Are they significant? Does it matter whether they are or aren't? We answer these questions in this section by giving an explanation of the difference between one-tailed and two-tailed t tests and discussing how t tests can be used to obtain power in research.

One-Tailed Versus Two-Tailed t Tests

At this point, refer again to Table A.5 in Appendix A (the tabled values of t to which you compare the values calculated). Remember, you decide the probability level (we have been using .05), calculate the degrees of freedom for t, and read the tabled t value at the column (probability)-by-row (df) intersection. If your calculated t exceeds the tabled value, it is significant at the specified alpha and degrees of freedom. This table is used for a *two-tailed* t *test* because we assume that the difference between the two means could favor either mean. Sometimes, Group 1 will be better than Group 2 or, at worst, no poorer than Group 2. In this case, the test is a *one-tailed* t *test*, that is, it can go only one direction. Then, when looking at Table A.5, the .05 level is .10, .025 is .05, and .01 is .02. However, generally we are not so sure of our results that we can employ the one-tailed t table.

t Tests and Power in Research

In chapter 5, power was mentioned as the probability of rejecting the null hypothesis when the null hypothesis is false. To obtain power in research is very desirable, as the odds of rejecting a false null hypothesis are increased. The independent t test is used here to explain the three ways to obtain power. However, these ways apply to all types of experimental research.

Consider the formula for the independent t test:

$$t = \frac{M_1 - M_2}{\sqrt{\dfrac{s_1^2}{n_1} + \dfrac{s_2^2}{n_2}}} \quad \begin{matrix} 1 \\ 2 \\ 3 \end{matrix}$$

Note that we have placed numbers (1, 2, 3) beside the three horizontal levels of this formula. These three levels represent what can be manipulated to increase or decrease power.

The first level ($M_1 - M_2$) gives power if we can increase the difference between M_1 and M_2. You should see that if the second and third levels remain the same, a larger difference between the means increases the size of the t ratio, which increases the odds of rejecting the null hypothesis and thus increases power. How can the difference between the means be increased? The logical answer is by applying stronger, more concentrated treatments. These treatments should move the means of the experimental and the control groups farther apart. This results in less overlap in their distributions.

The second level is s_1^2, s_2^2, or the variances (s^2) for each of the two groups. Recall that the standard deviation represents the spread of the scores about the mean. If this spread becomes smaller (scores distributed more closely about the mean), the variance is also smaller. Because the variance term is in the denominator of the t test, if the first and the third levels remain the same, the t ratio will become larger, thus increasing the odds of rejecting the null hypothesis and increasing power. How can the standard deviation and thereby the variance be made smaller? The answer is to apply the treatments more consistently. The more consistently the treatments are applied to each subject, the more the subjects will become similar in response on the dependent variable. This groups the distribution more tightly around the group means, thus reducing the standard deviation.

Finally, the third level (n_1, n_2) is the number of subjects in each group. If n_1 and n_2 are increased and the first and second levels remain the same, the denominator will become smaller (note n is divided into s^2), and the t ratio larger, thus increasing the odds of rejecting the null hypothesis and obtaining power. Obviously, n_1 and n_2 can be increased by placing additional subjects in each group.

Of course, power may also be influenced by varying alpha (i.e., if alpha is set at .10 as opposed to .05, increased power is attained). But in doing this, we increase the risk of rejecting a true null hypothesis.

In summary, power is desirable to obtain because it increases the odds of rejecting a false null hypothesis. Power may be obtained by using strong treatments, administering those treatments consistently, using as many subjects as feasible, or varying alpha. But remember, there is always a second question even in the most powerful experiments. After the null hypothesis is rejected, the strength (meaningfulness) of the effects must be evaluated.

The t ratio has a numerator and a denominator. From a theoretical point of view, the numerator is regarded as *true variance*, or the real difference between the means. The denominator is considered *error variance*, or variation about the mean. Thus, the t ratio is

$$t = \frac{\text{true variance}}{\text{error variance}}$$

where true variance $= M_1 - M_2$ and error variance $= \sqrt{s_1^2/n_1 + s_2^2/n_2}$. If no real differences exist between the groups, true variance = error variance, or the ratio between the two is true variance/error variance, or 1. When a significant t ratio is found, we are really saying that true variance exceeds error variance to a certain degree. The degree needed for significance is dependent on the number of subjects (df) and the alpha level established.

The estimate of the strength of the relationship (ω^2) between the independent and dependent variables is represented by the ratio of true variance to total variance.

$$\omega^2 = \frac{\text{true variance}}{\text{total variance}}$$

Thus, ω^2 represents the proportion of the total variance that is due to the treatments (true variance).

RELATIONSHIP OF t AND r

As we mentioned previously, our separation of statistical techniques into the two categories of relationships among variables (chapter 6) and differences among groups (this chapter) is an artificial one because both sets of techniques are based on the general linear model. A brief demonstration with t and r should make the point. However, the concept can be extended into the more sophisticated techniques discussed in chapter 6, later in this chapter, and in chapter 8 (Understanding Multivariate Techniques).

Table 7.4 provides an example of the relationship between t and r. Note that Group 1 has a set of scores (dependent variable) for 5 subjects as does Group 2. We have calculated the mean and standard deviation of each group by the previously provided formulas and then conducted an independent t test. The two groups are significantly different, $t(8) = 5.00$. We then assigned each subject a dummy code (either 1 or 0) that stands for his or her group. If we treat the dummy-coded variable as X and the dependent variable as Y and ignore group membership (10 subjects with two variables), then the correlation formula used earlier can be applied to the data. The resulting correlation is .87. By applying a t test to r, t is 5.0, the same as the t test done on the group means. The point is that r represents the relationship between the independent and dependent variables (in fact, r^2 is a biased estimator of ω^2) and the test of r (i.e., the t test) evaluates the reliability (significance) of the relationship. Appendix B provides an example of an independent t test using the data from Table 7.4.

We are not trying to confuse you. There are three sources of variance (true variance + error variance = total variance). The t test is the ratio of true variance to error variance, whereas r is the square root of the proportion of total variance accounted for by true variance. To get t from r only means manipulating the variance components in a slightly different way. This is because all parametric correlational and differences-among-groups techniques are based on the general linear model. This result can easily be shown to exist in the more advanced statistical techniques (for a thorough treatment of this topic, see Pedhazur, 1982).

Table 7.4 Comparison of *t* and *r*

	Group 1			Group 2	
Dummy code	Dependent variable		Dummy code	Dependent variable	
1	1		0	6	
1	2		0	7	
1	3		0	8	
1	4		0	9	
1	5		0	10	
Σ 5	15		0	40	
M ...	3		...	8	
s ...	1.58		...	1.58	

$$t = \frac{M_1 - M_2}{\sqrt{\dfrac{s_1^2}{n_1}+\dfrac{s_2^2}{n_2}}} = \frac{3 - 8}{\sqrt{\dfrac{1.58^2}{5} + \dfrac{1.58^2}{5}}} = 5.0$$

$df = (n_1 + n_2) - 2 = 8$

$t(8) = 5.0, p < .05$

$$r = \frac{N\Sigma XY - (\Sigma X)(\Sigma Y)}{\sqrt{N\Sigma X^2 - (\Sigma X)^2}\sqrt{N\Sigma Y^2 - (\Sigma Y)^2}} = \frac{10(15) - (5)(55)}{\sqrt{10(5) - 25}\sqrt{10(385) - 3{,}025}} = \frac{12.5}{14.4} = .87$$

$$t = \sqrt{\frac{r^2}{(1 - r^2)/(N - 2)}} = \sqrt{\frac{.87^2}{(1 - .87^2)/(10 - 2)}} = \sqrt{\frac{.757}{.030}} = 5.0$$

You need to understand this basic concept because it is becoming increasingly common for researchers to use regression techniques to analyze what has been traditionally termed experimental data. These data have usually been analyzed by techniques discussed in this chapter. We have, however, demonstrated that what is traditional is not required. What is important is that the data have been appropriately analyzed to answer the following two basic questions:

- Are the groups significantly different?
- Does the independent variable account for a meaningful proportion of the variance in the dependent variable?

Significance is always evaluated as the ratio of true variance to error variance, whereas percent variance accounted for is always the ratio of true variance to total variance.

ANALYSIS OF VARIANCE

Using *t* tests is a good way to determine differences between two groups. Often, though, experimenters work with more than two groups. A method of determining differences among them is needed in those cases. This section explains how analysis of variance is used to determine differences among two or more groups.

Simple Analysis of Variance

The concept of simple (sometimes called one-way but seldom considered simple by graduate students) *analysis of variance (ANOVA)* is an extension of the independent *t* test. In fact, *t* is just a special case of simple ANOVA in which there are two groups. *Simple ANOVA* allows the evaluation of the null hypothesis among two or more group means with the restriction that the two or more groups are levels of the same independent variable. In an earlier example, we suggested a *t* test was appropriate to test between the means of two groups who trained at 40% and 70% of $\dot{V}O_2$max. This represents two levels (40% and 70%) of one independent variable (intensity of training). In fact, simple ANOVA and its statistic symbol, the *F* ratio, could just as easily have been used. But what would happen if there were more than two levels of the independent variable, for example, 40%, 60%, and 80% of $\dot{V}O_2$max? Simple ANOVA could be used in this situation to test the null hypothesis that $M_1 = M_2 = M_3 = 0$, or that the difference among the three group means is not significant.

Why not do a *t* test between the 40% and 60% groups, a second *t* test between the 40% and 80% groups, and a third *t* test between the 60% and 80% groups? The reason is because this would violate an assumption relative to the established alpha level (let it be $p < .05$). The .05 level means 1 chance in 20 of a chance difference, assuming that the subjects on which the statistical test are made are from independent random samples. In our case, this is not true—each group has been used in two comparisons (e.g., 40% vs. 60% and 40% vs. 80%) rather than only one. Thus, we have increased the chances of making a Type I error (i.e., alpha is no longer .05). Making this type of comparison, in which the same group's mean is used more than once, is an example of increasing the experimentwise error rate. Simple ANOVA allows all three group means to be compared simultaneously, thus keeping alpha at the designated level of .05.

Calculating Simple ANOVA

Table 7.5 provides the formulas for calculating simple ANOVA and the *F* ratio. This method, the so-called ABC method, is rather simple:

$A = \Sigma X^2$: This means to square each subject's score, sum these squared scores (regardless of which group the subject is in), and set the total equal to A.

$B = (\Sigma X)^2 / N$: For this value, we sum each subject's score (regardless of group), square the sum, divide by the total number of subjects, and set the answer equal to B.

$C = (\Sigma X_1)^2 / n_1 + (\Sigma X_2)^2 / n_2 + \ldots + (\Sigma X_i)^2 / n_i$: This requires that we sum each subject's score in Group 1, square the sum, and divide by the number of subjects in Group 1; do the same for the scores in Group 2 and so on for however many groups (*i*) there are; then, set the answer to C.

Next, fill in the summary table for ANOVA using *A*, *B*, and *C*. Thus, the between-groups (true variance) sum of squares (*SS*) is equal to $C - B$; the between-groups degrees of freedom (*df*) is the number of groups minus one ($k - 1$); the between-groups variance or mean square (MS_B) is the between-groups sum of squares divided by the between-groups degrees of freedom. The same follows when the source is within groups (error variance) and then for the total. The *F* ratio is MS_B/MS_W.

Table 7.6 provides an example for which the formulas in Table 7.5 are used. The scores from Groups 1, 2, and 3 are the sums of two judges' skill ratings for a particular series of movements. The groups are randomly formed from 15 junior high school students. Group 1 was taught with videotape and used individual corrections by the teacher while the student viewed the videotape. Group 2 was taught with videotape, but only general group corrections were made while students viewed the tape. Group 3 was taught by the teacher without the benefit of videotape equipment. From looking at the formulas in Table 7.5, you should be able to see how each number in Table 7.6 was calculated.

Your main interest in Table 7.6, after you make sure you understand how the numbers were obtained, is in the *F* ratio of 10.00. Table A.6 in Appendix A contains tabled *F* values for the .05 and .01 levels of significance. Although the numbers in this table are obtained the same way as in the *t* table, you use the table in a slightly different way. Note in Table 7.6, that the *F* ratio is obtained by dividing MS_B by MS_W. The term MS_B has 2 *df* associated with it (numerator) and the MS_W 12 *df* (denominator). Notice also that the *F* table (Table A.6) has degrees of freedom across the top (numerator) and down the left-hand column (denominator). For our *F* of 10.00, read down the 2-*df* column to the 12-*df* row; there are two numbers where the row and the column intersect. The top number (3.88) in light print is the tabled

Table 7.5 Formulas for Calculating Simple ANOVA

$$A = \Sigma X^2$$
$$B = \frac{(\Sigma X)^2}{N}$$
$$C = \frac{(\Sigma X_1)^2}{n_1} + \frac{(\Sigma X_2)^2}{n_2} + \ldots + \frac{(\Sigma X_i)^2}{n_i}$$

Summary table for ANOVA

Source	SS	df	MS	F
Between (true)	$C - B$	$k - 1$	$(C - B)/(k - 1)$	MS_B/MS_W
Within (error)	$A - C$	$N - k$	$(A - C)/(N - k)$	
Total	$A - B$	$N - 1$		

Note. X = a subject's score, N = total number of subjects, n = number of subjects in a group, k = number of groups, SS = sum of squares, df = degrees of freedom, MS = mean square.

Table 7.6 A Simple ANOVA

	Group 1		Group 2		Group 3	
	X	X^2	X	X^2	X	X^2
	12	144	9	81	6	36
	10	100	7	49	7	49
	11	121	6	36	2	4
	7	49	9	81	3	9
	10	100	4	16	2	4
Σ	50	514	35	263	20	102
M	10	. . .	7	. . .	4	. . .

$A = \Sigma X^2 = 514 + 263 + 102 = 879$
$B = (\Sigma X)^2/N = (50 + 35 + 20)^2/15 = (105)^2/15 = 11{,}025/15 = 735$
$C = (\Sigma X_1)^2/n_1 + (\Sigma X_2)^2/n_2 + (\Sigma X_3)^2/n_3 = (50)^2/5 + (35)^2/5 + (20)^2/5$
$\quad = 2{,}500/5 + 1{,}225/5 + 400/5 = 825$

Summary table for ANOVA

Source	SS	df	MS	F
Between	90	2	45.0	10.00*
Within	54	12	4.5	. . .
Total	144	14	. . .	. . .

*$p < .05$.

F for the .05 level, whereas the bottom number (**6.93**) in dark print is the tabled F for the .01 level. If our alpha had been established as .05, then you can see that our F value of 10.00 is larger than the tabled value of .05 (actually, it is also larger than .01), so our F is significant and could be written in the text of an article as $F(2, 12) = 10.00$, $p < .05$ (read "F with 2 and 12 degrees of freedom equals 10.00 and is significant at less than the .05 level"). A computer program to calculate simple (one-way) ANOVA is provided in Appendix B. Following the listing of this program is a sample printout using the data from Table 7.6.

Follow-Up Testing

We now know that significant differences exist among the three group means (Group 1 = 10, Group 2 = 7, and Group 3 = 4). However, we do not know whether all three groups differ (e.g., whether 1 and 2 differ from 3 but not from each other). Thus, we next perform a follow-up test. One way to do this is to use t tests between Groups 1 and 2, 1 and 3, and 2 and 3. However, the same problem that we discussed earlier still exists with alpha. Several follow-up tests protect the experiment-wise error rate. These methods include Scheffé, Newman-Keuls, Duncan's, and several others. Each of the tests is calculated in a slightly different way, but they all are conceptually similar to the *t* test in that they identify which groups differ from each other. The Scheffé method is the most conservative, which means it identifies fewer significant differences. Duncan's is the most liberal, identifying more significant differences. Newman-Keuls falls between the other two.

For our purposes, one example should suffice, so we demonstrate the use of the Newman-Keuls method of making multiple comparisons among means. Table 7.7 arranges the means from highest (10) to lowest (4) (the means could also be arranged from lowest to highest). By following steps 1-8, you can see that all three groups differ from one another, *p* < .05. We could conclude that the techniques used in Group 1 were better than those used in Groups 2 and 3 and that the techniques used in Group 2 were better than those used in Group 3.

Look more carefully at Table A.7 in Appendix A. Note that as the means are further apart in terms of size, a greater difference is required for significance. This is what protects alpha in a technique of this type. You should plan for the type of multiple range test to be used if significant differences are obtained in the ANOVA. These are called *post hoc comparisons*, which means that you make the comparisons after finding a significant *F* ratio. Some people refer to this as data snooping (you snoop around to see which groups differ).

Table 7.7 Newman-Keuls Test Applied to Data From Table 7.6

Group	M	2	3
1	10	3.16*	6.32*
2	7	. . .	3.16*
3	4	. . .	. . .

Step 1: Calculate error term: $E = \sqrt{MS_w/n} = \sqrt{4.5/5} = .95$.

Step 2: Order the means from highest to lowest: 10, 7, 4.

Step 3: Calculate the differences between the means: 3, 6, 3.

Step 4: Divide the difference by E and enter in table above: $3/.95 = 3.16$, $6/.95 = 6.32$, $3/.95 = 3.16$.

Step 5: Calculate the steps between means; this is the number of means in the ordered set—Group 1 to 2 is two steps, Group 1 to 3 is three steps, Group 2 to 3 is two steps. The number of steps is called k.

Step 6: The *df* for error is 12 (see Table 7.6).

Step 7: Enter the Studentized range table (Table A.7 in Appendix A) with k and 12 *df* depending on which groups are being compared—Groups 1 and 2 would be 2 and 12 *df*, Groups 1 and 3 would be 3 and 12 *df*, and Groups 2 and 3 would be 2 and 12 *df*.

Step 8: Compare value calculated for table above with value in Table A.5 at alpha .05 (for this example) and * the differences that are larger than the tabled value.

*p < .05.

The researcher may also use *planned comparisons* to test for differences among groups. Planned comparisons are a priori in nature; that is, they are planned before the experiment. Thus, an experimenter might postulate a test between two of the groups before the experiment because in theory this particular comparison is important and should be significant. However, the number of planned comparisons in an experiment should be small relative to the total number of possible comparisons.

Meaningfulness of Results

Now that we know that F is significant and have followed it up to see which groups differ, we should answer our second question: What percent variance is accounted for by our treatments, or how meaningful are our results? One way to get a quick idea is to refer to Table 7.6 and put true variance over total variance: SS_{true}/SS_{total} = 90/144 = .625, or 62.5% of the variance is accounted for by the treatments. Although this is sufficient for a quick estimate, it is biased. The more accurate way is to use the following formula from Tolson (1980):

$$\omega^2 = \frac{[F(k-1)] - (k-1)}{[F(k-1)] + (N-k) + 1} \tag{7.12}$$

where F = the F ratio, k = the number of groups, and N = the total number of subjects. If we do this with the data from Table 7.6, then we have

$$\omega^2 = \frac{[10.00(3-1)] - (3-1)}{[10.00(3-1)] + (15-3) + 1} = \frac{18}{33} = .545$$

Thus, ω^2 indicates that 54.5% of the total variance is accounted for by the treatments.

Putting our statistics together, we could say that the treatments were significant, $F(2, 12) = 10.00$, $p < .05$, and accounted for a meaningful proportion of the variance ($\omega^2 = 54.5\%$). In addition, a follow-up Newman-Keuls test indicate that all three groups were different ($p < .05$), with Group 1 showing the best performance and Group 3 the poorest.

Summarizing Simple ANOVA

One final point to recall before leaving our discussion of simple ANOVA is that t was a special case of F when there were only two levels of the independent variable (two groups). In fact, this relationship is exact, $t^2 = F$. Table 7.8 provides a specific example (within rounding error). In other words, there is very little need for t, as F will handle two or more groups. However, t remains in use because it was developed first, being the simplest case of F.

Table 7.8 Comparison of t and F

	Experimental group				Control group		
	X	$(X - M)^2$	X^2		X	$(X - M)^2$	X^2
	2	.09	4		8	4	64
	4	2.89	16		7	1	49
	3	.49	9		5	1	25
	3	.49	9		4	4	16
	2	.09	4		7	1	49
	1	1.69	1		5	1	25
	1	1.69	1		6	0	36
Σ	16	7.43	44		42	12	264
M	2.3	. . .	. . .		6.0	. . .	. . .
s	1.11	. . .	. . .		1.41	. . .	. . .

$$t = \frac{M_1 - M_2}{\sqrt{(s_1^2/n_1) + (s_2^2/n_2)}} = \frac{2.3 - 6}{\sqrt{(1.11^2/7) + (1.41^2/7)}} = \frac{3.7}{.68} = 5.44$$

$A = \Sigma X^2 = 44 + 264 = 308$

$B = (\Sigma X)^2/N = (58)^2/14 = 240.29$

$C = (\Sigma X_1)^2/n_1 + (\Sigma X_2)^2/n_2 = (16)^2/7 + (42)^2/7 = 36.57 + 252 = 288.57$

Summary table for ANOVA

Source	SS	df	MS	F
Between	48.28	1	48.28	29.80
Within	19.43	12	1.62	. . .
Total	67.71	13	. . .	. . .

$t^2 = F$, $(5.44)^2 = 29.8$, $29.6 \cong 29.8$ (within rounding error)

Factorial ANOVA

Up to this point, examples of two levels (*t*) or two or more levels (simple ANOVA) of one independent variable have been discussed. In fact, what has occurred is that all other independent variables have been controlled except the single independent variable to be manipulated and its effect on a dependent variable. This is called the Law of the Independent Variable. But, in fact, we can manipulate more than one independent variable and statistically evaluate the effects on a dependent variable. This procedure is called *factorial ANOVA*, meaning that there is more than one factor or independent variable. Theoretically, a factorial ANOVA may have any number of factors (two or more) and any number of levels within a factor (two or more). However, we seldom encounter ANOVAs with more than three or four factors. This is another good place to apply the KISS principle (Keep It Simple, Stupid).

Calculating Factorial ANOVA

For our purpose we consider only a two-way factorial ANOVA, meaning the use of only two independent variables. There would be two main effects and one interaction. *Main effects* are tests of each independent variable when the other is disregarded. Look at Table 7.9 and note that the first independent variable (IV_1) has three levels, labeled A_1, A_2, and A_3. Assume that these three levels represent the intensity of training: 40%, 60%, and 80% of $\dot{V}O_2$max for 20 min per day for a 12-week period. The second independent variable (IV_2) represents frequency of training: 2 days per week (B_1) versus 3 days per week (B_2). We can test IV_1 by comparing the row means (M_{A_1}, M_{A_2}, M_{A_3}) because IV_2 (B_1 and B_2) is equally represented at each level of A. That is, for each level of A, two groups (one training 2 days and one 3 days per week) are included. Thus, frequency of training is held constant to allow the test of intensity of training by the F_A ratio.

The same holds true for IV_2, frequency of training. By looking at the column means (M_{B_1} and M_{B_2}), you can see that the three levels of A (IV_1), intensity of training, are equally represented in the two levels of B. Therefore, the main effect of frequency of training can be tested by the F_B ratio.

In a study of this type, the main interest usually lies in the interaction. We want to know whether the effect of the levels of A depends on or changes across the levels of B, that is whether the effect of intensity of training depends on (interacts with) the frequency of training. This effect is tested by the F_{AB} ratio, which evaluates the six cell means: $M_{A_1B_1}$, $M_{A_1B_2}$, $M_{A_2B_1}$, $M_{A_2B_2}$, $M_{A_3B_1}$, and $M_{A_3B_2}$. Unless some special circumstance exists, interest in the testing of main effects is usually limited by the presence of a significant interaction, which means that what happens in one independent variable depends on the level of the other. Thus, normally it makes little sense to evaluate main effects when the interaction is significant.

This particular factorial ANOVA is labeled as a 3 (Intensity of Training) × 2 (Frequency of Training) ANOVA (read "3-by-2 ANOVA"). As the bottom of Table 7.9 indicates, the true variance can be divided into three parts:

- true variance due to A (intensity of training),
- true variance due to B (frequency of training), and
- true variance due to the interaction of A and B.

Table 7.9 Factorial (3 × 2) ANOVA Model

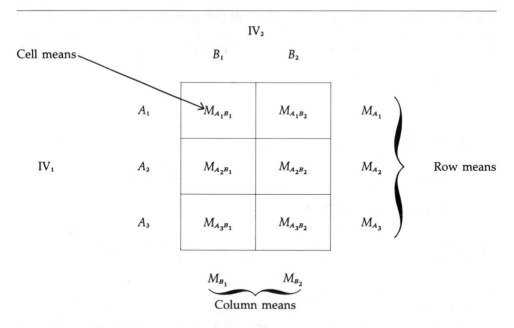

IV_1—main effect is the test of the row means by F_A.
IV_2—main effect is the test of the column means by F_B.
The interaction is the test of the six cell means by F_{AB}.

F_A = (true variance due to A)/(error variance)
F_B = (true variance due to B)/(error variance)
F_{AB} = (true variance due to A × B)/(error variance)

Each of these true variance components is tested against (divided by) error variance to form the three F ratios for this ANOVA. Each of these Fs will have its own set of degrees of freedom so that it can be checked for significance in the F table in Appendix A.

Table 7.10 gives the ABC method for calculating a two-way factorial ANOVA. Table 7.11 then provides an example using intensity of training and frequency of training as the independent variables and distance covered on the 12-min run as the dependent variable. Thirty subjects are randomly assigned to one of the six groups (ns = 5). Thus, this is a 3 × 2 ANOVA. The test for intensity is significant, $F(2, 24) = 161.57$, $p < .05$.

This F is then followed up with a Newman-Keuls test, and we see that the 80% group performed significantly better than both the 60% and the 40% group (Table 7.12), whereas the 60% group was significantly better than the 40% group.

The test for frequency of training is also significant, $F(1, 24) = 448.00$, $p < .05$. However, no follow-up is required for this independent variable because there are

Table 7.10 The ABC Method for Calculating a Two-Way Factorial ANOVA

$A = \Sigma X^2$
$B = (\Sigma X)^2/N$
$C \text{ (rows)} = [(\Sigma X_{r_1})^2 + (\Sigma X_{r_2})^2 + \ldots + (\Sigma X_{r_i})^2]/n_{r_1}$
$D \text{ (columns)} = [(\Sigma X_{c_1})^2 + (\Sigma X_{c_2})^2 + \ldots + (\Sigma X_{c_j})^2]/n_{c_1}$
$E \ (r \times c) = [(\Sigma X_{\text{cell}_1})^2 + (\Sigma X_{\text{cell}_2})^2 + \ldots + (\Sigma X_{\text{cell}_k})^2]/n_{\text{cell}_1}$

Summary table for ANOVA

Source	SS	df	MS	F
Rows (IV$_1$)	$C - B$	$r - 1$	SS_R/df_R	MS_R/MS_E
Columns (IV$_2$)	$D - B$	$c - 1$	SS_C/df_C	MS_C/MS_E
R × C	$(E - B) - (C - B) - (D - B)$	$(r - 1)(c - 1)$	SS_{RC}/df_{RC}	MS_{RC}/MS_E
Error	$(A - B) - (E - B)$	$(N - 1) - (r - 1) +$ $(c - 1) + (r - 1)(c - 1)$	SS_E/df_E	
Total	$A - B$	$N - 1$		

where r = number of rows or levels of IV$_1$
c = number of columns or levels of IV$_2$

only two levels (thus, in a factorial, t^2 approximately equals F). All that is necessary is to note that the 3-day-per-week condition ($M = 3772.3$) produces significantly better performance than the 2-day-per-week condition ($M = 3055.3$).

Finally, the test for the $A \times B$ interaction is significant, $F(2, 24) = 113.40$, $p <$ .05. Thus, what happens with intensity of training depends on the frequency of the training. Figure 7.1 is a plot of this interaction. You can see that the three intensities of training are very similar in effect on the 12-min run when training is 2 days per week. However, the 80% level is clearly the best at 3 days per week, and the 60% level is better than the 40% level. The 40% level is very similar to all three intensities at the 2 days per week training frequency. In looking at this interaction, we might conclude that training 2 days per week or at 40% of $\dot{V}O_2$max is not very effective. However, if the frequency of training is at least 3 days per week and at intensities of 60% of $\dot{V}O_2$max or higher, significant cardiorespiratory benefits (as measured by the 12-min run) occur.

As you can see, all we have done to follow up the significant interaction is to verbally describe the plot in Figure 7.1. Considerable disagreement exists among researchers about how to follow up significant interactions. Some researchers use a multiple comparison of means test (such as Newman-Keuls) to contrast the interaction cell means. However, these multiple comparison tests were developed for contrasting levels within an independent variable and not for cell means across two or more independent variables; thus, their use may be inappropriate. Other researchers use a follow-up called a test of simple main effects. In our example, this indicates that a multiple comparison test should be applied to the three cell means within

Table 7.11 An Example of a Two-Way Factorial ANOVA

		IV_2 (frequency of exercise)				
		2 d/wk		3 d/wk		
		X	X^2	X	X^2	
		2,940	8,643,600	2,980	8,880,400	
		3,070	9,424,900	3,160	9,985,600	
	40%	3,100	9,610,000	3,025	9,150,625	$\Sigma X_{r_1} = 30{,}285$
		2,925	8,555,625	3,045	9,272,025	
		3,050	9,302,500	2,990	8,940,100	
		X	X^2	X	X^2	
IV_1		3,150	9,922,500	3,720	13,838,400	
(intensity		3,020	9,120,400	3,630	13,176,900	
of	60%	2,990	8,940,100	3,570	12,744,900	$\Sigma X_{r_2} = 33{,}510$
exercise)		3,050	9,302,500	3,690	13,616,100	
		2,980	8,880,400	3,710	13,764,100	
		X	X^2	X	X^2	
		3,170	10,048,900	3,920	15,366,400	
		3,120	9,734,400	4,040	16,321,600	
	80%	3,050	9,302,500	4,110	16,892,100	$\Sigma X_{r_3} = 35{,}620$
		3,110	9,672,100	4,005	16,040,025	
		3,105	9,641,025	3,990	15,920,100	

$$\Sigma X_{c_1} = 45{,}830 \qquad \Sigma X_{c_2} = 53{,}585$$

$A = \Sigma X^2 = 8{,}643{,}600 + 9{,}424{,}900 + \ldots + 15{,}920{,}100 = 334{,}010{,}825$

$B = (\Sigma X)^2/N = (2{,}940 + 3{,}070 + 3{,}100 + \ldots + 3{,}990)^2/30 = 329{,}444{,}741$

$C = [(\Sigma X_{r_1})^2 + (\Sigma X_{r_2})^2 + (\Sigma X_{r_3})^2]/n_{r_1} = [(30{,}285)^2 + (33{,}510)^2 + (35{,}620)^2]/10 = 330{,}888{,}573$

$D = [(\Sigma X_{c_1})^2 + (\Sigma X_{c_2})^2]/n_{c_1} = [(45{,}830)^2 + (53{,}585)^2]/15 = 331{,}449{,}408$

$E = [(\Sigma X_{cell_1})^2 + (\Sigma X_{cell_2})^2 + \ldots + (\Sigma X_{cell_k})^2]/n_{cell_1}$

$= [(15{,}085)^2 + (15{,}200)^2 + (15{,}190)^2 + (18{,}320)^2 + (15{,}555)^2 + (20{,}065)^2]/5 = 333{,}903{,}595$

Summary table for ANOVA

Source	SS	df	MS	F
Rows (A)	1,443,832	2	721,916	161.57*
Columns (B)	2,004,667	1	2,004,667	448.68*
A × B	1,010,355	2	505,177	113.07*
Error	107,230	24	4,468	. . .
Total	4,566,084	29	. . .	. . .

*$p < .05$.

Table 7.12 Newman-Keuls Follow-Up to Significant Main Effect F From Table 7.11

Group	M	2	3
1 40%	3,028.5	15.26*	25.24*
2 60%	3,351.0	. . .	9.98*
3 80%	3,562.0	. . .	. . .

$E\ =\sqrt{MS_E/n}\ =\sqrt{4,468/10}\ =\ 21.14$

$t_{12} = (3,028.5 - 3,351)/21.14 = 322.5/21.14 = 15.26$

$t_{13} = (3,028.5 - 3,526)/21.14 = 533.5/21.14 = 25.24$

$t_{23} = (3,351 - 3,562)/21.14 = 211/21.14 = 9.98$

*$p < .05$.

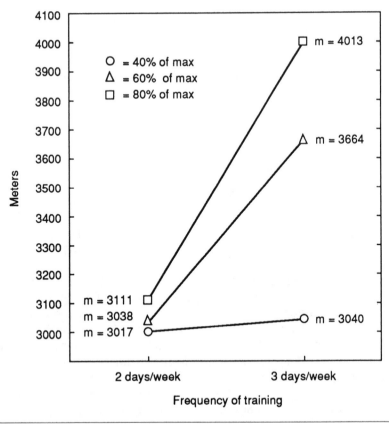

Figure 7.1 The plot of the interaction for a two-way factorial ANOVA.

the levels of the independent variable of B. That is, the three levels of intensity are tested against one another at the 2-day-per-week training and then at the 3-day-per-week training. If the interaction is to be followed up with a statistical test, simple main effects would be the preferred technique.

Our preference for evaluating an interaction is to do as we have done: plot the interaction and describe it. This takes into account the true nature of an interaction; that is, what happens in one independent variable depends on the other. However, you are likely to encounter all these ways of testing interactions (and probably some others) as you read the research literature. Just remember that the researcher is trying to show you how the two or more independent variables interact. Also, remember that follow-ups on main effects are usually unnecessary (or at least the interpretation must be qualified) when the interaction is significant. Although we have done the follow-ups in this example to help you better understand the procedures, the follow-ups would be of limited interest in the presence of a significant and meaningful interaction.

Appendix B contains a computer program to calculate a two-way factorial ANOVA. Following the listing of this program is a sample printout using the data from Table 7.11.

Meaningfulness of Results

We have now answered the first statistical question about a factorial ANOVA: What are the significant effects? As in previous examples, we now turn to the meaningfulness of the effects, or what percent of the variance in the dependent variable is accounted for by the independent variables and their interaction? The three formulas that follow (from Tolson, 1980) provide the ω^2 test for each component of ANOVA:

$$\omega_A^2 = \frac{(p-1)F_A - (p-1)}{(p-1)F_A + (q-1)F_B + (p-1)(q-1)F_{AB} + (N-pq) + 1}$$

$$\omega_B^2 = \frac{(q-1)F_B - (q-1)}{(p-1)F_A + (q-1)F_B + (p-1)(q-1)F_{AB} + (N-pq) + 1} \qquad (7.13)$$

$$\omega_{AB}^2 = \frac{(p-1)(q-1)F_{AB} - (p-1)(q-1)}{(p-1)F_A + (q-1)F_B + (p-1)(q-1)F_{AB} + (N-pq) + 1}$$

where p = the number of levels of A, and q = the number of levels of B. These formulas involve the proportion of true variance to total variance. Note that once you calculate total variance, that value remains the same for the test of all three proportions. In Table 7.13 we have applied Formula 7.13 to the Fs calculated in Table 7.12. Each ω^2 represents the percent variance accounted for by that component of the ANOVA model. The ω^2 can be summed to estimate the percent of the total variance that is true variance. Of course, effect sizes can be calculated according to the previous formulas (7.7 and 7.8) for any two means that you want to compare whether the means are from main effects or interactions.

Table 7.13 The Calculation of ω^2 for the F Ratios From Table 7.11

$$\omega_A^2 = \frac{(3-1)161.57 - (3-1)}{(3-1)161.57 + (2-1)448.00 + (3-1)(2-1)113.07 + (30-6) + 1}$$

$$= \frac{2(161.57) - 2}{(2)161.57 + (1)448.00 + (2)(1)113.07 + 24 + 1}$$

$$= \frac{321.14}{323.14 + 448.00 + 226.14 + 25} = \frac{447}{1,022.28} = .31$$

$$\omega_B^2 = \frac{(2-1)448.00 - (2-1)}{1,022.28} = \frac{447}{1,022.28} = .44$$

$$\omega_{AB}^2 = \frac{(3-1)(2-1)113.07 - (3-1)(2-1)}{1,022.28} = \frac{226.14 - 2}{1,022.28} = \frac{224.14}{1,022.28} = .22$$

Thus, the independent variable of intensity accounts for 31% of the true variance; the independent variable of frequency accounts for 44% of the true variance; the interaction accounts for 22% of the true variance; and the total true variance is 97%.

Summarizing Factorial ANOVA

Our discussion of simple and factorial ANOVA has dealt with studies in which the levels of the independent variables have the subjects randomly assigned. This is not always the case. Frequently, levels of the independent variable may be categorical (also called classification) in nature. For example, we could do a simple ANOVA in which the levels (or groups) of the independent variable involve novice and expert tennis players. Or, in the previously presented factorial ANOVA, we could look at the effects of intensity of training (40%, 60%, and 80% of $\dot{V}O_2max$) 3 days per week, 20 min per day for 12 weeks as one independent variable (three levels) and have the other independent variable be categorical (e.g., gender). That is, we would be interested in whether intensity of training affected males and females differently. The levels of the first independent variable have subjects randomly assigned, whereas subjects cannot be randomly assigned to the categorical variable (one is either male or female). Another common use of categorical variables involves age levels. A study might look at the effects of the levels of a treatment independent variable (where subjects are randomly assigned) on 6-, 9-, and 12-year-old females. Clearly, the interest in this type of factorial ANOVA is the interaction: Does the effectiveness of treatment differ according to the age of the child?

Repeated Measures ANOVA

Much of the research in physical education, exercise science, and sport science involves studies that measure the same dependent variable more than once. For example, a study in sport psychology might investigate whether athletes' state anxiety (how nervous they feel at the time) is different after than before a game. Thus, a state-anxiety inventory would be given just preceding and immediately following the game. The question of interest is, Does state anxiety change significantly from before to after the game? A dependent *t* test could be used to see whether significant changes occurred. This is the simplest case of *repeated measures ANOVA*.

Another study might have subjects measured on the dependent variable on several occasions. Suppose we wanted to know whether children (between ages 6 and 8) would increase the distance they threw a ball using an overhand throwing pattern. We decide to measure the children's distance throw every 3 months during the 2 years of the study. Thus, the children were assessed eight times on how far each could throw. We now have eight repeated measures on the same children. We would use a simple ANOVA with repeated measures on the one factor. Basically, the repeated measures is used as eight levels of the independent variable, which is time (24 months). This analysis may also be referred to as a *split-plot ANOVA* or *subject × trials ANOVA*. They both mean the same thing.

The most frequent use of repeated measures involves a factorial ANOVA, in which one or more of the factors (independent variables) are repeated measures. An example is an investigation of the effects of knowledge of results (KR) on skilled motor performance. There are three groups of subjects (three levels of independent variable) who receive varying types of KR (no KR, short or long of the target, and number of centimeters short or long of the target). The task is to position a handle that slides back and forth on a trackway (called a linear slide) as close to the target as possible. But the subjects are blindfolded, so they cannot see the target. They have only verbal KR to correct their estimates of where the target is located along the trackway.

In this type of study, subjects are usually given multiple trials (assume 30 trials in this example) so that the effects of the quality of KR can be judged. The score on each trial is error from the target in centimeters. This type of study is frequently analyzed as a two-way factorial ANOVA with repeated measures on the second factor. Thus a 3 (Levels of KR) × 30 (Trials) ANOVA with error as the dependent variable is used to analyze the data. The first independent variable (levels of KR) is a true one (three groups are randomly formed). The second independent variable (30 trials) is repeated measures. Sometimes this ANOVA is called a two-way factorial ANOVA with one between-subjects factor (levels of KR) and one within-subjects factor (30 repeated trials). Although an *F* ratio is calculated for each independent variable, the major focus is usually on the interaction. For example, do the groups change at different rates across the trials?

Advantages of Repeated Measures

Repeated measures designs have three advantages (Pedhazur, 1982):

- They provide the experimenter the opportunity to control for individual differences among subjects, probably the largest source of variation in most studies. In between-subject designs (completely randomized), the variation among subjects goes into the error term. Of course, this tends to reduce the *F* ratio unless it is offset by a large number of subjects. Remember, the error term of the F ratio consists of dividing the variation among subjects by the degrees of freedom (which is based on the number of subjects). In repeated measures designs, variation from individual differences can be identified and separated from the error term, thereby reducing it and increasing power.

- As you can deduce from the first advantage, repeated measures designs are more economical in that fewer subjects are required.
- Repeated measures designs allow the study of a phenomenon across time. This is particularly important in studies of change in, for example, learning, fatigue, forgetting, performance, and aging.

Problems of Repeated Measures

However, several problems adversely affect repeated measures designs, including the following:

- **Carryover effects.** Treatments given earlier influence those given later.
- **Practice effects.** Subjects get better at the task (dependent variable) as a result of repeated trials in addition to the treatment (also called the testing effect).
- **Fatigue.** Subjects' performance is adversely influenced by fatigue (or boredom).
- **Sensitization.** Subjects' awareness of the treatment is heightened because of repeated exposure.

Note that some of these problems may be the variables of interest in repeated measures designs. Carryover effects may interest the researcher of learning, whereas increased fatigue over trials may be of major interest to an exercise physiologist.

The tricky part of repeated measures designs involves how to analyze the data statistically. We have already mentioned ANOVA models with repeated measures as one way to analyze the data. Unfortunately, these repeated measures ANOVAs have assumptions in addition to the ones we have given for all techniques. For a long time, statisticians thought that a major assumption, called *compound symmetry*, was required, all the variables within a group must have equal variances, all the correlations among variables must be equal, and the covariance matrices of all groups must be equal. These assumptions are seldom met in repeated measures studies, particularly those in physical education, exercise science, and sport science (Stamm & Safrit, 1975). However, these assumptions have been shown to be unnecessarily strict (for a discussion, see Schutz & Gessaroli, 1987). The correct assumption is called *sphericity*: The repeated measures, "when transformed by a set of orthonormal weights, are uncorrelated with each other and have equal variances" (Schutz & Gessaroli, 1987, p. 134). If the design has a between-subjects factor, the pooled data (across all subjects) must exhibit sphericity. How well the data meet these assumptions is best estimated by a statistic called epsilon (ϵ). Epsilon ranges from 1.0 (perfect sphericity, the assumption is met) to 0.0 (complete violation). An epsilon above .75 is desirable in repeated measures experiments. Most of the widely used statistical packages (SPSSx and BIMED) have repeated measures programs that provide both estimates of epsilon and tests that should be used to evaluate the F ratio for the repeated measures factors in the designs. The failure to meet this assumption results in an increase in Type I error; that is, the alpha level may be considerably larger than the researcher intended. Several statisticians (Davidson, 1972; Harris, 1985; Morrow & Frankiewicz, 1979) have suggested that multivariate techniques are the more appropriate means of analysis. However, two additional points are important (Pedhazur, 1982):

- When the assumptions are met, the ANOVA with repeated measures is more powerful than the multivariate tests.
- If the number of subjects is small, only the ANOVA repeated measures test can be used.

If you are contemplating conducting a study that uses a repeated measures design, then an additional source of reading should be helpful to you. Schutz and Gessaroli (1987) provide a tutorial on the use of repeated measures for univariate and multivariate data that gives a sound rationale for making decisions as well as specific examples of how the data may be analyzed and evaluated.

Calculating Repeated Measures

Table 7.14 provides the formulas (ABC method) used to calculate a one-way ANOVA with repeated measures. This analysis may also be called a Subject × Trials ANOVA, or a two-way ANOVA with 1 subject per cell. An example of these calculations is provided in Table 7.15. The example used here is the data from Table 7.6, in which Groups 1, 2, and 3 are labeled across the top. Note in Table 7.15 that the group designation has been changed to Trials 1, 2, and 3. Thus, where previously (Table 7.6)

Table 7.14 The ABC Method for Calculating One-Way Repeated Measures ANOVA

$A = \Sigma X^2$
$B = (\Sigma X)^2/N$
$C \text{ (subjects)} = [(\Sigma X_{r_1})^2 + (\Sigma X_{r_2})^2 + \ldots + (\Sigma X_{r_i})^2]/n_{r_1}$
$D \text{ (trials)} = [(\Sigma X_{c_1})^2 + (\Sigma X_{c_2})^2 + \ldots + (\Sigma X_{c_j})^2]/n_{c_1}$

Summary table for ANOVA

Source	SS	df	MS	F
Subjects	$C - B$	$r - 1$	SS_S/df_S	MS_S/MS_R
Trials	$D - B$	$c - 1$	SS_T/df_T	MS_T/MS_R
Residual	$(A - B) - (C - B) + (D - B)$	$(r - 1)(c - 1)$	SS_R/df_R	. . .
Total	$A - B$	$N - 1$	. . .	. . .

where r = number of subjects
c = number of trials
N = total number of scores (no. subjects × no. trials)

Table 7.15   Repeated Measures ANOVA

Subjects	Trial 1		Trial 2		Trial 3	
	X	X^2	X	X^2	X	X^2
1	12	144	9	81	6	36
2	10	100	7	49	7	49
3	11	121	6	36	2	4
4	7	49	9	81	3	9
5	10	100	4	16	2	4
Total	50	514	35	263	20	102
M	10	. . .	7	. . .	4	. . .

$A = \Sigma X^2 = 514 + 263 + 102 = 879$

$B = (\Sigma X)^2/N = (50 + 35 + 20)^2/15 = (105)^2/15 = 11{,}025/15 = 735$

$C = [(\Sigma X_{r_1})^2 + (\Sigma X_{r_2})^2 + \ldots + (\Sigma X_{r_i})^2]/n_{r_1}$
$= [(12 + 9 + 6)^2 + (10 + 7 + 7)^2 + (11 + 6 + 2)^2 + (7 + 9 + 3)^2 + (10 + 4 + 2)^2]/3$
$= [27^2 + 24^2 + 19^2 + 19^2 + 16^2]/3 = 2{,}283/3 = 761.00$

$D = [(\Sigma X_{c_1})^2 + (\Sigma X_{c_2})^2 + \ldots + (\Sigma X_{c_j})^2]/n_{c_1}$
$= [50^2 + 35^2 + 20^2]/5 = 4{,}125/5 = 825.00$

Summary table for ANOVA

Source	SS	df	MS	F
Subjects	26.00	4	. . .	. . .
Trials	90.00	2	45.00	12.86*
Residual	28.00	8	3.50	. . .
Total	144.00	14	. . .	. . .

Note. $\epsilon = 1.00$; no adjustment of *df*s when $\epsilon = 1.0$.

*$p < .05$.

we had three groups of 5 subjects ($n = 15$), we now have 5 subjects, each measured on three trials of a task. The reason for doing this is that when Tables 7.15 and 7.6 are compared, you can see why the repeated measures design results in increased economy. Notice that the total sum of squares and degrees of freedom are the same. Also, the between effect (Table 7.6) and trials effect (Table 7.15) are the same. However, the sum of squares for the within effect (error) in Table 7.6 has been divided into two components in the repeated measures analysis (Table 7.15). The residual effect (estimating error) has a sum of squares of 28.00 with 8 *df*, and the subjects' effect has a sum of squares of 26.00 with 4 *df*. This results in an *F* ratio for the repeated measures ANOVA (Table 7.15) being larger than that for the simple ANOVA (Table 7.6) despite having only one third the number of subjects. The sum of squares for subjects in Table 7.15 is not tested and simply represents the normal variation among subjects. Thus, across the three trials, the subjects' mean performance decreased significantly (Trial 1 = 10, Trial 2 = 7, and Trial 3 = 4). This analysis has all the strengths and weaknesses previously discussed.

Table 7.15 includes the epsilon estimate from this analysis, which was obtained by running the computer program for this problem in Appendix B. If epsilon is less than 1.00, the degrees of freedom would have been adjusted according to $df \times \epsilon$ = adjusted df. This is done for the degrees of freedom in both the numerator and the denominator of any F ratio that includes the repeated measures factor.

A very conservative approach to this adjustment (called Geisser/Greenhouse correction) can also be done (Stamm & Safrit, 1975) as follows:

$$\theta = 1/(k - 1) \qquad (7.14)$$

where k = the number of repeated measures. Then the degrees of freedom for trials are multiplied by this value, $\theta(k - 1)$, as well as the degrees of freedom for error, $\theta(n - 1)(k - 1)$. These adjusted degrees of freedom (to the nearest whole df) are used to look up the F ratio in the F table. If the F ratio is significant under the conservative test, then the effect likely is a real one. However, this procedure was advocated several years ago, and, with the tests of the repeated measures designs now available, a computer program providing the epsilon estimate is more appropriate.

ANALYSIS OF COVARIANCE

Analysis of covariance (ANCOVA) is a combination of regression and ANOVA. The technique is used to adjust the dependent variable for some distractor variable (called the *covariate*).

Using ANCOVA

Suppose we want to evaluate the effects of a training program to develop leg power on the time required to run 50 yd. However, we know that reaction time (RT) will influence the 50-yd dash time because those who begin more quickly after the start signal have an advantage. We form two groups, measure RT in each group, train one with our power development program while the other serves as a control group, and measure each subject's time for running 50 yd. This is a study in which ANCOVA might be used to analyze the data. There is an independent variable with two levels (power training and control), a dependent variable (50-yd dash), and an important distractor variable, or covariate (RT).

Analysis of covariance is a two-step process in which an adjustment is first made for the 50-yd-dash score of each subject according to his or her RT. A correlation (r) is calculated between RT and the time in the 50-yd dash. The resulting prediction equation, 50-yd-dash time = $a + (b)RT$ (same as $\tilde{Y} = a + bX$), is used to calculate each subject's predicted 50-yd-dash time ($\tilde{Y}$). The difference between the actual 50-yd-dash time (Y) and the predicted time ($\tilde{Y}$) is called the residual ($Y - \tilde{Y}$). A simple

ANOVA is then calculated using each subject's residual score as the dependent variable* (1 *df* for within sums of squares is lost because of the correlation). This allows an evaluation of 50-yd-dash speed with RT controlled.

Analysis of covariance can be used in factorial situations and with more than one covariate. The results are evaluated as in ANOVA except one or more distractor variables have been controlled. Also, ANCOVA is frequently used in situations in which a pretest is given, some treatment applied, and then a posttest given. The pretest is used as the covariate in this type of analysis. Note that in the preceding section (Repeated Measures ANOVA) we indicated that this same situation could be analyzed by repeated measures. In addition, ANCOVA is used when comparing intact groups because the groups' performances (dependent variable) can be adjusted for distractor variables (covariates) on which they differ.

Limitations of ANCOVA

Although ANCOVA may seem to be the answer to many problems, its use does have limitations. In particular, its use to adjust final performance for initial differences can result in misleading interpretations (Lord, 1969). In addition, if the correlations between the covariate and the dependent variable are not equal across the treatment groups, standard ANCOVA (there are nonstandard ANCOVA techniques) is inappropriate.

EXPERIMENTWISE ERROR RATE

Sometimes several comparisons are made on different dependent variables while using the same subjects. In most cases, use of a multivariate technique (discussed in the next chapter) is the appropriate solution. However, when dependent variables are combinations of other dependent variables (e.g., cardiac output is Heart Rate × Stroke Volume), a multivariate model using all three dependent variables is inappropriate. (This book is not the appropriate place to explain why. For more detail, see Thomas, 1977.) Thus, an ANOVA among three groups might be calculated separately for each dependent measure (i.e., three ANOVAs). The problem is that this procedure results in increasing the alpha that has been established for the experiment. One of two solutions is appropriate for adjusting alpha. The first is called the Bonferroni technique and simply divides the alpha level by the number of comparisons to be made:

$$\alpha_{EW} = \alpha/c \tag{7.15}$$

where α_{EW} = alpha corrected for the experimentwise error rate, α = alpha, and c = the number of comparisons. In our example, if α = .05 and c = 3, then the

---

*Actually, the procedure is slightly different, but the concept is the same.

alpha for each comparison is .05/3, or .017. This means that the F ratio would have to reach an alpha of .017 to be declared significant.

The second option is to leave the overall alpha at .05 but to calculate the upper limit that the alpha might be:

$$\alpha_{UL} = 1 - (1 - \alpha)^k \qquad (7.16)$$

where α_{UL} = alpha (upper limit) and k = the number of groups. Again, using our example, $\alpha_{UL} = 1 - (1 - .05)^3 = .14$. Thus, the hypotheses are really being tested somewhere between an alpha of .05 if the dependent variables are perfectly correlated and .14 if they are independent. In instances where researchers make multiple comparisons using the same subjects, they should either adjust alpha to the experimentwise rate, or at least report the upper limit on their alpha.

> In instances where researchers make multiple comparisons using the same subjects, they should either adjust alpha to the experimentwise rate, or at least report the upper limit on their alpha.

SUMMARY

This chapter has presented techniques used in situations in which differences among groups are the focus of attention. Basically, these techniques are categorized into two groups:

- A t test is used to determine how a group differs from a population, how two groups differ, how one group changes from one occasion to the next, and how several means differ (the multiple range tests).
- ANOVA shows differences among the levels of one independent variable (simple ANOVA), among the levels of two or more independent variables (factorial ANOVA), and among levels of independent variables when there is a distractor variable or covariate (ANCOVA).

Table 7.16 provides an overall look at the techniques of this chapter and chapter 6 (relationships among variables) with regard to their appropriate use. Note that there are techniques for relationships among variables that parallel each of the techniques for differences among groups. In fact, the relationship between t and r that was demonstrated earlier in this chapter holds, as ANOVA techniques are the equivalent of multiple regression. Each of the techniques evaluates our two basic questions: Is the effect or relationship significant? and, Is the effect or relationship meaningful?

Some of the ideas presented here are complex and may not be easily understood in one reading. We provide some suggested readings and problems at the end of this chapter that should be helpful. If you do not feel confident in your understanding of this material, reread the chapter, do the problems, and consult some of the suggested readings. This is important because information in Parts III and IV will assume that you understand Part II.

Table 7.16 Comparison of Statistical Techniques From Chapters 6 and 7

Description	Differences among groups	Relationships among variables
1 IV (2 levels) → 1 dv	Independent t test	. . .
1 predictor → 1 criterion	. . .	Pearson r
1 IV (2 or more levels) → 1 dv	Simple ANOVA	. . .
2 or more IVs → 1 dv	Factorial ANOVA	. . .
2 or more predictors → 1 criterion	. . .	Multiple regression

Problems

1. t test
   a. Critique the statistical part of a study that uses an independent t test.
   b. Calculate ω^2 for t in this study.
   c. Find a study that uses a multiple range test (Newman-Keuls, Duncan's, or Scheffé) as a follow-up to ANOVA and critique the use of this test.
   d. Table 7.17 provides a problem and data set for a t test. Answer the questions at the bottom of the table.

2. ANOVA
   a. Critique the statistical part of a study that uses simple ANOVA. Calculate ω^2 for F.
   b. Critique the statistical part of a study that uses a two-way factorial ANOVA. Calculate ω^2 for each factor and the interaction.
   c. Critique a repeated measures study that uses ANOVA.

SUGGESTED READINGS

General

Ferguson, G.A. (1971). *Statistical analysis in psychology and education* (3rd ed.). New York: McGraw-Hill.

Keppel, G. (1982). *Design and analysis: A researcher's handbook*. New Jersey: Prentice Hall.

Kirk, R.E. (1982). *Experimental design: Procedures for the behavioral sciences*. Belmont, CA: Brooks/Cole.

Pedhazur, E.J. (1982). *Multiple regression in behavioral research*. New York: Holt, Rinehart and Winston.

Winer, B.J. (1971). *Statistical principles in experimental design*. New York: McGraw-Hill.

Repeated Measures

Schutz, R.W., & Gessaroli, M.E. (1987). The analysis of repeated measures designs involving multiple dependent variables. *Research Quarterly for Exercise and Sport*, 58, 132-149.

Table 7.17 Example for Problem 1d

Differences between groups

Two groups of 7-year-old children are asked to jog 35 m down a string placed on the ground. Then they are asked to reproduce the distance jogged on a second string placed at a right angle to the first. One group (experimental) is cued before they begin that the best way to remember the distance is to count the number of steps. The control is just told to remember as best they can. Below is the error in meters each subject made when estimating the 35 m distance jogged on the second trial.

Experimental group		Control group	
S_1	2.55	S_8	7.68
S_2	3.62	S_9	6.80
S_3	3.42	S_{10}	5.68
S_4	2.86	S_{11}	3.97
S_5	2.00	S_{12}	7.23
S_6	1.08	S_{13}	5.48
S_7	1.16	S_{14}	6.03

Questions

1. Are the two groups significantly different (alpha = .05)?
2. What percent variance is accounted for by the treatment?
3. Place the following statistics into a table: M and s for each group; t; df; ω^2.
4. Did the use of a counting strategy produce a reliable and meaningful performance difference for the experimental group when compared to the control group? Justify your answer.

Chapter 8

□

Understanding Multivariate Techniques

Up to this point we have discussed experimental research examples in which there were one or more independent variables but only one dependent variable. Multivariate cases have one or more independent variables and two or more dependent variables. For example, it seems more likely that when independent variables are manipulated, they influence more than one thing. The multivariate case allows for more than one dependent variable. To use techniques that allow only one dependent variable (called *univariate techniques*) repeatedly when there are several dependent variables increases the experimentwise error rate in the same way as doing multiple *t* tests instead of simple ANOVA when there are more than two groups.

In evaluating relationships among variables, we have discussed having one predictor and one criterion (regression) and several predictors and one criterion (multiple regression). As with multivariate techniques for experimental data, correlational data often have several predictors and several criteria; sometimes, whether variables are predictors or criteria is not so clear.

> Using techniques that allow only one dependent variable repeatedly when there are several increases the experimentwise error rate in the same way as doing multiple *t* tests instead of simple ANOVA when there are more than two groups.

In this chapter we provide you with a conceptual understanding of various multivariate techniques frequently found in the physical education, exercise science, and sport science literature. Techniques often used in experimental studies are

- discriminant analysis,
- multivariate ANOVA (and special cases with repeated measures designs), and
- multivariate ANCOVA.

In correlational studies, techniques often used include

- canonical correlation,
- factor analysis, and
- structural modeling (often called path analysis or LISREL).

Remember, however, that the general linear model still underlies all the techniques, and we are still attempting to learn two things: Is what is being evaluated significant (reliable)? and, How meaningful are significant findings?

DISCRIMINANT ANALYSIS

This technique is used when there is one independent variable (two or more levels) and two or more dependent variables. The technique is a combination of multiple regression and simple ANOVA. In effect, discriminant analysis uses a combination of the dependent variable to predict the independent variable, which in this case is group membership. In the discussion of multiple regression in chapter 6, several predictor variables were used in a linear combination to predict a criterion variable. In essence, discriminant analysis does the same thing except that several dependent variables are used in a linear combination to predict group membership. This prediction of group membership is the equivalent of discriminating among the groups (recall how t could be calculated by r). The same methods used in multiple regression to identify the important predictors are used in discriminant analysis. These include forward, backward, and stepwise selection techniques.

Forward, Backward, and Stepwise Selection

As mentioned previously, the forward selection technique enters the dependent variables in the order of their importance; that is, the dependent variable that contributes the most to separation of the groups (discriminates among or predicts group membership the best) is entered first. By correlation techniques, the effect of the first dependent variable on all others is removed, and the dependent variable that contributes the next greatest amount to separation of the groups is entered at Step 2. This procedure continues until all dependent variables have been entered or until some criterion for stopping the process (established by the researcher) is met.

The backward selection procedure is similar except that all the dependent variables are entered and the one contributing the least to group separation is removed. This continues until the only variables remaining are those that contribute significantly to the separation of the groups. The stepwise technique is similar to forward selection except that at each step all the dependent variables are evaluated to see whether each still contributes to group separation. If a dependent variable does not contribute, it is stepped out (removed) from the linear combination.

An Example of Discriminant Analysis

Table 8.1 provides an example of the use of discriminant analysis with a forward selection technique for choosing significant dependent variables. In this study (Tew & Wood, 1980), varsity football players were classified into three groups: offensive and defensive backs, offensive and defensive linemen, and linebackers and receivers. Data were collected for 28 athletes in each group ($N = 84$) on seven variables: 40-yd dash, 12-min run, shuttle run, vertical jump, standing long jump, bench press, and squat. Discriminant analysis was applied to determine how many of the seven dependent variables were needed to separate (predict) the three groups of football players. The top of Table 8.1 shows the seven original variables with the R^2s (estimates of percent variance accounted for) and the Fs for each variable. This F is only a simple

ANOVA on this variable for the three groups. As you can see, the three groups are significantly different ($p < .05$) on all seven variables. The question not answered is, What is the relationship among these seven variables for the 84 athletes? For example, the shuttle run (which requires speed) would be expected to relate highly to the 40-yd dash.

Table 8.1 Example of the Use of Discriminant Analysis (Forward Selection Technique)

Variable	Original variables ($df = 2, 81$)		Probability
	R^2	F	
40-yd dash	.36	23.11	.0001
12-min run	.08	3.65	.03
Shuttle run	.21	10.48	.0001
Vertical jump	.30	17.25	.0001
Standing long jump	.27	14.85	.0001
Bench press	.39	25.90	.0001
Squat	.13	5.87	.004

Forward selection summary			
Step	Variable entered	F to enter	Probability of F	Average squared canonical correlation
1	Bench press	25.90	.0001	.20
2	40-yd dash	28.22	.0001	.34
3	Vertical jump	3.21	.05	.35

$F(6, 158) = 19.46, p < .0001$

Variable	Variables not in the equation ($df = 2, 78$)		Probability
	R^2	F	
12-min run	.03	1.19	.31
Shuttle run	.00	0.05	.95
Standing long jump	.02	0.94	.40
Squat	.06	2.42	.10

Applying Discriminant Analysis

In applying discriminant analysis, we set two criteria for the statistical computer program, namely, to include the variable at each step with the largest F ratio and to stop when no remaining variable has an F significant at $p < .05$. By looking at the original variables in Table 8.1, you can see which one will be entered at Step 1. The bench press is entered because it has the biggest F (25.90). The program then uses a semipartial correlation procedure to remove the effects of the bench press from the remaining six dependent variables. Note that the 40-yd dash is included next at Step 2. If you looked at the computer printout (not provided here), you would see that the 40-yd dash has the largest F (28.22) at Step 2 (you should now be looking at forward selection summary in the middle of Table 8.1). At Step 3 the vertical jump is entered ($F = 3.21$, $p < .05$) because it has the largest F among the remaining five dependent variables when they are adjusted for the bench press and the 40-yd dash. At this point, none of the four remaining dependent variables had significant Fs, so the program provides the overall test of the composite of the dependent variables' (bench press, 40-yd dash, and vertical jump) ability to separate the three groupings of players, $F(6, 158) = 19.46$, $p < .0001$. On the right of the forward selection summary is the averaged squared canonical correlation, which is cumulative at each step. This is an estimation of the percent variance accounted for (20% with the first variable, 34% with the first and second variables, and 35% with all three). At the bottom of Table 8.1 are the dependent variables not included in the discriminant analysis equation. Note that none of the remaining four dependent variables are significant in their ability to separate the three groups when the effects of the bench press, 40-yd dash, and vertical jump are removed from them. This means that the characteristics underlying performance in the three dependent variables included are the same characteristics underlying performance in the four not included. This seems to be a reasonably good explanation except for the 12-min run. But note that it did not discriminate very effectively among the groups to begin with ($F = 3.65$, $p < .03$, 8% variance accounted for). This really addresses the issue of why the 12-min run would be expected to discriminate among football players, as their training regimens are not designed to develop cardiovascular endurance.

Following Up Discriminant Analysis

We might want to follow up the discriminant analysis with univariate techniques to determine which groups actually differed from one another on each of the three dependent variables included. There are several ways to approach this follow-up, but for simplicity, consider the fact that you could perform the Newman-Keuls test among the three groups on the first dependent variable. Then, ANCOVA could be done among the three groups on the second dependent variable using the first dependent variable as a covariate. This would provide adjusted means (means of the second dependent variable corrected for the first) on the second dependent variable. A Newman-Keuls test could be done among the adjusted means using the adjusted mean square for error. This procedure is continued through each dependent variable using the previously stepped-in dependent variables as covariates and is called a *step down* F *technique*. There are also other ways to follow up discriminant analysis.

Summarizing Discriminant Analysis

As you can see, we have used discriminant analysis in a situation in which the three groups were intact (i.e., not randomly formed). This is a very common application of discriminant analysis. However, discriminant analysis does not overcome the need to randomly form the groups if determination of cause-and-effect is the purpose of the research.

Discriminant analysis can also be used to place people into groups. We could write a prediction equation—$\tilde{Y} = a +$ bench press (B_1) + 40-yd dash (B_2) + vertical jump (B_3)—that could be used to classify players as backs, linemen, and linebackers and receivers. However, given that only 35% of the variance is accounted for in this model, the usefulness of this prediction equation could be questioned. Of course, football coaches would love to find a valid and reliable equation of this type because the tests could be given to high school athletes to predict those players who might be successful at the various positions on college teams.

MULTIVARIATE ANALYSIS OF VARIANCE

From an intuitive point of view, *multivariate analysis of variance* (*MANOVA*) is a rather straightforward extension of ANOVA, the only difference being that the F tests of the independent variables and interactions are based on a linear composite of several dependent variables. There is no need to consider simple MANOVA, as this is discriminant analysis (one independent variable with two or more levels and two or more dependent variables).

Using MANOVA

The mathematics are rather complex for factorial MANOVA, but the idea is relatively simple. A combination (linear composite) of the dependent variables is made that will maximally separate (predict) the levels of the first independent variable. Then a combination of the dependent variables is made that will maximally separate the levels of the second independent variable and so on. Note that the combination to separate the second independent variable may be different from the combination to separate the first. However, certain statistical computer programs offer the option of using the same linear combination for all independent variables and interactions. Finally, the combination of dependent variables that maximizes the interactions is calculated. Each of the tests of independent variables and interactions has an associated F and degrees of freedom that is interpreted as F for ANOVA. There are several ways to obtain this F in MANOVA: Wilks's lambda, greatest characteristic root, Roa's F-approximation, and others. We point this out only because authors sometimes identify how the MANOVA Fs were obtained. For your purposes, these distinctions are not important: Consider only that the MANOVA F ratios are similar to ANOVA F ratios.

Once MANOVA has been used, a significant linear composite of dependent variables is identified as separating the levels of the independent variable. Then, the question of importance usually is, Which of the dependent variables contributes significantly to this separation? One of many ways to answer this question is to use discriminant analysis and the stepdown F procedures discussed in the previous section as follow-up techniques. This works well for the main effects but not so well for interactions. Interactions in MANOVA are most frequently handled by calculating factorial ANOVA for each dependent variable, although this procedure fails to take the relationships among the dependent variables into account.

An Example of MANOVA

As an example of the use and follow-up of MANOVA, consider an experiment reported by French and Thomas (1987). One of the aspects of this study was to evaluate the influence of two groupings of age level (8- to 10-year-olds and 11- to 12-year-olds) and level of expertise (expert and novice players within each age level) on basketball knowledge and performance. A basketball knowledge test and two basketball skills tests (shooting and dribbling) were given to all the children. Following is French and Thomas's description of these particular results:

A 2 × 2 (Age League × Expert/Novice) MANOVA was conducted on the scores of the knowledge test and both skill tests. The results of the MANOVA indicated significant main effects for age league, $F(3, 50) = 5.81$, $p < .01$, expert/novice, $F(3, 50) = 28.01$, $p < .01$, but no significant interaction. These main effects were followed up by a stepdown procedure using a forward selection discriminant analysis. The alpha level used as a basis for stepping in variables was set at .05. The discriminant analysis for age league revealed that knowledge was stepped in first, $F(1, 54) = 8.31$, $p < .01$. Neither skill test was entered. Older children ($M = 79.5$) possessed more knowledge than younger children ($M = 64.9$). The discriminant analysis for expert/novice revealed shooting was stepped in first, $F(1, 54) = 61.40$, $p < .01$, knowledge second, $F(1, 53) = 5.51$, $p < .05$, and dribbling was not entered. Child experts ($M = 47.2$) performed significantly better than novices ($M = 25.7$) in shooting skill. The adjusted means for knowledge showed that child experts ($M = 77.1$) possessed more basketball knowledge than novices ($M = 64.2$). (p. 22)

MULTIVARIATE ANALYSIS OF COVARIANCE

Conceptually, *multivariate analysis of covariance (MANCOVA)* represents the same extension of ANCOVA that MANOVA did for ANOVA. In MANCOVA there are two or more independent variables, two or more dependent variables, and one or more covariates. Recall how ANCOVA was done (chapter 7). A variable was used to adjust the dependent variable by correlation, and then ANOVA was calculated on the adjusted dependent variable. In MANCOVA each dependent variable is adjusted for one or more variables (covariates); then, a linear composite is formed from the adjusted dependent variables that best discriminates among the levels of each independent variable, just as in MANOVA. Follow-up procedures are the same as in MANOVA except that the linear composite of adjusted dependent variables is used. This technique is seldom used and typically used incorrectly. Normally, there is no reason to adjust a dependent variable for a linear composite of covariates. We have purposely not provided an example of the use of MANCOVA from the exercise and sport science literature. MANCOVA is a fine technique if you understand what it does and you specifically want to test for that. However, many researchers have a misunderstanding of the application of MANCOVA and do not use it properly.

REPEATED MEASURES
WITH MULTIPLE DEPENDENT VARIABLES

Sometimes, experiments have multiple dependent variables that are measured on more than one occasion (over time). For example, in an exercise adherance study, both physiological and psychological variables might be measured once per week for a 15-week training program. If there were two training groups (different levels of training) and a control group (each with 15 subjects), all of which were measured every week (i.e., 15 times) on two psychological and three physiological measures, we have a design that is three levels of exercise × 15 trials (3×15) for five dependent variables. This design offers several options for analysis.

We could do five 3×15 ANOVAs with repeated measures on the second factor. In this case, we would follow the repeated measures procedures described in chapter 7. However, we would be inflating the alpha by doing multiple analyses on the same subjects. Of course, the alpha could be adjusted by the Bonferroni technique ($\alpha = .05/5 = .01$), but this fails to take into account the relationships among the dependent variables, which might be substantial.

Schutz and Gessaroli (1987) have provided an excellent tutorial on how to handle this problem. The following brief discussion is taken from their study, but if you are using this design and analysis, you should read their complete study and example. There are two options for this analysis: multivariate mixed model (MMM) analysis and doubly multivariate (DM) analysis. Which is used depends on the assumptions that your data meet. Using the study previously described (3 levels of exercise × 15 trials for five dependent variables), the MMM analysis treats the independent variable (levels of exercise) as a true multivariate case by forming a linear composite of the five dependent variables to discriminate among the levels of the independent variable. If this composite is significant, it can be followed up by the stepdown F procedures discussed previously (for an alternative procedure, see Schutz and Gessaroli, 1987). For the repeated measures factor (and interaction), a linear composite is formed for each trial, and the linear composite at each trial is treated as a regular repeated measures analysis. This means that the sphericity assumption must be met as previously described and that epsilon can be used to test this assumption with the same standards described in chapter 7. The interpretation of the resulting F ratio for main effects for groups, trials, and the Group × Trial interaction are the same as in other designs. The question usually posed here is, Do the groups change at different rates across the trials on the linear composite of dependent variables? This is the preferred analysis if the sphericity assumption can be met because most authors believe it offers more power. However, this is a difficult assumption to meet, especially if there are more than two or three dependent variables measured on more than three to five trials.

The DM analysis does not require that the sphericity assumption be met. The analysis is the same for the independent variable of exercise; however, in the repeated measures part of the analysis, a linear composite is formed not only of the dependent variables at each trial but also of the 15 trials (which are themselves linear composites), thus the name DM. However, the interpretations of the Fs for the two main effects and interaction remain essentially the same, and follow-ups become more complex.

CANONICAL CORRELATION

Previously (chapter 6), we discussed correlation in which there was one dependent (or criterion) variable and one independent (or predictor) variable (zero-order correlation, r) and in which there was one dependent variable and two or more independent variables (multiple regression). There is also a correlational technique that can determine the relationship in which there are two or more dependent variables (criteria) and two or more independent variables (predictors). This technique is called *canonical correlation*.

In essence, there are two linear combinations: one of Y variables and one of X variables. These composites are weighted in such a way that the maximum possible correlation is achieved. This is the canonical correlation (R_c), and R_c^2 is the estimated amount of common association (shared variance) between the two linear composites of these variables. This is similar to multiple regression, in which the X variables were weighted in terms of their linear combination effects.

Canonical correlation is sometimes used in an exploratory manner to find out which variables might best be manipulated for use as the independent variables, and which will best show results as dependent variables. For example, suppose we have several physical characteristics for a group of athletes, such as height, weight, percent fat, and several performance measures of power, speed, endurance, and aerobic capacity. We may wish to find which among the physical characteristics are best suited to act as predictor variables and which of the performance variables are most appropriate to serve as a criterion. Canonical correlation will identify the best solution, and multiple regression is sometimes used to follow up for interpretation and prediction purposes.

For example, McPherson and Thomas (1989) studied expert and novice children tennis players at two age levels (10- to 11-year-olds and 12- to 13-year-olds). They measured tennis knowledge and tennis skill (serve and ground strokes) in these players and then videotaped the children as they played six games. The videotapes were coded for three qualities of game performance (control, decisions, and execution). They were interested in the relationship between tennis knowledge and skill (predictor variables) and several aspects of game performance (criterion variables) and used canonical correlation to evaluate this relationship. Following is a description of their results:

> The canonical correlation to examine the relation of knowledge and groundstroke skill and the components of tennis play following the serve . . . revealed one significant function, $R_c = .79$, $F(6, 70) = 7.58$, $p < .01$. The standardized canonical coefficients indicated that both knowledge (0.42) and groundstrokes (0.69) were important in the relation to decisions (0.65) and execution (0.41). (p. 198)

McPherson and Thomas used canonical correlation to establish the general nature of the relationships between knowledge, skill, and game performance before they analyzed in more detail how expert and novice children organize tennis knowledge differently.

FACTOR ANALYSIS

Many performance variables are used to describe people's behavior. Often it is useful to reduce a large set of performance measures to a more basic and manageable structure. We have already discussed the likelihood that two performance measures might to some extent measure the same underlying characteristic. This represents the degree to which they are correlated. *Factor analysis* is an approach to reducing a set of measures to their basic (underlying) structures. There are numerous procedures grouped under the general topic of factor analysis. We do not discuss in detail the various techniques but do provide a general explanation that allows you to read and understand any study that uses factor analysis.

Using Factor Analysis

Factor analysis is performed on a group of individuals on whom a series of measures have been taken. The researcher usually wants to describe a reduced number of underlying constructs and possibly select the one or two best measures of each construct. Factor analysis begins by calculating an intercorrelation matrix of all the measures used (correlation between all possible pairs of variables; thus, if eight measures were made, the correlation would be determined between variables 1 and 2, 1 and 3, and so on for a total of 28 correlations). The goal of factor analysis is to discover the principal factors that underlie a group of measures and describe the relation of each measure to the principal factor. Thus, the computer program first provides a choice about how many factors to use. The more the tests have high *load-*

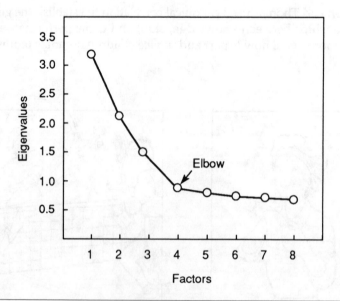

Figure 8.1 Scree curve for factor analysis.

ings (correlations) on a factor, the more important the factor is in accounting for the total variance of the tests.

There are rules of thumb about how many factors to use, the best of which is called a *scree curve*. Figure 8.1 shows a scree curve for a factor analysis. The *y*-axis is called *eigenvalues* (the correlation of each test with that factor squared and summed), and the *x*-axis is the number of factors (and is equal initially to the number of variables). You decide to keep the number of factors before the elbow of the scree curve (note that the scree curve has the greatest bend after three factors). These factors are then rotated according to a criterion to maximize the tests' loadings and to minimize the relation among factors (this is called *orthogonal*, or *varimax, rotation*). Or the researcher may decide to allow the factors to correlate with one another (called *oblique rotation*). The researcher then decides what represents a significant loading (correlation with a factor): .4 is often used, but the choice is arbitrary.

An Example of Factor Analysis

Table 8.2 is an example of a factor analysis of a sports orientation questionnaire (Gill & Deeter, 1988) that was administered to a group of subjects. Gill and Deeter did both varimax and oblique rotations (columns under each of the three factors of Competitiveness, Goal, and Win). The numbers in each column represent the correlation of each item with the hypothesized factor. Ideally, the authors wanted each item to load heavily (correlate highly) on the one factor that the item was designed to measure and to load to a low degree on the other two factors. A solution such as this is called a *simple structure*. As you can see, the structure is fairly simple for the Competitiveness and Goal factors, but the loadings are not so clear-cut for the Win factors. Gill and Deeter reported a clear bend in the scree curve after the third factor (thus, they rotated the three factors presented in Table 8.2). You can see in Table 8.2 that the first factor accounts for 33.5% of the total variance, the second factor for 10.8%, and the third factor for 5.3%. The total variance accounted for in this solution is 49.6%.

Table 8.2 Factor Weights for Sports Orientation Questionnaire Items From Varimax and Oblique Rotations

| | Competitiveness | | Goal | | Win | |
Item	Varimax	Oblique	Varimax	Obique	Varimax	Oblique
Competitiveness						
I am a competitive person	.71	.74	.05	.18	.21	.34
I try my hardest to win	.75	.78	.10	.24	.21	.34
I am a determined competitor	.77	.79	.12	.26	.09	.22

(Cont.)

Table 8.2 (Continued)

| | Factors | | | | | |
| Item | Competitiveness | | Goal | | Win | |
	Varimax	Oblique	Varimax	Obique	Varimax	Oblique
I want to be the best every time I compete	.54	.62	.24	.33	.27	.34
I look forward to competing	.82	.83	.10	.25	.11	.25
I thrive on competition	.74	.80	.12	.26	.31	.42
My goal is to be the best athlete possible	.68	.74	.23	.36	.22	.32
I enjoy competing against others	.79	.80	.07	.22	.17	.30
I want to be successful in sports	.71	.75	.17	.30	.18	.29
I work hard to be successful in sports	.73	.78	.28	.41	.10	.20
The best test of my ability is competing against others	.69	.72	.06	.19	.23	.35
I look forward to the opportunity to test my skills in competition	.79	.80	.16	.30	.08	−.21
I perform my best when I am competing against an opponent	.64	.70	.12	.24	.34	.44
Goal						
I set goals for myself when I compete	.35	.46	.58	.64	.04	.04
I am most competitive when I try to achieve personal goals	.01	.11	.50	.50	−.04	−.09
I try hardest when I have a specific goal	.01	.15	.64	.63	.01	−.07
Reaching personal performance goals is very important to me	.08	.24	.77	.77	.04	−.04
The best way to determine my ability is to set a goal and try to reach it	.03	.15	.61	.60	.01	−.07
Performing to the best of my ability is very important to me	.27	.37	.57	.61	−.03	−.05
Win						
Winning is important	.50	.62	.16	.26	.57	.63
Scoring more points than my opponent is very important to me	.38	.50	.10	.18	.59	.63
I hate to lose	.27	.43	.19	.24	.69	.70
The only time I am satisfied is when I win	.17	.28	−.09	−.04	.70	.73
Losing upsets me	.20	.33	.02	.07	.72	.74
I have the most fun when I win	.44	.52	.06	.14	.47	.54
Percent variance	33.5		10.8		5.3	
Cumulative percent variance	33.5		44.3		49.6	

Note. Adapted by permission from *Research Quarterly for Exercise and Sport*, Sept. 1988, **59**, 3, p. 196. *RQ* is a publication of the American Alliance for Health, Physical Education, Recreation and Dance, 1900 Association Dr., Reston, VA 22091.

Additional Types of Factor Analysis

There are other types of factor analysis. The one previously discussed is often called *exploratory factor analysis*. Once a pattern is identified, the researcher may want to see whether the structure fits a new data set from a different sample. Solutions such as the previous one can sometimes be very sample specific, especially if a unique group (e.g., athletes) is used. Thus, Gill and Deeter took the solution and applied it to two new samples in a *confirmatory factor analysis*. In this approach, an important element is how well the proposed solution fits the new sample. Several ways of determining this are available, and Gill and Deeter report most of them (coefficient of determination, chi-square, chi-square/*df* ratio, goodness of fit, and root mean square residuals). All the statistics supported that the three-factor model was a good one.

Numerous other approaches to factor analysis exist, but the previous example should enable you to follow what the researchers are doing. They should provide you with a good description of the following:

- The solution selected
- How the number of factors selected to be rotated was determined
- How the rotation was done
- What was considered a significant loading

It is also important to have a large number of subjects for factor analysis (some suggest at least 10 per variable). Remember also that solutions tend to be very specific to the sample on which they were determined, so a battery established by factor analysis on one sample may not prove useful on a different sample (e.g., college sample to sample of college athletes, adults to children, etc.).

> Solutions tend to be very specific to the sample on which they were determined.

STRUCTURAL MODELING

Path analysis and linear structural modeling (LISREL) are structural, or causal, modeling techniques that are used to explain the way certain characteristics relate to one another and attempt to imply cause. You should remember from the discussion in chapter 7 that cause-and-effect is not a statistical result, but a logical one. That is, if the experimenter can argue theoretically that changing a certain characteristic should result in a specific change in behavior, and if the actual experiment (and statistical analysis) support this hypothesis, then cause is often inferred for a particular independent variable on a dependent variable. Of course, this is true only if all other possible influences have been controlled.

The way variables influence one another is not always clear; for example, $X \rightarrow Y \rightarrow Z$, or $X \leftarrow Y \rightarrow Z$. In the first case, X influences Y, which in turn influences Z; however, in the second case, Y influences both X and Z. This is a very simple explanation. Path analysis and LISREL allow a more complex modeling of the way variables influence one another. But all you can say about these models is that they are either consistent or inconsistent with the data. Whether this infers cause-and-effect depends on other things (e.g., control of all other variables, careful treatments, logical hypotheses, valid theories).

Path Analysis

Path analysis uses correlations among all the variables (much like multiple regression) to estimate the linkages among measures where the experimenter has a rationale for how these measures should influence one another. Path analysis labels two types of variables: *exogenous*, whose variance is explained by factors outside the model, and *endogenous*, whose variance is explained by exogenous variables, other variables within the model, or both.

Often, researchers assume that the flow of cause to effect is in one direction, and arrows are used to depict this flow (see Figure 8.2). Path analysis is rarely used anymore since the evolution of LISREL.

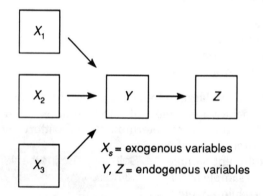

X_s = exogenous variables

Y, Z = endogenous variables

Figure 8.2 Example of a structural model with the flow of influence in one direction.

Linear Structural Relations

Linear structural relations, or *LISREL*, is an approach to structural modeling that has gained widespread use, particularly among social scientists. It is much like path analysis, except path analysis assumes that all variables are measured without error. Of course, this is a very weak assumption, as we know all types of errors creep into real data (measurement error, coding errors, testing errors, etc.). The best way for you to gain a basic understanding of LISREL is through an example (Greenockle, Lee, & Lomax, 1990) from the physical education literature. These researchers were interested in describing the relationship between student characteristics and exercise behavior. Figure 8.3 shows how they found this relationship to be in a sample of 10 intact high school physical education classes in which the teacher had agreed to teach a specific physical fitness unit. They measured four background variables on the students: past activity level, perception of father's activity level, perception of mother's activity level, and knowledge of physical fitness. Two measures of attitude toward exercise were taken from a valid and reliable questionnaire. Two subjective norm measures were obtained from the same questionnaire, which indicated subjects' perceptions concerning how others felt about the subjects' exercise behavior. One measure of intention to exercise was obtained. Five exercise behaviors were measured: jogging, fitness test score, percent participation, heart rate, and perceived exertion. The technique of LISREL was used because it allows related measures to be grouped together (as in factor analysis) into components (e.g., exercise behavior) and shows the relationships among the components in terms of magnitude and direction. The estimates of each component are grouped together in a linear equation (using their factor loadings). Then a series of general linear equations (as in multiple regression) shows the relationships among the components. ''The general intent of the analysis is to reconstruct the observed correlation matrix as well as possible by imposing a theoretical structure on the data'' (Greenockle et al., 1990, p. 63). Model fitting indexes are used to assess the nature of the fit. These are similar to those discussed previously for confirmatory factor analysis: chi-square and goodness of fit. The results of the study by Greenockle et al. indicated ''the prediction of exercise behavior by attitude and subjective norm to be significantly mediated

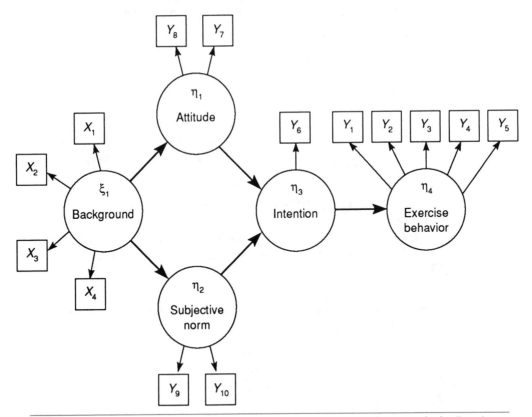

Figure 8.3 LISREL Model. Adapted by permission from *Research Quarterly for Exercise and Sport*, March, 1990, **69**, pp. 59-69. *RQ* is a publication of the American Alliance for Health, Physical Education, Recreation and Dance, 1900 Association Dr., Reston, VA 22091.

by intention'' (p. 59). You can see, then, that structural modeling techniques provide a way to evaluate the very complex relationships that exist in real-world data. By establishing the directions that certain relationships go, stronger inferences can be made about which characteristics are likely to cause other characteristics.

SUMMARY

The multivariate techniques discussed here are mathematically complex. However, we think you can gain enough understanding from the explanations offered to read a research study using one of these techniques and to follow what happens. The techniques were grouped as experimental (discriminant analysis, MANOVA, MANCOVA, and repeated measures) and correlational (canonical, factor analysis, and structural modeling). However, as we have noted several times, whether cause-and-effect exists depends very little on statistics but mostly on logical, theoretical, and design rationale.

Problems

1. Locate a study that used discriminant analysis and briefly describe how it was used to address the purpose of the study. Identify any follow-up procedures that were used.
2. Locate a study that used MANOVA in its data analysis. Identify the independent and the dependent variables.
3. Locate a study that used canonical correlation in its data analysis. Identify the dependent variables (criteria) and the independent variables (predictors).

SUGGESTED READING

Schutz, R.W., & Gessaroli, M.E. (1987). The analysis of repeated measures designs involving multiple dependent variables. *Research Quarterly for Exercise and Sport*, **58**, 132-149.

Chapter 9

□

Nonparametric Techniques

In the preceding chapters, various parametric statistics have been described. As you recall, parametric statistics make assumptions about the distribution with regard to normality and homogeneity of variance. Another category of statistics is called nonparametric statistics. This category is also referred to as *distribution-free statistics* because there are no assumptions made about the distribution of scores.

Nonparametric statistics are quite versatile in that they can deal with ranked scores and categories. This can be a definite advantage when the investigator is dealing with variables that do not lend themselves to precise, interval-type data (that are more likely to meet parametric assumptions), such as categories of responses on questionnaires and various affective behavior rating instruments. Data from qualitative research are often numerical counts of events that can be effectively analyzed with nonparametric statistics.

The main drawback to nonparametric statistics is that they may be less powerful in detecting a false null hypothesis. Thus, if the basic assumptions of a parametric test can be met, a parametric statistic is usually recommended because it is more efficient. However, when the researcher knows that a set of data does not meet the assumptions of normality and homogeneity of variance, or when the only type of scores available are ranks or frequencies of occurrence, the researcher should use nonparametric tests. Many nonparametric methods are available. We describe a few of the more common ones.

> The main drawback to nonparametric statistics is that they are less powerful in detecting a false null hypothesis. Thus, if the basic assumptions of a parametric test can be met, a parametric statistic is usually recommended because it is more efficient.

CHI-SQUARE

Data are often classified into categories, such as gender, age, grade level, treatment groups, or some other *nominal* (categorical) *measure*. A researcher is sometimes interested in evaluating whether the number of cases in each category is different from what would be expected on the basis of chance, some known source of information (such as census data), or some other rational hypothesis about the distribution of cases in the population. *Chi-square* is a technique that provides a statistical test as to the significance of the discrepancy between the observed and the expected results.

For example, tennis coach Roger Rabbitfoot believes in jinxes. He believes that one court at his university is definitely unlucky for his team. He kept records of matches on four courts over the years and is convinced that his team has lost significantly more matches on court number 4 than on any other. Roger set out to prove his point by comparing the number of losses on each of the four courts. The same number of matches had been played on each court, and his team lost a total of 120 individual matches on these courts over the time period. Theoretically, it would be expected that each court would have one fourth, or 30, of the losses. The observed frequencies and the expected frequencies are shown in Table 9.1.

The formula for chi-square (χ^2) is

$$\chi^2 = \Sigma[(O - E)^2/E] \tag{9.1}$$

where O = the observed frequency and E = the expected frequency. Thus, the expected frequency in each cell is subtracted from the observed (or obtained) frequency. This difference is then squared (which means all differences will be positive), and these values are divided by the expected frequency for their respective cells and are then summed. The resulting chi square is then interpreted for significance by consulting Table A.8 in Appendix A. Because there are four courts (or cells), the number of degrees of freedom (df) is $c - 1 = 3$. The researcher finds the critical value for 3 df, which is 7.82 for the .05 probability level. Roger's calculated value of 7.19 is less than this, so the null hypothesis that there were no differences among the four courts in the number of losses is not rejected. The observed differences could be attributed to sampling error. Roger probably still believes in his heart that he is right (called cardiac research).

Table 9.1 Observed and Expected Numbers of Losses at Four Tennis Courts

| | \multicolumn{5}{c}{Court number} | | | | |
	1	2	3	4	Total
Observed	24	34	22	40	120
Expected	30	30	30	30	120

Court	$O - E$	$(O - E)^2$	$(O - E)^2/E$
1	−6	36	1.20
2	+4	16	0.53
3	−8	64	2.13
4	+10	100	3.33
		$\chi^2 =$	7.19

Note. $\chi^2 = 7.82$ at .05 level (3 df).

COURT#1   COURT#2   COURT#3   COURT#4

In some cases, the expected frequencies for classifications can be obtained from existing sources of information, such as in the following example. A new assistant professor, Nancy Niceperson, is assigned to teach the large sections of an introduction to physical education. After a few semesters, the department chairperson hears rumors that Dr. Niceperson is too lenient in her grading practices, so he uses chi-square to compare the grades of the 240 students with the department's prescribed normal curve grade distribution: 3.5% A's and F's, 24% B's and D's, and 45% C's. If Dr. Niceperson were adhering to this normal curve distribution, then she would be expected to have given 8 A's and 8 F's (3.5% × 240), 58 B's and 58 D's (24% × 240), and 108 C's (45% × 240). The observed frequencies (Nancy's grades) and the expected frequencies (the department's mandated distribution) are shown in Table 9.2.

The chairperson, who is always fair, does not want to make a wrong decision, so he decides to use the .01 level of probability. Table A.8 shows that for 4 *df* (there are five grades, or cells), a chi-square of 13.28 is needed for significance at the .01 level. The obtained chi-square of 46.46 exceeds this value, indicating a significant deviation from the expected grade distribution. Clearly, Nancy's grades show too many A's and B's and too few D's and F's. The chairperson did the only fair thing by firing her on the spot.

The Contingency Table

Often a problem involves two or more categories of occurrences and two or more groups (a two-way classification). A common example is in the analysis of the results of questionnaires or attitude inventories in which there are several categories of responses (e.g., agree, no opinion, disagree) and two or more groups of respondents (e.g., exercise adherents and nonadherents). This type of two-way classification is called a *contingency table*.

To illustrate, Table 9.3 shows the responses of a group of athletes and a group of nonathletes to the following statement on a sportsmanship inventory: "A baseball player who traps a fly ball between the ground and his glove should tell the

Table 9.2 Observed and Expected Grade Distribution

	A (3.5%)	B (24%)	Grade C (45%)	D (24%)	F (3.5%)	Total
Observed	21	75	114	28	2	240
Expected	8	58	108	58	8	240

Grade	$O - E$	$(O - E)^2$	$(O - E)^2/E$
A	13	169	21.13
B	17	289	4.98
C	6	36	0.33
D	−30	900	15.52
F	−6	36	4.50
		$\chi^2 =$	46.46

Note. $\chi^2 = 13.28$ at .01 level (4 *df*).

umpire that he did not catch it." In the previous examples of one-way classification, the expected frequencies were determined by some type of rational hypothesis or source of information. In a contingency table, the expected values are computed from the marginal totals. For example, the total number of respondents who agreed with the statement was 144. Because there are 450 people in all, then 144/450, or 32% of the total group, agreed with the statement. Thus, if there were no difference between athletes and nonathletes on sportsmanship (the null hypothesis) as reflected by this statement, then 32% of the athletes ($32 \times 200 = 64$) and 32% of the nonathletes ($32 \times 250 = 80$) would be the expected frequencies for these two cells.

A much faster method of calculating these expected frequencies is simply to multiply the column total by the row total for each cell and divide by the total number (N). So, in the previous examples for the athletes who agreed with the statement, it would be $144 \times 200/450$, or 64; for the nonathletes-agree cell, it would be $144 \times 250/450$, or 80. All the cell values can be determined in this way. Chi-square is computed in the same manner as in the examples of one-way classification.

The degrees of freedom for a contingency table is $(r - 1)(c - 1)$, where r stands for rows and c for columns. In this case, we have two rows and three columns, so $df = (2 - 1)(3 - 1) = 2$. As before, the investigator then looks up the tabled value for significance (in this study, the investigator had decided on the .01 level) and sees that a chi-square of 9.21 is needed. The obtained chi-square of 79.29 is clearly significant. This tells us that the null hypothesis is rejected: there is a significant difference between athletes and nonathletes in their responses to the statement. After inspecting the table, we could conclude that a significantly greater proportion of

**Table 9.3 A 3 × 2 Contingency Table on Responses
of Athletes and Nonathletes to Sportsmanship Statement**

	Agree	No opinion	Disagree	Total
Athletes				
Observed	30	46	124	200
Expected	(64)	(56)	(80)	(200)
Nonathletes				
Observed	114	80	56	250
Expected	(80)	(70)	(100)	(250)
Totals	144	126	180	450

$O - E$	$(O - E)^2$	$(O - E)^2/E$
−34	1,156	18.06
34	1,156	14.45
−10	100	1.79
10	100	1.43
44	1,936	24.20
−44	1,936	19.36
	$\chi^2 =$	79.29

Note. $\chi^2 = 9.21$ at .01 level (2 *df*).

nonathletes agreed that the player should tell the umpire he had trapped the ball and, conversely, that a higher proportion of athletes felt he should not.

Restrictions in Using Chi-Square

Although we indicated that nonparametric statistics do not require the same assumptions concerning the population as do parametric statistics, there are some restrictions in using this technique. The observations must be independent and the categories mutually exclusive. By this we mean that an observation in any category should not be related to or dependent on other observations in other categories. You could, for example, ask 50 people about their activity preferences. If each gave three preferences, you would not be justified in using a total (N) of 150 because the preferences of any subject would likely be related and the chi-square inflated. Moreover, an observation can be placed in only one category. The observed frequencies are exactly that—they are numbers of occurrences. Ratios and percentages are not appropriate. Another related point is that the total of the expected frequencies and the total of the observed frequencies for any classification must be the same. In Table 9.3, for example, notice that the total of the expected frequencies for athletes is the same as the total of the observed frequencies. The same is also seen for non-athletes and for the column totals.

Chi-square is usually not applicable for small samples. The expected frequency for any cell should not be less than 1.0. Furthermore, some statisticians claim that no more than 20% of the cells can have expected values of less than 5. Opinions vary

> Observations must be independent and the categories mutually exclusive. An observation in any category should not be related to or dependent on other observations in other categories.

on this, however. Some say no cell should have less than 5, whereas other statisticians would allow as many as 40%. A common tactic in cases with several cells with expected frequencies less than 5 is to combine adjacent categories, therefore increasing the expected values.

There is widespread agreement among researchers that a 2 × 2 contingency table should have a so-called correction for continuity. This correction, usually referred to as *Yates' correction for continuity*, is to subtract 0.5 from the difference between the observed and the expected frequencies for each cell before it is squared:

$$\text{Corrected } \chi^2 = \Sigma[(O - E - 0.5)^2/E] \tag{9.2}$$

Another limitation imposed on the 2 × 2 contingency table is that the total number (N) should be at least 20.

Finally, it should go without saying that the expected distribution should be logical and established before the data are collected. In other words, the researcher decides on the hypothesis (probability, equal occurrence, census data, etc.) before the analysis. The researcher is not allowed to look over the distribution and then conjure up an expected distribution that would fit his or her hypothesis.

MANN-WHITNEY *U* TEST

The Mann-Whitney *U* test is analogous to the parametric independent *t* test. The *U* test is one of the more powerful of the nonparametric tests. It can be used with very small or fairly large groups and requires only ordinal (rank) measurement. We can use this test when we have two independent groups and one dependent variable.

There is more than one way to compute the Mann-Whitney *U* test. We demonstrate only the ranking method that is recommended for larger groups because the counting procedure for small groups is too time consuming if you have, say, 20 or more scores.

Suppose a researcher wishes to test the hypothesis that experienced teachers require less time (duration of eye fixation) than novice teachers while observing skill performance. A group of golf teachers with over 10 yr of experience are compared to a group of novice golf teachers. Both groups observe the same individuals performing a golf drive. An eye movement recorder is used to measure the duration of eye fixation in milliseconds (ms). The scores for the 11 experienced and 12 novice teachers are shown in Table 9.4. The median time for experienced golf teachers is 117 ms and 128 ms for novice teachers.

The steps in the Mann-Whitney U test are as follows:

1. Rank the scores for both groups (all 23 teachers). We ranked the shortest time as 1 and the longest as 23. Of course, we must maintain their group identities in the ranking process. When you have ties in ranks, you give each score the average of the ranks they occupy. For example, in Table 9.4, two people have scores of 114, which occupy the 5th and the 6th ranks. So, we give each person the average of those two ranks (5.5), and the next rank is now 7. Three teachers had scores of 120, which occupy the 9th, 10th, and 11th ranks. Therefore, all three are given the middle rank (10), and the next rank is 12.

2. Sum the ranks for each group. You can check your accuracy in ranking by using the formula $N(N + 1)/2$, where N is the total number of scores in all groups combined. In this example, it would be $23(23 + 1)/2 = 276$, which agrees with the sum of the ranks of Group 1 (81.5) plus the sum of Group 2 (194.5), or 276.

3. Calculate U. The difference between the groups will be maximum when there is little overlap between samples. In other words, if there is no overlap, then all measurements for one sample would be greater than the other. On the other hand, if the null hypothesis is true, scores from the two groups will be mixed, in which

Table 9.4 Mann-Whitney U Test of Expert and Novice Golf Teachers on Duration of Eye Fixation

Group 1 Experienced ($n = 11$) Raw score (ms)	Rank	Group 2 Novice ($n = 12$) Raw score (ms)	Rank
111	4	130	19
114	5.5	123	12
120	10	124	13
101	1	138	21
118	8	142	23
128	17	120	10
125	14	127	15.5
117	7	140	22
106	2	136	20
120	10	129	18
110	3	127	15.5
		114	5.5
	$\Sigma R_1 = 81.5$		$\Sigma R_2 = 194.5$

case the ranks of one sample will be greater than the other sample about half the time and the same for the other sample. Thus, U would be near $(n_1)(n_2)/2$ if there is no difference between groups. Conversely, a real difference between groups will show a high U for one group and a low U for the other. The formula for calculating U for Group 1 follows:

$$U = n_1 n_2 + [n_1(n_1 + 1)/2] - \Sigma R_1 \tag{9.3}$$

where n_1 = the number of subjects in Group 1, n_2 = the number of subjects in Group 2, and ΣR_1 = the sum of ranks for Group 1.

In our example, U for Group 1 is

$$U = (11)(12) + [11(11 + 1)/2] - 81.5 = 116.5$$

The formula for U for Group 2 is

$$U = n_1 n_2 + [n_2(n_2 + 1)/2] - \Sigma R_2 \tag{9.4}$$

In our example, U for Group 2 is

$$U = (11)(12) + [12(12 + 1)/2] - 194.5 = 15.5$$

4. Determine probability. This can be accomplished either by consulting a table of U values (for the smaller of the two Us) or by calculating z and consulting a table of areas of the standard normal probability curve (Table A.2). The U tables are used with small samples. If samples are of moderate size (say 10 or more in each sample), the sampling distribution of U will be approximately normal, and the calculation of z is appropriate. Most statistics textbooks contain U tables if you want to use the Mann-Whitney U test with very small samples.

The calculation of z is as follows:

$$z = \frac{U - (n_1)(n_2)/2}{\sqrt{n_1 n_2(n_1 + n_2 + 1)/12}} \tag{9.5}$$

Substituting the values from Table 9.4, we calculate z using the U for Group 1:

$$z = \frac{116.5 - (11)(12)/2}{\sqrt{(11 \times 12)(11 + 12 + 1)/12}}$$

$$= \frac{116.5 - 66}{\sqrt{(132)(24)/12}}$$

$$= \frac{50.5}{\sqrt{264}}$$

$$= 50.5/16.25 = 3.11$$

It does not matter which U is used. If we had used the U for Group 2, the resulting z would be -3.11. So the absolute value of z is the same (only the sign is different).

Consult Table A.2 and find the z for 3.11. We see that the probability that a difference this large would occur by chance is less than .01%. Thus, there appears to be a real difference between the two groups of teachers on duration of eye fixation, with experienced teachers demonstrating significantly less time than the novice golf teachers.

WILCOXON MATCHED-PAIRS SIGNED-RANKS TEST

You recall from chapter 7 that there are studies in which one has matched groups, or the same group of people being tested twice on a dependent measure, and the investigator wants to know whether the difference between the matched groups (or the change in scores for the same subjects) is significant. In such situations, the independent t test is not appropriate, and the researcher must use a dependent t test (or repeated measures ANOVA). The same principle applies in nonparametric statistics. The researcher would not be correct in using a test such as the Mann-Whitney U test with dependent (paired) groups.

The Wilcoxon matched-pair signed-ranks test is a powerful nonparametric test for comparing related samples. In the Wilcoxon test, the size of the difference between scores (such as between pre- and posttest scores) is determined and ranked.

An example illustrates the steps and the interpretation of this test. A researcher, Dr. Marlo Perkins, believes that adventure programs are conducive to raising one's self-concept. She gathers scores on a self-concept scale for a group of boys before and after an adventure activity program (Table 9.5). She wishes to assess whether they gained in self-concept. So, in this case, she is using a one-tailed test because she is hypothesizing a positive change and is not interested in any changes that might occur in the opposite direction. (Note: This example is to illustrate the Wilcoxon statistical test and is not intended as a model for experimental design.) In such a case, other influences certainly could explain changes in self-concept other than the adventure program. A control group would definitely add validity to such a study. Unfortunately, Dr. Perkins never read this book.

1. Determine the differences (column 3) by subtracting the pretest scores from the posttest scores. Of course, some differences are positive and some negative. In two cases, no change in score occurred. Therefore, these two are dropped from further analysis because they would have no influence.

2. Rank the differences *without* regard to sign (column 4). We started with the lowest difference, and we see that three people have a difference of one ($+1$, -1, -1). As before, because they occupy the first three ranks, each is given the average rank of 2.

3. Place the appropriate sign in front of the ranks (column 5).

4. Determine if there are more plus or minus ranks and enter the smaller number in column 6. These ranks are summed, which is designated as T.

5. Test the T statistic for significance. With a small N (less than 25), Table A.9 is consulted. Because two sets of scores that had no change were dropped, N is

Table 9.5 Self-Concept Scores Before and After an Adventure Program

Subject	(1) Pre	(2) Post	(3) Differences (D)	(4) Rank D	(5) Signed R	(6) Fewest
A	33	36	+3	6.5	+6.5	. . .
B	30	31	+1	2	+2	. . .
C	40	37	−3	6.5	−6.5	−6.5
D	27	36	+9	13	+13	. . .
E	18	24	+6	10	+10	. . .
F	26	25	−1	2	−2	−2
G	35	35	0	. . .	. . .	. . .
H	20	16	−4	8	−8	−8
I	38	33	−5	9	−9	−9
J	16	24	+8	12	+12	. . .
K	26	28	+2	4.5	+4.5	. . .
L	21	20	−1	2	−2	−2
M	18	20	+2	4.5	+4.5	. . .
N	24	24	0	. . .	. . .	. . .
O	11	18	+7	11	+11	. . .

$$T = 27.5$$

13. Dr. Perkins had specified in advance that she would be using the significance level of .01. Consulting Table A.9 with an N of 13, we see that a T of 13 or less is necessary to reject the null hypothesis at the .01 level for a one-tailed test. Consequently, Dr. Perkins sadly concludes that no significant gains in self-concept followed participation in the adventure program.

6. **With a sample size of greater than 25, compute z and consult Table A.2 for the critical value.** We use the data in Table 9.5 to demonstrate the calculation of z:

$$z = \frac{T - N(N+1)/4}{\sqrt{N(N+1)[2(N+1)]/24}}$$

$$= \frac{27.5 - 13(13+1)/4}{\sqrt{13(13+1)[2(13+1)]/24}} \tag{9.6}$$

$$= \frac{-18}{14.57}$$

$$= -1.24$$

The sign of the z does not matter. Table A.2 shows a probability of 0.11 for the one-tailed test (not significant).

KRUSKAL-WALLIS ANOVA BY RANKS

The Kruskal-Wallis test is a nonparametric test of group differences when there are more than two independent groups. This is comparable to one-way ANOVA in parametric statistics. The data are converted to ranks for the analysis.

An Example of Kruskal-Wallis

To illustrate this technique, we use the example at the beginning of chapter 1 concerning the effectiveness of aerobic dance and jogging on loss of fat as measured by the sum of skinfolds. A control group was also used in which the subjects did not engage in any exercise program but were measured before and after the 10-week period. For the purpose of this analysis we use small numbers of subjects in each group and assume that our data were skewed, thus prompting the use of a nonparametric test. Table 9.6 shows the scores for the three groups. The scores represent the loss of fat; thus, negative numbers are "good," and positive numbers represent gains in fatness and are "bad."

1. **Combine all scores and rank them.** The poorest score (a gain of fatness of 20 mm in skinfold thickness) is given a rank of 1 and the best score (a loss of 32 mm) the highest rank of 21. As in previous examples, ties are given the average ranking.

2. **Place the overall ranking for individuals next to their raw scores and sum the rankings for each group.** It should be obvious by now that if the null hypothesis is true, the average rank for each group would be the same. In other words, any differences in scores would be attributable to sampling error. We see that the average

Table 9.6 Kruskal-Wallis ANOVA of Comparison of Exercise Programs on Loss of Fatness

Aerobic dance (n = 8)		Jogging (n = 7)		Control (n = 6)	
Score	Rank	Score	Rank	Score	Rank
-10	10	-25	15.5	+10	3
-29	19	-31	20	-5	7
-8	8	-19	12	+20	1
-32	21	0	6	-10	10
-22	14	-28	18	+9	4
-25	15.5	-27	17	+13	2
+2	5	-10	10	. . .	. . .
-20	13	. . .	. . .	. . .	. . .
ΣR = 105.5		ΣR = 98.5		ΣR = 27	
$\bar{R}$ = 13.2		$\bar{R}$ = 14.1		$\bar{R}$ = 4.5	

ranks for the three groups are as follows: aerobic dance (13.2), jogging (14.1), and control (4.5).

3. Test for the significance of the differences among the groups by the Kruskal-Wallis test (H):

$$H = [12/N(N + 1)] \cdot \Sigma[(\Sigma R_i)^2/n_i] - 3(N + 1) \qquad (9.7)$$

where N = the total number of scores, ΣR^2 = the sum of the squared sum of ranks for the three groups, and n = the number of scores in a group.

4. Do the simple computations. For each group we need to square the sum of ranks and divide by the number of scores in that group; we then sum R_i^2/n for all three groups:

$$\frac{(105.5)^2}{8} + \frac{(98.5)^2}{7} + \frac{(27)^2}{6} = 2,898.8$$

This sum is multiplied by $12/N(N + 1)$:

$$[12/21(21 + 1)] \times 2,898.8 = .026 \times 2,898.8 = 75.37$$

from which we subtract $3(N + 1)$:

$$75.37 - 3(21 + 1) = 75.37 - 66 = 9.37$$

5. When there are at least 5 subjects in each group, test H by chi-square with df = k − 1 (where k is group). If there are 5 or fewer subjects in each group, use a special table. If there is a large number of tied ranks (e.g., over 25%), a correction for H should be calculated (Siegel, 1956). Because we have sufficient numbers in each group, we consult Table A.8 and see that the tabled chi-square value at the .05 level for 2 df is 5.99. As our value of 9.37 surpasses that, we can conclude that there are significant differences among the groups.

Follow-Up Comparisons

When we described one-way ANOVA in chapter 7, you will remember that when F is significant, a follow-up procedure (e.g., Newman-Keuls) is used to find where the differences are. A similar procedure can be performed to test the differences between the average ranks.

This procedure allows the investigator to make all possible pairwise comparisons while holding the overall alpha level at a specified value. In our example in Table 9.6, suppose we wish to make all possible comparisons while holding the overall alpha level to .05 or less. With three groups, three comparisons are possible of $k(k − 1)/2$. We set the confidence level for each comparison. First, we can use the Bonferroni technique and divide the alpha level (.05) by the number of comparisons (3), which results in .017. Consulting Table A.2, we find the z value that corresponds to this percent of area in the tails of the distribution and find the z value of 2.39. This will be multiplied by the standard error of difference (*SE*) between any two samples:

$$SE_{\bar{R}_1-\bar{R}_2} = \sqrt{[N(N + 1)/12] \cdot (1/n_1 + 1/n_2)} \qquad (9.8)$$

where N = the total sample size and n the size of the groups being compared.

For our three comparisons, the standard error of differences are as follows:

aerobic dance (A) versus jogging (J):

$$SE_{\bar{R}_A-\bar{R}_J} = \sqrt{[21(21 + 1)/12](1/8 + 1/7)} = 3.21$$

aerobic dance (A) versus control (C):

$$SE_{\bar{R}_A-\bar{R}_C} = \sqrt{[21(21 + 1)/12](1/8 + 1/6)} = 3.35$$

jogging (J) versus control (C):

$$SE_{\bar{R}_J-\bar{R}_C} = \sqrt{[21(21 + 1)/12](1/7 + 1/6)} = 3.45$$

The confidence interval can now be established for each comparison. The confidence interval equals the observed difference between groups plus or minus z for .017, or 2.39 ($SE_{R_1-R_2}$):

aerobic dance versus jogging:

$$\bar{R}_A(13.2) - \bar{R}_J(14.1) \pm (2.39)(3.21) = 0.9 \pm 7.67 = -6.77 \text{ to } 8.57$$

aerobic dance versus control:

$$\bar{R}_A(13.2) - \bar{R}_C(4.5) \pm (2.39)(3.35) = 8.7 \pm 8.01 = 0.69 \text{ to } 16.71$$

jogging versus control:

$$\bar{R}_J(14.1) - \bar{R}_C(4.5) \pm (2.39)(3.45) = 9.6 \pm 8.25 = 1.35 \text{ to } 17.85$$

A comparison is considered statistically significant when the confidence interval does not include zero. In the previous comparisons, the significant differences are in the two comparisons involving the control group with the exercise groups. So, we conclude that both the aerobic dance and the jogging groups result in significant reductions in fatness and that there is no difference between the two types of exercise in this regard.

FRIEDMAN TWO-WAY ANOVA BY RANKS

The Friedman test is analogous to repeated measures ANOVA in parametric statistics. The scores are ranked, and chi-square is used as the test of significance. An example will explain the steps in the analysis.

A group of 12 people have been measured for percent fat by three different methods: (a) hydrostatic weighing, (b) total body water, and (c) potassium-40. The investigator wishes to discover whether there is any difference among the three methods. The values for Methods a, b, and c for the 12 subjects are shown in Table 9.7.

The three scores for each individual are converted to ranks from 1 to 3. Subject 1, for example, has percent fat values of 16.0, 15.7, and 15.2 for Methods a, b, and c, respectively. Method c yields the lowest percent, so it is ranked 1, the next lowest (b) is ranked 2, and Method a is ranked 3. This procedure is followed for the rest of the subjects (ranks are also shown in the table). The familiar procedure of averaging tied ranks is followed.

The ranks for each column are summed. Under the null hypothesis, these sums should be about the same because the ranks should be evenly distributed over all three methods. On the other hand, if one method shows consistently low percent fat values, for example, it would have more ranks of 1, and the result would be a lower sum of ranks.

The Friedman two-way ANOVA by ranks yields a chi-square with $k - 1$ df. The formula is as follows:

$$\chi^2 = [12/Nk(k + 1)][\Sigma(\Sigma R)^2] - 3N(k + 1) \tag{9.9}$$

where N = the total subjects (number of rows), k = the number of columns, and $\Sigma(R)^2$ = the sum of the squared column totals.

Table 9.7 Data for Friedman Two-Way ANOVA Comparing Three Methods of Estimating Percent Fat

Subject	Method a	Method b	c	R(a)	Ranks R(b)	R(c)
1	16.0	15.7	15.2	3	2	1
2	11.6	10.9	11.5	3	1	2
3	18.1	18.0	17.6	3	2	1
4	16.3	16.8	17.0	1	2	3
5	12.0	13.1	12.8	1	3	2
6	12.5	12.2	12.3	3	1	2
7	9.3	8.8	9.0	3	1	2
8	18.8	17.5	18.0	3	1	2
9	19.2	19.7	19.7	1	2.5	2.5
10	22.3	22.8	21.6	2	3	1
11	20.7	20.3	19.6	3	2	1
12	24.1	23.7	24.4	2	1	3
		Sums of ranks =		28	21.5	22.5

The computations for our example are as follows:

$$\chi^2 = [12/12(3)(3 + 1)][(28)^2 + (21.5)^2 + (22.5)^2] - 3(12)(3+1)$$
$$= (12/144)(784 + 462.25 + 506.25) - 144$$
$$= .083(1,752.5) - 144 = 1.46$$

From Table A.8, with $k - 1$ df, the chi-square needed for significance at the .05 level is 5.99. Therefore, we conclude that there are no significant differences among the three methods of estimating percent fat.

A special table (Siegel, 1956) of critical values of chi-square is needed if one uses very small samples (e.g., $k = 3$ and $N < 10$ or $k = 4$ and $N < 5$).

SPEARMAN RANK-DIFFERENCE CORRELATION

There are times when an investigator wishes to determine the relationship between variables when the assumptions of parametric statistics cannot be met or perhaps when precise measurements are not available. If the data can be converted to ranks, the Spearman rank-difference method can be used to find the correlation between two sets of ranks. It is a quick and simple process:

$$r_s = 1 - 6\Sigma D^2/[N(N^2 - 1)] \tag{9.10}$$

where ΣD^2 = the sum of the squared differences between ranks and N = the number of pairs of ranks.

To demonstrate the method, suppose an English teacher ranked 10 boys on social behavior in class. The basketball coach ranked the same 10 boys on his perception of their social behavior in sport participation. The research question is, Are social behaviors of boys perceived similarly across various contexts (e.g., English class and basketball practice)? Table 9.8 contains the data for the rank-difference method.

We substitute the ΣD^2 and the N values in Formula 9.10 as follows:

$$r_s = 1 - 6(148)/10(100 - 1)$$
$$= 1 - 888/990$$
$$= 1 - .897$$
$$r_s = .10$$

Table A.10 contains the values of r_s that are necessary for significance at the .05 and .01 levels. We enter the table with our N of 10 and find the tabled values for r_s at the .05 level to be .65. Because our r_s is much lower than that, we are forced to conclude that our coefficient is not significantly different from zero, and social behavior appears to be specific to the setting rather than a general trait.

Table 9.8 The Spearman Rank-Difference Correlation of Two Ratings of Social Behavior

Student	Classroom	Athletics	D	D^2
A	4	1	3	9
B	6	9	−3	9
C	8	8	0	0
D	1	6	−5	25
E	7	2	5	25
F	3	4	−1	1
G	9	3	6	36
H	5	10	−5	25
I	2	5	−3	9
J	10	7	3	9
				$\Sigma D^2 = 148$

The Spearman r_s can be computed on variables in which one or both of the values are interval measurements. The measurements simply must be converted to ranks. Of course, tied ranks are averaged. In a negative correlation, ΣD^2 is very large, so the fraction to be subtracted from 1 is greater than 1, which results in a negative r_s.

The Spearman r_s and the Pearson r will not necessarily yield the same coefficient for the same data, especially if there are a number of tied ranks. Also, because r_s is based on ranks that are not continuous or normally distributed, the coefficient may differ from Pearson r. However, the Spearman r_s is a valuable tool for special cases in which r cannot or should not be used.

OTHER INDEXES OF ASSOCIATION

Several correlational techniques can be used in situations in which data are discrete (i.e., not continuous).

Contingency Coefficient

You can compute the relationship between dichotomous variables such as gender and race by the use of a *contingency coefficient*. The test of significance is the chi-square. You recall that we described the contingency table in this chapter for use in detecting differences between groups or sets of data. The contingency table can also be used to determine relationships. You can have any number of rows and columns in a contingency table. After the chi-square is computed, the contingency coefficient can be computed:

$$C = \sqrt{\chi^2/N + \chi^2} \qquad (9.11)$$

If χ^2 is significant, C is also significant. The direction of the relationship is established by examining the data. There are several limitations concerning the ability of the contingency coefficient to estimate correlation. In general, one needs several categories and a large number of observations to obtain a reasonable estimate.

Multivariate Contingency Tables: The Loglinear Model

Categorical data can be analyzed in combination with other variables. In other words, contingency tables can be studied in more than only two dimensions. Therefore, one can identify associations among many variables, for example, the interrelationships among age, gender, skill level, and teaching method. This would be similar to parametric multivariate analysis except that in continuous quantitative data, variables are expressed as linear composites. However, with categorical variables, the researcher deals with contributions to the expected frequencies within each cell of the multivariate contingency table. Any given cell represents the intersection of many marginal proportions.

Loglinear models are used to analyze multivariate contingency tables. Relative frequencies are transformed to logarithms, which are additive and similar to sum of squares in analysis of variance. Main effects and interactions can be tested for significance. The probability of membership in a particular category can be predicted as a function of membership in other categories using a logistic regression equation and is based on the log odds of membership (called a *logit*).

The loglinear model has considerable potential application in qualitative research (Schutz, 1989). This type of analysis is attracting much attention from researchers and theoreticians. The loglinear analysis provides a means for sophisticated study of the interrelationships among categorical variables. Readers who are interested in pursuing this topic are directed to the text by Kennedy (1983).

SUMMARY

In this chapter we have presented some of the nonparametric tests that can be used as alternatives to corresponding parametric tests. It would be a mistake to conclude that nonparametric tests are inferior to or less scientific than parametric tests. Often a nonparametric test provides an answer to the question of interest at a satisfactory level of significance. Remember that just because a nonparametric test is easy to compute does not mean that something more has to be done before it can be considered fit to be reported.

It is true that nonparametric tests are usually less powerful than the corresponding parametric test. However, if the nonparametric test produces a significant rejection of the null hypothesis, why should one feel compelled to use the parametric counterpart? Certainly, one should use the parametric test if more power is needed, but nonparametric tests are legitimate statistical procedures and are appropriate whenever the assumptions about the populations being sampled do not meet the criteria for parametric tests.

Table 9.9 provides a summary of the nonparametric statistics described in this chapter and their application with regard to the type of data (ordinal or nominal), the nature of the sample (independent or dependent), and the number of groups and correlational techniques.

Table 9.9 Summary of Nonparametric Tests

Comparisons of nominal (category) data	
One classification:	Chi-square
Two or more classifications:	Contingency tables

Comparisons with ordinal (ranked) data		
	Independent groups	*Dependent groups*
Two groups:	Mann-Whitney *U* test	Wilcoxon matched pair
More than two groups:	Kruskal-Wallis ANOVA	Friedman ANOVA

Correlations	
Ordinal (rank) data:	Spearman rank difference
Nominal (category) data (two classifications):	Contingency coefficient
Nominal (category) data (more than two classifications):	Loglinear analysis

Problems

1. Compute chi-square for the following contingency table of activity preferences of men ($n = 110$) and women ($n = 90$). Determine the significance of the chi-square at the .01 level using Table A.8. When calculating the expected values, round off to whole numbers of expected frequencies.

    a. Write a brief interpretation of your results.

    b. What would be the critical value for significance at the .05 level if you had five rows and four columns?

	Racquetball	Weight training	Aerobic dance
Men	35	45	30
Women	28	13	49

2. Critique the statistical part of a study that uses chi-square in the analysis.
3. Find whether there is a significant difference among the following four groups using the Kruskal-Wallis ANOVA method. First convert the scores to ranks (smallest score = 1) and then determine the significance at the .05 level.

Group 1	Group 2	Group 3	Group 4
52	36	32	51
42	37	44	54
51	40	32	46
44	49	45	43
60	50	38	58
39	32	. . .	41
. . .	30	. . .	35

SUGGESTED READINGS

Bartz, A.E. (1976). *Basic statistical concepts in education and the behavioral sciences.* Minneapolis: Burgess.

Conover, W.J. (1971). *Practical nonparametric statistics.* New York: Wiley.

Morehouse, C.A., & Stull, G.A. (1975). *Statistical principles and procedures with applications for physical education.* Philadelphia: Lea & Febiger.

Siegel, S. (1956). *Nonparametric statistics for the behavioral sciences.* New York: McGraw-Hill.

PART III

Types of Research

Research may be divided into five basic categories: analytical, descriptive, experimental, qualitative, and creative (the last category includes art and dance but is not presented in this book). Chapter 10 discusses historical research, which is a type of analytical research that answers questions through the use of past knowledge and events. Substantial changes have occurred in recent years in the reporting of historical research, particularly regarding the integration of the events of interest with other related events. In this chapter, Nancy Struna provides an excellent overview of historical research methods. Note that this chapter is written in University of Chicago style because that is the style most commonly used in reporting historical research. Chapter 11 is a nice overview of another type of analytical research that can

be applied to physical activity—philosophic methods. Kathy Pearson does a fine job of explaining and grouping philosophic research methods, and uses various examples to identify the strengths and weaknesses of these methods. Chapter 12 presents meta-analysis, another type of analytical research that focuses on the shortcomings of the typical literature analysis. Meta-analysis is a more useful solution in analyzing a large body of literature. Although several other types of research are considered analytical, historical, philosophic, and meta-analysis are the most common and useful in physical education, exercise science, and sport science.

Chapter 13 discusses descriptive research and focuses on the present, showing the relationship among people, events, performances, and so on as they now exist. Included as descriptive research are surveys, case studies, correlational studies, developmental studies, and observational studies.

Chapter 14 introduces experimental research, which deals with future events or the establishment of cause-and-effect. What independent variables can be manipulated to create change in the future in a certain dependent variable? After discussing how difficult cause-and-effect is to establish, the chapter is divided according to the strengths of various designs: preexperimental, true experimental, and quasi-experimental. Our purpose is to illustrate which designs and principles are best suited for controlling for the various sources of invalidity that threaten experimental research.

Finally, chapter 15 is an overview of qualitative research techniques, which are finding increased use in physical education, exercise science, and sport science. The assumptions underlying qualitative research differ from types of research that adhere to the traditional scientific method. That does not mean qualitative research is not science (i.e., systematic inquiry); however, the techniques for acquiring and analyzing knowledge differ from the typical steps in the scientific method. This chapter discusses differences in the quantitative and qualitative paradigms, procedures used in qualitative research, and interpretation and theory construction.

If you are either a producer or a consumer of research in physical education, exercise science, and sport science, you must gain an understanding of accepted techniques for solving problems systematically. The following six chapters attempt to provide the basic underpinnings of research planning. Many of the research types reported here are closely associated with the appropriate statistical analyses previously presented. Frequent references to the appropriate statistics will be made as the many types of research are discussed. Use the knowledge gained from the previous section to understand this application. An understanding of the relationship between the correct type of design and the appropriate statistical analysis is one you should begin acquiring as soon as possible.

Chapter 10

□

Historical Research

Nancy L. Struna

The ways of the historian often mystify the scientist. First, the historian studies the past rather than the present, and the reality of the past is often elusive. Further, the historian can rarely be as certain about past relationships, causes, or consequences as can the scientist, for he or she just cannot isolate variables as concisely and independently. Finally, the historian writes differently from the scientist. A historical report has no distinct sections on purpose, methods, results, and conclusions; and the "telling a story" format of the historical study can mask the systematic, rational procedures that produced it.

The historian's work need not, however, be so mysterious; for history, if not exactly a science, is certainly sciencelike. The historian, who attempts to describe and explain change and continuity in human experience in the past, undertakes many of the tasks that characterize scientific research. He or she carefully derives questions from the literature, thoroughly gathers and translates evidence (data), and tests inferences. Also, like the scientist, the historian works to disprove rather than to prove findings and requires that his or her mind be "trained in a discipline of attentive disbelief."[1]

The similarities between historical and scientific research are many, and these will become clearer as this chapter proceeds. There is, however, one significant difference that requires some comment. This is about the roles of *law* and *theory*. In traditional science, laws and theories are generalizations about natural phenomena. Laws describe what some "thing" is, and the relationships of the components are often expressed mathematically. A theory builds on such a description, but it also proposes to explain a phenomenon. Moreover, if a scientific theory is adequate, it will also be predictive in that it will account for future or further occurrences.

Many historians, on the other hand, do not view social phenomena—or, consequently, laws and theories—as scientists do natural phenomena. One of the prevailing assumptions in historical scholarship is that humans, who are rational beings, make and give meaning to social phenomena. Their thoughts and actions, as well as the individual character of experience and meaning, are neither predetermined nor predictable. This "human agency" thus diminishes the probability of "covering laws" as well as the predictive function of theory.[2] So the role of theory in history is limited to accounting for (both describing and explaining) particular events and processes. One such social theory that historians of sport and leisure have employed is that of modernization.[3] This maintains that "progressive increases in per capita productivity set in motion" a whole series of

The author wishes to thank Jane Clark, University of Maryland, and Stephen Hardy, University of New Hampshire, for their thoughtful comments on earlier drafts of this chapter. Their criticisms and suggestions improved the work immensely.

changes common to a range of human institutions and activity.[4] Modernization thus describes and, to some extent, explains how a society became what it did. However, it also works only in particular societies. Consequently, a social theory like modernization does not predict events and processes as scientific theories do.[5]

Some historians discount the role of theory in historical research even further, for many reasons. Most of these scholars do, however, expect to produce meaningful generalizations from the historical evidence, or data. But rather than employing the word "theory," they use the terms "model" or "conceptual framework." Moreover, such models or conceptual frameworks do draw on social science theories. So, in effect, few historians proceed to or from the evidence of the past without some attention to theory and without some regard for theoretical generalizations. If a study of the past did not produce such generalizations, it would not be a history.[6]

THE HISTORIAN BEGINS

The possibilities and limits of theory in history are probably not the first issues a graduate student would think about as he or she begins to study historical research. The discussion of social theory does, however, serve two purposes. First, it helps students to understand why history is sciencelike and not science. Second, it introduces students to the kinds of issues that face working historians. There are many such issues, and how one resolves them affects how and what one sees in the past. Three other issues are particularly crucial to one's conception of the past. First, how does social change proceed? Is change gradual, progressive, and cumulative, or, in a word, evolutionary? Second, what is historical evidence, and will it "speak" to the historian?[7] Finally, when one

is investigating past sports, exercise programs, or leisure practices, what is one really studying?

Paradigms

The answers to questions about such things as the nature of historical change, evidence, and subject are a part of what Thomas Kuhn, in *The Structure of Scientific Revolutions*, has called the researcher's paradigm. Synonyms for paradigm include research *perspective, tradition*, and, in the historian's ordinary language, *approach*, and they all say the same thing. A paradigm encompasses beliefs and assumptions about every part of the researcher's work, including what evidence is, what the significant questions are, the role of theory, and interpretive tools and rules. All researchers, scientists, and historians have such a body of beliefs that result from the things one has thought about in the course of his or her research.[8]

Beginning students of history will probably not be able to define an integrated, logically consistent paradigm. Most historians readily admit that it takes them a long time to do so, and this is one of the reasons why they maintain that they become good historians only in the second halves of their careers. So, I introduce the notion of paradigms to help students start to think about the things that historians think about and the beliefs that bear on the "doing" of history.

Secondary Sources

From a practical standpoint, secondary sources, or the existing literature, are the history student's true beginning point, as they are for all researchers. The secondary literature includes the existing body of books, articles, and other media (such as films or tape recordings) that are histories in contrast to the primary, or firsthand, sources that contain the actual evidence. In the literature, a student will become more aware of the nature and effect of researchers' paradigms. One may read about the "evolution" of a club, conflicting accounts of a given event or person's life, or a different view of history than the one presented in this chapter. Each is a matter of the unstated paradigm. But students will take other information from the secondary sources as well.

Today, historians of sport and leisure, physical education, and exercise science have a vast array of secondary literature on which to draw. In fact, we actually have several literatures. First, of course, is direct literature: monographs, anthologies, journal articles, films, encyclopedias about the history of sport and health, and so on.[9] There is also an ever-widening body of ancillary literature that derives both from traditional disciplines (history, anthropology, sociology, political science, and economics, among others) and from the newer, often interdisciplinary fields such as American studies, women's studies, Afro-American studies, public policy, and management. Individual topics may require a student to examine the literature in medicine, law, and other fields as well.

Students will often not know precisely what their secondary literature consists of until they have begun to dig for background reading on their topics. Most students generally start their studies of history with a general area of interest, such as some thing, person, or era about which or whom they wish to know more (the amorphous "topic"). One's advisor will undoubtedly suggest some books and articles for the student to read and understand so that he or she can begin to realize what is already known about this topic. But graduate advisors will invariably encourage the student to do precisely what they do to locate the literature: use the computer searches to proceed systematically through various literature banks. Not too many years ago, students sought secondary literature through various published indexes, such as *America: History and Life*; *Education Index*; and *Social Science Abstracts*. Today, however, students can define a string of key words and search on-line data bases, such as the Online Computer Library Center Union Catalog (OCLC) and the Research Libraries Information Network (RLIN), which register the catalog records of many contributing libraries.[10]

What does one take from this secondary literature? The simple answer is, as much as possible. At one level, a student reads as much as possible on a topic so that he or she knows what other scholars do and do not know about that topic. At another level, a student reads the literature to understand both the broader society that affected the subject and the conceptual frameworks and social theories that will bear on any conclusions. Finally, the student reads the literature to uncover sources of evidence. In historical research, evidence is discussed in the text, but the actual identification and location of that evidence usually appears in the notes and appendices. For this reason, historians often study the notes as long and hard as they do the body of an article or book.

The history student's eventual success or failure often hinges on how thoroughly he or she is grounded in the literature. This literature will assist the student in shaping the approach or framework (or paradigm) that directs the research. It will direct the student to the data and the many ways of interrogating the evidence. And, perhaps most important (at least as one begins to investigate the past), the literature will help the student to refine and transform the original amorphous topic into a researchable question.

Questions

All research is about answering questions, and on this point history is exactly like science. But one issue critical to the life of the historian may raise the stake of the question in historical research: the issue of objectivity. Not too many years ago, historians would find themselves on one of two sides of a debate about objectivity. Either they were objective or they were not. The "nots" were known as subjectivists or relativists.[11] Today, however, most working historians admit that they will be more or less objective, or at least relatively objective. Beginning with questions helps the historian to operate with more rather than less objectivity, or, in simple terms, as an open-minded detective. Questions about what one will find encourage this open-mindedness, whereas propositions about what one wants or expects to find do not.

So how does a student develop a good beginning question, and what criteria can one apply to distinguish a good question from a bad one? On the general matter of questions, the French historian Henri-Irenee Marrou offered some sage advice: "There is an unlimited number of different questions to which the documents can provide answers." However, he cautioned, one must ask each question of the past "properly."[12] And that proper questioning of the past begins with the secondary sources. A good question, at the very least, is one grounded in and derived from the literature; the unknown it focuses on is thus clear, as is the significance of the question. But a good question is something more as well. It is also answerable.[13]

Let us work through two examples that will move us from the vague topic to the good beginning question. The first example, for which there is a good deal of secondary literature, involves the topic of baseball in the late nineteenth century. The student comes to this topic in the "normal" way, that is, from personal interest, from some knowledge of the literature, or both. In the beginning the advisor will probably tell the student to narrow the topic so that it becomes "doable" in the span of the graduate experience. The student, in turn, focuses on a given city or town where he or she has access to records and will not spend a fortune traveling and on a particular set of years, or a period. At this point, or perhaps up to this point, the student will read the histories of baseball, the history of the particular city or region, and the more general histories of the period. From all this, the student will conclude that his or her town did have a baseball club by 1865, that the town (say Cleveland, Ohio) did have a rapidly expanding population and industrial base by the same date, and that baseball was still controlled by players in loosely linked clubs. The student can now delimit the topic with a set of questions that are answerable and most of which test the conclusions offered in the literature. Who were the earliest members of the Cleveland baseball club? Was baseball a middle-class, upper-class, or working-class sport? Where did they play, and what rules did they use? Did baseball provide a refuge from their industrial work, or did it replicate the players' work lives?

> Beginning with questions helps the historian to operate with more rather than less objectivity, or, in simple terms, as an open-minded detective.

The second topic presents a bit more of a challenge because nothing has been written about it. The topic is the women's high school athletic association in a state, in this case Louisiana. In the beginning the student knows only that the organization first appeared about 1925. Still, he or she begins (just as the student in the previous example did) in the literature. The topic itself suggests the background reading, for every word in that topic has a literature: social histories of the 1920s (and subsequent decades), women's and gender histories, organized athletics, histories of schools and education, and Louisiana history. From all this, the student learns nothing about the particular athletic federation but much about the issues concerning competition for girls and women, the occupational and social expectations and roles for women, the other organizations that women formed, and the changing curriculum, population, and context of high schools in Louisiana. The logical transformation of topic to questions can now occur. Who were the organizers? What goals did they have? What ac-

tivities and what kinds of competitive format did they incorporate? When were different (or additional) sports introduced? What were the relationships of athletic competitions to other physical education, health, and recreational programs? What was the structure of the association? What were the relationships of the association to other governing structures within the school and community? Questions such as these will be precursors to some bigger questions: How did the association change over time? What social factors affected the organization? How did the association affect the broader student and school life, especially gender relations? Why did it come into being?

Designing the Research

Once a student has replaced the vague topic with specific, beginning questions, he or she can begin to construct a research design. This is not a phrase that working historians frequently use, and the apparent lack of discussion about constructing the design of the study may be one of the things that mystifies scientists about the work of their colleagues in history. But good historians do design their research, even if such designs lack the formulaic precision found in experimental designs. A design in historical research is precisely what it is in scientific research: a systematic, even hierarchical, layout of the questions and a plan for answering them. In science there are three broad categories of designs:

- Description, which produces a statement of what is or was some thing and from which variables are identified
- Correlation, which examines relationships among variables
- Experimentation, which examines one set of relationships (cause-and-effect)

Most historians reduce this list to two designs on the basis of the questions asked:

description (what happened) and analysis (how and why something happened).[14] The first broad historical design category is virtually the same as descriptive scientific research. The second plan parallels the correlational and cause-and-effect research in science minus the experimentation.[15]

How does a student decide which design —descriptive or analytic—he or she should undertake? The critical factors should be, of course, the existing literature and the questions one wishes to answer. If virtually nothing is known about a particular event, person, or program, then a good descriptive history is in order. Good descriptive history, which is distinct from a *chronicle* (a listing of happenings in time) or *antiquarianism* (the collecting of old things), is also an appropriate goal for students who are just learning to ask historical questions and to work with evidence. But just as is the case in science, descriptive research in history has its limits. Students who wish to explore beyond the "whats" to the "hows" and "whys" will develop analytic designs even if this means doing some descriptive work as well. Doctoral students especially, who can expect publishable books from their dissertations, should look to the existing literature for models of analytic histories. Such recently published models include monographs such as Melvin Adelman's *A Sporting Time: New York City and the Rise of Modern Athletics, 1820-1870* and Martha Verbrugge's *Able-Bodied Womanhood: Personal Health and Social Change in Nineteenth-Century Boston.*[16] Such comprehensive, analytic histories stand as the wave of the future.

DESCRIPTIVE HISTORY

The world's oceans present us with a useful analogy for understanding descriptive history. Today, scientists know much about these huge bodies of water: their depths, their total sizes, the plants and animals that live in them, and even the courses that ships need to travel across them. Not too many centuries ago, however, the oceans were truly uncharted seas, a situation that made captains and navigators double as mapmakers. Today, much of the past of sport, exercise, education, athletics, health, and leisure is like those uncharted seas of old; and, like earlier ocean travelers, one who makes that journey to the past becomes a mapmaker. In short, the goal of a descriptive history is to construct a "map" of past experience.

A good map locates roads and landmarks, and this is precisely what good *descriptive history* does. It locates in time and place a person, a trend, an event, or an organization in the past by providing answers to particular questions. Such questions are many, but they include where something took place or someone lived, when an event happened or a person lived, who a person was, and what an organization or program was. In effect, descriptive history identifies as fully as possible a set of experiences in the past.

Identifying the appropriate questions is the first step in designing a descriptive study, as the earlier discussion of questions suggested. A student begins with a broad topic, say the history of intercollegiate athletics at Arizona State University. Then he or she digests the secondary literature on intercollegiate athletics, higher education, the state, and the university. This literature reveals that nobody really knows anything about ASU athletics, so questions formulated to produce a map of the experiences are needed. When did competition emerge? Where did the matches occur? In what sports did the competitors participate? Who (in terms of class, gender, etc.) were the competitors and the opponents? Were officials and spectators present (and, if so, who were they)? The result will resemble a richly detailed map of the people, places, and matches.

However, because this is a historical study, the map will also contain a particular set of markers, or the periods or time phases that "contain" events within time and indicate change over time.[17] To produce these patterns in time, the student will need to ask a second set of questions that draw directly from the secondary literature; for example, When were different sports and opponents added to the athletic program? and, What was the course of incorporation of athletics within the broader life of the university? What were the economic and demographic characteristics of the student body over time?

The secondary literature, however, suggests more than just another set of questions to be asked about the ASU experience. Because it also offers answers to these questions in the form of conclusions about the patterns of athletic experience at other institutions, it also provides the student with hypotheses to test. Logically deduced, just as are scientific hypotheses, these broad statements of probability in the case of intercollegiate athletics may be as follows. Initially, the students created, funded, and organized athletics; eventually, as athletics began to compete with students' academic responsibilities and to draw alumni support, faculty and administrators sought to become actors on the athletic stage; and, even later, departments of athletics became embroiled in racial, class, and gender controversies. All these statements constitute the student's final "story," which is the goal of descriptive history.

ANALYTIC HISTORY

In effect, what the student has done to design this descriptive study is to develop two sets of questions about ASU athletics. The first set includes the ones that will result in the student's knowing "what" happened at ASU. The second set will enable the investigator to make sense of the ASU experiences both in terms of patterns within and over time and in terms of the existing literature. What the student has not done, however, is to pose questions about the relationships among experiences and the factors, or variables, that affected them. Such questions are the domain of *analytic history*, our second type of history, which focuses on how something occurred and even why someone did something. The analytic historian, in other words, begins with the map (or description) of experiences, breaks apart and relates the constituents of those experiences, and ends with "making sense" of the entire scene.

If we continue with the example of intercollegiate athletics at Arizona State University, we can design an analytic investigation. Assume, if you will, that one of the conclusions of the previous description is that by about 1920 the types of sports included in the athletic program had changed. The earliest forms, football and basketball for men, now existed alongside rodeo, riflery, swimming, a distinctive women's version of basketball, track, and so on. The questions thus become, How did this situation come to be? and, Why did the athletic program diversify?

The answers are not simple, nor are they arrived at simply. A simple-sounding "how" question, which asks about the process of the experience, is one of the most difficult to answer in historical research. A "why" question, which focuses on the cause, is even more difficult to answer. Before one can even begin to answer the "how" questions, a student needs to identify clearly all the variables—the agents and the social factors and structures—that operated in the process of change. In the case of the ASU athletic program (as the prior descriptive history established), the variables include three main groups of actors (students, alumni, and faculty and administrators), the beliefs and interests of each group, and the social setting and structures in which they existed. It is the relationships among these three main sets of variables, then, that the student needs to be able to analyze if he or she is to answer the "how" question.

Thus, our initial question of how this situation came to be needs to be restated as a series of answerable subquestions about relationships and changes in relationships within and across time. Such questions might include the following: What was the relationship between the changing ethnic and gender composition of the student body and the emergence of new forms of sport? How did students react to (or act on) faculty efforts to monitor the times and funding of competition? What was the relationship between alumni and students or between administrators and alumni? What was the relationship between the university's teams and the broader community and government officials?

At this point the student of biophysical science would probably be able to identify the "predictor" variable and proceed to test for cause-and-effect in the laboratory by conducting a controlled experiment. The science student would then be able to answer the question of what caused a given phenomenon, our "why" question. Students of history, however, will find that the trip from determining relationships among variables in a given set of past experiences to determining cause is much more difficult, even in a quantitative study.[18] In fact, looking for a single cause may be an impossible task for several reasons. The primary reason is a theoretical one in that historical experiences and events are "massive clusters" of behavior and thought, only some of which may even have been "known" to the historical actors.[19] Put another way, unlike some natural science phenomena, social phenomena are com-plexes of human action, thoughts and beliefs, social factors, and consequences (both intended and unintended). The final form of any given event or experience is something more and perhaps even something other than its components. The second reason is a methodological one: Historians cannot be certain that they have uncovered all the evidence of any given event or person. Consequently, descriptions and explanations will fall short of "absolute truth" no matter how well refined and valid the interpretive schemes and techniques may be.

So we are left expecting the answer to our "why" question to be inexact. Why did the ASU athletic program broaden about 1920? The probable cause or causes will lie within the relationships among students, faculty, alumni, and other supporters of the university. Clearly, the historian cannot "control" for student "effect," nor can one isolate the alumni as a group and apply different "treatments" to them. Moreover, we do not yet have the means to separate and then recombine in an experimental fashion all the variables that affect human experience in the past: class, gender, motive, received traditions, social structures, and so on. Theoretically informed and methodologically driven, then, the student analyst produces a complex explanation, or even a complex of explanations, that takes the shape of a true logical inference.

WORKING WITH THE EVIDENCE

The preceding discussion may have left the impression that historical research depends almost entirely on the kinds of questions one asks. In the real world of the historian, however, nothing could be further from the truth. A student will, of course, use questions to structure his or her study. But questions require answers; and answers require evidence, or, in the scientist's terms, data. Moreover, the evidence that one identifies and uses will affect the increasingly specific questions that one asks. Located in primary sources, or firsthand accounts, historical evidence is truly the determinant in the research process.[20]

What is historical evidence, or data? In *Truth in History*, Oscar Handlin offered what is perhaps the simplest and clearest definition: Evidence is "everything made or recalled."[21] Each "thing" is a piece of the past, and such pieces come in many forms: artifacts, such as equipment and clothes; photographs; oral tales and reminiscences; numerical evidence, such as prize money and census accounts; and literary materials, such as letters, laws, and written stories. The evidence that a student will use depends, of course, on the questions that he or she is asking. The questions also determine whether a student uses qualitative, quantitative, or both forms of evidence.[22] However, about one thing there is no "depending": There can be no answers to questions without evidence. Just as a physiologist must have raw data about the heart rate to answer questions about cardiovascular condition, or just as the psychologist must have records of brain activity to study hemispheric dominance, the historian must have information created and constructed by his or her subjects in the past.

> Located in primary sources, or firsthand accounts, historical evidence is truly the determinant of the research process.

Locating Primary Sources

Before a student can begin to work with evidence, he or she needs to identify the sources that may contain the evidence. To locate where historical sources may exist (usually in distinct kinds of "laboratories" such as archives, libraries, or privately run collections), the student can proceed in a number of ways. If one is working on a particular sport, recreational facility, curricular program, or any other project that is locale specific, he or she may go directly to the catalogs or indexes, for the holdings of the local historical society (state or town), to the college or university archives, to a hall of fame, or to an organization's archives and library. Some of these are identified in Appendix 1 at the end of this chapter. A student may also draw on the on-line data bases noted earlier and on published catalogs, such as the *National Union Catalog of Manuscripts*, that exist in most university libraries. Students will also find that many newspapers, censuses, and government records have indexes to help them locate potential information and that many topical bibliographies of sources are published.

Historical Criticism

Once a student has located existing primary sources, even though the actual identification will probably not yet be complete, he or she begins to criticize the sources. This is an evaluative process that has two steps. The first step determines the form of the material: Is a given artifact or document really a source of evidence? This phase of the evaluation, called *external criticism*, establishes the authenticity of the source. A student has only to think about Watergate or the Iran-Contra affair to realize why the historian must establish a source as an authentic "witness" to the past. For any number of reasons, people in the past (who were the makers of all historical evidence) could, and have been known to, forge documents. More common than outright forgeries, however, are the unintended errors that may have resulted when some time or person intervened between the actual occurrence of an event and the time when a record of the event or person actually appeared. So historians either must know how to establish that a record is really a record of what it purports to be (through a technique like carbon-14 dating for very old artifacts or through textual and stylistic analysis for documents) or must rely on experts to perform these tests. The simple point, of course, is that a piece of evidence must be the genuine article![23]

The second kind of test that historians apply to firsthand records is called *internal criticism*. This examination deals with the nature of the source, specifically whether a now-determined genuine artifact or document is credible. Internal criticism thus involves matters of consistency and accuracy and, at one level, is comparable to the scientist's efforts to establish validity.[24] Just as the scientist must establish the adequacy and "truth" of a test, instrument, or construct, so the historian must determine both

whether an observation or some other form of record is believable and what the context and perspective of the record is. Historians who use quantitative data and sampling techniques will actually use the same techniques to establish validity that biophysical scientists do. Investigators who rely on more traditional data sources, especially literary documents, cannot approach the mathematical precision of validity coefficients, but they do ask appropriate questions systematically. In fact, there are certain rules a student should apply in the process of internally criticizing a document. One is the *rule of context*, which maintains that a word must be understood in relation to the words that precede and follow it, and not in relation to the historian's own contemporary usage. Reading sentences and paragraphs requires the same guidelines of sequence and connotation. A second guideline is the *rule of perspective*, which encourages the student to ask who (or what agency or group) left the record, what a source's relationship to an event or group was, and even how the source collected the information. Finally, there is the *rule of omission* or *free editing*, which holds that most historical sources —whether official records, newspaper accounts, diaries, or formal agreements—are not accounts of complete scenes. The minutes of an NCAA meeting, a photograph of a home run, a day's diary entry by someone like Albert Spalding or Senda Berenson, and even a census or map records some things and leaves out others. Diarists may omit things that happened or words that were spoken in the course of a day, and the editor of a meeting's minutes or of a newspaper report may use different words, leave out entire sections of a report, or even purposefully misrepresent conversations and actions.[25] Thus, because sources may omit information, whether intentionally or not, the historian needs to use more than one source to view any event, program, or person in the past, in much the same way as a biomechanist will use three cameras to view one movement from different angles.

Reading the Evidence

The location and criticism of historical sources are important tasks that all historians perform over and over again. These tasks, however, are not ends in themselves. A newspaper, for example, is a source of information about the past, just as an EMG record is a source of information about muscle contractions. And, like the EMG firing pattern, the newspaper text or picture requires a "reading." In short, a student needs to know what information the newspaper (or any historical source) contains.

To accomplish this, the student will ask a relatively simple question of each piece of information: What is this evidence evidence of? Consider a practical example—a health and physical education curriculum from 1950. Most students in physical education, exercise science, and sport science are familiar with curricula, which lay out goals, activities, and learning outcomes. But about what or whom can a curriculum really inform us? Is it evidence of what went on in the classroom? Is it evidence of all the thoughts about health and physical education that the writers may have held? Or is it evidence of the state of health and physical education in the country? The answer, of course, is none of the above. Insofar as it was written in behavioral terms, the health and physical education curriculum is nothing more or less than evidence of a set of expected behaviors. Moreover, it is evidence of behaviors expected by the writers.

Students will see that all historical sources provide us with evidence that is narrow in scope once they ask what the evidence is evidence of. Typical newspaper accounts of a ballgame, for example, provide us with a portion of the reporter's observations rather than

a comprehensive picture of all that occurred in the contest. The same is true of diaries and letters. Rulebooks provide information about what behaviors should or should not occur, but they do not tell us about what behaviors actually did or did not occur. Likewise, numerical evidence can inform us of only certain things. A salary figure, for example, informs us only of dollars paid to a player, not what the value of the athlete was. The number of fans at an event tells us how many people were present, not whether the event was popular.[26]

Determining what the evidence is evidence of invariably leads a student to one of two conclusions. Either the evidence is "right," meaning both adequate and appropriate, or it is not. If the evidence is adequate and appropriate, then the student can proceed to answer the research questions. However, if the evidence is not right, the student faces a dilemma. This situation might have occurred with our health education curriculum had we expected it to be evidence of behaviors in the classroom. It is also a situation that can and frequently does occur when historians have asked questions about beliefs, attitudes, values, processes, and conditions. Most of our common forms of evidence, whether literary or numerical, provide data about what people did or said rather than about what they believed. Consequently, unless a historian makes some hard-to-establish assumptions about the relationships between what one saw or did and what one believed, he or she will find that most historical sources do not provide the right information about an individual's or a society's beliefs and attitudes.

There are several options for resolving this dilemma. First, a student can change the questions. Second, he or she can retain the question and search for other, appropriate sources of evidence. Finally, one can "translate" what is evidence of one thing (usually behavior) into evidence of another thing, such as beliefs or other concepts. This is an inferential process that requires the careful construction of "indicators" and the testing of relationships. It is also a process about which historians can learn much from their peers in science, who frequently investigate what they cannot directly observe. Physiologists, for example, examine cardiovascular fitness, a condition that cannot be directly observed or measured. So they have developed and validated an inferred indicator: expired air. In studying aggression, psychologists have proceeded similarly. They cannot observe and measure aggression directly, but they can observe and measure one inferred indicator: violent acts.

Constructs and inferential relationships are important to historians when they wish to examine concepts, values, or attitudes that cannot be directly observed. Social class is such a concept. It is also a complex of behaviors and attitudes about which no one piece of evidence is direct evidence. Historical sources do, however, provide numerous and appropriate indicators (occupation, income, goods purchased and used, club membership, and so on) that altogether may be inferred as evidence of class. Indicators and inferences are also essential to the study of beliefs and values, as in the case of research on the beliefs of members of health clubs. A student may suspect that particular beliefs (in good health, fitness, and even beauty) may have influenced or perhaps even caused people to join a given club. The hypothesis is not directly testable, however, because of the nature of the evidence. All the records of the clubs and even of the members (daily logs, accounts, equipment used and purchased, exercise regimens, and diaries) are readable only as evidence of what the members did, not what they believed. Again, the student must infer a relationship between the observed and the unobservable and, of course, test it.

In part because of the critical role of inferences in historical description and explanation, other information about a person, an event, or a team becomes essential to the historian. This other information will often be in sources that may at first seem tangential to a student's major sources. In the previous example of the research about beliefs of health club members, one might not think that evidence about members' occupations, the other activities and groups in which they participated, their eating habits and medical histories, and their neighborhoods (among other things) would be particularly important, but it is. Only with this evidence can a student test the inferences about beliefs that he or she has produced from the health club behavior data. If the student projected a belief in fitness as one of the factors (perhaps even as a motive) for a subject's membership in the health club, he or she must test that belief in other behavioral situations, and the evidence for this lies in this other information. If no such evidence is forthcoming or if there is counterevidence (if the subject drank heavily, ate high-cholesterol food, or did not regularly see a doctor), the student will need to look for a "new" belief within the health club behaviors. In effect, this seemingly tangential evidence did not bear out the inferred relationship between behavior and belief.[27]

> Constructs and inferential relationships are important to historians when they wish to examine concepts, values, or attitudes that cannot be directly observed.

CONTEXT

This tangential evidence is important in historical research for another reason as well. It is a part of the context in which a historical subject lived or a historical process occurred and in which sport, recreation, or health experiences and processes need to be placed if they are to be understood. Context refers to the ensemble of data about a person, an event, or a period. Rather than background material, in other words, *context* refers to the total network of facts and meanings. The term is so important in historical research that one scholar has defined history as the "discipline of context."[28]

Context figures in many tasks that the historian performs. Students may recall the rule of context discussed in the section on internal criticism. They may also recognize the allusions to context in the paragraphs on indicators and inference. But it is in the reading of evidence that the importance of context becomes most obvious, as one extended example should reveal. The source here is a typical literary document, the *American Turf Register and Sporting Magazine*, which was an urban journal published in the 1820s and 1830s. The particular article, "The Great Foot Race" (reprinted in Appendix 2), is an account of a pedestrian race held at the Union Course racetrack on Long Island in June 1835.[29] Besides the kind of race and its site, the article contains information about the distance covered (ten miles), the number of competitors (nine), some descriptive information about the runners (name, age, weight, occupation, and dress), the order in which they ran, the prize money ($1,300), and the time for each mile achieved by the winner.

From this evidence, we can construct a description of the event. Nine men, ranging in age from twenty-two to thirty-three and of various manual occupations, competed against one another over a distance of ten miles on what was normally a horse track on a Friday in June 1835. The winner, Henry Stannard, covered the distance in the prescribed time (just under an hour) and won the purse of $1,300 in the presence of a crowd estimated at between 16,000 and 20,000. This

is all the information we can read with any certainty in this account.

The rest of the information in the article is in bits and pieces and generally in the form of judgments and suggestions by the reporter. For example, the first sentence of the piece introduced the event as the "great trial of human capabilities." We cannot accept that at face value; the phrase may even have been a literary device employed by the writer to interest readers. The report also mentions that a tenth runner, Francis Smith, had appeared but did not run because he had not entered his name "by a certain day," a reason that may or may not be true; the runner was a black man, who may have been excluded on the grounds of race. The report also indicates that another man, John Cox Stevens, was particularly active in the race; he even rode around the track with Stannard. But Stevens's exact role remains unclear. Finally, we cannot be certain that the purse represented the sum total of Stannard's winnings and that he was the only one who "won" money. The reporter also noted that betting, even by the runners, was a part of the scene.

So, beyond the earlier bare-bones and not very telling description of this event, we cannot proceed from this article. As a consequence, many fairly simple questions must go unanswered: Was pedestrianism common? Was the $1,300 purse typical, or was it a large one? Was this really a "great race"? Was Smith prevented from running because of his late entry or because of his race? Was the crowd large? Answers to these questions hinge on the student's willingness to read the evidence in relation to or in conjunction with other pieces of evidence. The first question, for example, requires data on other races—in fact, a counting of them and a numerical comparison to other sport and public events in this period. The second question can be answered only by a comparison of this purse to other purses and to the annual incomes of similar working men. The last question, Was the crowd large? requires a major shift in the evidential base from qualitative to quantitative evidence. Descriptive statistics from both sport and nonsport crowds are essential; inferential statistics would be more informative. The remaining questions as well demand additional data on other sports, events, and social practices of the times.

The significance of this practice of reading the evidence in its full and appropriate context should not be underestimated. The evidence becomes drab and lifeless when it is divorced from the network of facts and meanings in which any given piece of evidence about a sport, health practice, or recreational program originally existed. To picture such a situation, consider a ball. Unless a student places a ball in the context of a game played by real people who hit and threw and caught it, it exists only as a round object. Taken out of its context, a ball becomes just another bit of rubber, cloth packing, or animal bladder. Considering your own life as a graduate student might even make the point a bit more dramatically. Taken out of the context of graduate school, in a particular place at a particular time in your life, much of what you do (like reading this chapter) would make absolutely no sense to anyone, even to you! So, like you, if historians are to achieve their goal of making sense of the past, they must place their subjects in context.

SOME FINAL THOUGHTS

We now have all the components for the making of a good history. From the secondary literature, we have derived our research questions: significant ones, telling ones, and answerable ones. We have laid out the questions in a logical, hierarchical order and have identified the evidence needed to answer

them. We have located and criticized the sources, and we have spent hours reading and determining the context for the evidence. We have, in effect, been both scientist and detective. So, are we finished?

Not quite! The historian is not finished until he or she makes sense of whatever piece of the past one has investigated. This is clearly a matter of constructing a case, a theme, or, perhaps more pointedly, an argument. With everything done so far—the questions raised and the evidence read and interrogated—the historian now assumes the guise of both architect and prosecuting attorney.

> The significance of this practice of reading the evidence in its full and appropriate context should not be underestimated.

The construction of a history demands an answer to one final question: So what happened here? Another way of asking this is, So what does all this mean? Regardless of how one poses it, this question needs an answer before a student can begin to write. Like the architect, who would not presume to build a house before he or she knew what the house would look like, the historian would not presume to write the story before he or she was certain of its context and meaning.

With the story line, theme, or central argument clear, the student now begins to operate like a prosecuting attorney. The task is a fairly simple one, at least compared to some of the other things he or she has already done. It is to build the case: to present the evidence and interpretations clearly and logically. This is primarily a matter of seeing the patterns within the evidence—patterns across time and patterns of experience. Once again, there is no magical formula for ferreting out the patterns. One needs to read his or her evidence thoroughly, put it aside, and think about its meaning and relationships.

The building of a historical case also requires the ordering and connecting of these patterns. No prosecuting attorney would take a case to court until the sequence of events was clear and until he or she knew which evidence to produce when. So it is with the historian's case. An outline or some other form of flowchart will help, and this may take many forms. Some scholars jot down words, some use symbols, and others write out whole sentences or even paragraphs. But the net effect is the same; that is, the student has a blueprint to guide his or her writing.

Writing, or composing the story, is the final task in the doing of history. It is also a skill that, like most others, takes practice. Some people develop the skill more readily than do others; some historians even maintain that writing is a more complicated skill than are many of the other tasks they undertake. About one fact related to writing, however, most historians (and most scientists) will agree: Good writing is nothing more or less than good thinking. So, if the student has done good thinking about the questions, the evidence, the "case," and the patterns, he or she should find good writing a bit easier.

The writing of history deserves a more extended treatment than the one presented here. It actually warrants several volumes of material, but that is not in the purview of this book or this chapter. There are many books that students can consult about the writing of history.[30] There is not, however, such an extensive literature on historical research that is especially oriented to graduate students in physical education, exercise science, and sport science. I hope this chapter provided that orientation. Perhaps only time—and good history—will tell.

SUMMARY

History is the systematic study of change and continuity in past human affairs. The historian carefully derives questions, gathers and interrogates evidence (data), and frames and tests inferences. He or she also incorporates and tests social theories and operates within distinctive research paradigms or conceptual frameworks. Questions important to the historian include the following:

- How does social change proceed?
- How did people in the past use sport and exercise practices to construct categories such as gender and class?
- Why did particular forms of sport and exercise emerge at particular times, and what cultural meanings did they have?
- In what ways did sport, health, and exercise affect the social structures and economic and political systems?

Secondary sources—the written accounts of others—provide the beginning point for historians to develop questions and the design of the research. The construction of viable answers, however, requires primary evidence, which one subjects to both internal and external criticism, and context. This matter of reading the evidence in its full and appropriate context is essential to historical research. Finally, the historian must make sense of his or her conclusions by answering the question, So what happened here?

Problems

1. Select a historical article from the *Journal of Sport History*. Summarize the arguments that the author made, identify the evidence that he or she used, and analyze how the author used the evidence to make the arguments.

2. Locate one of the serials identified in Appendix 1. Read one article in it about sport, health, or exercise. What kind of evidence does this article contain, and about what questions does this evidence provide information? What can this evidence *not* tell us anything about?

Appendix 1

□

Selected Historical Sources

COLLECTIONS

Source	Location
AAHPERD Archives Extensive material on physical education, exercise, sport programs, etc.	Reston, Va.
Avery Brundage Collection Some 310 boxes, more than 100 scrapbooks; Brichford Guide to the collection	University of Illinois (Urbana-Champaign, IL)
YMCA Library	St. Paul, Minn.
International Sports and Games Research Collection	University of Notre Dame (South Bend, Ind.)
National Baseball Library Individual files for all players (many topics); runs of personal papers	Cooperstown, N.Y.
Albert Spalding Collection Henry Chadwick Scrapbooks; Harry Wright Notebooks; runs of Spalding Guides and instruction books	New York Public Library

These sources are provided courtesy of Professor Stephen Hardy, University of New Hampshire. Dr. Hardy collected the sources from various scholars around the country, developed the bibliography, and presented it at the AAHPERD national convention, April 1989.

Sporting Books Collection	Princeton University (Princeton, N.J.), Firestone Library
Basketball Hall of Fame	Springfield, Mass.
National Track Hall of Fame Historical Library 15,000 items, including programs, rulebooks, and statistical guides	Butler University (Indianapolis), Irwin Library Rare Book Room
Pro Football Hall of Fame Archives	Canton, Ohio
Strong Museum and Library Extensive collection of nineteenth and early twentieth century papers, artifacts, books, etc. relating to exercise and health movements	Rochester, N.Y.
College and university archives Often rich in material about sport, exercise, and athletics	Individual institution archives
City, county, or town historical societies Contain records, artifacts, diaries, and papers of all kinds relating to exercise, sport, and recreation	Individual state, county, or city archives

GOVERNMENTAL OR ORGANIZATION DOCUMENTS

Source	*Location*
NCAA Proceedings, 1906 to present Official records and debates	NCAA headquarters (Mission, Kans.) and university libraries
Records of governing bodies AAU, NCAA, Big 10, NHL, NFL, or any governing body from which one may request information	Organization headquarters and archives
Public statutes and legislative records For any historical period; these are published and usually indexed	State and local archives
State and federal tax lists and censuses Contain economic and demographic data; typically published and indexed	State archives and libraries

Probate records
    Estate inventories, court cases, wills,
    and land records for demographic and
    economic analyses
	Individual state, county, or city archives

Court records
    Contain legal data as well as informa-
    tion about sport and exercise practices
    and attitudes; occasionally indexed
	Individual state and county archives

MANUSCRIPTS

Source	*Location*
Walter Byers Papers About 40 boxes now being processed	NCAA headquarters (Mission, Kans.)
Amos Alonzo Stagg Papers Runs for years ca. 1892-1933	University of Chicago Archives

Walter Camp Papers
    Covers collegiate and amateur sports;
    includes 100-page index, 1876-1925
	Yale University Archives (New Haven,
	Conn.); available on microfilm

E. M. Hartwell Papers
    One of the founders of the profession
    of physical education
	Johns Hopkins University (Baltimore,
	Md.), Eisenhower Library, Special Col-
	lection

Edward Hitchcock Jr. Room
    Correspondence, papers, and early
    books and journals in physical edu-
    cation
	Amherst College (Amherst, Mass.), Frost
	Library

Lou Henry Hoover Papers
    Leader in the organization and promo-
    tion of sport for girls and women
	Herbert Hoover Library

Arthur H. Steinhaus Papers
    One of founders of the American Col-
    lege of Sports Medicine; 40 boxes
	University of Tennessee Library,
	Knoxville

Senda Berenson Papers	Smith College Archives (Northampton, Mass.)
Joe Louis Scrapbooks	University of Michigan Archives (Ann Arbor)

Branch Rickey Papers
    Cover all aspects of Rickey's life in baseball, especially the business side

Library of Congress (Washington, D.C.)

Papers of U.S. presidents
    For example, Theodore Roosevelt on the football issue, Dwight Eisenhower on Jesse Owens, and Gerald Ford on amateur sports (often there are some real gems)

Presidential Libraries

Papers of university presidents
    Typically contain material on athletics and physical education

Individual institutional archives

SERIALS

Source	Location
The Afro-American (1892+) Reports on Afro-American sports, especially in the East	Enoch Pratt Library (Baltimore, Md.); available on microfilm
American Turf Register and Sporting Magazine Early nineteenth century magazine focusing on outdoor field sports and racing	American Periodical Series microfilm; National Agricultural Library (Beltsville, Md.); originals
Boston Medical and Surgical Journal Early history of exercise, fitness, and health issues in the nineteenth century	National Library of Medicine (Bethesda, Md.); University of Chicago, Crerar Library
Clipper (New York, 1853-1924) Sporting newspaper from the mid-nineteenth century and on; later became *Variety*; Henry Chadwick wrote extensively for it	New York Public Library; available on microfilm
Country Life (1901-1917) Covered elite sports, clubs, and resorts	Various libraries
Foreign Language Press Survey WPA project; translations include aspects of social life related to sport	University of Chicago; Chicago Public Library

Frank Leslie's Illustrated (1854-1904)	Various libraries
Journal of Health (1829-1833)	American Periodical Series microfilm
Journal of Health and Physical Education; Journal of Health, Physical Education, Recreation and Dance; Journal of Physical Education and Recreation; etc.	AAHPERD Archives (Reston, Va.); various libraries
Local newspapers At any level; often contain important details of everyday life and practices	Local public libraries and historical societies
New York Times (1851+) Increasing coverage of all sports over time; tends toward bourgeois practices; indexed	Available on microfilm
Outing Magazine (1888-1923)	Various libraries
The Playground (1907+) Professional journal covers play and recreation issues; became *Recreation*	Various libraries
Spirit of the Times (1831-1903) Excellent coverage of a range of sports across social classes	Available on microfilm
Sporting Life (1883-1922)	Available on microfilm
The Sporting News (1886+)	Available on microfilm
Sports Illustrated (1954+)	Various libraries
The Sportswoman (1924-1936) Published by the U.S. Field Hockey Association; also considered lacrosse and some general issues about sports for women	Scattered in various college and university libraries, including those of Vassar (Poughkeepsie, N.Y.), Bryn Mawr (Bryn Mawr, Pa.), Smith (Northampton, Mass.), and the University of Pennsylvania (Philadelphia)

Appendix 2

□

The Great Foot Race

The great trial of human capabilities, in going ten miles within the hour, for $1,000, to which $300 was added, took place on Friday, on the Union Course, Long Island; and we are pleased to state, that the feat was accomplished twelve seconds within the time, by a native born and bred American farmer, Henry Stannard, of Killingworth, Connecticut. Two others went the ten miles—one a Prussian, in a half a minute over; the other an Irishman, in one minute and three quarters over the time.

As early as nine o'clock, many hundreds had crossed the river to witness the race, and from that time until near two, the road between Brooklyn and the course presented a continuous line, (and in many places a double line) of carriages of all descriptions, from the humble sand cart to the splendid barouche and four; and by two o'clock, it is computed that there were at least from sixteen to twenty thousand persons on the course. The day, though fine, being windy, delayed the start until nineteen minutes before two, when nine candidates appeared in front of the stand, dressed in various colors, and started at the sound of a drum.

The following are the names, &c. of the competitors, in the order in which they entered themselves:

Henry Stannard, a farmer, aged twenty-four years, born in Killingworth, Connecticut. He is six feet one inch in height, and weighed one hundred and sixty-five pounds. He was dressed in black silk pantaloons,

American Turf Register and Sporting Magazine 6 (June 1835): 518-20.

white shirt, no jacket, vest, or cap, black leather belt and flesh colored slippers.

Charles R. Wall, a brewer, aged eighteen years, born in Brooklyn. His height was five feet ten and a half inches, and he weighed one hundred and forty-nine pounds.

Henry Sutton, a house painter, aged twenty-three years, born in Rahway, New Jersey. Height five feet seven inches; weight one hundred and thirty-three pounds. He wore a yellow shirt and cap, buff breeches, white stockings and red slippers.

George W. Glauer, rope-maker, aged twenty-seven, born in Elberfeldt, Prussia. Height five feet six and a half inches; weight one hundred and forty-five pounds. He had on an elegant dress of white silk, with a pink stripe and cap to match; pink slippers and red belt.

Isaac S. Downes, a basket-maker, aged twenty-seven, born at Brookhaven, Suffolk county. Height five feet five and a half inches; weight one hundred and fifty pounds. He was dressed in a white shirt, white pantaloons, blue stripe, blue belt, no shoes or stockings.

John Mallard, a farmer, aged thirty-three, born at Exeter, Otsego Co., New York. Height five feet seven and a half inches; weight one hundred and thirty pounds. Dress, blue calico, no cap, shoes or stockings.

William Vermilyea, shoemaker, aged twenty-two years, born in New York. Height five feet ten and a half inches; weight one hundred and fifty pounds. Dressed in green calico, with black belt; no shoes or stockings.

Patrick Mahony, a porter, aged thirty-three, born in Kenmar county, Kerry, Ireland.

Height five feet six inches. Weight one hundred and thirty pounds. Dress, a green gauze shirt, blue stripe calico breeches, blue belt, white stockings, and black slippers.

John M'Gargy, a butcher, aged twenty-six, born at Harlaem. Height five feet ten inches. Weight one hundred and sixty pounds. Dressed in shirt, pink stripe calico trowsers, no shoes or stockings.

There was a tenth candidate, a black man, named Francis Smith, aged twenty-five, born in Manchester, Virginia. Mr. Stevens was willing that this man should run; but as he had not complied with the regulation requiring his name to be entered by a certain day, he was excluded from contesting the race.

The men all started well, and kept together for the first mile, except Mahony, who headed the others several yards, and Mallard, who fell behind after the first half mile. At the end of the second mile, one gave in; at the end of the fourth mile, two more gave up; in the fifth, a fourth man fell; at the end of the fifth mile, a fifth man gave in; during the eight mile, Downes, one of the fastest, and decidedly the handsomest runner, hurt his foot, and gave in at the termination of that mile, leaving but three competitors, who all held out the distance.

The following is the order in which each man came up to the judges' stand at the close of each mile.

	Miles									
	1st.	2d.	3d.	4th.	5th.	6th.	7th.	8th.	9th.	10th.
Stannard,	3	4	3	3	3	2	2	1	1	1
Glauer,	2	2	1	1	2	3	3	3	2	2
Mahony,	1	1	5	5	5	4	4	4	3	3
Downes,	5	3	2	2	1	1	1	2	gave in.	
McGargy,	6	7	7	7	4	gave in.				
Wall,	4	5	4	4	gave in.					
Sutton,	8	8	6	6	gave in.					
Mallard,	9	9	8	8	fell and gave in.					
Vermilyea,	7	6	gave in.							

The following is the time in which each mile was performed by Stannard, the winner. Mahony, the Irishman, did the first mile in five minutes twenty-four seconds.

	Min.	Sec.
1st mile,	5	36
2d ''	5	45
3d ''	5	58
4th ''	6	25
5th ''	6	2
6th ''	6	3
7th ''	6	1
8th ''	6	3
9th ''	5	57
10th ''	5	54
	59	44

The betting on the ground both before and after starting, was pretty even, and large sums were staked both for and against time. Downes was undoubtedly the general favorite; and was well known in the neighborhood; he did the eight miles in forty-eight and a half minutes; he had been well trained under his father, who in his thirty-ninth year, performed seventeen miles in one hour and forty-five minutes; accomplishing the first twelve and a half miles in one hour and fifteen minutes.

Mallard was known to be an excellent runner; he had performed sixteen miles in one hour and forty-nine minutes, stopping during the time to change his shoes. He was not sober when he started, and he fell in the fifth mile.

The German had performed the distance between New York and Harlaem, and returned thence (twelve miles) in seventy minutes; his friends were very sanguine of his success. He betted nearly $300 that he would win the prize. He was within the time until the sixth mile, and he performed the ten miles in one hour and twenty-seven seconds. He was four seconds behind time in the eighth mile. Part of the distance he carried a pocket handkerchief in his mouth.

Mahony, the Irishman, had undergone no training whatever; he left his porter's cart in Water street, went over to the course, ran the first mile in less than five and a half minutes; at the end of the sixth mile he was one minute and a quarter behind; at the end of the eighth mile two minutes behind; at the ninth he was three minutes behind, and he performed the ten miles in sixty-one and three quarter minutes. On the 25th of last month, this man ran eight miles in forty-one minutes fifty-six seconds. M'Gargy was out of condition; but he did the five miles in thirty-two and a half minutes. Vermilyea was very thin and in a wreched state of health; he travelled thirty-eight miles on foot, on Tuesday last,

to be here in time to enter, and the next day performed eight miles in forty-six minutes; he is an excellent runner, but gave in at the end of the second mile from a pain in the side; he was also thrown down by a man crossing the course in the first mile. Wall and Sutton ran remarkably well, but gave in at the end of the fourth mile for want of training.

Stannard, the winner, we understand, has been in good training for a month. He is a powerful stalwart young man, and did not seem at all fatigued at the termination of the race. He was greatly indebted to Mr. Stevens, for his success; Mr. S. rode round the course with him the whole distance, and kept cheering him on, and cautioning him against over-exertion in the early part of the race; at the end of the sixth mile, he made him stop and take a little brandy and water, after which his foot was on the mile mark just as the thirty-six minutes were expired; and as the trumpet sounded he jumped forward gracefully, and cheerfully exclaimed "Here am I to time;" and he was within the time every mile. After the race was over, he mounted a horse and rode round the course in search of Mr. Richard Jackson, who held his overcoat. He was called up to the stand and his success (and the reward of $1,300) was announced to him, and he was invited to dine with the Club; to which he replied in a short speech thanking Mr. Stevens, and the gentlemen of the Club for the attention shewn to the runners generally throughout the task. After this, it was announced by Mr. King, the President of the Jockey Club, that the German and the Irishman, who had both performed the ten miles, though not within the time, would receive $200 each.

We are happy to state that none of the men seemed to feel any inconvenience from their exertions; every thing went off remarkably satisfactory, nor did we hear of the slightest accident the whole day. After the foot race was over, a purse of $300, two mile heats, for all ages, was run for by the following horses, and decided as under:

	1st.	2d.
Tarquin	1	1
Post Boy	2	3
Columbia Taylor	3	dist.
Rival	4	2
Ajax	5	dist.
Sir Alfred	6	d'rn.

The first heat was performed in three minutes forty-seven seconds—the second in three minutes fifty seconds.

During the running of this match, a written paper was handed to Mr. King, stating that two native Americans were willing to attempt to walk five hundred miles without eating or drinking, as soon as a purse of $500 should be made up.

The day was remarkably fine, but the wind blew very strongly on the course, and considering the vast amount of money (in bets, &c.) at stake, Mr. Stevens felt uncertain at first how to act, and decided to postpone the race; but the general opinion and desire seem to be against any postponement, and he yielded to this. The result on this account was most fortunate. The race was won handsomely; although when it wanted but twenty eight seconds to the hour, bets at five to three were offered, and taken, that the task would not be accomplished. It is certain that if the wind had not been so high, Stannard would have performed the ten miles in fifty-seven minutes.

NOTES

[These notes represent the substance and style of notes as they would appear in a research manuscript according to *The Chicago Manual of Style* (13th ed.). Direct quotations are cited immediately, whereas the citations for information and ideas borrowed and adapted from one or more sources, either secondary or primary, occur at the end of a sentence or paragraph. Some additional discursive material may also appear in a note.]

1. E. P. Thompson, *The Poverty of Theory and Other Essays* (New York, 1978), 28-29.

2. For readily available and readable discussions of theoretical differences between natural and social phenomena, see R. Gerald Glassford, "Methodological Reconsiderations: The Shifting Paradigm," *Quest* 39 (Fall 1987): 295-312; and Roberta J. Park, "Hermeneutics, Semiotics, and the 19th-Century Quest for a Corporeal Self," *Quest* 38 (Spring 1986): 33-49. About social theory, human agency, and other issues related to theory, see Gordon S. Wood, "Intellectual History and the Social Sciences," in *New Directions in American Intellectual History*, ed. John Higham and Paul Conkin (Baltimore, 1979); Alex Callinicos, *Making History* (Ithaca, N.Y., 1988); Anthony Giddens, *The Constitution of Society* (Berkeley, Calif., 1984); idem., *Sociology: A Brief but Critical Introduction* (New York, 1987), 11-12; Peter Burke, *Sociology and History* (London, 1980); Eric Monkkonen, "The Challenge of Quantitative History," *Historical Methods* 17 (Summer 1984): 89-90; and Carey B. Joynt and Nicholas Rescher, "The Problem of Uniqueness in History," *History and Theory* 2 (1961): 150-62.

3. See, for example, Allen Guttmann, *From Ritual to Record: The Nature of*

Modern Sport (New York, 1978); and Melvin Adelman, *A Sporting Time: New York City and the Rise of Modern Athletics, 1820-1870* (Urbana, Ill., 1986).

4. Joyce Appleby, "Modernization Theory and the Formation of Modern Social Theories in England and America," *Comparative Studies in Society and History* 20 (1978): 261.

5. One of the earliest discussions remains appropriate: Peter N. Stearns, "Modernization and Social History: Some Suggestions and a Muted Cheer," *Journal of Social History* 14 (Winter 1980): 189-210.

6. Maurice Mandelbaum, *The Anatomy of Historical Knowledge* (Baltimore, 1977).

7. On the dilemmas associated with thinking about the evidence, see Stephen R. Humphrey, "The Historian, His Documents, and Elementary Modes of Historical Thought," *History and Theory* 19 (1980): 1-20. Students may find that reading some histories will help them to see how and why these questions and the answers to them do affect a historian's writing. So, for what may well be the classic example of both history as an evolutionary process and evidence speaking for itself, see Ronald A. Smith, *Sports and Freedom: The Rise of Big-Time College Athletics* (New York, 1988). For an alternative model of historical experience (one that incorporates change and persistence, or continuity), see Elliott Gorn, *The Manly Art: Bare-Knuckle Prize Fighting in America* (Ithaca, N.Y., 1986). A position on the evidence that is opposite to Smith's—that it will not reveal anything until something has been asked of it—is evident in Nancy L. Struna, "Sport and Society in Early America," *International Journal of the History of Sport* 5 (December 1988): 292-311.

8. Thomas Kuhn, *The Structure of Scientific Revolutions* (Chicago, 1962). About the implications of Kuhn's work for history and the social sciences, see Barry Barnes, *T. S. Kuhn and Social Science* (New York, 1982); and David Hollinger, "T. S. Kuhn's Theory of Science and Its Implications for History," *American Historical Review* 78 (April 1973): 370-93.

9. Reviews of the literature on the history of sport, leisure, and health can be very helpful to students and working historians alike. General reviews include Melvin L. Adelman, "Academicians and American Athletics: A Decade of Progress," *Journal of Sport History* 10 (Spring 1980): 80-106; Stephen Hardy and Alan Ingham, "Games, Structures, and Agency: Historians on the American Play Movement," *Journal of Social History* 17 (Winter 1983): 285-301; Roberta J. Park, "Research and Scholarship in the History of Physical Education and Sport," *Research Quarterly for Exercise and Sport* 54 (June 1983): 93-103; and Nancy L. Struna, "In 'Glorious Disarray': The Literature of American Sport History," *Research Quarterly for Exercise and Sport* 56 (June 1986): 151-60.

10. See, for example, Joyce Duncan Falk, "OCLC and RLIN: Research Libraries at the Scholar's Fingertips," American Historical Association Newsletter *Perspectives* 27 (May/June 1989): 1, 11-13, 17. See also Robert L. Oakman, *Computer Methods for Literary Research* (Athens, Ga., 1984).

11. This debate really commenced over a century ago with the introduction of so-called scientific history by the German scholar Leopold Von Ranke, who maintained that objective history, history "written as it really happened," was both possible and necessary. Wilhelm Dilthey just as clearly stated the

opposing position—the subjectivist, or interpretivist, position—which was predicated on his view that the "historical world was a text to be deciphered." Later relativists raised the level of the debate by establishing a clear role for the present; the past had meanings for, and could be used to solve problems in, the present. This issue of the objective versus the subjective has some bearing on questions about theory in history and on the nature of evidence (see n. 2 above). See also John R. Hall, "Temporality, Social Action, and the Problem of Quantification in Historical Analysis," *Historical Methods* 17 (Fall 1984): 206-18.

12. Henri-Irenee Marrou, *The Meaning of History*, trans. Robert J. Olsen (Baltimore, 1967), 76-77.

13. For a more extended discussion of the question-deriving process, see Nancy L. Struna, "E. P. Thompson's Notion of 'Context' and the Writing of Physical Education and Sport History," *Quest* 38 (Spring 1986): 24-27.

14. Description and analysis are the common categories of historical research presented in methodology books, such as those by Robert Shafer, *A Guide to Historical Method*, 3rd ed. (Homewood, Ill., 1980); and Jacques Barzun and Henry F. Graff, *The Modern Researcher*, 3rd ed. (New York, 1977). Two other terms, however—*narration* and *explanation*—often make their way into such discussions and can confound one's understanding of historical designs. *Narration*, or *narrative history*, does not mean the same thing as *description*. *Narration* refers to a mode of historical thought, specifically the recounting of something in the past. Narration will, then, take place in the creation of a de-

scriptive history. But so may *explanation*, if the word is used in the general sense of "making clear." Both the narrative and the explanatory modes of thought may appear in analytic histories. See Robert F. Atkinson, *Knowledge and Explanation in History* (Ithaca, N.Y., 1978); Mandelbaum, *The Anatomy of Historical Knowledge*; Dale H. Porter, *The Emergence of the Past: A Theory of Historical Explanation* (Chicago, 1981); and Allan Megill, "Recounting the Past: 'Description,' Explanation, and Narrative in Historiography," *American Historical Review* 94 (June 1989): 627-53.

15. Some historians also describe a third design, *synthetic history*, that builds primarily on existing histories (secondary sources) to produce overarching generalizations. See Thomas Bender, "Wholes and Parts: The Need for Synthesis in American History," *Journal of American History* 73 (June 1986): 120-36.

16. See note 3 above and Martha Verbrugge, *Able-Bodied Womanhood: Personal Health and Social Change in Nineteenth-Century Boston* (New York, 1988).

17. Fernand Braudel, *On History*, trans. Sarah Matthews (Chicago, 1980), 25-54; Humphrey, "The Historian, His Documents"; Hall, "Temporality, Social Action."

18. Carole Shammas, "Dealing with Dichotomous Dependent Variables," *Historical Methods* 14 (Winter 1981): 47-51; Michael D. Ornstein, "Discrete Multivariate Analysis: An Example from the 1871 Canadian Census," *Historical Methods* 16 (Summer 1983): 101-8; David P. Gagan, Peter J. George, and Ernest H. Oksanen, "On Regression Models with Observation-Specific

Dummy Variables," *Historical Methods* 19 (Winter 1986): 5-8.

19. Dale H. Porter, "History as Process," *History and Theory* 14 (1975): 297-313.

20. Thompson, *Poverty of Theory*, 27-28. In Thompson's exact words, "A historian is entitled . . . to make a provisional assumption . . . that the evidence which he handles has a 'real' (determinant) existence independent of its existence within the forms of thought, that this evidence is witness to a real historical process, and that this process (or some approximate understanding of it) is the object of historical knowledge." However, he continued, "The historical evidence is there . . . not to disclose its own meaning but to be interrogated" (pp. 28-29).

21. Oscar Handlin, *Truth in History* (Cambridge, Mass., 1979), 120.

22. Quantitative (numerical) evidence is slowly but surely finding its way into historical research in sport studies. Much more needs to be used, particularly in cases for which historians want to establish conditions, extent of change, and social class. The most helpful journal about quantitative techniques in history is *Historical Methods* (cited in nn. 2, 11, 18, and 27).

23. One classic case of a document of questionable authenticity that had a major, longstanding impact on the history of a sport was a diagram of a baseball field, presumably authored by Abner Doubleday when he was a schoolboy in 1839. Abner Graves, who claimed to have been a classmate and eyewitness, included the diagram in a letter to the Mills Commission, which had been set up to establish the "origin" of baseball in 1907. The commission accepted the diagram and Graves's testimony as "proof" that Doubleday had "invented" the game.

Shafer, *A Guide to Historical Method*, 127-47; Handlin, *Truth in History*, 111-24. For a marvelous (and humorous) discussion of a suspect document and the problems it created, see John D. Milligan, "The Treatment of an Historical Source," *History and Theory* 18 (1979): 177-96.

24. Shafer, *A Guide to Historical Method*, 149-70; Handlin, *Truth in History*, 124-44.

25. Shafer, *A Guide to Historical Method*, 150-58.

26. Handlin, *Truth in History*, 165-226.

27. Adrian Wilson, "Inferring Attitudes from Behavior," *Historical Methods* 14 (Summer 1981): 143-44.

28. E. P. Thompson, "Anthropology and the Discipline of Historical Context," *Midland History* 3 (Spring 1972): 41-55.

29. "The Great Foot Race," *American Turf Register and Sporting Magazine* 6 (June 1835): 518-20.

30. See, for example, Savoie Lottinville, *The Rhetoric of History* (Norman, Okla., 1976); and Henry W. Fowler and F. G. Fowler, *The King's English* (Oxford, 1954).

Chapter 11

□

Methods of Philosophic Inquiry in Physical Activity

Kathleen M. Pearson

On the heels of Franklin Henry's (1964) signal reference to physical education as an academic discipline, the Big Ten Body of Knowledge Project (Zeigler & McCristal, 1967) identified philosophy as one of the six areas of scholarly endeavor in physical education and sport. These events brought a flurry of activity to specify what constituted the methods of research in philosophy of physical education and sport. A brief review of this activity, which continues to this day, reveals the need for an ordinary language approach to these methods of inquiry.

Table 11.1 exemplifies works on philosophic inquiry into sport and physical education that have been published during the past several decades. Unfortunately, most of this material is couched in language that assumes some familiarity with the philosophic enterprise, making it quite helpful to working sport philosophers but fairly useless for teachers of general research methods or for students who attempt to read independently. Osterhoudt (1978) admitted this limitation:

> It is further the case that few uninitiated readers are likely to profit much from an unaided reading of the book. A fully satisfactory understanding may well wait upon the interpretative assistance of one already familiar with the subject. (p. xviii)

Many years of teaching the philosophy of physical education and sport have convinced

Table 11.1 Overview of Works on Philosophic Inquiry Into Physical Activity

Authors	Nature of work
Pearson, 1968, 1972	Identified a taxonomy of 3 categories (construct, system, and concept analysis) and 12 subcategories of activity in philosophy of general education
Fraleigh, 1970	Used case studies to exemplify three types of philosophic inquiry: theory building, structural analysis, and phenomenology
Zeigler, 1970	Advocated that a philosopher speculate about the nature of the universe and life, set forth a systematic plan for living, or approach the research task analytically
Osterhoudt, 1972	Reviewed the literature and found that all studies in the philosophy of sport fell into the three categories identified by Pearson (1968)
Gerber, 1972	Edited a text with selected articles on philosophy of sport and physical activity, briefly describing methods employed in the articles
Hyland, 1974	Advocated an approach of responsive openness

(Cont.)

Table 11.1 (Continued)

Authors	Nature of work
Kretchmar, 1974	Advocated studying the philosophy of sport from a personal experience perspective using phenomenological analysis
Pearson, 1974	Advocated a constructive exchange of ideas rather than arguing for the superiority of one or another mode of inquiry
Osterhoudt, 1974	Proposed an overview of the usual distinctions in philosophic method in hopes of leading to further discussion and reflection
Gerber and Morgan, 1979	Edited second edition of Gerber (1972)
Bressman and Pieter (1985)	Described the philosophic processes of edification and theory building, advocating these as fruitful avenues for studying human movement.

me that our colleagues who teach general research methods are fuzzy about just what philosophers do. As a result, students come from research courses partially prepared to do or understand other research techniques, but still in the dark concerning the philosophic enterprise as it is applied to physical education and sport. I don't fault these colleagues for this situation; the review in Table 11.1 suggests that philosophers of sport and physical education may have been acting as their own worst enemies. Because we have been gearing our works for other philosophers, or writing in a manner that requires a philosopher's intervention to be fully understood, we may have created a closed circle and hampered our own cause. The writings of the authors discussed have been quite scholarly and helpful to those already initiated into the "cult," and as contributing scholars the authors are to be commended. Without such scholarly endeavor, Gerber and Morgan (1979) could not have commented in the preface to the second edition of their text that "the situation in 1979 is markedly different. The philosophic study of sport and the body is now a vigorous, well-developed and recognized field of study" (p. v).

But the need remains to explain in plain English what it means to do philosophy of sport and physical education. In recognition of this need, the international Philosophic Society for the Study of Sport formed a Pedagogy Committee to find ways to improve the teaching of philosophy of sport. Fraleigh's (1970) observation that we are vulnerable to the charge that anything goes in philosophic research still may be somewhat true today.

The remainder of this chapter is an attempt to fill the gap in communication between the philosopher of sport and physical education and students in research methods. In attempting this task I describe nine ways of doing philosophic inquiry within the following general headings:

- Identifying concept-unifying agents
- Working from models or paradigms
- Language analysis
- Phenomenology

Although my examples are from sport and physical education, the methods apply equally to philosophic study in allied professions such as recreation and health.

A word of caution to the reader. The methods I describe do not represent a closed system. That is, philosophic inquiry is open-ended; the methods presented here are merely representative and do not exhaust the possibilities. Quite the opposite is true. If something you are reading does not fit into one of the methods described here, try to dis-

cern the philosopher's strategy. And if you wish to explore a philosophic problem that does not lend itself to any of the methods presented here consider inventing a strategy for shedding light on the problem. The nine ways of doing philosophy of sport and physical education that follow are merely an attempt in ordinary language to open the door for those who wish to understand or engage in the philosophic enterprise.

IDENTIFYING CONCEPT-UNIFYING AGENTS

The three methods presented in this section share the aim of trying to discover what agents serve to unify a given concept. A philosopher using one of these methods might ask a question like this: Why are some activities intuitively considered sport while others are not? In other words, what is it that unifies or ties together those activities commonly accepted as sportlike? (The concept might just as easily be "game," "play," etc. In any case, the philosopher is searching for the unifying agent or agents.)

> The methods I describe do not represent a closed system. The methods presented here are merely representative and do not exhaust the possibilities.

Identifying Necessary and Sufficient Conditions

The philosopher who approaches a task from this stance is attempting to set forth necessary and sufficient conditions for defining a class of things. The difference between conditions that are necessary and those that are sufficient might be demonstrated as follows. For a living creature to belong to the class known as birds, it should have no more than two legs. This is a necessary condition; however, it is not sufficient for defining birds. Human beings, for example, meet the same condition. So other conditions must be added such that, taken together, they are broad enough to include all that might be properly called birds and narrow enough to exclude all nonbirds. When a philosopher had succeeded in identifying these conditions, he or she could claim to have set forth the necessary and sufficient conditions for defining that class of things known as birds.

Identifying Conditions

Properly identifying these conditions is extremely difficult, for there always seem to be borderline cases. This approach to doing philosophy of physical education and sport has come under attack (McBride, 1975), but it is considered by some to be quite legitimate, if not vital, to the philosophic enterprise. Suits (1978), for example, attempted to set forth the necessary and sufficient conditions to define game playing. He argued that all game-playing activities were unique in possessing the following characteristics (necessary and sufficient conditions):

- The activity is directed at bringing about a specific state of affairs.
- In the attempt to bring about this state of affairs, the players' attempts are confined to using only means permitted by the rules.
- The means permitted by the rules are more limited in scope than they would be in the absence of the rules.
- The sole reason for accepting the limitations imposed by the rules is to make possible such activity. (p. 41)

These four conditions, according to Suits, were broad enough to include all game-playing activities and narrow enough to exclude all non-game-playing activities.

Testing the Validity of Conditions

The validity of necessary and sufficient conditions is determined by the tests of *narrowness* and *broadness*. The conditions must be neither too narrow (ruling out legitimate activities) nor too broad (admitting illegitimate activities). McBride (1979) argued that Suits's conditions suffered from both of those defects. He pointed to a game called Sun-Earth-Moon and stated that Suits's conditions were too narrow to allow this activity to be included as game playing. On the other hand, he said, activities such as "high jumping, footracing, and mountain climbing are not ordinarily thought of as games and yet they fit the criteria of the definition in all respects" (p. 63). Thus, according to McBride, Suits's so-called necessary and sufficient conditions were not valid for defining game playing.

Consult the original works of both Suits and McBride to see if you understand the technique used by Suits and the criticism leveled by McBride. Has Suits succeeded in identifying the unifying agents for the concept of game playing? Does the activity Sun-Earth-Moon fit what we would ordinarily call a game, as McBride argued? Do high jumping, footracing, and mountain climbing fit the criteria, and if so, can we make a case for including them as game-playing activities?

Other works that attempt to identify necessary and sufficient conditions include Delattre (1975), Hutslar (1981), Jeu (1972), Meier (1988), Osterhoudt (1977), Pate (1988), Suits (1979; 1988), and Tangen (1985).

Developing Taxonomies

Some philosophers, rather than develop necessary and sufficient conditions for a class of things, attempt to develop a *taxonomy*, or classification system. You already are familiar with systems for classifying subject matter in physical education (team sports, individual sports, dance, aquatics, and the like). Indeed, my very effort to identify here some ways of doing philosophy of sport and physical education is an attempt to develop a taxonomy.

A taxonomy can be either closed or open-ended. For a closed taxonomy, the philosopher begins with a set of necessary and sufficient conditions (perhaps developed by another philosopher) for a thing to belong to a particular class. Within this closed system, the philosopher then attempts to set forth subcategories for all of the activities that fall within those conditions.

More often philosophers prefer to develop open-ended taxonomies, which leave room for additional categories or subcategories as these might come to light. This approach seems more useful for fluid concepts such as sport and games, because new forms are continually being developed, and open-ended taxonomies allow for this evolution. Philosophers who develop open-ended taxonomies make no claim to meeting the tests of broadness and narrowness integral to the necessary and sufficient conditions approach.

Caillois (1979) developed an open-ended taxonomy for classifying games. Considering all games, both physical and mental, he attempted to discover "a principle of classification capable of subsuming them under a small number of well-defined categories" (p. 30). He proposed four, depending on whether competition, chance, simulation, or vertigo played the dominant role in a particular game. He dubbed these categories agon, alea, mimicry, and ilinx, respectively. *Agon* is a classification for games in which competition is dominant, such as many sports. *Alea* designates games in which the player has no control over the outcome and in which fate or luck is dominant, such as dice games, roulette, and lotteries. *Mimicry* consists of games in which players make believe or try to make other believe that they are someone other than themselves. Games of alea could not fall into this category, but agon games might. A judgment would be required about whether agon or mimicry was dominant to classify the game. A game like charades might require this judgment, whereas children's games in which the aim is to imitate adults would clearly be classified as mimicry. *Ilinx*, the fourth classification, includes games based on "the pursuit of vertigo and which consist of an attempt to momentarily destroy

the stability of perception" (p. 35). Caillois suggested this category might include games such as tightrope walking and children's twirling until they are dizzy.

It is important to note the difference between this attempt to clarify the nature of games and the approach of identifying necessary and sufficient conditions. Caillois makes no claim that his classification system includes all games or that it excludes all nongame activities. He readily admits that other activities might fall into these categories. His only claim is that many games do, indeed, fall into the categories he has suggested. Other philosophers who have tried to formulate taxonomies include Duncan (1983), Goldberger & Moyer (1982), Hoch (1985), Loy (1968), Morgan (1977), and Zeigler (1983).

Family Resemblance Approach

In trying to discover why certain activities are clearly considered game, sport, physical education, recreation, and the like but others are rejected as properly fitting these classifications, some philosophers have turned to Wittgenstein's (1953/1958) *family resemblance theory*. Despairing of finding necessary and sufficient conditions for an activity to be classified as a game and rejecting the notion that there is some essential feature common to all games, Wittgenstein suggested that games share a kind of family resemblance. Malcolm (1967) described Wittgenstein's position as follows.

Consider the various kinds of games there are (for example, board games, card games, ball games) and the variety within each kind. If we pick out a feature common to two games, we shall find that it is absent from some other place in the spectrum of games. Not all games are amusing, not all involve winning or losing, not all require competition between players, and so on. What makes all of them games, what gives unity to those activities, is not some feature present in all games but a multitude of relationships "overlapping and criss-crossing."

One can often see a striking resemblance between several generations of the same family. Studying them at close hand one may find that there is no feature common to all the family. The eyes or the build or the temperament are not always the same. The family resemblance is due to many features that "overlap and criss-cross." The unity of games is like a family resemblance. (p. 335)

Several scholars have ventured into this mode of inquiry for doing philosophy of sport and physical education. Fogelin (1972) tried to analyze sport as a concept. He hypothesized that sport is one of many concepts that do not "mark out an area of things sharing a common essence, but instead they collect together a family of things sharing a system of overlapping features" (p. 59). This very vagueness, Fogelin asserted, is what makes sport so interesting. He stated, "It is not a damned shame that the concept of sports constitutes a diverse system of overlapping notions; it is precisely this fact that makes it more interesting, say, than the concept of a prime number" (p. 60).

Fogelin attempted to demonstrate schematically the family resemblance theory applied to sport. He identified different sports as S_1, S_2, and so on, and the features possessed by each as A, B, C, D, and the like. His scheme appeared (p. 59) as follows:

S_1	S_2	S_3	S_4	S_5
A	B	C	D	D
B	C	D	E	A
C	D	E	F	B

It is apparent from the scheme that no two sports have exactly the same features. Various features of each sport are shared with some other sports, but not all. There does seem to be, according to Fogelin, a system of overlapping features that constitutes the family resemblance.

Fogelin pointed out that this scheme illustrates how we usually make one of two mistakes when we attempt to analyze a complex concept such as sport. Either we assume beforehand that there must be a common feature running through all sport and willfully disregard some legitimate cases, or we become obsessed with certain cases and make them paradigms. For example, if we decide that Feature B is the essential feature that runs through all sport, we would include S_1, S_2, and S_5 in the concept of sport and arbitrarily, and many times contrary to our intuition, exclude S_3 and S_4. On the other hand, we might decide that S_1 is the paradigm case and thereby S_2, S_3, and S_5 are counted as sport, but S_4 is rejected as not really being a sport because it has none of the features of S_1. Fogelin closed his case against the attempt to find a common essence where none exists as follows:

Perhaps the time will come when theorists will find it easy to control their conceptual apparatus, but my hunch is that Kant was right and that there is a natural tendency of human beings to abuse their conceptual apparatus in an attempt to make it yield substantive truth. I have tried not to do this in this paper, and that is why I have nothing profound to tell you. (p. 61)

Manser (1967) and Zeigler (1973a) have also applied the family resemblance theory to sport and physical education.

WORKING FROM PARADIGMS

Two additional types of philosophic inquiry in sport and physical education can be made after one is exposed to a model, or paradigm, set forth by another philosopher: goodness of fit and the implications, or extrapolations, approach.

Goodness of Fit

The *goodness-of-fit* approach to philosophic inquiry is used to determine whether some activity or object can be shown to properly fit a certain paradigm. Usually (but not always) the paradigm sets forth the necessary and sufficient conditions for classification. For example, it might define the necessary and sufficient conditions for an activity to be classified as game playing (as in the case of Suits's work, 1978, described earlier), as an object of art, as an aesthetic experience, and the like. The philosopher then tests the goodness of fit between that paradigm and some activity or object.

An Example of Goodness of Fit

Keenan (1973), interested in whether the athletic contest might be shown to be an instance of Aristotle's paradigm for tragic drama, set out to test whether the necessary and sufficient conditions set forth by Aristotle were present in the athletic contest.

The first task for one using the goodness-of-fit approach is to set forth clearly and accurately the components of the original paradigm. This is important so that others can properly assess the merits, or validity, of the conclusions drawn about goodness of fit. Keenan carefully described the components of Aristotle's paradigm for tragic drama: plot, character, thought and diction, and melody and spectacle.

The next obligation of the philosopher using this approach is to test the thing in question (in this case, the athletic contest) against each of the components of the paradigm. Keenan had to analyze the athletic contest to determine if each of the four conditions set forth by Aristotle was present. Keenan performed this task and reported four findings. First, the will to win in the athletic contest properly fits the plot component of Aristotle's paradigm for tragic drama. Because each athlete brings to the contest the will to win and not everyone can win, the plot is set for the drama to unfold. Second, the skill of the players in the athletic contest brings greatness to their roles and properly fits the character component of Aristotle's paradigm. As the plot unfolds, each player skillfully fulfills his or her assigned role and thus brings greatness to that character and to the drama. Third, as the drama progresses, the thoughts of the players and coaches are "spoken" through the skilled and strategic movements of the players, and thus the thought and diction components of Aristotle's paradigm become evident. Finally, although the athletic contest does have music and spectacle, which properly fit Aristotle's melody and spectacle components, Keenan asserted that these components were not necessary to the true artistic depiction of tragic drama.

Based on this analysis of the goodness of fit between Aristotle's paradigm and the athletic contest, Keenan concluded that the athletic contest can indeed be properly classified as an artistic depiction of tragic drama. His conclusion carries the inherent declaration that the athletic contest is an art form (theater) or at least a work of art (drama).

Analysis of Goodness of Fit

Three different types of conclusions might result from a goodness-of-fit analysis. An unbiased analysis leaves the way open for any one of the three.

It might be found (as in Keenan's work) that the phenomenon does properly fit all of the components of the paradigm. The philosopher then concludes that the phenomenon is correctly categorized as an instance of the sort exemplified by the paradigm.

On the other hand, it might be found that the phenomenon does not fit one or more of the components of the paradigm. In this case the philosopher ordinarily concludes that the phenomenon is not an instance of the sort that fits the paradigm.

The philosopher might argue, however, when the phenomenon in question does not fit one or more of the components of the paradigm that those components are unnecessary to the paradigm's integrity. In this case, the philosopher concludes that the phenomenon is correctly categorized as an instance of the sort supposedly represented by the paradigm, arguing that the necessary and sufficient conditions set forth by the paradigm fail the test of narrowness and exclude phenomena that ought to be included.

The goodness-of-fit approach to doing philosophy has been quite popular; you can find additional examples in Arnold (1986), Gerber (1979), Kleinman (1977), Lenk (1976), Reid (1970), and Roberts (1986).

Implications (Extrapolations) Approach

The method of doing philosophy frequently referred to as the *implications approach* might be more descriptively labeled the *extrapolations approach*. This mode of inquiry is appropriate when a philosopher wishes to perform a logical extrapolation from a given paradigm. This method differs from goodness of fit in that the philosopher, following exposure to a paradigm, does not test how well a phenomenon fits the model but instead attempts to answer this question: If the phenomenon in question were to conform to this paradigm, what would its features be? That is to say, the philosopher does not try to test what the phenomenon (sport, physi-

cal education, etc.) *is* against the features of a paradigm, but rather sets forth what the phenomenon would or should be if it were to conform to the paradigm. If the philosopher advocates the paradigm, the analysis delineates what the phenomenon *should* be like to conform to the paradigm. If the philosopher assumes an impartial stance, the analysis delineates what the phenomenon *would* be like if it were to fit the features of the paradigm.

A noted pioneer in applying this approach to sport and physical education is Earle F. Zeigler. The monumental works in which he has extrapolated the meanings of the major philosophies for physical education, sport, health, and recreation are classics and remain some of the finest teaching tools in the field. Several of his works are listed in the references at the end of this section.

After being exposed to Rawls's theory of justice, Keenan (1975) became interested in the theory's meaning for conduct in sport. Keenan sought to discover from an impartial stance what sport conduct would be like if it were to conform to Rawls's theory. His first task was to describe clearly and accurately the relevant aspects of the concepts of the original position and the veil of ignorance as they appeared in Rawls's theory of justice as fairness.

Keenan explained the *original position* as "the hypothetical situation in which we all independently seek fulfillment of our personal interests and desires" (p. 112). Given this original position, according to Rawls, some sort of social cooperation is needed to avoid the certain chaos that would result from all of us egotistically pursuing our own best interests. Keenan introduced the reader to the principle that Rawls suggested govern our decisions: "All social values . . . are to be distributed equally unless an unequal distribution of any, or all, of these values is to everyone's advantage" (p. 112).

The next important component in Rawls's paradigm of justice as fairness is a means by which this principle might be implemented justly. Keenan explained that to implement the principle fairly, according to Rawls, we must all operate from "behind a hypothetical *veil of ignorance* which limits knowledge of class position, status, economic worth, natural abilities and assets, and the like" (p. 113). That is, we must all take the stance that we do not know who we will be in the society that will operate by the rules we establish and the decisions we make.

Having completed the first step of inquiry (describing relevant features of the paradigm), Keenan proceeded to the next step. He turned to the phenomenon to be analyzed —sport—and attempted to perform a logical extrapolation of Rawls's paradigm for conduct in sport. Keenan argued that Rawls's paradigm applied to sport leads to the following conclusions.

Once the rules for sport are set forth by persons operating behind the veil of ignorance, all are free to pursue their own ends within the framework of those rules. Further, if cheating occurs in any form among sport participants, those persons simply fail to adopt the concept of and the morality of justice as fairness set forth by Rawls.

In summary, someone using the extrapolations approach to philosophic inquiry must accurately describe the relevant features of the chosen paradigm and then carefully perform a logical extrapolation of its meaning as applied to a given phenomenon (in this case, sport). The philosopher then sets forth the findings and conclusions that result from that extrapolation. Keenan chose to take a neutral stance concerning Rawls's paradigm, but had he taken the stance of an advocate, he likely would have included evaluative remarks about those who do and do not adopt Rawls's principle of justice as fairness when they participate in sport.

This mode of inquiry has probably been used more than any other by those who engage in philosophy of physical education and sport. Representative works include Abe (1986), Arnold (1988), Bain (1988), Kleinman (1979), Morgan (1977), Pearson (1979), Ravizza & Daruty (1985), Simon (1984), and Zeigler (1964 and 1973b).

LANGUAGE ANALYSIS

The language analyst examines terms common to an enterprise, such as sport and physical education, to detect contradictory or confusing uses of terms. If confusion or contradiction is discovered, the analyst may go a step further and suggest means for clearing up the difficulties. The philosopher who does *language analysis* thus becomes somewhat of a therapist. According to Altson (1967):

> He must help us, the perplexed, to see the steps by which we have unwittingly slipped from sense into nonsense; he must lead us back to the ordinary use of these words, on which their intelligibility depends, thus relieving the conceptual cramps into which we have fallen. (p. 387)

One who undertakes language analysis must be careful not to distort meanings when words and phrases are removed from context. It is also important that the original sources be cited so that readers can go to them and judge the validity of the analyst's findings if they wish.

Very few comprehensive studies have been completed in physical education using language analysis, and a great deal of work probably remains. Colvin (1977) was somewhat of a pioneer in her comprehensive language analysis of the concept of basic locomotor skills in elementary physical education. She examined the language used by textbook authors to discover the amount of agreement on what constituted the class of movements referred to as basic locomotor skills. First Colvin identified the names of several skills that were generally agreed to be basic locomotor skills. She then attempted to tease out similarities and differences in the ways authors described those skills. Finally, she made recommendations for clearing up some of the confusion that exists about basic locomotor skills.

One of the first responsibilities of a language analyst is to show why consistency concerning the concept under analysis is desirable. Colvin suggested that because the development of basic or fundamental skills is a primary concern of elementary physical educators, there should be some kind of consensus on what constitutes this class of skills. She also pointed out that a lack of agreement results in inconsistent preparation of elementary physical educators, and that further confusion results from differences over how each of these skills should be described and performed. She summed up her position as follows:

If we are to avoid an utter sea of confusion there should be certain agreed-upon commonalities among the many persons whose labors are devoted to describing and/or prescribing programs in human movement for children. The alternative to these commonalities, it seems to me, is inevitable verbal chaos—a state which mitigates against the very things for which educators presumably strive. (p. 12)

A second responsibility of the language analyst is to present a rationale for selecting works to be reviewed, guarding against bias. Colvin stated her rationale this way:

A certain amount of variety as to general types of elementary physical education books was sought. Most were of the broad inclusive type but there were several in each of the more specific areas of motor learning, dance and movement education. Also, in order to keep the results current, only books published within the last ten years were included. (p. 9)

Having established a need for the analysis and a rationale for the data sources, the next task of the analyst is to carefully scrutinize each work and record pertinent data. Colvin found that eight movements—run, walk, jump, hop, leap, skip, gallop, and slide—were most frequently mentioned as basic locomotor skills. (Five other movements were mentioned in at least one of the 21 texts reviewed, indicating some disagreement concerning which skills were basic. Because of their infrequent inclusion, Colvin excluded them from further analysis.)

The most difficult part of language analysis is comparing and contrasting how terms are used. Some analysts start with this step. For example, one might choose the term "physical fitness" and analyze the various meanings attached to it. Colvin performed this task for the eight movements she identified.

The analyst must take care to cite the authors who used each description (meaning) for a given term so that the analyst's findings and conclusions can be verified by the reader. Colvin did an excellent job of weaving her sources into her analysis as examples of the confusion over how children should perform the eight basic locomotor skills.

For example, there was some agreement in the descriptions of the run, but also some rather basic differences. Three authors indicated that when one runs at full speed, only the balls of the feet touch the ground. But another author cited studies that found that sprinters' heels do touch the ground and that we should avoid teaching sprinters to "run on their toes" because it interferes with mechanical leg action (p. 10).

Colvin found the greatest differences in descriptions to be for the slide. Most authors described the slide as occurring on the feet and being like a gallop, except done in a sideways direction. Some authors, however, described the slide as occurring on other body parts. One author presented this very puzzling description: "A slide is similar to the skip in that it combines both a step and a hop in a rhythmical manner. Only one leg, however, maintains the leading position. Sliding is executed in a sideward direction" (p. 12). Colvin found it difficult to conceptualize this movement in view of the earlier descriptions of the walk and the hop in the same text.

After data have been collected and analyzed and the findings presented, the analyst should present recommendations. Colvin concluded her analysis by recommending the following, based on her findings:

Basic motor skills should be divided first into locomotor and non-locomotor movements.

Locomotor movements should be further subdivided into those that occur on the feet (foot) and those that occur on other body parts.

Descriptions of basic movements should include enough detail that readers can determine what the normal pattern for children should be.

Some term such as elevating or springing should be used as the major term, and jumping, hopping and leaping should be subsumed under this major heading.

A hop should consist of taking off from one foot and landing on the same foot; a leap might be described as taking off from one foot (more forcefully than when running) and landing on the other foot; a jump should entail taking off from one or two feet and landing on two feet, and since it is very uncommon, taking off from two feet and landing on one foot should be omitted as a basic movement.

Both a gallop and a slide should be described as a combination of walk and run rather than walk and leap. (pp. 12-13)

In a later in-depth analysis of the term "slide," Colvin (1978) found that authors described the slide in distinctly different ways. It seems likely, in light of this finding, that children would not understand the exact nature of a slide even after exposure to physical education classes. One can hardly imagine a mathematics teacher asking students to perform addition (a basic mathematics skill) and, depending on which text the students or the teacher had read, some might perform addition, some subtraction, and still others division.

In summary, the language analyst must first establish a need for the analysis and present some rationale for the sources of data to be analyzed. The sources must then be carefully scrutinized and the data accurately recorded. Next the data should be analyzed for agreement, contradictions, and inconsistencies. Finally, based on these findings, recommendations should be made for resolving some of the confusion.

Certainly Colvin's work provides evidence that there is a need for this type of analysis and clarification. Several pioneering works using language analysis in sport and physical education are Colvin (1978), Fox (1975), Spencer-Kraus (1969), Wertz (1981), and Zeigler (1979).

After data have been collected and analyzed and the findings presented, the analyst should present recommendations.

PHENOMENOLOGY

The term *phenomenology* designates inquiries that try to describe consciousness of experience. These inquiries differ in terms of how close the philosopher is to the actual experience. Studies where the examiner remains far from the experience can usually be subjected to external verification, whereas those where the examiner is more closely involved are verified internally, or subjectively. Three different types of phenomenological inquiry are described here: The first is open to external verification, the second can be partially verified from an external perspective, and the third must be verified internally (subjectively).

Analyzing Experiences Described by Others

One of the most popular subjects for analyzing experiences described by others has been

what some have referred to as the "perfect moment," the "complete moment," or the "peak experience" in sport. Several scholars have analyzed descriptions of such moments to try and discover commonalities to all of the experiences or a general condition shared by most of them. Descriptions are collected either by searching relevant literature or by using an interview technique.

Ravizza (1977) interviewed 20 athletes in an attempt to discover what their peak experiences might have in common. He reported that there appeared to be 13 closely related qualities that the athletes shared during these peak experiences. It is important if others are to confirm a researcher's findings that not only the survey instrument but also the data that resulted from its use be included in the report.

Osbourne (1979) reviewed appropriate literature to collect his data concerning the perfect moment. He hypothesized that these moments are most likely to occur when the athlete is not mentally focused on the competitive aspect of the activity. After collecting and analyzing athletes' published descriptions of these moments, Osbourne reported that, indeed, the athletes were typically not focused on competition when these moments occurred. Unlike Ravizza, who was searching for essences (commonalities) present in all peak experiences, Osbourne was attempting to discover whether a single quality was always present. Although several of the athletes Osbourne interviewed did seem to be focused on the competitive aspect during their peak experiences, most were not, so Osbourne accepted his hypothesis. Anyone using this technique should include all descriptions studied in their original forms so readers can verify the philosopher's conclusions. Another example of this mode of inquiry can be found in Progen (1981).

Analyzing One's Own Experience

An analysis of the philosopher's own experience usually proceeds through three stages:

1. The phenomenon of conscious experience is described through conscious reflection.
2. The philosopher attempts to identify a commonality or commonalities to the experiences described.
3. The investigator attempts to separate a phenomenon (commonality) from all consideration of its presence or nonpresence in any particular context.

The final stage allows the philosopher to reflect on his or her consciousness of the phenomenon as a "given" and to understand the characteristics of that consciousness.

Kretchmar (1971) used this mode of inquiry in his phenomenological analysis of the "Other" in sport. His analysis proceeded through the three stages described.

Through reflection, Kretchmar attempted to describe his experiences of the Other in the sports of cross-country, baseball, and basketball. This part of the analysis revealed that the Others most commonly experienced were the opponents, teammates, officials, coaches or managers, and spectators. The opponents (other persons as well as inanimate objects, times, distances, and so forth) seemed to be the most dominant Other, and the spectator the least dominant. Experience of the Other occurred either as an object ("thing") or as an undifferentiated part of the whole experience, and as such not distinct from oneself.

The second stage was an attempt to discover phenomena common to the experiences of the Other in sport. Kretchmar isolated arbitrariness, opposition, and relevant facticity as phenomena distinguishing the sport experience from other experiences. Of these, Kretchmar concluded that only opposition demanded a consideration of Otherness.

The third and last part of the analysis was to isolate the concept of opposition from any consideration of its presence or nonpresence in any given experience or situation. By reflecting on the concept of opposition as a "given," Kretchmar attempted to uncover and describe concepts that are necessary for the possibility of opposition. He discussed concepts of spatiality and temporality and the issue of "doing" something in relationship to the Other. At the completion of this third stage of the analysis of the Other in the sport experience he concluded that "the phenomenon of opposition requires the presence of an Other. The Other in sport is recognized by what he does. Man, in sport, establishes his own identity in relationship to the Other" (p. 133).

The verifiability of the descriptions in Stage 1 of this mode of inquiry is completely subjective. The validity of the descriptions depends on the philosopher's ability to recount the experience faithfully. Stage 2 is somewhat more public in nature because the reader can look for problems in the logic used to discover commonalities and either affirm or cast doubt on the findings. Because during the third stage the phenomenon is separated from any part of lived history, the findings from this stage must be validated subjectively. Thus, one of the three stages can be verified externally and the other two are verified subjectively. Stoll (1982) explicated this mode of inquiry as an alternative approach to sport history.

Experiential Description

Whereas Kretchmar included description, analysis, and reduction, Kleinman (1970) urged that we omit Stages 2 and 3 from phenomenological inquiry. He believed that each step beyond the description moves us further from the actual lived experiences and thus further from the phenomenon as it was experienced. He also asserted that meaningful level of existence stands the greatest chance of being revealed through experiential description. He did caution, however, that there is little hope, even through experiential description, of capturing experience as it has been experienced. Instead, experiential description attempts only to grasp the significance of experience. In other words, Kleinman suggested, meaningful experience is probably ineffable, somehow too overpowering to be expressed in words.

Welter (1978) agreed with Kleinman's assertion that analysis and reduction move us away from the actual lived experience. She did not agree, however, that meaningful lived experience is ineffable. She suggested that the seeming ineffability could be overcome through experiential description. Earlier attempts had failed, she believed, because the philosophers had made one of two errors. Some, such as Ravizza (1977), had attempted to capture the experience by analyzing the descriptions of others, thus shattering those experiences into bits and pieces in attempts

to discover essences or characteristics. Others, such as Kretchmar (1971), in dividing their energies into three parts—description, analysis, and reduction—diluted their concentration on the important description phase of their work.

Welter attempted to test the hypothesis that it is possible to describe complete moments in sport in a way that adequately expresses those moments as the athletes were conscious of them. Welter felt the philosopher must concentrate on description alone and avoid the tendency to look for commonalities. Each experience is complete unto itself and must be described as a whole, with no important element omitted and with no reference made to anything outside the experience itself. Only through direct awareness of particular experiences in their totality could the problem of ineffability be overcome.

Over a period of months Welter immersed herself one by one in seven complete moments she had experienced in volleyball, softball, and track. She described this phase of her method as follows:

> The seven descriptions of complete moments were accomplished by directly confronting a particular moment in its totality, as a separate entity. The writer attempted to accurately and honestly express the moment as it was experienced by her. This was repeated for each complete moment in each sport. The intent in each case was to express the moment, not necessarily as it might have appeared to occur, but as it was actually experienced by the athlete. (p. 32)

In the second phase of her method Welter reviewed the descriptions and either rejected or accepted the hypothesis that the seeming ineffability of the experience had been overcome. Her criterion was whether she was able to recognize the experience as it occurred originally. If she did recognize the experience in her description of it, she accepted the hypothesis. If some essential part seemed to be missing or inadequately described, she rejected the hypothesis. This, according to Schmitt (1967), is the only way to assess the accuracy of phenomenological descriptions. The experiencer is the only one who can judge the adequacy of the description of an experience. If she or he can recognize the experience in all of its essential qualities, then the description is accurate and valid.

Welter was able to accept her hypotheses for five of the seven descriptions. In cases of acceptance the philosopher need only state that she or he recognized an experience in its essential qualities as it actually originally occurred. Welter rejected her hypothesis for two of her descriptions. In such cases the philosopher should attempt to explain what part of the experience seemed to be missing or inadequately described.

Two rather lengthy quotes (reprinted by permission) from Welter should offer a better feel for this type of inquiry. The first is her explanation for rejecting the hypothesis for one of her descriptions. The entire explanation is included to give you a sense of the honesty and candidness necessary.

As I reread it, the entire description seemed somewhat artificial. I reworked this description word by word until I was satisfied, but by that time I was so involved in the experience, and had relived it so many times in such a short period, that probably one word would have adequately described it for me, because one word in the state of mind I was in would have brought all the feelings of the moment back to me.

One problem with this description is that it does not flow in the same way that the experience flowed. I was trying so hard to find the exact words that I wanted that it seems to be *just* words. Also I was concerned because I did not know who might be reading the description, and I had never shared the experience with anyone. This was reflected in the description. For example, when I originally wrote the second paragraph, I tried to describe how my relationship to the ball changed so that we almost seemed to become one. The original description almost seemed to suggest that I was having some strange kind of love affair with the ball. So, although that description might have been more honest, and perhaps even have satisfactorily expressed the relationship, I changed it to try to make it more acceptable.

While writing this description I was too much aware of the difficulties I thought I needed to overcome. For example, I was concerned about somehow meshing the tiny details of the experience with the overall feelings I had. At one point I thought I might be describing my movements as a coach or physical educator, using too many facts (knees bent, elbows locked), and not enough feelings (what it felt like). I noticed I was beginning to moralize and explain. I was afraid of deviating too much from the normal (the love affair with the ball). I did not want to sound conceited. At times I became aware that I was writing for the people that I knew would be reading the description. Had I ignored these "difficulties" as I saw them, and just written, perhaps the description would have been satisfactory. (pp. 36-38)

Welter was more successful with the next description. She accepted the hypothesis for it because she recognized the experience as she was conscious of it at the time of its happening. In keeping with Welter's belief that subjective experience cannot be adequately expressed or understood through analysis and that "viewing *parts* of complete moments rather than viewing the total moment as experienced by the athlete compounds the problem of ineffability" (p. 17), I have reproduced the description in full. The absence of reference to anything outside the experience itself is in keeping with the need to confront the experience as an entity in itself when engaging in this mode of inquiry.

Once, while playing for my college softball team, I had an experience that will keep me playing softball forever just for the chance that it might happen again. We were playing Fort Hays, Kansas against a team of comparable skill and experience. It was toward the beginning of the season of my senior year and we had just had what I believed to be a positive change in the coaching staff. I was looking forward to the game and the season and was excited to be playing again under those circumstances. It felt so good to be outdoors on a nice spring evening with people I cared about and playing a game I loved, that I was enjoying it as I enjoy few things. I could not think of anything that I would rather be doing. Rather than worrying about the technical aspects of the game, I was allowing myself the rare pleasure of enjoying the evening and myself and playing as I had as a child. I was playing center field and was getting some action and hoping for more. I loved playing center field because I loved to run, and I always hoped for long fly balls that I had to run and run to get to and then could just barely reach.

I think we won the game and I played well, but I really only remember one play. A ball was hit deep over my right shoulder, so deep that I knew I would have to turn and take my eyes from the ball and just run to the spot where I thought it would land, if I was to have

any chance to get a glove on it. Because I was feeling so good about playing and was really alert and excited about the game, I turned and was running almost as the ball was hit. I took one quick look at it to judge where it was headed and then turned my back and just ran. It felt so good to be running, and suddenly I realized that I was not even straining to get to the ball. Power and grace combined, and with no conscious direction or effort I was running as I had never run before. Pure speed, that I had only dreamed about before, was suddenly present in my earthly body, seemingly disdainful of all the windsprints and leg presses I had done in the past as I had struggled to force this feeling. But now it all seemed so very natural. I could have laughed at the irony of it—for years I had struggled while coaches gave instructions and I ran extra sprints after practice and read books on proper technique and daydreamed of the ultimate run—a perfect, flowing, intricate combination of power and grace and efficiency. I thought I had come close many times in races and workouts, but something was always missing; it was never quite complete for some reason. And suddenly, here in a game that I was playing simply to celebrate the evening and myself and my favorite sport, it appeared by surprise and I felt that I was being gently chided for thinking that I could make it happen. It was so easy. I seemed to be *made* to run. My purpose for being seemed to be to chase balls hit out of reach and to run and run anyway and reach and stretch farther than muscles allowed and just barely hang on to balls that were sure base hits. And it was too easy. Surely something I wanted so badly should cause some pain. At least the strain should be felt in some way; at least it should be seen in the tightening of the jaw in a moment of intense concentration. Surely I needed to do something besides enjoy the feeling of my body moving in a way that I had never been able to *make* it move before. But it seemed to require nothing of me but that I not resist. I was as a bird in flight that swoops and soars, playing important personal games with the run and the sand and the sea. All that mattered was the moment and the act itself. I wanted to run that way forever.

Without breaking stride I looked back over my left shoulder and caught sight of the ball, gently moving in an arc toward the spot to which I was still running. It moved slowly, almost floating, and I saw the seams as the ball slowly rotated. All that existed at the moment was my body and the ball. My body was still moving with its new-found efficiency, so incredibly powerful and graceful that it seemed to have transcended human boundaries and to be moving in some other dimension. And the ball that had been hit so hard was almost floating in the warm night air. I was aware only of my body and the ball and the space around. My mind seemed strangely free, floating along, watching everything happen, watching the action unfold. I felt myself reach up and out as far as I could and watched the ball settle into the pocket of my glove. I felt the pressure of the ball against the leather of my glove as it pressed against the palm of my hand. I could not have run any faster or reached any farther. It was the best effort that I could have made, and it had been made without any effort on my part. I enjoyed the moment as I had never enjoyed other moments when I was busy directing the action and giving myself in-

structions on technique. I enjoyed the moment in the same way that I had enjoyed sandlot games as a child when I did not know how to direct the action. In a way those games were similar to this moment because they had also been celebrations that allowed me a glimpse of my true potential. But this time there was no incomplete, yearning feeling, no desire to go just a little farther and a little faster the next time. I was satisfied. I had reached my potential. The moment was complete. (pp. 49-52)

Of the three phenomenological approaches described, Welter's remains closest to the actual lived experience. This approach can only be verified subjectively—only the experiencer can judge the adequacy of each description.

Studer's (1977) work is another example of experiential description in sport and physical education. Because so little has been attempted, the possibilities for gaining insight into sport and physical education through experiential description are really unknown.

SUMMARY

Philosophic inquiry is a process for shedding light on the nature and significance of physical activity. Of the nine representative methods of doing philosophy of sport and physical activity explained, three are techniques for identifying concept-unifying agents. By identifying necessary and sufficient conditions, one attempts to define a class of things. The conditions must be broad enough to include all things properly fitting the class and narrow enough to exclude all others. Developing taxonomies is a technique for subdividing items in a class. A taxonomy may be either closed or open-ended. Those who practice the family resemblance approach try to demonstrate that the members of a class do not share given features but instead have a multitude of family resemblances that overlap and crisscross.

Two methods of philosophic inquiry are defined in the section working from paradigms. In the goodness-of-fit technique, the philosopher attempts to determine whether an activity can be shown to properly fit the parameters of a given paradigm, "testing the fit" between the paradigm and activity in question. In the implications approach, one tries to perform a logical extrapolation of a paradigm in order to describe what an activity would or should be like if it were to conform to that paradigm.

A language analyst tries to detect contradictory or confusing uses of terms. The technique includes identifying terms, searching and analyzing relevant sources, and suggesting improvements for how terms are used.

The phenomenologist attempts to describe consciousness of experience in one of three ways: analyzing the experiences described by others, analyzing one's own consciousness of experience, or engaging in experiential description. These modes of inquiry differ in how close the investigator is to the experience being described.

The philosophic enterprise is open-minded and should always leave room for new methodological categories and subcategories; you are encouraged to invent new strategies for investigation and to try to decipher the techniques used by those whose works fail to fit the methods described.

Problems

The nine philosophic methods in the chapter are clustered under four major headings.

1. Read one of the studies that are cited at the end of each method. Describe how the procedures used parallel those used in the example presented for that method. Describe how the procedures differ from those in the example.
2. Select a different major heading. Read a study cited at the end of one of the methods under that heading, and explain why the study was cited there.

Chapter 12

□

Meta-Analysis

An analysis of the literature is a part of all types of research. The scholar is always aware of past events and how they influence current research. Sometimes, however, the literature review stands by itself as a research paper, one that involves the analysis, evaluation, and integration of the published literature. As mentioned in chapter 1, a number of journals consist entirely of literature review papers, and nearly all research journals publish review papers occasionally.

All the procedures discussed in detail in chapter 2 apply to the literature analysis. The difference is that the purpose here is to use the literature for empirical and theoretical conclusions rather than to document the need for a particular research problem. A good literature analysis will result in several tangible conclusions and should spark interest in future directions for research. Sometimes a literature analysis will lead to a revision or to the proposal of a theory. The point is that a literature analysis is not simply a summary of the related literature; it is a logical type of research that leads to valid conclusions, hypothesis evaluations, and the revision and proposal of theory.

> A literature analysis is not simply a summary of the related literature; it is a logical type of research that leads to valid conclusions, hypothesis evaluations, and the revision and proposal of theory.

The approach to a literature analysis is like any other type of research. The researcher must clearly specify the procedures that are to be followed. Unfortunately, the literature review paper seldom specifies the procedures the author used. Thus, the basis for the many decisions made about individual papers is usually unknown to the reader. Of course, this makes an objective evaluation of a literature review nearly impossible. Questions that are important yet usually unanswered in the typical review of literature include the following:

- How thorough was the literature search? Did it include a computer search and hand search? In a computer search, what were the descriptors used? Which journals were searched? Were theses and dissertations searched and included?
- On what basis were studies included or excluded from the written review? Were theses and dissertations arbitrarily excluded? Did the author make decisions about inclusion or exclusion on the basis of the perceived internal validity of the research, on sample size, on research design, or on appropriate statistical analysis?
- How did the author arrive at a particular conclusion? Was it based on the number of studies supporting or refuting the conclusion (called vote counting)? Were these studies weighted differentially according to sample size, meaningfulness of the results, quality of the journal, and internal validity of the study?

Many more questions could be asked about the decisions made in the typical literature review paper, for good research involves a systematic method of problem solving. However, in most literature reviews the author's systematic method remains unknown to the reader, thus prohibiting an objective evaluation of these decisions.

In recent years, several attempts have been made to solve the problems associated with literature reviews. The most notable of these attempts was made in a paper by Glass (1976) and followed up with a book by Glass et al. (1981), who proposed a technique called meta-analysis.

PURPOSE OF META-ANALYSIS

Meta-analysis involves two procedures lacking in previous literature reviews. First, a definitive methodology is reported concerning the decisions in a literature analysis. Second, the results of various studies are quantified to a standard metric that allows the use of statistical techniques as a means of analysis. Here are the steps in a meta-analysis:

1. The identification of a problem
2. A literature search by specified means
3. A review of identified studies to determine inclusion or exclusion
4. A careful reading and evaluation to identify and code important study characteristics
5. The calculation of effect size
6. The application of appropriate statistical techniques
7. The reporting of all these steps and of the outcomes in a review paper

Of course, one of the major problems in a literature review paper is the number of studies that must be considered. To some extent, analyzing all these studies is like trying to make sense of all the data points in a single study. However, within a study, statistical techniques are used to reduce the data to make them understandable. The procedures of meta-analysis are very similar. The findings within individual studies are considered the data points to use in a statistical analysis across the findings of many studies.

How, then, can findings based on different designs, data collection techniques, dependent variables, and statistical analysis be compared? Glass addressed this issue by using an estimate he calls effect size (ES, or the symbol Δ). Note that we discussed this general concept in chapter 7 as a way of judging the meaningfulness of group differences. ES is determined by the following formula:

$$ES = \frac{M_E - M_C}{s_C} \qquad (12.1)$$

where M_E = the mean of the experimental group, M_C = the mean of the control group, and s_C = the standard deviation of the control group. Note that this formula places the difference between the experimental and control groups in control group standard deviation units. For example, if M_E = 15, M_C = 12, and s_C = 5, then ES = (15 − 12)/5 = .60. The experimental group's performance exceeded the control group's performance by .60 of a standard deviation. If this were done across several studies addressing a common problem, the findings of the studies would be in a common metric, ES (Δ), which could be compared. The mean and standard deviations of ES could be calculated from several studies. This would allow a statement about the average ES of a particular type of treatment.

Suppose we wanted to know whether a particular treatment affects males and females differently. In searching the literature, we find 15 studies on males comparing the treatment effects and 12 studies on females. We could calculate an ES for each of the 27 studies and the mean (and standard deviation) of the ES for males (n = 15) and females

($n = 12$). An independent t test could then be used to see whether the average ES differed for males and females. If the t values were significant and the average ES for the females was greater, we could conclude that the treatment had more effect on females than on males. Glass et al. (1981) provided considerable detail on the methods of meta-analysis, including literature search strategies, how to calculate ES from the statistics reported in various studies, suggestions for how and what to code from studies, and examples of the use of meta-analysis.

Certainly, meta-analysis is not the answer to all the problems associated with literature reviews. But Glass has provided an objective way to evaluate the literature. Recent advances (Hedges, 1981, 1982a, b; Hedges & Olkin, 1980) in studying the statistical properties of ES have contributed considerably to the appropriate use of meta-analysis. The text by Hedges and Olkin (1985) provides a complete accounting of the procedures and statistical analyses appropriate for meta-analysis. A tutorial by Thomas and French (1986) is an overview of Hedges's (and colleagues') techniques and includes examples from physical education, exercise science, and sport science.

EXAMPLES
OF META-ANALYSIS

Since Glass's (1976) original proposal of the meta-analysis technique, several meta-analyses have been published, including a few in physical education, exercise science, and sport science. A brief overview of some of these studies should identify the value of meta-analysis.

In a meta-analysis on the effects of perceptual-motor training for improving academic, cognitive, or perceptual-motor performance, Kavale and Mattson (1983) reported a distinct lack of success for perceptual-motor training in the 180 studies included. The largest ES they found was .198, and it was associated with the 83 studies rated low in internal validity. In fact, in studies with high internal validity, the trained subjects did worse. Thus, perceptual-motor training does not appear useful for any type of outcome (academic, cognitive, or perceptual-motor) for any type of subject (normal, educable mentally retarded, trainable mentally retarded, slow learner, culturally disadvantaged, learning disabled, reading disabled, or motor disabled) at any age level (preschool, kindergarten, primary grades, middle grades, junior high school, or high school).

Sparling (1980) reported a meta-analysis of ES differences between males and females for maximal oxygen uptake ($\dot{V}O_2max$). One of the most interesting findings was that when ES was averaged across studies, it was reduced when corrections were made for the differing body compositions of males and females. When $\dot{V}O_2max$ was expressed as liters per minute (l/min), 66% of the variance was explained by knowing the subject's gender; when $\dot{V}O_2max$ was expressed as ml/min • kg BW (body weight), the explained variance was reduced to 49%; and when expressed as ml/min • kg FFW (fat-free weight), the explained variance was reduced to 35%. Thus, the advantage of males over females in $\dot{V}O_2max$ is reduced when corrected for body weight and is reduced even more when corrected for fat-free weight.

In a meta-analysis on the effects of exercise on blood lipids and lipoproteins, Tran, Weltman, Glass, and Mood (1983) reported an analysis of 66 training studies involving a total of 2,925 subjects. They found significant relationships between training and beneficial changes in blood lipids and lipoproteins: "Initial levels, age, length of training, intensity, $\dot{V}O_2max$, body weight, and percent fat have been shown . . . to interact with exercise and serum lipids and lipo-protein changes'' (p. 400).

Feltz and Landers (1983) reported a meta-analysis of the effects of mental practice on motor skill learning and performance. From 60 studies they calculated an average ES of .48, less than one half of a standard deviation unit. They concluded that mentally practicing a motor skill is slightly better than not practicing one at all.

In studying gender differences in motor performance across childhood and adolescence, Thomas and French (1985) reported findings from 64 studies based on 31,444 subjects. They found motor performance differences to be related to age in 12 of the 20 motor tasks. These 12 tasks followed four general types of curves across age. Figure 12.1 shows one typical type of curve for three tasks (long jump, shuttle run, and grip strength). The differences are moderate (about .5-.75 standard deviation units) before puberty but then increase dramatically during and following puberty (over 1.5 standard deviation units). They concluded that the differences before puberty were likely to be induced by environmental factors (differential treatment by parents, teachers, coaches, and peers) but that they represented an interaction of biology and environment beginning at puberty. Note the difference between the curves in Figures 12.1 and 12.2. Effect sizes for throwing performance are 1.5 standard deviation units at ages 3-4 and increase constantly across childhood and adolescence until the differences are 3.5 standard deviation units by age 18. Thomas and French suggested that differences that were so large so early in life might have some basis in biology and in the influence of cultural treatments and expectations for girls and boys.

Crews and Landers (1987) reported a meta-analysis of the relation between aerobic fitness and psychosocial stressors. They had 34 studies including 1,449 subjects and reported that reduced psychosocial stress was

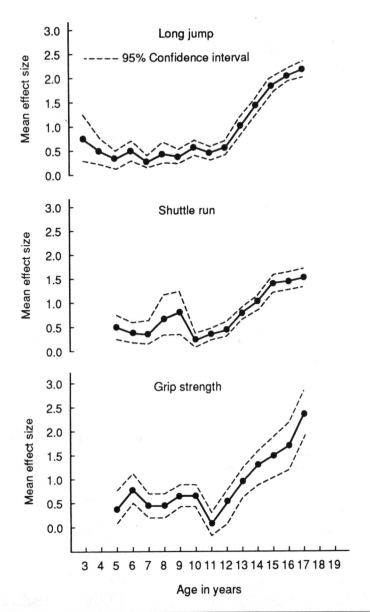

Figure 12.1 ES for three motor performance tasks. *Note.* Dotted lines are confidence intervals.

found in more aerobically fit subjects (ES = .48) when they were compared to less fit subjects or baseline measures. This effect was reliable regardless of the types of physiological or psychological measures used. In addition, none of the moderator variables (e.g., study and subject characteristics, methodological characteristics, and stressor characteristics) were important for this finding as the ES's were homogeneous.

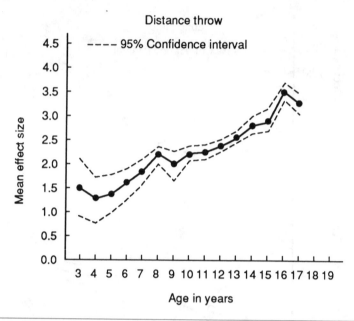

Figure 12.2 ES by age and gender for throwing for distance. *Note.* Dotted lines are confidence intervals.

These examples have been used to illustrate the value of the meta-analysis approach (for additional reading, the last two—Thomas and French, and Crews and Landers—are useful because they applied the more recent techniques of Hedges et al.). In the perceptual-motor meta-analysis, the controversial issue of the value of this type of training appears resolved: no benefit. In the meta-analysis of gender differences in $\dot{V}O_2$max, these large differences appear to be accounted for in large part by differences in body composition rather than any differences in underlying mechanisms. Also, exercise appears to have a positive effect on cholesterol and its components. Mental practice is better than no practice, but not by much. Gender differences in motor performance before puberty appear mainly environmentally induced, but throwing may be a skill for which biology plays a greater role before puberty. Finally, higher levels of aerobic fitness appear to be associated with lower levels of psychosocial stress.

Meta-analysis, when applied appropriately and interpreted carefully, offers a means of reducing a large quantity of studies to underlying principles. These principles can become the bases for program development, future research, and theory testing as well as various practical applications, such as practice and training.

METHODOLOGICAL CONSIDERATIONS

Thomas and French (1986) published a tutorial and example of meta-analysis, part of which is adapted here to take you through the important steps and issues in a meta-analysis. We thank Karen French and the *Research Quarterly for Exercise and Sport* for allowing us to adapt part of this paper.

Meta-Analysis:
Criticisms and Questions

Although meta-analysis has been a widely used technique in the last few years, considerable controversy exists concerning the validity of meta-analysis (e.g., Carlberg et al., 1984; Slavin, 1984a, b). Among the most severe criticisms of meta-analysis is for its combination of findings from studies representing different measurement scales, methodologies, and experimental designs. This criticism of "mixing of apples and oranges" was compounded by the results of early meta-analyses using the methods of Glass (1977), which tended to reveal few differences in ES's, even between studies in which internal validity and methodological control clearly varied. Hedges (1981, 1982) and Hedges and Olkin (1983, 1985) extended the original work of Glass (1977) and proposed a new set of techniques and statistical tests specifically designed to address the following major questions and criticisms of meta-analysis:

- What should be used as the standard deviation when calculating an ES?
- Because sample ES's are biased estimators of the population of ES's, how can this bias be corrected?
- Should ES's be weighted for their sample size?
- Are all ES's in a sample from the same population of ES's? This is the "apples and oranges" issue: Is the sample of ES's homogeneous?
- What are appropriate statistical tests for analyzing ES's?
- If a sample of ES's includes outliers, how can they be identified?

In the following sections, we address each of these questions, provide you with a basic summary of the theoretical basis for the statistical procedures introduced by Hedges (1981, 1982) and Hedges and Olkin (1983, 1985), and provide some suggestions for the application of these techniques in physical education, exercise science, and sport science research.

> Meta-analysis, when applied appropriately and interpreted carefully, offers a means of reducing a large quantity of studies to underlying principles.

Choice of Standard Deviation for the Effect Size

Originally, Glass et al. (1981) proposed the use of the control group's standard deviation as the most appropriate measure of group variability. From an intuitive perspective, the control group's variability represents the "normal" variation in an untreated population. The control group's standard deviation also has the advantage of assigning equal ES's to equal treatment means when a study contains two or more experimental groups that have heterogeneous variances. Therefore, the control group's standard deviation serves as a common standard metric from which treatment differences can be compared.

In most cases, estimates of the group variance are homogeneous. Hedges (1981) argued that a pooled estimate of the variance provides a more precise estimate of the population variance. (The square root of the pooled estimate of the variance is the pooled estimate of the standard deviation.) One advantage of pooling variances is an increase in the degrees of freedom associated with the estimate of variance. The pooled estimate Hedges (1981) suggested is given in Formula 12.2. Note that the variance of each group is weighted by the sample size of that group in a way that is similar to the procedure used in t tests with unequal ns. The formula is

$$s_P = \sqrt{\frac{(N_E - 1)\, s_E^2 + (N_C - 1)\, s_C^2}{N_E + N_C - 2}} \quad (12.2)$$

where N_E = the sample size of the experimental group (Group 1), N_C = the sample size of the control group (Group 2), s_E^2 = the variance of the experimental group (Group 1), and s_C^2 = the variance of the control group (Group 2).

Many studies involve tests of effects between or among categorical variables (e.g., race and gender) where there is no control condition. Early meta-analyses used an average of the standard deviations of the groups compared (Glass & Smith, 1979; Hyde, 1981; Smith, 1980). Hedges and Olkin (1985) have suggested using the square root of the weighted pooled variance ($\sqrt{s_P^2}$) as the estimate of the standard deviation (for an example using gender differences in motor performance, see Thomas & French, 1985).

There are cases in which the variance for the groups is heterogeneous. Glass et al. (1981) have shown that ES's are biased when the group variances are unequal. Because parametric tests are based on the assumption of equal variances, ES's calculated from t and ANOVA may be biased if the group variances are unequal.

Researchers should evaluate whether heterogeneous variances are a common phenomenon in the area of research for the meta-analysis. We have encountered unequal variances when comparing the motor performance of children of different age levels (French & Thomas, 1984). We offer these suggestions. When the ES compares an experimental group and a control group and the group variances are unequal, use the standard deviation of the control group to calculate the ES in all studies. If the ES compares two groups (such as age or gender) in which there is no clear control condition, we believe

the weighted pooled estimate suggested by Hedges (1981) is the best choice.

Distribution Theory for ES Estimators

Hedges (1981) has provided a theoretical and structural model for the use of ES as an estimator of treatment effects. An individual ES may be viewed as a sample statistic that estimates the population of possible treatment effects within a given experiment.

Hedges (1981) has shown that the variance of an individual ES may be directly calculated from the following formula:

$$\text{var}\,(ES_i) = \frac{N_E + N_C}{N_E N_C} + \frac{ES_i^2}{2(N_E + N_C)}$$
$$(12.3)$$

where N_E = the sample size of the experimental group (Group 1), N_C = the sample size of the control group (Group 2), and ES_i = the estimate of ES. Note that the variability associated with the sample statistic, or ES, is a function of the value of the ES and the sample size. An ES based on a large sample has a smaller variance than an ES based on a small sample. Therefore, ES's based on large samples are more precise estimates of the population parameter of treatment effects.

Hedges (1981) also demonstrated that ES's are positively biased in small samples; however, the bias is 20% or less when the sample size exceeds 20. A virtually unbiased estimate of ES can be obtained by multiplying the ES by the correction factor given in the following formula*:

$$c = 1 - \frac{3}{4m - 9} \quad (12.4)$$

where $m = N_E + N_C - 2$ when a pooled estimate is used as the standard deviation,

---

*This formula is correct here, but was printed incorrectly in Thomas and French (1983).

$m = N_1 + N_2 - 2$ if a pooled estimate is used in a categorical model, or $m = N_C - 1$ when the control group standard deviation is used.

Each ES should be corrected before averaging or further analysis. If ES's are not corrected before averaging, the average of even a large number of ES's remains biased and simply estimates an incorrect value more precisely (Hedges, 1981). Early meta-analyses in exercise and sport (Feltz & Landers, 1983; Sparling, 1980) did not correct each ES for small sample bias. The ES's reported in these studies are most likely slight overestimates.

Although the individual ES estimate can be corrected for bias, the variability associated with the estimate remains a function of the sample size. Thus, as stated before, ES's with large samples are more precise estimates than ES's with small samples. Hedges (1981) and Hedges and Olkin (1985) introduced statistical techniques that weight each ES on the basis of the reciprocal of its variance (for more detail, see Thomas & French, 1986). Therefore, ES's that are more accurate receive more weight in each analysis.

Tests of Homogeneity

Meta-analysis has been criticized for mixing apples and oranges, or combining studies with different measurement scales, designs, and methodologies. No appropriate test existed to determine whether all the ES's were estimating the same population treatment effect until Hedges (1982) introduced his test for homogeneity. The homogeneity statistic, H, is specifically designed to test the null hypothesis, H_0: $ES_1 = ES_2 = \ldots = ES_i$. This is equivalent to saying that all ES's tested come from the same population of ES's.

The statistic H is the weighted sum of squared deviations of ES's from the overall weighted mean. The contribution of each ES to the overall mean is weighted by the reciprocal of its variance. Effect sizes with smaller variances receive more weight in the calculation of the overall mean. Under the null hypothesis, H has a chi-square distribution with $N - 1$ degrees of freedom, where N equals the number of ES's.

When the null hypothesis is not rejected, all ES's are similar and represent a similar measure of treatment effectiveness. In this case, the researcher should report the homogeneity statistic indicating that ES's are homogeneous and use the weighted mean ES with confidence intervals for interpretation. If the null hypothesis is rejected, ES's are not homogeneous and do not represent a similar measure of treatment effectiveness, or grouping. Two methods have been proposed by Hedges (1982) and Hedges and Olkin (1983) to examine explanatory models for ES's.

Analysis of Variance

The first method is analogous to ANOVA, in which the sum of squares for the total H statistic is partitioned into sum of squares between or among groups of ES's (H_B) and sum of squares within groups of ES's (H_W). Each sum of squares may be tested as a chi-square with $k - 1$ df for H_B and $N - k - 1$ df for H_W (where N = the number of ES's and k = the number of groups). Therefore, a test can be conducted for between- or among-group differences (H_B), and a test can be conducted to determine whether all ES's within a group are homogeneous (H_W). Further discussion of the categorical model is presented in Hedges (1982) and Hedges and Olkin (1985).

Weighted Regression

The second method proposed by Hedges and Olkin (1983) to fit an explanatory model to ES data is a weighted regression technique. We have chosen to present a more detailed discussion of the regression techniques for several reasons. First, one of the meta-analyses discussed previously in exercise and sport has used regression techniques to analyze ES (Thomas & French, 1985). Second, it is common for a continuous variable to influence ES. Third, often more than one study characteristic influences ES. This is especially true when there is a large number of ES's. The regression procedures can accommodate a larger number of variables in the analysis without inflating the alpha level of the statistical test. Conducting many tests using the categorical or ANOVA-like procedures results in alpha inflation. The researcher would need to report the experimentwise error rate or adjust the alpha level using the Bonferroni technique. Fourth, categorical variables can easily be dummy or effect coded and entered into the regression procedures. For example, published versus unpublished papers can be dummy coded and entered into the regression. Thus, it is not necessary to conduct a separate analysis for categorical variables.

Each ES is weighted by the inverse of its variance in the weighted regression technique. Most mainframe statistical packages (e.g., SAS, SPSS, BMDP) have an option to perform weighted regression. Thus, the computations may be done easily on any mainframe computer system.

The sum of squares total for the regression is equivalent to the homogeneity statistic, H. It is partitioned into sum of squares regression and sum of squares error. The *sum of squares for regression* gives a test of the regression (H_R). The sum of squares regression is tested as a chi-square with $df = p$, where p equals the number of predictor variables. The sum of squares error provides a test of model specifications (H_E). The sum of squares error is tested as a chi-square with $df = N - p - 1$, where N equals the number of ES's and p equals the number of predictor variables. The test of model specification evaluates the deviation of the ES's from the regression model. A nonsignificant test of model specification indicates that the ES's do not deviate substantially from the regression model. A significant test for model specification indicates that one or more ES's deviate substantially from the regression model. Ideally, the researcher wants the H_R for regression to be significant and the H_E for model specification to be nonsignificant.

When the test for model specification is significant, one or more ES's do not follow the specified regression. In many cases, the ES's that do not follow the same pattern may indicate other characteristics that may add to the model (e.g., published vs. unpublished studies). Moreover, some ES's may represent *outliers* (unrepresentative scores). In either case, the use of outlier techniques is helpful in identifying these ES's.

Test for Outliers

Hedges and Olkin (1985) have outlined procedures to identify outliers in categorical and regression models. We use an example from a regression model (for more information concerning the categorical model, see Hedges and Olkin, 1985, chapter 7).

Outliers in regression models may be identified by examining the residuals of the regression equation. The absolute value of the residuals is standardized to z scores by subtracting the mean and dividing by the standard deviation. Effect sizes with standardized residuals larger than 2 can be considered outliers, as they fall outside 95% of the distribution.

According to Hedges and Olkin (1985), each ES makes a contribution to the regression model. The outliers identified by standardized residuals may vary depending on which ES's are in the model at the time. Hedges and Olkin (1985) have suggested computing standardized residuals multiple times with a different ES deleted from the model each time the residuals are computed.

For example, if one has 10 ES's, standardized residuals would be computed 10 times with a different ES deleted from the model each time. However, some of our preliminary work has suggested that if more than 20 ES's are included in the regression model, the value of going through all possible combinations of deleting ES's from the model may be limited. Simply calculate the residuals with all the ES's in the model, standardize the residuals, and declare any ES with a z score larger than 2 as an outlier.

Other Considerations

Sometimes all the information needed to calculate an ES is not available in a research report. Both Glass et al. (1981) and Hedges and Olkin (1985) have provided ways to estimate ES's from standard statistics (e.g., t, F, and r). However, on occasion only the statement that two groups do not differ significantly will be reported. What should the meta-analyst do? To drop the study is to bias the results of the meta-analysis toward significant differences. Thomas and French (1985) inserted a *zero ES*, using the rationale that no significant differences means the differences did not reliably differ from zero. However, Thomas and French (1985) had few zero ES's. Using many zero ES's may cause problems in the analysis of homogeneity by making the studies look overly consistent. Hedges (1984) suggested a correction factor that adjusts for this problem. Regardless of the solution selected, the meta-analyst must cope with this issue and select a logical solution.

TUTORIAL EXAMPLE OF META-ANALYSIS

The following example is a subset of data from Thomas and French (1985) for gender differences in throwing velocity across age.

The example is presented so that the procedures involved in each step are given.

Selection of Studies

To identify a set of studies that examined gender differences in motor performance, Thomas and French conducted a computer search using ERIC and Psychology Information to identify studies that compared the performance of males and females across age levels. A number of journals in exercise, sport, and psychology were searched by hand (see Thomas & French, 1985). Although the total meta-analysis had 64 studies on 20 tasks that met all the criteria for inclusion, only 5 of these studies were on throwing velocity. The studies used for this example are listed in the note to Table 12.1.

Coded Characteristics of the Studies

The age of the subjects was the primary variable that was hypothesized to be related to ES, the magnitude of which was predicted to change across age levels.

Calculation of Effect Size

Thirteen ES's were calculated from the five studies. Each ES was calculated by subtracting the mean of the female group's performance from the mean of the male group's performance and dividing by the pooled weighted standard deviation (Formula 12.2). Therefore, a positive ES indicates that males throw with greater velocity than females. Each ES was multiplied by the appropriate correction factor (Formula 12.4) to correct for small sample bias (Hedges, 1981). In addition, the variance of each ES and the reciprocal of the variance of each ES were calculated from Formula 12.3. Table 12.1 provides a summary of these calculations.

Table 12.1 Summary Information for the Five Studies

Study #	ES #	Male M	Male s	Male N	Female M	Female s	Female N	Pooled s (weighted)	Uncorrected ES	Corrected ES	Variance of ES	Inverse of the variance of ES
1	1	35.7	7.0	10	27.4	4.5	9	6.0	1.39	1.33	.258	3.88
1	2	41.4	7.8	10	30.9	3.0	9	6.0	1.74	1.66	.284	3.52
1	3	44.7	7.1	10	34.9	1.3	9	5.2	1.87	1.79	.295	3.39
2	4	35.3	7.0	12	26.2	4.2	12	5.8	1.58	1.52	.215	4.65
3	5	38.8	7.8	22	28.7	8.3	17	8.0	1.25	1.23	.124	8.08
3	6	44.3	8.3	22	31.6	8.3	17	8.3	1.53	1.50	.133	7.51
3	7	49.6	8.3	22	34.6	8.9	17	8.6	1.75	1.72	.142	7.04
3	8	77.6	10.1	22	55.9	11.3	17	10.6	2.04	2.00	.155	6.43
4	9	46.3	7.3	28	30.8	4.6	25	6.2	2.51	2.47	.133	7.50
5	10	51.5	6.6	35	34.8	4.1	35	5.5	3.03	3.00	.122	8.22
5	11	57.3	5.5	33	40.5	5.3	36	5.4	3.11	3.07	.127	7.89
5	12	63.6	7.1	39	41.6	6.5	38	6.8	3.23	3.20	.118	8.45
5	13	69.0	5.0	37	50.4	5.1	37	5.0	3.63	3.64	.144	6.95

Note. Study 1: Roberton, Halverson, Langendorfer, and Williams (1979); Study 2: Halverson, Roberton, Safrit, and Roberts (1977); Study 3: Halverson et al. (1982); Study 4: Maples (1977); Study 5: Glassow, Halverson, and Rarick (1965).

Test for Homogeneity

The first step in the analysis of these data was to conduct the test for homogeneity to determine whether all ES's were similar. The H statistic was significant, $\chi^2(12) = 53.88$, $p < .05$. A significant portion of the variance remains unexplained because the H statistic was significant. The age of the subject was predicted to be related to ES; therefore, age may account for a major portion of the variance. A weighted regression was chosen as a method of analysis because age is a continuous variable. Effect size was regressed on the age of the subject. The test for regression was significant, $\chi^2(1) = 24.49$, $p < .05$. The test for model specification that tests the homogeneity of ES's around the regression line was significant, $\chi^2(11) = 29.72$, $p < .05$. Therefore, one or more ES's deviated significantly from the regression line.

Because the test for model specification was significant, a test for outliers in the regression was conducted following the procedures outlined by Hedges and Olkin (1985). We have tried to simplify the discussion of the outlier tests. The regression equation was calculated 13 times, and one ES was deleted from the model on each calculation. The H_R for regression and the H_E for model specification for each of the 13 regressions are given in Table 12.2. The χ_R^2 for regression and the χ_E^2 for model specification listed on the same line as an ES correspond to the χ_R^2 for regression and the χ_E^2 for model specification calculated, and that ES was deleted from the model. Therefore, on the first line, the χ_R^2 for regression is 21.24 and the χ_E^2 for model specification is 29.33 when the first ES (1.33) was deleted from the regression. The *absolute values* of the residuals from the regression were computed and converted to z scores by subtracting the mean and dividing by the standard deviation. Rather than present the standardized residuals calculated

13 times with one ES deleted from the model each time, we present the standardized residuals for each ES with all ES's included in the regression equation in Table 12.2. The standardized residual for ES #8 (2.779) is greater than 2 and can be considered an outlier. Furthermore, a significant reduction in the sum of squares for model specification (H_E) was found when ES #8 was deleted from the model, $\chi_E^2(10) = 11.25$, $p > .05$. Also, the χ_R^2 for regression increased to 42.42. Note that the χ_R^2 for regression and the χ_E^2 for model specification did not change very much when the other ES's were individually deleted from the regression calculations. Thus, the ES's are homogeneous around the regression line when ES #8 is not included in the model.

Once an ES has been identified as an outlier, it is important to examine why it may be an outlier. An outlier could indicate other characteristics that should be added to the model. In our example, the ES identified as an outlier was considerably lower at age 12

Table 12.2 Standardized Residuals

ES #	Age	ES	H_R (1)	H_E (10)	Residual
1	6	1.33	21.24	29.33	−0.652
2	7	1.66	23.34	29.48	−0.801
3	8	1.79	24.25	29.11	−0.272
4	5	1.52	21.87	29.54	−1.060
5	6	1.23	16.42	28.05	−0.331
6	7	1.50	20.99	28.22	−0.266
7	8	1.71	23.88	27.91	−0.042
8	12	2.00	42.42	11.25	2.779
9	8	2.47	24.79	29.11	−0.747
10	8	3.00	25.58	23.80	1.012
11	9	3.07	22.02	26.62	0.312
12	10	3.20	18.42	27.83	−0.232
13	11	3.64	13.56	26.48	0.301

Note. With all effect sizes in the regression model, H_R (1) = 24.49 and H_E (11) = 29.72.

(2.00) than those at ages 10 and 11 (3.20 and 3.64, respectively) when the ES between males and females would be expected to increase with age. Throwing velocity for the ES at age 12 was measured by a velocimeter. The study that included ES's at ages 10 and 11 used a film analysis to obtain a measure of velocity. Thus, the ES at age 12 may be lower than the ES's at 10 and 11 because of a difference in the way throwing velocity was measured. The final model (outlier deleted) revealed that the test for regression was significant, $\chi_R^2(1) = 42.42$, $p < .05$, and the test for model specification nonsignificant, $\chi_E^2(10) = 11.25$, $p > .05$.

Figure 12.3 is a plot of the mean ES's at each age with their 95% confidence intervals, which we reported in a more comprehensive paper (Thomas & French, 1985). We chose to report the mean ES at each age. One could also use a figure with the regression line and each individual ES plotted around the regres-

sion line. We felt that the mean ES with confidence interval retained a better representation of the original data. This was especially true with the other motor tasks we reported (Thomas & French, 1985), as these had a much greater number of ES's.

As you can see from Figure 12.3, gender differences in throwing velocity are large even for preschool children (1.5 standard deviation units) and increase in a linear manner during childhood and early adolescence, when the differences are greater than 3.5 standard deviation units. Thus, boys throw with much greater velocity than girls at a very early age, and this advantage continues to increase as boys and girls age.

Although there are differences in the treatment of boys and girls, gender differences in throwing velocity as large as 1.5 standard deviation units at age 3 to 4 are unlikely to be completely environmentally caused. Thomas and French (1985) discussed other

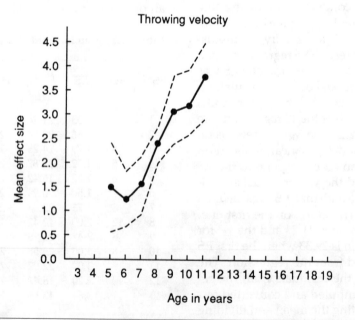

Figure 12.3 ES by age and gender for throwing for velocity.

research that suggests that biological variables may contribute to the large gender difference in throwing velocity. However, the fact that the gender difference continues to increase in childhood and adolescence is probably a combination of biological and environmental influences.

One advantage of using meta-analysis to examine gender differences in motor performance across age is that the magnitude of these differences can be determined. Thomas and French (1985) calculated ES's for a number of motor tasks. No gender difference was found in performance on certain tasks. On other tasks, the gender difference was small before puberty and increased after puberty. Large gender differences in throwing velocity and throwing distance existed before puberty and increased in magnitude following puberty. Overall, the magnitude of gender differences across age was dependent on the type of task examined. These comparisons would not be possible using the traditional qualitative review of literature.

A FINAL POINT

One issue remaining unaddressed by methodological literature on meta-analysis is the likely correlation among multiple ES's drawn from one study. For example, in our data (Table 12.1), three ES's were drawn from Study 1, four ES's from Study 3, and four ES's from Study 5. In this particular case, the ES's can be expected to be independent because each is based on the difference between female and male throwing performance at a different age level. However, one of these studies (Study 5) contained other motor performance characteristics (e.g., running and jumping) tested on the same children. Might the ES's be correlated because they are based on the same children's performance?

This problem is equivalent to the problems in a single study with multiple measures on the same subject. Certainly the variables might be correlated. The meta-analyst might select one or two alternatives. We (Thomas & French, 1985) chose to argue that previous research and theory had shown the variables to have little or no correlation; thus, they could be considered independent. If the variables are correlated, the meta-analyst should at least adjust the experimentwise error rate (see chapter 7).

SUMMARY

A literature analysis is not just a summary of studies arranged in some kind of sequence. It should be structured, analytical, and critical and lead to specific conclusions. The meta-analysis is a definitive methodology that quantifies results and allows statistical techniques to be used as a means of analysis.

The meta-analysis explicitly details how the search was done, the sources, the choices made regarding inclusion or exclusion, the coding of study characteristics, and the analytical procedures. The basis of a meta-analysis is the effect size, which transforms differences between experimental and control groups' performances to a common metric, which is expressed in standard deviation units.

The meta-analysis technique has been widely used in recent years. A number of meta-analyses have been done in physical education, exercise science, and sport science. The meta-analysis offers a means of reducing large quantities of studies to underlying principles. We used a tutorial as an example of a meta-analysis to illustrate the various steps. Refinements in technique continue to be made regarding the choice of the standard deviation to be used in calculating an effect size, the weighting of effect sizes for sample bias, tests for outliers, and the statistical procedures that can be used for the analysis.

Problem

Select a possible problem (e.g., gender differences in running speed, effects of weight training on males and females, or influence of training at 60% of $\dot{V}O_2max$ vs. 80% of $\dot{V}O_2max$). Find five studies that compare the characteristics you select (e.g., males and females). Make sure each study has the means and standard deviations for the variables of interest. Calculate the ES for each study and correct it for bias. Calculate the average ES for the five studies and their pooled standard deviations. Interpret this finding.

SUGGESTED READINGS

Samples of Meta-Analysis

Crews, D.J., & Landers, D.M. (1987). A meta-analytic review of aerobic fitness and reactivity to psychosocial stressors. *Medicine and Science in Sports and Exercise*, **19** (Suppl. 5), 114-120.

Thomas, J.R., & French, K.E. (1985). Gender differences across age in motor performance: A meta-analysis. *Psychological Bulletin*, **98**, 260-282.

Additional Readings on Meta-Analysis

Glass, G.V., McGaw, B., & Smith, M. (1981). *Meta-analysis in social research*. Beverly Hills, CA: Sage.

Hedges, L.V., & Olkin, I. (1985). *Statistical methods for meta-analysis*. Orlando, FL: Academic Press.

Thomas, J.R., & French, K.E. (1986). The use of meta-analysis in exercise and sport: A tutorial. *Research Quarterly for Exercise and Sport*, **57**, 196-204.

Chapter 13

☐

Descriptive Research

Descriptive research is a study of status that is widely used in education and the behavioral sciences. Its value is based on the premise that problems can be solved and practices improved through objective and thorough observation, analysis, and description. Several techniques or methods of problem solving fall into the category of descriptive research.

The most common descriptive research method is the survey, which includes questionnaires, interviews, and normative surveys. Developmental research is also descriptive. Through cross-sectional and longitudinal studies, researchers investigate the interaction of growth and maturation and of learning and performance variables. The case study is descriptive research and is widely used in a number of fields. A type of case study is the job analysis. Observational research and correlational studies constitute other forms of descriptive research. Observational research is a method of obtaining quantitative and qualitative data about people and situations, and correlational studies determine and analyze relationships. Predictions are also generated from correlational research.

This chapter discusses some of the characteristics and basic procedures of the various types of descriptive research.

THE SURVEY

The *survey* is generally broad in scope. The researcher usually seeks to determine present practices (or opinions) of a specified population. The survey is a widely used research tool in education, psychology, sociology, and physical activity. The questionnaire, the interview, and the normative survey are the three main types of surveys.

The Questionnaire

The questionnaire and the interview are the same except for the method of questioning. The procedures for developing questionnaire and interview items are similar. Consequently, much of the discussion regarding the steps in the construction of the questionnaire also pertains to the interview.

> The very obvious limitation to the questionnaire is that the results are simply what people say they do or what they say they believe or like and dislike.

The *questionnaire* is used to obtain information by asking subjects to respond to questions rather than by observing their behavior. The very obvious limitation to the questionnaire is that the results are simply what people say they do or what they say they believe or like and dislike. However, certain information can be obtained only in this manner, and so it is imperative that the questionnaire is planned and prepared carefully to ensure the most valid results.

The several steps in the survey research process include the following:

1. Determining the objectives
2. Delimiting the sample of respondents
3. Constructing the questionnaire
4. Conducting a pilot study
5. Writing the cover letter
6. Sending the questionnaire
7. Sending out the follow-ups
8. Analyzing the results
9. Preparing the research report

Determining the Objectives

This step may seem too obvious to mention, yet countless questionnaires have been prepared without clearly defined objectives. In fact, this may primarily account for the low esteem in which survey research is sometimes held. The investigator must have a clear understanding as to what information is needed and how each item will be analyzed. As with any research, the analysis is determined in the planning phase of the study, not after the data have been gathered.

The researcher must decide on the questionnaire's specific purposes: What information is wanted? How will the responses be analyzed? Will they merely be described by listing the percentages of subjects who responded in certain ways, or will the responses of one group be compared with those of another?

Thus, one of the most common mistakes made in constructing a questionnaire is not specifying the variables to be analyzed. In some cases, when the investigator fails to list the variables, questions unrelated to the objectives are asked. In other cases, the investigator forgets to ask pertinent questions. For example, in a survey of curricular offerings in physical education, if one of the objectives is to compare the offerings on the basis of how physical education is scheduled, the respondent must be asked about the sched-

uling. If male teachers are to be compared with female teachers, then gender must be indicated, and so on. What is to be analyzed must be made clear.

Delimiting the Sample

Most researchers who use questionnaires have in mind a specific population to be sampled. Obviously, the subjects selected must be the ones who have the answers to the questions. In other words, the investigator must be knowledgeable about who can supply what information. If information about policy decisions is desired, the subjects should be those involved in making such decisions.

Sometimes the source used in selecting the sample is inadequate. For example, some professional associations are made up of teachers, administrators, professors, and other allied professional workers. Thus, this association's membership is not a good choice as subjects for a study that is geared only for public school teachers. Unless there is some screening mechanism as to place of employment, many incomplete questionnaires will be returned because the questions were not applicable.

The representativeness of the sample is an important consideration. Stratified random sampling, as discussed in chapter 5, is sometimes used. In a questionnaire surveying the recreational preferences of a university student body, the sample should reflect the proportion of students at the different class levels. Thus, if 35% of the students are freshmen, 30% are sophomores, 20% are juniors, and 15% are seniors, then the sample should be selected according to those percentages. Similarly, if a researcher is studying school program offerings and 60% of the schools in the state have less than 200 students enrolled, then 60% of the sample should be from such schools.

The selection of the sample should be based on the variables specified to be studied.

Certainly, this affects the generalizability of the results. If an investigator specifies that the study deals with just one sex, one educational level, or one institution, and so on, then the population is narrowly defined, and it may be easy to select a representative sample of that specific population. However, the generalizations that can be made from the results are also restricted to that specific population. On the other hand, if the researcher is aiming the questionnaire at all of a specific population (e.g., all athletic directors or all fitness instructors), then the generalizability is enhanced, but the sampling procedures are made more difficult; thus, a larger sample size is required.

Sample size is important from two standpoints: (a) for adequacy in representing a population and (b) for practical considerations of time and cost. Certain formulas can be used to determine adequacy of sample size (Tuckman, 1978, p. 232). These formulas involve probability levels and the amount of sampling error deemed acceptable. The practical considerations of time and cost need attention within the planning phase of the study. Surprisingly, students often ignore these considerations until they are forced to sit down with a calculator and tabulate the costs of printing, initial mailing (which includes self-addressed, stamped return envelopes), follow-ups, scoring, and data analysis. Sometimes the costs are so substantial that a sponsoring agency or grant must be found to subsidize the study, or else the project must be narrowed or abandoned entirely. Time is also important with regard to the variability of subjects, possible seasonal influences, and various deadlines.

Constructing the Questionnaire

The notion that constructing a questionnaire is easy is a fallacy. Questions are not simply "thought up." Anyone who prepares a questionnaire and asks someone to read it soon discovers that it is not such an easy task after all. Those questions that were so clear and concise to the writer are often met with misinterpretation, perplexed frowns, and sometimes even raucous laughter.

Continually asking yourself, What specific objective is this question measuring? is one of the most valuable guidelines for writing questions. Then ask, How am I going to analyze the response? While you are writing questions, it is a good idea to prepare a blank table that includes the categories of responses, comparisons, and other breakdowns of data analysis so that you can readily determine exactly how each item will be handled and how each will contribute to the objectives of the study.

> Continually asking yourself, What specific objective is this question measuring? is one of the most valuable guidelines for writing questions.

Next, you must decide on the format for the questions, some examples of which follow.

Open-ended questions. *Open-ended questions,* such as "How do you like your job?" or "What aspects of your job do you like?" may be the easiest for the investigator to write. Such questions allow the respondent considerable latitude to express feelings and to expand on ideas. However, the several drawbacks to open-ended questions usually make them less desirable than closed questions. For example, most respondents do not like open-ended questions. For that matter, most people do not like questionnaires because they feel they are encroachments on their time. Also, open-ended questions require more time to answer than closed questions. Another drawback is the limited control as to the nature of the response: The respondent often rambles and strays from the question. Also, open-question responses are difficult to synthesize and to group into categories.

Sometimes open-ended questions are used to construct closed questions. Student evaluations, or questionnaires, are often developed by having students list all the things they like and dislike about a course. From such lists, closed questions are constructed by categorizing the open-question responses.

Closed questions. *Closed questions* come in a variety of forms (some of the measurement scales are covered in more detail in chapter 18.) A few of the more commonly used closed questions are rankings, scaled items, and categorical responses.

A *ranking* forces the subject to place responses in a rank order according to some criterion. As a result, value judgments are made, and the rankings can be summed and analyzed quantitatively. An example of a rank-order response question follows.

Rank the following activities with regard to how you like to spend leisure time. Use numbers 1-5, with 1 being the most preferred and 5 the least preferred.

___ Reading

___ Watching television

___ Arts and crafts

___ Vigorous sports such as tennis and racquetball

___ Mild exercise activity such as walking

Scaled items are one of the most commonly used types of closed questions. Subjects are asked to indicate the strength of their agreement or disagreement with some statement or to cite the relative frequency of some behavior, as in the following example:

Indicate the frequency with which you are involved in committee meetings and assignments during the academic year.

Rarely   Some-   Often   Frequently
          times

The *Likert scale* is a 5-point scale in which there is an assumption of equal intervals between responses:

In a required physical education program, students should be required to take at least one dance class.

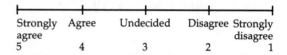

Strongly   Agree   Undecided   Disagree   Strongly
agree   disagree
5   4   3   2   1

The difference between "strongly agree" and "agree" is considered equivalent to the difference between "disagree" and "strongly disagree," and so on. Thus, the scaled responses can be treated with parametric statistics (although many researchers do not do so). Different response words can be used in scaled responses, such as "excellent," "good," "fair," "poor," "very poor," "very important," "important," "not very important," "of no importance," and so on.

Categorical responses offer the subject only two choices. Usually, the responses are "yes" and "no" or "true" and "false." An obvious limitation of categorical responses is the lack of other options such as "sometimes" or "it depends." Categorical responses do not require as much time to administer as scaled responses but also do not provide as much information as to the subject's degree of agreement or frequency of behavior.

Sometimes questions in questionnaires are keyed to the responses of other items. For example, a question might ask whether the respondent's institution offers a doctoral degree. If the subject answered ''yes,'' then he or she would be directed to answer subsequent questions about the doctoral program. If the subject answered ''no,'' the subject would be directed either to stop or to move on to the next section.

Borg and Gall (1983) have offered the following rules for constructing questionnaire items:

- The items must be clearly worded so that the items mean the same to all respondents. Avoid words that have no precise meaning, such as ''usually,'' ''most,'' and ''generally.''
- Use short questions rather than long questions because they are easier to understand.
- Do not use items that have two or more separate ideas in the same question; for example, ''Although everyone should learn how to swim, passing a swimming test should not be a requirement for graduation from college.'' This item cannot really be answered because a person might agree with the first part of the sentence but not the last or vice versa. Another example is, ''Does your department require an entrance examination for master's and doctoral students?'' This is confusing because the department may have such an examination for doctoral students but not for master's students or vice versa. If the response choices are only ''yes'' and ''no,'' a ''no'' response would indicate no examination for either program, and a ''yes'' response would mean exams for both. This should be a two-part question.
- Avoid using negative items such as ''Physical education should not be taught by coaches.'' Negative items are often confusing, and the negative word

is sometimes overlooked, causing the individual to answer in exactly the opposite way.

- Avoid technical language and jargon. Attempt to achieve clarity and the same meaning for everyone.
- Be careful that you do not bias the answer or lead the respondent to answer in a certain way. Sometimes questions can be stated in such a way that the person knows what is the ''right'' response. For example, you would know what response was expected if you encountered the question ''Since teachers work so hard, should they receive higher salaries?'' The same advice applies to the problem of threatening questions. If the respondent perceives certain items to be threatening, he or she will probably not return the questionnaire. A questionnaire on grading practices, for example, may be viewed as threatening because poor grading practices would indicate that the teachers are not doing a good job. Thus, a teacher who feels threatened either may not return the questionnaire or may give responses that seem to be ''right answers.''

Appearance and Design. Finally, the entire appearance and format of the questionnaire can have a significant bearing on the return rate. Questionnaires that appear to be poorly organized and prepared are likely to be ''filed'' in the wastebasket. Remember, many people have negative attitudes toward questionnaires, so anything that the researcher can do to overcome this negative attitude will enhance the likelihood of the questionnaire being answered. Some of the suggestions in this regard are merely cosmetic, such as the use of colored paper or an artistic design. Even little things, such as having dotted lines from the questionnaire item to the response options or grouping related items together, may pay big dividends.

The questionnaire should provide the name and address of the investigator. It is especially important that the instructions for answering the questions are clear and complete and that examples are provided for any items that are anticipated as being difficult to understand.

The first few questions should be easy to answer; the respondent is more likely to start answering easy questions and is also more apt to complete the questionnaire once he or she is committed. A poor strategy is to begin with questions that require considerable thought or time to gather information. In this regard, every effort should be made to make difficult questions as convenient to answer as possible. For example, questions that ask for enrollment figures, size of faculty, number of graduate assistants, and so on can often ask for responses in ranges (e.g., 1-10, 11-20, 21-30). First, you will probably group the responses for analysis purposes anyway. Second, the respondent can often answer range-type questions without having to consult the records or at least can supply the answers more quickly. An even more basic question to ask yourself is, Do I really need that information? or, Does it pertain to my objectives? Unfortunately, some investigators simply ask for information off the top of their heads with no consideration as to the time required to supply the answer or as to whether the information is relevant.

A general rule is that short questionnaires are more effective than long ones. According to Borg and Gall (1983), an analysis of 98 questionnaire studies showed that, on average, each page added to a questionnaire reduced the number of returns by about 0.5%. Because many people are prejudiced against questionnaires, the cover letter (which will be discussed later) and the size and appearance of the questionnaire are crucial. A

lengthy questionnaire requiring voluminous information will very likely be put aside until later if not discarded immediately.

The Pilot Study

A *pilot study* is recommended for any type of research but is imperative with a survey. Actually, the designer of a questionnaire may be well advised to do two pilot studies. The first trial run consists simply of asking a few colleagues or acquaintances to read over the questionnaire. These people can provide valuable critiques about the questionnaire format, content, expression and importance of items, and whether questions should be added or deleted.

After revising the questionnaire in accordance with the criticisms obtained in the first trial run, a sample of respondents are selected who are a part of the intended population for the second pilot study. The questionnaire is administered, and the results are subjected to item analysis (discussed in chapter 18). In some questionnaires, correlations may be run between scores on each item and the whole test to see whether the items are measuring what they are intended to measure. In all cases, responses are examined to determine whether the items seem clear and appropriate. First, questions that are answered the same by all the sample need to be evaluated; they probably lack discrimination. Those responses that are quite unexpected may indicate that the questions are poorly worded. Some rewording and other changes might also be necessary if the subjects, who might be sensitive to some questions, do not respond to them. Furthermore, the pilot study will determine whether the instructions are adequate.

A trial run of the analysis of results should always be accomplished in the pilot study. The researcher can see whether the items can be analyzed in a meaningful way and then ascertain whether some changes may be warranted for easier analysis. This is one of the most profitable outcomes of the pilot study. Of course, if substantial changes are mandated by the results of the pilot study, another pilot study is recommended to determine whether the questionnaire is ready for initial mailing.

The Cover Letter

Unquestionably, the success of the initial mailing depends largely on the effectiveness of the *cover letter* that accompanies the questionnaire. Although it has several purposes, a good cover letter should still be brief and to the point.

The cover letter should explain the purposes and importance of the survey. In other words, it should convince the respondent of the worth of the study. If the purposes are explained in a succinct and professional manner (and if the purposes are worthy of study), the respondent will likely become interested in the problem and will be inclined to cooperate.

An effective cover letter should also indicate a brief and tactful assurance of confidentiality, specifying how the respondent's privacy and anonymity will be maintained. In this regard, if anonymity is to be emphasized, then the respondent's name should not be typed on the cover letter because this might create doubt about the sincerity of the pledge of confidentiality. Therefore, a code number is a much better method of identification.

Furthermore, the cover letter should make an appeal to the importance of the respondent's cooperation. Some use of subtle flattery may be desirable with reference to the respondent's professional status and the importance of his or her response. This must be done tactfully, however, and used only when appropriate. In this situation, the person's name and address should appear on the cover letter. Preferably, a word processor should be used so that the letters look as if they were individually typed. It is insulting to try to convince persons that they have been handpicked for their expertise and valued opinions when the letters are addressed "Dear Occupant."

If the survey is endorsed by recognized agencies, associations, or institutions, specify this in the cover letter. If possible, use the organization's or institution's letterhead stationery. Respondents will be much more cooperative if some respected person or organization is supporting the study. Also acknowledge whether financial support is being given and by whom. Identify yourself by name and position. If the study is part of your thesis or dissertation, give your advisor's name. Sometimes it is advantageous if the department chairperson or dean of the college signs the letter. Then, to increase the response rate, contact subjects by letter, card, or telephone, asking for their participation in the survey. Provided the purposes of the study are worthwhile, it is usually effective at this time to offer the respondent a summary of the results. However, be sure that you follow through with your promise.

Because a questionnaire is an imposition on a person's time, strategies involving rewards and incentives are sometimes used in an effort to amuse or involve the respondent. Some questionnaires include money (perhaps a dollar) as a token of appreciation. This may appeal to a person's integrity and evoke cooperation. Then again, you may just be out a dollar. The disadvantage is that inflation plays havoc with the effects of such rewards. A quarter may have been effective years ago, whereas one or more dollars may be required to elicit the same "sense of guilt" for not responding.

The cover letter should request that the questionnaire be returned by a certain date. (This information should be specified on the questionnaire also.) When establishing the date of the return data, consider such things as the respondent's schedule of responsibilities, vacations, and so forth. Be reasonable in the time you allow the person to respond; however, with questionnaires it is advisable

not to give the respondent too much time because of the tendency to put it aside and later forget it. One week is ample time for the respondent to answer (in addition to the mailing time).

The appearance of the cover letter is just as important as the appearance of the questionnaire. Grammatical errors, misspelled words, sloppy erasures, and improper spacing and format give the respondent the impression that the author does not attach much importance to details and that the study will probably be poorly done.

Researchers have tried a number of subtle and tactful approaches to establish rapport with the respondent. Some have tried a very solemn appeal to the monumental importance of the survey, some have attempted casual humor, and others have tried a homespun, folksy approach. Obviously, the success of any approach depends on the skill of the writer and the receptiveness of the reader. Any of these attempts can backfire.

A number of years ago, one of this book's authors (Nelson) received from the head of his department a note to which a letter like this was attached:

Dear Dr. _____

It has been said: "There are two kinds of information, knowing it or knowing where to find it." I asked three men you know, Doctors Eeney, Meeney, and Moe, a certain question and each said: "Sorry. I don't know his name." But they came back with the helpful suggestion—to write to you.

Now for the question: What is the name of the person in your department or school who is in charge of your graduate program in physical education? . . .

Cordially yours,

Harry Homespun

The department head answered the letter; then, shortly thereafter, this letter arrived:

Dear Dr. Nelson:

Your good work in administering a graduate program is well known throughout our profession. Even though there are many knotty problems, everyone wants to upgrade the resources for graduate studies. But how? Because of your scholarly approach, my associates Doctors Eeney, Meeney, and Moe suggested that I write to you.

Knowledgeable leaders, like you, tell us of the ever-present struggle between physical education and the cultural lag. . . .

It has been said: "If you want to get something important done, ask a busy person." My associates tell me you are busier than a bird dog in tall grass. They also say that you have a high regard for excellence. . . . If you could find it convenient to return your checked copy on or before May 1, you might help reduce the cultural lag.

Cordially yours,

Harry Homespun

About a month later, another letter arrived:

Dear Dr. Nelson:

You're a great help. Your prompt reply was like a major league catcher, brilliantly fielded and efficiently returned. Many thanks.

Professional people in your position represent a storehouse of knowledge. Consequently, there is additional information which only you can supply. Please go over the enclosed checksheet, . . .

Your timely help is appreciated. Your good work has preceeded [sic] our correspondence. . . .

Keep up the good work.

Cordially yours,

Harry Homespun

We have, of course, omitted the main parts of the letters concerning what was being studied and what the instructions specified, but these parts were generally well done. About a year later another questionnaire arrived with the following cover letter:

Dear Dr. Nelson:

Your excellent leadership in administering graduate programs is well known throughout the profession. Because of your genuine interest in upgrading our mutual field of endeavor, my advisors Doctors Eeney, Meeney and Moe suggested that I correspond directly with you.

Scholarly graduate administrators and advisors like you often come in contact with the problems of standards. Your considered judgment is solicited in this study to arrive at some common criteria for evaluating graduate programs. . . .

Cordially yours,

Fred Folksy

Then came another letter:

Dear Dr. Nelson:

Your prompt return of the checked statements is greatly appreciated. My advisors Doctors Eeney, Meeney and Moe were certainly correct when they indicated you would gladly cooperate in this survey.

It has been said: "If you want to get something important done, ask a busy person." My associates tell me that you are busier than a bird dog in tall grass. . . .

If you could find it convenient to return your checked copy . . . you would help us reduce the cultural lag in our profession. . . .

Cordially yours,

Fred Folksy

It is safe to assume that these two graduate students had the same research methods course at the same institution. Most likely, in the discussion of the survey method, some examples of cover letters were given with different approaches. Professors Eeney, Meeney, and Moe would undoubtedly be embarrassed if they knew that the two students had written such nearly identical letters.

In most respects, the cover letters contained the essential information, and the topics were worthwhile. The authors were simply too heavy-handed in their attempts at a down-home approach, and their efforts to flatter the respondent regarding the respondent's expertise were rather obviously lacking in subtlety. The remarkable thing was that a bird dog helped reduce cultural lag.

Table 13.1 is an example of a cover letter for a questionnaire that dealt with a potentially threatening topic. The letter effectively explains to the respondent how confidentiality will be assured. Table 13.2 shows a cover letter that focuses on the importance of the topic and on the agencies endorsing the study. It also tactfully appeals to the respondent's ego.

Sending the Questionnaire

The investigator needs to carefully consider the best time for the initial mailing. Such considerations include holidays, vacations, and especially busy times of the year. A self-addressed, stamped envelope should be included. It is almost an insult to ask the respondent to answer the questionnaire and then to address an envelope and furnish a stamp to mail it back.

Other matters regarding the mailing of the questionnaire, such as establishing the date to be returned, have been covered in previous sections. The initial mailing represents a substantial cost to the sender. Securing a sponsor to underwrite or defray expenses and using

Table 13.1 Sample Cover Letter

Dear _____

Your participation in a national survey of perceived leader behavior in physical education is needed. As a doctoral student in physical education at the University of Georgia, I am conducting this study to compare and contrast male and female faculty members' perceptions of their male and female department heads' leader behavior. This institution was randomly selected to take part in this research project. Your department head has already been contacted and expressed willingness to take part in the study. I am now asking randomly selected faculty members from your institution to become involved. Your name was one of those selected to ask to participate by answering the enclosed questionnaires.

Participation will require approximately 15 minutes of your time to answer both questionnaires that will be used and to fill out an information sheet. The questionnaires and instructions as to how they are to be completed have been included with this letter in the hopes you will agree to be a participant. There is no evaluation intended or implied with this study. The instruments used describe the perceived leader behavior of the administrator. The analysis of the data will be utilized in group mean scores. Following the completion of the survey and the statistical analysis of the data, I will gladly send you a summary of the findings. All data will be dealt with confidentially and no institution or individual taking part in the study will be identified.

Hopefully, you will find time in your busy schedule to participate in this study. Thank you for your time and participation. I look forward to your early response.

Sincerely,

Kay A. Johnson

Clifford G. Lewis
Major Professor

Enclosures: 5

Note. Reprinted by permission of C.G. Lewis.

Follow-Up Procedures

This should not come as a big shock, but it is unlikely that you will get 100% return on the initial mailing. A follow-up letter is nearly always needed, and this can be done in many different ways. One approach is to wait several days after the expected return date and then to send another letter with another copy of the questionnaire and another self-addressed, stamped envelope to those who have not responded. (This is expensive, of course.) An alternative is to simply send a postcard, reminding the subject that the completed questionnaire has not been received. Then, after a few weeks send another letter, questionnaire, and self-addressed, stamped envelope. Follow-ups are effective. In a number of cases, the person has forgotten to respond, and a mere reminder will prompt a return. Other nonrespondents who had not planned to return the questionnaire may be influenced by the researcher's efforts in reiterating the significance of the study and the importance of his or her input.

The follow-up letter should be tactful. The person should not be chastised for not responding. The best approach is to write as though the person would have responded had it not been for some oversight or mistake on the part of the investigator (for an example of a follow-up letter, see Table 13.3).

Table 13.2 Sample Cover Letter

Dear _____

The responsibilities that I have in providing leadership in physical education for a large school district have caused me to give consideration to the approach needed to achieve acceptable objectives of physical fitness in the secondary boys' physical education program.

Through the cooperation of the San Diego Unified School District, the School of Education and the Physical Education Department of the University of California, Los Angeles, and the Bureau of Health Education, Physical Education and Recreation of the California State Department of Education, I am undertaking a study in the area of physical fitness. Representatives of the President's Council on Physical Fitness have said this information would be most valuable for them also. The purpose of the study is to establish criteria that can be utilized in planning activities in physical education classes for secondary aged boys (12-18) to develop and maintain selected aspects of physical fitness. The selected aspects to be considered are those commonly referred to as cardiorespiratory endurance (stamina), muscular strength and endurance, and flexibility. The information gained will be used in program planning by helping to answer such questions as these: What part of the physical education lesson should be spent on specific fitness activities (such as calisthenics, interval running, weight training, etc.) and what part of the lesson should be spent on sports and games of our culture (such as basketball, volleyball, softball, track, tennis, gymnastics, dance instruction, etc.)? What guidelines should be established in planning the specifics of physical fitness work? What physical fitness activities should be used?

A committee of exercise physiologists nominated you as a person who is qualified to comment on this topic because of your recognized position as a leader and your research in the area of physical fitness. It would be most appreciated if you would answer the enclosed questions and return them in the envelope provided at your earliest convenience. A summary of the answers will be returned to you.

Sincerely yours,

Asahel E. Hayes
Physical Education Specialist

AEH:sh
Encs.

Note. Reprinted by permission of Curriculum Services Division, San Diego City Schools.

Table 13.3 Sample Follow-Up Letter

Dear _____

I sent a questionnaire regarding criteria for planning physical fitness work in physical education classes to you a few weeks ago and have not heard from you. As you can appreciate, it is important that we obtain response from everyone possible inasmuch as only a few select individuals were contacted. Our school district is planning an immediate study and updating of its physical education program based on the results of this study so it is of vital concern.

The questionnaire was sent during the summer when you may have been away from your office. I have included another copy, however, and it would be most helpful if you could take from 30-45 minutes to give your opinions on the information requested.

Thank you so much for your cooperation.

Sincerely yours,

Asahel E. Hayes
Physical Education Specialist

AEH:ew
Encs.

Note. Reprinted by permission of Curriculum Services Division, San Diego City Schools.

Follow-ups increase the percentage of returns. Tuckman (1978) reported that ordinarily about one or two thirds of the questionnaires are returned during the first month. After this, about 10%-25% can be obtained through follow-up techniques. Most studies aim for at least a 75%-90% return rate.

Sometimes a second follow-up is carried out, usually by means of a postcard. Occasionally, telephone calls are made to nonrespondents. If a significant number (e.g., over 20%) of persons do not return the questionnaire, a serious threat is posed to the validity of the results. The overriding concern is that these nonrespondents may represent a different population than the respondents.

This is especially likely when the questionnaire deals with some sensitive area. For example, surveys about program offerings and grading practices are often not returned by schools with inadequate programs and poor grading practices. Thus, the obtained responses are apt to be biased in favor of the better programs and better teachers.

In cases in which over 20% of the questionnaires are not returned, it is recommended that a sample of the nonrespondents be surveyed. Of course, this is not easy. If people have ignored the initial mailing and one or two follow-ups, the chances are not good that they will respond to another request, but it is worth a try. The preferred technique is to randomly select a small number (e.g., 5%-10%) of the nonrespondents by using the table of random numbers (this technique is sometimes called "double-dipping"). Then contact is made either by telephone or by a special cover letter. After the responses have been obtained, comparisons are made between the answers of the nonrespondents and the answers of the subjects who responded initially. If the responses are similar, you can assume that the nonrespondents are not different from those who replied. If there are differences, then you need to either try to get a greater percentage of the nonrespondents or be sure that these differences are noted and discussed in the research report.

Analyzing the Results and Preparing the Report

These last steps are discussed in chapter 20, which deals with the results and discussion sections of the research report. The main consideration here is that the method of analysis must be decided on in the planning phase of the study. Many surveys are analyzed merely by tallying the responses to the various items and reporting the percentage of the subjects that answered one way and the percentage that answered another way. Often, not much in the way of meaningful interpretation can be gained. For example, when the researcher states simply that 18% of the respondents strongly agreed with some statement, 29% agreed, 26% disagreed, 17% strongly disagreed, and 10% had no opinion, the reader's reaction may be, "So what?" Surveys must be designed and analyzed with the same care and scientific insight as experimental studies.

The Delphi Method

The *Delphi survey method* uses questionnaires but in a different manner than the typical questionnaire survey. The Delphi technique uses a series of questionnaires in such a way that the respondents finally reach a consensus about the subject. It is basically a method of using expert opinion to help make decisions about practices, needs, and goals.

The procedures include the selection of the experts, or the informed persons who are to respond to the series of questionnaires. A set of statements or questions is prepared for consideration. The first stage in the Delphi technique, called a *round*, is mostly exploratory. The respondents are asked their opinions and evaluations on various issues, goals, and so on. Open-ended questions may be included that allow the subjects to express their views and opinions.

The questionnaire is then revised as a result of the first round and sent to the respondents, asking them to reconsider their answers in light of the analysis of all respondents to the first questionnaire. Subsequent rounds are carried out, and the "panel of experts" are given summaries of previous results and asked to revise their responses if appropriate. The group's consensus about the issue is finally achieved through the series of rounds of analysis and subsequent considered judgments. Anonymity is a prominent feature of the Delphi method, and the consensus of recognized experts in the field provides a viable means of arriving at decisions concerning important issues.

The Interview

As mentioned earlier, the steps for the *interview* and the questionnaire are basically the same. The focus here is only on the differences.

Preparing for the Interview

The most obvious difference between the questionnaire and the interview is in the gathering of the data. In this respect, the interview is more valid because the responses are apt to be more reliable; also, there is a much greater percentage of returns.

The selection of subjects should be done in the same manner as the questionnaire in terms of sampling techniques. Generally, the interview uses smaller samples, especially when a graduate student is doing the survey. Cooperation must be secured by contacting the subjects selected for interviewing. If some of the chosen subjects refuse to be interviewed, the researcher must consider possible bias to the results, as was done with nonrespondents in a questionnaire study.

To effectively conduct an interview takes a great deal of preparation. Graduate students sometimes have the impression that anyone can do it. The same procedures used with the questionnaire are followed in preparing the items, with which the interviewer must be very familiar. The researcher must carefully rehearse the interview techniques. One of the sources of invalidity is that the interviewer tends to improve with experience, and thus the results of earlier interviews may differ from interviews conducted later in the study. A pilot study is very important. The interviewer can make sure the vocabulary level is appropriate and that the questions will be equally meaningful given the ages and educational backgrounds of the subjects who are surveyed.

Training is required in making initial contact and presenting the verbal cover letter by phone. At the meeting, the interviewer must establish rapport and make the person feel at ease. If a tape recorder will be used, permission must be obtained. If a tape recorder will not be used, then the interviewer must have an efficient system of coding the responses without consuming too much time and appearing to be taking dictation. The interviewer must not inject his or her own bias into the conversation and certainly should not argue with the respondent. Although there are many advantages of the interview over the questionnaire with regard to the flexibility of the questioning, there is also the danger of straying from the questions and getting off the subject. The interviewer must tactfully keep the respondent from rambling, and this requires skill.

The key to getting good information is to ask good questions. We have all been impressed by watching really good interviewers on television. What makes them good? There is no single answer to this question. Certainly, the personality of the interviewer is a factor, but good interviewers have quite different personalities. Some are even rather obnoxious. Some are friendly and supportive with the interviewees, some seem to badger the people, and some play the devil's advocate in their questioning. Good interviewers do not ask yes-or-no questions, they do not ask multiple questions in a single question, and they try to avoid inserting their own points of view. Table 13.4 contains some basic types of questions and some examples. See if you recognize these approaches from interviews you have seen on television.

The interview has the following advantages over the questionnaire:

- The interview is more adaptable. Questions can be rephrased and further questions asked.
- The interview is more versatile with regard to the personality and receptiveness of the respondent.
- The interviewer can observe how the person responds and can thus achieve greater insight into the sensitivity of the topic and the intensity of feelings from

Table 13.4 Four Questions Used in the Interview Process

Type of question	Example
Hypothetical: Asks what the respondent might do or what it might be like in a certain situation; it usually begins with "What if" or "Suppose"	Suppose this is my first day of student teaching. What would it be like?
Devil's advocate: Challenges the respondent to consider an opposing view	Some people would say that professional education courses are of no value for the student-teaching experience. What would you say to them?
Ideal position: Asks the respondent to describe an ideal situation	What do you think the ideal prestudent-teaching and teaching programs should be like?
Interpretive: Advances tentative interpretation of what the respondent has been saying and asks for a reaction	Would you say that the student-teaching experience is different from what you expected?

Note. From Merriam (1988, p. 80). Copyright 1988 by Jossey-Bass. Adapted by permission.

the respondent. This can considerably add to the validity of the results as it is one of the greatest threats to validity in questionnaire studies.

- Because each person is contacted before the interview, interviews have a greater rate of return. Moreover, people tend to be more willing to talk than to fill out a questionnaire. A certain amount of ego is involved because a person feels more flattered to be interviewed than only being sent a questionnaire.

The Telephone Interview

Interviewing by telephone is becoming more prevalent. Some of the advantages of telephone interviewing over face-to-face interviewing follow:

- Telephone interviewing is less expensive. The use of WATS lines and other reduced-cost plans greatly lessens the costs of conducting an interview study. One study (Graves & Kahn, 1979) reported that telephone interviews cost about half as much as personal interviews.
- The interviewer can work from a central location, which facilitates the monitoring and the quality control of the interviews and provides a better opportunity for using computer-assisted interviewing techniques (Borg & Gall, 1983).
- Many people are more easily reached by telephone than by personal visitation.
- The telephone interview enables the researcher to reach a wide geographical area, which is a limitation of the personal interview. This advantage also can increase the validity of the sampling.
- There is some evidence that persons will respond more candidly to sensitive questions over the telephone than in personal interviews, in which the presence of the interviewer may inhibit some responses.

The use of the microcomputer in telephone interviewing provides an excellent means of data collection and analysis. Microcomputers can be used in several ways in the data-gathering process. For example, the microcomputer displays the questions for the interviewer to ask, and then the interviewer types the subject's responses. Each response triggers the next question, thus eliminating the turning of many pages and the likelihood of asking inappropriate questions. This is most helpful when some responses are linked to further questions that may be on a page other than the actual questionnaire. In addition, the responses are stored for analysis (thus reducing scoring errors), and the stored responses can then be called out for statistical analysis.

An obvious limitation of telephone interviewing is that some people do not have telephones. Although this needs to be considered (especially in sampling the poor), the percentage of adults who do not have telephones is actually quite small. The problem of unlisted numbers can be mostly overcome by using a table of random numbers to select the four numbers after the three-number exchange. You can reach both listed and unlisted numbers by this method. Dillman (1978) has provided a comprehensive discussion of the relative advantages and disadvantages of the telephone survey.

The Normative Survey

The *normative survey* is not described in most research methods textbooks. As is implied in the name, this method involves establishing norms for abilities, performances, beliefs, and attitudes. A cross-sectional approach is used in that samples of people of different ages, genders, and other classifications are selected and measured.

The steps in the normative survey are generally the same as in the questionnaire, the basic difference being in the manner in which the data are collected. The researcher selects the most appropriate tests to measure the desired performances or abilities, such as the components of physical fitness.

The American Alliance for Health, Physical Education, Recreation and Dance (AAHPERD) has sponsored several normative surveys. Probably the most notable was the Youth Fitness Test (see AAHPER, 1958), conducted in response to the furor caused by the results of the Kraus-Weber test (Kraus & Hirschland, 1954), which had revealed that American children were inferior to European children in minimum muscular fitness. The Youth Fitness Test was originally given to 8,500 boys and girls in a nationwide sample. Follow-up testing was done, and the norms were updated in 1965 and 1975.

In the AAHPER normative survey, a seven-item motor fitness test battery was determined by a committee. The University of Michigan Survey Research Center selected a representative sample of boys and girls in Grades 5-12. Initial contact was made requesting each school's cooperation. Directions for giving the test items were prepared, and physical education teachers in various parts of the country were selected and trained to administer and supervise the testing.

In any normative survey, it is important that the testing be administered in a rigidly standardized manner. Deviations in the way measurements are taken give meaningless results. The data from the survey are collected and analyzed by some norming method, such as percentiles, T scores, or stanines. Norms are constructed for the different categories of age, sex, and so on.

In addition, AAHPERD conducted a sport skills testing project, which involved establishing norms for skills of boys and girls of different ages in a number of sports. The National Children and Youth Fitness Study (Phase I, 1985; Phase II, 1987) was a norma-tive survey that resulted in norms for a health-related physical fitness test. The test battery included measures of cardiovascular condition (distance run), body composition (skinfolds), the strength and endurance of the abdominal muscles (sit-ups) and the arm and shoulder muscles (pull-ups and modified pull-ups), and the flexibility of the muscles of the posterior thigh and lower back (sit-and-reach).

> In any normative survey, it is important that the testing be administered in a rigidly standardized manner. Deviations in the way measurements are taken give meaningless results.

Sometimes comparisons are made between the norms of different populations. In other studies, the major purpose is simply to establish norms. The primary drawbacks to any normative survey are in the selection of tests to measure the behavior in question and the standardization of testing procedures in the gathering of the data. The problem with the selection of the testing instrument is the danger of generalizing on the basis of specific tests. For example, if one test item (such as pull-ups) is used to measure a particular component (strength), too much importance may be placed on the score. In other words, pull-ups are decidedly influenced (adversely) by body weight and primarily involve the arm and shoulder muscle groups. Strength in other parts of the body is not being assessed, and the assumption cannot be made that a person who does well (or poorly) in pull-ups would perform the same way in other strength tests.

This question of test selection is important in any type of research. The standardization of testing procedures is essential for establishing norms. However, when a normative survey involves a number of different testers from different parts of the country, this becomes a source of possible measurement error. Published test descriptions simply cannot address all the aspects of test administration and the ways of handling the many problems of interpreting procedures that arise. Extensive training of testers is the answer, but this is often impossible from a logistical standpoint.

DEVELOPMENTAL RESEARCH

Developmental research implies the study of changes in behavior across the lifespan. Although much of the developmental research has focused on infancy, childhood, and adolescence, research on senior citizens and even across the total human lifespan is increasingly common.

Longitudinal and Cross-Sectional Designs

The focus of developmental research involves cross-age comparisons. For example, children at ages 6, 8, and 10 could be compared on how far they can jump; or, adults at 45, 55, and 65 could be compared on their knowledge of the effects of obesity on life expectancy. Both of these are developmental studies. One of the major characteristics of developmental studies is whether the same subjects are followed over time (longitudinal design) or whether different subjects are selected at each age level (cross-sectional design).

Longitudinal studies are powerful because the changes in behavior across the timespan of interest are within the same subjects. However, longitudinal designs are time consuming. A longitudinal study of children's jumping performance at ages 6, 8, and 10 obviously requires 4 years to complete.

That is probably not a very wise choice of designs for a master's thesis. Longitudinal designs have additional problems besides the time required to complete them. First, over the several years of the study, some of the subjects are likely to move away when parents change jobs; or school districts may rezone attendance, causing the subjects to be spread out over several schools. In longitudinal studies of senior citizens, some will die over the course of the study. The problem with a loss of subjects is knowing whether the sample characteristics remain the same when subjects are lost. For example, when children are lost from the sample when parents change jobs, is the sample then composed of children of lower socioeconomic levels because the more affluent parents move? Furthermore, if obesity is related to longevity, are older citizens more likely to be less obese and consequently have increased knowledge because the more obese subjects with less knowledge have died? Thus, knowledge about obesity may not be changing from ages 45 to 65; rather, the sample is changing.

Another problem with longitudinal designs is that subjects become increasingly familiar with the test items, and the items may cause changes in behavior. The knowledge inventory on obesity may prompt subjects to seek information about obesity, thus changing their knowledge, attitudes, and behaviors. Therefore, the next time they complete the knowledge inventory, they have gained knowledge. However, this gain of knowledge is the result of having been exposed to the test earlier and might not have occurred without that exposure.

Cross-sectional studies are usually less time consuming to carry out. These studies involve testing several age-groups (e.g., 6, 8, and 10) at the same point in time. Although cross-sectional studies are more time efficient than longitudinal studies, a problem called *cohorts* exists: Are all the age-groups really from the same population (group of cohorts)? Asked another way, are environmental circumstances that affect jumping performance the same today for 6-year-olds as when the 10-year-olds were 6 or have physical education programs improved over this 4-year span so that 6-year-olds receive more instruction and practice in jumping than the 10-year-olds did when they were 6? If the latter is the case, then we are not looking at the development of jumping performance but rather at some uninterpretable interaction between "normal" development and the effects of instruction. The cohort problem exists in all cross-sectional studies.

An example of a longitudinal developmental study is that of Halverson, Roberton, and Langendorfer (1982), who studied the throwing velocity of the overarm throw of children from early elementary school through junior high school. Thomas et al. (1983) provided an example of a cross-sectional developmental study in which they looked at the development of memory for distance information by selecting different age-groups. Then they compared the effects of a practiced strategy for remembering distance at each age level to show that the appropriate use of strategy reduces age differences in remembering distance. Each of these studies suffers from the specific defects associated with the type of developmental design. Halverson et al. (1982) had a loss of subjects over the several years of the study, whereas Thomas et al. could not establish if their younger subjects were more familiar with memory strategies than the older subjects were when they were younger.

Although both longitudinal and cross-sectional designs have some problems, they are the only means available to study development. Thus, both are needed and are important parts of the research process. These two types of designs are considered descriptive research. However, either may be

considered experimental research (chapter 14); that is, an independent variable may be manipulated within an age-group. In the Thomas et al. (1983) study, the use of strategy was manipulated within each of the three age-groups. Thus, age was a categorical variable, whereas strategy was a true independent variable. This point is addressed here because developmental research will not be covered in chapter 14 on experimental research.

Methodological Problems

Whether the developmental research is longitudinal or cross-sectional, a number of methodological problems exist (for a more detailed discussion, see Thomas, 1984).

Unrepresentative Scores

One of the most common problems is an unrepresentative score. These scores, called outliers, occur in all research but are particularly problematic at the extremes of developmental research (children and senior citizens). Outliers frequently result from shorter attention spans, distraction, and lack of motivation to do the task. The best way to handle these unrepresentative scores is to

1. plan the testing situation within a reasonable time limit that accounts for attention span,
2. set up the testing situation where distractions cannot occur, and
3. be aware of what an unrepresentative score is and retest when one occurs.

The last thing a researcher wants to do is use unrepresentative scores. Therefore, outliers not detected at testing should be found when the distribution of the data is studied. There are several ways to test for these extreme and unrepresentative scores (e.g., see Barnett & Lewis, 1978). The most important fact is that the developmental researcher should expect and plan for handling outliers in the data set.

Semantics

A second problem in developmental research involves semantics. Selecting the words to use in explaining the task to various age-groups of children is a formidable one. If the researcher is not careful, older children will perform better than younger children, only because they grasp the idea of what to do more quickly. Although the standard rule in good research is to give identical instructions to all the subjects, this rule must be bent for developmental studies with children. The researcher must explain the testing situation in a way the subject can understand, and tangible evidence must be obtained that the variously aged subjects did understand the testing situation before the test was conducted. This frequently involves having the subject demonstrate the activity to some criterion level of performance before collecting the data.

A good example of this problem involved a group of early elementary school children taking a computer course through a continuing education program at a local college. The children were doing fine until the teacher (a college instructor of computer science) began to write instructions on the blackboard. Then everyone stopped working. Finally, one of the children whispered to the teacher, "Some of us can't read cursive." After the teacher printed the instructions in block letters, all the children happily returned to their computing work (Chronicle of Higher Education, 1983).

Lack of Reliability

A third developmental research problem involves the lack of reliability in younger children's performances. When a performance score is obtained for a child, it should be a reliable one; that is, if the child is tested again, the performance score should be about the same. Obtaining reliable performance is frequently a problem with younger children for many of the same reasons that outliers occur. Of course, making sure the child understands the task must be the first consideration and maintaining motivation the second. A task that can be made fun and enjoyable is more likely to elicit a consistent performance. This can be done by the use of cartoon figures, encouragement, and rewards (for some ideas on how cartoon figures can be used to improve motivation on many gross motor tasks, see Herkowitz, 1984). The developmental researcher should maintain frequent reliability checks during testing sessions (for appropriate techniques, see chapter 16).

Statistical Problems

The final developmental problem to mention is a statistical one. A frequent means of making cross-age comparisons is to use ANOVA, an assumption of which (see chapter 7) is that the groups being compared have equal variances (spread of scores about the mean). This assumption may often be violated in making cross-age comparisons. Depending on the nature of the task, older children may have considerably larger or smaller variances than younger children. A developmental researcher should be aware of this potential issue and some of the solutions. In particular, pilot work using the tasks of interest in the research should provide insight into this problem.

Protecting Subjects

The protection of human subjects in research was discussed in chapter 4. Of course, this protection also pertains to children. Permission of parents or guardians is required for minors to participate in research. This permission should be obtained in the way it is for adult subjects, except that the explanation and consent forms are given to the parents or guardians. When minors are old enough to understand the methodology, their consent should also be obtained. This means explaining the purpose of the research in terms children can understand. Most public and private schools have their own requirements concerning approval of research studies.

The normal sequence of events involves

- planning the research;
- acquiring approval of the university's committee for protection of human subjects;
- locating and getting the approval of the school system, the school involved, and the teachers; and
- getting the approval of parents and, when appropriate, students.

You can see that a good deal of paperwork is required. Thus, beginning the process well in advance of the time you plan to begin data collection is necessary.

Summarizing Developmental Research

In summary, developmental research is an important type of study that generally involves either longitudinal or cross-sectional designs. Each design has some flaws, but each also has strengths that the other lacks. In particular, the researcher must be aware of several methodological problems existing in developmental studies. Although developmental studies have been presented in this chapter on descriptive research, they frequently may be experimental or quasi-experimental in nature. Finally, the researcher must be especially careful in protecting the rights of children as subjects in developmental research.

THE CASE STUDY

In the case study, the researcher strives for an in-depth understanding of a single situation or phenomenon. This technique is used in many fields, including anthropology, clinical psychology, sociology, medicine, political science, speech pathology, and various educational areas such as disciplinary problems and reading difficulties. It has been used considerably in the health sciences and to some extent in exercise science, sport science, and physical education.

The *case study* is a form of descriptive research. Whereas the survey method obtains a rather limited amount of information about many subjects, the case study gathers a large amount of information about one or a few subjects. Although the study consists of a rigorous, detailed examination of a single case, the underlying assumption is that this case is an example of many other such cases. Consequently, through the in-depth study of a single case, a greater understanding about similar cases is achieved. This is not to say, however, that the purpose of case studies is to make generalizations. On the contrary, drawing inferences about a population from a case study is not justifiable. On the other hand, the findings of a number of case studies may play a part in the inductive reasoning that is involved in the development of a theory.

The case study is not confined to the study of an individual but can be used in research involving programs, institutions, organizations, political structures, communities, and situations. The case study is used in qualitative research in dealing with critical problems of practice and extending the knowledge base of the various aspects of education, physical education, exercise science, and sport science (qualitative research is discussed in chapter 15).

Information about case study methodology is rather difficult to find. As Merriam (1988) observed, material on case study research strategies can be found everywhere and nowhere. Methodological material on case study research is scattered about in journal articles, conference proceedings, and research reports of the many different fields that use this form of research. A brief summary of the weaknesses and strengths of the technique can usually be found in most research methods textbooks. Moreover, most research methods courses do not deal with the case study except in a very cursory manner.

Consequently, most students do not consider the case study approach as a means of solving research problems, and those who do attempt case studies must either find someone to tutor them or else spend a great deal of time locating methodological material in the various journals and other sources. Frustration in trying to find substantive material about case study research in an educational setting prompted Merriam (1988) to write her interesting and informative text *Case Study Research in Education*.

Types of Case Studies

In many ways, case study research is similar to other forms of research. It involves the identification of the problem, the collection of data, and the analysis and reporting of results. As with other research techniques, the approach and the analysis depend on the nature of the research problem. Case studies can be descriptive, interpretive, or evaluative.

Descriptive Studies

A descriptive case study presents a detailed picture of the phenomena but does not attempt to test or build theoretical models. Sometimes, descriptive case studies are historical in nature, and sometimes they are done for the purpose of achieving a better understanding of the present status. Descriptive case studies frequently serve as an initial step or data base for subsequent comparative research and theory building (Merriam, 1988).

Interpretive Studies

Interpretive case studies also employ description, but the major focus is to interpret the data in an effort to classify and conceptualize the information and perhaps theorize about the phenomena. For example, a researcher might use the case study approach to reach greater understanding about the cognitive processes involved in sport.

Evaluative Studies

Evaluative case studies also involve description and interpretation, but the primary purpose is to use the data to evaluate the merit of some practice, program, movement, or event. The efficacy of this type of case study relies on the competence of the researcher to use the available information to make judgments (Guba & Lincoln, 1981). The case study approach enables a more in-depth, holistic approach to the problem than may be possible with survey studies.

Case Study Subjects

Subjects in a case study depend, of course, on the problem being studied. The subject (or case) may be a person (student, teacher, or coach), a program (Little League baseball), an institution (a one-room school), a project (Basic Stuff), or a concept (mainstreaming). In most cases, random sampling is not used because the purpose of a case study is not to estimate some population value but to select subjects from which one can learn the most. Chein (1981) used the term *purposive sampling*. Goetz and LeCompte (1984) referred to this concept as *criterion-based sampling*. The researcher establishes criteria necessary for being included in the study, then finds a sample that meets the criteria. Criteria may include age, years of experience, evidence of level of expertise, and situation and environment. The subject, or case, may be one classroom that meets certain criteria or a state that is involved in a specific program.

Characteristics of the Case Study

The case study involves the collection and analysis of many sources of information. In some respects, the case study has some of the same features found in historical research. Although it consists of intensive study of a single unit, it may be that the case study's ultimate worth is an insight and knowledge of a general nature and improved practices. The generalizability of a case study is ultimately related to what the reader is trying to learn from it (Kennedy, 1979). The case study approach is probably most frequently used in trying to understand why something has gone wrong.

Gathering and Analyzing Data

The case study is very flexible as to the amount and type of data that are gathered as well as to the procedures used in gathering the data. Thus, the steps in the methodology are not distinct or uniform with all case studies.

Data for case studies can be interviews, observations, or documents. It is not uncommon for a case study to employ all three types of data. A case study involving a child, for example, may include interviews with the child and the child's teachers and parents. The researcher may systematically observe the child in the class or in some other setting. Documents could include medical examination reports, physical performance test scores,

achievement test results, grades, interest inventories, scholastic aptitude tests, teacher anecdotal records, and autobiographies. As noted previously, some case studies are mainly descriptive, others focus on interpretation, and others are evaluative. Some case studies propose and test hypotheses, whereas some attempt to build theories through inductive processes.

Analysis of data in a case study is a formidable task because of the nature of the data and the massive amount of information to analyze. According to Merriam (1988), data collection and analysis continues and intensifies after the data have been collected. The data must be sorted, categorized, and interpreted. As in any research, the ultimate value of a study rests on the insight, sensitivity, and integrity of the researcher, who, in the case study, is the primary instrument in the collection and analysis of the data. This is both a strength and a weakness. It is a weakness if the researcher fails to use the appropriate sources of information. The researcher can also be guilty of either oversimplifying the situation or exaggerating the actual state of affairs (Guba & Lincoln, 1981). On the other hand, a competent researcher can use the case study to provide a thorough, holistic account of a complex problem.

Application in Physical Education

Several case studies in physical education were directed by H. Harrison Clarke at the University of Oregon (Clarke & Clarke, 1970). The studies dealt with persons of low (and high) fitness levels. Most of the studies sought to discover factors that may contribute to low fitness or the substrength individual. A remarkable example of the case study approach and effective follow-up was seen in a demonstration project undertaken by Frederick Rand Roger and Fred E. Palmer (Clarke, 1967, 1968). Twenty junior high school boys with the lowest physical fitness scores were studied as to the cause of low fitness. Information used included somatotype, IQ, academic scholarship, medical history, and status. A follow-up project involved individual attention and special class meetings. Through exercises, improved health habits, medical referrals, and counseling, vast improvements were reported in fitness, scholarship, and behavior. An example of a recent case study was in the area of pedagogy by Werner and Rink (1989), who described the teaching behaviors of four teachers.

One of the principal advantages of the case study approach is that it can be fruitful in formulating new ideas and hypotheses about problem areas, especially areas for which there is no clear-cut structure or model. The researcher selects the case study method because of the nature of the research questions being asked. The case study, when used effectively, can play an important role in contributing to knowledge in our field.

JOB ANALYSIS

A *job analysis* could be considered a type of case study. It is a technique designed to determine the nature of a particular job and the types of training, preparation, skills, and attitudes necessary for success in the job.

Job analyses are regularly done in fields such as counseling and vocational training. There have been a few such studies in physical education, exercise science, and sport science that have dealt with administrative positions, intramural duties, and coaching and teaching responsibilities.

The procedures vary in conducting a job analysis. The objective is to obtain as much relevant information as possible about the job and the job requirements. One method is to observe someone in the particular occupation. Of course, this is time consuming and

probably bothersome for the person in the job. Nevertheless, the procedure is recommended because the researcher can acquire a kind of vicarious on-the-job experience and gain valuable insight into the whole atmosphere connected with the occupation. A limitation to this method is the lack of sufficient time to observe all facets of the job, particularly seasonal duties and responsibilities.

Questionnaires and interviews are effective job analysis techniques to use to elicit a person's responses to the kinds of duties performed, the types and degree of preparation required or recommended for accomplishing the tasks, and the perceived advantages and disadvantages of the job.

The limitations of the job analysis as a research technique include the fallibility of memory and self-reports. There may be a tendency to accent either the positive or the negative aspects of the job, depending on the time, the circumstances, and the subject. Also, there is the danger that the approach can be too mechanical, thus neglecting some of the more abstract aspects of the job and its requirements.

OBSERVATIONAL RESEARCH

Observation is used in a variety of research endeavors. It provides a means of collecting data and is a descriptive method of researching certain problems. In the questionnaire and interview techniques, the researcher relies on self-reports as to how the subject behaves or what the subject believes. A weakness of self-reports is that persons may not be candid as to what they really do or feel and may give what they perceive to be socially desirable responses. An alternative descriptive research technique is for the researcher to observe subjects' behavior and use qualitative or quantitative analysis of the observations. Some educators claim that this yields more accurate data. There are, of course, several limitations to observational research.

Basic considerations in observational research include the following:

- What behaviors will be observed?
- Who will be observed?
- Where will the observations be conducted?
- How many observations will be made?
- When will the observations be made?
- How will the observations be scored and evaluated?

Many other considerations are connected to these basic ones. Depending on the problem and the setting, each individual investigation has its own unique procedures. Therefore, only the basic considerations can be discussed in rather general terms.

What Behaviors Will Be Observed?

This consideration relates to the statement of the problem and to the operational definitions. For example, a study on teacher effectiveness must have clearly defined observational measures of teacher effectiveness. Definite behaviors must be observed, for example, the extent to which the teacher asks students questions. Some other aspects of teacher effectiveness include giving individual attention, demonstrating skills, dressing appropriately for activities, and starting class on time. The researcher, in determining what behaviors will be observed, must also limit the scope of the observations to make the study manageable.

Who Will Be Observed?

As with any study, the population from which samples will be drawn must be determined. Will the study focus only on elemen-

tary school teachers? Which grades? Will the study include only physical education specialists, or will it also include classroom teachers who teach physical education? There is also the question about the number of teachers who will be observed. Will the study include observations of students in addition to teachers? In other words, the researcher must describe precisely who the subjects of the study will be.

Where Will the Observations Be Conducted?

The setting for the observations must be considered in addition to the basic considerations regarding the size of the sample and the geographical area. Will the setting be unnatural or natural? Using an unnatural setting means bringing the subject to a laboratory, room, or other locale for the observations.

There are some advantages to an unnatural setting in terms of control and of freedom from distractions. For example, a one-way mirror is advantageous for observation as it removes the influence of the observer on the behavior of the subject. That behavior is affected by the presence of an observer is also shown in classroom situations. When the observer first arrives, the students (and perhaps the teacher) are curious about the observer's presence. Consequently, they may behave differently than they would if the observer were not there. The teacher may also act differently, possibly by perceiving the observer as a threat or being aware of the purpose of the observations. In any case, the researcher should not make observations on the initial visit. Allowing the subjects to become gradually accustomed to the observer's presence is best.

Whether the subject will be observed alone or in a group is also related to setting. In a natural setting, such as the playground or classroom, the subject may behave more typically, but there will also likely be more extraneous influences on behavior.

How Many Observations Will Be Made?

As with most measurements, the more observations, the better, due to the increased reliability gained when more trials or observations are used. However, there are obvious practical considerations with respect to feasibility; therefore, the researcher must decide on how many observations may realistically be made.

Many factors determine the decision of how many observations will be made. First are the operationally defined behaviors in question and the time constraints of the study itself. For example, if a person is studying the amount of activity or participation of students in a physical education class, several considerations must be made. First, the type of activity unit and the number of units encompassed in the study must be decided on in the planning phase of the study. The number of observations for each activity is dependent on the particular stage of learning in the unit, whether in the introductory phase, the practice stage, the playing stage, and so on. This must be specified in the operational definitions, of course, but both the length of the unit and the subsequent length of each stage within each unit play major roles in determining the number of observations that are feasible.

Another factor to consider is the number of observers. If only one person is doing the observations, either the number of students (subjects) being observed or the number of observations per subject (or both) will be restricted. To attempt to generalize from observing a few subjects on a few occasions as to their "typical" behavior is hazardous.

Some types of behavior may not be manifested very frequently. Sportsmanship, aggression, leadership, and other traits (as operationally defined) are not readily observable because of the lack of opportunity to display such traits (among other things). The occasion must present itself, and the elements of the situation must materialize in a way that the student has the opportunity to react. Consequently, the number of observations is bound to be extremely limited if left to chance occurrence. On the other hand, situations that are contrived to provoke certain behavior are often unsuccessful because of their artificiality.

We cannot say how many observations are necessary but can only warn against too few observations; thus, we recommend a combination of feasibility and measurement considerations. This question is readdressed in the discussion on scoring and evaluating observations.

> To attempt to generalize from observing a few subjects on a few occasions as to their "typical" behavior is hazardous.

When Will the Observations Be Made?

You can easily observe that all the basic considerations being discussed are related and overlap with one another. The determination of when to make the observations includes decisions about time of day, day of the week, phase in the learning experience, season, and other time factors.

In reference to our previous example of observing the amount of student activity in a physical education course, different results would be expected if the observations were made at the beginning of the unit than if they were made at the end. Also, allowing the subjects to get used to the situation so that the observational procedures do not interfere with normal activity is another consideration. In observing student teachers, for example, differences would certainly be expected if some were observed at the beginning of their student-teaching experience and others at the end of the semester.

Graduate students encounter major problems with regard to time and observational research. They find it difficult to spend the time necessary to make a sufficient number of observations to provide reliable results. Furthermore, graduate students usually must gather the data by themselves, making it much more time consuming than if other observers were available.

How Will the Observations Be Scored and Evaluated?

A number of techniques are employed for recording observational data. Great strides have been made in recent years in this respect. The use of microcomputers and other computer-assisted event-recording methods have alleviated many of the technical problems that plagued observational research in the past. Significant advancements will undoubtedly be made in the future in the speed and accuracy of entering and analyzing data.

Some of the more commonly used procedures for recording observational data include

- narrative, or continual recording;
- tallying, or frequency counting;
- the interval method; and
- the duration method.

The *narrative*, or *continual recording*, *method* involves the researcher recording in a series of sentences the occurrences he or she observes as they happen. This is the slowest and least efficient method of recording. The

observer must be able to select the most important information to record because everything that occurs in a given situation cannot possibly be recorded. Probably the best use of this technique is in helping to develop more efficient recording instruments. The researcher first uses the continuous method and then develops categories for future recording from the narrative.

The *tallying*, or *frequency counting*, *method* involves recording each time a certain behavior occurs. The behavior must be clearly defined. The frequency counts are made within a certain time frame, such as the number of occurrences in 10 minutes or 30 minutes per session.

The *interval method* is used when the researcher wishes to record whether the behavior in question occurs in a certain interval of time. This method is useful when it is difficult to count individual occurrences. One of the leading standardized systems for interval recording is the Flanders' Interaction Analysis System (Flanders, 1970), in which the observer records the behavior of the subject according to 10 specific behavior classifications within each time interval. All classroom behavior can be classified into 1 of the 10 categories. In the simplest interval system, the observer merely records whether the subject exhibits the prescribed behavior in a given interval of time. Sometimes the time intervals are selected randomly or on some fixed basis rather than by continuous observation. Thus, a form of time sampling can be employed.

The *Academic Learning Time in Physical Education (ALT-PE)* is an observational instrument developed by Siedentop and graduate students at Ohio State University (Siedentop, Birdwell, & Metzler, 1979; Siedentop, Trousignant, & Parker, 1982) for use in physical education. It entails time sampling in which a child is observed for a specified period of time, and the child's activities during that time period are coded. The recording system encompasses (a) the setting or learning environment established by the teacher; (b) the content of the instruction, such as skills, practice, knowledge, and game playing; (c) the responses of the learner whether engaged or not engaged in the content of the lesson; and (d) the difficulty of the responses when the learner is engaged in the activity.

The *Cheffers' Adaptation of the Flanders' Interaction Analysis System (CAFIAS)* was developed by Cheffers (1972/1973) to allow systematic observation of physical education classes and classroom situations. The CAFIAS provides a device for coding nonverbal behavior through a double category system so that any behavior can be categorized as verbal, nonverbal, or both. The CAFIAS permits the coding of the class as a whole when the entire class is functioning as one unit, when the class is divided into small groups, or when the students are working individually or independently with no teacher influence.

The *duration method* involves some timed behavior. The researcher uses a stopwatch or other timing device to record how much time a subject spends engaged in a particular behavior. A number of studies have used this method in observing student time on-task and off-task. In the previous example about the amount of activity in a physical education class, a researcher could simply record the amount of time a student spends in actual participation or the amount of time spent standing in line or waiting to perform. The researcher usually observes a subject for a given unit of time (e.g., a class period), starting and stopping a stopwatch as the behavior starts and stops so that a cumulative time on-task (or off-task) is recorded.

Videotape

A potentially invaluable instrument for observational research is the videotape. Its greatest advantage is that the researcher need not worry about recording observations at the time the behavior is occurring. Furthermore, it is possible for a number of persons to be observed at one time. For example, teachers and students can be observed simultaneously, which is difficult in normal observational techniques. In addition, the videotape can be replayed as often as needed to evaluate the behavior, and a permanent record can be retained.

The use of videotape does have some disadvantages. It is expensive, the filming requires a significant degree of technical competence for lighting and positioning, and it may be cumbersome at times to follow the action. The presence of a camera may also alter behavior to the extent that the subjects do not behave normally. However, if the disadvantages can be resolved, videotaping can be an effective process for observational research.

Weaknesses in Observational Research

Problems and limitations of observational research include the following:

- A primary danger in observational research lies in the operational definitions of the study. The behaviors must be carefully defined to be observable. Consequently, the actions may be so restricted that they do not depict the critical behavior. For example, teacher effectiveness encompasses many behaviors, and to observe only the number of times the teacher asked questions or gave individual attention may be inadequate samples of effectiveness.
- Effectively using observation forms requires much practice. Inadequate training, therefore, represents a major pitfall in this form of research. Also, there are difficulties encountered in trying to ob-

serve too many things. Often, the observation form is too ambitious for one person to use.

- Certain behaviors cannot be evaluated as finely as some of the observation forms dictate. A common mistake is to ask the observer to make discriminations that are too precise, thus reducing the reliability of the ratings.
- The presence of the observer almost always affects the behavior of the subjects. The researcher must be aware of this and try to reduce the amount of disturbance.
- Generally, observational research is greatly expedited by having more than one observer. Failure to use more than one observer results in decreased efficiency and objectivity.
- As with other forms of descriptive research, there must be sufficient numbers of subjects and observations per subject to have adequate internal and external validity. A study with only a handful of subjects on which a small number of observations are made before and after some treatment intervention contributes little to the body of knowledge concerning teacher-student behavior analysis.

OTHER UNOBTRUSIVE RESEARCH MEASURES

There are multiple methods of gathering information about people other than questionnaires, case studies, and observation. Webb, Campbell, Schwartz, and Sechrest (1966) discussed different approaches that they term "unobtrusive measures." Some examples they mentioned include the replacement rate for floor tiles around museum exhibits as a measure of relative popularity of exhibits. The degree of fear caused by telling ghost stories to children has been assessed by

observing the shrinking diameter of the circle of seated children. Dilation of the pupils of the eyes has been used as an index of fear and interest. Boredom has been measured by the amount of fidgeting movements in an audience. The rate of library withdrawals of fiction and nonfiction books has been studied to determine the impact of television in communities. Children's interest in Christmas has been demonstrated by the size of their drawings of Santa Claus and the amount of distortion in the figures.

In some of the methods (such as those just mentioned), the experimenter is not present when the data are being produced. There are conditions, however, when the researcher is present but still acts in a nonreactive manner. In other words, the subjects are not aware that the researcher is gathering data. For example, a researcher in psychology measured the degree of acceptance of strangers among delinquent boys by measuring the distance maintained between a delinquent boy and a new boy whom the researcher introduced to the delinquent subject. Sometimes, the researcher intervenes to speed up the action or force the data but in a manner that does not attract attention to the method. In studying the cathartic effect of activity on aggression, Ryan (1970) had an accomplice behave in an obnoxious manner and then measured the amount of electric shock the subjects administered to that accomplice and to "innocent" bystanders. Other researchers have intervened by causing subjects to fail or succeed so that responses to winning and losing in competitive situations could be observed.

Unobtrusive measures also include a multitude of records such as birth certificates, political and judicial records, actuarial records, magazines, newspapers, archives, and inscriptions on tombstones. An interesting use of city records (Webb et al., 1966) was the analysis of city water pressure as an index of television viewing interest. Immediately after a television show, the water pressure dropped as drinks were obtained and toilets flushed. Mabley (1963) presented data on Chicago's water pressure on the day of an exciting Rose Bowl game that showed a drastic drop in pressure at the time of the game's end.

The issue of ethics arises in some forms of unobtrusive measures with regard to the invasion of privacy. Informed-consent compliance has placed considerable restraints on certain research practices, such as those that involve entrapment and experiments that aim to induce heightened anxiety.

CORRELATIONAL RESEARCH

Correlational research is descriptive in that it explores relationships that exist among variables. Sometimes predictions are made on the basis of the relationships, but correlation cannot determine cause-and-effect. The basic difference between experimental research and correlational research is that the latter does not cause something to happen. There is no manipulation of variables or experimental treatments administered. The basic design of correlational research is to collect data on two or more variables on the same subjects and to determine the relationships among the variables. But, of course, the researcher should have a sound rationale for exploring the relationships.

Different correlational techniques were discussed in chapter 6 through examples of situations that lend themselves to correlational research. The two main purposes for doing a correlational study are to analyze the relationships among variables and to predict.

Steps in Correlational Research

The steps in a correlational study are similar to those used in other research methods. The problem is first defined and delimited. The selection of the variables to be correlated is of critical importance. Many studies have failed in this regard. Regardless of how sophisticated the statistical analysis may be, the statistical technique can deal only with the variables that are entered, thus the saying "Garbage in, garbage out." The validity of a study that seeks to identify basic components or factors of fitness hinges on the identification of the variables to be analyzed. A researcher who wishes to discriminate between starters and substitutes in a sport is faced with the crucial task of determining which physiological or psychological variables are the important determinants of success. The researcher must lean heavily on past research in defining and delimiting the problem.

Subjects are selected from the pertinent population using recommended sampling procedures. The magnitude and even the direction of a correlation coefficient can vary greatly, depending on the sample used. Remember that correlations show only the degree of relationship between variables, not the cause of the relationship. Consequently, because of other contributing factors, one might obtain a correlation of .90 between two variables in a sample of young children and one of .10 between the same variables in adults or vice versa. Chapter 6 used examples of how factors such as age can influence certain relationships. Another aspect of correlation is that the size of the correlation coefficient depends to a considerable extent on the spread of the scores.

A sample that is fairly homogeneous in certain traits seldom will yield a high correlation between variables associated with those traits. For example, the correlation between a distance run and maximal oxygen consumption with a sample of elite track athletes will almost invariably be low because the athletes are so similar; there is not enough variability to permit a high correlation because

the scores on the two measurements are too uniform. If you included some less trained subjects in the sample, the size of the correlation coefficient would increase dramatically.

In prediction studies, the subjects must be representative of the population for whom the study is directed. One of the major drawbacks to prediction studies is that the prediction formulas are often sample specific, which means that a formula's accuracy is greatest (or maybe only acceptable) when it is applied to the particular sample on whom it was developed. Chapter 16 discusses this shrinkage phenomenon as well as cross-validation, which is used to counteract shrinkage.

The collection of data requires the same careful attention to detail and standardization that all research designs do. A variety of methods for collecting data may be used, such as physical performance tests, anthropometric measurements, pencil-and-paper inventories, questionnaires, and observational techniques. The scores must be quantified, however, to be correlated.

Analysis of the data can be performed by a number of statistical techniques. Sometimes the researcher wishes to use simple correlation or partial correlation to study how variables, either by themselves or in a linear composite of variables, are associated with some criterion performance or behavior. Factor analysis is a data-reduction method that helps determine whether relationships among a number of variables can be reduced to smaller combinations of factors or common components. Path analysis is a technique used to test some theoretical model about causal relationships between three or more variables.

Prediction studies usually employ multiple regression because the accuracy of predicting some criterion behavior is nearly always improved by using more than one predictor variable. Discriminant analysis is a technique used to predict group membership, and canonical correlation is a method for predicting a combination of several criterion variables from several predictor variables.

Limitations of Correlational Research

Limitations of correlational research include those of both planning and analysis. We have already pointed out the importance of the identification of pertinent variables and the selection of proper tests to measure those variables. There should be hypotheses based on previous research and theoretical considerations, rather than simply correlating a set of measurements to see what happens. The selection of an inadequate measure to use as a criterion in a prediction study is a common weakness. For example, a criterion of success in some endeavor is often difficult to operationally define.

A basic mistake in correlational research is to assume cause-and-effect rather than simply association. In prediction studies, researchers sometimes fail to use proper cross-validation procedures. As stated in chapter 6, a researcher can rely too much on statistical significance and not enough on the meaningfulness of the size of correlation coefficients.

SUMMARY

Descriptive research encompasses many different techniques. The techniques are measures of status, although some might seek opinions or even future projections in the responses.

The most common descriptive research technique is the survey, which includes questionnaires and interviews. The two are very similar except for the method of asking questions. The questionnaire is a valuable tool for obtaining information over a wide geographical area. A good cover letter is important in getting cooperation. One or two follow-ups are often necessary to secure an adequate representation of the respondents. Interviews usually yield more valid data because of the personal contact and the opportunity to make sure that respondents understand the questions. Telephone interviews are becoming increasingly popular. They have most of the advantages of face-to-face interviews plus flexibility to involve more subjects over a larger geographical area. The Delphi survey technique uses a series of questionnaires in such a way that the respondents eventually reach a consensus about the topic. It is frequently used to survey expert opinion in an effort to help make decisions about practices, needs, and goals.

The normative survey is designed to obtain norms for abilities, performances, beliefs, and attitudes. The various AAHPERD fitness tests developed over the years are examples of normative surveys. In all surveys, representative sampling is extremely important.

Developmental research seeks to study growth measures and changes in behavior over a period of years. In a longitudinal design the same subjects are followed over time. When different subjects are sampled at different age levels, the design is cross-sectional. Of paramount importance in developmental research is whether the subjects are representative of their populations and their performances. A developmental study may involve experimental treatment, with the researcher attempting to determine the interaction of some treatment with age.

In a case study, the researcher attempts to gather a lot of information about one or a few subjects (cases). Through in-depth study of a single case, a greater understanding about other similar cases is achieved. Case studies can be descriptive, interpretive, or evaluative. One of the principal advantages of the case study approach is that it can lead to the formulation of ideas and hypotheses about problem areas.

The job analysis is a type of case study in which extensive information is gathered and evaluated regarding job conditions, duties and responsibilities, and the types of training, preparation, skills, and attitudes that are necessary for success in a certain job.

Observational research is a descriptive technique that involves the qualitative and quantitative analysis of observed behaviors. Unlike the survey method, which relies on self-reports as to how a subject behaves, observational research attempts to study what a person actually does. Behavior is usually coded as to what occurs, when, how often, and how long. Standardized observation instruments such as the ALT-PE and the CAFIAS are frequently used. Researchers often videotape their subjects to record and store the observations for later analysis.

Some studies use unobtrusive measures in which the subjects are unaware that the researcher is gathering data. For example, instead of (or in addition to) asking a person how much he or she smokes, the researcher might count the cigarette butts in an ashtray after a certain time period. Although the methods may be interesting and innovative, there may be constraints due to ethical considerations such as invasion of privacy and entrapment.

Correlational research examines relationships among variables. Sometimes the relationships are used for prediction. Although correlations are often used in conjunction with experimental research, the study of relationships is descriptive in that it does not involve the manipulation of variables. A major pitfall in correlational research is to assume that because variables are related, one causes another.

Problems

1. Locate a thesis (or dissertation) that uses a questionnaire to gather data. Briefly summarize the methodology, such as the procedures used in constructing and administering the questionnaire, the selection of the subjects, any follow-up techniques, and so on.
2. Locate two developmental studies—one cross-sectional and one longitudinal—and answer the following questions about each:

   a. Is the study descriptive or experimental?
   b. What age levels are studied?
   c. What are the independent and dependent variables?
   d. What statistics are used to make cross-age comparisons?
   e. Do the variances (standard deviations squared) of the dependent variables appear to differ across age levels? Have the authors considered this? How?
   f. Does the study try to justify loss of subjects (longitudinal) or the cohort problem (cross-sectional)? How?

3. Write a brief abstract of a case study found in the literature. Indicate the problem, the sources of information used, and the findings.
4. Find an observational study in the literature and write a critique of the article, concentrating on the methodology.
5. Locate and write a brief abstract of a correlational research study.

Chapter 14

□

Experimental Research

Experimental research attempts to establish cause-and-effect relationships. That is, an independent variable is manipulated to judge its effect upon a dependent variable. However, the process of establishing cause-and-effect is a difficult one. We have already discussed the fact that just because two variables are correlated does not mean one causes the other. However, cause-and-effect cannot exist unless two variables are correlated. Therefore, correlational research is frequently used before conducting experimental research. We may do an investigation to see whether two variables are related before trying to manipulate one to change the other.

Also, remember that cause-and-effect is not established by statistics. Statistical techniques can only reject the null hypothesis (establish that groups are significantly different) and identify the percent variance in the dependent variable accounted for by the independent variable or the effect size; neither of these procedures establishes cause-and-effect. Cause-and-effect can be established only by the application of logical thinking to well-designed experiments. This logical process establishes that there is no other reasonable explanation for the changes in the dependent variable except the manipulation done as the independent variable. The application of this logic is made possible by the following:

- The selection of a good theoretical framework
- The application of an appropriate experimental design

- The use of the correct statistical model and analyses
- The proper selection and control of the independent variable
- The appropriate selection and measurement of the dependent variable
- The use of appropriate subjects
- The correct interpretation of the results

In this chapter we discuss experimental designs by explaining how you can recognize and control sources of invalidity and threats to both internal and external validity. We also explain several types of experimental designs. Before going any further into this chapter, use the glossary to review the following terms used throughout the discussion:

- Independent variable
- Dependent variable
- Categorical variable
- Control variable
- Extraneous variable

SOURCES OF INVALIDITY

All the types of designs we discuss have strengths and weaknesses that pose threats to the validity of the research design, as stated so well by Campbell and Stanley (1963):

Fundamental . . . is a distinction between internal validity and external validity. Internal validity is the basic minimum without which any experiment is uninterpretable: Did in fact the experimental treatments make a difference in this specific experimental instance? External validity asks the question of generalizability: To what populations, settings, or treatment variables can this effect be generalized? (p. 5)

Both internal and external validity are important in experiments. However, they are frequently at odds in the planning and designing of research. Gaining internal validity involves controlling all variables so that the researcher can eliminate all rival hypotheses as explanations for the outcomes observed. Yet in controlling and constraining the research setting to gain internal validity, the researcher places the generalization (external validity) of the findings in jeopardy. In studies with strong internal validity, the answer to the question of to whom, what, or where can the findings be generalized may be very uncertain. This is because in ecologically valid (real-world) settings, everything is not controlled and may not operate in the same way as in the controlled, laboratory context. Thus, the researcher is left with a dilemma: Is it most important to be certain that the manipulation of the independent variable caused the observed changes in the dependent variable, or is it most important to be able to generalize the results to other populations, settings, and so on? We cannot provide an easy answer to that question, which is often debated at scientific meetings and in the literature (e.g., see Martens, 1979, 1987; Siedentop, 1980; Thomas, 1980; Thomas et al., 1986).

> The purpose of quasi designs is to fit the design to settings more like the real world while still controlling as many of the threats to internal validity as possible.

To expect any single experiment to meet all research design considerations is unreasonable. A more realistic approach is to

identify the specific goals and limitations of the research effort. Is internal validity or external validity the more important issue? Once that is decided, the researcher can plan the research with one type of validity as the major focus while maintaining as much of the other type of validity as possible. Another recourse is to plan a series of experiments in which the first experiment would have strong internal validity even at the expense of external validity. If the first experiment identified that changes in the dependent measure are the result of manipulating the independent variable, subsequent experiments could be designed with increasing external validity even at the expense of internal validity. This would allow evaluation of the treatment in settings more like the real world.

THREATS TO INTERNAL VALIDITY

Campbell and Stanley (1963) identified eight threats to the internal validity of experiments (see Table 14.1). If these threats are uncontrolled, the change in the dependent variable may be difficult to attribute to the manipulation of the independent variable.

Table 14.1 Eight Threats to Internal Validity

1. *History*—events occurring during the experiment that are not part of the treatment
2. *Maturation*—processes within the subjects that operate as a result of time passing, for example, aging, fatigue, hunger
3. *Testing*—the effects of one test on subsequent administrations of the same test
4. *Instrumentation*—changes in instrument calibration, including lack of agreement within and between observers
5. *Statistical regression*—the fact that groups selected on the basis of extreme scores are not as extreme on a subsequent testing
6. *Selection biases*—identification of comparison groups in other than a random manner

7. *Experimental mortality*—loss of subjects from comparison groups due to nonrandom reasons
8. *Selection-maturation interaction*—specific to nonequivalent group designs where the passage of time might affect one group but not the other

---

Note. From Campbell-Stanley: *Experimental and Quasi-Experimental Designs for Research*, pp. 5-6. Copyright © 1963 by the American Educational Research Association. Used by permission of Houghton Mifflin Company.

History

A history threat means that some unintended event occurred during the treatment period. For example, if a study was evaluating the effects of a semester of physical education on the physical fitness of fifth graders, the fact that 60% of the children participated in a recreational soccer program would constitute a history threat to internal validity. The soccer program is also likely to produce benefits to physical fitness that would be difficult to separate from the benefits of the physical education program.

Maturation

Maturation as a threat to internal validity is most often associated with aging. This threat occurs frequently in designs in which one group is tested on several occasions over a long period of time. Elementary physical education teachers frequently encounter this source of invalidity when they give a physical fitness test in the early fall and again in the late spring. The children nearly always do better in the spring. The teacher would like to claim that the physical education program was the cause. Unfortunately, maturation is a plausible rival hypothesis for the observed increase; that is, the children have grown larger and stronger and thus probably run faster, jump higher, and throw farther.

Testing

A testing threat is the effect that taking a test once has on taking it again. For example, if a group of athletes were administered a 50-item multiple-choice test to evaluate their knowledge about steroids today and again 2 days later, the athletes would do better the second time even though no treatment intervened. Taking the test once helps in taking it again. The same effect is present in physical performance tests, especially if the subjects are not allowed to practice the test a few times. If a class of beginners in tennis hits 20 forehand shots delivered to them from a ball machine today and again 3 days later, the subjects will, in general, do better the second time. They learned something from performing the test the first time.

Instrumentation

Instrumentation is a problem frequently faced in exercise science research. Suppose the researcher uses a spring-loaded device to measure strength. Unless the spring is calibrated regularly, it decreases in tension with use. Thus, the same amount of applied force will produce increased readings of strength. Instrumentation also applies to research using observers. Unless training and regular checks occur, the same observer may systematically vary his or her ratings across time or subjects (called observer drift), or different observers may not rate the same performance in the same way.

Statistical Regression

Statistical regression may occur when groups are not randomly formed but are selected on the basis of an extreme score on some measure. For example, if a group of children have their behavior on a playground recorded on an activity scale (very active to very inactive) and two groups are formed—one of very active children and one of very inactive children—statistical regression is likely to occur when the children are next observed on the playground. The children who were very active will be less active (although still active), and the very inactive children will be more active. In other words, both groups will regress (move from the extremes) toward the overall average. This phenomenon reflects only the fact that a subject's true score tends to vary about the mean. If extreme scores are used, the subject is observed on the high (or low) side of a typical performance. The next performance is usually not as extreme; thus, when scores are averaged across groups, the high group on the particular attribute appears to get worse, whereas the low group appears to get better. Statistical regression is a particular problem in studies that attempt to compare highly skilled with less skilled subjects, highly anxious versus less anxious subjects, and so on.

Selection Bias

Selection biases occur when groups are formed on some basis other than random assignment. Thus, when treatments are administered, the rival hypothesis that the differences are due to initial selection biases is always present; that is, the groups were different to begin with rather than as a result of the treatments. Showing that the groups were not different at the beginning on the dependent variable does not overcome this shortcoming. Any number of other unmeasured variables on which the groups differ might explain the treatment effect. Borg and Gall (1983) asked important questions that apply to selection (or sampling bias):

Did the study use volunteers? Use of volunteers is common in research in exercise, sport, and physical education. Yet volunteers are often not representative of any-

one but other volunteers. They may differ considerably from non-volunteers in motivation for the experimental task and setting.

Are subjects extremely nonrepresentative of the population? Often we are unable to select subjects at random for our studies, but it is very useful if we at least believe (and can demonstrate) that they represent some larger group from our culture. (pp. 205-206)

Experimental Mortality

Experimental mortality refers to the loss of subjects from the treatment groups. Even when groups are randomly formed, this threat to internal validity may occur. Subjects may remain in an experimental group receiving a fitness program because it is fun, whereas subjects in the control group become bored, lose interest, and drop out of the study.

Selection-Maturation Interaction

A selection-maturation interaction occurs only in specific types of designs. In these designs, one group is identified because of some specific characteristic, whereas the other group lacks this characteristic. An example might be the differences between expert and novice tennis players. Although they differ on skill, they may also differ on socioeconomic status. Experts may be more likely to come from families with greater incomes and could therefore afford to join country clubs where they received good instruction and a lot of practice and tournament experiences.

Additional Threats

Any of these eight threats to internal validity may reduce the researcher's ability to claim

that the manipulation of the independent variable produced the changes in the dependent variable. The various experimental designs and how they control (or fail to control) the threats to internal validity are discussed later in this chapter.

One additional threat to internal validity not mentioned by Campbell and Stanley (1963) has been identified. *Expectancy* (Rosenthal, 1966) refers to experimenters or testers anticipating that certain subjects will perform better. This effect, although usually unconscious on the part of the experimenters, occurs where subjects or experimental conditions are clearly labeled. For example, testers will rate "skilled" subjects better than "unskilled" subjects regardless of treatment. This effect is also evident in observational studies in which the observers will rate posttest better than pretest performance because they expect change. Or, if the experimental and control groups are identified, observers will rate the experimental group better than the control without any treatment occurring. The expectancy effect may influence the subjects also. For example, in a youth-sport study, coaches may actually cause poorer

performance in substitutes (compared to starters) because the substitutes realize the coach treats them differently (e.g., the coach may show less concern about incorrect practice trials).

THREATS TO EXTERNAL VALIDITY

Campbell and Stanley (1963) have identified four threats to external validity, or the ability to generalize results to other subjects, settings, measures, and so on. These four threats are summarized in Table 14.2.

Table 14.2 Four Threats to External Validity

1. *Reactive or interactive effects of testing*—the fact that the pretest may make the subject more aware of or sensitive to the upcoming treatment. This results in the treatment's not being as effective without the pretest.
2. *Interaction of selection biases and the experimental treatment*—when a group is selected on some

(Cont.)

Table 14.2 (Continued)

characteristic, the treatment may work only on groups possessing that characteristic.

3. *Reactive effects of experimental arrangements*—the fact that treatments that are effective in very constrained situations (e.g., laboratories) may not be effective in less constrained (more like real-world) settings.

4. *Multiple-treatment interference*—when subjects receive more than one treatment, the effects of previous treatments may influence subsequent ones.

Note. From Campbell-Stanley: *Experimental and Quasi-Experimental Designs for Research*, pp. 5-6. Copyright © 1963 by the American Educational Research Association. Used by permission of Houghton Mifflin Company.

Reactive or Interactive Effects of Testing

Reactive or interactive effects of testing may be a problem in any design with a pretest. Suppose a fitness program is to be the experimental treatment. If a physical fitness test is administered to the sample first, the subjects in the experimental group might realize that their levels of fitness are low and be particularly motivated to follow the prescribed program closely. However, in an unpretested population, the program might not be as effective because the subjects would be unaware of their low levels of physical fitness.

Interaction of Selection Bias and Experimental Treatment

The interaction of selection biases and the experimental treatment may prohibit the generalization of the results to subjects lacking the particular characteristics (bias). For example, a drug education program might be quite effective in changing the attitudes toward drug use of college freshmen. This same program would probably lack effective-

ness for third-year medical students because they would be very familiar with drugs and their appropriate uses.

Reactive Effects of Experimental Arrangements

Reactive effects of experimental arrangements are a persistent problem for laboratory-based research (e.g., in exercise physiology, biomechanics, motor control, and learning). In these cases, is the researcher investigating an effect, process, or outcome that is specific to the laboratory and cannot be generalized to other settings? We have referred to this earlier as ecological validity. For example, in a study employing high-speed cinematography, the skill to be filmed must be performed in a certain place and joints marked for later analysis. Is the skill performed in the same way during participation in a sport? One specific type of reactive behavior has been labeled the *Hawthorne effect* (Brown, 1954). This refers to the fact that subjects' performances change when attention is paid to the subjects. This may be a threat to both internal and external validity, as it is likely to produce better treatment effects and reduce the ability to generalize the results.

Multiple-Treatment Interference

Multiple-treatment interference is most frequently a problem when the same subjects are exposed to more than one level of the treatment. Suppose subjects are going to learn to move to the hitting position in volleyball using a lead step or a crossover step. We want to know which step gets the subjects in a good hitting position most quickly. If the subjects attempt both types of steps, the learning of one might interfere with (or enhance) learning the other. Thus, the researcher's ability to generalize the findings may be confounded by the use of multiple treatments. A better design might have been to have two separate groups, each of which learns one of the techniques.

The ability to generalize findings from research to other subjects or situations is a question of random sampling more than any other. Do the subjects, treatments, tests, and situations represent any larger populations? Although a few of the experimental designs discussed next control certain threats to external validity, in general the researcher controls these threats by the way the sample, treatments, situations, and tests are selected.

CONTROLLING THREATS TO VALIDITY

Threats to internal and external validity are controlled in different ways and by specific techniques. In this section we describe useful approaches to solving these problems in the design of experiments.

Internal Validity

Many of the threats to internal validity are controlled by equating the subjects in the experimental and control groups. This is most often done by random assignment of subjects to groups.

Randomization

As mentioned in chapter 5, randomization allows the assumption that the groups do not differ at the beginning of the experiment. The randomization process controls for history up to the point of the experiment; that is, the researcher can assume that past events are equally distributed among groups. It does not control for history effects during the experiment if experimental and control subjects are treated at different times or places. Only the researcher can make sure that no events, beside the treatment, occur in one group and not the others.

Randomization also controls for maturation, as the passage of time would be equivalent in all groups. Statistical regression is controlled because it operates only when groups are not randomly formed. Both selection biases and selection-maturation interaction are controlled because these threats occur only when groups are not randomly formed.

Sometimes ways other than random assignment of subjects to groups are used to attempt to control threats to internal validity. The matched-pair technique equates pairs of subjects on some characteristic and then randomly assigns the pairs to groups. The researcher might want very tight control on previous experience in strength training. Thus, subjects would be matched on this characteristic and then randomly assigned to the experimental and control groups.

A matched-group technique may also be used. This involves assigning subjects to experimental and control groups so that the group means are equivalent on some variable. This is generally regarded as an unacceptable procedure because the groups may not be equivalent on other, unmeasured variables that could affect the outcome of the research.

In within-subjects designs, the subjects are used as their own controls. This means each subject receives both the experimental and the control treatment. In this type of design, the order of treatments should be counterbalanced; that is, half the subjects should receive the experimental treatment first and then the control, and the other half the control first and then the experimental. If there are three levels of the independent variable (1 = control, 2 = experimental A, 3 = experimental B), the six possible combinations should be identified (1-2-3, 1-3-2, 2-1-3, 2-3-1, 3-1-2, 3-2-1) and subjects randomly assigned to order. As the number of treatment levels administered to the same subjects becomes larger than 3 or 4, experimenters may assign a random order of the treatments to each subject rather than counterbalancing treatments.

Three of the threats to internal validity remain uncontrolled by the randomization process. Reactive or interactive threats of testing can be controlled only by elimination of the pretest. However, it can be evaluated by two of the designs: randomized groups pretest/posttest and Solomon four-group (discussed later in this chapter).

Test Reliability

Instrumentation cannot be controlled or evaluated by any design. Only the experimenter can control this threat to internal validity. Part IV (Measurement) goes into some detail on techniques for controlling the instrumentation threat. Of particular significance is test reliability. Whether the measurement is obtained from a laboratory device (oxygen analyzer), motor performance test (standing long jump), attitude-rating scale (feelings about drug use), observer (coding percentage of time a child is active), knowl-edge test (basketball strategy), or survey (available sport facilities), the answer must be a consistent one. This frequently involves the assessment of test reliability across situations, between and within testers or observers, and within subjects. The validity of the instrument (does it measure what it was intended to measure?) must also be established to control for instrumentation problems. The total process of establishing appropriate instrumentation for research is called *psychometrics*. One final point about instrumentation is called the *halo effect*. This occurs in ratings of several skills on the same individual. Raters seeing a skilled performance on one task are likely to rate the subject higher on subsequent tasks regardless of the level of skill displayed. In effect, the skilled behavior has rubbed off (created a "halo") on later performance.

Subject Retention

Experimental mortality is not controlled by any type of experimental design. Only the ex-

THE JUDGES' BOX

9 FT   10 FT   11 FT

perimenter, by seeing that subjects are not lost (at all, if possible) from groups, can control this. Many of these problems can be handled in advance of the research by carefully explaining the research to the subjects and the need for them to follow through with the project. (During the experiment itself, begging, pleading, and crying sometimes work.)

Placebos, Blind, and Double-Blind Setups

Other ways of controlling threats to internal validity include *placebos* and *blind* and *double-blind setups*. A placebo is used to evaluate whether the treatment effect is real or whether it is due to some psychological effect. Frequently, a control condition in which subjects receive the same attention and interaction with the experimenter is used, but the treatment administered does not relate to performance on the dependent variable.

A blind study is one in which the subject does not know whether he or she is receiving the experimental or the control treatment. In a double-blind study, neither the subject nor the tester knows which treatment the subject is receiving. The triple-blind test has also been reported (R.F., 1983): The subject does not know what he or she is getting, the experimenter does not know what he or she is giving, and the investigator does not know what he or she is doing. We can only hope the triple-blind test finds limited use in our field.

All these techniques (except the triple-blind test) are useful in controlling Hawthorne, expectancy, and halo effects as well as what we call the *Avis effect* (a recent version of the John Henry effect), or the fact that subjects in the control group may try harder simply because they are in the control group.

A good example of the use of these techniques for controlling psychological effects is the use of steroids to build strength in athletes. A number of studies were done to evaluate the effects of steroids. To combat the fact that athletes may get stronger because they think they should when using steroids, a placebo (another pill that looks just like the steroid) is used. The athletes are blind as to whether they receive the placebo. In a double blind, the athlete, the person dispensing the steroids (or placebo), and the testers would all be blind to which group received the steroids. Unfortunately, until recently these procedures had not worked very well in this specific type of study because taking large quantities of steroids made the athlete's urine smell bad. Thus, the athlete knew whether he or she was receiving the steroid or the placebo.

External Validity

External validity is generally controlled by selecting the subjects, treatments, experimental situation, and tests to be representative of some larger population. Of course, random selection is the key to controlling most of the threats to external validity. Remember, more than the subjects may be randomly selected. For example, the levels of treatment can be randomly selected from the possible levels, and experimental situations can be selected from possible situations.

As previously noted, the idea of generalizing the situation is called ecological validity. Although the results of a particular treatment can be generalized to a larger group if the sample is representative, this generalization may apply only to the specific situation in the experiment. If the experiment is conducted under controlled laboratory conditions, then the findings may apply only under controlled laboratory conditions. Frequently, the experimenter hopes the findings will generalize to real-world exercise, sport, industrial, or instructional settings. Whether the outcomes will generalize in this way depends largely on how the subjects perceive the study, and this influences the way subjects respond to study characteristics. The question of interest here is, Does the study have enough characteristics of real-world settings so that subjects respond as if they are in the real world? That is, Is there ecological validity? This is not an easy question to answer and has resulted in a number of scholars advocating that more research in physical education, exercise science, and sport science be conducted in field settings (e.g., Costill, 1985; Martens, 1987; Thomas et al., 1986).

Reactive or interactive effects of testing can be evaluated by the Solomon four-group design (discussed later in this chapter). Interaction of selection biases and the experimental treatment is controlled by random selection of subjects. Reactive effects of experimental arrangements can be controlled only by the researcher (this is again the issue of ecological validity). Multiple-treatment interference may be partially controlled by counterbalancing treatments across subjects. But only the researcher can control whether the treatments will still interfere. That decision is based on knowledge about the treatment rather than the type of experimental design.

> Random selection is the key to controlling most of the threats to external validity.

TYPES OF DESIGNS

This section (much of which is taken from Campbell & Stanley, 1963) is divided into three categories: preexperimental designs, true experimental designs, and quasi-experimental designs. We use the following notation:

- R: This signifies random assignment of subjects to groups.

- O: This signifies an observation or test (subscripts refer to the order of testing; i.e., O_1 is the first time a test is given and O_2 the second).
- T: This signifies that a treatment is applied (the terms T_1 and T_2 on different lines refer to different treatments; terms on the same line mean that the treatment is administered more than once); a blank space means that the group is a control.
- ---: A dotted line between groups means that the groups are used intact rather than being randomly formed.

Preexperimental Designs

These three designs are called *preexperimental designs* because they control very few of the sources of invalidity. None of the designs have random assignment of subjects to groups.

1. One-Shot Study

In this design a group of subjects receives a treatment followed by a test to evaluate the treatment:

$$T \quad O$$

This design fails all the tests of good research. All that can be said is that at a certain point in time this group of subjects performed at a certain level. In no way can the level of performance (O) be attributed to the treatment (T).

2. One-Group Pretest-Posttest Design

This design, although very weak, is better than Design 1. At least we can observe whether any change in performance has occurred:

$$O_1 \quad T \quad O_2$$

If O_2 is better than O_1, we can say that the subjects improved. For example, Bill Biceps (a qualified exercise instructor) conducted an exercise test at a health club. Subjects then trained 3 days per week, 40 minutes per day, at 70% of their estimated $\dot{V}O_2$max for 12 weeks. After the training period subjects retook the exercise test and significantly improved their scores. Can Mr. Biceps conclude that the exercise program caused the changes in the exercise test performance he observed? Unfortunately, this design does not allow us to say why the subjects improved. Certainly, it could be due to the treatment, but it could also be due to history. Some event other than the treatment (T) may have occurred between the pretest (O_1) and the posttest (O_2). Maturation is a rival hypothesis. The subjects may have gotten better (or worse) over time. Testing is a rival hypothesis; the increase at O_2 may be the result only of experience with the test at O_1. If the group being tested is selected for some specific reason, then any of the treatments involving selection biases could occur. This design is most frequently analyzed by the dependent t test to evaluate whether significant change occurred between O_1 and O_2.

3. Static Group Comparison

This design compares two groups, one of which receives the treatment and one of which does not:

$$\frac{T \qquad O_1}{O_2}$$

However, the dotted line between the groups indicates that the groups were not equivalent when the study began. Most frequently, this means that the groups were selected intact rather than being randomly formed. This leaves one in the position of being unable to determine whether any differences between O_1 and O_2 are caused by T, as O_1 and O_2 might have been different only because the groups differed initially. This design is subject to invalidity because of selection biases and the selection-maturation interaction. A t test for independent groups is used to evaluate whether O_1 and O_2 differ significantly. However, even if they do differ, the difference cannot be attributed to T.

Designs, 1, 2, and 3 are not valid means of answering research questions (see Table 14.3). They do not represent experiments because the change in the dependent variable cannot be attributed to manipulation of the independent variable. Generally, you will not encounter these preexperimental designs in research journals, and we hope you will not find (or produce) theses or dissertations using these designs. Designs 1, 2, and 3 represent much wasted effort because little or nothing can be concluded from the findings. If you submit studies using these designs to research journals, you are likely to receive rejection letters similar to one Snoopy (from the "Peanuts" comic strip) received: Dear Researcher, Thank you for submitting your paper to our research journal. To save time, we are enclosing two rejection letters—one for this paper and one for the next one you send.

True Experimental Designs

These are called *true experimental designs* because the groups are randomly formed, allowing the assumption that they were equivalent at the beginning of the research. This controls for past (but not present) history, maturation (should occur equally in the groups), testing, and all sources of invalidity that are based on nonequivalency of groups (statistical regression, selection biases, and selection-maturation interaction). However, only the experimenter can make sure that

Table 14.3 Preexperimental Designs and Their Control of the Threats to Validity

Validity threat	One-shot study	One-group pretest and posttest	Static group
Internal			
History	–	–	+
Maturation	–	–	?
Testing		–	+
Instrumentation		–	+
Statistical regression		?	+
Selection	–	+	–
Experimental mortality	–	+	–
Selection × Maturation		–	–
Expectancy	?	?	?
External			
Testing × Treatment		–	
Selection biases × Treatment	–	–	–
Experimental arrangements		?	
Multiple treatments			

Note. + = strength, – = weakness, = not relevant, ? = questionable. From Campbell and Stanley (1963).

nothing happens to one group (beside the treatment) and not the other (present history), that scores on the dependent measure do not vary as a result of instrumentation problems, and that the loss of subjects is not different between the groups (experimental mortality).

4. Randomized-Groups Design

Note that this design is very similar to Design 3 except that the groups are randomly formed:

$$R \quad T \quad O_1$$
$$R \qquad\quad O_2$$

If the researcher controls the threats to internal validity not controlled by randomization, then this design allows the conclusion that significant differences between O_1 and O_2 are due to T. An independent t test is used to analyze the difference between O_1 and O_2.

This design, as depicted, represents two levels of one independent variable. It may be extended to any number of levels of an independent variable:

$$R \quad T_1 \quad O_1$$
$$R \quad T_2 \quad O_2$$
$$R \qquad\quad O_3$$

In this case, three levels of the independent variable exist, where one is the control and T_1 and T_2 represent two levels of treatment. This design can be analyzed by simple ANOVA, which contrasts the dependent variable (O_1, O_2, O_3) as measured in the three groups. For example, T_1 is training at 70% of $\dot{V}O_2$max, T_2 is training at 40% of $\dot{V}O_2$max, and the control is not training. The variables O_1, O_2, and O_3 are the measures of cardiorespiratory fitness (12-min run) in each group taken at the end of the training.

This design may also be extended into a factorial design; that is, more than one independent variable could be considered. Table 14.4 provides an example of a factorial design. Independent variable 1 (IV_1) has three levels (A_1, A_2, A_3), and independent variable 2 (IV_2) has two levels (B_1, B_2). This results in six cells (A_1B_1, A_1B_2, A_2B_1, A_2B_2, A_3B_1, A_3B_2), to which subjects are randomly assigned. At the end of the treatments, each cell is tested on the dependent variable (O_1, O_2, O_3, O_4, O_5, O_6). This design is analyzed by a 3×2 factorial ANOVA that tests the effects of IV_1 (F_A), IV_2 (F_B), and their interaction (F_{AB}).

This design may also be extended to an increased number of independent variables (three, four, or more) and retain all the controls for internal validity previously discussed. Sometimes this design is used with a categorical independent variable. Looking again at Table 14.4, suppose that IV_2 (B_1, B_2) represented two age levels. Clearly, the levels of B could not be randomly formed. The design would appear as follows:

$$\begin{array}{cccc} & R & A_1 & O_1 \\ B_1 & R & A_2 & O_2 \\ & R & A_3 & O_3 \\ \hline & R & A_1 & O_4 \\ B_2 & R & A_2 & O_5 \\ & R & A_3 & O_6 \end{array}$$

The levels of A are randomly formed within B, but the levels of B cannot be randomly formed. This no longer qualifies completely as a true experimental design but is frequently used in physical education, exercise science, and sport science. This design is analyzed in a 3×2 ANOVA, but the interpretation of results must be done more conservatively.

Any of the versions of Design 4 may also have more than one dependent variable. Although the consideration of the design remains the same, the statistical analysis becomes multivariate. Where two or more levels of one independent variable exist but

Table 14.4 Extension of Design 4 Into a Factorial Design

		IV$_2$	
		B_1	B_2
	A_1	A_1B_1	A_1B_2
IV$_1$	A_2	A_2B_1	A_2B_2
	A_3	A_3B_1	A_3B_2
R		A_1B_1	O_1
R		A_1B_2	O_2
R		A_2B_1	O_3
R		A_2B_2	O_4
R		A_3B_1	O_5
R		A_3B_2	O_6

Note. Analyzed in a 3×2 factorial ANOVA. F_A = main effect of A; F_B = main effect of B; F_{AB} = interaction of A and B.

several dependent variables are present, discriminant analysis is the appropriate multivariate statistic. In the factorial versions of this design (two or more independent variables), if multiple dependent variables are used, then MANOVA is the appropriate analysis.

5. Pretest-Posttest Randomized-Groups Design

In this design the groups are randomly formed, but both groups are given a pretest as well as a posttest. This design is labeled as follows:

$$R \quad O_1 \quad T \quad O_2$$
$$R \quad O_3 \qquad O_4$$

The major purpose of this type of design is to determine the amount of change produced by the treatment; that is, does the experimental group change more than the control group? This design threatens internal validity of testing, but the threat is controlled, as the comparison of O_3 to O_4 in the control group includes the testing effect as well as the comparison of O_1 to O_2 in the experimental group. Thus, although the testing effect cannot be evaluated in this design, it is controlled.

This design is used frequently in physical education, exercise science, and sport science, but its analysis is rather complex. There are at least three common ways used to do a statistical analysis of this design. First, a factorial repeated measures ANOVA can be used. One factor (between subjects) is the treatment versus no treatment, whereas the second factor is pretest versus posttest (within subjects or repeated measures). However, the interest in this design is usually the interaction: Do the groups change at different rates from pretest to posttest? If you choose a repeated measures ANOVA for this design (in our opinion the best choice), pay close attention to our discussion of repeated measures in chapters 7 and 8 (multivariate issues in repeated measures). A second analysis is to use simple ANCOVA with the pretest for each group (O_1 and O_3) used to adjust the posttest (O_2 and O_4). Recall that there are some problems with using the pretest as a covariate (see chapter 7's discussion of ANCOVA). Finally, the experimenter could subtract each subject's pretest value from the posttest value (called a *gain score*) and perform a simple ANOVA (or, with only two groups, an independent *t* test) using each subject's gain score as the dependent variable. Each of these techniques has strengths and weaknesses, but you will find all three used in the literature.

In this design the important question is, Does one group change more than the other group? Although this issue is frequently called the analysis of gain scores, a more appropriate label is the assessment of change. Clearly, in a learning study the change is expected to be gain. But in an exercise physiology study, the change might be decreased performance caused by fatigue. Regardless, the issues are the same. How can this change be assessed appropriately?

The easiest answer is to obtain a change score by subtracting the pretest from the posttest. Although this is intuitively attractive, it does have some problems. First, these change scores tend to be unreliable. Second, the subjects who begin low in performance can improve more easily than those who begin with high scores. Thus, initial score is negatively correlated with the change score. How would you like your tennis performance evaluated on change if your initial score was high (e.g., 5 successful forehand drives out of 10 trials) compared with a friend who began with a low score initially (e.g., 1 out of 10 successful hits)? If you improved to 7 out of 10 on the final test and your friend improved to 5 out of 10 (the level of your initial score), your friend has improved twice as much as you have (a gain of 4 vs. 2 successful hits).

The issues involved in the proper measurement of change are complex ones, and we cannot treat these issues here. However, much has been written on this topic. We suggest you read Schmidt (1988, chapter 11) about this problem in motor learning and performance or, for more complete coverage, see Harris (1963).

This design may also be extended into more complex forms. First, more than two (pretest and posttest) repeated measures can be used. This is common in the areas of motor learning and control. Two randomly formed groups of subjects might be measured 20, 30, or 40 or more times as they learn a task. The two groups might differ in the information they are given after each trial. Thus, if 30 trials are given, the design is a 2 (Groups) × 30 (Trials), and a 2 × 30 ANOVA with repeated measures on the second factor (Trials) might be the statistical analysis. Remember from chapter 7 that it is very difficult to meet the assumptions for a repeated measures ANOVA with many repeated measures. Thus, in designs like these, trials may be blocked (e.g., several trials averaged, reducing the number of repeated measures) or one of the multivariate repeated measures analyses can be used (see chapter 8).

Sometimes the design is extended in other ways. For example, we could take the design in Table 14.4 (a 2 × 3 factorial) and add a third factor of a pretest and a posttest. This would result in a three-way factorial with repeated measures on the third factor.

All the versions of this design are subject to the first threat to external validity: reactive or interactive effects of testing. The pretest may make the subject more sensitive to the treatment and thus reduce the ability to generalize the findings to an unpretested population.

6. Solomon Four-Group Design

This design is the only true design to specifically evaluate one of the threats to external validity: reactive or interactive effects of testing. The design is depicted as follows:

$$
\begin{array}{cccc}
R & O_1 & T & O_2 \\
R & O_3 & & O_4 \\
R & & T & O_5 \\
R & & & O_6
\end{array}
$$

As you can judge, this design is a combination of Designs 4 and 5. The purpose is explicitly to determine whether the pretest results in increased sensitivity of the subjects to the treatment. This design allows a replication of the treatment effect (is $O_2 > O_4$ and is $O_5 > O_6$), an assessment of the amount of change due to the treatment (is $[O_2 - O_1] > [O_4 - O_3]$), an evaluation of the testing effect (is $O_4 > O_6$), and an assessment of whether the pretest interacts with the treatment (is $O_2 > O_5$). Thus, this is a very powerful experimental design. Unfortunately, it is also an inefficient design as twice as many subjects are required. This results in very limited use, especially among graduate students doing theses and dissertations. In addition, no good way exists to analyze this design statistically. The best alternative (this one does not use all the data) is a 2 × 2 ANOVA set up as follows:

	No T	T
Pretested	O_4	O_2
Unpretested	O_6	O_5

Thus, IV_1 has two levels (pretested and unpretested), and IV_2 has two levels (no treatment and treatment). In the ANOVA, the F ratio for IV_1 establishes the effects of pretesting, the F for IV_2 establishes the effects of the treatment, and the F for interaction evaluates the external validity threat of interaction of the pretest with the treatment. Table 14.5 summarizes the control of threats to validity of experimental designs.

Quasi-Experimental Designs

Not all research in which an independent variable is manipulated fits clearly into one of the true experimental designs. As researchers attempt to increase external and ecological validity, the careful and complete control of the true designs becomes

Table 14.5 True Experimental Designs and Their Control of the Threats to Validity

Validity threat	Randomized groups	Pretest-posttest randomized groups	Solomon four-group
Internal			
History	+	+	+
Maturation	+	+	+
Testing	+	+	+
Instrumentation	+	+	+
Statistical regression	+	+	+
Selection	+	+	+
Experimental mortality	+	+	+
Selection × Maturation	+	+	+
Expectancy	?	?	?
External			
Testing × Treatment	–	+	+
Selection biases × Treatment	?	?	?
Experimental arrangements	?	?	?
Multiple treatments			

Note. + = strength, – = weakness, = not relevant, ? = questionable. From Campbell and Stanley (1963).

increasingly difficult if not impossible. The purpose of quasi designs is to fit the design to settings more like the real world while still controlling as many of the threats to internal validity as possible. The use of these types of designs in physical education, exercise science, and sport science and in other areas (e.g., education, psychology, and sociology) has increased considerably in recent years. Perhaps the most authoritative text on quasi-experimental designs is that by Cook and Campbell (1979).

7. Time Series Designs

This design has only one group but attempts to show that the change that occurs when the treatment is interjected differs from the times when it is not. This design may be depicted as follows:

$$O_1 \quad O_2 \quad O_3 \quad O_4 \quad T \quad O_5 \quad O_6 \quad O_7 \quad O_8$$

The basis for claiming that the treatment causes the effect is that a constant rate of change can be established from O_1 to O_4 and from O_5 to O_8 but that this rate of change varies between O_4 and O_5. For example, in Figure 14.1, lines A, B, and C suggest that the insertion of the treatment (T) results in a visible change across observations, whereas lines D, E, F, and G indicate that the treatment has no reliable effect.

The typical statistical analyses previously discussed do not fit time series designs very well. For example, a repeated measures ANOVA with appropriate follow-ups applied to line C in Figure 14.1 might indicate that all observations (O_1-O_8) differ significantly even though we see that the rate of increase changes between O_4 and O_5. We do not present the details, but statistical techniques are available to test both the slopes and the intercepts in time series designs.

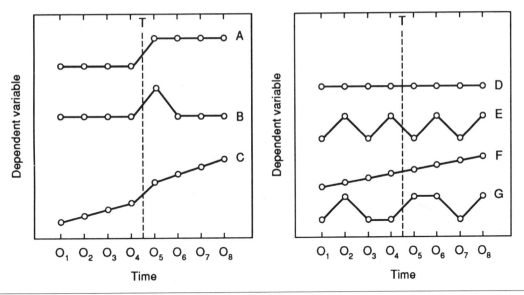

Figure 14.1 Examples of times series changes. From Campbell-Stanley: *Experimental and Quasi-Experimental Designs for Research*, p. 38. Copyright © 1963 by the American Educational Research Association. Used by permission of Houghton Mifflin Company.

> Gaining internal validity involves controlling all variables so that the researcher can eliminate all rival hypotheses as explanations for the outcomes observed.

This type of design appears to control for a number of the threats to internal validity. For example, maturation would appear to be constant between observations. Testing effects can also be evaluated, although they could be difficult to separate from maturation. Selection biases also appear to be controlled because the same subjects are used at each observation. Of course, history, instrumentation, and mortality are controlled only to the extent that the researcher controls them. On pages 314-315 is a humorous example of a time series design.

8. Reversal Design

This type of design is increasingly used in school settings and is depicted as follows:

$$O_1 \quad O_2 \quad T_1 \quad O_3 \quad O_4 \quad T_2 \quad O_5 \quad O_6$$

The purpose here (as with the time series) is to determine a baseline measure (O_1-O_2), evaluate the treatment (O_2-O_3), return to baseline (O_3-O_4), evaluate the treatment (O_4-O_5), and return to baseline (O_5-O_6).

In Figure 14.2, lines such as A, B, and C suggest that the insertion of the treatment is effective, whereas lines such as D, E, and F do not support a treatment effect. Statistical analyses for reversal designs also need to be tests of the slopes and intercepts of the lines among various observations.

One final point is applicable to Designs 7 and 8. We have discussed these designs as if one group is measured repeatedly over time; however, the format of these two designs is also used in single-subject research. Instead of one group being followed across all the time periods, a single subject is followed. But many more observations (data points) are needed when these designs are used for single-subject research. However, single-subject designs do not lend themselves to statistical analysis.

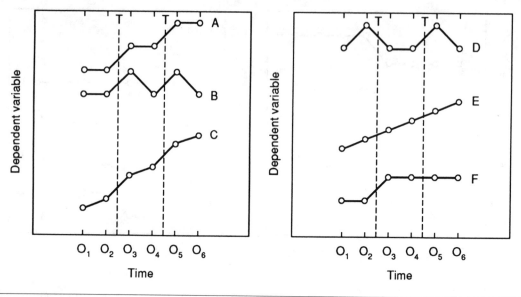

Figure 14.2 Examples of changes across time in reversal designs.

---

7 ± 2: Miller Must Have Been An Assistant Professor

Jerry R. Thomas

Summary.—Miller's magical number for memory span (7 ± 2) is humorously brought to task because of its inability to predict the everyday performance of teenagers, graduate students, and full professors. Explanations are provided for the deficits in memory performance of these subgroups during lifespan development.

Miller's (1956) classic paper identifying the memory span as 7 ± 2 items must have omitted using full professors as subjects, at least based on an *n* of 1, namely me. I have frequently heard clinical psychologists accused of going into psychology to study their own problems. Maybe that is a more valid explanation than bringing Miller's work to task. For years my graduate students have said that I study memory for movement because (a) I have little or no memory, and (b) I lose my spatial orientation just walking around the block. However, I prefer to think that

Miller's results only apply to a subsample of the population—6- to 10-yr.-old children, college students, and new assistant professors. Six- to 10-yr.-old children never forget anything you promised to do (or even things you said maybe . . .). However, as soon as they approach the teen years, their memory spans drop to less than 1 unit of information.

Teenagers cannot remember to make their beds as they are getting out of them. Evidently, nothing ever happens to teenagers at school, although I prefer to think that they just cannot recall anything that happened.

When these teenagers with little memory capacity go to college, an amazing transition in memory occurs. Between the freshman and senior years, the young adults' memory capacity increases at least 7 ± 2 units of information. Loosely defined, this means *they know everything*; conversely, parents know nothing.

After working a few years and coming back to graduate school, memory facility is somewhat reduced. Graduate students have a memory capacity of 3 ± 1 units of information: (a) They know that they are graduate students; (b) They remember to pick up their graduate assistantship paycheck; (c) They remember to attend their graduate seminars. The ± 1 refers to the fact that they occasionally remember to do the reading for the seminar (+ 1) but they sometimes forget to come to class (− 1).

As soon as graduate students receive their PhDs, Miller's magical number (7 ± 2) is again a good predictor of memory—new assistant professors know everything. However, movement through the academic ranks gradually reduces capacity to remember until the average capacity of full professors (and parents) is reached, 2 ± 1 units of information. A full professor can remember (a) he is a full professor and (b) his paycheck comes regularly. The ± 1 refers to the fact that the full professor sometimes remembers that he has graduate students (+ 1) but occasionally forgets to pick up the regular paycheck (− 1).

Based on the failure of this model to meet the assumptions of stage theory (i.e., one should never regress to an earlier stage), we must assume that this uneven transition in memory states (see Fig. 1) is environmentally induced.

But how can the environment cause these wide variations in memory performance? First, I believe we have to assume that Miller is correct about the structural maximum of memory performance because the deficits are not confined to a single point in the lifespan (i.e., teenagers, graduate students, full professors). The question of interest then becomes, *what causes such a serious depression in memory performance for teenagers, graduate*

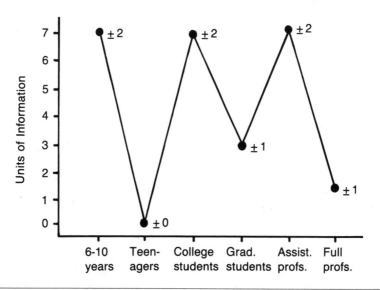

Figure 1. Maximum number of units of information retained in memory across the lifespan.

students, and full professors? Given my extensive study of memory as well as personal experience with all the stages, I can deduce the answer.

For teenagers the drop to about 0 memory with no variance is an interaction of carbonated soft drinks, junk food, and other boys or girls (whichever sex the teenager in question is not). This interaction is not a simple one and has an indirect effect, that is, this interaction causes pimples and the need for braces, both of which are very distracting in and of themselves. Taken in combination with Mom saying "wash your face" and "brush your teeth," all of the teenager's memory capacity is occupied.

The deficit that occurs for graduate students is easy to explain. Three factors are involved. First, the graduate student is expected to work full-time (either as a research or teaching assistant) for one-third or less of normal pay, a very distracting and disconcerting circumstance. Second, the graduate student is expected to study and do research day and night. One's major professor assumes graduate students do not need sleep.

Finally, the graduate student's major professor is continually nagging him or her to read this paper, collect these data, write this paper, and work on his or her dissertation. In combination, these items reduce memory capacity.

But why does the full professor who seems to have everything going for him or her show such poor memory performance? Full professors have a living wage (according to some), cars that run, houses with real furniture, tenure, graduate students to do the work, and time to play golf and tennis. What could possibly explain the deficit in memory performance? Answering that question is the easiest of all:

GRADUATE STUDENTS AND TEEN-AGERS!

REFERENCE

Miller, G. (1956) The magical number seven, plus or minus two: some limits on our capacity for processing information. *Psychological Review, 63*, 81-97.

From "7 ± 2: Miller Must Have Been an Assistant Professor" by J.R. Thomas, 1987, *NASPSPA Newsletter*, **12**(1), pp. 10-11. Adapted by permission.

9. Nonequivalent Control Group

This design is frequently used in real-world settings where groups cannot be randomly formed. The design is as follows:

$$\begin{array}{ccc} O_1 & T & O_2 \\ \hline O_3 & & O_4 \end{array}$$

You will recognize this as Design 5 without randomization. Frequently, researchers will compare O_1 to O_3 and declare the groups equivalent if this comparison is not significant. Unfortunately, because the groups do not differ on the pretest does not mean they are not different on any number of unmeasured characteristics that could affect the outcome of the research.

If the groups differ when compared (O_1 vs. O_3), ANCOVA is usually employed to adjust O_2 and O_4 for initial differences. Although this design is frequently used, we believe that Designs 7 and 8 are much stronger quasi-experimental designs for investigating intact situations.

10. Ex Post Facto Design

In its simplest case, this is Design 3 but with the treatment not under the control of the experimenter. For example, we frequently compare the characteristic of athletes versus nonathletes, skilled players versus unskilled players, and expert performers versus novice performers. In effect, we are searching for variables that discriminate among these groups. Our interest usually resides in questions like, Did these variables influence the way these groups became different? Of course, this design cannot answer this question, but it may provide interesting characteristics for manipulation in other experimental designs.

11. Switched Replication Design

This design (Cook & Campbell, 1979) can be either true or quasi depending on whether levels are subjects or groups.

Levels (Subjects or groups)	Trials 1	2	3	4	5
1	O_1 T	O_2	O_3	O_4	O_5
2	O_6	O_7 T	O_8	O_9	O_{10}
3	O_{11}	O_{12}	O_{13} T	O_{14}	O_{15}
4	O_{16}	O_{17}	O_{18}	O_{19} T	O_{20}

If subjects are randomly assigned to levels 1 to 4, the design is a true one. If levels 1 to 4 are different "intact" groups (e.g., tennis players—college, high school, and two age levels of youth leagues), then the design is quasi. Any number of levels beyond two can be used, but the number of trials must be one greater than the number of levels.

This design has two strong features: The treatment is replicated several times, and long-term treatment effects can be evaluated. There is no standard statistical anaylsis for this design, but various ANOVAs with repeated measures could be used. Or the de-

sign might be analyzed by fitting regression lines to each level and testing how the slopes change.

This design might be particularly useful in research on sport teams where teams could be different levels or where different players within a team could be assigned to the various levels. (Thanks to Sandy Braver, Department of Psychology at Arizona State University, for this idea.)

There are other quasi-experimental designs, but the ones discussed here are the most frequently used types. Of course, quasi designs never quite control internal validity as well as do true designs; but they do allow us to conduct investigations either when true designs cannot be used or when the use of a true design significantly reduces external validity. Table 14.6 summarizes the control of threats to validity of quasi-experimental designs.

SUMMARY

In experimental research one or more independent variables (the treatment) are manipulated to assess the effects on one or more dependent variables (the response that is measured). Research studies are concerned with both internal and external validity. Internal validity pertains to controlling factors as required so that the results can be attributed to the treatment. Threats to internal validity include history, maturation, testing, instrumentation, statistical regression, selection biases, experimental mortality, selection-maturation interaction, and expectancy.

External validity is the ability to generalize the results to other subjects and other settings. Four threats to external validity were discussed: reactive or interactive effects of testing, the interaction of selection biases and the experimental treatment, reactive effects of experimental arrangements, and multiple-treatment interference. It is nearly impossible

Table 14.6 Quasi-Experimental Designs and Their Control of the Threats to Validity

Validity threat	Time series	Nonequivalent control	Reversal	Ex post facto
Internal				
History	−	−	−	?
Maturation	+	+	+	?
Testing	+	+	+	
Instrumentation	?	+	?	
Statistical regression	+	?	+	
Selection	+	+	+	−
Experimental mortality	+	+	+	
Selection × Maturation	+	−	+	−
Expectancy	?	?	?	?
External				
Testing × Treatment	−	−	?	−
Selection biases × Treatment	?	?	?	?
Experimental arrangements	?	?	?	?
Multiple treatments			?	

Note. + = strength, − = weakness, = not relevant, ? = questionable. From Campbell and Stanley (1963).

to have high degrees of both internal and external validity. The rigid controls needed for internal validity make it difficult to generalize the results to the real world. Conversely, studies with high external validity usually are weak in internal validity. Random selection of subjects and random assignment to treatments are the most powerful means of controlling most threats to internal and external validity.

Three types of experimental designs were described. Preexperimental designs are weak in that they can control very few sources of invalidity. True experimental designs are characterized by random formulation of groups, which allows the assumption that the groups were equivalent at the beginning of the study. The randomized groups, the pretest-posttest randomized groups, and the Solomon four-group designs were included under the category of true experimental designs.

Quasi-experimental designs are often used when it is too difficult or impossible to use true experimental designs or when a true design significantly limits external validity. Time series designs, the reversal design, the nonequivalent control group design, the ex post facto design, and the switched replication design were identified as quasi-experimental designs that are frequently used in experimental research.

Problems

Locate two research papers in refereed journals in your area of interest. One paper should have a true experimental design and the other a quasi-experimental design. Answer the following questions about each.

1. Describe the type of design. Draw a picture of it, using the notation from

this chapter. How many independent variables are there? How many levels of each? What are they? How many dependent variables? What are they?

2. What type of statistical analysis was used? Explain how it fits the design.

3. Identify the threats to internal validity that are controlled and uncontrolled. Explain each.

4. Identify the controlled and uncontrolled threats to external validity. Explain each.

Chapter 15

□

Qualitative Research

Qualitative research in physical education, exercise science, and sport science is relatively new. Researchers in education began adapting ethnographic research design to educational settings in the United States in the 1970s (Goetz & LeCompte, 1984), and significant qualitative research in physical education has been conducted more recently, mainly in the 1980s. In fact, it was not until 1989 that an invited essay/tutorial on qualitative research (Locke, 1989) was published in the Review and Commentary section of the *Research Quarterly for Exercise and Sport*.

The qualitative method of research is not new, however, in other fields. It has been employed in anthropology, psychology, and sociology for many years. This general form of research has been called a variety of names, including ethnographic, naturalistic, interpretive, grounded, phenomenological, subjective, and participant observational. Although the approaches are all slightly different, each "bears strong family resemblance to the others" (Erickson, 1986, p. 119).

For those of you who have never heard of qualitative research, it might be beneficial to review your courses or readings in anthropology. Nearly everyone has heard of classic ethnographic studies (even if you have never heard them referred to as ethnographic), such as the famous cultural research Margaret Mead conducted when she lived in the Samoai Islands in the South Pacific. Mead interviewed the Samoans at length about their society, their traditions, and their beliefs. This is an example of qualitative research. You do not need to live among natives in a remote, exotic land to do it, however. The qualitative research we refer to in this chapter is done mainly in everyday settings, such as schools, gymnasiums, sport facilities, fitness centers, and hospitals.

It could be argued that the term "qualitative research" may be too restrictive in that it seems to denote the absence of anything quantitative; however, this is certainly not the case. Nonetheless, qualitative research seems to be the term used most often in our field.

Our discussion of qualitative research focuses on the interpretive method as opposed to the so-called thick, rich description that characterized early research in anthropology, psychology, and sociology. This latter approach involves a very long and detailed account of the entity or incident and was espoused by Franz Boas, who is considered the "father" of cultural anthropology. In rejecting the armchair speculation that typified the late-19th-century work, Boas insisted that the researcher not only collect his or her own data but that it be reported with as little comment or interpretation as possible (cited in Kirk & Miller, 1986). We believe that the most significant feature of qualitative research is the interpretive content rather than an overconcern about procedure.

Erickson (1986) argues that the technique of narrative description (sometimes referred to as "writing like crazy") does not necessarily mean the research being conducted is interpretive or qualitative.

It is not our intention to present a comprehensive review of qualitative research. One reason is that we do not have the space to do so, as this text is designed primarily to survey various methods of research. Despite our assertion that qualitative research is quite new in our field, a comprehensive review would still be a major undertaking because we would need to draw from many related fields. Moreover, there is considerable disagreement among qualitative researchers concerning their methodologies and theoretical presuppositions that would need to be addressed. You can gain a solid appreciation regarding the scope of qualitative research, the different approaches to data collection, and their theoretical foundations by consulting, for example, Jacob (1987, 1988) and the references in essays such as those of Erickson (1986) and Locke (1989). Readable single-source texts include those of Bogdan and Biklen (1982), Goetz and LeCompte (1984), and Lincoln and Guba (1985).

THE QUANTITATIVE-QUALITATIVE QUANDARY

Much has been written on the debate over the comparative merits of quantitative and qualitative approaches to problem solving, so we do not discuss it here. Locke (1989) observed that the debate in our field comes at a point where the same dispute is winding down in other areas. So, instead of relating some of the arguments about which method is better, let us simply contrast some main differences between quantitative and qualitative research.

Qualitative research is often depicted as being the antithesis of the more traditional quantitative methods, such as experimental and survey research. Quantitative research methods typically involve precise measurements, rigid control of variables (often in a laboratory setting), and statistical analyses. Qualitative research methods generally include field observations, case studies, ethnography, and narrative reports (Linn, 1986).

Quantitative research tends to focus on analysis (i.e., taking apart and examining components of a phenomenon), whereas qualitative research seeks to understand the meaning of an experience to the participants in a particular setting and how the components mesh together to form a whole. Some of the basic characteristics of quantitative and qualitative research are contrasted in Table 15.1.

Notice that in qualitative research the focus is on the "essence" of the phenomena; the view of the world is a function of one's perception and is highly subjective. The objectives are primarily description, understanding, and meaning. The researcher does not manipulate variables through experimental treatments but rather is interested more in process than in product. The researcher observes and gathers data in the field, that is, the natural setting. There are no preconceived hypotheses, which characterize quantitative research. Rather, qualitative research strives to develop hypotheses from the observations. In other words, qualitative research emphasizes induction, whereas quantitative research largely emphasizes deduction.

In quantitative research, the researcher tries very hard to keep out of the data gathering process through the use of laboratory measurements, questionnaires, and other so-called objective instruments. The quantitative data are then usually analyzed by statistical formulas, with computations performed by computers. However, the researcher is the primary instrument for data collection and analysis in qualitative research, which is very subjective in this sense. The researcher is interacting with the subjects, and the sensitivity and perception of the researcher play crucial roles in procuring and processing the observations and responses.

Table 15.1 Characteristics of Qualitative and Quantitative Research

Point of comparison	Qualitative research	Quantitative research
Focus of research	Quality (nature, essence)	Quantity (how much, how many)
Philosophical roots	Phenomenology, symbolic interaction	Positivism, logical empiricism
Associated phrases	Fieldwork, ethnographic, naturalistic, grounded, subjective	Experimental, empirical, statistical
Goals of investigation	Understanding, description, discovery, hypothesis generating	Prediction, control, description, confirmation, hypothesis testing
Design characteristics	Flexible, evolving, emergent	Predetermined, structured
Setting	Natural, familiar	Unfamiliar, artificial
Sample	Small, nonrandom, theoretical	Large, random, representative
Data collection	Researcher as primary instrument, interviews, observations	Inanimate instruments (scales, tests, surveys, questionnaires, computers)
Mode of analysis	Inductive (by researcher)	Deductive (by statistical methods)
Findings	Comprehensive, holistic, expansive	Precise, narrow, reductionist

PROCEDURES IN QUALITATIVE RESEARCH

It should go without saying that there are many variations in the way qualitative research is done. Consequently, the procedures outlined in this section should be viewed simply as an attempt to provide an orientation for readers who are basically unfamiliar with qualitative research. As with any type of research, the novice will benefit the most from reading completed studies that have used particular methods.

Defining the Problem

We will not spend much time defining the problem because we have talked about this step before, and it does not differ appreciably from that of other research methods. We emphasized that several possible methods can be used for any research problem. The differ-

ent methods can yield different information about the problem. Thus, when the researcher decides to use qualitative research as opposed to some other design, the decision is based on what he or she wants to know about the problem (for more discussion on this point, see chapter 1).

Formulating Hypotheses and the Theoretical Framework

In highlighting some of the differences between quantitative and qualitative research, we stated that qualitative research usually builds hypotheses and theories in an inductive manner, that is, as a result of the observations. Quantitative research often begins with research hypotheses that are subsequently tested. Thus, it is not uncommon for a qualitative study to not have stated hypotheses in the first part (or chapter) of the report. As explained by Goetz and LeCompte

(1984), although research ultimately may hope to discover causal relationships, ethnographers commonly avoid assuming a priori relationships. However, some studies are designed to confirm or refine hypotheses that have been developed in previous research. In such studies, hypotheses are stated in the first part of the report. The researcher then proceeds to modify, refine, confirm, or reject them.

Data Collection

There are several components in collecting data for qualitative research, just as there are in quantitative research. Training and pilot work are still necessary, and so is selecting subjects appropriately. In addition you need to gain access to the field setting and become as unobtrusive as possible in your collection of data.

Training and Pilot Work

In qualitative research the investigator is the instrument for collecting and analyzing the data. It is imperative, then, that the researcher is adequately prepared. Certainly course work, fieldwork reports, and advice and interaction with one's advisor are helpful, but ultimately the only way to become competent is through hands-on experience. In the classic anthropological tradition, fieldwork is essentially unteachable (Erickson, 1986). One arrives with an open mind, a pad and pencil, a safari jacket, and a hunting knife. Romantic as this may seem, modern-day professional preparation is more structured, and clinical experience is usually acquired through projects under the direction of an advisor.

As always, pilot work is essential, and fieldwork experience in a setting similar to that of the proposed study is recommended. If the researcher has prior experience in the field setting (e.g., as an instructor, a coach, or a player), it will certainly be helpful in

most respects. However, Locke (1989) made a good point while describing the phases of a qualitative study about familiarity, in that it tends to spawn "an almost irresistible flood of personal judgments" (p. 7) that, if not recognized and controlled, could become a significant threat to the integrity of the data.

Selection of Subjects

Basically, the selection of subjects for a qualitative study is the same as described for the case study in chapter 13. Qualitative research studies do not attempt to make inferences from their subjects to some larger population. Rather, the subjects are selected because they have certain characteristics. Obviously, there are pragmatic reasons concerning the location and the availability of subjects because in nearly every case numerous other sites and subjects with similar characteristics exist.

Probability sampling is not used, simply because there is no way to estimate the probability that each subject has of being selected and no assurance that each subject has some chance of being included (Chein, 1981). Instead, the selection of subjects in qualitative research is purposive, which in essence means that a sample is selected from which one can learn the most. The researcher may be looking for subjects with certain levels of expertise or experience. Goetz and LeCompte (1984) used the term "criterion-based sampling," in which the researcher establishes certain criteria or standards that must be met before a subject can be included in the investigation. In essence, then, the selection of subjects in qualitative research involves consideration of where to observe, when to observe, whom to observe, and what to observe (Burgess, 1982).

Entry

The researcher must have access to the field setting to conduct a qualitative study. Moreover, the researcher must be able to observe and interview the subjects at the appropriate time and location. These mundane details may seem somewhat trivial in the overall scheme of things in the mystical world of research, but nothing is more important than site entry. In any type of research you must have access to the data, whether it is source material in historical research or subjects in an experimental or a survey study. However, the problem can be of greater magnitude in qualitative research than in most other methods. The researcher is not simply borrowing the subjects for a short time for some measurements or taking a little class time to administer a questionnaire. In qualitative research, the investigator is often at the site for days, weeks, or months. This "outsider" is listening, watching, coding, and videotaping, as well as imposing on the time of the teacher (or coach, or whomever) and the students (players and participants) for interviews.

We are intentionally belaboring this point because it is so important. Obviously, it takes diplomacy, personality, and artful persuasion to gain site entry. Frankly, some people just cannot do this. Even when entry is achieved, some studies have failed to do what they intended because the investigator "rubbed people the wrong way" and the subjects were not motivated to cooperate fully.

Thus, the negotiation of gaining access to the subjects in their naturalistic setting is important and complex. It starts with the first contact by telephone or letter, extends through data collection, and continues after the researcher has left the site (Erickson, 1986).

Before we discuss some of the aspects of data collection, we should elaborate a little more on the topic of cooperation with the subjects. Rapport is everything. The subjects must feel that they can trust you, or else they will not give you the information you are after. Obviously, formal informed consent must be obtained and the stipulations embodied in the whole concept of informed consent observed.

There are a number of ethical considerations in qualitative research, simply because of the intensive personal contact with the subjects. Thus, the subjects need to know that provisions will be followed to safeguard their rights of privacy and to guarantee anonymity. If, for some reason, it is impossible to keep information confidential, this must be made clear. The researcher must have given a great deal of thought to these matters before data collection and must be able to explain the purpose and significance of the study effectively and convey the importance of subject cooperation in language that the subjects can understand. One of the largest obstacles in the quest for natural behavior and candor on the part of the subjects is their suspicion that the researcher will be evaluating them in some way. The researcher must be very convincing in this regard. The most successful studies are those in which the subjects feel as though they are a part of the project. In other words, a collaborative relationship should be established.

Methods of Data Collection

The most common sources of data collection in qualitative research are interviews, observations, and researcher-designed instruments (Goetz & LeCompte, 1984). The methodology is planned and pilot-tested before the actual study.

The researcher will typically have some type of framework (subpurposes perhaps) that determines and guides the nature of the data collection. For example, one phase of the research might pertain to the manner in which expert and nonexpert sport performers perceive various aspects of a game. This phase could involve having the subject describe his or her perceptions of what is taking place in a specific scenario. A second phase of the study might focus on the interactive thought processes and decisions of the two groups of subjects while they are playing. The data for this phase could be obtained from filming the subjects in action and then interviewing the subjects while they are watching their performances on videotape. Still another aspect of the study could be directed at the knowledge structure of the subjects, which could be determined by a researcher-constructed instrument.

Interviews. The interview is undoubtedly the most common source of data in qualitative studies. The person-to-person format is most prevalent, but occasionally group interviews are conducted. Interviews range from the highly structured style in which questions are determined before the interview to the open-ended, conversational format. In qualitative research, the highly structured format is used primarily to gather sociodemographic information. For the most part, however, interviews are more open-ended and less structured (Merriam, 1988). Frequently, the interviewer will ask the same questions of all the subjects, but the order of the questions, the exact wording, and the type of follow-up questions may vary considerably.

It requires skill and experience to be a good interviewer. We emphasized earlier that the researcher must first establish rapport with the subjects. If the subjects do not trust the researcher, they will not open up and describe their true feelings, thoughts, and intentions. Complete rapport is established over time as people get to know and trust one another. However, one facet of skill in interviewing is being able to ask questions in such a way that the respondent feels that he or she can talk freely. Kirk and Miller (1986) described their field research in Peru, where they attempted to ascertain the knowledge of urban, lower-middle-class people about coca, the organic source of cocaine. Coca is legal and widely available there.

In their initial attempts to ask the people to tell them about coca, they received the same culturally approved answers from all the subjects. It was only after they changed their style of asking less sensible questions (e.g., How did you find out you didn't like coca?) that the Peruvians opened up and elaborated on their knowledge of (and sometimes their personal commitment to) coca. Kirk and Miller made a good point about asking the right questions and the value of using different approaches. Indeed, this is a basic argument for the validity of qualitative research.

Skill in interviewing takes practice. Ways to develop such skill include videotaping one's own performance in conducting an interview, observing experienced interviewers, role playing, and peer critiquing. It is very important that the interviewer appear nonjudgmental. This can be difficult in situations in which the subject's views are quite different from those of the interviewer. The interviewer must be alert to both verbal and nonverbal messages and flexible in rephrasing and pursuing certain lines of questioning. The researcher must be able to ask questions so that the subject understands what is being asked. One must be able to use wording that is clear and meaningful to the respondent. Above all, the interviewer has to be a good listener.

The use of a tape recorder is undoubtedly the most common method of recording interview data as it has the obvious advantage of preserving the entire interview for later analysis. Although some subjects may experience nervousness in talking while being taped, this uneasiness usually disappears in a short time. The main drawback with tape recording is equipment malfunctions. This is vexing and frustrating when it happens during the interview, but it is devastating when it happens afterward when you are trying to replay and analyze the interview. Certainly, it is wise to always have fresh batteries and to make sure the recorder is working proper-ly early in the interview. It is also recom-mended that about halfway through the interview you stop and play back some tape to see whether the person is speaking into the microphone loudly and clearly enough and whether you are getting the data. The subjects (especially children) love to hear themselves speak, so playing back the tape for them serves as motivation also. Remem-ber, however, that machines can always malfunction.

Videotaping seems to be the best method because you not only hear what the subject said but also preserve nonverbal behavior. Videotape is not used much because it is awkward and intrusive. However, it will probably become more prevalent as techni-cal advances continue to be made.

Taking notes during the interview is another frequently used method. Sometimes it is used in addition to recording, primarily when the interviewer wishes to denote cer-tain points of emphasis or make additional notations. Taking notes without taping has the drawback of not being able to record all

that is said. It also keeps the interviewer very busy, interfering with one's thoughts and ob-servations while the subject is talking. In highly structured interviews and when using some type of formal instrument, the inter-viewer can more easily take notes by check-ing and writing short responses than he or she can in a probing, less structured inter-view format.

The least preferred technique is trying to remember and write down afterward what was said in the interview. The drawbacks are many, and this method is seldom used.

Observation. Earlier studies relied on direct observation with note taking and coding of certain categories of behavior. More recently, videotaping has been the method of choice. The videotape can observe all of a subject's behavior and preserve it for later analysis. If desired, sounds associated with the observa-tions can simultaneously be recorded, as can comments by the researcher. The newer cameras are lightweight and capable of ob-taining remarkably clear pictures in natural lighting.

One of the major drawbacks to observation methods is obtrusiveness. A stranger with a camera or pad and pencil is recording people's natural behavior. A key word here is "stranger." The task of a qualitative researcher is to make sure that the subjects get accustomed to having the researcher (and video camera) around. For example, the researcher may want to practice or pretend to film in the setting for at least a couple of days before the initial filming.

In an artificial setting, one-way mirrors and observation rooms can be used. In a natural setting, it would be nice if one could use a "Candid Camera" ploy, such as hiding a camera in a stuffed moose head (in a gym?). Locke (1989) has observed that most naturalistic field studies are reports of what goes on when a visitor is present. The important question is, How important and limiting is this? Locke suggested ways of suppressing reactivity, such as both being in the setting long enough so that the visitor is no longer considered as a novelty and being as unobtrusive as possible in everything from dress to choice of location in a room.

Other Data-Recording Devices. There are many sources of data in qualitative research. We have mentioned researcher-constructed behavior-coding inventories. Self-reports of knowledge and attitude also are occasionally used. Their use is limited, simply because of the inherent limitations of such formal self-reports with regard to a truly qualitative study. We also mentioned the use of scenarios, which usually are developed by the researcher. The subject's responses provide his or her perceptions, interpretations, and awareness of the total situation and the interplay of the actors in the scenario.

Other recording devices include notebooks, narrative field logs, and diaries, which record the researcher's reactions, concerns, and speculations during the course of the data collection. Printed materials such as course syllabi, team rosters, evaluation reports, subject notes, and photographs of the setting and situations are examples of document data used in qualitative research.

Data Analysis

Data analysis in qualitative research is quite different from conventional quantitative research. First, analysis is done during as well as after data collection. During data collection the researcher is sorting and organizing data and speculating and developing tentative hypotheses to guide and direct him or her to other sources and types of data. Qualitative research is often done in a manner somewhat similar to multiple experiment research, in which discoveries made during the study shape and direct each successive phase of the study. Thus, simultaneous data collection and analysis allows the researcher to direct the data-collection stage more effectively. Analysis then becomes more intensive after the data have been collected (Merriam, 1988).

Another basic difference between quantitative and qualitative data analysis is that qualitative data are generally presented by words, descriptions, and images, whereas quantitative analysis is typically presented through numbers.

The analysis of data in a qualitative study can take different forms, depending on the nature of the investigation and the defined purposes. Consequently, one cannot go into great depth in discussing analysis without tying it to a specific study. Therefore, we summarized the general phases of analysis synthesized from descriptions in several qualitative research texts. The general phases include sorting and analysis during data collection, analysis and categorization, and interpretation and theory construction.

Sorting and Analysis During Data Collection

The simultaneous collection and analysis of data is an important feature of qualitative research. It enables the researcher to focus better on certain questions and, in turn, to direct the data collection more effectively. Although the researcher has specific questions in mind when the data collection is begun, very likely changes and shifts in focus will be made as the data unfold.

The researcher needs to keep in close touch with the data. It is a foolish mistake to wait until after the data are collected to analyze them. Decisions must be made with regard to scope and direction, or the researcher may be left with a mass of data that are unfocused, repetitious, and overwhelming in the sheer volume of material that needs to be processed (Merriam, 1988). Also, there could be gaps in the data because the researcher is so close to the data that he or she may not realize that some needed evidence was not collected.

The researcher typically writes many observer comments to stimulate critical thinking about what is being observed. The researcher should not be merely a human recording machine. New ideas should be tried out, and one should think about how certain data relate to the larger theoretical, methodological, and substantive issues (Bogdan & Biklen, 1982). However, it is a good idea to periodically review one's proposal to make sure the investigation is not straying from the original questions that must be addressed in the final report (Goetz & LeCompte, 1984).

Analysis and Categorization

Analysis is the process of making sense out of one's data. Goetz and LeCompte (1984) have recommended that the researcher read the data again before analysis to ensure com-

> It is a good idea to periodically review one's proposal to make sure the investigation is not straying from the original questions that must be addressed in the final report.

pleteness and to generate analytic categories. This is the beginning of the stages of organizing, abstracting, integrating, and synthesizing, which ultimately permit the researcher to report what has been seen and heard. An outline may be developed to search for patterns that can be transformed into categories.

The qualitative researcher faces a formidable task in sorting the data for content analysis. Obviously, there are many types of categories that can be devised with any given set of data, depending on the problem being studied. For example, a researcher could categorize observations of a physical education class in terms of management style by the teacher; another category could relate to social interaction among the students; another category could deal with sex differences in behavior or treatment; and another could be based on verbal and nonverbal instructional behavior. Categories can range in complexity from relatively simple units of behavior types to conceptual typologies or theories (Merriam, 1988).

Researchers use different data-sorting techniques. Index cards and file folders have been widely used for years. Computers can be programmed to store, sort, and retrieve data. First, interview transcripts, notes, and observations are entered into the computer. Then, after themes (categories) have been designated, the researcher can retrieve sets of data that have been sorted by category.

Categorization of data is one of the key facets of true qualitative research. The researcher, instead of using mere description, may use descriptive data as examples of the concepts that are being advanced. The data need to be studied and categorized so that the researcher can retrieve and analyze information across categories as part of the inductive process.

Interpretation and Theory Construction

When the data have been organized and sorted, the researcher then attempts to merge them into a holistic portrayal of the phenomenon. An acknowledged basic goal of qualitative research is to vividly reconstruct the events that happened during the fieldwork.

The Analytic Narrative. This reconstruction may (in some studies) be largely a descriptive narrative organized chronologically or topically. In our concept of qualitative research, however, we support the position voiced by Goetz and LeCompte (1984) that researchers who merely describe fail to do justice to their data. Goetz and LeCompte maintain that by leaving readers to their own conclusions, one risks misinterpretation and perhaps trivialization of the data by readers who are unable to make the implied connections. They further suggest (p. 196) that the researcher who can find no implications beyond the data should never have undertaken the study in the first place.

The *analytic narrative* is the foundation of qualitative research. Researchers (especially novices) are often reluctant to take the bold action needed to assign meaning to the data. Erickson (1986) has suggested that to stimulate analysis early in the process one should force oneself to make an assertion, choose an excerpt from the field notes that substantiates the assertion, and then write a *narrative vignette* that portrays the validity of the assertion. The researcher, in the process of making decisions concerning the event to report and the descriptive terms to use, becomes more explicitly aware of the perspectives that are emerging from the data. This awareness thus stimulates and facilitates further critical reflection.

The narrative vignette is one of the fundamental characteristics of qualitative research. As opposed to the typical analysis sections in quantitative research studies (which are about as interesting as watching paint dry), the vignette captures the reader's attention, thereby helping the researcher make his or her point. It gives the reader a sense of "being there." A well-written description of a situation can convey a sense of holistic meaning that is definitely advantageous in providing evidence for the various assertions of the researcher. Locke (1989), in characterizing qualitative research, has stated that the researcher can describe the physical education scene so vividly that "you can smell the lockers and hear the thud of running feet" (p. 4). Griffin and Templin (1989) provide the following example of a vignette:

> The second period physical education class at Big City Middle School is playing soccer. The teacher has placed two piles of sweatshirts at each end of a large open field to serve as goals. There are no field markings. Four boys run up and down the field following the ball. Several other students stand silently in their assigned position until the ball comes near, then they move tentatively toward the ball to kick it away. Three girls stand talking in a tight circle near the far end of the field. They are startled when the ball rolls into their group, and two boys yell at them to get out of the way. They do and then regroup after the ball and the boys go to the other side of the field. Two boys, who have not touched the ball during the class, engage in a playful wrestling match near one goal. The teacher stands in the center of the field with a whistle in his mouth. He hasn't said anything since he divided students into

teams at the beginning of class. He has blown the whistle twice to call fouls. The students play around him as if he were not there. A bell rings and all the students drop their pinneys where they are and start toward the school building. Belatedly, the teacher blows his whistle to end the game and begins to move around the field picking up pinneys.

After class, as we walk back to the building, the teacher says, ''These kids are wild. If you can just run off some of their energy, they don't get into so much trouble in school. This group especially, not too many smarts (taps his temple), don't get into much game strategy.'' (He sees a boy and girl from the class standing near the door of the girls' locker room talking.) He yells, ''Johnson, get your butt to the shower and stop bothering the ladies.'' He smiles at me. ''You've got to be on them all the time.'' He looks up and sighs, ''Well, two [classes] down, three to go.'' (p. 399)

We caution you, however, that Locke and other scholars do not hold that richness of detail alone is what makes a narrative vignette valid. Siedentop (1989) has warned that whether data are to be trusted should not be based on the narrative skills of the researcher. According to Erickson (1986), a valid account is not simply a description but an analysis:

> A story can be an accurate report of a series of events, yet not portray the meaning of the actions from the perspectives taken by the actors in the event. . . . It is the combination of richness and interpretive perspective that makes the account valid. (p. 150)

Vignettes are not left to stand by themselves. The researcher should make interpretive connections between narrative vignettes and other forms of description, such as direct quotes and quantitative materials.

Direct quotes from interviews with the subjects taken from field notes and audio- or videotapes are another form of vignette that enriches the analysis and furnishes documentation for the researcher's point of view. Direct quotes from different individuals may serve to demonstrate agreement (or disagreement) about some phenomenon. Direct quotes from the same people on different occasions may provide evidence that certain events are typical or could demonstrate a pattern or trend in perceptions over time.

For example, Nelson (1988), trying to illustrate differences in the thought processes of students taught by expert and novice teachers, used quotes to document her assertion that students of novice teachers tended to think about procedures and organization more than content:

> **Interviewer:** What are you thinking at this point in the lesson?
>
> **Student:** I didn't know what to do. I thought we were going to run around the gym.
>
> **Student:** I was thinking are we all going to be in the same group. (p. 58)

In contrast, thoughts of students of expert teachers were more related to the lesson content:

> **Interviewer:** What are you thinking at this point in the lesson?
>
> **Student:** He was showing us how it [heart rate] would change after we did aerobics.
>
> **Student:** I was thinking about how to . . . uh, make sure I was adding correctly to get the right score and everything like that. (p. 59)

It is usually emphasized in qualitative research that one should communicate one's perspective clearly to the reader. The narrative's function is to present the researcher's interpretive point in a clear and meaningful manner.

Quantitative Analysis

Although we have tended to emphasize the differences between qualitative and quantitative research, we do not want you to conclude that there are no (or should not be any) quantitative features in a qualitative study (and vice versa). Actually, qualitative research can use a wide range of quantitative analyses, from simple frequency tables to multivariate statistical techniques.

Frequency tables are not uncommon at all. Raw frequencies of occurrences are used to reduce data. This is especially appropriate in studies that use some type of observational instrument that codes designated categories of behavior. The frequencies are often converted to percentages to show the extent of certain behaviors or to make comparative statements.

Frequency data in qualitative research are often nominal measures. Thus, contingency tables are sometimes used to demonstrate data patterns. Nonparametric statistics are usually the most appropriate type of statistical analysis because of the difficulty in making the necessary assumptions for parametric statistics. Miles and Huberman (1984) have described a number of methods that can be used in coding, analyzing, and interpreting qualitative data. In his commentary on Locke's (1989) study, Schutz (1989) maintained that there are a number of both nonmathematical and mathematical ways of analyzing qualitative data. He cited the "systematic network analysis" strategy proposed by Bliss and colleagues as being a viable nonmathematical method that produces a pictorial representation (tree diagram) of the manner by which coded categories are related "which are independent and which are conditional on the choice of others" (p. 33).

Among the mathematical procedures, Schutz highlighted loglinear analysis as having relevance for qualitative data analysis. Although qualitative variables are nominally scaled, the frequency of occurrence lends itself to quantitative analysis by contingency tables and to subsequent procedures similar to factorial ANOVA. "The log-linear analysis transforms the relative frequencies to logarithms which yield an additive model similar to the additivity of the Sum of Squares in ANOVA" (Schutz, 1989, p. 34).

The main point we are trying to make here is that qualitative research does not exclude quantitative analysis. One of the negative features or outcomes of arguments that support or defend particular methods is that the reader fails to see points of convergence among different methods. The researcher should always be alert and amenable to using any methods that could yield meaningful information. Remember, the major purpose of any analysis is to make the most sense out of the data.

Triangulation of Data

The term *triangulation*, borrowed from the field of surveying, refers to the use of more than one source of data to substantiate a researcher's conclusion. Triangulation provides a means by which qualitative researchers test the strength of their interpretations. It is a means used to establish validity and reliability in qualitative research (see chapter 16). In its most basic sense, triangulation is a way of increasing confidence in one's findings. Intuitively, it makes sense that the more evidence one has, the more likely one's conclusions are valid. Triangulation is not a simple concept. There are different types of triangulation, and in some cases triangulation can act to increase error rather than reduce it.

Denzin, cited in Fielding and Fielding (1986), classified triangulation into four types:

- data,
- investigator,
- method, and
- theory.

Data triangulation refers to data sources (oneself, informants, interviews, observations, documents, and different times and settings). Investigator triangulation can be "within-method" or "between-method." The former refers to the same approach being used more than once and the latter to different methods being applied to the same situation. Theory triangulation is a phase of analysis in which a situation is examined from the standpoint of different competing theories (Fielding & Fielding, 1986). Perhaps a simple example of source triangulation may assure you that we are not talking about anything mysterious or esoteric here. Say that a study is addressing the success of a coach. Multiple sources of data (triangulation) could include interviews with the coach, colleagues, players, parents of the players, and administrators.

Generally, triangulation is valuable because of the increased quality control achieved by combining methods, observers, and data sources. However, it is naive to think that merely combining different kinds of data will "unproblematically add up to produce a more complete picture" (Hammersley & Atkinson, 1983, p. 199). There is the definite likelihood that multiple methods may serve to magnify error. In other words, each method has some error associated with it, and some methods have more than others. This has a multiplying effect. The different methods must be weighed and considered in terms of their relative biases and limitations. Moreover, although theoretical triangulation can provide a more complete picture, it does not necessarily reduce bias. Thus, an important aspect of triangulation is to consider the relationships of the different kinds of data to counteract the threat to validity of each.

The concept of *convergence* is embodied in triangulation. Convergence is what you might imagine triangulation would accomplish. It is analogous to robustness in factor analysis in that, if the same results appear with different methodological techniques, it probably is not simply the product of the method. Convergence strengthens the evidence.

Theory Construction

Our use of the terms "theory" and "theorizing" should not unduly alarm graduate students and discourage them from undertaking qualitative research. We are not talking about developing a model on the scale of the theory of relativity here. *Theorizing*, according to Goetz and LeCompte (1984), is a cognitive process of discovering abstract categories and the relationships among those categories. A theory is an explanation of some aspect of practice that permits the researcher to draw inferences about future events. This process is a fundamental tool to develop or confirm explanations. One processes information, compares the findings with past experience and sets of values, and then makes decisions. The decisions may not be correct, so one may then need to revise the theory or model in such cases.

Data analysis depends on theorizing. The tasks of theorizing are "perceiving; comparing, contrasting, aggregating, and ordering; establishing linkages and relationships; and speculating" (Goetz & LeCompte, 1984, p. 167). Perceiving involves the consideration of all sources of data and all aspects of the phenomena being studied. Of course, this takes place during data collection as well as afterward. The perceptual process of determining which specific factors to analyze guides the collection of data.

The tasks of comparing, contrasting, aggregating, and ordering are primary functions in qualitative research. The researcher decides which units are similar and dissimilar and what is important about the differences and similarities. Analytic description cannot occur until the researcher builds the categories of like and unlike properties and carries out a systematic content analysis of the data.

Establishing linkages and relationships constitutes a kind of detective work that qualitative researchers do in the theorizing process. The researcher uses both inductive and deductive methods of establishing relationships ''while developing a theory or hypothesis that is grounded in the data'' (Goetz & LeCompte, 1984, p. 172).

Speculation is often depicted as the key to hypothesizing and developing theories. It requires the researcher to play with the data and make inferences. The researcher must go beyond the data and predict what will happen in the future. Speculation is a basic component of the inductive process. *Negative case selection* is also used in theorizing. In this procedure, the researcher looks for exceptions to the hypothesized construct. The exceptions require either a reformulation of the hypothesis, a redefinition of the phenomenon, or a qualification of the circumstances.

Establishing hypotheses requires evidence to make an educated guess about some phenomenon. The researcher tests the hypothesis and then modifies and refines it until the hypothesis either is rejected or is accepted as being a suitable explanation. Taylor and Bogdan (1984) have set forth some steps in analytic induction. The researcher roughly defines the phenomenon and formulates an explanatory hypothesis that may be based on the data, the literature, or the researcher's experience and intuition. The researcher tests the hypothesis with one or more cases. Negative cases are also sought to disprove the hypothesis. Whenever the data do not fit the hypothesis, the researcher goes back to the drawing board and reformulates the hypothesis or redefines the phenomenon. This process continues until the hypothesis seems to hold up over a broad range of cases. Tested hypotheses evolve into theories, which are generalizable and can explain a large number of phenomena.

A theory based on and evolving from data is called a *grounded theory* (Glaser & Strauss, 1967). In applied research, grounded theories are considered to be the best at explaining observed phenomena, understanding relationships, and drawing inferences about future activities.

The Written Report

There is no standard (or ''correct'') format for a qualitative research report, just as there are no rigorously adhered-to formats for any other type of research. Here we simply mention some main components of a qualitative research report and their placement in the report. Your department or university may have a definite order of components that you must follow.

The components of a qualitative study are similar to those of other conventional research reports. The first part introduces the problem and provides background and related literature. A description of method is an integral part of the report. Although this section is not as extensive in a journal article as in a thesis, it is usually much more extensive than in other forms of research. The reasons are obvious. The methodology is integrally related to the analysis and is also very important in terms of validity and reliability.

The analysis and discussion section forms a major proportion of the report. Charts, tables, and figures are contained in this section and must be integrated into the narrative. A major contributor to the bulk of this section is the description that is contained in a qualitative study. As we discussed previously, narrative vignettes and direct quotes are basic to this type of research. The qualitative study strives to provide enough detail to show the reader that the author's conclusions make sense (Firestone, 1987). The author is faced with a delicate problem in terms of finding a balance between the rich description materials and the analysis and interpretation. Some writers include too much description to illustrate their points, and some use too little. Researchers have suggested that 60%-70% of the report be descriptive material and that 30%-40% should be devoted to the conceptual framework (Merriam, 1988). Definitely, some balance is needed, and the task requires judgment in deciding which evidence to include to illustrate one's ideas.

It is doubtful that any graduate student is under the false impression that doing qualitative research is a quick-and-easy technique. To emphasize this point, we call your attention to Table 15.2, which lists some of the trials and tribulations that happened to one doctoral student in only the data collection phase of the study.

Table 15.2 List of Funny Things That Happened During the Collection of Qualitative Data

1. On two occasions, reported to gymnasium (carrying camera, TV monitor, tape recorder, and notes) to find door locked. Had to walk all the way around the building—once in the rain.
2. Reported to school to collect data to find classes wouldn't be held because of:
   a. a donut sale
   b. teacher was ill (twice)
   c. Christmas music rehearsal
3. Interview with teacher interrupted by principal due to crisis over a parent and a charity clothing sale. Interview postponed.
4. Tape recorder became inoperable during interview.
5. Tape recorder became inoperable while transcribing. Had to repeat interviews.
6. Group tape-recording session had to be rescheduled because of complete loss of control when a third-grade student belched into the microphone.
7. Had to buy own camera because department's camera was inoperable.
8. Broke own camera. Repair took two weeks.
9. Had to use participating school's TV monitor but couldn't find proper cord. Interviews had to be rescheduled.
10. While the grad student was making backup tapes, the VCR with original data tape was stolen. Police nabbed the culprit and data were recovered, but the graduate student was comatose.

INTERNAL AND EXTERNAL VALIDITY IN QUALITATIVE RESEARCH

All types of research must address the concepts of internal and external validity. Lincoln and Guba (1985) have suggested that the term *truth value* be used instead of internal validity and that the term *transferability* be used for external validity. In previous chapters we have tried to make the point that some types of research designs are stronger in internal validity and others stronger in external validity. Furthermore, the two concepts may work in opposition to each other in that tight controls to increase internal validity reduce the generalizability of the findings and, conversely, that designs that strive for external validity suffer from threats to internal validity.

Internal Validity

Although experimental laboratory research is often depicted as being the epitome of internal validity, some researchers contend that qualitative research is also high in internal validity. Merriam (1988) has stated that internal validity deals with the question of how one's findings match reality. In other words, do the findings capture what is really there? Reality is viewed as holistic, multidimensional, and ever-changing. Thus, the qualitative researcher is primarily interested in perspectives rather than truth per se (Taylor & Bogdan, 1984). Ratcliff (1983) has argued that there are only notions of validity and that committing oneself to a particular notion of validity can lead to a *Type III error* (solving the wrong problem) or a *Type IV error* (solving a problem that is not worth solving).

Goetz and LeCompte (1984) have taken a more conventional approach to internal validity. They believe that qualitative research faces some of the same threats to internal validity as other types of research. History, for example, is seen as a threat to qualitative research. The researcher should try to establish baseline data and determine which data remain stable over time and which data

change. Systematic replication and comparisons with baseline data can help control not only for the threat of history but also for that of maturation.

Observer effects represent a significant threat to internal validity in qualitative research. Observer effects must be considered in light of specific contexts. The threat can be greatly reduced by the firsthand presence of the researcher over time. Unobtrusiveness, honesty, and constructive personal relationships with the subjects will enhance internal validity. Locke (1989) has emphasized that qualitative researchers should learn to be wary of subjects who occasionally do not tell the truth (for any of several reasons) and thus can become skilled at penetrating false data.

Selection and regression problems face the qualitative researcher just as in experimental research. The qualitative researcher does not usually have any treatment effects to isolate, but he or she must analyze the data carefully in light of the specificity of the participants.

Spurious conclusions can result from bias and contamination of the data. The researcher needs to examine the data carefully and make good use of corroborative sources of data and thorough analytical techniques.

Merriam (1988) listed six basic strategies to ensure internal validity. The strategies include

- triangulation,
- plausibility checks of taking data and interpretations back to the subjects,
- long-term data collection and repeated observations,
- peer examination and evaluation of one's findings,
- involving the participants in all phases of the research, and
- clarifying the researcher's own bias and theoretical orientation at the outset of the study.

External Validity

The generalizability of this method of research has often been questioned because of the small number of subjects and the lack of random sampling in the typical qualitative research study. Some qualitative researchers have attempted to meet this criticism in the traditional sense with multicase or cross-case methods (Yin, 1984). On the other hand, Erickson (1986) maintained that generalizable knowledge is inappropriate for qualitative research and that one should concentrate on "concrete universals" arrived at through specific cases and then compare them with the specifics of other similar cases. What one learns from a specific situation is transferable.

One of the strongest intuitive arguments for external validity in qualitative research is the concept of *user generalizability*. The user (reader) evaluates the findings of the carefully described and interpreted study and asks what things apply to his or her situation. It is contended that this is a common practice in medicine and law. Thus, generalizing is left to those who can apply the findings to their own situations. Locke (1989) stated that, given the rich contextual description, most readers can easily recognize which situations apply to their own and that the strong recognition of application by the reader is in no way an inferior measure of external validity. Goetz and LeCompte (1984) used the term "transferability" to refer to the degree to which the qualitative researcher uses and communicates the theoretical frameworks, definitions, and research techniques that are accessible to and understood by other researchers in the same or related fields.

CONCLUDING REMARKS

The relatively recent attention given qualitative research in the fields of physical educa-

tion, exercise science, and sport science (along with the lively discussions and arguments between qualitative and quantitative advocates) is viewed by some to be an insult to the integrity and tradition of qualitative research. Qualitative research is not some brand-new, unsubstantiated method of inquiry. Interpretive, participant observational fieldwork has been used in the social sciences as a research method for over 70 years (Erickson, 1986). Siedentop (1989), commenting on this fact, stated that ethnographic methodology has long been accepted and even honored. He then asks why there is the current flap about qualitative research in physical education.

One point of contention is that qualitative research does not report evidence of validity and reliability in the traditional sense. Kirk and Miller (1986) have stated that because qualitative research is based on different assumptions about reality and uses a different paradigm, there should be different conceptualizations of validity and reliability. To the qualitative researcher, reality is assumed to be holistic, multidimensional, and ever-changing rather than a single, fixed, objective phenomenon waiting to be discovered (Merriam, 1988):

> Unlike experimental designs where validity and reliability are accounted for before the investigation, rigor in a qualitative study derives from the researcher's presence, the nature of the interaction between researcher and participants, the triangulation of data, the interpretation of perceptions, and rich, thick description. (p. 120)

Answers to questions about what is happening here may seem trivial at first glance. On further inspection, however, we see that it is not, as everyday life is largely invisible to us because of familiarity and its contradictions. Often we do not realize the patterns of our actions as we perform them. Anthropologist Clyde Kluckhohn said that the fish would be the last creature to discover water. Locke (1987) added that the last person to understand the dynamics of a gym class might well be a physical educator. What is happening can become visible and can be documented systematically.

> To the qualitative researcher, reality is assumed to be holistic, multidimensional, and ever-changing rather than a single, fixed, objective phenomenon waiting to be discovered.

We should point out that qualitative research is by no means confined to the area of pedagogy. It is easy to get that impression because of the ever-increasing volume of literature on qualitative research in educational journals and textbooks. Qualitative research has a great deal of application in the study of the sociological aspect of sport. Bain (1989) observed that two of the earliest qualitative research studies published in the *Research Quarterly for Exercise and Sport* were on this topic. Sage (1989) cited several qualitative studies on sports dealing with Little League baseball, bodybuilding, soccer, surfing, and coaching.

In a provocative essay dealing with the science of human behavior, Martens (1987) questioned the basic assumptions of orthodox science. A longtime critic of the conventional experimental approach to sport psychology as the only way to conduct research, Martens presented a convincing argument and appeal for qualitative paradigms and the emphasis on experiential knowledge.

The focus of this chapter has been on interpretive qualitative research. Bain (1989) has mentioned another approach called *critical theory*, the main difference between the

two approaches lying in the goals of the research. Interpretive research is largely value free, whereas critical theory research is value based. In other words, in critical theory the aim is to give the research subjects the insight necessary to make choices that will improve their lives. Bain also stated that critical research is usually grounded in feminism, neo-Marxism, or the empowering pedagogy of Freire. Each of these theoretical perspectives challenges the status quo and strives for greater equality. Very little research in critical theory has been done in exercise and sport science and physical education. However, a number of obvious issues in sport with regard to women, race, and exploitation of athletes would lend themselves to this form of research.

The debates between the quantitative and the qualitative researchers will undoubtedly continue for a while, but it is hoped that they will rise above the name-calling stage (e.g., the "number crunchers" vs. the "navel gazers") and address the issues and problems in a professional and constructive manner.

Actually, the boundaries between quantitative and qualitative methodologies sometimes get blurred and break down when subjected to scrutiny. It seems advantageous for the profession and for research in general to capitalize on the strengths of both methods rather than argue about the differences. The quantitative researcher must make a number of qualitative decisions regarding the question, design, measurements, analytical procedures, and interpretations to emphasize. Similarly, the qualitative researcher often finds certain quantitative summaries, classifications, and analyses to be useful (Linn, 1986). Kidder and Fine (cited in Merriam, 1988) stated that there is nothing mysterious about combining quantitative and qualitative measures. This is, in fact, a form of triangulation that enhances the validity and reliability of one's study. Sage (1989) pointed out that there is a growing maturity in physical education, exercise science, and sport science with regard to drawing concepts, theories, and methods from all the social sciences as well as the humanities.

The fact is that qualitative research is a legitimate means of addressing certain questions in our field. There has been a remarkable growth of increasingly sophisticated methods to guide qualitative researchers. We should take advantage of the work that has been done in other fields and try to extend the boundaries of knowledge by our own contributions. Locke (1989) has provided a fitting concluding statement regarding the place of qualitative research in our field: It should be done, it will be done, and it is important that it be done well.

SUMMARY

Qualitative research methods include field observations, case studies, ethnography, and narrative reports. The researcher gathers data in the natural setting such as the gymnasium, the classroom, the fitness center, or the sport facility.

Qualitative research does not have the preconceived hypotheses that characterize quantitative research. Inductive reasoning is stressed, whereby the researcher seeks to develop hypotheses from observations. The focus is on the "essence" of the phenomena. The sensitivity and perception of the researcher play important roles in collecting and analyzing the data.

The importance of gaining access to the data in the field setting was stressed. Establishing rapport and gaining the trust and confidence of the subjects are essential. The most common sources of data collection are observations and interviews. Analysis of data in qualitative research is done during data collection as well as afterward. The researcher must sort and organize the data and develop tentative hypotheses that serve to guide and direct him or her to other sources and types of data.

Data analysis involves organizing, abstracting, integrating, and synthesizing. The analytic narrative is the foundation of qualitative research. The narrative vignette gives the reader a sense of being present for the observation; it conveys a sense of holistic meaning to the situation. It is not unusual for a qualitative study to include quantitative analysis.

Triangulation of data is used to establish validity and reliability. Data triangulation includes multiple sources of data, different investigators, and different methods. In theory triangulation, the situation is examined from different theoretical standpoints.

The qualitative researcher often attempts to construct a theory through the inductive process to explain relationships among categories of data. A theory that evolves from data is called a grounded theory. In the written report, the qualitative researcher must achieve a balance between rich description and analysis and interpretation.

Internal and external validity are important concepts in qualitative research just as they are in other research methods. Internal validity is the ability of the researcher to capture "what is really there." One of the most effective tools in achieving internal validity is the intensive firsthand presence of the researcher over an extended time. Triangulation of data, unobtrusiveness, honesty, and constructive personal relationships with the subjects all contribute significantly to internal validity.

One of the strongest arguments for external validity of qualitative research is user generalizability. In other words, the reader of the study evaluates the descriptions and analysis and determines what things apply to his or her situation.

Qualitative research is a viable approach to solving problems in our field. It has a great deal of application in pedagogy in physical education, exercise science, and sport science. Answers to the question of "what is happening here" can best be obtained in natural settings through the systematic observation and interaction methodology of qualitative research.

Problem

Locate a qualitative study and write an abstract of approximately 300 words on the methods used in gathering the data (observation, interviews, etc.) and in presenting the results (narrative vignettes, quotes, tables, etc.).

SUGGESTED READINGS

Refer to the Review and Commentary section of the *Research Quarterly for Exercise and Sport*, **60** (March 1989). A review/tutorial is written by Larry Locke, with commentaries by Bain, Sage, Schutz, and Siedentop.

Locke, L.F. Qualitative research as a form of scientific inquiry in sport and physical education (pp. 1-20).

Bain, L.L. Interpretive and critical research in sport and physical education (pp. 21-24).

Sage, G.H. A commentary on qualitative research as a form of scientific inquiry in sport and physical education (pp. 25-29).

Schutz, R.W. Qualitative research: Comments and controversies (pp. 30-35).

Siedentop, D. Do the lockers really smell? (pp. 36-41).

Other suggested readings include two qualitative studies, one in physical education and one in sport.

Griffin, P.S. (1985). Teacher perceptions of and reactions to equity problems in a middle school physical education program. *Research Quarterly for Exercise and Sport*, **56**, 103-110.

Sage, G.H. (1989). Becoming a high school coach: From playing sports to coaching. *Research Quarterly for Exercise and Sport*, **60**, 81-92.

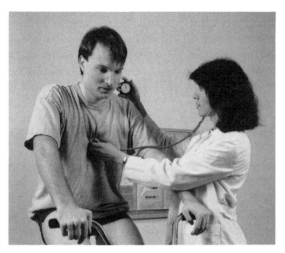

PART IV

Measurement

A basic step in the scientific method of problem solving is the collection of data; therefore, an understanding of measurement theory is necessary. Although measurement is discussed here as a research tool, measurement itself is an area of research. The measurement specialist in physical education, exercise science, and sport science, for example, is concerned with test reliability theory and the analysis of the measurement process regardless of what aspect of psychomotor performance is being measured. In this part, three chapters are devoted to measurement as it applies to the types of research commonly performed in physical education, exercise science, and sport science.

Chapter 16 explains the fundamental criteria for judging the quality of measures used in collecting research data: validity and reliability. *Validity* is the degree to which a test

or instrument measures what it purports to measure. The different forms of validity—logical, content, criterion, and construct—are described. Ways by which the different types of validity may be established are also explained. Reliability refers to the consistency and dependability of a measure. A test must be reliable to be valid. Several techniques are presented by which coefficients of reliability may be calculated for different types of measures. The validity and reliability of qualitative research are also discussed.

Chapters 17 and 18 are devoted to the main categories of measures used in research in physical education, exercise science, and sport science: physical (e.g., height and weight), movement (either the movement itself or some representation of it), and written. Chapter 17 summarizes some of the dependent variables used in research on movement and the various problems associated with such measures. This chapter makes no attempt to deal with the meaningful research questions about movement but only presents some of the measurements used as dependent variables. No two people (not even the authors, Thomas and Nelson) can adequately present the research questions from the various specialties within physical education, exercise science, and sport science. This book is concerned with research methods (in this case, methods used in measuring movement), not the content or knowledge base of movement. Thus, the focus here is not to suggest research questions about movement but rather to show the ways movement has frequently been measured. Psychophysiological measurements include physical fitness assessment, the physiological responses to exercise, and the measurement of psychomotor parameters. Motor behavior measurements include the evaluation of basic movement patterns, sport skills and motor

learning, and performance laboratory measures. Biomechanical measurements, such as cinematography and electromyography, are briefly discussed, as are the characteristics and problems associated with observational measurement techniques.

Many studies in physical education, exercise science, and sport science use written responses to gather research data. Chapter 18 addresses the measurement of affective behaviors such as attitude, personality traits, anxiety, self-concept, and sportsmanship. The types of responses used in affective behavior measurement and rating scales in general are discussed as to their strengths and weaknesses. Attention is given to the measurement of knowledge and to techniques for evaluating test items as to difficulty and discrimination. Finally, an introduction to item response theory is presented as a relatively new and promising advance in analyzing test data to obtain more information about the abilities of the examinees.

Chapter 16

□

Validity and Reliability

The validity of an experiment has been discussed on numerous occasions in this book. Various sources of invalidity, such as history, instrumentation, testing, and maturation, were explained in chapter 14. Validity in this sense refers to whether the results can be attributed to the experimental variables rather than to extraneous variables (internal validity) and whether the results can be generalized beyond the particular experiment (external validity).

In gathering the data on which the results are based, we are also greatly concerned with the validity of the measurements we are using. If, for example, a study seeks to compare training methods for producing strength gains, the researcher must have a valid measure of strength to be able to evaluate the effects of the training methods. Validity of measurement, then, indicates the degree to which the test, or instrument, measures what it is supposed to measure. Thus, validity refers to the soundness of the interpretation of a test, the most important consideration in measurement.

An integral part of validity is reliability, which pertains to the consistency, or repeatability, of a measure. A test cannot be considered valid if it is not reliable. In other words, if the test is not consistent—if you cannot depend on successive trials to yield the same results—then the test cannot be trusted. Of course, a test could be reliable but not valid, but it could never be valid if it were not reliable. For example, weighing oneself repeatedly on a broken scale would give reliable results but not valid ones.

VALIDITY OF MEASUREMENT IN RESEARCH

There are different purposes for using certain measures. Consequently, there are different kinds of validity. According to the American Psychological Association (APA) and the American Educational Research Association (AERA), the four basic types of validity are

- logical,
- content,
- criterion, and
- construct.

You notice logical validity was listed as a separate type of validity; however, the APA and the AERA consider logical validity as a special case of content validity. Because our main concern in this book is measurement for research purposes, logical, content, criterion, and construct validity are discussed only briefly. A more comprehensive discussion would be necessary if we were directing our attention to the evaluation of educational objectives.

> If the test is not consistent, then the test cannot be trusted. Of course, a test could be reliable but not valid, but it could never be valid if it were not reliable.

Logical Validity

Logical validity is sometimes referred to as *face validity*, although some measurement experts eschew that term. *Logical validity* is claimed when the measure obviously involves the performance being measured. In other words, it means that the test is valid by definition. A static balance test that consists of balancing on one foot has logical validity. A speed-of-movement test, in which the person is timed in running a specified distance, must be considered to have logical validity. Occasionally, logical validity is used in research studies, but a researcher would prefer to have more objective evidence as to the validity of measurement.

Content Validity

Content validity pertains almost exclusively to learning in educational settings. A test has content validity if it adequately samples what was covered in the course. As with logical validity, there is no statistical evidence that can be supplied for content validity. The teacher should prepare a table of specifications (sometimes called a test blueprint) before making out the test. The topics and course objectives, as well as the relative degree of emphasis that was accorded each, can then be keyed to a corresponding number of questions pertaining to each area.

Criterion Validity

Measurements used in research studies frequently are validated against some criterion. Actually, *criterion validity* is used in two main contexts: concurrent validity and predictive validity.

Concurrent Validity

Concurrent validity involves a measuring instrument being correlated with some criterion that is administered at about the same time (i.e., concurrently). Many physical performance measures are validated in this manner. Several criterion measures that are popularly used include an already validated or accepted measure, judges' ratings and tournament results, and some other observable performance criterion. Usually, concurrent validity is employed when the researcher wishes to substitute a shorter, more easily administered test for a criterion that is more difficult to measure.

To illustrate: Maximal oxygen consumption is regarded as the most valid measure of cardiorespiratory fitness. However, it requires a laboratory, expensive equipment, and considerable time for testing; furthermore, only one person can be tested at a time. Let us assume that a researcher, Douglas Bag, wishes to screen subjects as to their fitness levels before assigning them to experimental treatments. Rather than using such an elaborate test as maximal oxygen consumption, Douglas determines it would be advantageous to give a shorter, more easily administered measure. He would like to use a stair-walking test he has devised. To determine whether it is a valid measure of cardiorespiratory fitness, he could administer both the maximal oxygen consumption test and the stair-walking test to a group of subjects (from the same population as will be used in the study) and correlate the results of the two tests. If there is a satisfactory relationship, Doug can conclude that his stair-walking test is valid.

Written tests may also be validated in this way. For example, a researcher might wish to use a more practical group intelligence test than one such as the lengthy Stanford-Binet, which must be administered individually.

Judges' ratings serve as criterion measures for some tests (sport skills are sometimes validated this way). A great amount of time and effort is required to secure competent judges, provide for practice in the use of the rating scale, test for agreement among judges, arrange for the subjects to be viewed a sufficient number of trials, and so on. Consequently, judges' ratings cannot be used routinely to evaluate performances. The use of some skills tests would be more economical. Furthermore, the skills tests usually provide knowledge of results and measures of progress for the students. The skills tests could be initially validated, however, by giving the test and having judges rate the subjects on those skills. A validity coefficient can be obtained by correlating the scores on the skills tests with the judges' ratings.

Choice of the criterion is critical in the concurrent validity method. All the correlation can tell you is the degree of relationship between a measure and the criterion. If the criterion is not adequate, then the concurrent validity coefficient is of little consequence.

Predictive Validity

Predictive validity involves the use of a criterion to be predicted. In many cases the criterion is some later behavior, such as when entrance examinations are used to predict later success. Suppose that a physical education faculty wished to develop a test that could be given in beginning gymnastics classes to predict success in advanced classes. The test would be administered to students while they were in beginner courses. At the end of the advanced course, those test results would be correlated with the criterion of success (grades, ratings, etc.). In trying to predict a certain behavior, one should try to ascertain whether there is a known "base rate" for that behavior. For example, someone might attempt to construct a test that would predict girls who might develop bulimia at a university. Suppose that the incidence of bulimia is 10% of the female population at that school. Knowing this, one could be correct 90% of the time in predicting that no one in the sample will be bulimic. If the base rate is very low or very high, a predictive measure may have little practical value because the increase in predictability will be negligible.

Chapters 6 and 13 discussed aspects of prediction in correlational research. Multiple regression is often used because several predictors are likely to have a greater validity coefficient than the correlation between any one test and the criterion. Previously, we

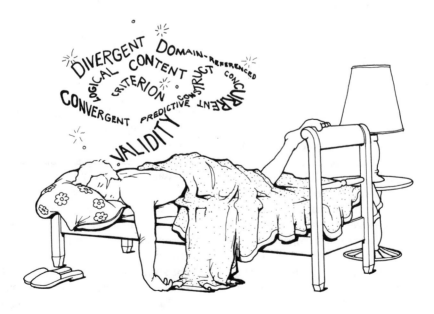

used the example of the prediction of percent fat from skinfold measurements. The criterion—percent fat—is measured by the underwater (hydrostatic) weighing technique. A number of skinfold measures are taken, and multiple regression is used to determine the best prediction equation. The researcher hopes to be able to use the skinfold measures in the future if the prediction formula demonstrates an acceptable validity coefficient.

One of the limitations of such studies is that the validity tends to decrease when the prediction formula is used with a new sample. This tendency is called *shrinkage*. Common sense suggests that shrinkage is more likely when a small sample is used in the original study and particularly when the number of predictors is large. In fact, if enough predictor variables (equal to the number of subjects) are added to the multiple regression equation, one can achieve perfect prediction. The problem is that the correlations are unique to the sample, and when the results are applied to another sample (even similar to the first one), the relationship does not hold. Consequently, the validity coefficient decreases substantially (i.e., shrinkage occurs).

A technique that is recommended to help estimate shrinkage is *cross-validation*. In this technique, the same tests are given to a new sample from the same population to check whether the formula is accurate. For example, a researcher might administer the criterion measure and predictor tests to a sample of 200 subjects. Then, using 100 of the subjects, he or she would calculate a multiple regression to develop a prediction formula. This formula is then applied to the other 100 subjects to see how accurately it predicts the criterion for these subjects. Because the researcher has the actual criterion measures on these subjects, the amount of shrinkage can be ascertained by correlating (Pearson r) the predicted scores with the actual scores. A comparison of the R^2 from the multiple

prediction with the r^2 between the actual and the predicted criteria yields an estimate of shrinkage.

Construct Validity

Many human characteristics are not directly observable. Rather, they are hypothetical constructs that carry a number of associated meanings concerning how a person who possesses the trait or traits to a high degree would behave differently from someone who possesses a low degree of the trait or traits. Anxiety, intelligence, sportsmanship, creativity, and attitude are a few such hypothetical constructs. Because these traits are not directly observable, measurement poses a problem. *Construct validity* is the degree to which a test measures a hypothetical construct and is usually established by relating the test results to some behavior. For example, a number of behaviors are expected of someone with a high degree of sportsmanship. This person might be expected to compliment the opponent on shots made during a tennis match. As an indication of construct validity, a test maker could compare the number of times the person scoring high on a test of sportsmanship complimented the opponent with the number of times a person scoring lower on the test did so.

The *known group difference method* is sometimes used in establishing construct validity. For example, construct validity of a test of anaerobic power could be demonstrated by comparing test scores of sprinters and jumpers with distance runners. Sprinting and jumping require anaerobic power to a greater extent than distance running. Therefore, the tester could determine whether the test differentiates between the two kinds of track performers. If the sprinters and jumpers score significantly higher than the distance runners, this would provide some evidence that the test measures anaerobic power.

An experimental approach is occasionally used in demonstrating construct validity. For example, a test of cardiovascular fitness might be assumed to have construct validity if it reflected gains in fitness following a conditioning program. Similarly, the originator of a motor skills test could demonstrate construct validity with regard to its sensitivity in differentiating between groups of instructed and noninstructed children.

Correlation can also be used in establishing construct validity. Hypothesized structures or dimensions of the trait being tested are sometimes formulated and verified with factor analysis. Correlation is also used when the tester wishes to examine relationships between constructs, for example, when it is hypothesized that someone with high scores on the test being developed (e.g., cardiovascular fitness) should also do well on some total physical fitness scale. Conversely, persons with low scores on the cardiovascular test would do poorly on the fitness test.

Validity Generalization

In the discussion on criterion validity, we mentioned the problem of population (or situation) specificity, whereby the prediction is most accurate for the sample that was used in developing the formula. For example, a researcher develops a formula for predicting percent body fat from skinfold measures for young adult females. If you look at the literature on this topic you will see that a rather large number of researchers have done this particular study and that a variety of correlation coefficients have been obtained between skinfold measurements and a criterion of percent fat (such as derived from underwater weighing).

A pertinent question is, Just how generalizable is the prediction of percent body fat from skinfold measurements? How valid is the prediction when you wish to look at other ages, such as older or younger females? What about using athletic and nonathletic women? What about predicting for males? Certainly, a person does not want to have to compute a new criterion-predictor formula every time he or she wants to predict percent fat. Validity generalization is a statistical model designed to address this problem.

Validity generalization was developed by Schmidt, Hunter, and Urry (1976). The method uses the concepts of meta-analysis (see chapter 12) for generalizing the results of many studies employing the same criterion-predictor combinations. Patterson (1989) has provided a clear and readable summary and application of the method in exercise science.

As with any innovative idea, there is controversy about validity generalization and its assumptions. One drawback is that one needs a very large number of studies (samples) to achieve adequate power. Nevertheless, it is a potentially valuable tool for estimating validity generalizability and has widespread applications in certain tests.

Validity in Criterion-Referenced Measurement

The methods discussed so far relate to norm-referenced measurement. Research studies also use criterion-referenced measurement, in which a test purports to establish that subjects have achieved certain levels of proficiency or development. For example, a developmental study may wish to establish that the subjects have reached mature behavior in some motor task such as throwing or jumping.

Domain-Referenced Validity.   A test is used that contains the essential components (or objectives) of that task weighted as to their importance. This is *domain-referenced validity*. It is usually validated by using a pool of judges and measurement specialists to assess the representativeness of items and item bias (Safrit, 1989). Written tests may also be validated in this manner, for example, when a researcher wishes to establish that the subjects possessed suitable knowledge about a topic. Safrit (1989) listed the steps for demonstrating domain-referenced validity in written tests.

Decision Accuracy. Another approach to validity of criterion-referenced tests (besides domain-referenced ones) is *decision accuracy*. This approach involves decisions of mastery-nonmastery classifications. Contingency tables are generally used in this procedure.

An example of a study in exercise science that dealt with decision accuracy is that by Washburn and Safrit (cited in Safrit, 1989). This study assessed the validity of an aerobic capacity cutoff score for U.S. Forest Service firefighters. The study involved three analytical procedures to test the cutoff decision score: the calculation of the outcome probabilities (c) in a contingency table, calculation of the phi coefficient, and a utility analysis to determine relative weighting. Cross-validation was performed.

Item Response Theory. In some tests (mostly of the cognitive type), cutoff scores on a mastery test can be established by the use of *item response theory*, also referred to as *latent trait theory*. This approach can be used to select the optimal test items that will yield the most precise information about the individual's mastery of material (see Spray, 1987, 1989; further discussion on item response theory can be found in chapter 18).

Validity in Qualitative Research

Chapter 15 discussed internal and external validity of qualitative research. In the present chapter we are concerned with the validity of the observations or of data collection. The validity of the measurements in quantitative research is based on underlying premises or theories. In some cases, it is a physical principle, such as the density of fat or fat-free mass. The accuracy of measurements can be judged in relation to the underlying principle. Consider the principle that fat-free mass has a density of 1.10 g/cc. We would then certainly conclude that a measured total body density of 1.10 g/cc for an individual is inaccurate because it would indicate that the person had no fat at all (of course, the underlying principle or theory can be incorrect).

In exercise science, maximal oxygen consumption is considered to be the most valid criterion of aerobic capacity. It is often used as the criterion when other tests attempt to predict aerobic capacity. Researchers do not try to validate the criterion but rather assume that it is "correct" (has theoretical validity). In a study that uses a measure such as maximal oxygen consumption, the researcher is usually concerned only with reliability. Thus, one assumes that the measure is valid, and the proof of accuracy is whether one can get consistent results.

The point here is that criterion validity is somewhat circular because one cannot claim theoretical validity unless the criterion itself is theoretically valid. Moreover, theoretical validity is difficult to establish by methods other than qualitative research. Actually, the whole concept of validity is tied to definitions, which are made by people. We are reminded of a quote attributed to Willie Nelson, the colorful country-western star, regarding his ownership of a golf course. Someone asked what the course's par was, and Nelson replied that it was anything he wanted it to be. He elaborated, "This hole here, for example, is a par 46, and yesterday I birdied the sucker."

The qualitative researcher does not usually attempt to provide numerical evidence of the validity of the observations. "The issue of validity is not a matter of methodological hair splitting about the fifth decimal point, but a question of whether the researcher sees what he or she thinks he or she sees" (Kirk & Miller, 1986, p. 21).

The qualitative researcher is constantly doing something comparable to hypothesis testing. The researcher's perceptions are continuously checked against possible alternatives or sources of error. When the hypothesis is incorrect, the researcher will usually find out about it (Kirk & Miller, 1986).

Reliability does not assure validity in qualitative research any more than in quantitative research. You can get the same answers to the same questions consistently, but the answers may not be correct. Whereas the criticism often levied at qualitative research is the lack of supporting numerical data, the qualitative researcher counters that the quantitative researcher tends to simply accept results without question and tests them for significance. The qualitative researcher, on the other hand, will suspect faulty data and then search for the error.

In chapter 15 we defined the Type III error as that of asking the wrong questions. This is probably the cause of most validity problems in qualitative research. However, through multiple sources of data and simultaneous analysis with the data collection, the qualitative researcher contends that his or her interpretations of the data are valid. Just as the interview is considered by most to be more valid than the questionnaire, the intensive firsthand presence of the researcher is the strongest support for validity in the data-gathering process in qualitative research.

RELIABILITY OF MEASUREMENT IN RESEARCH

A measure that does not yield consistent results is not valid because you cannot depend on the results. The degree of consistency of

a test is reliability. Test reliability is sometimes discussed in terms of observed score, true score, and error score.

A test score obtained on an individual is the *observed score*. It is not known whether this is a true assessment of this person's ability or performance. There may well be measurement error involved pertaining to the test directions, the instrumentation, the scoring, or the emotional-physical state of the subject. Thus, an observed score theoretically consists of the person's *true score* and *error score*. Expressed in terms of score variance, the observed score variance consists of true score variance plus error variance. The goal of the tester is to remove error to yield the true score. The coefficient of reliability is the ratio of true score variance to observed score variance. Because true score variance is never known, it is estimated by subtracting error variance from observed score variance. Thus, the reliability coefficient reflects the degree to which the measurement is free of error variance.

Just as the interview is considered by most to be more valid than the questionnaire, the intensive firsthand presence of the researcher is the strongest support for validity in the data gathering process in qualitative research.

Sources of Measurement Error

Measurement error can come from four sources: the subject, the testing, the scoring, and the instrumentation. Measurement error associated with the subject includes many factors, including mood, motivation, fatigue, health, fluctuations in memory (and performance), previous practice, specific knowledge, and familiarity with the test items.

Errors in testing are those that can arise due to the lack of clarity or completeness in the directions, to whether the instructions are rigidly followed, to whether supplementary directions or motivation is applied, and so forth. Errors in scoring relate to the competence, experience, and dedication of the scorers as well as to the nature of the scoring itself. The extent to which the scorer is familiar with the behavior being tested and the test items can greatly affect the accuracy of the scoring. Carelessness and inattention to detail produce measurement error. Measurement error due to instrumentation includes obvious causes such as inaccuracy and lack of calibration of mechanical and electronic equipment. It also refers to the inadequacy of tests in discriminating between abilities and to the difficulty of scoring some tests.

Expressing Reliability Through Correlation

The degree of reliability is expressed by a correlation coefficient, ranging from 0.00 to 1.00. The closer the coefficient is to 1.00, the less error variance it reflects and the more the true score is assessed. Reliability is established several ways, which are summarized in the next section. The type of correlation technique used in computing the reliability coefficient differs from that used in establishing validity. Pearson r is often referred to as *interclass correlation*. This is used in correlating two different variables (bivariate statistic), such as in determining validity where judges' ratings are correlated with scores on a skill test. However, interclass correlation is not appropriate in establishing reliability because the same variable is being correlated. When a test is given twice, the scores on the first test administration are correlated with the scores on the second administration to determine the degree of consistency. In this case, the two test scores are for the same variable;

so interclass correlation should not be used. Rather, *intraclass correlation* is the appropriate statistical technique. This method uses ANOVA to obtain the reliability coefficient.

Interclass Correlation

There are three main weaknesses of Pearson r (interclass correlation) for reliability determination. The first is that, as mentioned previously, the Pearson r is a bivariate statistic, whereas reliability involves univariate measures. Second, in Pearson r, the computations are limited to only two scores, X and Y. Often, however, more than two trials are given, and the tester is concerned with the reliability of multiple trials. For example, if a test specifies three trials, the researcher must either give three more trials and use the average or best score of each set of trials for the correlations or perhaps correlate the first trial with the second, the first with the third, and the second with the third. In the first case, extra trials must be given only for reliability; in the second case, multiple correlations often lose meaningfulness. Finally, the interclass correlation does not provide a thorough examination of different sources of variability on multiple trials. For example, changes in means and standard deviations from trial to trial cannot be considered in the Pearson r method but can be analyzed with intraclass correlation.

Intraclass Correlation

Intraclass correlation provides estimates of systematic and error variance. For example, systematic differences among trials can be examined. The last trials may differ significantly from the first trials because of a learning phenomenon or fatigue effect (or both). If the tester is aware of this, then perhaps initial (or final) trials can be excluded or the point at which performance levels off can be used as the score. In other words, through

ANOVA the tester is able to truly examine test performance from trial to trial and then decide on the most reliable testing schedule.

An example of intraclass correlation (R) is given in Table 16.1. The example consists of three trials. The procedures leading to the calculation of R are the same as those of the simple ANOVA with repeated measures presented in chapter 7.

Refer to Table 7.14 for the formulas used in calculating the necessary sums of squares (SS) and mean squares (MS). Using those formulas, we calculate the total sum of squares to be 27.6. The sum of squares for subjects is 14.9 and that for trials 7.6. We can then calculate the residual sum of squares by subtraction and get 5.1. Next, we compute the mean squares for subjects, trials, and residual by the formulas in the table:

MS for subjects = 3.73
MS for trials = 3.80
MS for residual (error) = .64

Table 16.1 Summary of ANOVA for Reliability Estimation (3 Trials)

Student	Trial 1	Trial 2	Trial 3
A	3	3	4
B	4	6	6
C	2	3	4
D	1	3	4
E	2	4	2
	$M=2.4$	$M=3.8$	$M=4.0$

Summary of ANOVA

Source	SS	df	MS	F
Subjects	14.9	4	3.73	. . .
Trials	7.6	2	3.80	5.94*
Residual	5.1	8	.64	. . .

*$p < .05$.

Calculating F.   You can determine any significant differences among the three trials by calculating the F for trials as in Table 7.14. Then enter Table A.6 in Appendix A and read down the 2-df column to the 8-df row. Our F of 5.94 is found to be greater than the tabled F of 4.46 for the .05 level of probability. Thus, there are significant differences among trials. At this point we need to recognize that there are different opinions as to what should be done with trial differences (Baumgartner & Jackson, 1987; Johnson & Nelson, 1986; Safrit, 1976). Some test authorities argue that the test performance should be consistent from one trial to the next and that any trial-to-trial variance should be attributed simply to measurement error. If we decide to do this, the formula for R is

$$R = (MS_S - MS_E) / MS_S \qquad (16.1)$$

in which MS_S = the mean squares for subjects (from Table 16.1) and MS_E = the mean squares for error, which is computed as follows:

$$\frac{SS \text{ for trials} + SS \text{ for interaction}}{df \text{ for trials} + df \text{ for interaction}}$$

$$= \frac{7.6 + 5.1}{2 + 8}$$

$$= 1.27$$

The R is thus calculated: $R = (3.73 - 1.27) / 3.73 = .66$

Discarding Trials.   Another way of dealing with significant trial differences is to discard the trial or trials that are noticeably different from the others (Baumgartner & Jackson, 1987). Then a second ANOVA is conducted on the remaining trials and another F test computed. If F is nonsignificant, R is calculated using Formula 16.1, in which trial variance is considered measurement error. If F is still significant, additional trials are discarded, and another ANOVA is conducted. The purpose of this method is to find a measurement schedule that is free of trial differences (nonsignificant F that yields the largest possible criterion score) and that is most reliable. This method is especially appealing when there is an apparent trend in trial differences, as when a learning phenomenon (or release of inhibitions) is evident in the initial trial or trials. For example, if five trials on a performance test yielded scores of 15, 18, 23, 25, and 24, one might discard the first two trials and compute another analysis on the last three trials. Similarly, a fatigue effect may be evidenced by a decrease in the final trials in some types of tests.

In the example in Table 16.1, note that Trial 1 is considerably lower than Trials 2 and 3. So, we discard the first trial and compute another ANOVA on Trials 2 and 3 (results are shown in Table 16.2). The F for trials in the table is nonsignificant, so we compute R with Formula 16.1: $R = (2.85 - .7) / 2.85 = .75$.

Note that we computed MS_E (.7) by combining the sum of squares for trials and residual and dividing by their respective degrees of freedom: $(.1 + 3.4) / (1 + 4) = .7$. We see that R is considerably higher when we discarded the first trial.

Ignoring Trial-to-Trial Variance. A third approach is simply to not consider trial-to-trial variance as measurement error and to compute R as follows:

$$R = (MS_S - MS_{res}) / MS_S \qquad (16.2)$$

Table 16.2 Summary of ANOVA for Reliability Estimation (2 Trials)

Source	SS	df	MS	F
Subjects	11.4	4	2.85	...
Trials	.1	1	.10	.11
Residual	3.4	4	.85	...

Using the data in Table 16.1, we calculate R as follows: $R = (3.73 - .64) / 3.73 = .88$.

In this approach, trial-to-trial variance is not considered as true score variance or error score variance. Consequently, R is notably higher than it was in the previous approaches because all trial-to-trial variance is removed. Although some measurement authorities advocate this approach, it does not seem to follow the theory that observed score variance equals true score variance plus error score variance. Other measurement specialists argue that every source of variance not attributable to subjects should be considered error score variance (Safrit, 1976). Although we do not intend to enter into the argument, we do believe it should be of interest to the researcher (tester) to ascertain whether there are trial-to-trial differences. Consequently, if significant differences are found, the tester can decide whether it seems appropriate to eliminate some trials (as with a learning trend) or whether to simply consider trial-to-trial differences as measurement error.

Intertester reliability is determined the same way. Thus, the objectivity of judges or different testers is analyzed by intraclass R and judge-to-judge variance calculated in the same way as trial-to-trial variance. Of course, more complex ANOVA designs can be used in which trial-to-trial, day-to-day, and judge-to-judge sources of variance all can be identified. Baumgartner (1989) and Safrit (1976) discussed some of the models that can be used for establishing reliability.

METHODS OF ESTABLISHING RELIABILITY

It is easier to establish reliability than validity. We first look at three types of coefficients of reliability: stability, alternate forms, and internal consistency.

Stability

The coefficient of *stability* is determined by the test-retest method on separate days. This method is frequently used with fitness and motor performance measures but rarely with pencil-and-paper tests. This is the most severe test of consistency because the errors associated with measurement are likely to be more pronounced when the two test administrations are separated by a day or more.

In the *test-retest method*, the test is given one day and then administered the same way a day or so later. The time interval may be governed to some extent by how strenuous the test is and whether more than a day's rest is needed. Of course, the time interval cannot be so long that actual changes in ability, maturation, or learning occur between the two test administrations.

Intraclass correlation is used to compute the coefficient of stability of the scores on the two tests. Through ANOVA procedures, the tester can determine the amount of variance accounted for by the separate days of testing as well as test trial differences, subject differences, and error variance.

Alternate Forms

The *alternate-forms method* of establishing reliability involves the construction of two tests, both of which supposedly sample the same material. This method is sometimes referred to as the *parallel-form method* or the *equivalence method*.

The two tests are given to the same subjects. Ordinarily, there is some time interval between the two administrations. The scores on the two tests are then correlated to obtain a reliability coefficient. The alternate-forms method is a widely used technique with standardized tests, such as those of achievement and scholastic aptitude. The method is rarely used with physical performance tests, proba-

bly because it is more difficult to construct two different sets of good physical test items than it is to write two sets of questions.

Some test experts maintain that, theoretically, the alternate-forms method is the preferred method. Any test is only a sample of test items from a universe of possible test items. Thus, the degree of relationship between two such samples should yield the best estimate of reliability.

Internal Consistency

An *internal consistency* reliability coefficient can be obtained by any of several methods. Some of the commonly used methods are the same-day test-retest, the split-half method, the Kuder-Richardson method of rational equivalence, and the coefficient alpha technique.

Same-Day Test-Retest

The *same-day test-retest method* is used almost exclusively with physical performance tests as practice effects and recall tend to produce spuriously high correlations when this technique is used with written tests. The test-retest on the same day results in a higher reliability coefficient than does a test-retest on separate days. One would certainly expect more consistency of performance within the same time period than on different days. Intraclass correlation is used to analyze trial-to-trial (internal) consistency.

Split Half

The *split-half technique* is the most widely used method of determining internal consistency. This method is commonly used in written tests and occasionally in performance tests that require numerous trials. The test is divided in two, and the two halves are then correlated. A test could be divided into first and second halves, but this is usually not deemed satisfactory. Sometimes a person tires near the end of the test, and sometimes easier questions are placed in the first half. Usually, the odd-numbered questions are compared with the even-numbered ones. That is, the number of odd-numbered questions a person got correct is correlated with the number of correct answers on the even-numbered questions.

Because the correlation is between the two halves of the test, the reliability coefficient represents only half the size of the total test; that is, behavior is sampled only half as thoroughly. Thus, a step-up procedure, the *Spearman-Brown prophecy formula*, is used to estimate the reliability for the entire test because the total test is based on twice the sample of behavior (twice the number of items). The formula is as follows:

$$\text{corrected reliability coefficient} = \frac{2 \times \text{reliability for 1/2 test}}{1.00 + \text{reliability for 1/2 test}}$$

If, for example, the correlation between the even-numbered items and the odd-numbered items was .85, the corrected reliability coefficient would be

$$\frac{2 \times .85}{1.00 + .85} = \frac{1.70}{1.85} = .92$$

The *Kuder-Richardson (K-R) method of rational equivalence* can be used for items that are scored dichotomously (e.g., right or wrong). Only one test administration is required, and no correlation is calculated. Two formulas, known as K-R 20 and K-R 21, are the most widely used. The resulting coefficient represents an average of all possible split-half reliability coefficients.

The K-R 20 is considered by many test experts to be the best for determining reliability. The K-R 21 is a simplified version of the K-R 20. It is so easily and quickly computed that it is very applicable to the teacher (or re-searcher) for "homemade" tests. The K-R 21 formula is:

$$\text{K-R } 21 = 1.00 - \frac{M(n - M)}{n(s^2)}$$

where M = the mean score for the test, n = the number of test items, and s^2 (standard deviation squared) = the test variance. The Kuder-Richardson formulas generally result in lower reliability coefficients than other methods. One can assume, then, that the coefficient represents a minimum reliability estimate.

Coefficient alpha is a form of the K-R 20 formula that can be used for test items that are not scored dichotomously, but it can be used with ordinal data. The alpha coefficient, usually referred to as the *Cronbach alpha coefficient* (see Cronbach, 1951), is applicable to multiple trial tests. The coefficient alpha yields an estimate of reliability that is equivalent to intraclass reliability when interval data are used. Coefficient alpha gives the proportion of total variance that is associated with, or accounted for by, the trial covariances. It is rather easily calculated by finding the sum of the variances for trials and then computing the variance for the total.

INTERTESTER RELIABILITY (OBJECTIVITY)

A form of reliability that pertains to the testers is called *intertester reliability*, or often *objectivity*. This facet of reliability is the degree to which different testers can achieve the same scores on the same subjects.

In general, most teachers and students prefer objective over subjective measures because so much depends on how valid and reliable the measures are. Objective measures are not automatically better than subjective ones, but they do yield quantitative scores that are more "visible" and that, statistically, can be handled more easily. In most research techniques, objective measurements are a must.

The degree of objectivity (intertester reliability) can be established by having more than one tester gather data; then the scores are analyzed with intraclass correlation techniques to obtain an intertester reliability coefficient. It is possible to assess a number of sources of variance in one analysis, such as variance due to testers, trials, days, subjects, and error (for discussion of the calculations involved, see Safrit, 1976).

Intertester reliability is more critical in some areas of measurement than in others. For example, anthropometric measurements (such as skinfolds and body circumferences and diameters) are subject to considerable intertester variability.

Generalizability Theory

Earlier in this chapter we said that intertester reliability is determined the same way as intraclass reliability. An extension of intraclass reliability is *generalizability theory* (*G theory*). This model enables the researcher to identify sources of error in estimating reliability of scores on a test. To illustrate, in the measurement of strength, we can think of numerous variables that affect the reliability of the scores. Among these are the subjects and their ages, genders, and levels of experience; the tester; the types of instruments used; the types of contraction; and the muscle groups being studied.

The G theory employs two approaches, the G study and the D study. The *G study* uses repeated measures ANOVA to help identify the relative importance of different sources of variance that contribute to measurement error. In the *D study*, the researcher calculates generalizability coefficients for the study's various components. The combined results of the G and the D studies provide the researcher with an optimal measurement format for collecting the data. Morrow (1989) has provided an excellent description and tutorial for G theory, and Wood and Safrit (1987) compared different multivariate models in estimating reliability of a test battery. Generalizability theory should play an increasingly important role in estimating test reliability in the future.

Reliability in Criterion-Referenced Measurements

In criterion-referenced measurements, the tests are not designed to discriminate among subjects' abilities; instead, they are often used for screening and measuring competencies (Safrit, 1986). The statistical methods used to establish reliability with criterion-referenced measurements are different than those used with norm-referenced tests. Both are concerned with consistency, but criterion-referenced tests try to consistently replicate a person's domain (or true) score independently of other persons' performances (Looney, 1989).

Hambleton and Novick (1973) first proposed the *proportion of agreement index* to assess the consistency of correct decisions. The index is now usually corrected for chance. Looney (1989) has described and discussed the various procedures involved as well as estimates for single-test administration.

Reliability in Qualitative Research

In qualitative research, one cannot very well replicate the data-gathering process simply for the purpose of establishing reliability. The subjects would probably think the researcher was suffering from senility if he or she tried to interview the same people with the same questions twice on the same day. However, qualitative researchers sometimes do ask the same questions of different (but similar) subjects and occasionally interview the same subjects over time as evidence of consistency, or agreement.

We repeat that repeatability is not validity because repeatable results may be repeatedly wrong. Furthermore, a large number of people saying the same thing does not guarantee that what is said is real. Merriam (1988, p. 171) gave a good example, that an audience's account of a magician is not as reliable as that of one stagehand who watched the show from behind the curtain.

The researcher can become more reliable through practice. Triangulation can also work to increase reliability. The reliability of the data can be enhanced by using various techniques and sources.

Goetz and LeCompte (1984) interpreted reliability as the extent to which studies can be replicated. That is, can a researcher using the same methods obtain the same results as those obtained in a prior study? They point out that the difficulties of replication in

qualitative research stem from the fact that a study takes place in natural settings and is often undertaken for the purpose of recording processes of change. Reliability in qualitative research can be examined from the standpoint of external reliability and internal reliability.

> Repeatability is not validity because repeatable results may be repeatedly wrong.

External Reliability

External reliability refers to the content of the data. Goetz and LeCompte (1984) discussed five major problems associated with external reliability: researcher status, choice of subjects, social situations and conditions, analytic constructs and premises, and methods of data collection and analysis.

Researcher status relates to the role of the researcher in the group. Is the researcher a participant observer or a nonparticipant

observer? Is the researcher considered a friend or some sort of evaluator? Margaret Mead's data on adolescent sexual behavior in Samoan society were challenged by Daniel Freeman, who also studied Samoan society many years later (Agar, 1986). The discrepancy in their findings may be due largely to the researcher's status position. Mead was a young woman at the time she talked with the Samoan adolescent girls. Freeman's status was more that of a distinguished visitor when he conducted much of his study with male parents. Clearly, the researcher's role and status within the group should be described.

Choice of subjects is closely related to the role of the researcher. The nature of the data will certainly be greatly influenced by the source. In the previous discussion concerning Mead and Freeman, one can easily understand how there could be discrepancies when Mead's subjects were largely adolescent females and Freeman's subjects male parents. The researcher needs to carefully describe both the characteristics of the subjects and the rationale for their selection (Kirk & Miller, 1986).

Social situations and conditions can have a significant bearing on what information the subjects are willing to reveal. A subject may speak freely under some conditions but be quite guarded when asked the same questions in another context. The presence of others is obviously a factor that can affect what people say. The researcher's description of the social situations and conditions is an important aspect of external reliability.

Analytic constructs and premises refer to the manner in which the researcher defines and categorizes the data. Some concepts and operational definitions are constant from the inception of the proposal, whereas others change as the data unfold.

Methods of data collection and analysis must be carefully described if the content of the data is to be assessed. All the details as to how observations were gathered and recorded, how interviews were conducted, and how multiple sources of data were integrated into the study need to be delineated. Of equal or more importance is the necessity of specifying and discussing the general strategies employed in analyzing the data. The credibility of the data is closely tied to the clarity and thoroughness of the accounts of how the data were examined and synthesized (Goetz & LeCompte, 1984).

Internal Reliability

Internal reliability concerns interobserver agreement. In other words, what is the extent of agreement among different observers concerning the description of events? According to Goetz and LeCompte (1984), qualitative researchers use any of the following strategies to reduce threats to internal reliability: low-inference descriptors, multiple researchers, participant researchers, peer examination, and mechanically recorded data.

''Low-inference descriptors'' relates to the method of rich, thick description used in data collection. Verbatim accounts of conversations and complete field notes provide reviewers with the means for judging the researcher's findings.

Multiple researchers are involved in a team effort. This sometimes occurs when researchers in different geographical areas collaborate on a study. In such studies that have more than one researcher, it is imperative that all team members are extensively trained in the methods of observation and descriptive techniques.

Participant researchers are local observers who confirm what has been seen and recorded. This is not done to any great extent in our field.

Peer examination involves having colleagues corroborate a researcher's findings. This may be informally done by asking people to evaluate one's study, and it is a standard practice when an article is submitted for publication. The manuscript is reviewed by qualified researchers in that area.

Mechanically recorded data offer an effective means of assessing internal reliability in a qualitative study. The use of tape recorders, photographs, and videotapes is a fairly common practice, and other qualified researchers can be asked to examine the data. In this process it is essential that all observers are carefully trained and that they adhere closely to the same coding procedures. Interobserver reliability can be established in some qualitative research studies by having other competent people evaluate or code the behavior of the same subjects. Videotapes are advantageous because more judges can be used and the evaluations done at any time and as many times as desired. A percent of agreement can be computed by dividing the number of agreements between raters by the total number of coded behaviors. Observer ''drift'' is often tested by checking interobserver values at the beginning, middle, and end of the data collection. If desired, intraobserver reliability can be established by having the researcher evaluate the same videotapes on another occasion. However, this is usually done as a training procedure before conducting the study.

Finally, some qualitative research experts maintain that reliability evidence is not necessary if internal validity can be demonstrated. Guba and Lincoln (1981) used the logic that it is impossible to have internal validity without reliability. Therefore, reliability is simultaneously demonstrated.

STANDARD ERROR OF MEASUREMENT

Part II touched on the concept of standard error several times with regard to t and F tests

and to interpreting significance levels. It also gave attention to the standard error of prediction in correlational research.

The standard error of measurement is an important concept in interpreting the results of measurement. Sometimes we get too carried away with the aura of scientific data collection and fail to realize that there is always the possibility of measurement error. For example, maximal oxygen consumption ($\dot{V}O_2max$) has been mentioned several times in this book as the most valid measure of cardiorespiratory fitness. Field tests are frequently validated through correlation with $\dot{V}O_2max$. We must be careful, however, not to consider $\dot{V}O_2max$ as a perfect test that is error free. Every test yields only observed scores; we can obtain only estimates of a person's true score.

It is much better to think of test scores as falling within a range that contains the true score. The formula for the standard error of measurement ($S_{y \cdot x}$) is

$$S_{y \cdot x} = s\sqrt{1.00 - r} \qquad (16.5)$$

where s = the standard deviation of the scores and r = the reliability coefficient for the test. In the measurement of percent body fat for female adults, assume that the standard deviation is 5.6% and the test-retest correlation .83. The standard error of measurement would be

$$S_{y \cdot x} = 5.6\sqrt{1.00 - .83} = 2.3\%$$

Assume further that a particular woman's measured percent fat is 22.4%. We can use the standard error of measurement to estimate a range within which her true percent fat probably falls.

Standard errors are assumed to be normally distributed and are interpreted in the same way as standard deviations. About two-thirds (actually 68.26%) of all test scores will fall within plus or minus one standard error of measurement of their true scores. In other words, there is a 68% chance that a person's true score will be found within a range of the obtained score plus or minus the standard error of measurement. In the example of the woman who had an obtained score of 22.4% fat, chances are 2 in 3 that her true percent fat is 22.4% ± 2.3% (standard error of measurement) or somewhere between 20.1% and 24.7%.

We can be more confident if we multiply the standard error of measurement by 2 because about 95% (95.44%) of the time the true score can be expected to be found within a range of the observed score plus or minus two times the standard error of measurement. Thus, in the present example, we can be about 95% sure that the woman's true percent fat will be 22.4% ± 4.6% (± 2.3% × 2), that is, between 17.8% and 27.0%.

From the formula we see that the standard error of measurement is governed by the variability of the test scores and the reliability of the test. If we had a higher reliability coefficient, the error of measurement would obviously decrease. In the present example, if the reliability coefficient was .95, the standard error of measurement would be only

"Boy! He's taller than I thought!"

1.3%; or, with the same reliability (.83) but with a smaller standard deviation, such as 4%, the standard error of measurement would be 1.7%.

Remember the concept of standard error of measurement when you are interpreting test scores. As indicated earlier, people sometimes have absolutely blind faith in some measurements, particularly if the measurements appear to be scientific. With percent fat estimation from skinfold thicknesses, for example, we need to keep in mind that error is connected not only with the skinfold measurements but also with the criterion that these measurements are predicting, that is, the density obtained from underwater weighing and the determination of percent fat from the body density values. Yet we have observed people accepting as gospel that they have a certain amount of fat because someone measured a few skinfolds. Newspapers have reported that some athletes have only 1% fat. This would be impossible from a physiological standpoint. Moreover, it is possible to obtain a predicted *negative* percent fat from regression equations. Please do not misunderstand. We are not condemning skinfold measurements but are simply trying to emphasize that all measurements are susceptible to errors and that common sense, coupled with knowledge of the concept of standard error of measurement, can help us better understand and interpret the results of measurements. The measurement specialists in Figure 16.1 seem to be happily unaware of measurement error of any kind, standard or unstandard.

SCALES OF MEASUREMENT

Interval scale measures and ordinal data have been mentioned several times in the discussion of statistics and measurement. There are basically four types of scales: nominal, ordinal, interval, and ratio.

Nominal

When scores are grouped into categories, or classes, the result is a *nominal scale*, or a classification by name. Scores of boys and girls can be assigned to two mutually exclusive groups, which means that no score can fall in more than one classification. Because the nominal scale classification is for identification only, there is no differentiation as to order or magnitude of differences between groups. Examples of nominal scales include such categories as gender and race.

Sometimes a researcher creates groups on the basis of some measurement criterion. For example, subjects might be categorized as high or low anxious on the basis of an anxiety measure. High-, average-, and low-fitness groupings and highly skilled and poorly skilled classifications are other such examples. In these cases, the classifications are not strictly nominal because there is some kind of distinction regarding order. Such scales could be considered somewhere between nominal and ordinal.

Ordinal

Ordinal scales are ranks. They provide more information than do nominal data. The highest ordinal number is better than the next highest, which in turn is better than the third highest. With an ordinal scale, we do not know how much better one score is than another. Therefore, we must use caution in making comparisons. For example, John is 6 inches taller than Joe, and Joe is a half inch taller than Bob. Yet, by merely ranking them, we have John first, Joe second, and Bob third, and the ordinal difference between the first and second ranks is the same as that between the second and third. We cannot assume equal intervals between ranks in terms of their actual raw scores.

Percentiles are ordinal numbers; thus, a teacher should not try to average percentiles or interpolate between two percentile ranks. A score falling between the 60th and the 65th percentiles should not be assigned a value of 62.5 because it cannot be assumed that the scores are evenly distributed between those two percentile ranks.

Interval

Interval scales provide not only the order between scores but also the magnitude of the distance between them. A score of 35 sit-ups is not only higher than a score of 25: it is 10 sit-ups higher. Similarly, a difference between 35 and 25 sit-ups is the same absolute difference as that between 25 and 15. Interval scoring enables us to interpret performances with standard scores (discussed later in this chapter).

Ratio

Ratio scales have all the properties of the other three scales plus a true zero value, which represents a complete absence of the characteristic. An interval measure does not have a true zero. A common example frequently used to distinguish between the interval and the ratio scales is the IQ scale, the scores of which are interval because there is no "zero intelligence." We cannot say that an IQ of 160 is twice as high as an IQ of 80 because zero on the IQ scale is an arbitrary point. We can say only that a score of 160 is 80 points higher than a score of 80.

On the other hand, measures of force, time, and distance are ratio scales because they have true zero points. A force of 50 lb is twice as high as one of 25 lb. A jump of 20 ft is twice as far as one of 10 ft. Actually, although a number of the measures used in physical education, exercise science, and sport science are ratio scales, they are treated the same as interval scores. For example, even though distance is a ratio scale, the relative differences between performances may not be equal. The 2-in. difference between high jumps of 7 ft 2 in. and 7 ft is probably more significant than the 2-in. difference between jumps of 5 ft 2 in. and 5 ft.

STANDARD SCORES

Direct comparisons of scores are not possible without having some point of reference. Is a score of 46 cm on the vertical jump as good as a score of 25 push-ups? How can you compare centimeters and repetitions? If we know that the class mean for the vertical jump is 40 cm and that 20 is the mean for push-ups, we know that the performances of 46 cm and 25 push-ups are better than average, but how much better? Is one performance better than the other?

One way to compare the performances is to convert each score to a standard score. A standard score is a score expressed in terms of standard deviations from the mean. Standard scores are interval scores because the standard deviation is a constant interval unit throughout the scale. We now discuss how to determine standard scores by using z scores, T scales, and stanines.

z Scores and T Scales

The basic standard score is the z score. The z scale converts raw scores to a mean of zero and to a standard deviation of 1.0. The formula is

$$z = (X - M) / s \qquad (16.6)$$

Suppose that the mean and standard deviation for vertical jump scores are 40 and 6 cm,

respectively, and for push-ups 20 and 5, respectively. Thus, a score of 46 cm for the vertical jump is a z score of $+ 1.00$: $z = (46 - 40) / 6 = 6 / 6 = 1.00$.

A score of 25 push-ups is also a z score of $+ 1.00$: $z = (25 - 20) / 5 = 5 / 5 = 1.00$.

We see that the person performed exactly the same on the two tests. Both performances were 1 s above the mean. Similarly, scores of different students can be compared on the same test by z scores. A person jumping 37 cm has a z score of $- .05$, a student who jumps 44 cm has a z score of 0.67, and so on. All standard scores are based on the z score. However, because z scores are expressed in decimals and have positive and negative numbers, they are not as easy to work with as are some of the other scales. The T *scale*, for example, sets the mean at 50 and the standard deviation at 10. This removes the decimal and makes all scores positive. A score 1 s above the mean ($z = 1.0$) is a T score of 60. A score 1 s below the mean ($z = -1.0$) is a T score of 40. Because over 99% (99.73%) of the scores fall between ± 3 s, it is rare to have T scores less than 20 ($z = -3.0$) and over 80 ($z = 3.0$). Some standardized tests that use different transformations of means and standard deviations using the z-score distribution are shown in Table 16.3.

Table 16.3 Standardized Means and Standard Deviations of Well-Known Tests

Scale	M	s
Graduate Record Examination	500	100z
Stanford-Binet IQ	100	16z
College Entrance Examination	500	100z
National Teachers Examination	500	100z
Wechsler IQ	100	15z

Stanines

Stanines are another type of standard score. The word stanine is derived from the words "standard" and "nine" because there are nine standard score units. The mean of the stanine scale is 5, and the standard deviation is 2. The percentages of the distribution for the nine stanines are as follows:

Stanine	Percent
1	4
2	7
3	12
4	17
5	20
6	17
7	12
8	7
9	4

The decision as to which standard score to use depends on the nature of the research study and the extent of interpretation required for the test takers. In essence, then, it is a matter of choice in light of the use of the measures.

SUMMARY

In this chapter we discussed the concepts of validity and reliability of measurements and how they apply to research. Criterion validity (which includes both concurrent and predictive validity), and construct validity are two of the most commonly used methods of validating measures used in research studies. One of the problems often identified regarding predictive measures is population or situation specificity. A current area of interest among measurement specialists is validity generalization, which attempts to estimate the generalizability of the results of different studies on the same topic.

The methods used in validating norm-referenced measurements are not applicable to criterion-referenced measurements. Methods used to establish domain-referenced validity and decision accuracy were identified.

Qualitative research has special problems regarding validity. Considerable discussion was devoted to some of the issues raised concerning data collection in qualitative research studies and some of the arguments and approaches used to address the problems.

The topic of test reliability has prompted hundreds of studies and innumerable discussions among test theorists and researchers. The reason for this interest is that a measure that does not yield consistent results can not be valid. The topic is quite complex. The classical test theory (CTT) views reliability in terms of observed scores, true scores, and error scores, and the coefficient of reliability is the ratio of true score variance to observed score variance. Thus, the reliability coefficient reflects the degree to which the measure is free of error variance. The rationale for using intraclass R instead of r for reliability was presented, as well as the computational procedures for intraclass R. Various methods of estimating reliability were mentioned such as stability, alternate forms, and internal consistency. Generalizability theory (G theory) is an extension of intraclass reliability that enables the researcher to identify sources of error in estimating reliability of scores on a test. Reliability techniques used in criterion-referenced measurements were summarized, and concerns regarding reliability in qualitative research were addressed.

The concept of standard error of measurement was discussed. Standard error is determined by the variability of the test scores and the reliability of the test. It is very important for all users of measurements to understand and appreciate their limitations, and that a score should be viewed as an estimate of the true score which probably falls within a range of scores.

There are basically four types of scales of measurement: nominal, ordinal, interval, and ratio. Standard scores allow direct comparisons of scores of different tests and types of scoring. The basic standard score is the z score, which interprets any score in terms of standard deviations from the mean.

Problems

1. Briefly describe two ways that evidence of construct validity could be shown for either a motor performance test (such as throwing), a test of power, or a test of manipulative skill. How could criterion validity be shown in your example?

2. Find in a research journal a study that used a written test (for example, an attitude inventory). Describe how the author reported the reliability of the instrument. What is another technique that could have been used to establish reliability?

3. A researcher develops a prediction formula for estimating maximal oxygen consumption from the results of a mile run. The standard error of estimate (prediction) is 3 milliliters per kilogram of body weight per minute ($ml \cdot kg^{-1} \cdot min^{-1}$). Let's say that a man who runs the mile in 8 minutes is predicted to have a maximal oxygen consumption score of 50 $ml \cdot kg^{-1} \cdot min^{-1}$. Interpret this in terms of the standard error of estimate. In other words, how "sure" is this prediction? Briefly describe how the researcher could use cross-validation in the development of this prediction formula.

Chapter 17

□

Measuring Movement

This chapter summarizes some of the ways that movement has been measured for use as a dependent variable in research. We present the manner in which different experimental variables are measured independently of the research questions that might be asked about movement. Any attempt to summarize the appropriate research questions in the various areas of physical education, exercise science, and sport science is impossible. Thus, this chapter presents some of the ways movement has been measured and some methodological difficulties associated with these measurements.

PSYCHOPHYSIOLOGICAL MEASUREMENT

A great deal of evaluation and research in physical education is directed at psychophysiological performance. Physical fitness assessment occupies considerable interest among exercise physiologists and physical education teachers. The measurement of basic motor abilities and skills pertaining to sport has also prompted much study over the years. We briefly summarize some of the methods of measuring various psychophysiological parameters.

Measurement of Physical Fitness

There is no universal definition of physical fitness. It is, after all, a matter of professional opinion. By now the concept of health-related physical fitness is widely accepted by authors on fitness, by exercise specialists, by medical personnel, and, by and large, in physical education. All the components of physical fitness supposedly have direct health implications for everyone and not only for athletes or other special populations. Nearly everyone agrees that three of the components of health-related fitness are cardiorespiratory endurance, muscular strength, and muscular endurance. Flexibility and body composition are two other components commonly included. However, there is some disagreement among physical fitness authorities as to whether these two parameters meet all the criteria for physical fitness components. We have no intention of entering into the debate or even discussing it. We simply talk about the measurement of the five areas wherever they belong.

> Any attempt to summarize the appropriate research questions in the various areas of physical education, exercise science, and sport science is impossible.

Cardiorespiratory Measures

The measurement of cardiorespiratory fitness can be separated basically into laboratory measures and field measures. However, these two categories can be divided even further into what might be called "poor man's" laboratory measures and pseudoscientific field measures.

Maximal Oxygen Consumption. Maximal oxygen consumption ($\dot{V}O_2$max) is generally considered to be the most valid measure of cardiovascular fitness, or aerobic capacity. The procedure involves exercising to exhaustion using a standardized workout, usually on a treadmill or bicycle ergometer because the speed and resistance of the exercise can be regulated. A number of methods, or protocols, are used for progressively increasing the work load, depending on the subject's level of fitness and other considerations. The subject is fitted with a mouthpiece, to which a hose is attached. As he or she exercises, the expired air is measured for volume and analyzed for oxygen and carbon dioxide content. The rate of oxygen consumption increases with an increasing work load to a point at which the rate of oxygen consumption levels off. This is the person's aerobic capacity. Other criteria include a respiratory quotient greater than 1.15, or when the subject is unwilling to do a greater work load (Heinert, Serfass, & Stull, 1988). Aerobic capacity is usually measured in milliliters of oxygen per kilogram of body weight per minute.

Modern instrumentation and computers enable the researcher to instantly obtain a variety of measures, a process that once took a great deal of time and painstaking calculations. Of course, this instrumentation is very expensive. The expense, the time required, and the inability to test but one person at a time prohibit the measurement of maximal oxygen consumption in the field. Therefore, other methods requiring less expensive equipment, less time, and less effort have been devised.

Submaximal Tests. Many of you have probably been tested on a submaximal test of cardiorespiratory fitness in an exercise physiology class or a test-and-measurement laboratory class. Such tests usually entail riding a bicycle ergometer for a specified time. Pulse rate is the only measurement taken. Then a nomogram is consulted or a chart is used to predict your aerobic capacity. These tests are

what we referred to as poor man's laboratory techniques because they require only a bicycle ergometer and a stopwatch to time the pulse.

Distance Run. The most commonly used field tests are distance runs. The length of the distance run has been a subject of many investigations. It appears that a distance requiring about 5 or more minutes is needed for acceptable validity. The validity of distance runs is usually established by correlating performance on the run with maximal oxygen consumption.

The distance run is appealing as a measure because a number of people can be tested at the same time and because the test is familiar and does not require much skill (although running definitely requires practice to learn optimal pace). Years ago, people would not run except in an emergency, and thus distance-run tests were quite short (e.g., 300, 440, or 600 yd). Research has indicated that these distances are too short and rely too heavily on speed to adequately measure cardiorespiratory fitness. Because of the popularity of jogging and the national interest in aerobics, longer distances, such as the 1- or 2-mi and the 9- or 12-min runs, are now commonly used.

A few years ago, step tests were popular. These are considered field measures because they require very little equipment and lend themselves to mass testing. We were referring to these kinds of *step tests* when we mentioned pseudoscientific field tests because they involve a physiological measurement (pulse counting). A number of step tests have been developed, ranging from very vigorous to moderately strenuous exercise. In most of the tests, the pulse is taken after exercise. Step tests, like distance runs, have construct validity. However, step tests are measuring only one aspect of cardiorespiratory fitness, and high correlations have usually not been found using maximal oxygen consumption as the criterion.

Strength and Endurance Measures

We combine our discussion of strength and endurance measures simply because they are usually combined in field tests, not because they are the same thing.

Relationship Between Strength and Endurance. The relationship between strength and endurance varies greatly, depending on several factors, such as absolute and relative strength and endurance, body weight, and body composition. For example, strength and endurance have a high positive correlation if we are talking about *absolute strength* and absolute endurance ("absolute" means that no consideration is given to body size or maximum strength). To illustrate, suppose that everyone in a sample is required to lift a 25-lb weight as many times as possible. The stronger person will find this easier than a weaker person because it represents a lighter load for the stronger person. Thus, a high positive correlation would be found between strength and endurance. If, however, everyone's maximum strength is determined and then a weight to lift is assigned (e.g., 25% of maximum strength), the correlation will change drastically. In some cases there will be no correlation between strength and endurance, and in other studies negative correlations will be found.

Strength and endurance can be measured precisely and separately in the laboratory. To the layperson, strength and endurance are very "simple" because everyone intuitively knows what they are. However, both abilities are actually complex. For example, there are different manifestations of strength (and strength training), such as isotonic, isometric, and isokinetic. We have already mentioned absolute strength. *Relative strength* is the ability to exert maximum force (isotonically, isometrically, or isokinetically) in relation to a person's size. With absolute strength, larger persons tend to be stronger than smaller persons. With relative strength, a small person may be as strong as or stronger than a larger individual if strength is measured in relation to size.

Measuring Strength. Various instruments, such as dynamometers and tensiometers, have been used for years to measure strength. Of course, lifting weights is an objective measure of strength. The term "1 RM" means the maximum amount of weight a person can lift once (1 RM = one repetition maximum). Because weight training has become an integral part of conditioning programs in athletics, the availability of weights for physical education programs and measurement has also increased. Several weight-training devices (machines) are available that can be used to measure strength and endurance. Isokinetic dynamometers are widely used in research and rehabilitation to assess and develop strength and endurance in isolated muscle groups.

Measuring Endurance. *Muscular endurance* is the ability to persevere in working against a submaximal resistance. In the laboratory, endurance is usually measured by having a subject exercise a particular muscle group until some criterion of exhaustion is reached. The movement is carefully controlled so that only the muscle group under study is allowed to work. The weight or resistance used depends on whether the task is to be absolute or relative endurance. For example, a researcher might determine the subject's maximal strength of a muscle group (e.g., elbow flexors) and then have the subject exercise at a set cadence to exhaustion with a weight that represents a proportion of the maximal strength. The subject is strapped to the table

in such a way that only the elbow flexors can operate in lifting the weight. The cadence is established with a metronome. The criterion of exhaustion is when the subject cannot maintain the cadence on two successive trials (Nelson, 1978). Isokinetic dynamometers are versatile in endurance research in that the researcher can isolate muscle groups and visually determine on a graph the point at which the subject, through repeated contractions, reaches a particular percentage of maximal force. The instrument can also be interfaced with a personal computer to provide prompts of when to exert force, to measure the maximal force on each movement, to record and display the readings on the screen, and to store data for later analysis (Yoon, 1988).

Barbells and free weights can also be used for endurance testing, as can some of the weight-training machines on the market. Muscular endurance can also be measured isometrically by having a subject hold a weight or exert a given amount of force against a dynamometer or other measuring device for as long as possible.

Some field tests include items that are aimed primarily at muscular endurance, such as squat thrusts and squat jumps. One of the difficulties with these tests is deciding on a time limit. If you do not set a time limit, the task causes a great deal of muscle soreness and increases the risk of injury. If you do set a time limit, agility enters into the task because it takes skillful movement of the body to perform the exercise repetitively in a certain time span.

Measuring the Combination of Strength and Endurance. Fitness tests that have been developed for the armed forces, public schools, colleges, and various organizations have traditionally included items that supposedly combine strength and endurance. Pull-ups, push-ups, the flexed-arm hang, and sit-ups are among the more popular test items of this kind. One of the contributing reasons for selecting these items is that field tests strive to choose items that are well known and that require little, if any, equipment. Items such as pull-ups are relative strength (and endurance) items because the subject must raise and lower his or her own body weight. One of the main objections to a test item such as pull-ups is that it cannot be called a test of both strength and endurance if the person can do only one or two. In this case it is a strength item because it represents maximal resistance. Remember, the definition of endurance specifies submaximal resistance that will allow repeated movements (or sustained force). Consequently, you cannot conclude that a person has no endurance if he or she lacks the strength to do the task more than once. Furthermore, if a boy cannot do a single pull-up, do you conclude that he lacks both strength and endurance? A further problem with items such as pull-ups is that most of the scores cluster at the low end of the scale; thus, the distribution is skewed rather than normally distributed.

Administering Strength and Endurance Tests. The administration of strength and endurance tests is surprisingly difficult because there are so many ways a person can do them incorrectly. When a subject performs a "simple" sit-up with hands clasped behind the head and knees bent, the tester must make sure the hands stay clasped. In attempting to develop a little bounce and momentum, the subject tries to omit touching the elbows to the mat each time. As fatigue enters into the exercise, the knees start to straighten, and the person does not sit up completely to touch the thigh. Furthermore, in a timed event the subject is apt to sacrifice desirable form for speed, resulting in a straight-back sit-up instead of the desired curl-up. Thus, it is safe to conclude that these well-known, "simple" test items of strength and endurance are anything but simple.

Flexibility Measures

Advocates of *flexibility* as a component of health-related physical fitness point to the importance of flexibility in avoiding injury due to sudden strains or movements. One of the inevitable results of inactivity (and thus aging) is the loss of flexibility, which hinders mobility. Athletic coaches and trainers have become acutely aware of the importance of flexibility in training and conditioning programs to avoid injury and promote more efficient movement. How much flexibility is needed? Is too much flexibility harmful? These questions are still unanswered. One thing known is that flexibility is highly specific, which means that a person who is flexible enough to bend and touch the toes easily may be quite inflexible in another part of the body, such as in the movement of the shoulders. Therefore, the results of a single test of flexibility in a fitness test battery cannot be generalized to indicate total flexibility. However, this is true for a test of any kind of ability, whether it be strength, power, or balance.

Flexibility has been measured in a variety of ways. The *sit-and-reach* is probably one of the oldest and best known tests. This item produced the greatest number of failures in the Kraus-Weber test of minimum muscular fitness. Through years of clinical experience, Kraus and Weber found that lack of flexibility in the back of the legs and in the back contributed significantly to problems of lower back pain. This is one of the principal reasons for the inclusion of the sit-and-reach test in the AAHPERD Physical Best Test (AAHPERD, 1989). Other simple field measures of flexibility include those of shoulder elevation, ankle flexibility, trunk and neck extension, and arm movement backward and sideward (see Johnson & Nelson, 1986).

The Leighton flexometer measures range of motion in degrees and is one of the more scientific instruments for evaluating flexibility. It has a weighted dial and a weighted pointer that attach to a segment of the body by means of a strap. Both the dial and the pointer rotate freely around a ball-bearing–supported axle. At the starting position, the dial is locked. The body segment is then moved to its extreme limit. The pointer follows the movement and is then locked for reading (Sigerseth, 1970). Therapists have used the *goniometer* for years in measuring the loss and recovery of flexibility in joints due to injury and rehabilitation. The *electrogoniometer* is another instrument that has been used for research purposes.

Body Composition Measures

The analysis of body composition has become very popular in recent years because of the urging of physicians, who have long recognized the association of obesity with a number of diseases and other health problems.

Body composition measurement refers to the leanness-to-fatness ratio. Lean body weight is composed of muscle, bone, and all other tissues except fat. Fat weight consists of fat contained subcutaneously and internally. Many laboratory and field methods are available for assessing body composition.

Among the laboratory methods, *hydrostatic* (underwater) *weighing* is the most commonly used. Body density is estimated by calculating the body's loss of weight underwater. The resulting body density is then put into a formula to compute percent fat. Formulas for converting density to percent fat are based on the difference in density of fat and lean body tissues. The underwater weighing procedures require a tank of water or a swim-

ming pool and a method for measuring residual lung volume, body weight in air, and body weight underwater. The temperature of the water must also be measured because the density of water varies with temperature. Density is mass (or weight) per unit volume. The weight is simply the individual's body weight in air (i.e., on land). Volume is estimated by subtracting the person's weight underwater from his or her weight on land. This value is divided by the density of water, corrected for the temperature of the water at the time of weighing. Subtracted from this is the residual lung volume and the estimated volume of air in the gastrointestinal tract (Behnke & Wilmore, 1974). Other laboratory methods for determining body composition include volume displacement, potassium-40, ultrasound, magnetic resonance imaging, helium dilution, radiographic analysis, and body water content.

Field methods consist mostly of the measurement of skinfold thickness, body circumferences, and skeletal diameters. Of these three, skinfold measurements are most commonly used. Recently, the principles of body impedance have been applied to the measurement of body composition (Segal, Gutin, Presta, Wang, & Van Itallie, 1985). This method is based on the concept that electrical conductivity is much greater in fat-free mass than in fat tissue because of the larger electrolyte content of lean tissue. Predictions of percent fat are often made from these measurements by using the results of hydrostatic weighing or some other laboratory technique as the criterion.

Skinfold thicknesses are taken at different body sites by the use of calipers. The accuracy of predicting percent fat from skinfold measures (and other anthropometric measurements) is subject to considerable measurement error. A great deal of practice and exacting care is required for accurate results. Skinfold measurements are included in the AAHPERD Physical Best Test (AAHPERD, 1989).

Measurement of Psychomotor Parameters

When introducing physical fitness measurement earlier in this chapter, we spoke of the acknowledged difference between fitness components, about which everyone should be concerned (health related), and certain fitness parameters, which are needed primarily for skilled performances, such as in athletics and dance. These components include power, speed, reaction time, agility, balance, kinesthetic perception, and coordination.

Power Measures

In many sports, power is considered to be the most important physical attribute. However, power is not simply a combination of strength and speed. (Many coaches have been disappointed by this misconception.) Rather, power involves the skillful coordination of strength and speed. An individual may be tremendously strong and may move quickly but still may lack the explosive power of another individual with less strength and less speed. There is definite skill involved in being able to exert force with lightning speed.

Power is technically defined as the change in work divided by the change in time, or the time rate of change of work. You should recall from your physics classes that work is the product of force times distance. This product, divided by time, is power.

Most of the tests of power commonly used in the schools (e.g., the vertical jump and standing long jump) do not include the three components of force, distance, and time. In fact, distance is the only measure usually obtained. Occasionally, for research purposes, performance scores are adjusted for body weight to calculate the actual work performed. A heavy person is generally penalized when a jump is scored only by distance jumped. Yet, a heavier person may have performed more work than a lighter person even though the latter had jumped farther. Keep in mind that we are speaking primarily about measurement for research purposes. Certainly, in basketball, the maximum height jumped is the most important consideration, not a person's body weight.

> Power is not simply a combination of strength and speed. Rather, power involves the skillful coordination of strength and speed.

Margaria, Aghems, and Rovelli (1966) developed a test that has been used to a considerable extent in research studies. It involves running up a flight of stairs two steps at a time as rapidly as possible. The time required to run up six or eight (or any number) stairs is recorded. Consequently, all three components of power are measured. The height of each stair times the number of stairs climbed determines distance. This is multiplied by the person's body weight to obtain the amount of work performed. Time is divided into work to yield a power score, which is then sometimes converted to horsepower. Construct validity has been established with, for example, sprinters, who scored higher than distance runners.

The vertical jump has sometimes been scored in power units. The time factor can be determined in various ways, such as measuring the amount of time in the air and using the acceleration of free-falling bodies. The vertical jump, regardless of how it is measured, still represents a rough but valid indication of athletic power.

Speed of Movement and Reaction Time Measures

Speed of movement can be measured accurately with the use of an electronic timer. The extent of the movement depends on the nature of the research project. In some studies, total body movement (such as running speed) is measured. In other studies, speed of movement might entail only a finger movement or the blink of an eye. Speed of movement is defined as the time elapsed from the point of initiation of the movement to the completion of the movement.

Speed of movement is often studied along with *reaction time*, which is the time elapsed from the presentation of a stimulus (such as a sound, a touch, or a flash of light) until the initiation of the response. In a race such as the 40-yd dash, reaction time would be the time from the stimulus (e.g., the firing of the starter's pistol) until the runner started to move (as in exerting pressure against the starting blocks). Speed of movement begins from the exertion of pressure until the subject reaches the 40-yd mark.

Reaction time has been measured with regard to many characteristics. For example, reaction time has been found to increase as the responses become more complex (Christina, Fischman, Vercruyssen, & Anson, 1982). Moreover, reaction time has been "fractionated" into *premotor time*, or *PMT* (the central component), and *motor time*, or *MT* (the peripheral component). The PMT is the interval between the time the stimulus is presented until the first action potential in the muscle manifests, whereas MT is the interval between the first muscle action potential and the initiation of the movement. Electromyography is used to fractionate PMT and MT (Sidaway, 1988). The electrical activity is rather quiet during the PMT interval; then, a burst of activity signals the onset of MT.

Apparently, a very low relationship exists between PMT and MT.

Agility Measures

Agility has been included in a number of applied research studies in physical education. It involves the accuracy and speed of changing direction while moving. Agility need not involve running but can also include movement of the body, such as scrambling up and down or jumping or hopping for accuracy (Chelladurai, 1976). In some tests, agility and power are closely associated, such as when a person must sprint a short distance and then change direction and sprint again.

In other agility tasks, power is not involved at all. In some tests, fitness components such as flexibility and endurance can enter into the performance, whereas in others coordination is the primary factor.

Agility performance is highly specific to the task. Correlations between agility tests are notoriously low. For example, a shuttle run (involving a short sprint, a stop, and a change of direction), a zigzag run (dodging around obstacles), and a squat thrust (moving rapidly from a standing position to a squat, then to a push-up position, and back to standing) are all recognized agility tests. The correlations among these tests are so low that there is virtually no generality at all. In other words, a person might be good at one task and poor or average at another. Here again one must be careful in drawing conclusions on a person's agility from only one test in a fitness battery. There is no such thing as general agility. Research in a specific sport should select (or construct) an agility test that involves the types of movements required for that sport rather than some so-called standard agility test. For example, agility in basketball requires quick direction changes, with or without a basketball. Thus, for an agility test to be useful in predicting or measuring basketball skill, it must test for that characteristic.

Balance Measures

Balancing ability depends on kinesthetic sensations, visual perception, and the mechanisms in the semicircular canals. Of the different kinds of balance, two major categories are static and dynamic. *Static balance* refers to the ability to hold a stationary position, whereas *dynamic balance* is the ability to maintain equilibrium while moving. As with many abilities, balance is highly specific to the task. There is virtually no relationship between static and dynamic balance.

Balance tasks have been used considerably in research, particularly in motor learning and performance studies. The stabilometer and the freestanding ladder-climb tests are commonly used. The *stabilometer* consists of a platform on which the subject attempts to stand while keeping the sides from tilting and touching the floor. The stabilometer is usually scored electronically so that the time is stopped or an error is recorded whenever the sides touch the floor. Platform balancing apparatus have been designed to measure postural adjustments in balancing. Layne and Abraham (1987) used such a platform. Each movement of the board activates electrical switches that produce a signal to be recorded on tape. In the freestanding ladder-climb task, the subject attempts to climb as far as possible before the ladder falls over. There is no cause for alarm because the ladder is only a few feet high (e.g., 5 ft). Often the ladder climb is scored electronically. For example, a score might be registered when the ladder tilts a certain number of degrees from the vertical position.

Balance beam tests have frequently been used in perceptual motor learning studies and research with mentally retarded and brain-damaged subjects. The height, width, and configuration of the beams can vary greatly, depending on the age and ability levels of the subjects. The subject may be asked to move forward, backward, or sideward along the beam. The score is usually the point in time at which the subject steps off the beam.

Balance tests are rarely used in motor fitness test batteries. Simple field tests sometimes used in the schools are the diver's stance, the stork stand, the Bass sticks, the sideward leap, and various positional tasks such as the squat stand and the headstand. Another type of balancing task involves balancing objects on the hand or the head.

Kinesthetic Measures

Kinesthetic ability tests were researched quite heavily years ago (Scott, 1955; Wiebe, 1954). Very few studies have been done recently on the topic of *kinesthetic measurement*. Kinesthetic perception tests have included short jumps for accuracy with the eyes open or closed; balancing tasks with the eyes closed; throws or kicks at a target with the eyes closed or the target obscured; positional tasks, such as moving the arm to a certain distance or angle; and tasks that involve recognizing and exerting a specific amount of force, such as one-half maximal hand-gripping force. The major limitation of kinesthetic tests is their low reliability. Some possible reasons for this include (a) the heavy reliance in normal activities on vision, which when removed in the experimental task greatly disrupts kinesthetic performance; and (b) the novelty of the task, coupled with an insufficient number of trials in which to demonstrate kinesthetic ability. A number of motor learning and control research studies use tasks that involve kinesthetic awareness.

The linear positioning slide (described later) is frequently used to measure kinesthetic spatial location (see, e.g., Reeve & Mainor, 1983).

Coordination Measures

It is readily acknowledged that coordination is an integral component of skill-related fitness and performance. However, in accordance with the concept of specificity, there is no such thing as general, or all-around, coordination. Often-heard comments such as ''so-and-so is well coordinated'' are actually based on rather limited observations. Researchers gave up years ago trying to measure general coordination and motor ability.

The measurement of coordination in research studies is necessarily restricted to some observational definition of eye-hand or eye-foot coordination with respect to particular tasks. Ball-throwing, kicking, dance-steps, and locomotor tasks have been used as measures of coordination for research purposes. Juggling is a classic eye-hand coordination

activity that has often been used in motor learning experiments. The Mashburn task, which uses an elaborate testing apparatus, requires the subject to use the hands and feet simultaneously while tracking a target. The task is a continuous, three-dimensional procedure, with independent dimensions being the right-left position of foot pedals and the forward-backward and right-left position of an aircraft-type control stick. Target locations of the controls are presented on a display, and the subject must position the controls so that each control position matches the corresponding target location (Lewis, McAllister, & Adams, 1951). A type of this instrument was developed in World War II for screening and training pilots. Some researchers have suggested that this was the beginning of research in motor learning (see the historical overview of physical education research in chapter 1).

Many manipulative tasks have been used in motor-learning research studies involving eye-hand coordination (e.g., pegboards, ro-

tary pursuit apparatus, and even children's games). Coordination measures have generally claimed logical validity, and the nature of coordination probably lends itself well to the establishment of construct validity.

Motor Behavior Measurements

Motor behavior generally deals with the acquisition and control of motor skills. Types of measurements include tests of basic movement patterns, sport skills tests, and laboratory measures. The distinctions among the measurements discussed here and in other parts of this chapter are not nearly as clearcut as our simplified discussion makes them appear. In addition, the measurements obtained are generally of two types: process and product. For example, in throwing, the outcome of the throw (how far and how accurate) can be measured (product), or the mechanics of the throwing movement can be analyzed (process). Here we present mainly the outcomes, or product measurements; we discuss process, or movement form (mechanics) assessments, later in this chapter. Nevertheless, the two cannot be separated. We want to know not only whether a movement pattern produced a quality outcome but also what was correct about the pattern and what needs to be altered.

Basic Movement Patterns

Our interest in basic movement patterns lies mostly with preschool and elementary school children. At these levels, teachers focus on the development of movement patterns in general rather than in the specific sport context. Thus, tests frequently include throwing and kicking balls for distance and accuracy, catching, striking with implements, and jumping. Tests are constructed to measure these skills for children aged 9 years and above. Checklist and rating scales are useful

for younger children because of the inconsistency of young children's performance (for a more detailed discussion, see Thomas & Thomas, 1983). Because throwing, catching, striking, and jumping are important skills in the sports of our culture, these skills are those most emphasized in teaching and testing children. The tests usually measure the outcomes of performance in time, distance, accuracy, or successful attempts. Many of the tests have been standardized and contain norms that are reported in publications on testing and measurement in physical education (e.g., Johnson & Nelson, 1986).

Sport Skills Tests

These tests measure many of the same characteristics of performance that tests of basic movement patterns do. However, performance is measured with the equipment and in the context of the specific sport (i.e., any implements used in the sport and in situations that are similar to ones encountered in the sport). For example, striking may be assessed in baseball as the number of successful hits out of a specific number of trials when the ball is projected by a pitching machine at 70 mph. Control of the soccer ball may be measured by a dribbling test through a series of direction changes. A kick for distance may involve punting a football. Again, most publications on testing and measurement provide many examples of these tests, reliability and validity information, and sometimes norms. In addition, AAHPERD has developed a sport skills test series for use by teachers.

Laboratory Measures

Many novel tasks have been developed for laboratory use in studying the acquisition and control of motor skills. Novelty is important in these tasks to control for prior experience. If none of the subjects has experience in performing the specific skill, then everyone begins at the same point in the skill acquisition process.

Motor Behavior Tasks. Following is a list of some frequently used tasks in motor behavior laboratories:

• **Pursuit rotor** (Figure 17.1)—This is a continuous tracking device much like a phonograph turntable. The task is to keep a hand-held stylus on a small circle located on the rotating disk. The stylus and disk are connected to a clock, which records the amount of time the stylus remains in contact with the small circle during a specified time interval.

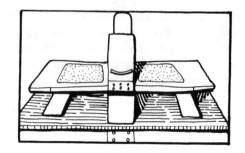

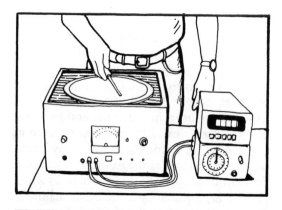

Figure 17.1 Pursuit rotor tracking.

Figure 17.2 a, the stabilometer; b, taking the stabilometer test.

• **Stabilometer** (Figure 17.2)—This is simply a platform centered on a fulcrum, much like a seesaw. The subject stands with both feet on the platform (one on either side of the fulcrum) and attempts to maintain the platform in a level (balanced) position. The score is either the number of times the platform touches the base on either side (errors) or the time the platform is kept in balance.

• **Anticipation timer** (Figure 17.3)—This consists of a trackway that is several feet long with small lights mounted at close intervals down the trackway. A controlling device causes lights to turn on and off consecutively down the trackway, simulating movement. The speed of this movement is determined by how rapidly the lights are turned on and off. The subject's task is to press a hand-held button when the last light turns on and off (simulated movement is at the end of the trackway). The score is the error in milliseconds that the button is pressed either too early or too late.

Figure 17.3 Anticipation timer.

• **Linear slide** (Figure 17.4)—This permits a task in which the subject moves a nearly frictionless handle down a trackway. The subject's task may be to move to some specified location (in which case the subject is usually blindfolded) or to move a certain distance in a criterion time (e.g., 400 cm in 40 ms). The score is the error in centimeters (either short or long) from the location or the error in milliseconds (either fast or slow) for the time to move the specified distance.

Figure 17.4 The linear slide.

• **Tapping board** (Figure 17.5)—This device has two metal circles (can be any size; but, as an example, assume 2 cm in diameter) mounted a certain distance apart (e.g., 18 cm). The subject uses a metal stylus to tap back and forth between the two circles as rapidly as possible. The circles and stylus are connected to a counter, which records the number of touches during a specified time period.

Figure 17.5 Tapping board.

Note that the outcomes of these tasks may be total time, total errors, directional error (long or short), timing error (fast or slow), or frequency of occurrence. In particular, long and short directional errors and fast and slow timing errors have generated interesting issues in measurement.

Reaction Time. Reaction time was discussed earlier in this chapter but it is appropriate to discuss it again here because it is also frequently used as a laboratory task. A reaction time task may be designed in which the subject is asked to respond to a stimulus by moving from a home key to one of several other keys. The amount of time it takes for the subject to release the home key after the stimulus is the reaction time. Reaction time varies as a function of the need for planning in the upcoming movement, number of choices of movements, direction of movement, and length of movement. Thus, reaction time seems useful as an index of motor planning or motor programming.

Obtaining Performance Estimates. If several subjects are given several trials on either the linear slide or the anticipation timer, then they are likely to have scores that are short or fast (labeled negative, or minus) and long or slow (labeled positive, or plus). A number of ways exist to obtain a performance estimate from these scores. Table 17.1 defines and gives examples of four common ways.

Absolute error (AE) was the most common way of reporting performance error until Schutz and Roy (1973) pointed out that AE was some undefined linear composite of *constant error (CE)* and *variable error (VE)*. Schutz and Roy recommended that AE no longer be used and that CE be used to reflect bias (i.e., did the subject tend to undershoot or overshoot the target?) and that VE be used to represent variability in performance. (A low VE means consistent estimation and high VE inconsistent estimation.) However, it soon became apparent that CE was not a good error estimate to average across subjects; that is, if some subjects undershoot on the average and others overshoot, the sign (±) of their scores tend to cancel and yield a group mean of zero. Schutz (1979) then suggested the use of absolute constant error (|CE|) to solve this problem. Earlier, Henry (1974) had advocated that one error score had the advantage of simplicity but, because AE was undefined, that researchers should use a defined composite error he called E.

$$E = \sqrt{CE^2 + VE^2} \qquad (17.1)$$

Beginning in the late 1970s, numerous statistical studies were done on the qualities of the error measures as dependent variables (see, e.g., Gessaroli & Schutz, 1983; Safrit, Spray, & Diewert, 1980; Schutz, 1979).

Table 17.1 Ways of Estimating Error Scores

Subject	X_1	X_2	X_3	X_4
			Trial	
Tom	+7	−4	−6	+3
Sam	−11	−2	+8	+3
Bill	−6	−3	−1	+3
John	+2	−1	−3	+1

AE—called absolute error. For each subject the scores are summed disregarding the sign and then divided by the number of scores, i.e., AE = $\Sigma|X|/N$. Thus, Tom's AE for the four trials is $(7 + 4 + 6 + 3)/4 = 20/4 = 5$.

CE—called constant error. The scores are summed (using the sign) for each subject and divided by the number of scores, i.e., CE = $\Sigma X/N$. Sam's CE is $[(-11 - 2) + (8 + 3)]/4 = (-13 + 11)/4 = -2/4 = -.50$.

|CE|—called absolute constant error. CE is calculated, then the absolute value is taken, i.e., |CE| = $|\Sigma X/N|$. Bill's |CE| is $|(-6 - 3 - 1 + 3)/4| = |-7/4| = 1.75$.

VE—called variable error. VE is the standard deviation of a subject's average CE score, i.e., VE = $\sqrt{\Sigma(X - M)^2/N}$. John's score is CE = $[(2 + 1) + (-1 - 3)]/4 = (3 - 4)/4 = -1/4 = -.25$.

$$VE = \sqrt{[(2 - .25)^2 + (-1 - .25)^2 + (-3 - .25)^2 + (1 - .25)^2]/4}$$
$$= \sqrt{(3.06 + 1.56 + 10.56 + .56)/4} = \sqrt{3.94} = 1.98$$

The most commonly used error scores today are |CE| and VE, although all of them are used on occasion. Laabs (1980) suggested that CE (and thus probably |CE|) represents perceptual judgment in memory, whereas VE represents the strength of the memory trace for a movement. Thus, VE could be used to measure learning and forgetting. It seems to be a particularly useful measure because it represents variability of performance. Therefore, beginners should have larger VE scores than more skilled performers, and younger children should have larger VE scores than older children.

Biomechanical Measurements

Biomechanics has been defined as "the application of the physical laws of motion to the study of biological systems" (Burdett, 1983, p. 2). Measurements to quantify movements have resulted from three specific sources: high-speed cinematography, force transducers, and electromyography. *High-speed cinematography* is the most widely used. Early studies used a single camera that allowed two-dimensional analysis. More recent advances use two (or more) cameras, which allow motion to be studied in three dimensions. These techniques are increasingly being applied to sport skills. Movements are then analyzed frame by frame for displacements of body segments as well as for their velocities and accelerations. Standard formulas of physics are applied to quantify measures. More sophisticated systems are interfaced with high-speed computers for rapid and detailed analysis. Even more refined and detailed video-recording systems are now being used.

Force transducers are used to measure the forces exerted during motor performance, including both the reactions between a runner's or jumper's feet and the ground and the forces exerted against equipment, such as

bicycles and weights. The transducers are interfaced with computer equipment (usually by an analog-to-digital converter) for faster and more thorough analysis.

Electromyography (*EMG*) is a technique that is bringing biomechanics and motor learning and control closer together. This technique uses skin or muscle electrodes to pick up electrical activity caused by muscle contraction during movement. This allows assessment of synchronous and asynchronous firing patterns in motor units during activity. The firing pattern determines the force exerted by the muscle as well as the timing. Of great interest is the difference in electrical patterns between skilled and novice performers, the changes that occur as a novice acquires skill over many practice trials, or the consistency of the EMG pattern during various movement speeds. Electromyographical signals are read directly into computers or can be recorded as pen displacements on a strip recorder.

Observational Measurement

Most of the measures of movement discussed have been acquired in relatively constrained settings, that is, testing situations or laboratories. Sometimes measurements are made by recording observations in real-world settings, such as during physical education classes or sport participation. This involves the use or development of some sort of coding instrument. Most frequently, the instrument has a series of categories into which the various motor behaviors may be coded. The behaviors are observed using such techniques as event recording, time sampling, and duration recording.

An example of an event-recording instrument for sport is the *Coaches Behavioral Assessment Scale* (*CBAS*) developed by Smith, Smoll, and Hunt (1977). The purpose of this scale is to record the reactive and spontaneous behaviors of the coach to actions of players during games (football, soccer, baseball, and basketball have all been used). The scale has eight categories of reactive behaviors and four categories of spontaneous behaviors. While watching the sport contest, the researcher codes any event of coach-player interaction that occurs (for a more detailed description and references, see the chapter by Smoll and Smith in Thomas, 1984).

The Academic Learning Time in Physical Education (ALT-PE) instrument, developed by Siedentop et al. (1979, 1982), is an example of time sampling. The researcher observes a child for certain lengths of time at specified intervals, for example, 10 s of watching and 10 s of rest. The activities in which the child engages during the 10 s are coded. This allows estimates of time on-task, time listening, and time waiting for a turn. Duration techniques are similar in format. However, the researcher's purpose is to record the length of time a subject spends on a particular event.

In these types of scales, as with any measure, validity and reliability are important. However, it is usually considerably more difficult to obtain consistency in recording children's activities in a physical education class or sport than recording error measurements from a laboratory task such as the linear slide. The researcher must be concerned about two types of consistency: first, that an observer records an event the same way each time and, second, that two observers record the same event the same way.

Video-recording instrumentation is of tremendous value in observational research. If the activity of interest can be videotaped, then observers can be more sure of their recording techniques because performance can be viewed more than once. However, considerable cost is involved.

In observational measurement, blind and double-blind techniques are particularly useful. Observers tend to code experimental and control groups and pre- and posttests differently if they know this information. Videotapes are particularly useful here because order and group assignment can be randomized to keep the observer naive to the time period and treatment condition.

Observational researchers are always concerned about the consistency of coders. Typically, coders are trained to a criterion level of reliability, and then reliability checks are made regularly during the project. A common way of estimating reliability among coders is called *interobserver agreement (IOA)*, which uses the following formula:

$$IOA = \frac{agreements}{(agreements + disagreements)}$$

Agreements are commonly coded behaviors, whereas disagreements are behaviors coded differently. IOA is typically reported as the percent of agreements.

USING COMPUTERS IN MEASURING MOVEMENT

Whereas any type of computer can be used in measuring movement, microcomputers are the most commonly used. These computers may be used in three ways: controlling the data-collection situation, recording the data, and analyzing the data.

Controlling the Data-Collection Situation

Programs are frequently written for microcomputers that either partially or completely control the testing session. In a motor behavior experiment, the task might be to make either a long or a short movement when a stimulus light appears. A computer program can be written that works as follows:

1. The experimenter loads the program into the microcomputer before the subject arrives in the testing situation.
2. When the subject arrives, the experimenter enters his or her name, I.D. number, and any other pertinent characteristics, such as age, gender, handedness, and which group the subject is in.
3. The computer then displays a picture of the task and written instructions concerning how the subject is to perform.
4. The computer provides a set number of practice trials. After each trial, the subject is provided knowledge of results about his or her reaction time and movement time.
5. The computer controls all aspects of the experimental testing session, including the flashing of the warning light, flashing the movement signal, randomizing the interval between the warning and the movement signals, controlling the interval between trials, providing knowledge of results at a precise point between trials, and even retesting a trial if a reaction or movement time is outside a specified range.

Computers are typically used in exercise physiology laboratories for regulating the conditions of the exercise (e.g., speed and elevation of the treadmill) and controlling the time intervals for the various measurements that are taken during the exercise bout.

Recording the Data

In the previously described situation, the microcomputer is also used to record the data after each trial. However, sometimes the micro might be used to record data but not to control the data-collection situation. For example, an observer could enter data directly into a micro while observing a physical education class. If a program were written to handle data from the ALT-PE coding instrument (Siedentop et al., 1979; 1982), the entries could be made into a micro as easily as onto a code sheet.

Analyzing the Data

The micro may be used partly or completely to analyze the data (for statistical programs that are available for use on microcomputers, see Appendix B). The micro can also be used to send the data to a larger, mainframe computer for statistical analysis. This is done by interfacing the micro with the mainframe by a phone line. Normally, this requires special hardware (modem) and software (a special program for either the micro or the mainframe). However, most computer centers are adaptable to this need.

Summarizing Computer Use in Measuring Movement

Remember, these are only examples of the uses of microcomputers. Innovative researchers and technicians have found hundreds of unique ways to use micros in controlling, recording, and analyzing research. The advantages are easily seen in the time saved, the reduction in the number of errors, and the increased sophistication of experiments. As an example, a number of errors can be made in obtaining the data from the instrumentation used in the analysis. For example, if instrumentation is done by hand, the experimenter could read the instrument incorrectly, record the data incorrectly, transfer the data to a code sheet incorrectly, or enter the data for analysis improperly. All these sources of error are controlled when a micro is used to record and analyze the data.

The limitations in using microcomputers are easily observed. First, micros cost money. Second, once the micro is obtained, it must be interfaced with the equipment, and programs must be written to control the experimental situation. Because these programs may be unique to the experiment being conducted, they may not be available commercially. Thus, the technical support must be obtained so that the micro can be used effectively. Finally, micros are not maintenance free, and they continually use supplies such as diskettes as well as more advanced programs and additional hardware.

SUMMARY

This chapter has provided some examples of the ways movement may be measured. Included have been measurements of physical fitness, motor abilities, basic movement skills, sport skills, and laboratory tasks for motor behavior. Biomechanical and observational measurements have also been included. Neither these categories nor the examples within the categories are meant to be inclusive. However, we feel that examples are sometimes helpful in understanding concepts.

Problem

Find a measure of movement used in research in exercise and sport science or physical education that is not covered in this chapter and complete the following:

a. Identify the study in which it appears (cite the reference in APA style).
b. Describe the measure of movement.
c. Explain how the measure is scored.
d. Report any evidence of validity and reliability provided.
e. Summarize what was found in the study with regard to the measure you selected.

Chapter 18

☐

Measuring Written Responses

Much of the research conducted in physical education, exercise science, and sport science involves measurement of written (and oral) responses. Research questions frequently deal with affective behavior, which includes attitudes, interests, emotional states, and personality and psychological traits. This chapter considers some of these affective behavior measures and examines various types of responses that are used in such pencil-and-paper tests and some characteristics of rating scales. Attention is also given to item analysis in written tests of knowledge, as well as item response theory (IRT) as an alternative to classical test theory.

MEASUREMENT OF AFFECTIVE BEHAVIOR

A variety of behaviors fall into the category of affective behavior, including attitudes, personality, anxiety, self-concept, social behavior, and sportsmanship. A recent discussion of the construction, strengths, and weaknesses of affective tests, as well as scaling, is presented by Nelson (1989).

Attitude

A large number of attitude inventories have been developed. Undoubtedly, many of the test developers feel there is a direct link between attitude and behavior. For example, if a person has a favorable attitude toward physical activities, that person will participate in such activities. Research, however, has seldom substantiated this link between attitude and behavior, although such a link seems logical.

Researchers usually try to locate an instrument that has already been validated and that is an accepted measure of attitude rather than having to construct one. Finding a published test that closely pertains to the research topic is a problem. Another problem is that often the researcher wants to determine whether some treatment will bring about a change in attitude. A source of invalidity discussed in chapter 14 is the reactive effects of testing. The pretest sensitizes the subject to the attitudes in question and this may promote a change rather than the treatment.

Another problem (mentioned in chapter 13) inherent in any self-report inventory is whether the person is truthful. It is usually quite evident what a given response indicates. For example, a person is asked to indicate his or her degree of agreement or disagreement to the statement, "Regular exercise is an important part of our daily lives." The individual may perceive that the socially desirable response is to agree with this statement regardless of his or her true feelings. Some respondents deliberately distort their answers to appear "good" (or "bad"). Tests sometimes use so-called filler items to make the true purpose of the instrument less visible. For example, a test designer might include several unrelated items, like "Going to the opera is a desirable social activity," to disguise the fact that the instrument is designed to measure attitude about exercise. This is especially important when social desirability considerations may be biasing factors.

When a researcher seeks to find an attitude instrument to use in a study, validity and reliability must, of course, be primary considerations. Unfortunately, published attitude scales have not always been constructed in a scientific manner, and limited information is provided about validity and reliability. Actually, reliability can be established rather easily as far as methodology is concerned. (We are not saying that attitude scales are easily made reliable.) Validity is usually the problem because of the failure to develop a satisfactory theoretical model for the attitude construct.

Attitudes toward physical education, sport, and exercise have been measured in numerous studies. An example of a well-constructed attitude inventory is Kenyon's (1968) *Attitude Toward Physical Activity (ATPA) Inventory*. The theoretical model for the ATPA hinges on the premise that attitude toward activity is relatively stable and that positive attitudes are manifested by active participation or by watching others perform (passive involvement). Content validity was established by factor analysis and expert opinion. Construct validity was also established through the group difference method.

On the other hand, the *Physical Estimation and Attraction Scale (PEAS)* is based on the theory that attitude toward activity is modifiable by participation in physical activity (Sonstroem, 1978). The PEAS was constructed with sound procedures, and construct validity has been demonstrated by a number of research studies. Thus, a researcher who is planning a study to assess changes in attitude through some planned activity would be advised to use the PEAS rather than the ATPA because the latter is based on the theoretical framework that attitude is difficult to change.

Construct validity in attitude inventories can be established by comparing different groups who supposedly would be expected to reflect different attitudes. For example, boys of high and low fitness were found to differ significantly in both the estimation and the attraction items of the PEAS test. Construct validity in attitude inventories and other affective measures often includes convergent validity and discriminant validity procedures. *Convergent validity* involves correlations between measures of the same construct. For example, if someone constructed an attitude inventory, it would be expected that other general attitude inventories (or dimensions of attitude) would correlate moderately to highly with it. In *divergent*, or *discriminant*, *validity*, the assumption is that the measure in question should not correlate with measures of different constructs. For example, in the ATPA, the dimension of attitude toward physical activity as a social experience would not be expected to correlate highly with a dimension such as pursuit of vertigo.

Personality

A large number of research studies in physical education and sport have attempted to explore the relationship between personality traits and various aspects of athletic performance. Interest in this topic can be attributed to several factors, including the great deal of public attention that is focused on athletics. Athletes are obviously "special" people with regard to physical characteristics. Beyond that, however, is the hypothesis that athletes have certain personality traits that distinguish them from nonathletes.

Areas of Investigation of Personality Traits of Athletes

One area of investigation has been to identify personality traits that might be uniquely characteristic of athletes in different sports. For example, do persons who gravitate toward vigorous contact sports differ in personality from those individuals who prefer noncontact sports? That is, is there a "football type" or a "bowler type"? Are superior athletes different than average athletes in certain personality traits? Can participation in competitive sport modify one's personality structure? Moreover, do athletes within a sport differ on some traits that, if known, could point to different coaching strategies, or perhaps be used to screen and predict those athletes who will be "hard" to coach or who will lack certain qualities associated with success?

Persons with a strong interest in sports, such as former coaches and players, have been greatly attracted to the study of personality and athletics. Having a strong interest in athletics does not compensate for a lack of preparation and experience in psychological evaluation. Unfortunately, there have been numerous cases of ignorance about personality structure and misuse of personality measuring instruments. Many well-intentioned but unprepared graduate students have undertaken theses and dissertations that have purported to investigate the personality structure of athletes.

Instruments for Measuring Personality Traits

We have repeatedly emphasized the point that measuring instruments are not infallible; there is always the likelihood of measurement error, and when the measuring instrument is being used by someone who is not knowledgeable about the parameter being measured, the chance of error is magnified. It is true that some pencil-and-paper personality trait inventories are easily administered and objectively scored. The problem arises with the interpretation, however. What does it mean when groups differ significantly on traits such as protension or autia? The mere reporting of the presence or lack of significant differences in personality traits has very little meaningfulness. Alderman (1974) has stated, "Too often, intuitive jumps are made between very ordinary information and highly complex behavioral explanations without realizing the limitations and restrictions that many of our personality inventories possess" (p. 128).

> Measuring instruments are not infallible; there is always the likelihood of measurement error, and when the instrument is being used by someone who is not knowledgeable about the parameter being measured, the chance of error is magnified.

The aspiring researcher in this area needs to know which traits can be expected to produce specific motivational states and which are not likely to have any effect. Moreover, some traits are more independent of other traits, whereas some overlap and operate in conjunction with certain others. Consistency of behaviors that manifest particular traits is impossible to achieve over a variety of situations. People simply react differently to different situations, and, although a person may exhibit self-confidence or dominance in some situations, that same individual may be quite the opposite in other situations. The point is that personality is very complex. Elaborate theories have been developed in attempting to explain human behavior through personality constructs. A graduate student is naive indeed to think that the scores on a single instrument given to a sample of subjects on one occasion by an untrained tester will yield a great deal of generalizable conclusions about such a complex concept as personality structure. The study of personality is not futile, however. On the contrary, there is persuasive evidence that certain special populations, such as superior athletes, do have unique and identifiable personality profiles. We are simply emphasizing the complexity of personality dynamics and the need for adequate scholarly preparation of the researcher.

Of the several pen-and-paper personality inventories on the market, the *Cattell 16 Personality Factor (PF) Questionnaire* has been used most frequently in research studies concerning the personality profiles of athletes and participants in physical activity.

Sport-Specific Affective Measures

Recently, sport psychologists have recognized the value of sport-specific measures of various behaviors and perceptions. Much of the impetus for this approach can be traced to Martens's work on competitive anxiety (discussed in the next section).

Some of the sport-specific measures that have been developed relate to group cohesiveness (Carron, Widmeyer, & Brawley, 1985), intrinsic and extrinsic motivation (Weiss, Bredemeier, & Shewchuck, 1985), confidence (Vealey, 1986), and sport achievement orientation (Gill & Deeter, 1988). The rationale for the sport-specific approach is that general measures of achievement, anxi-

ety, motivation, and other traits do not have high validity for sport situations. These recent studies in test development indicate a commitment on the part of sport psychologists to develop measures of affective behavior that are multidimensional and specific to the competitive environment.

Anxiety

The measurement of anxiety in our field has been concentrated primarily in the areas of sport psychology and motor learning because of the recognized implications of anxiety level on motor performance. Spielberger (1966) is generally credited with differentiating between two types of anxiety: state and trait. *State anxiety* is an immediate emotional state of apprehension and tension in accordance with a specific situation, whereas *trait anxiety* is more of a general tendency to be anxious. Thus, trait anxiety is a rather stable characteristic of an individual. Persons with high trait anxiety are prone to perceive more situations as threatening and to respond with different degrees of state anxiety.

This distinction is important to the researcher who is planning to assess changes in anxiety produced by a particular stressful situation. If a trait anxiety inventory is selected, then, by definition, one should not expect a change. Until Spielberger developed his A-state and A-trait anxiety scales, such studies were virtually doomed from the start as far as measurable changes in anxiety were concerned.

In light of the importance of specificity, Martens (1977) developed a sport-specific trait anxiety inventory, the *Sport Competition Anxiety Test (SCAT)*, which he found to be a better predictor of trait anxiety in a sport context when compared with general trait anxiety scales. Martens found satisfactory reliability and convincing evidence of content and construct validity for SCAT when it was used within the context of his model of competition.

Self-Concept

Self-concept is a personality trait that has prompted numerous studies in nearly all our areas. Other terms that have been used either synonymously with or as a facet of self-concept include self-image, self-confidence, self-esteem, and self-regard. A major premise for the interest in this area is that the manner in which persons see themselves has a high relationship with achievement. Furthermore, it is hypothesized that self-concept can be modified by certain types of experiences, especially those that provide positive reinforcement.

Of particular interest to persons in movement-oriented fields is the influence of body image on total self-concept. Researchers have attempted to assess the effects of weight loss on obese individuals as to changes in their body images. Several projective tests and self-report scales have been constructed to measure body image. However, the projective tests cannot be objectively scored, making them inappropriate for persons other than psychologists. The Tennessee Self-Concept Scale (Fitts, 1965) has been widely used in research in exercise and sport science. It measures eight dimensions of self-concept and provides a total overall self-esteem score.

The effects of different types of recreational activities and experiences on self-concept have been investigated numerous times. For example, activities such as rock climbing and adventure programs have been studied to determine whether participation in such ''risk-type'' activities can bring about favorable changes in self-concept.

Some of the problems encountered here are similar to those we have alluded to in other research. The primary consideration is in test selection. A test that is constructed on the premise that self-concept is a stable personality trait should not be used in a study in which changes in self-concept are expected. In other words, the researcher needs to select a measure that views self-concept as a dimension that is amenable to change.

Social Behavior

Interest in social behavior is logical because physical educators generally list social development as one of the main objectives of physical education. However, the amount of interest in developing social behavior measuring instruments has diminished through the years. An example of an early social behavior rating scale is the *Cowell Social Adjustment Index* (Cowell, 1958). Major stumbling blocks in attempts to measure social behavior have been the lack of clear-cut definitions as to what social behavior consists of and the lack of acceptable validity and reliability coefficients. Behavior measurement is usually performed by some type of rating scale. The problems associated with such ratings are discussed in chapter 13 in the section ''Observational Research,'' and limitations of rating scales in general are described later in the present chapter. We are simply acknowledging that this area of research is included in affective behavior measurement.

Fair Play

One of the espoused goals included under the objective of promoting desirable social qualities in physical education and sport is the development of a sense of fair play. A great amount of lip service has been given to this goal, and claims have been made that physical education and sports contribute to the development of fair play; however, almost no evidence exists to prove this occurs.

Investigators have used a cross-sectional approach in comparing samples of older children with younger children in an attempt to yield evidence that participation in organized physical activity and competition develops good sportsmanship. Some researchers have compared professional players with amateurs, and others have looked at the effect of university size on the sportsmanship of athletes within the different institutions.

The research results have been confusing, to say the least. Some evidence has shown that the longer one participates in sports, the poorer the quality of sportsmanship. Some of the contradictions in findings may be attributed to the means of assessing sportsmanship. One method involves the use of rating scales. Operationally defining observable sportsmanship poses a problem, as does the lack of sufficient opportunities to display the behavior. Pencil-and-paper tests of sportsmanship have been mostly of a situational format in which a given situation is described and the respondent asked to indicate whether the course of action is appropriate. The *Lakie Attitude Toward Athletic Competition Scale* (Lakie, 1964) is an example of such an instrument.

The main drawback to the sport-situation approach is that the respondent can easily pick out which answer is the desired one. In addition, the described situation is often one that may not contribute to fair play in the strict interpretation of the act but that is an accepted practice in the sport. For example, although blocking the base path in baseball is illegal, catchers are taught to do this when trying to tag a runner sliding into home plate. Thus, an experienced player would not view this action as violating a sense of fair play, whereas a person unfamiliar with the game would answer correctly because blocking the base path is a violation of the rules. The situational approach is probably the most feasible for pencil-and-paper inventories, but much work needs to be done to develop truly valid and reliable research instruments.

TYPES OF RESPONSES

In measuring affective behavior, a variety of scales are used to quantify the responses. Three of the more commonly used scales are the Likert scale, the semantic differential scale, and the Thurstone-type scales.

The Likert Scale

The Likert scale was referred to in chapter 13 in connection with survey research techniques. It is usually a 5- or 7-point scale with assumed equal intervals between points. The Likert scale is used to assess the degree of agreement or disagreement with statements and is widely used in attitude inventories. An example of a Likert scale item follows:

I prefer quiet recreational activities such as chess, cards, or checkers rather than activities such as running, tennis, or basketball.

| Strongly Agree | Agree | Undecided | Disagree | Strongly Disagree |

A principal advantage of scaled responses such as the Likert is that it permits a wider choice of expression than items such as "always," "never," "yes," or "no." The five, seven, or more intervals help increase the reliability of the instrument (for more comprehensive information concerning the Likert, semantic differential, and other scales, see Edwards, 1957, or Nunnaly, 1978).

The Semantic Differential

The *semantic differential scale* employs bipolar adjectives at each end of a 7-point scale. The respondent is asked to make judgments about certain concepts. The scale is based on the importance of language in reflecting a person's feelings. A sample of a semantic differential item follows.

The Coach

1. creative	: : : : : : :	unoriginal
2. supportive	: : : : : : :	critical
3. fair	: : : : : : :	unfair

The 1-7 scale between adjectives is scored with 7 being the most positive judgment. Factor analysis studies have rather consistently identified the same three dimensions being assessed by the semantic differential technique: evaluation (e.g., fair-unfair), potency (e.g., powerful-feeble), and activity (e.g., dynamic-static).

Thurstone-Type Scales

The *Thurstone-type scales* were the first to use judges to determine comparative weightings for psychological stimuli. The respondent expresses agreement or disagreement with a series of statements. In developing Thurstone scales, each of the items is first scaled by a panel of judges. The judges rate each statement with a numerical value from 1 to 11, with 11 reflecting the most positive attitude. The median score of the judges for each item is then used to weight the statements for use in scoring.

An example of a statement as it would appear on the tester's manual follows.

1. Physical education should be required in the elementary school. (9.1)

The final score (9.1) is the sum of all the weighted scores divided by the number of "agree" items. The Thurstone-type scales are more difficult to construct than the Likert and semantic differential scales because of the involvement of the judges.

Rating Scales

Rating scales are sometimes used in research to evaluate performance. For example, in a study that compares different strategies in teaching diving, the dependent variable (diving skill) would most likely be derived from expert ratings because diving does not lend itself to objective skill tests. Thus, after the experimental treatments have been applied, persons knowledgeable in diving rate all the subjects on their diving skills. To do this in a systematic and structured manner, the raters need to have some kind of scale with which to assess skill levels in different parts or phases of the performance.

A self-rating scale concerning an individual's perceived efforts during exercise that has been widely used in research is the *Ratings of Perceived Exertion (RPE)* scale by Borg (1962). The underlying rationale for the scale is that the many physiological indicators of exertion are combined and integrated into a whole, or gestalt, of subjective feeling of physical effort. This feeling of perceived exertion was quantified by Borg into a scale with numbers ranging from 6 to 20, reflecting a range of exertion from "very, very light" to "very, very hard."

Types of Rating Scales

There are different kinds of rating scales. Some scales use numerical ratings, some use checklists, some have verbal cues associated with numerical ratings, some require forced choices, and still others use rankings. Some scales are relatively simple, whereas others are rather complex. Regardless of the degree

of complexity, however, practice in using the scale is imperative.

When more than one judge is asked to rate performances, some common standards must be set. Training sessions with videotaped performances of persons of different levels of ability are very helpful in establishing standard frames of reference before judging the actual performances of the subjects in the study. (Intertester agreement and reliability were discussed in chapters 16 and 17.)

Rating Errors

Despite efforts to make ratings as objective as possible, there are inherent pitfalls in the process. Some of the recognized errors in rating include leniency, central tendency, the halo effect, proximity, observer bias, and observer expectation.

Leniency is the tendency for observers to be overly generous in their ratings. This error is less likely to occur in research than in evaluating peers (e.g., co-workers). Thorough training of raters is the best means of reducing leniency.

Central tendency errors result from the inclination of the rater to give an inordinate number of ratings in the middle of the scale, avoiding the extremes of the scale. Several reasons are attributed to this. Sometimes it may be due in part to ego needs or status. For example, the judge is acting in the role of an expert and, perhaps unconsciously, may grade good performers as average to indicate that he or she is accustomed to seeing better performances. Sometimes, errors of central tendency are due to the observer's wanting to "leave room" for better future performances. A common complaint in large gymnastics, diving, and skating competitions is that the performers scheduled early in the meet are scored lower for comparable performances than athletes scheduled later in the competition.

Central tendency error at the other end of the scale is the inclination to avoid assigning very low scores and is likely due to a judge's reluctance to be too harsh (wanting to "give the poor devil a break"). It is, of course, a form of leniency.

The halo effect is the commonly observed tendency for a rater to allow previous impressions or knowledge about a certain individual to influence ratings on all that individual's behaviors. For example, knowing that an individual excels in one or more activities, a judge may rate that person highly on all other activities. The halo effect perhaps is not the most appropriate term because negative impressions of a person tend to lead to lower ratings in subsequent performances.

Proximity errors are often the result of overly detailed rating scales, the lack of sufficient familiarity with the rating criteria, or both. Proximity errors are manifested when the rater tends to rate behaviors that are listed close together as more nearly the same than when the behaviors are separated some distance on the scale. For example, if the qualities "active" and "friendly" were listed adjacent to each other on the scale, proximity errors would result if raters evaluated performers as being more similar on those characteristics than if the two were listed several lines apart on the rating scale. Of course, if the rater does not have adequate knowledge about all facets of the behavior, he or she may not be able to distinguish between different behaviors that logically should be placed close together on the scale. Thus, the different phases of behavior are rated the same.

Observer bias errors are a function of the judge's own characteristics and prejudices. For example, a person who has a low regard for movement education may also tend to rate students from such a program too low. Racial, sexual, and philosophical biases are potential sources of rating errors. Observer bias errors are directional in that they produce errors that are consistently too high or too low.

Observer expectation errors can operate in various ways, often stemming from other sources of errors such as the halo effect and observer bias. Observer expectations can contaminate the ratings in that a person who expects certain behaviors will be inclined to see evidence of those behaviors and interpret observations in the "expected" direction.

Research has demonstrated the powerful phenomenon of expectation in classroom situations in which teachers are told that some children are gifted or slow learners. The teachers tend to treat the pupils accordingly, giving more attention and patience to the "gifted" and less time and attention to the "slow learners."

In the research setting, potential observer expectation errors are likely when the observer knows what the experimental hypotheses are and is thus inclined to watch for these outcomes more closely than if he or she were unaware of the expected outcomes. The double-blind experimental technique described in chapter 14 and elsewhere is useful in controlling for expectation errors. In the double-blind method, the observers are not aware of which subjects received which treatments. They also should not know which performances are the pretest and which are the posttest.

In summary, rating errors are always potentially present. The researcher must be aware of them and strive to eliminate or reduce them. One of the ways to minimize rating errors is to define the behavior to be rated as objectively as possible. In other words, avoid having the observer make many value judgments. Another suggestion is to keep observers "ignorant" of the hypotheses and of who received what. Bias and expectation can be minimized if the observer is given no information about the subjects' past achievements, intelligence, social status, and other characteristics. The most important precaution the researcher can take is to train the observers adequately to achieve high levels of accuracy and interrater reliability.

> The most important precaution the researcher can take is to train the observers adequately to achieve high levels of accuracy and intertester reliability.

KNOWLEDGE TESTING

Obviously, the measurement of knowledge is a fundamental part of the educational thrusts in physical education, exercise science, and sport science. However, the construction of knowledge tests is relevant for research purposes as well. Most pencil-and-paper measuring instruments used in research involve similar procedures in establishing validity and reliability. These procedures were summarized in chapter 16. Consequently, our attention is directed primarily to item analysis techniques (for a discussion of measurement methodology for knowledge tests, see Mood, 1989).

Item Analysis

The purpose of *item analysis* is to determine which items are suitable and which need to be rewritten or discarded. Two important facets of item analysis are the difficulty of the test items and the power to discriminate between different levels of achievement.

Item Difficulty

In most cases, the analysis of the test item (*item difficulty*) is easily accomplished. One simply divides the number of persons who correctly answered the item by the total number of people who responded to the item. For example, if 80 people answered an item, and 60 answered it correctly, the item would have a difficulty index of .75 (60/80). A "hard" item has a low difficulty index; that is, if only 8 of 80 answered it correctly, the index is 8/80,

or .10. Most test authorities recommend that questions with difficulty indices below .10 or over .90 should be eliminated. The best questions are those that have difficulty indices around .50. Occasionally, a test maker may wish to set a specific difficulty index for screening purposes. For example, if only the top 30% of a group of applicants are to be chosen, this could be accomplished by using questions with difficulty indices of .30. Questions that everyone answers correctly or that everyone misses provide no information about people differences in norm-referenced measurement scales.

Item Discrimination

Item discrimination, or the degree to which test items discriminate between persons who did well on the entire test and those who did poorly, is an important consideration in analyzing test items. There are a number of ways to compute an *index of discrimination*. The simplest way is to divide the completed tests into a high group and a low group on the basis of scores and then use the following formula:

$$\text{Index of Discrimination} = (NH - NL)/N$$

(18.1)

where NH = number of high scorers who answered the item correctly, NL = the number of low scorers who answered the item correctly, and N = the number in either the high or the low group. To illustrate, if we have 30 in the high group and 30 in the low group, and 20 of the high scorers answered an item correctly and 10 of the low scorers answered it correctly, the index of discrimination would be .33: $(20 - 10)/30 = 10/30 = .33$.

Various percentages of high and low scorers are used in determining discrimination indices, such as the upper and lower 25%, 30%, or 33%. The Flanagan method uses the upper and the lower 27%. The proportion of each group answering each item correctly is calculated; then a table of normalized biserial coefficients is consulted to obtain the item reliability coefficient. Thus, item reliability is the relationship between responses to each item and total performance on the test.

If approximately the same proportion of high scorers answer an item correctly as did the low scorers, the item is not discriminating. Most test makers strive for an index of discrimination of .20 or higher for each item. Obviously, a negative index of discrimination would be unacceptable. In fact, when this happens, the question needs to be examined closely to see whether something in the wording is throwing off the high scorers.

Types of Knowledge Test Items

The most common types of test items are completion, essay, matching, alternate choice, and multiple choice. Each type of question has its strengths and weaknesses (these are discussed in detail in measurement and evaluation textbooks).

Knowledge tests have been used in research studies concerning facts and fallacies about diet and exercise, game rules and strategies, basic knowledge pertaining to different subject areas, and other topics. Knowledge testing in such research studies invariably uses objective items, such as multiple choice or alternate choice. Matching test items are objective, but they are time consuming and limited as to the effective number of items that can be presented.

Multiple-choice items are considered by testing authorities as the most reliable of the test items. Good multiple-choice items are difficult to write. The stem should be presented clearly and concisely, and the alternatives must be meaningful and attractive. Poor alternatives simply limit the choices and can reduce multiple-choice items to alternate-choice items.

The number of alternatives influences reliability. The more choices, the greater the reliability because the likelihood of getting the correct answer by chance is reduced. However, as you increase the number of alternatives, practical considerations (e.g., time required for testing) negate the advantage. Between three and five choices are recommended.

Alternate-choice items, such as true-false, are used occasionally in research studies. This type of item has been criticized for various reasons, but often the weaknesses cited can be minimized by careful test construction. Alternate-choice items are less reliable than multiple-choice tests of the same length. However, more alternate-choice items can be given in a set time period, and this can increase the test reliability. The items are easier to write than those of multiple choice, but considerable skill is required to write good test questions. With care, alternate-choice tests can be employed to assess knowledge effectively.

ITEM RESPONSE THEORY

Most of the information concerning the validity, reliability, and item analysis thus far pertains to what is called *classical test theory (CTT)*. There have been some radical changes recently in the study of the measurement of cognitive and affective behaviors. The advance that has received the most attention in the educational and psychological literature is *item response theory (IRT)*.

Characteristics of IRT

Whereas in the CTT inferences are made about items and student abilities from total *test* score information, IRT, as the name implies, attempts to estimate an examinee's ability on the basis of his or her responses on test *items*. Classical test theory requires only a few assumptions with regard to the observed scores and the true scores of individuals on a test. Group statistics pertaining to the total score on a particular test for the total group being examined are used to make generalizations to an equivalent test and population. The estimate of error is assumed to be the same for all individuals.

Item response theory is based on stronger assumptions than CTT. The two major ones are unidimensionality and local independence. Unidimensionality means that a single ability or trait is being measured. This ability is not directly measurable, so IRT is sometimes referred to as *latent trait theory* (for an introduction to IRT and some of its applications, see Spray, 1989). According to Spray, the real advantage of IRT is that the measurement of an examinee's ability from responses to test items is not limited to a particular test. Rather, it can be measured by any collection of test items that are considered to be measuring the same trait.

In traditional CTT, item difficulty is measured as a function of the total group. In IRT, item difficulty is fixed and can be assessed relative to an examinee's ability level. Thus, the probability of an examinee with a particular ability level making a correct response to an item can be mathematically described by an *item characteristic curve (ICC)*. The ICC is a nonlinear regression for any item that increases from left to right, indicating an increase in the probability of a correct response with increased ability, or latent trait. The item difficulty remains constant regardless of the group of examinees (*parameter invariance*). The item's discriminating power is indicated by the steepness of the curve. The ICC can be analyzed in relation to the difficulty of the item, the discriminating power of the item, and a so-called guessing parameter.

Application for IRT

Space limitations (and lack of knowledge by the authors) prohibit a detailed description and discussion of IRT. It is not a simple concept, and complex computer programs are required. Large sample sizes are needed for item calibration and ability estimates. The IRT model has been the subject of intense research in psychology and education for a number of years. It definitely has potential application for assessment problems in physical education, exercise science, and sport science.

Spray (1989) has described several ways IRT can be used: item banking, adaptive testing, mastery testing, attitude assessment, and psychomotor assessment. *Item banking* is the creation of large pools of test items that can be used for constructing tests that have certain characteristics with regard to the precision of estimating latent ability.

Adaptive testing, sometimes called *tailored testing*, refers to selecting items that will best fit (items neither too difficult nor too easy) the ability level of each individual. This function must be done on a computer by using items drawn from an item bank.

In criterion-referenced measurement, tests are constructed that use a cutoff score to indicate the proportion of items that should be answered correctly to represent mastery of the subject matter. Item response theory can be used to select the optimal number of items that will yield the most precise indication of mastery for an examinee. In other words, subjects of different ability levels would require different numbers of items.

Item response theory has considerable potential application for assessing attitudes and other affective behaviors. Models of IRT have been proposed that will estimate the attitude or trait parameter of each respondent on an interval scale regardless of the ordinal nature of the scale. A score for each trait level is available for each category of each item. Changes in attitude or other traits over time can also be assessed with IRT models. To date, few affective measuring instruments have been constructed using IRT procedures. In our field, Tew (1988) used IRT methods in the construction of a sport-specific test of mental imagery.

The potential use of IRT for psychomotor assessment has been postulated (Spray, 1987) but has not yet been demonstrated to any extent. The nature of motor performance tests is different from written tests in terms of the numbers of items and trials. Also, some of the assumptions (particularly local independence) of IRT are not easily accommodated in psychomotor testing. Preliminary research on the application of IRT to motor performance has been conducted by Safrit, Costa, and Cohen (1989). More research will undoubtedly be done on the application of IRT models to our field.

SUMMARY

Physical education, exercise science, and sport science frequently use research measures involving written responses to test written knowledge as well as affective attributes like attitudes, interests, emotional states, and psychological characteristics. Many general measures of these constructs have been used over the years (e.g., Cattell 16 Personality Factor Questionnaire, Spielberger State-Trait Anxiety Inventory). However, more recently, specific sport and exercise tests have been developed for affective measures such as the Physical Estimation and Attraction Scale, Sport Achievement Orientation Inventory, and Sport Competition Anxiety Test.

Responses on many of these scales are solicited using widely accepted formats, such as the Likert scale (usually a 5-point scale ranging from strongly agree to strongly disagree) and the semantic differential scale (a 7-point scale anchored at the extremes by bipolar adjectives). When using scales like these, researchers must be aware of specific problems like rating errors, leniency, central tendency, halo effects, proximity, observer bias, and observer expectation.

Knowledge testing requires that the researcher use item analysis techniques for short answer responses. The difficulty and discrimination must be established for each test item so the quality of the knowledge test can be determined.

Item response theory (also called latent trait theory) is an approach different from classical test theory. It allows item difficulty to be fixed so that the subject's ability level can be determined. Item response theory is useful in tailoring tests for adaptive testing, mastery testing, attitude assessment, and psychomotor assessment.

Problem

Identify an affective measure used in research in exercise and sport science or physical education not presented in this chapter and complete the following:

a. Identify the study in which it appears (cite the reference in APA style).
b. Describe the affective measure.
c. Explain how the measure is scored.
d. Report any evidence of validity and reliability provided.
e. Summarize what was found in the study with regard to the measure you selected.

Writing the Research Report

Part I discussed the research proposal, its purpose, and the structure of the different parts. Parts II through IV provided the details needed to understand and conduct research, including statistics, types of research, and measurement. Finally, this section completes the research process with instructions on how to prepare the research report. You may also want to refer to chapter 2, which discussed some rules and recommendations for writing the review of literature, for this is an important part of the research report.

Chapter 19 briefly examines all the parts of the research proposal that have been discussed throughout several chapters. In addition, we offer some of our thoughts about the nature of the meeting to review the research proposal.

The final two chapters focus on the final written research report. Up to now every-

thing has involved how to understand other research and how to develop a plan for your own research. Chapter 20 helps you organize and write the results and discussion chapters (or sections) of your research. Suggestions are also provided on how to prepare tables, figures, and illustrations and where to place them in the research report.

Finally, chapter 21 offers some suggestions about traditional and alternative ways of organizing and writing theses and dissertations. In addition, a brief section on writing for scientific journals and a short discourse on preparing and giving oral presentations are presented. To conclude, ethical considerations among researchers and between graduate students and their major professors are discussed.

Chapter 19

□

The Proposal

Basically, the *research proposal* contains the definition, scope, and significance of the problem and the methodology that will be used to solve it. In a four-chapter thesis or dissertation (introduction, method, results, and discussion), the proposal consists of the first two chapters. In studies using a five-chapter format, in which the review of literature is the second, the proposal encompasses the first three sections. If the alternative style (basically for preparing an article for a journal) of preparing the thesis or dissertation (advocated in chapter 21) is used, then the proposal consists of the introduction and method chapters, appropriate tables, figures, and appendices (e.g., scoresheets, cover letters, questionnaires, sample informed-consent forms, and pilot study data).

One of the goals of this book has been to help prepare a student develop a research proposal. We have already discussed the contents of the proposal. Chapters 2 through 4 of this book pertain specifically to the body of the research proposal. Other chapters relate to various facets of planning a study with regard to the hypotheses, measurements, designs, and statistical analyses. Thus, this chapter attempts to bring the proposal together. We also spend some time discussing the proposal meeting and committee actions. Finally, we touch on basic considerations involved in grant proposals, specifically, how they differ from thesis and dissertation proposals.

CHAPTER 1: INTRODUCTION

The student's most important task is to convince the committee (whether it be the proposal committee, a journal reviewer, or a reviewing committee for a granting agency) that the problem is important and worth investigating. The first chapter should do this, and it should also attract the reader's interest to the problem. The review of literature provides background information and a critique of the previous research done on the topic, pointing out weaknesses, conflicts, and areas needing study. A concise statement of the problem informs the reader of the exact purpose, that is, what the researcher intends to do.

Hypotheses are advanced on the basis of previous research and perhaps some theoretical model. Furthermore, operational definitions serve to inform the reader exactly how the researcher is using certain terms. Operational definitions must be observable and must generally relate to the dependent and independent variables. Basic assumptions are also stated and serve to specify certain conditions and premises that must exist for the study to proceed. Limitations are possible shortcomings or influences that are acknowledged by the researcher and are generally the result of the delimitations to the study that are imposed by the investigator. The first chapter concludes with a statement about the significance of the study, which can be judged from either a basic or an applied research standpoint. The significance section emphasizes contradictory findings and limitations of previous research and the ways in which the proposed study will contribute to further knowledge about the research topic (see Part I of this book for elaboration).

Chapter 3 of this book covered most of the parts included in the proposal's introduction chapter. Chapter 2 concerned the literature review, and chapter 1 included a discussion on the inductive and deductive reasoning processes used in developing the problem and formulating hypotheses.

Innumerable hours are involved in preparing the first chapter (introduction) of the proposal, especially with respect to the literature search and the formulation of the problem. The student usually depends heavily on help from an advisor and from completed studies for examples of format and description.

Before we continue with our discussion, however, we need to mention that you should write your proposal in the future tense. You will state that so many subjects *will be* selected and that certain procedures *will be* carried out. Theoretically, if the proposal is carefully planned and well written, you need only to change the tense from future to past to have the first two chapters of the thesis or dissertation. Realistically, however, numerous revisions will probably be made between the proposal and the final version.

To reiterate, the importance of the study and its contribution to the profession is the main focus of the first chapter in the proposal, and this constitutes the basis for approval or disapproval.

CHAPTER 2: METHOD

Assuming that the review of literature is included in the first chapter, the second (method) chapter of the proposal is frequently the focus of most of the questions from committee members in the proposal meeting (the proposal meeting is discussed in the next section). In the method chapter, the student must clearly describe how the data will be collected in order to solve the problem set forth in the first chapter. The student needs to specify who the subjects will be and how they will be chosen, how many subjects will be selected, any special characteristics of importance, how the subjects' rights and privacy will be protected, and how informed consent will be obtained. The measurements that will be used are detailed and the validity and reliability of the measures documented. Next, the procedures are described. If, for example, the study is a survey, the measurement instruments are discussed as to the steps in construction and validation. If the study is an experimental one, the treatments (or experimental programs) are described explicitly along with the control procedures that will be exercised. Finally, the experimental design and planned statistical analysis of the data are delineated in this chapter.

Periodically, we have emphasized the importance of conducting pilot studies before gathering data. If pilot work has been done, it should be described and the results reported. Often the committee members have major concerns about such questions as whether the treatments can produce meaningful changes, whether the measurements are accurate and can reliably discriminate between subjects, and whether the investigator can satisfactorily perform the measurements and administer the treatments. The pilot study should provide answers to these questions.

We recommended in chapter 4 that the student use the literature to help determine the methodology. Answers to questions about whether certain treatment conditions are sufficiently long, intense, and frequent to produce anticipated changes in behavior can be defended by results of previous studies.

THE PROPOSAL PROCESS

We have reiterated the contents of the proposal: the introduction (including the review of literature) and the methods that are going to be used. Fundamentally, the proposed purpose—in conjunction with pertinent background information, plausible hypotheses, operational definitions, and delimitations—is the factor that will determine whether the study is worthwhile. Consequently, the first chapter is instrumental in stimulating interest in the problem and establishing the rationale and significance of the study. Thus, the committee's decision to approve or disapprove rests primarily with the persuasiveness exhibited in the first chapter.

Actually, however, the basic decision about the merit of the topic should already have been made before the proposal meeting. In other words, we believe that the student should consult with the advisor and most (if not all) of the committee members to reach a consensus about the worth of the study before the proposal meeting is scheduled. If the majority of the committee is not convinced that the study is worthwhile, a formal proposal meeting should not be held. You may have a problem if you get your proposal returned with a checklist such as that in Table 19.1.

The Proposal Committee

Let us digress a moment to discuss the composition of the proposal committee. The structure of committees and the number of committee members will vary from one institution to another. It is probably safe to say that most thesis committees consist of at least three members and most dissertation com-

Table 19.1 A Checklist for Thesis or Dissertation Proposal Evaluation

Interim Thesis/Dissertation Evaluation

Dear _____:

Greetings! I regret that my busy schedule prohibits me from rendering a detailed written evaluation of your thesis/dissertation. However, I have checked the appropriate actions or comments that apply to your proposal.

— If at first you don't succeed, try, try again.
— Don't sell your research methods textbook (Thomas & Nelson, of course); you'll need to take the course again.
— You were not required to write your paper in a foreign language (Burmese, or whatever it was).
— I couldn't read beyond the third page; one does not have to eat a whole pie to know it is bad.
— I hear they are hiring at Sam's Diner.
— May I have your permission to use your proposal as an example next semester when I teach research methods?
— Have you paid your tuition and fees yet? If not . . .
— Please call my secretary and arrange an appointment with me. Consider taking a tranquilizer before you arrive.
— I have been serving on thesis/dissertation committees for over 15 years and can now honestly say that I've seen it all.

mittees at least five. The major and minor professors are included in these numbers, although the master's student is often not required to have a minor. Other members should be chosen on the basis of their

> The proposed purpose—in conjunction with pertinent background information, plausible hypotheses, operational definitions, and delimitations—are the factors that will determine whether the study is worthwhile.

knowledge about the subject or expertise in other aspects of the research, such as design and statistical analysis. Sometimes the institution or department specifies a certain number of the committee that must be from inside or outside the department. Usually, there is no maximum to the number of committee members allowed.

In regard to the topic of premeeting support, we strongly recommend that the student, with the help and advice of the major professor, get general approval and support for the problem itself from at least two of the three thesis committee members (or three of the five dissertation committee members). This support is tentative, of course, and final approval is contingent on the refinements that might be needed and on the adequacy of the methodology.

The formal committee meeting is not the place for planning the study. This should have been thoroughly done beforehand. In this regard, some graduate programs have so-called preproposal meetings for the purpose of brainstorming and informally reaching an agreement on the efficacy of the proposed topic. This kind of meeting, in effect, functions to garner support from the committee before a great deal of time and effort are spent on a fruitless endeavor. The student prepares and distributes an outline of the purpose and basic procedures before the meeting. The student should have spent considerable time in consultation with the advisor (and probably at least another committee member) and should have searched the literature sufficiently to be adequately prepared to present a sound case for the study. The preproposal meeting is not just a "bull" session in which the student is fishing for basic ideas. At the same time, the informality of the occasion does allow a good interchange of ideas and suggestions.

Preparing the Proposal

The formal proposal should be carefully prepared. If the proposal is poorly typed and contains errors of grammar, spelling, and format, an unfavorable impression is created with the committee members. This may lead to a feeling among the committee that the student lacks the interest, motivation, or desire to do the proposed research. With the availability of microcomputers and word processors there is no reason for a student to present a poorly prepared proposal. Also, because spell-checking routines are available on most word-processing packages, these should always be used. Remember, however, that a spell-checking routine will not identify the use of an incorrect word that is spelled correctly. Also be aware that most campuses have high-quality printers (e.g., lasers) available that a student may gain access to for printing good copies of proposals to be distributed to committee members.

Committee members should not ignore errors in proposals with the idea that the student will correct these later. Doing so may lead the student to assume that carelessness is acceptable in data collection or in the final written thesis or dissertation. Copies of the proposal should be given to the committee members well in advance of the meeting. The advance number of days is usually specified by the department or university.

The Proposal Meeting

In the typical proposal meeting, the student is asked to briefly summarize the rationale for the study, its significance, and the methodology (good visual aids enhance this presentation). The remainder of the session consists of questioning by the committee members. Assuming that the topic is acceptable, the

questions concern mainly the methods and the competence of the student who will conduct the study. The student should exhibit tactful confidence in presenting the proposal. A common mistake students make is to be so humble and pliable that they agree to every suggestion made, even those that radically change the study. The advisor should help ward off these ''helpful'' suggestions, but the student must also be able to respectfully defend the scope of the study and the methodology. If adequate planning has gone into the proposal, the student (with the assistance of the major professor) should be able to recognize useful suggestions and defend against those that seem to offer minimal aid.

Once the proposal is approved, most institutions treat it as a contract in that the committee expects the study to be done in the manner specified in the proposal. Moreover, the student can assume that if the study is conducted and analyzed as planned and is well written, it will be approved. If any unforeseen changes are required during the course of the study, they must be approved by the advisor. Substantial changes usually must be reviewed by some or all of the committee.

PROPOSALS FOR GRANTING AGENCIES

All sources of grants, whether governmental agencies or private foundations, require research proposals so that they can decide which projects to fund and the extent to which to fund them. The granting agencies nearly always publish guidelines for applicants to follow in preparing proposals.

The writing of the proposal is of paramount importance. The researcher rarely gets a chance to explain or to defend the purpose or procedures. Thus, the decision is based entirely on the written proposal. The basic format for a grant proposal is similar to the thesis or dissertation proposal. However, some additional types of information are required, as are some procedural deviations.

We cannot emphasize too strongly the importance of following the guidelines. Granting agencies tolerate little (if any) deviation from their directions. All sections of the application must be addressed and deadlines strictly followed. Frequently, a statement of intent to submit a proposal is required a month or so before the proposal is filed.

Grant proposals include

- a statement of the problem,
- its relevance to one of the specified priorities of the granting agency, and
- the methodology to be followed.

A limited review of literature is often required to demonstrate familiarity with previous research. Occasionally, the funding agency will impose some restrictions with regard to design and methods. For example, it is not uncommon for an agency to prohibit control groups if the treatment is hypothesized to be effective. In other words, the agency may not want any persons to be denied treatment. This can pose some problems for the researcher in scientifically evaluating the outcomes of the project.

Because every granting agency has stipulations regarding the types of programs it can and cannot fund, a detailed budget is required, as is a justification for each budget item.

In addition, the competence of the researcher has to be documented. Each researcher must attach a vita, and often a written statement is required pertaining to appropriate preparation, experience, and accomplishments. The adequacy of facilities and sources of support must also be addressed.

Letters of support are occasionally encouraged. These are included in the appendix. Numerous copies of the proposal are usually

required. The proposal is evaluated by a panel of reviewers in accordance with certain criteria regarding the contribution to knowledge, relevance, significance, and soundness of design and methodology.

The preparation of a grant proposal is a time-consuming and exacting process. Several types of information are specified, and time is needed to gather the information and state it in the manner prescribed by the guidelines. One is advised to begin preparing the proposal as soon as the guidelines are available.

Finally, it is usually wise to contact the granting agency before preparing and submitting a proposal. Seldom are proposals funded that are submitted without some prior contact with the granting agency. Finding out the agency's interests and needs is a time-saving venture for the researcher. Often, a visit to, or an extended phone conversation with, the research officer is advisable. Looking at proposals previously funded by the agency or seeking guidance from researchers who have been funded is helpful.

> We cannot emphasize too strongly the importance of following the guidelines. Granting agencies tolerate little (if any) deviation from their directions.

INTERNAL PROPOSALS

Many colleges and universities (particularly larger research universities) offer internal funding for graduate student research. Although these grants usually are not large, they do offer helpful support for research. These typically require a two- to five-page proposal that has the support of the major professor and often the department chairperson. The contents usually include an abstract, a short narrative focusing on the proposed methodology and why the research is important, and a budget. Notices that internal funding is available are routinely posted or advertised around the college or university. A good place to find out is at your graduate school office.

SUMMARY

The research proposal describes the definition, scope, and significance of a problem and the methodology to be used to study it. The proposal is essentially the plan for the study. The introduction provides the background and literature for the problem, the problem statement, hypotheses, definitions, assumptions and limitations, and the significance of

the study. The method section describes the subjects, instrumentation, procedures, and design and analysis.

These two chapters are presented by a student to his or her research committee as the plan for inquiry. The student's committee determines the worth of the study, suggests needed alterations, and ultimately must agree that the study should be done. The proposal must be carefully prepared with appropriate pilot work so that the committee is convinced that the student can complete the research plan.

Proposals to granting agencies are similar but are typically required to have specific lengths and formats. Students are advised to talk with outside agencies and more experienced grant-writers before preparing and submitting proposals. Many colleges and universities have internal grants for which graduate students can apply to support thesis and dissertation research.

Problem

Find out the steps for writing a thesis or dissertation proposal at your school. List them in chronological order, including selection of a major professor and committee, preparing a proposal, and getting the proposal approved. Explain the process at each step.

SUGGESTED READING

Locke, L.F., Spirduso, W.W., & Silverman, S.J. (1987). *Proposals that work: A guide for planning dissertations and grant proposals* (2nd ed.). Newbury Park, CA: Sage.

Chapter 20

□

Results and Discussion

At the end of chapter 4 we promised we would discuss later the final chapters of the thesis or dissertation. Those chapters are the results and discussion.

Results mean what you found and *discussion* explains what the results mean. In theses and dissertations, the results and discussion usually are separate chapters. In journal papers they are sometimes combined. We discuss these chapters here as separate chapters in a research report.

CHAPTER 3: RESULTS

The results report what your research has found. This is the most important part of the research report. The introduction and literature review indicate why you will conduct the research, the method explains how you will do it, and the results discuss your contribution to knowledge, that is, what you found. The results should be concise and effectively organized and should include appropriate tables and figures.

Because there is no one correct way to present all results sections, the results may be organized in various ways. The best way may be to address each of the tested hypotheses. On other occasions, the results may be organized around the dependent variables of interest. In some cases, you may want to show first that certain standard and expected effects have been replicated before you go on to discuss other findings. For example, in developmental studies of motor performance tasks, older children are better than younger

ones. The researcher may want to report the replication of this effect before proceeding to other results.

Some items should always be reported in the results. The means and standard deviations for all dependent variables under all conditions should be included. These are basic descriptive data that allow other researchers to evaluate your findings. The data should be presented in one table if possible. Sometimes only the means and standard deviations of important findings are included in the results chapter. However, all the remaining means and standard deviations should be included in the appendix.

The results chapter should also use tables and figures to display appropriate findings. Figures are particularly useful for percentage data, interactions, or summarizing related findings. Only the important tables and figures should be included in the results chapter; the remaining ones should be placed in the appendix.

Statistical information should be summarized in the text where possible. Statistics of ANOVA and MANOVA should always be summarized in the text and complete tables relegated to the appendix. Above all, the statistics reported should be meaningful. Day (1983) reported a classic case that read

33 1/3% of the mice used in this experiment were cured by the test drug; 33 1/3% of the test population were unaffected by the drug and remained in a moribund condition; the third mouse got away. (p. 35)

Sometimes tables are a better way to present this information. If the perfect scientific paper is ever written, the results section will read, ''The results are shown in Table 1'' (Day, 1983, p. 36). However, this does not mean that the results chapter should be comprised mostly of tables and figures. It is very disconcerting to have to thumb through eight tables and figures between two pages of text. But even worse is to have to turn 50 pages to the appendix to find a necessary table or figure. Read what you have written. Are all the important facts there? Have you provided more information than the reader can absorb?

Do not be redundant and repetitive in the results. A common error is to include a table or figure in the results and then repeat it in the text. It is appropriate to describe tables and figures in a general way or to point out particularly important facts, but do not repeat every finding. However, as Day (1983) has reported, some writers are so concerned with reducing verbiage that they lose track of antecedents, particularly *it*:

''The left leg became numb at times and she walked it off. . . . On her second day, the knee was better, and on the third day it had completely disappeared.'' The antecedent for both its was presumably ''the numbness,'' but I rather think that the wording in both instances was a result of dumbness. (p. 36)

CHAPTER 4: DISCUSSION

Although the results are the most important part of the research report, the discussion is the most difficult to write. There are no cute tricks or clear-cut ways to organize the discussion, but there are some rules that define what to include:

- Discuss your results—not what you wish they were but what they are.
- Relate your results back to the introduction, previous literature, and hypotheses.
- Explain how your results fit within theory.
- Interpret your findings.
- Recommend or suggest applications of your findings.
- Summarize and state your conclusions with appropriate supporting evidence.

In particular, the discussion should point out factual relationships among variables and situations, thus leading to a presentation of the significance of the research. If after reading your discussion the reader says ''So what,'' then you have failed in your research reporting.

The discussion should also point out any methodological problems that occurred in the research. However, a methodological cop-out to explain the results is unacceptable. If you did not find predicted outcomes and you resort to methodological failure as an explanation, *you did not do sufficient pilot work*.

Graduate students sometimes want their results to sound wonderful and to solve all the problems of the world. Thus, in their discussions they often make claims well beyond what their data indicate. Your major professor and committee are likely to know a lot about your topic and therefore are unlikely to be fooled by these claims. They can see the data and read the results. They know what you have found and the claims that can be made. A much better strategy is to make your points effectively in your discussion and not try to generalize these points into grandiose ideas that will solve humanity's major problems. Write so that your limited contribution of knowledge is highlighted; if you make broader claims, knowledgeable readers are likely to discount the importance of the legitimate findings of your research.

> If you did not find predicted outcomes and you resort to methodological failure as an explanation, *you did not do sufficient pilot work*.

Another point about writing your discussion is to write so that reasonably informed and intelligent people can understand what you have found. Do not use a thesaurus to replace your normal vocabulary with multisyllabic words and complex sentences. Your

writing should not look like the following examples (Day, 1983, p. 149), which by translating you can probably recognize as some well-known sayings:

1. As a case in point, other authorities have proposed that slumbering canines are best left in a recumbent position.
2. It has been posited that a high degree of curiosity proved lethal to a feline.
3. There is a large body of experimental evidence which clearly indicates that smaller members of the genus *Mus* tend to engage in recreational activity while the feline is remote from the locale.
4. From time immemorial, it has been known that the ingestion of an "apple" (i.e., the pome fruit of any tree of the genus *Malus*, said fruit being usually round in shape and red, yellow, or greenish in color) on a diurnal basis will with absolute certainty keep a primary member of the health care establishment absent from one's local environment.
5. Even with the most sophisticated experimental protocol, it is exceedingly unlikely that you can instill in a superannuated canine the capacity to perform novel feats of legerdemain.
6. A sedimentary conglomerate in motion down a declivity gains no addition of mossy material.
7. The resultant experimental data indicate that there is no utility in belaboring a deceased equine.

Your discussion can generally be guided by the following questions taken from the *Publication Manual of the American Psychological Association* (APA, 1983, p. 28):

• What have I contributed here?
• How has my study helped to resolve the original problem?

• What conclusions and theoretical implications can I draw from my study?

The responses to these questions are the core of your contribution, and readers have a right to clear, unambiguous, and direct answers.

MULTIPLE EXPERIMENTS

Graduate students are conducting more research that involves multiple experiments. These experiments may ask several related questions about a particular problem or may be built on one another with the outcomes of the first leading to questions for the second. This is a very positive trend, but it sometimes leads to problems within the traditional thesis or dissertation format. Chapter 21 discusses traditional and alternative ways of organizing theses and dissertations. However, within the traditional framework, multiple experiments are probably best handled by separate chapters.

The first chapter includes the introduction, theoretical framework, literature review, general statement of the research problem, and related definitions and delimitations. Subsequent chapters present each experiment. Each of these chapters includes a brief introduction, a discussion of the specific problem and hypotheses, and method, results, and discussion sections. The final chapter is a general discussion in which the experiments are tied together. It contains the features of the discussion previously presented.

PREPARING TABLES

The first question is, Do you need a table? There is no easy answer to this question, but two characteristics are important: Is the material more easily understood in a table?

and, Does the table interfere with reading the results? Once you decide you need a table (all numbers do not require tables), follow these basic rules:

- Like characteristics should read vertically in the table.
- Make the headings of tables clear.
- A table should be understandable without referring to the text.

Table 20.1 is an example of a useless table that could be more easily presented in the text. This table can be handled in one sentence: "The experimental group ($M = 17.3$, $s = 4.7$) was significantly better than the control group ($M = 12.1$, $s = 3.9$), $t(28) = 3.31$, $p < .05$." Table 20.2 is also unnecessary. From the 10 comparisons among group means, only 1 was significant. The values in the table are the equivalent of t tests. This table can also be presented in one sentence: "The Scheffé test was used to make comparisons among the age-group means, and the only significant difference was between the youngest (7-year-olds) and oldest (15-year-olds) groups, $t = 8.63$, $p < .05$."

We have borrowed an example of a useful table (see Table 20.3) from Safrit and Wood (1983). As you can see, like characteristics appear vertically. Also, an extensive

Table 20.1 Useless Table Number 1

Means, Standard Deviations, and t Test for Distance Cartwheeled While Blindfolded

Groups	N	M	s	t
Experimental	15	17.3 m	4.7 m	3.31*
Control	15	12.1 m	3.9 m	

*$p < .05$.

Table 20.2 Useless Table Number 2

Scheffé's Test for Differences Among Age Levels in Ability to Wiggle Their Ears

Age	7	9	11	13	15
7	—	1.20	1.08	1.79	8.63*
9		—	1.32	1.42	1.57
11			—	1.58	1.01
13				—	0.61
15					—

*$p < .05$.

amount of text would be required to present these same results, yet they are easy to understand in this brief table.

One final point involves reporting numbers either in tables or in the text. Report numerical information only to the precision to which it was measured. For example, if you measure a jump to the nearest centimeter, to report that subjects, on average, jumped 34.753 cm is unnecessary. This reflects only mindless copying of numbers from computer printouts or calculator readouts. At most you would report the number as 34.8 cm, but we prefer rounding to the preciseness of measurement (i.e., 35 cm). Although jumping could have been measured to a more precise level than the nearest centimeter, it was not. Sometimes attempts at preciseness become humorous, bringing to mind the report that the average American family has 2.4 children. (We thought children came only in whole units!) In the first example, the jump could have been measured in more precise units. In the latter example, a single child is the smallest (most discrete) unit of measurement available.

The same mindless reporting of statistical numbers also occurs. Because computer

Table 20.3 Example of a Useful Table

Characteristics of Users and Nonusers
HRFT Pilot Survey

	Users	Nonusers
Gender		
Male	4 (36.4%)	33 (62.3%)
Female	7 (63.6%)	20 (37.7%)
Age		
20-25	1 (09.1%)	2 (03.8%)
25-30	1 (09.1%)	8 (15.1%)
30-35	5 (45.5%)	9 (17.0%)
35-40	1 (09.1%)	7 (13.2%)
40 and over	3 (27.2%)	27 (50.9%)
Type of school		
Elementary	1 (09.1%)	18 (34.0%)
Middle	0 (00.0%)	18 (34.0%)
Junior-senior high	1 (09.1%)	0 (00.0%)
High	9 (81.8%)	17 (32.0%)
Student population		
0-100	0 (00.0%)	0 (00.0%)
100-500	1 (09.1%)	17 (33.3%)
500-1,000	0 (00.0%)	16 (31.4%)
1,000-1,500	1 (09.1%)	1 (02.0%)
Over 1,500	9 (81.8%)	17 (33.3%)

Note. From Safrit and Wood (1983). Reprinted by permission from *Research Quarterly for Exercise and Sport*, *54*, p. 205. *RQ* is a publication of the American Alliance for Health, Physical Education, Recreation and Dance, 1900 Association Dr., Reston, VA 22091.

printouts carry the statistics and probabilities to five or more places beyond the decimal does not mean the numbers should be reported to that level. Two or (at most) three places are adequate. However, this can result in rather odd probabilities: $t(22) = 14.73$, $p < .000$. Now, $p < .000$ means no chance of error; this cannot occur because, if there is no chance of error, how can it be a probability? What happened is that the exact probability was something like $p < .00023$ and the researcher rounded it back to $p < .000$.

You cannot do this. As indicated earlier, we believe it is more appropriate to report whether the probability exceeded the alpha set for the experiment (e.g., $p < .05$). However, if the researcher insists on reporting the probability to some level beyond alpha, a "1" or a higher number must always be the last term in the probability. The previous example ($p < .00023$), if reported to three decimals, should read $p < .001$.

Although the mindless use of numbers frequently occurs, sometimes other items are reported that are just as mindless. In reviewing for a research journal, one of us encountered a study in which a group of children were given a 12-week treatment. The author reported the mean age and standard deviation of the children before and after the 12-week treatment. Not surprisingly, the children had all aged 12 weeks. In addition, the author calculated a t test between the pre- and the post-treatment means for age that was, of course, significant. That is, the fact that the children had aged 12 weeks during the 12-week period was a reliable finding.

PREPARING FIGURES AND ILLUSTRATIONS

Many of the suggestions about table construction also apply to figures and illustrations because a figure is only another way to present a table. An important question regarding whether to use a table or a figure is, Does the reader need the actual numbers, or is a picture of the results more useful? A more important question may be, Do you need either? Can the data be presented more concisely and easily in the text? Figures and tables do not add scientific validity to your research report. In fact, they may only clutter the results. Day (1983) suggested a reasonable means for deciding whether to use a table or a figure: "If the data show pronounced trends making an interesting picture, use a graph. If the numbers just sit there, with no exciting trend in evidence, a table should be satisfactory'' (p. 56).

Several other considerations are important in preparing figures. Selection of the type of figure is somewhat arbitrary. Bar graphs seem particularly useful to present percentage and frequency data. Also, bar graphs can present more information without appearing so cluttered. Figures are quite useful in presenting interactions and data points that change over time (or across multiple trials).

Of course, the dependent variable is placed on the y-axis and some independent or categorical variable on the x-axis. If you have more than one independent variable, how do you decide which to put on the x-axis? We have already partially answered that question. If time or multiple trials are used, put them on the x-axis. For example, if a study found an interaction on the dependent variable between age level (7-, 9-, 11-, 13-, and 15-year-old males) and the treatment (experimental versus control), age with five

levels is usually the more appropriate choice for the x-axis. Note that this is a general rule, but specific circumstances may dictate otherwise. A good example of the use of a figure to present an interaction is shown in Figure 20.1. Note that both age and time are independent variables, so time is placed on the x-axis.

> An important question regarding whether to use a table or a figure is, Does the reader need the actual numbers, or is a picture of the results more useful? A more important question may be, Do you need either?

Figure 20.2 is a good example of a useless figure. The results can be summarized in two sentences: ''During acquisition, all three groups reduced their frequency of errors but did not differ significantly from one another. At retention, Experimental Group 2 further reduced its number of errors, whereas

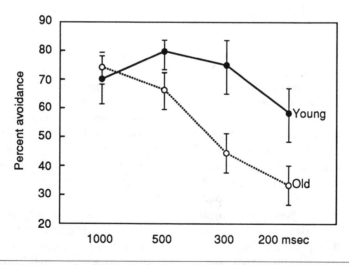

Figure 20.1 Appropriate use of a figure to depict an interaction. From Spirduso (1983). Reprinted by permission from *Research Quarterly for Exercise and Sport*, **54**, p. 211. *RQ* is a publication of the American Alliance for Health, Physical Education, Recreation and Dance, 1900 Association Drive, Reston, VA 22091.

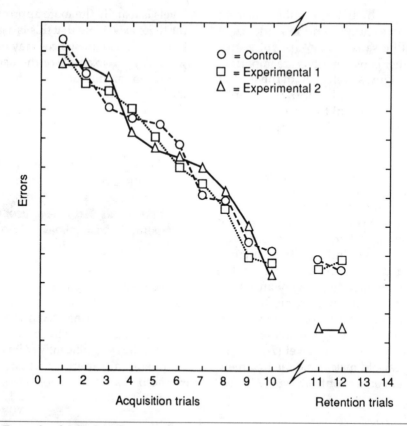

Figure 20.2 Example of a useless figure.

Experimental Group 1 and the Controls remained at the same level." Also, when results of different groups follow a very similar pattern, a figure frequently appears cluttered.

One final consideration is the construction of the y-axis. In general, between 8 and 12 intervals encompassing the range of means is useful. Do not extend the y-axis outside the range of means because this wastes space. Again, consider whether you need a figure at all. Often, theses and dissertations include drawings such as that in Figure 20.3. Looking at that figure, you immediately see a strong and significant interaction between knowledge of results (KR) and goal setting. Now look at the y-axis, on which the depen-

dent variable is shown. Note that the scores are given to the nearest hundredth of a second. Actually, there is less than a half-second (0.50) difference among the four groups on a task in which average performance is about 18 seconds. In fact, this interaction is not significant and clearly accounts for little variance. It should merely be reported as nonsignificant with no figure included. The researcher made the interaction only appear important by the scale used on the y-axis.

Illustrations (photographs and line drawings) are also used in research reporting. Most frequently, illustrations are of experimental arrangements and equipment. They should not be used when the equipment is of a standard design or make; a brief descrip-

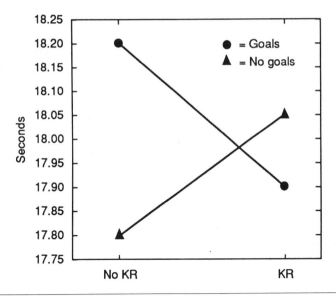

Figure 20.3 A nonsignificant interaction made to appear significant by the scale of the dependent variable.

tion will suffice. Any unusual arrangement or novel equipment should be described and either a picture or line drawing included. If specifications and relationships are important to include within the illustration rather than in the text, a line drawing is preferable because it can be more easily labeled.

Remember, as a general rule, tables, figures, and illustrations are appropriate for the results chapter but not the discussion. An exception to this rule is a report of multiple experiments in which the general discussion chapter could contain a table or figure to display common findings or a summary across several experiments.

To review, when determining where tables, figures, and illustrations should appear—in the text or in the appendix—consider the following recommendations:

- Put important tables, figures, and illustrations in the text and all others in the appendix.
- Try not to clutter the results with too many tables, figures, and illustrations.

- Do not put summary tables for ANOVA and MANOVA in the results. Place the important statistics from these tables in the text and the tables in the appendix.

Remember also that all journals have prescribed formats and styles for articles submitted to them (e.g., those of the American Psychological Association or *Index Medicus*). These instructions for authors include directions for preparing tables and figures. Many of these decisions are arbitrary. Read and look at what you have written and then use common sense. Select the tables, figures, and illustrations that are needed to read and understand the results. Everything else goes in the appendix. The appropriate use of tables, figures, and illustrations can add to the interest and motivation of the reader.

As a general rule, tables, figures, and illustrations are appropriate for the results chapter but not the discussion.

SUMMARY

The results and discussion sections are written after the data have been collected and analyzed. The results tell what you found; the discussion explains what the results mean. The results are the most important part of the research. They represent the unique findings of your study and your contribution to knowledge. The discussion ties the findings back to the literature review, theory, and empirical findings from other studies. Your findings should be interpreted in the discussion. In the traditional format, the results are chapter 3 and the discussion is chapter 4. However, in multiple experiment studies, each experiment may best be reported in a separate chapter with its own brief introduction, method, results, and discussion. This is often followed by a chapter of general discussion of the multiple experiments.

Tables should be used in the discussion to summarize and present data when they are more effective than text presentation. Figures and illustrations are also used in the results, most frequently to demonstrate more dramatic findings.

Problems

Select a research report of interest from a refereed journal in your area of interest. Read the paper but concentrate on the results and discussion. Answer the following questions in a brief report.

1. Results:
   a. How is the results section organized?
   b. Compare the order of reported findings with the introduction, literature review, and statement of the problem. Do you see any relationships? What are they?
   c. What other way might the results have been organized? Would this be better or worse? Why?

2. Tables, figures, and illustrations:
   a. Are there any? How many of each?
   b. Why are they used? Could the data have been reported more easily in the text? When either a table or figure is used, would the other have been as good? Better? Why?

3. Discussion:
   a. How is the discussion organized?
   b. Are all results discussed?
   c. Is the discussion accurate in terms of the results?
   d. Are previous findings and theory woven into the discussion?
   e. Are all conclusions and supporting evidence clearly presented?
   f. Did the authors use any methodological cop-outs?

SUGGESTED READINGS

American Psychological Association. (1983). *Publication manual of the American Psychological Association* (3rd ed.). Washington, DC: Author.

Day, R.A. (1988). *How to write and publish a scientific paper* (3rd ed.). Phoenix: Oryx Press.

Chapter 21

□

Ways of Reporting Research

Our favorite author, Day (1983), provides an appropriate introduction to this chapter on ways of reporting research with the following quote:

> Scientific research is not complete until the results have been published. Therefore, a scientific paper is an essential part of the research process. Therefore, the writing of an accurate, understandable paper is just as important as the research itself. Therefore, the words in the paper should be weighed as carefully as the reagents in the laboratory. Therefore, the scientist must know how to use words. Therefore, the education of a scientist is not complete until the ability to publish has been established. (p. 158)

Chapter 19 covered the research proposal: how to write the introduction, the literature review, the problem statement, and the methodology for the thesis or dissertation. Chapter 20 explained how to organize and write the results and discussion sections. Effectively coordinating all this information into a thesis or a dissertation is the topic of concern in this chapter. Both the traditional style of organization and an alternative model, which we (Thomas, Nelson, & Magill, 1986) have developed, are presented. In addition, information about writing for publication in research journals, preparing abstracts, and presenting papers orally (including in a poster format) is included in this chapter.

UNETHICAL WAYS OF REPORTING RESEARCH

Before we explain the right way to prepare the thesis or dissertation, maybe we should tell you how *not* to do it.

Plagiarism

When you take stuff from one writer it's called plagiarism, but when you take it from many writers it's called research.
—Quoted from the Unknown Researcher (who published, but perished anyway)

Plagiarism means using the ideas, concepts, writings, and drawings of others as your own. Of course, this is completely unacceptable in the research process (including writing). Plagiarism carries severe penalties at all institutions. A researcher who plagiarizes work carries a stigma for life in his or her profession. No reward is worth the risk involved.

On occasion a graduate student or faculty member can inadvertently be involved in plagiarism. This generally occurs on work that is coauthored. If one author plagiarizes material, the other could be equally punished even though he or she is unaware of the plagiarism. Although there is no surefire means of protection (except never to work with anyone else), never allow a paper with your name on it to be submitted (or revised) unless you have seen the complete paper in its final form.

In scientific writing the originality of ideas is also important. Common practice is to circulate preprints and drafts of papers among scholars (which are often shared with graduate students) known to be working in a specific area. If ideas, methods, findings, and so on are borrowed from these, proper credit should always be given.

Dual Publication

Authors must also be careful about *dual publication*. Sometimes this is legitimate; for example, a scientific paper published by one journal may be reprinted by another journal or in a book of readings (this should always be noted). However, authors may not publish the same paper in more than one copyrighted original research journal. But what constitutes "the same paper"? Can more than one paper be written from the same data base? As with other concepts, the line is rather hazy. For example, Thomas (1986) indicated that

> frequently, new insights may be gained by evaluating previously reported data from a different perspective. However, reports of this type are always classed as research notes whether the re-analysis is undertaken by the original author or someone else. This does not mean that reports which use data from a number of studies (e.g., meta-analyses, power analyses) are classed as research notes. (pp. iii-iv)

Generally, good scientific practice is to publish all the appropriate data in a single primary publication. For example, if both psychological and physiological data were collected as a result of a specific experiment on training, publishing these separately may not be appropriate. Frequently, the main finding of interest will be in the interaction between psychological and physiological responses. But in other cases, the volume of data may be so large as to prohibit an inclusive paper. Sometimes the papers can be published as a series; at other times they may be completely separate.

Another type of example is large-scale studies in which a tremendous volume of data are collected (e.g., exercise epidemiology or pedagogical studies). Usually, data are selected from the computer files (or videotapes) to answer a specific set of related questions for a research report. Researchers may then use a different part (or even an overlapping part) of the data base to address another set of questions. This results in legitimate publications from the same data base. However, authors should identify that more than one paper have been produced from this data base. Researchers should follow these general types of rules, or they may be viewed as lacking scientific objectivity in their work and certainly as lacking in modesty (Day, 1983).

Most research journals require that the author include a statement that the paper has not been previously published or submitted elsewhere during the time the journal is considering it. Papers that have been published in one language may not be published as an original paper in a second language.

Copyright laws also apply to the use of tables and figures. If you use a table or figure from another source, you must get the permission of the copyright holder (for published papers usually the research journal) and cite it appropriately (e.g., used by permission of . . .).

Faking Data

If you read the current literature on scientific research, you are aware that scientists have on rare occasion been caught making up or altering research data. Of course this is completely unethical, and severe penalties are imposed on individuals who are caught. Pressures have been particularly intense in medically related research because such research is very expensive and requires outside funding. Often it seems easy to make a little change here or there or to say, "I only need a few more subjects, but I am running out of time." The odds of being detected in these types of actions are high, but even if you should get away with it, you will always know you did it and probably put other people at risk because of your actions.

TRADITIONAL FORMAT FOR WRITING THESES AND DISSERTATIONS

Again we quote Day (1983). His unwritten rule, although because he wrote it maybe it is no longer unwritten (somewhere in that statement is a limited amount of logic), is, "Write your thesis to please your major professor, if you can figure out what turns him [or her] on" (p. 125). Once this basic prin-

ciple is understood, we can offer some guidelines. But in case of doubt or conflict, return to that basic principle.

- Collect all the documents that outline university (or college) and departmental policy for theses and dissertations. Then actually read these documents, as someone at some level will eventually check to see whether you have followed them.
- Review the theses and dissertations of past graduate students whose work is well regarded by your institution. Identify common elements in their work, and pattern your work after theirs.
- Allow twice as much time as you think you need. Remember Murphy's Law: Whatever can go wrong will go wrong, and its special version, When several things can go wrong, the one that will go wrong is the one that will cause the greatest harm.

The thesis and dissertation have basically the same parts found in any scientific paper: an introduction and a literature review, and method, results, and discussion sections. Each of these parts becomes a chapter. Sometimes the introduction and the literature review are separate chapters, leading to five rather than four chapters. This format may vary in historical papers (see chapter 10) or multiple experiments (see chapter 20) or when your major professor says it should.

A section seldom mentioned in articles and books on preparing theses and dissertations is that of *acknowledgments*. You should acknowledge those people without whom the research would have been impossible. However, acknowledgments, as prepared by graduate students, take some odd turns. We saw one in which a woman acknowledged her ex-husband. She said that if he had not been so difficult to live with, she would never have gone back to the university and done graduate work. By doing that she found an area in which she had a tremendous interest, and this represented a significant change in her life. That is about the only positive statement we have ever heard about ex-spouses. Some other funny ones follow:

- My parents, husband, and children provided inspiration and support throughout, but I was able to complete my thesis anyway.
- My major professor, Dr. I.M. Published, coordinated the work and made an occasional contribution.
- Professor B.A. Snobb wants everyone to know he had nothing to do with this dissertation.
- Finally, we would like to thank our proofreader, I.D. Best, without whose hell; thes dcument wld net be pausible.

More seriously, you can acknowledge appropriate individuals, but keep the list short and to the point and do not be mushy. As in other areas, use correct English. In their acknowledgments, graduate students often use "wish" when they mean "want," as in "I wish to acknowledge I.B.A. Fink." Does that mean they might have acknowledged him if his contribution was not so lousy? The graduate student really wants to acknowledge him. But more appropriately, why not just say it: I acknowledge I.B.A. Fink.

In writing your thesis or dissertation, there are some ways to state information that are more appropriate than others. Table 21.1 offers some suggestions by Roger Soles (cited in Scherr, 1983) on recommended phrasing.

ALTERNATIVE FORMAT FOR WRITING THESES AND DISSERTATIONS

We devote considerable space here to what we call an *alternative format for thesis and dis-*sertation *writing*. The material in the following pages is reproduced from a paper we wrote with a colleague (Thomas et al., 1986). We acknowledge the contribution to this of Dr. Richard Magill from Louisiana State University, and we appreciate *Quest* (Human Kinetics) allowing us to adapt the paper for this book.

Introduction

Graduate education in the United States, especially at the doctoral level, was modeled after graduate education in Germany. The German university spirit of the search for knowledge and the concomitant emphasis on productive research were transplanted in large measure in America (Rudy, 1962). Although there have been some changes over the years in the requirements for the doctoral degree, the basic aims and expectations have in essence remained unaltered. The doctoral degree is conferred in recognition of a candidate's scholarship and research accomplishments in a specific field of learning through an original contribution of significant knowledge and ideas (Boyer, 1973).

Stated more simply, research is the foundation of the doctoral program, and the dissertation is the most distinctive aspect of the doctoral degree. It has been reported that the dissertation occupies an average of 39% of the time devoted to obtaining the degree (Porter, Chubin, Rossini, Boeckmann, & Connally, 1982). This percentage is an average of the full-time equivalent months of work on the PhD. Data are based on the fields of biochemistry, electrical engineering, psychology, physics, sociology, and zoology.

The thesis and the dissertation have several purposes, the major one being the contribution of new knowledge with scientific merit (American Psychological Association, 1959; Berelson, 1960; Porter & Wolfle, 1975).

Table 21.1 Thesis Guidelines

Don't say	Instead say
I have just found a way to add two and two the hard way.	I have just made a significant contribution to current methodological issues.
I have made a lot of mistakes in my life.	I have been fortunate to have had the opportunity to accumulate considerable experience.
Truthfully, I don't know what I am doing. But sooner or later I am bound to stumble on an acceptable answer.	Because of the complexity of the problem we had to employ the sophisticated Las Vegas technique, a converging Monte Carlo simulation.
Everybody knows what the answer is, so let's not waste a lot of time beating around the bush.	On the basis of a priori considerations involving Boolean logic and other advanced techniques, it was possible to narrow the relevant decision space considerably.
Because the original data did not give us the expected answer, we threw out data until we got the answer we wanted.	Exploratory estimates yielded wrong signs on some of the structural coefficients. However, closer scrutiny of the original data suggested that, in all probability, some of the data came from a different population. After discarding these data, logically consistent and statistically significant estimates were obtained.
I feel like taking a trip abroad without spending my own money.	It is our opinion that every agricultural economist has the moral responsibility to concern himself with international agricultural economics. I am ready to live up to this responsibility.
Things are going to change, but I don't have the slightest idea in which direction.	The next decade will see changes in the agricultural structure that will have dimensions and consistency never experienced hitherto anywhere in the world.
When I started this research I simply forgot to include taxation and inflation into the analysis. In retrospect, it is evident that an analysis of the problem without these variables is useless.	Taxation and inflation are two most important variables which must be considered in a complete analysis of this problem. However, inclusion of these two variables into this analysis was clearly beyond the scope of this study.
I wish I could understand what these journal articles are all about.	It is evident that our journal has come to the point where it contains mostly articles that do not address themselves to the real issues of today.
Neither evidence nor logic supports the conclusion I desire to draw.	Indirect evidence clearly supports our hypothesis. Our hypothesis is further supported by theoretical arguments advanced by Ricardo, Marshall, Keynes, Schultz, Heady, Leontief, Stigler, Fidel Castro, and others.

Note. From Scherr (1983, p. 152). Copyright 1983 by Blackwell Scientific. Adapted by permission.

A purpose typically cited in university bulletins is that it provides evidence of competency in planning, conducting, and reporting research. In terms of program objectives, the study is a valuable learning experience in that the thesis and the dissertation are functional exercises in executing the steps in the scientific method of problem solving. Even "ABDs" ("all-but-dones," or persons completing all work for the PhD except the dissertation) acknowledge the contribution that dissertations make to science and the scientific method (Jacks, Chubin, Porter, & Connally, 1983).

The importance of the dissemination of research results as an integral part of the research process is well established. It follows that one of the purposes of the dissertation is to serve as a vehicle to carry the results of independent investigation undertaken by the graduate student. Thus, the dissertation becomes part of the dissemination process. Porter et al. (1982) reported that dissertations do make substantial contributions to the knowledge base and that authors' published dissertations are cited more often than other papers they write.

However, despite the potential contribution that the dissertation can make to a field of study, the fact remains that only about one third to one half of the dissertations become available to the profession through publications (McPhie, 1960; Porter et al., 1982). There are, of course, several reasons why a dissertation does not get published. For one, despite the emphasis placed on research by the institutions, there are a considerable number of students for whom research is not an important aim. Porter et al. (1982) reported that 24% of the doctoral recipients surveyed expressed this feeling. Arlin (1977) went so far as to claim that most educators never do another piece of published research after they complete the master's thesis or doctoral dissertation. In addition, job placements after receiving the PhD place varying degrees of importance on research and publication. There is also the inescapable fact that not all dissertations are worthy of publication.

Conceivably, another contributing factor in the low rate of publication is the traditional style and format of the dissertation. Granted, the highly motivated new PhD will spend the time and effort to rewrite the dissertation into the proper format for journal review, but the less motivated student may not. The point is, why should dissertations and theses be written in a format that requires rewriting before publication if a vital part of the research process is publication of the research study (Day, 1983)?

> The thesis and the dissertation have several purposes, the major one being the contribution of new knowledge with scientific merit.

We contend that the traditional format of dissertations and theses is archaic. Doctoral students (especially those working with productive major professors) may have several scholarly refereed publications by the time the PhD is awarded. Should this person, who has shown that his or her previous work has scientific merit, be required to go through the ritual of writing a dissertation involving separate chapters that spell out every detail of the research process? It seems more logical to us to have the body of the dissertation prepared in the appropriate format and style for submission to a journal, which is the acceptable model for communicating results of research and scholarly works in the arts, sciences, and professions. This section suggests a format that accomplishes that purpose by restructuring the thesis and dissertation and explaining the contents of the various parts.

Limitations of Conventional Style

The conventional format of theses and dissertations typically contains four or five chapters. Traditionally, the chapters are intended to reflect the scientific method for solving problems: developing the problem and formulating the hypotheses, gathering the data, and analyzing and interpreting the results. These steps are typically embodied in chapters such as the introduction (which sometimes contains the literature review; at other times the literature review is a separate chapter), and the method, results, and discussion sections.

The thesis and the dissertation also have several introductory pages as prescribed by the institution, usually consisting of the title page, acknowledgments, abstract, table of contents, and lists of figures and tables. At the end of the study are the references and one or more appendices that contain items such as subject consent forms, tabular materials not presented in the text, more detailed descriptions of procedure, instructions to subjects, and raw data. A brief biographical sketch (the vita) is usually the last entry in the conventional thesis and dissertation.

The conventional format is, of course, steeped in scholastic tradition. In defense of this tradition, the discipline required to accomplish the steps involved in the scientific method usually is viewed as an educationally beneficial experience. Moreover, in most cases for the master's student, the thesis is the first research effort, and there may be merit in formally addressing such steps as operationally defining terms, delimiting the study, stating the basic assumptions, and justifying the significance of the study.

A more serious limitation of the conventional style relates to the dissemination of the results of the study, that is, publishing the manuscript in a research journal. Considerable rewriting is usually required to publish a thesis or dissertation because journal formats differ from those of conventional theses and dissertations. Granted, the information for the journal article is provided in the thesis and the dissertation, but a considerable amount of deleting, reorganizing, and consolidating is necessary to transform the study to journal format.

With regard to the dissertation, the student usually would like to publish this product of months (years) of time and painstaking effort. But in terms of expediency, the conventional format is decidedly counterproductive. The rewriting required may be made more difficult by the fact that the typical new PhD recipient immediately begins a new job that demands considerable time and energy. Unless the new PhD is motivated, the transformation of the conventional dissertation style to journal format may be delayed, sometimes indefinitely. Porter et al. (1982) claimed that new PhDs who fail to publish within 2 years subsequent to the awarding of the degree are unlikely to publish later.

The master's thesis is even more unlikely to be published. One reason is that the master's student generally does not consider publishing unless the major professor suggests it. Furthermore, the master's student is not as well prepared to write for publication as the doctoral student. Thus, the burden for publication is on the major professor, who, understandably, is often unwilling to spend the additional time necessary to supervise the rewriting of the study. Thus, most theses are not submitted for publication. Ironically, the time-honored, scholarly style of the conventional thesis and dissertation actually acts as an impediment to one of the

integral parts of the research process: the dissemination of the results.

Alternative Format

To be of value, an alternative format for theses and dissertations must overcome the limitations of the traditional format for reporting yet maintain the concept of a complete research report. The format we suggest has three major parts. Preliminary materials include such items as the title page, acknowledgments, and abstract. The body of the thesis and dissertation is a complete manuscript prepared in journal form. Included are the standard parts of a research report, such as the introduction, method, results, and discussion. The appendices include a more thorough literature review, additional information about method, and additional results. However, the alternative format, as we describe it, is more appropriate for reporting descriptive (e.g., surveys and correlational studies) and experimental research. The format requires some adjustments for reporting analytical research (e.g., historical and philosophical studies and meta-analysis) and qualitative studies.

Thus, parts of the thesis and dissertation using the alternative format would include the following:

Preliminary materials
   1.1 Title page
   1.2 Acknowledgments
   1.3 Abstract
   1.4 Table of contents
   1.5 List of tables
   1.6 List of figures

Body of the thesis or dissertation
   2.1 Introduction
   2.2 Method
   2.3 Results
   2.4 Discussion
   2.5 References
   2.6 Tables
   2.7 Figures

Appendices
   3.1 Extended literature review
   3.2 Additional methodology
   3.3 Additional results
   3.4 Additional materials

How can this format overcome the limitations of the traditional style? For both the master's and the doctoral student, a manuscript (body of the thesis or dissertation) is developed that is ready for journal submission. All that remains is to add the appropriate title page and abstract, and the paper can be sent to a suitable journal.

The advantage of this format for doctoral students should be apparent. Because PhDs who fail to publish their dissertations within 2 years are unlikely to continue publishing, encouraging publication by a more functional format is worthwhile. Especially when we consider that dissertations appear to make an important contribution to knowledge, the evaluation and subsequent publication of that knowledge through refereed journals is an important step to accomplish.

One final point before proceeding to the structure of the alternative format: The thesis or dissertation must follow a standard style manual. The three most common are the *Publication Manual of the American Psychological Association*, *Index Medicus*, and *The Chicago Manual of Style*. This format adapts nicely to any of these writing styles. A writing style is usually not a university-wide regulation, but frequently an academic department may adopt a particular style. If the alternative format is to be used, a department might want to allow more than one style. For example, many of the journals reporting exercise physiology and biomechanical studies use *Index Medicus*. Journals publishing papers in motor learning, control, and development; sport psychology and sociology; and professional preparation frequently use the APA manual. Journals that publish history and philosophy-of-sport papers may use *The Chicago Manual of Style*. It would be of considerable benefit for the graduate student to have the flexibility of choosing the style recommended by the journal to which the paper will be submitted.

Preliminary Materials

Most of this information will be mandated by the institution and usually appears at the beginning of the thesis or dissertation. Generally included are the title page, committee approval form, acknowledgments, dedication, abstract, table of contents, list of tables, and list of figures. Special considerations involved in preparing these specific pages are covered in other parts of this book. However, a slight change in the length of the abstract is recommended. Many institutions require that the abstract follow the form for *Dissertation Abstracts International*, which sets a 300-word maximum for the abstract length. Journals (and the style manuals mentioned previously) typically require abstracts between 100 and 150 words. If the thesis or dissertation writer keeps the abstract between 100 and 150 words, it can serve both requirements.

Body of the Thesis or Dissertation

This section should be a complete research report using the appropriate style for the journal to which it is to be submitted (or the style required by the department in which the work was done). Included are the introduction and literature review; method, results, and discussion sections; and references, tables, and figures. The author should keep the length within the bounds set by the journal. This is typically 15-25 pages for single experiments. Most journals allow additional pages for multiple experiments or unusually complex papers.

The thesis or dissertation author should consult several sources in preparing the body of the paper. One source is the journal to which submission is anticipated. Guidelines to authors and instructions regarding the appropriate style manual are typically published in journals (e.g., see each issue of *Research Quarterly for Exercise and Sport*). The author should read a number of similar papers in the selected journal to see how specific issues are handled (tables, figures, unusual citations, multiple experiments). In addition, the thesis or dissertation author should carefully follow the appropriate style manual.

Of course, the ultimate goal of this part of an alternative format for the thesis or dissertation is to enable the paper to be submitted to a journal as soon as possible. Improved format and better writing will not aid poor quality research. On the other hand, quality research can easily be hidden by a poor format that makes rewriting difficult, poor reporting that omits important information, or weak and boring writing that makes reading tedious. "Thus the scientist must not only 'do' science; he must 'write' science. Although good writing does not lead to the publication of bad science, bad writing can and often does prevent or delay the publication of good science" (Day, 1983, p. *x*). Research is not recognized in any formal sense as having been conducted until it has been shared with and evaluated by the academic community. As an additional point, there is no law (that we can locate) saying that the thesis or the dissertation must be written in such a way that the reader has difficulty staying awake.

Appendices

In the conventional format, the appendices primarily serve as a depository for nonessential information. To a degree this still characterizes what should be put in the appendices of the alternative format, but some additional features give them a unique worth. Usually, the number and content of the appendices are determined by the collective agreement of the student, the advisor, and the supervisory committee. In the alternate format we suggest four sections that provide a basis from which to develop the appendices. There may be other sections that could be included. However, we see these four as essential components of all appendices.

Each appendix should begin with an introductory narrative. These brief statements should describe what is in a particular section and how that information relates to the body of the thesis or dissertation. This enables the reader to get the most use of the information in the section.

Literature Review

The most important component of the appendices is a review of literature. The introduction in the body of the thesis or dissertation includes a discussion of related research, but it does so only with regard to presenting a minimum amount of information to establish an appropriate background for the one or more experiments that follow. One of the purposes of the thesis or dissertation is to allow the student an opportunity to demonstrate a knowledge of the research literature related to the topic of the thesis or dissertation. In the body of the alternative format, there is limited opportunity for this demonstration because journals typically have relatively brief, to-the-point introductions. A thorough, comprehensive literature review should be included as the first appendix to provide an appropriate mechanism for the student to demonstrate knowledge of the relevant literature. We recommend that this review also be written in journal style.

At least two additional purposes are served by including this literature review as an appendix. First, it provides an opportunity to have this information available for the student's committee members, some of whom may not be sufficiently familiar with the literature related to the thesis or dissertation. Second, if properly developed, this literature review can directly benefit the student by becoming a manuscript that can be submitted to a journal for publication.

The literature review contained in the appendices can take several forms, the most popular of which is probably the comprehensive review of the research literature that seeks to synthesize and evaluate research. This type of review makes connections among various research studies and establishes a strong foundation on which to build the thesis or dissertation research. This type of review also reveals how the research represented by the thesis or dissertation extends the existing body of knowledge related to the student's research topic.

A second form the appendix literature could take is a meta-analysis, which is a quantitative literature review that synthesizes previous research by analyzing results of many research studies by specified statistical methods. An example of a meta-analysis related to a physical education research topic can be seen in an article by Thomas and French (1985). A more complete discussion of meta-analysis can be found in chapter 12 of this book, in books by Glass et al. (1981) and Hedges and Olkin (1985), and in a paper by Thomas and French (1986).

Additional Method Information

A second important component of the appendices is the presentation of additional methodological information not included in the body of the thesis or dissertation. Journals encourage authors to provide method information that is brief yet sufficient to describe essential details related to the subjects, apparatus, and procedures used in the research. The disadvantage of journal articles is that often sufficient information is not provided to enable someone to replicate the study. In the alternative format for the thesis or dissertation, this useful additional information becomes an appendix. Information suitable for this section includes such material as more detailed characteristics of the subjects, more comprehensive experimental design information, fuller descriptions (and perhaps photographs) of tests or testing apparatus, copies of tests, inventories, or questionnaires, and specific instructions given to the subjects.

Additional Results Information

The third appendix should include additional information that is not essential for inclusion in the results section of the body. Editors of journals typically want only summary statements about the analyses and a minimum number of figures and tables. Thus, there is usually considerable material concerning the results that can be placed in the appendix, such as means and standard deviations, ANOVA tables, multiple correlation tables, validity and reliability information, and additional tables and figures.

Providing this type of information serves several purposes. First, it gives evidence that the data descriptions and analyses were properly done. Second, the student's committee members are given an opportunity to evaluate the statistical analyses and interpretations from the body of the thesis or dissertation. Third, other researchers are provided access to more detailed data and statistical information should they want it. For example, a researcher may want to include this thesis or dissertation in a meta-analysis. Because the additional results information presented in the appendix may have many future uses, its importance to the total thesis or dissertation cannot be overestimated.

Additional Materials

A fourth appendix could include a collection of information that is not appropriate for the body or the other appendices, such as human subjects committee approval form, individual subject's consent form, sample data recording forms, and perhaps the raw data from each subject. Also, detailed descriptions of any pilot work done before the study could be included in this or a separate appendix.

As can be seen from these descriptions, the appendices in the alternative format of a thesis or dissertation provide a mechanism for including information not contained in the body that may be significant for the student, the student's committee, and other researchers. It also provides a means for elaborating on some of the information in the body of the paper. Moreover, the comprehensive literature review provides the student with another possible publication. As a result, the appendices become meaningful and useful components of the total thesis or dissertation.

Examples of Alternative Format Dissertations

There are numerous alternative format dissertations available (e.g., French, 1985; Hardy, 1983; Lee, 1982; McPherson, 1987) on microform through *Dissertation Abstracts International*. These dissertations provide excellent examples of the format discussed here.

An unpublished thesis or dissertation remains information that is the exclusive domain of a few individuals. We established earlier that a vital part of the research process is the dissemination of knowledge. We maintain that a style and format should not impede this process. The proposed format accomplishes the traditional objectives of the thesis or dissertation yet facilitates the dissemination of knowledge.

JOURNAL WRITING

We highly recommend a work to which we have frequently referred in this book: *How to Write and Publish a Scientific Paper* (Day, 1983). In our opinion, this book is the researcher's best resource in preparing a paper for submission to a research journal. The book is short (181 pages), informative, readable, and funny. A new edition (Day, 1988) has been published, which is undoubtedly just as good as the other. But, like blue jeans and bedroom slippers, the older edition is more comfortable for us because we're more familiar with it. Although the small section here cannot replace the more thorough treatment given by Day, we do offer a few suggestions.

First, decide to which journal the research paper is to be submitted. Read its guidelines carefully and follow the recommended procedures. Guidelines usually explain the journal's publication style; how to prepare tables, figures, and illustrations; where to submit papers (and how many copies); acceptable lengths for papers; and sometimes estimated review time. Nearly all journals require that manuscripts not be submitted elsewhere simultaneously. To do so is unethical.

Journals follow a fairly standard procedure for papers that are submitted. One of your authors (Thomas) was editor-in-chief of *Research Quarterly for Exercise and Sport* for 6 years (1983-1989). Following is a description of what happens to a manuscript between submission to the editor and return to the author (the average time of this process for *RQES* is about 80 days):

1. The editor checks to see whether the paper is within the scope of the journal, is of appropriate length, and uses correct style. If any of these characteristics are inappropriate, it may be returned to the author.
2. The editor looks through the paper to determine that all appropriate materials are included (e.g., abstract, tables, and figures).
3. The editor reads the abstract, looks at the key words, and evaluates the reference list to identify potential reviewers.
4. Depending on the size of the journal, there may be sections (and section editors; e.g., *RQES* has 11 sections, including those for biomechanics, pedagogy, physiology, and psychology) or a board of associate editors. The editor places the paper in the appropriate section or with an appropriate associate editor.

5. The editor (sometimes in consultation with section or associate editors) assigns reviewers (usually two or three).
6. The reviewers and section editor (or associate editor) are mailed copies of the paper with review forms. They have a specific date by which they should complete the review.
7. The reviewers mail their reviews to the section editor (or associate editor). He or she reads and evaluates the paper and the reviews and makes a recommendation to the editor.
8. The editor reads the paper, the reviews, and the evaluations and writes the author concerning the paper's status. Usually the editor will outline the major reasons for the decision.

Smaller, more narrowly focused journals may not have section or associate editors, so manuscripts go directly back to the editor, who makes a publication decision. These decisions usually fall into three general categories (some journals have levels of the categories):

- Accept (sometimes with varying degrees of revision);
- Unacceptable (sometimes called rejected without bias), which means you can revise the paper and the editor will have it evaluated again; and
- Reject, which usually means the journal will no longer consider your paper.

The criteria used for reviews are fairly common and are represented by the questions in chapter 2 (Table 2.3). Rates for decisions to publish vary by the quality of the journal and the area of the paper and are frequently available: *RQES* accepts about 25% of the papers submitted (see the June 1988 issue for a more detailed description).

If this is your first paper, seek some advice from a more experienced author. This may be your major professor or another faculty member. Frequently, papers are rejected because they fail to provide important information. More experienced authors will pick up on this immediately. Journal editors and reviewers do not have time to teach you good scientific reporting. (Not everyone is fond of journal editors. One wag was reported to have said, "Editors have only one good characteristic—if they can understand a scientific paper, anyone can!" Another said, "Editors are in my opinion, a low form of life—inferior to the viruses and only slightly above academic deans" [Day, 1983, p. 80].) Teaching good reporting is the responsibility of your major professor, research methods courses, and books such as this one; but it is your responsibility to acquire the skill.

Do not be discouraged if your paper is rejected. All of us have had papers rejected, mostly early in our academic careers. Carefully evaluate the reviews and determine whether the paper can be salvaged. If it can, then rewrite it, taking into account the reviewer's and the editor's criticisms, and submit it to another journal. If it cannot be salvaged, learn from your mistakes. Occasionally, you may feel you have received an unfair review. If so, write back to the editor, point out the biases, and ask for another review by a different reviewer. Editors are generally open to this type of correspondence if it is handled in a professional way. However, opening with the sentence "Look what these stupid reviewers said" is unlikely to achieve success. Recognize that writing the editor is less likely to be successful if two or more reviewers have agreed on the important criticisms. Editors cannot be expert in every area, and they must rely on the recommendations of reviewers. If you find yourself resorting to this tactic very often, the problem is likely in your work.

As a final point in this part, we have noted the infrequency with which most scientific papers are read (of course, none of ours fall in that category). Some writers have speculated that only two to four people read the average paper completely. Is it possible that organizing the scientific paper differently might promote an increased audience? The answer might lie in a paper published in *Omni* magazine and included here as Table 21.2. The author, B.A. Realist (G. Benford), proposed a new organization to aid potential authors of scientific papers.

Table 21.2 Writing a Scientific Paper

Everyone knows that scientists write badly—everybody, that is, except scientists. They think they're merely being precise and orderly, and everyone else on the planet is either (a) illiterate, (b) sloppy, (c) a humanist, or (d) all of the above (Ref. 1). In some cases, of course, the individual scientist is not well acquainted with the English language. (In the opinion of English scientists, this explains the frequently unintelligible papers of Americans.)

The scientist is, by his reliance on the passive voice, hobbled, leading to sentences like this one, in which the subject is acted upon with lumpy nouns, without ever saying exactly whom the action is done by, so that the sentences get longer and longer as you read and never seem to end, even when there is clearly nothing more to say in the sentence, at which point the reader sometimes gets a meager little semicolon; this gives him a rest, so that he can go on and read another long phrase without really learning anything more, because the writer's hand has kept on moving even though his brain has long since been disengaged.

What to do? Trying to straighten a scientist's syntax is like trying to unsnarl week-old spaghetti, with some exceptions (see Ref. 2). It is far better to change the packaging of the sentences. Scientific papers are written like elaborate lab reports—first A, then B, on to C, plodding on to the conclusion. Such papers assume the reader is fascinated by the pearls of wisdom that ooze through the barnacle-laden sentences. The sad truth is that hardly anyone ever reads a paper all the way

through. A study by a British physics journal shows that the average number who finish the whole paper is 0.5—and that includes the author. Apparently, most scientists can't bear to reread their own work, much less read anyone else's.

In this paper a new scheme for paper organizing is proposed. It does not rely on weaning scientists away from the passive-voice construction, like that last one. Instead it relies on the way scientists actually read and on their motivation for reading papers.

While reading a scientific paper, scientists are led by two needs: (a) ego and (b) desire for information. Our research shows that ego always dominates. Therefore, papers should be organized to satisfy this. The preferred approach, one that makes the most of these insights, is as follows:

1. *Title*
2. *Author's name*
3. *References.* These must contain a broad spectrum of sources, mostly to ensure the greatest probability of naming the reader. Use as many multiauthor papers as possible to maximize the number of people who can be mentioned. A scientist will *always* pay greater attention to colleagues who cite him, if only to find where in the text he gets mentioned. Thus, the best strategy is to cite everybody you can, but then place the citations in the most unlikely places in the paper. Then the scientists have to read all or most of the paper carefully to find mention of them. They might even discover what the paper is about. A really high-risk alternative is to cite someone in the list of references but not in the text. Then he or she will read the whole paper, twice. The disadvantage, of course, is that the scientist will be livid with rage and frustration.
4. *Acknowledgments.* An important ego feeding ground. Thank the big names in your field, even if your sole contact with them was over coffee at some conference 3 years ago. The list should be lavish, implying close connections with the movers and shakers, but avoid mentioning dead people. They can do you no more good, and their rivals are still around. Finally, if space permits, include those who actually helped you. This part of the acknowledgments is purely optional.

5. *Grant reference.* Your grant-monitoring officer will always look for this. So stick it in early. Also, others will want to know what agency got suckered into paying for this stuff, so they can hit it up for grant money themselves.

6. *Introduction.* Here you explain what you plan to do. Promise a lot. Few will actually read the main text (see #8) to find out whether you actually do it. Fewer still will care.

7. *Conclusions.* Always overstate your results. Claim certainty where you have only the vaguest of suspicions.

8. *Main text.* With any luck, there will be no need to write this section. Everyone will have turned to the next paper to resume the search for his or her own name.

References

1. "Professorial Pathology," by E.U. Reka, A.B. Surd, and I.M. Pedant, *Journal of Academic Backstabbing*, Vol. 3, 1980.

2. *Explaining Asimov* (12 volumes), by the National Academy of Sciences, 1981.

Note. From Realist (G. Benford) (1982, p. 130). Copyright © 1982 by Omni Publications International, Ltd. Adapted by permission.

ABSTRACTS

Whether you are writing for a journal, using the traditional or alternative method of writing a thesis or dissertation, or are writing a paper to be presented at a conference, you will need to include an abstract. Abstracts for each purpose require slightly different orientations, but nearly all have constraints on length and form.

Thesis or Dissertation Abstracts

The abstract for your thesis or dissertation will probably have several specific constraints, including those of length, form, style, and location. First, consult your university or college regulations, then follow these carefully. With dissertations, this nearly always includes the form for submission to *Dissertation Abstracts International*. The exact headings, length, and margins are provided in a handout available from your graduate school office. In writing the abstract, consider who will read it. It will be located in computer searches by the title and key words. (The importance of these was discussed in chapter 1.) Write the abstract so the person reading it can determine whether he or she needs to look at the total thesis or dissertation. Important features are the theoretical framework, clear identification of the problem, who the subjects were, how measurements were made, and important and meaningful findings. Do not use all the space writing about your sophisticated statistical analyses or minor methodological problems.

Abstracts for Published Papers

An abstract for a published paper is much more brief. Usually, the length is 100 to 150 words. The important consideration is to get to the point: What was the problem? Who were the subjects? What did you find? The most useless statement encountered in these abstracts is "Results were discussed." Would anyone have expected that results would not be discussed?

Conference Abstracts

Abstracts for conferences are slightly different. Usually you are allowed a little more space because the reviewer must be convinced to accept your paper for presentation. In these abstracts, you should follow these procedures:

1. Write a short introduction to set up the problem statement.
2. State the problem.
3. Describe the methodology briefly, including
   a. subjects,
   b. instrumentation,

   c. procedures, and
   d. design and analysis.
4. Summarize the results.
5. Conclude with why the results are important.

Figure 21.1 shows an abstract developed by one of your authors (Thomas, 1989) that is used by the North American Society for Psychology of Sport and Physical Activity as a humorous sample for individuals submitting abstracts for the society's annual conference.

A critical part of a conference abstract is the results and their importance. If you do this in a vague, nondescript way, the reviewer may conclude that you have not completed the study. This is generally grounds for rejection. The conference planners cannot turn down other completed research when it is possible that yours will not be finished.

Finally, most conferences require that the paper be presented before publication. So, if you have a paper in review at a journal, it could be hazardous to submit it to a conference that is 8-12 months away. Also, many conferences require that the paper not have been previously presented. Be aware of this, and follow regulations. Violating these guidelines will never enhance your professional status, and other scholars will quickly become aware of it.

ORAL AND POSTER PRESENTATIONS

Once your conference paper is accepted, you are faced with presenting it. The presentation will be conducted either orally or in a poster session.

ABSTRACT SAMPLE
Please use the following style
for all abstracts.

I.M. Tenured and U. R. Promoted, JR's
South Fork School of Hard Knocks, Dallas,
TX 00001

How Motor Skill Research Can Get You a
Merit Raise

Current research suggests that merit raises
are directly related to the number of papers
faculty present and publish and inversely
related to the quality of the research...

.......The long term effect is to increase the
number of journals, conferences, and full
professors.

Figure 21.1 Sample conference abstract.

An abstract for a published paper is brief. The important consideration is to get to the point.

Oral Presentations

Oral presentations usually cause panic among graduate students and new faculty members. First, there is no way to get over this except to give several papers. But you can help assuage the feeling of apprehension and dread. Usually, the time allowed for oral research reports is 10-20 minutes, depending on the conference. You will be notified of the time limit when your paper is accepted. Because you must stay within the time limit and there is no way to present a complete report within this time limit, what do you do? We suggest that you present the essential features of the report using the following divisions for a 15-minute presentation:

- Introduction that cites a few important studies—3 minutes
- Statement of the problem—1 minute (use slides or an overhead)
- Method—3 minutes (slides or an overhead are helpful)
- Results—3 minutes (slides or overheads of figures)
- Discussion—2 minutes (slides or overheads of main points)
- Questions and discussion—3 minutes

Total—15 minutes

The most frequent errors in oral presentations are spending too much time on method and presenting results poorly. Proper use of slides (or overheads) is the key to an effective presentation, particularly in the results. Place a brief statement of the problem on a slide, and show it while you talk. A slide of the experimental arrangements reduces much of the excess verbiage in method. Always use slides to illustrate the results. A picture of the results (particularly figures and graphs) is much more effective than either tables or a verbal presentation. Keep the figures and graphs simple and concise. Have a pointer available to indicate significant features. Finally, remember Thomas and Nelson's Five Laws of Oral Presentations (Table 21.3). The way to avoid most of the problems associated with these laws is self-evident. One that may not be so evident is practicing your presentation. We get together the graduate students and faculty who are presenting papers at upcoming conferences and conduct practice sessions. Everyone presents his or her paper and has it timed. Then the audience asks questions and offers suggestions to clarify presentations and visual aids. The quality of the graduate students' presentations is generally improved and their confidence strengthened by the practice session.

Table 21.3 Thomas and Nelson's Five Laws of Oral Presentations

1. Something always goes wrong with the slide projector. More specifically,
   a. unless you check it beforehand, it will not work;
   b. either the electrical cord or the slide control cord (or both) will be too short;
   c. any slide not checked immediately before the presentation will be in upside down;
   d. if the projector has worked perfectly for the three previous presenters, the bulb will burn out during your presentation;
   e. every slide will require that the projector be refocused;
   f. a person getting up to leave after the previous paper will knock over the slide projector.
2. You will only drop your slide tray when you have the top off.
3. The screen will be too small for the room.
4. Your paper will be the last one scheduled during the conference. This will result in only the

(Cont.)

Table 21.3 (Continued)

moderator, you, and the previous presenter being there, the latter of whom will leave on completing his or her paper. Or conversely, your paper will be scheduled at 7:30 a.m., at which time you will be hung over and everyone else will still be in bed.

5. At your first presentation, the most prestigious scholar in your field will show up, be misquoted by you, and ask you a question.

Poster Presentations

The *poster session* is another way to give a paper at a conference. This involves the use of a large room in which presenters place summaries of their research on the wall or poster stands. The session is scheduled for a specific period of time, during which presenters stand by their work while anyone interested walks around, reads the material, and discusses items of interest with the presenters.

We prefer this format over oral presentations. The audience can look at the papers in which they are interested and have more detailed discussions with the authors. Within 75 minutes in a large room, 15-20 poster presentations can be made available. In contrast, 15-minute oral presentations allow only five presentations in 75 minutes. In addition, the audience must sit through several papers, often losing interest or creating a disturbance by arriving or leaving.

The presenter at a poster session should follow these guidelines:

- Know how much space is available for your materials.
- Provide the necessary equipment for attaching your materials to the wall (even

when the conference has indicated that supplies will be available).
- Mount your posters on contrasting backgrounds so they will be easily visible and will not blend into the backboards.
- Use figures and graphs where possible (as opposed to text and tables).
- Use large lettering for all text, numbers, and labels.

Clearly label the six parts of the poster presentation: introduction, statement of the problem, method, results (with figures and graphs), discussion and conclusions, and important references.

ETHICS AND THE RESEARCHER

Ethical considerations among researchers and ethical factors in the graduate student–major professor relationship are the two topics under discussion in this section. The major ethical issue among researchers involves joint research projects, or, more specifically, the publication and presentation of joint research efforts. As a general rule, the order of authorship for presentations and publications should be based on the contributions of the researchers to the project. The first, or senior, author is usually the researcher who developed the idea and the plan for the research. Second and third authors are normally listed in the order of their contributions.

Although this sounds easy enough, the decisions are difficult at times. Sometimes researchers make equal contributions and decide to flip a coin to determine who will be listed first. In fact, the order of authorship for this book was decided in that manner. We team-taught the research methods course for several years while we were on the faculty at Louisiana State University. We contributed equally to this book but, before we began, used a coin toss to decide who would be listed as first author (at the time Nelson was unaware of Thomas's extreme skill in games of chance; in subsequent years he has learned that lesson well). Note the phrase "before we began"—this is a good procedure to follow. Make the decisions about the order of authors at the beginning of a collaborative effort. This saves hard feelings among people later, when everyone may not agree on whose contribution was most important.

A second issue is who should be an author. Studies occasionally have more authors than subjects. In fact, sometimes the authors are also the subjects. When you look at what subjects must go through in some research studies, you can see why only a major professor's graduate students allow "that" to be done to them. Even then they insist on being an author as a reward. More seriously, here are two rules that should help define authorship:

• **Technicians do not necessarily become joint authors.** Graduate students sometimes feel that, because they collect the data, they should be coauthors. Only when graduate students contribute to the planning, analysis, and write-up of the research report are they entitled to be listed as coauthors. Even this rule does not apply to grants that pay graduate students for their work. A good major professor involves his or her graduate students in all aspects of his or her research program; thus, these students may frequently serve as coauthors as well as technicians.

• **Authorship should involve only those people who contribute directly to the specific research project.** This does not necessarily include the director of the laboratory or a graduate student's major professor. The only thing we advocate by the chain letter in Table 21.4 is the humor.

By ethical factors in the major professor–graduate student relationship, we mean that graduate students are colleagues and should be treated as such. If we want our students to be scholars when they complete their

Table 21.4 Chain Letter to Increase Publications

Dear Colleague:

We are sure you are aware of the importance of publications in establishing yourself and procuring grants, awards, and good-paying academic positions or chairpersonships. We have devised a way in which your curriculum vita can be greatly enhanced with very little effort.

This letter contains a list of names and addresses. Include the top two names as coauthors on your next scholarly paper. Then remove the top name and place your own name at the bottom of the list. Send the revised letter to five colleagues.

If these instructions are followed, by the time your name reaches the top of the list, you will have claim to coauthorship of 15,625 refereed publications. If you break this chain, your next 10 papers will be rejected as lacking in relevance to "real-world" behavior. Thus, you will be labeled as ecologically invalid by your peers.

Sincerely,

Jerry R. Thomas, Professor
Jack K. Nelson, Professor

List as coauthors
Jerry R. Thomas
Jack K. Nelson
I.M. Published
U.R. Tenured
C.D. Raise

graduate work, then we should treat them like scholars from the start, for graduate students do not become scholars on receipt of a degree. By the same token, graduate students must act like responsible scholars. This means producing careful, thorough, and quality work.

SELECTING A MAJOR PROFESSOR AND COMMITTEE

The three major concerns in this section are how to select a major professor and a committee, how to change major professors or committee members, and how to handle joint publications between you and your major professor.

Selecting a Major Professor

First, selection of a major professor depends on your area of interest. Frequently, master's students attend an institution because of convenience; however, doctoral students should select the institution they attend because of the quality of program and the faculty in their area of specialization. Do not make a hasty decision about your major professor. If you are already at the institution, carefully evaluate the specializations that are available in your interest areas. Ask questions about faculty and whether they publish in these areas. Read some of these publications and determine your interest. What financial support, such as laboratories and equipment, is given to these areas? Also, talk to graduate students in the areas. Finally, talk with the faculty members to determine how effectively you will be able to work with them.

We advocate a mentor model in preparing graduate students (particularly doctoral students) in physical education, exercise science, and sport science. For students to become good researchers (or good clinicians) requires a one-on-one student-faculty relationship. This means several things about graduate students and graduate faculty.

First, graduate students need to be full-time students to develop the research and clinical skills needed for success in research and teaching. They need to work with a mentor in his or her ongoing research program. This lends continuity to research efforts and pulls graduate students together into effective research teams. Theses and dissertation topics arise naturally from these types of settings. Additionally, more senior students become models and can offer assistance to novice graduate students. Expertise is acquired by watching experts, working with them, and then practicing the skills and techniques acquired.

Conversely, for a faculty member to be a good mentor, he or she must have an active, ongoing research program. This means that appropriate facilities and equipment must be available as well as time for the faculty member to devote to research and graduate student mentoring. Potential graduate students should investigate carefully the situations into which they will place themselves, especially if they have a major interest in research (for a good description of mentors, see Newell, 1987).

However, if you are not at the institution, find out which institutions offer the specialties in which you are interested. Write their graduate schools and departments, requesting information. Read the appropriate journals (over the past 5-10 years) and see which faculty are publishing. After you narrow down your list, find out about financial support and then plan a visit. Speak to the graduate coordinator for the department and the faculty in your area of interest. Sometimes you can meet some of the faculty at conventions, such as those of AAHPERD (national or district meetings), the American College of Sports Medicine, the International Society for Biomechanics, and the North American Society for Psychology of Sport and Physical Activity.

After you select a major professor, you must select a committee. Normally the master's or doctoral committee is selected in consultation with your major professor. The committee selected should be one that can contribute to the planning and evaluation of your work, not one that might be the easiest. It is preferable to wait a semester (quarter) or two (if you can) before selecting a final committee. This gives you the opportunity to have several potential committee members as teachers as well as allowing you to better evaluate your common interest.

Changing Your Major Professor

What happens, however, if you have a major professor (or committee member) who is not ideal for you? First, evaluate the reason. You need not be best friends, but it is important that you and your major professor are striving for the same goals. Sometimes students' interests change. Sometimes people just cannot get along. If handled professionally, however, this situation should not be a problem. Go to your major professor and explain the problem as you perceive it and offer him or her an opportunity to respond. Of course, the conflict may be on a more personal level. If so, use an objective and professional approach. If you cannot, or if this does not produce satisfactory results, the best recourse may be to seek the advice of the graduate coordinator or department chairperson.

Handling Joint Publications

The final concern deals with joint publications, specifically those between the major professor and the graduate student. Major professors do (and should) immediately begin to involve graduate students in the major professor's research program. When this happens, the general guidelines we sug-

gested earlier apply. However, two conflicting forces are at work. First, a professor's job is to foster and develop the scholarly ability of students. Second, however, pressure is increasing on faculty to publish so they can obtain the benefits of promotions, tenure, outside funding, and merit pay. Being the first (senior) author is of benefit in these endeavors. As a result, the faculty member wants to be selfless and to assist the student but feels the pressure to publish. This may not be a major issue for senior faculty, but it certainly is for the untenured assistant professor. As mentioned previously, there are no hard-and-fast rules other than that everyone agrees before the research is undertaken.

The thesis or dissertation is a special case. By definition, this is how the graduate student demonstrates his or her competence to receive the degree. Frequently, for the master's thesis, the major professor supplies the idea, design, and much of the writing and editing. In spite of this, we believe it should be regarded as the student's work. The dissertation should always be regarded as the student's work. However, second authorship for the major professor on either the thesis or the dissertation is acceptable under certain circumstances. The American Psychological Association has defined these circumstances adequately, and we recommend the use of the guidelines reported in Table 21.5.

SUMMARY

Chapters 19 and 20 focused on traditional ways of reporting research findings in the thesis and dissertation; however, additional reporting methods do exist. Students first need to understand how other peoples' work may be used appropriately. Plagiarism is the unacceptable use of someone else's work, particularly a failure to report that ideas, concepts, and writings have been borrowed.

**Table 21.5 APA Guidelines for
Joint Authorship in Dissertations**

APA Statement on Authorship of Research Papers

The ethics committee of the American Psychological Association this year adopted the following policy statement, for use in weighing complaints about crediting authors of scholarly reports.

- Only second authorship is acceptable for the dissertation supervisor.
- Second authorship may be considered obligatory if the supervisor designates the primary variables or makes major interpretive contributions or provides the data base.
- Second authorship is a courtesy if the supervisor designates the general area of concern or is substantially involved in the development of the design and measurement procedures, or substantially contributes to the write-up of the published report.
- Second authorship is not acceptable if the supervisor only provides encouragement, physical facilities, financial support, critiques, or editorial contributions.
- In all instances, agreement should be reviewed before the writing for publication is undertaken and at the time of the submission. If disagreements arise, they should be resolved by a third party using these guidelines.

The alternative format for theses and dissertations is a very useful way to report research. It has the advantage of being in the format for journal publication, one of the main ways used to evaluate scholarly work, yet it retains the essential characteristics of the complete reporting that is so valued in the thesis and dissertation. The alternative format is comprised of preliminary materials (e.g., title page, abstract), the body of the thesis or dissertation (e.g., introduction, method, results), and a set of appendices (e.g., extended literature review, additional results). The goal of this reporting style is to promote rapid publication of quality research.

Abstracts are frequently used as a form for submitting papers to scholarly meetings so they can be evaluated for possible presentation. Usually the abstract is limited in length and form according to the format prescribed by the scholarly group to whom it is submitted. If the abstracted paper is accepted for presentation, the form may be oral or poster. Oral presentations are usually 10 to 20 minutes long, and poster presentations are typically limited to a specific display space.

Finally, researchers need to be aware of the problems associated with joint authorship for publication. The order of authorship should be agreed on before research begins and is based on the contributions to the research project. Technicians are not necessarily coauthors; the decision depends on their contributions and the definitions of their jobs. The same applies to graduate students, who may or may not be coauthors on papers with their major professors. Graduate students should carefully evaluate their research and programmatic interests when selecting graduate programs and major professors.

Problems

1. Writing: Select a study from a journal and write a 150-word abstract in APA style (or whatever style your department uses).
2. Oral presentations: To emphasize the importance of time limits on oral presentations, we suggest that the professor organize the following presentations in class:

   a. Have each student select a published research study and prepare and present a 2-minute summary.

b. Do the same with another study but give a 5-minute summary.

3. Poster presentation: Have each student prepare a poster presentation of a research study from a journal. Put the posters around the classroom walls. Have students critique each poster (or some percentage of posters for larger classes).

SUGGESTED READINGS

Quest (Vol. 39, August 1987): This issue focuses on graduate programs in physical education, exercise science, and sport science. The entire issue is quite informative to potential master's and doctoral students. Articles of particular interest are by Newell (p. 88), Massengale (p. 97), Spirduso (p. 103), Thomas (p. 114), Spirduso and Lovett (p. 129), and King and Bandy (p. 153). Additional papers in this issue focus on specific types of graduate programs (e.g., teacher preparation and sport management) and may be of interest to specific students.

Day, R.A. (1988). *How to write and publish a scientific paper* (3rd ed.). Phoenix: Oryx Press.

Appendix A

□

Statistical Tables

Table A.1 Table of Random Numbers

22	17	68	65	84	68	95	23	92	35	87	02	22	57	51	61	09	43	95	06	58	24	82	03	47
19	36	27	59	46	13	79	93	37	55	39	77	32	77	09	85	52	05	30	62	47	83	51	62	74
16	77	23	02	77	09	61	87	25	21	28	06	24	25	93	16	71	13	59	78	23	05	47	47	25
78	43	76	71	61	20	44	90	32	64	97	67	63	99	61	46	38	03	93	22	69	81	21	99	21
03	28	28	26	08	73	37	32	04	05	69	30	16	09	05	88	69	58	28	99	35	07	44	75	47
93	22	53	64	39	07	10	63	76	35	87	03	04	79	88	08	13	13	85	51	55	34	57	72	69
78	76	58	54	74	92	38	70	96	92	52	06	79	79	45	82	63	18	27	44	69	66	92	19	09
23	68	35	26	00	99	53	93	61	28	52	70	05	48	34	56	65	05	61	86	90	92	10	70	80
15	39	25	70	99	93	86	52	77	65	15	33	59	05	28	22	87	26	07	47	86	96	98	29	06
58	71	96	30	24	18	46	23	34	27	85	13	99	24	44	49	18	09	79	49	74	16	32	23	02
57	35	27	33	72	24	53	63	94	09	41	10	76	47	91	44	04	95	49	66	39	60	04	59	81
48	50	86	54	48	22	06	34	72	52	82	21	15	65	20	33	29	94	71	11	15	91	29	12	03
61	96	48	95	03	07	16	39	33	66	98	56	10	56	79	77	21	30	27	12	90	49	22	23	62
36	93	89	41	26	29	70	83	63	51	99	74	20	52	36	87	09	41	15	09	98	60	16	03	03
18	87	00	42	31	57	90	12	02	07	23	47	37	17	31	54	08	01	88	63	39	41	88	92	10
88	56	53	27	59	33	35	72	67	47	77	34	55	45	70	08	18	27	38	90	16	95	86	70	75
09	72	95	84	29	49	41	31	06	70	42	38	06	45	18	64	84	73	31	65	52	53	37	97	15
12	96	88	17	31	65	19	69	02	83	60	75	86	90	68	24	64	19	35	51	56	61	87	39	12
85	94	57	24	16	92	09	84	38	76	22	00	27	69	85	29	81	94	78	70	21	94	47	90	12
38	64	43	59	98	98	77	87	68	07	91	51	67	62	44	40	98	05	93	78	23	32	65	41	18
53	44	09	42	72	00	41	86	79	79	68	47	22	00	20	35	55	31	51	51	00	83	63	22	55
40	76	66	26	84	57	99	99	90	37	36	63	32	08	58	37	40	13	68	97	87	64	81	07	83
02	17	79	18	05	12	59	52	57	02	22	07	90	47	03	28	14	11	30	79	20	69	22	40	98
95	17	82	06	53	31	51	10	96	46	92	06	88	07	77	56	11	50	81	69	40	23	72	51	39
35	76	22	42	92	96	11	83	44	80	34	68	35	48	77	33	42	40	90	60	73	96	53	97	86
26	29	13	56	41	85	47	04	66	08	34	72	57	59	13	82	43	80	46	15	38	26	61	70	04
77	80	20	75	82	72	82	32	99	90	63	95	73	76	63	89	73	44	99	05	48	67	26	43	18
46	40	66	44	52	91	36	74	43	53	30	82	13	54	00	78	45	63	98	35	55	03	36	67	68
37	56	08	18	09	77	53	84	46	47	31	91	18	95	58	24	16	74	11	53	44	10	13	85	57
61	65	61	68	66	37	27	47	39	19	84	83	70	07	48	53	21	40	06	71	95	06	79	88	54
93	43	69	64	07	34	18	04	52	35	56	27	09	24	86	61	85	53	83	45	19	90	70	99	00
21	96	60	12	99	11	20	99	45	18	48	13	93	55	34	18	37	79	49	90	65	97	38	20	46
95	20	47	97	97	27	37	83	28	71	00	06	41	41	74	45	89	09	39	84	51	67	11	52	49
97	86	21	78	73	10	65	81	92	59	58	76	17	14	97	04	76	62	16	17	17	95	70	45	80
69	92	06	34	13	59	71	74	17	32	27	55	10	24	19	23	71	82	13	74	63	52	52	01	41
04	31	17	21	56	33	73	99	19	87	26	72	39	27	67	53	77	57	68	93	60	61	97	22	61
61	06	98	03	91	87	14	77	43	96	43	00	65	98	50	45	60	33	01	07	98	99	46	50	47
85	93	85	86	88	72	87	08	62	40	16	06	10	89	20	23	21	34	74	97	76	38	03	29	63
21	74	32	47	45	73	96	07	94	52	09	65	90	77	47	25	76	16	19	33	53	05	70	53	30
15	69	53	82	80	79	96	23	53	10	65	39	07	16	29	45	33	02	43	70	02	87	40	41	45
02	89	08	04	49	20	21	14	68	86	87	63	93	95	17	11	29	01	95	80	35	14	97	35	33
87	18	15	89	79	85	43	01	72	73	08	61	74	51	69	89	74	39	82	15	94	51	33	41	67
98	83	71	94	22	59	97	50	99	52	08	52	85	08	40	87	80	61	65	31	91	51	80	32	44
10	08	58	21	66	72	68	49	29	31	89	85	84	46	06	59	73	19	85	23	65	09	29	75	63
47	90	56	10	08	88	02	84	27	83	42	29	72	23	19	66	56	45	65	79	20	71	53	20	25

22	85	61	68	90	49	64	92	85	44	16	40	12	89	88	50	14	49	81	06	01	82	77	45	12
67	80	43	79	33	12	83	11	41	16	25	58	19	68	70	77	02	54	00	52	53	43	37	15	26
27	62	50	96	72	79	44	61	40	15	14	53	40	65	39	27	31	58	50	28	11	39	03	34	25
33	78	80	87	15	38	30	06	38	21	14	47	47	07	26	54	96	87	53	32	40	36	40	96	76
13	13	92	66	99	47	24	49	57	74	32	25	43	62	17	10	97	11	69	84	99	63	22	32	98
10	27	53	96	23	71	50	54	36	23	54	31	04	82	98	04	14	12	15	09	26	78	25	47	47
28	41	50	61	88	64	85	27	20	18	83	36	36	05	56	39	71	65	09	62	94	76	62	11	89
34	21	42	57	02	59	19	18	97	48	80	30	03	30	98	05	24	67	70	07	84	97	50	87	46
61	81	77	23	23	82	82	11	54	08	53	28	70	58	96	44	07	39	55	43	42	34	43	39	28
61	15	18	13	54	16	86	20	26	88	90	74	80	55	09	14	53	90	51	17	52	01	63	01	59
91	76	21	64	64	44	91	13	32	97	75	31	62	66	54	84	80	32	75	77	56	08	25	70	29
00	97	79	08	06	37	30	28	59	85	53	56	68	53	40	01	74	39	59	73	30	19	99	85	48
36	46	18	34	94	75	20	80	27	77	78	91	69	16	00	08	43	18	73	68	67	69	61	34	25
88	98	99	60	50	65	95	79	42	94	93	62	40	89	96	43	56	47	71	66	46	76	29	67	02
04	37	59	87	21	05	02	03	24	17	47	97	81	56	51	92	34	86	01	82	55	51	33	12	91
63	62	06	34	41	94	21	78	55	09	72	76	45	16	94	29	95	81	83	83	79	88	01	97	30
78	47	23	53	90	34	41	92	45	71	09	23	70	70	07	12	38	92	79	43	14	85	11	47	23
87	68	62	15	43	53	14	36	59	25	54	47	33	70	15	59	24	48	40	35	50	03	42	99	36
47	60	92	10	77	88	59	53	11	52	66	25	69	07	04	48	68	64	71	06	61	65	70	22	12
56	88	87	59	41	65	28	04	67	53	95	79	88	37	31	50	41	06	94	76	81	83	17	16	33
02	57	45	86	67	73	43	07	34	48	44	26	87	93	29	77	09	61	67	84	06	69	44	77	75
31	54	14	13	17	48	62	11	90	60	68	12	93	64	28	46	24	79	16	76	14	60	25	51	01
28	50	16	43	36	28	97	85	58	99	67	22	52	76	23	24	70	36	54	54	59	28	61	71	96
63	29	62	66	50	02	63	45	52	38	67	63	47	54	75	83	24	78	43	20	92	63	13	47	48
45	65	58	26	51	76	96	59	38	72	86	57	45	71	46	44	67	76	14	55	44	88	01	62	12
39	65	36	63	70	77	45	85	50	51	74	13	39	35	22	30	53	36	02	95	49	34	88	73	61
73	71	98	16	04	29	18	94	51	23	76	51	94	84	86	79	93	96	38	63	08	58	25	58	94
72	20	56	20	11	72	65	71	08	86	79	57	95	13	91	97	48	72	66	48	09	71	17	24	89
75	17	26	99	76	89	37	20	70	01	77	31	61	95	46	26	97	05	73	51	53	33	18	72	87
37	48	60	82	29	81	30	15	39	14	48	38	75	93	29	06	87	37	78	48	45	56	00	84	47
68	08	02	80	72	83	71	46	30	49	89	17	95	88	29	02	39	56	03	46	97	74	06	56	17
14	23	98	61	67	70	52	85	01	50	01	84	02	78	43	10	62	98	19	41	18	83	99	47	99
49	08	96	21	44	25	27	99	41	28	07	41	08	34	66	19	42	74	39	91	41	96	53	78	72
78	37	06	08	43	63	61	62	42	29	39	68	95	10	96	09	24	23	00	62	56	12	80	73	16
37	21	34	17	68	68	96	83	23	56	32	84	60	15	31	44	73	67	34	77	91	15	79	74	58
14	29	09	34	04	87	83	07	55	07	76	58	30	83	64	87	29	25	58	84	86	50	60	00	25
58	43	28	06	36	49	52	83	51	14	47	56	91	29	34	05	87	31	06	95	12	45	57	09	09
10	43	67	29	70	80	62	80	03	42	10	80	21	38	84	90	56	35	03	09	43	12	74	49	14
44	38	88	39	54	86	97	37	44	22	00	95	01	31	76	17	16	29	56	63	38	78	94	49	81
90	69	59	19	51	85	39	52	85	13	07	28	37	07	61	11	16	36	27	03	78	86	72	04	95
41	47	10	25	62	97	05	31	03	61	20	26	36	31	62	68	69	86	95	44	84	95	48	46	45
91	94	14	63	19	75	89	11	47	11	31	56	34	19	09	79	57	92	36	59	14	93	87	81	40
80	06	54	18	66	09	18	94	06	19	98	40	07	17	81	22	45	44	84	11	24	62	20	42	31
67	72	77	63	48	84	08	31	55	58	24	33	45	77	58	80	45	67	93	82	75	70	16	08	24
59	40	24	13	27	79	26	88	86	30	01	31	60	10	39	53	58	47	70	93	85	81	56	39	38

(Cont.)

Table A.1 (Continued)

05	90	35	89	95	01	61	16	96	94	50	78	13	69	36	37	68	53	37	31	71	26	35	03	71
44	43	80	69	98	46	68	05	14	82	90	78	50	05	62	77	79	13	57	44	59	60	10	39	66
61	81	31	96	82	00	57	25	60	59	46	72	60	18	77	55	66	12	62	11	08	99	55	64	57
42	88	07	10	05	24	98	65	63	21	47	21	61	88	32	27	80	30	21	60	10	92	35	36	12
77	94	30	05	39	28	10	99	00	27	12	73	73	99	12	49	99	57	94	82	96	88	57	17	91
78	83	19	76	16	94	11	68	84	26	23	54	20	86	85	23	86	66	99	07	36	37	34	92	09
87	76	59	61	81	43	63	64	61	61	65	76	36	95	90	18	48	27	45	68	27	23	65	30	72
91	43	05	96	47	55	78	99	95	24	37	55	85	78	78	01	48	41	19	10	35	19	54	07	73
84	97	77	72	73	09	62	06	65	72	87	12	49	03	60	41	15	20	76	27	50	47	02	29	16
87	41	60	76	83	44	88	96	07	80	85	05	83	38	96	73	70	66	81	90	30	56	10	48	59

*Table A.1 is taken from Table XXXIII of Fisher, *Statistical Methods for Research Workers*, published by Oliver and Boyd, Ltd., Edinburgh, and is reproduced by permission of the author and the publisher.

Table A.2 The Standard Normal Curve

	One tail		Two tail	
z	π beyond	π remainder	π beyond	π remainder
0.00	0.5000	0.5000	1.0000	0.0000
0.01	0.4960	0.5040	0.9920	0.0080
0.02	0.4920	0.5080	0.9840	0.0160
0.03	0.4880	0.5120	0.9761	0.0239
0.04	0.4840	0.5160	0.9681	0.0319
0.05	0.4801	0.5199	0.9601	0.0399
0.06	0.4761	0.5239	0.9522	0.0478
0.07	0.4721	0.5279	0.9442	0.0558
0.08	0.4681	0.5319	0.9362	0.0638
0.09	0.4641	0.5359	0.9283	0.0717
0.10	0.4602	0.5398	0.9203	0.0797
0.11	0.4562	0.5438	0.9124	0.0876
0.12	0.4522	0.5478	0.9045	0.0955
0.13	0.4483	0.5517	0.8966	0.1034
0.14	0.4443	0.5557	0.8887	0.1113
0.15	0.4404	0.5596	0.8808	0.1192
0.16	0.4364	0.5636	0.8729	0.1271
0.17	0.4325	0.5675	0.8650	0.1350
0.18	0.4286	0.5714	0.8571	0.1429
0.19	0.4247	0.5753	0.8493	0.1507
0.20	0.4207	0.5793	0.8415	0.1585
0.21	0.4168	0.5832	0.8337	0.1663

	One tail		Two tail	
z	π beyond	π remainder	π beyond	π remainder
0.22	0.4129	0.5871	0.8259	0.1741
0.23	0.4090	0.5910	0.8181	0.1819
0.24	0.4052	0.5948	0.8103	0.1897
0.25	0.4013	0.5987	0.8026	0.1974
0.26	0.3974	0.6026	0.7949	0.2051
0.27	0.3936	0.6064	0.7872	0.2128
0.28	0.3897	0.6103	0.7795	0.2205
0.29	0.3859	0.6141	0.7718	0.2282
0.30	0.3821	0.6179	0.7642	0.2358
0.31	0.3783	0.6217	0.7566	0.2434
0.32	0.3745	0.6255	0.7490	0.2510
0.33	0.3707	0.6293	0.7414	0.2586
0.34	0.3669	0.6331	0.7339	0.2661
0.35	0.3632	0.6368	0.7263	0.2737
0.36	0.3594	0.6406	0.7188	0.2812
0.37	0.3557	0.6443	0.7114	0.2886
0.38	0.3520	0.6480	0.7039	0.2961
0.39	0.3483	0.6517	0.6965	0.3035
0.40	0.3446	0.6554	0.6892	0.3108
0.41	0.3409	0.6591	0.6818	0.3182
0.42	0.3372	0.6628	0.6745	0.3255
0.43	0.3336	0.6664	0.6672	0.3328
0.44	0.3300	0.6700	0.6599	0.3401
0.45	0.3264	0.6736	0.6527	0.3473
0.46	0.3228	0.6772	0.6455	0.3545
0.47	0.3192	0.6808	0.6384	0.3616
0.48	0.3156	0.6844	0.6312	0.3688
0.49	0.3121	0.6879	0.6241	0.3759
0.50	0.3085	0.6915	0.6171	0.3829
0.51	0.3050	0.6950	0.6101	0.3899
0.52	0.3015	0.8985	0.6031	0.3969
0.53	0.2981	0.7019	0.5961	0.4039
0.54	0.2946	0.7054	0.5892	0.4108
0.55	0.2912	0.7088	0.5823	0.4177
0.56	0.2877	0.7123	0.5755	0.4245
0.57	0.2843	0.7157	0.5687	0.4313
0.58	0.2810	0.7190	0.5619	0.4381
0.59	0.2776	0.7224	0.5552	0.4448
0.60	0.2743	0.7257	0.5485	0.4515
0.61	0.2709	0.7291	0.5419	0.4581

(Cont.)

Table A.2 (Continued)

z	One tail		Two tail	
	π beyond	π remainder	π beyond	π remainder
0.62	0.2676	0.7324	0.5353	0.4647
0.63	0.2643	0.7357	0.5287	0.4713
0.64	0.2611	0.7389	0.5222	0.4778
0.65	0.2578	0.7422	0.5157	0.4843
0.66	0.2546	0.7454	0.5093	0.4907
0.67	0.2514	0.7486	0.5029	0.4971
0.6745	0.25	0.75	0.50	0.50
0.68	0.2483	0.7517	0.4965	0.5035
0.69	0.2451	0.7549	0.4902	0.5098
0.70	0.2420	0.7580	0.4839	0.5161
0.71	0.2389	0.7611	0.4777	0.5223
0.72	0.2358	0.7642	0.4715	0.5285
0.73	0.2327	0.7673	0.4654	0.5346
0.74	0.2296	0.7704	0.4593	0.5407
0.75	0.2266	0.7734	0.4533	0.5467
0.76	0.2236	0.7764	0.4473	0.5527
0.77	0.2206	0.7794	0.4413	0.5587
0.78	0.2177	0.7823	0.4354	0.5646
0.79	0.2148	0.7852	0.4295	0.5705
0.80	0.2119	0.7881	0.4237	0.5763
0.81	0.2090	0.7910	0.4179	0.5821
0.82	0.2061	0.7939	0.4122	0.5878
0.83	0.2033	0.7967	0.4065	0.5935
0.84	0.2005	0.7995	0.4009	0.5991
0.8416	0.20	0.80	0.40	0.60
0.85	0.1997	0.8023	0.3953	0.6047
0.86	0.1949	0.8051	0.3898	0.6102
0.87	0.1922	0.8078	0.3843	0.6157
0.88	0.1894	0.8106	0.3789	0.6211
0.89	0.1867	0.8133	0.3735	0.6265
0.90	0.1841	0.8159	0.3681	0.6319
0.91	0.1814	0.8186	0.3628	0.6372
0.92	0.1788	0.8212	0.3576	0.6424
0.93	0.1762	0.8238	0.3524	0.6476
0.94	0.1736	0.8264	0.3472	0.6528
0.95	0.1711	0.8289	0.3421	0.6579
0.96	0.1685	0.8315	0.3371	0.6629
0.97	0.1660	0.8340	0.3320	0.6680
0.98	0.1635	0.8365	0.3271	0.6729
0.99	0.1611	0.8389	0.3222	0.6778

| z | One tail | | Two tail | |
	π beyond	π remainder	π beyond	π remainder
1.00	0.1587	0.8413	0.3173	0.6827
1.01	0.1562	0.8438	0.3125	0.6875
1.02	0.1539	0.8461	0.3077	0.6923
1.03	0.1515	0.8485	0.3030	0.6970
1.04	0.1492	0.8508	0.2983	0.7017
1.05	0.1469	0.8531	0.2937	0.7063
1.06	0.1446	0.8554	0.2891	0.7109
1.07	0.1423	0.8577	0.2846	0.7154
1.08	0.1401	0.8599	0.2801	0.7199
1.09	0.1379	0.6621	0.2757	0.7243
1.10	0.1357	0.8643	0.2713	0.7287
1.11	0.1335	0.8665	0.2670	0.7330
1.12	0.1314	0.8686	0.2627	0.7373
1.13	0.1292	0.8708	0.2585	0.7415
1.14	0.1271	0.8729	0.2543	0.7457
1.15	0.1251	0.8749	0.2501	0.7499
1.16	0.1230	0.8770	0.2460	0.7540
1.17	0.1210	0.8790	0.2420	0.7580
1.18	0.1190	0.8810	0.2380	0.7620
1.19	0.1170	0.8830	0.2340	0.7660
1.20	0.1151	0.8049	0.2301	0.7699
1.21	0.1131	0.8869	0.2263	0.7737
1.22	0.1112	0.8888	0.2225	0.7775
1.23	0.1093	0.8907	0.2187	0.7813
1.24	0.1075	0.8925	0.2150	0.7890
1.25	0.1056	0.8944	0.2113	0.7887
1.26	0.1038	0.8962	0.2077	0.7923
1.27	0.1020	0.8980	0.2041	0.7959
1.28	0.1003	0.8997	0.2005	0.7995
1.282	0.10	0.90	0.20	0.80
1.29	0.0985	0.9015	0.1971	0.8029
1.30	0.0968	0.9032	0.1936	0.8064
1.31	0.0951	0.9049	0.1902	0.8098
1.32	0.0934	0.9066	0.1868	0.8132
1.33	0.0918	0.9082	0.1835	0.8165
1.34	0.0901	0.9099	0.1802	0.8198
1.35	0.0885	0.9115	0.1770	0.8230
1.36	0.0869	0.9131	0.1738	0.8202
1.37	0.0853	0.9147	0.1707	0.8293
1.38	0.0838	0.9162	0.1676	0.8324

(Cont.)

Table A.2 (Continued)

z	One tail		Two tail	
	π beyond	π remainder	π beyond	π remainder
1.39	0.0823	0.9177	0.1645	0.8355
1.40	0.0808	0.9192	0.1615	0.8385
1.41	0.0793	0.9207	0.1585	0.8415
1.42	0.0778	0.9222	0.1556	0.8444
1.43	0.0764	0.9286	0.1527	0.8473
1.44	0.0749	0.9251	0.1499	0.8501
1.45	0.0735	0.9265	0.1471	0.8529
1.46	0.0721	0.9279	0.1443	0.8567
1.47	0.0708	0.9292	0.1416	0.8584
1.48	0.0694	0.9306	0.1389	0.8611
1.49	0.0681	0.9319	0.1362	0.8638
1.50	0.0668	0.9332	0.1336	0.8664
1.51	0.0655	0.9345	0.1310	0.8690
1.52	0.0643	0.9357	0.1285	0.8715
1.53	0.0630	0.9370	0.1260	0.8740
1.54	0.0618	0.9382	0.1236	0.8764
1.55	0.0606	0.9394	0.1211	0.8789
1.56	0.0594	0.9406	0.1188	0.8812
1.57	0.0582	0.9418	0.1164	0.8836
1.58	0.0571	0.9429	0.1141	0.8859
1.59	0.0559	0.9441	0.1118	0.8882
1.60	0.0548	0.9452	0.1096	0.8904
1.61	0.0537	0.9463	0.1074	0.8926
1.62	0.0526	0.9474	0.1052	0.8948
1.63	0.0516	0.9484	0.1031	0.8969
1.64	0.0505	0.9495	0.1010	0.8990
1.645	0.05	0.95	0.10	0.90
1.65	0.0495	0.9505	0.0989	0.9011
1.66	0.0485	0.9515	0.0969	0.9031
1.67	0.0475	0.9525	0.0949	0.9051
1.68	0.0465	0.9535	0.0930	0.9070
1.69	0.0455	0.9545	0.0910	0.9090
1.70	0.0446	0.9554	0.0891	0.9109
1.71	0.0436	0.9564	0.0873	0.9127
1.72	0.0427	0.9573	0.0854	0.9146
1.73	0.0418	0.9582	0.0836	0.9164
1.74	0.0409	0.9591	0.0819	0.9181
1.75	0.0401	0.9599	0.0801	0.9199
1.76	0.0392	0.9608	0.0784	0.9216
1.77	0.0384	0.9616	0.0767	0.9233

	One tail		Two tail	
z	π beyond	π remainder	π beyond	π remainder
1.78	0.0375	0.9625	0.0751	0.9249
1.79	0.0367	0.9633	0.0734	0.9266
1.80	0.0359	0.9641	0.0719	0.9281
1.81	0.0352	0.9649	0.0703	0.9297
1.82	0.0344	0.9656	0.0688	0.9312
1.83	0.0336	0.9664	0.0672	0.9328
1.84	0.0329	0.9671	0.0658	0.9342
1.85	0.0322	0.9678	0.0643	0.9357
1.86	0.0314	0.9686	0.0629	0.9371
1.87	0.0307	0.9693	0.0615	0.9385
1.88	0.0301	0.9699	0.0601	0.9399
1.89	0.0294	0.9706	0.0588	0.9412
1.90	0.0287	0.9713	0.0574	0.9426
1.91	0.0281	0.9719	0.0561	0.9439
1.92	0.0274	0.9726	0.0549	0.9451
1.93	0.0268	0.9732	0.0536	0.9464
1.94	0.0262	0.9738	0.0524	0.9476
1.95	0.0256	0.9744	0.0512	0.9488
1.960	0.025	0.975	0.05	0.95
1.97	0.0244	0.9756	0.0488	0.9512
1.98	0.0239	0.9761	0.0477	0.9523
1.99	0.0233	0.9767	0.0466	0.9534
2.00	0.0228	0.9772	0.0455	0.9545
2.01	0.0222	0.9778	0.0444	0.9556
2.02	0.0217	0.9783	0.0434	0.9566
2.03	0.0212	0.9788	0.0424	0.9576
2.04	0.0207	0.9793	0.0414	0.9586
2.05	0.0202	0.9798	0.0404	0.9596
2.054	0.02	0.98	0.04	0.96
2.06	0.0197	0.9803	0.0394	0.9606
2.07	0.0192	0.9808	0.0385	0.9615
2.08	0.0188	0.9812	0.0375	0.9625
2.09	0.0183	0.9817	0.0366	0.9634
2.10	0.0179	0.9821	0.0357	0.9643
2.11	0.0174	0.9826	0.0349	0.9651
2.12	0.0170	0.9830	0.0340	0.9660
2.13	0.0166	0.9834	0.0332	0.9668
2.14	0.0162	0.9838	0.0324	0.9676
2.15	0.0158	0.9842	0.0316	0.9684
2.16	0.0154	0.9846	0.0308	0.9692

(Cont.)

Table A.2 (Continued)

z	One tail		Two tail	
	π beyond	π remainder	π beyond	π remainder
2.17	0.0150	0.9850	0.0300	0.9700
2.18	0.0146	0.9854	0.0293	0.9707
2.19	0.0143	0.9857	0.0285	0.9715
2.20	0.0139	0.9661	0.0278	0.9722
2.21	0.0136	0.9864	0.0271	0.9729
2.22	0.0132	0.9868	0.0264	0.9736
2.23	0.0129	0.9871	0.0257	0.9743
2.24	0.0125	0.9875	0.0251	0.9749
2.25	0.0122	0.9878	0.0244	0.9756
2.26	0.0119	0.9881	0.0238	0.9762
2.27	0.0116	0.9884	0.0232	0.9768
2.28	0.0113	0.9887	0.0226	0.9774
2.29	0.0110	0.9890	0.0220	0.9780
2.30	0.0107	0.9893	0.0214	0.9786
2.31	0.0104	0.9896	0.0209	0.9791
2.32	0.0102	0.9898	0.0203	0.9797
2.326	0.01	0.99	0.02	0.98
2.33	0.0099	0.9901	0.0198	0.9802
2.34	0.0096	0.9904	0.0193	0.9807
2.35	0.0094	0.9906	0.0188	0.9812
2.36	0.0091	0.9909	0.0183	0.9817
2.37	0.0089	0.991	0.0178	0.9822
2.38	0.0087	0.9913	0.0173	0.9827
2.39	0.0084	0.9916	0.0168	0.9832
2.40	0.0082	0.9918	0.0164	0.9836
2.41	0.0080	0.9920	0.0160	0.9840
2.42	0.0078	0.9922	0.0155	0.9845
2.43	0.0075	0.9925	0.0151	0.9849
2.44	0.0073	0.9927	0.0147	0.9853
2.45	0.0071	0.9929	0.0143	0.9857
2.46	0.0069	0.9931	0.0139	0.9861
2.47	0.0068	0.9932	0.0135	0.9865
2.48	0.0066	0.9934	0.0131	0.9869
2.49	0.0064	0.9936	0.0128	0.9872
2.50	0.0062	0.9938	0.0124	0.9876
2.51	0.0060	0.9940	0.0121	0.9879
2.52	0.0059	0.9941	0.0117	0.9883
2.53	0.0057	0.9943	0.0114	0.9886
2.54	0.0055	0.9945	0.0111	0.9889
2.55	0.0054	0.9946	0.0108	0.9892

	One tail		Two tail	
z	π beyond	π remainder	π beyond	π remainder
2.56	0.0052	0.9948	0.0105	0.9895
2.57	0.0051	0.9949	0.0102	0.9898
2.576	0.005	0.995	0.01	0.99
2.58	0.0049	0.9951	0.0099	0.9901
2.59	0.0048	0.9952	0.0096	0.9904
2.60	0.0047	0.9953	0.0093	0.9907
2.61	0.0045	0.9955	0.0091	0.9909
2.62	0.0044	0.9956	0.0088	0.9912
2.63	0.0043	0.9957	0.0085	0.9915
2.64	0.0041	0.9959	0.0083	0.9917
2.65	0.0040	0.9960	0.0080	0.9920
2.70	0.0035	0.9965	0.0069	0.9931
2.75	0.0030	0.9970	0.0060	0.9940
2.80	0.0026	0.9974	0.0051	0.9949
2.85	0.0022	0.9978	0.0044	0.9956
2.90	0.0019	0.9981	0.0037	0.9963
2.95	0.0016	0.9984	0.0032	0.9968
3.00	0.0013	0.9987	0.0027	0.9973
3.05	0.0011	0.9989	0.0023	0.9977
3.090	0.001	0.999	0.002	0.998
3.10	0.0010	0.9990	0.0019	0.9981
3.15	0.0008	0.9992	0.0016	0.9984
3.20	0.0007	0.9993	0.0014	0.9988
3.25	0.0006	0.9994	0.0012	0.9986
3.291	0.0005	0.9995	0.001	0.999
3.30	0.0005	0.9995	0.0010	0.9990
3.35	0.0004	0.9996	0.0008	0.9992
3.40	0.0003	0.9997	0.0007	0.9993
3.45	0.0003	0.9997	0.0006	0.9994
3.50	0.0002	0.9998	0.0005	0.9995
3.55	0.0002	0.9998	0.0004	0.9996
3.60	0.0002	0.9998	0.0003	0.9997
3.65	0.0001	0.9999	0.0003	0.9997
3.719	0.0001	0.9999	0.0002	0.9998
3.80	0.0001	0.9999	0.0001	0.9999
3.891	0.00005	0.99995	0.0001	0.9999
4.000	0.00003	0.99997	0.00006	0.99994
4.265	0.00001	0.99999	0.00002	0.99998

*Adapted from Pearson, E.S., and Hartley, H.O.: Biometrika tables for statisticians, vol. 1, ed. 3, London, 1966, Cambridge University Press.

Table A.3 Critical Values of Correlation Coefficients

	Level of significance for one-tailed test				
	.05	.025	.01	.005	.0005
	Level of significance for two-tailed test				
df = N − 2	.10	.05	.02	.01	.001
1	.9877	.9969	.9995	.9999	1.0000
2	.9000	.9500	.9800	.9900	.9990
3	.8054	.8783	.9343	.9587	.9912
4	.7293	.8114	.8822	.9172	.9741
5	.6694	.7545	.8329	.8745	.9507
6	.6215	.7067	.7887	.8343	.9249
7	.5822	.6664	.7498	.7977	.8982
8	.5494	.6319	.7155	.7646	.8721
9	.5214	.6021	.6851	.7348	.8471
10	.4973	.5760	.6581	.7079	.8233
11	.4762	.5529	.6339	.6835	.8010
12	.4575	.5324	.6120	.6614	.7800
13	.4409	.5139	.5923	.6411	.7603
14	.4259	.4973	.5742	.6226	.7420
15	.4124	.4821	.5577	.6055	.7246
16	.4000	.4683	.5425	.5897	.7084
17	.3887	.4555	.5285	.5751	.6932
18	.3783	.4438	.5155	.5614	.6787
19	.3687	.4329	.5034	.5487	.6652
20	.3598	.4227	.4921	.5368	.6524
25	.3233	.3809	.4451	.4869	.5974
30	.2960	.3494	.4093	.4487	.5541
35	.2746	.3246	.3810	.4182	.5189
40	.2573	.3044	.3578	.3932	.4896
45	.2428	.2875	.3384	.3721	.4648
50	.2306	.2732	.3218	.3541	.4433
60	.2108	.2500	.2948	.3248	.4078
70	.1954	.2319	.2737	.3017	.3799
80	.1829	.2172	.2565	.2830	.3568
90	.1726	.2050	.2422	.2673	.3375
100	.1638	.1946	.2301	.2540	.3211

*Table A.3 is taken from Table VII of Fisher & Yates, *Statistical Tables for Biological, Agricultural and Medical Research*, published by Longman Group Ltd. London (previously published by Oliver and Boyd, Ltd., Edinburgh), and by permission of the authors and the publishers.

Table A.4 Transformation of r to z_r

r	z_r	r	z_r	r	z_r	r	z_r	r	z_r
.000	.000	.200	.203	.400	.424	.600	.693	.800	1.099
.005	.005	.205	.208	.405	.430	.605	.701	.805	1.113
.010	.010	.210	.213	.410	.436	.610	.709	.810	1.127
.015	.015	.215	.218	.415	.442	.615	.717	.815	1.142
.020	.020	.220	.224	.420	.448	.620	.725	.820	1.157
.025	.025	.225	.229	.425	.454	.625	.733	.825	1.172
.030	.030	.230	.234	.430	.460	.630	.741	.830	1.188
.035	.035	.235	.239	.435	.466	.635	.750	.835	1.204
.040	.040	.240	.245	.440	.472	.640	.758	.840	1.221
.045	.045	.245	.250	.445	.478	.645	.767	.845	1.238
.050	.050	.250	.255	.450	.485	.650	.775	.850	1.256
.055	.055	.255	.261	.455	.491	.655	.784	.855	1.274
.060	.060	.260	.266	.460	.497	.660	.793	.860	1.293
.065	.065	.265	.271	.465	.504	.665	.802	.865	1.313
.070	.070	.270	.277	.470	.510	.670	.811	.870	1.333
.075	.075	.275	.282	.475	.517	.675	.820	.875	1.354
.080	.080	.280	.288	.480	.523	.680	.829	.880	1.376
.085	.085	.285	.293	.485	.530	.685	.838	.885	1.398
.090	.090	.290	.299	.490	.536	.690	.848	.890	1.422
.095	.095	.295	.304	.495	.543	.695	.858	.895	1.447
.100	.100	.300	.310	.500	.549	.700	.867	.900	1.472
.105	.105	.305	.315	.505	.556	.705	.877	.905	1.499
.110	.110	.310	.321	.510	.563	.710	.887	.910	1.528
.115	.116	.315	.326	.515	.570	.715	.897	.915	1.557
.120	.121	.320	.332	.520	.576	.720	.908	.920	1.589
.125	.126	.325	.337	.525	.583	.725	.918	.925	1.623
.130	.131	.330	.343	.530	.590	.730	.929	.930	1.658
.135	.136	.335	.348	.535	.597	.735	.940	.935	1.697
.140	.141	.340	.354	.540	.604	.740	.950	.940	1.738
.145	.146	.345	.360	.545	.611	.745	.962	.945	1.783
.150	.151	.350	.365	.550	.618	.750	.973	.950	1.832
.155	.156	.355	.371	.555	.626	.755	.984	.955	1.886
.160	.161	.360	.377	.560	.633	.760	.996	.960	1.946
.165	.167	.365	.383	.565	.640	.765	1.008	.965	2.014
.170	.172	.370	.388	.570	.648	.770	1.020	.970	2.092
.175	.177	.375	.394	.575	.655	.775	1.033	.975	2.185
.180	.182	.380	.400	.580	.662	.780	1.045	.980	2.298
.185	.187	.385	.406	.585	.670	.785	1.058	.985	2.443
.190	.192	.390	.412	.590	.678	.790	1.071	.990	2.647
.195	.198	.395	.418	.595	.685	.795	1.085	.995	2.994

*Reprinted, by permission, from Allen L. Edwards, *Statistical methods*, 2nd ed., Holt, Rinehart, and Winston, Inc., New York, 1967.

Table A.5 Critical Values of *t*

df	Level of significance for one-tailed test					
	.10	.05	.025	.01	.005	.0005
	Level of significance for two-tailed test					
	.20	.10	.05	.02	.01	.001
1	3.078	6.314	12.706	31.821	63.657	636.619
2	1.886	2.920	4.303	6.965	9.925	31.598
3	1.638	2.353	3.182	4.541	5.841	12.941
4	1.533	2.132	2.776	3.747	4.604	8.610
5	1.476	2.015	2.571	3.365	4.032	6.859
6	1.440	1.943	2.447	3.143	3.707	5.959
7	1.415	1.895	2.365	2.998	3.499	5.405
8	1.397	1.860	2.306	2.896	3.355	5.041
9	1.383	1.833	2.262	2.821	3.250	4.781
10	1.372	1.812	2.228	2.764	3.169	4.587
11	1.363	1.796	2.201	2.718	3.106	4.437
12	1.356	1.782	2.179	2.681	3.055	4.318
13	1.350	1.771	2.160	2.650	3.012	4.221
14	1.345	1.761	2.145	2.624	2.977	4.140
15	1.341	1.753	2.131	2.602	2.947	4.073
16	1.337	1.746	2.120	2.583	2.921	4.015
17	1.333	1.740	2.110	2.567	2.898	3.965
18	1.330	1.734	2.101	2.552	2.878	3.922
19	1.328	1.729	2.093	2.539	2.861	3.883
20	1.325	1.725	2.086	2.528	2.845	3.850
21	1.323	1.721	2.080	2.518	2.831	3.819
22	1.321	1.717	2.074	2.508	2.819	3.792
23	1.319	1.714	2.069	2.500	2.807	3.767
24	1.318	1.711	2.064	2.492	2.797	3.745
25	1.316	1.708	2.060	2.485	2.787	3.725
26	1.315	1.706	2.056	2.479	2.779	3.707
27	1.314	1.703	2.052	2.473	2.771	3.690
28	1.313	1.701	2.048	2.467	2.763	3.674
29	1.311	1.699	2.045	2.462	2.756	3.659
30	1.310	1.697	2.042	2.457	2.750	3.646
40	1.303	1.684	2.021	2.423	2.704	3.551
60	1.296	1.671	2.000	2.390	2.660	3.460
120	1.289	1.658	1.980	2.358	2.617	3.373
∞	1.282	1.645	1.960	2.326	2.576	3.291

*Table A.5 is abridged from Table III of Fisher & Yates, *Statistical Tables for Biological, Agricultural and Medical Research*, published by Longman Group Ltd. London (previously published by Oliver and Boyd, Ltd., Edinburgh), and by permission of the authors and the publishers.

Table A.6 Critical Values of F

n_1 degrees of freedom (for greater mean square)

n_2	1	2	3	4	5	6	7	8	9	10	11	12	14	16	20	24	30	40	50	75	100	200	500	∞
1	161 4,052	200 4,999	216 5,403	225 5,625	230 5,764	234 5,859	237 5,928	239 5,981	241 6,022	242 6,056	243 6,082	244 6,106	245 6,142	246 6,169	248 6,208	249 6,234	250 6,258	251 6,286	252 6,302	253 6,323	253 6,334	254 6,352	254 6,361	254 6,366
2	18.51 98.49	19.00 99.00	19.16 99.17	19.25 99.25	19.30 99.30	19.33 99.33	19.36 99.34	19.37 99.36	19.38 99.38	19.39 99.40	19.40 99.41	19.41 99.42	19.42 99.43	19.43 99.44	19.44 99.45	19.45 99.46	19.46 99.47	19.47 99.48	19.47 99.48	19.48 99.49	19.49 99.49	19.49 99.49	19.50 99.50	19.50 99.50
3	10.13 34.12	9.55 30.82	9.28 29.46	9.12 28.71	9.01 28.24	8.94 27.91	8.88 27.67	8.84 27.49	8.81 27.34	8.78 27.23	8.76 27.13	8.74 27.05	8.71 26.92	8.69 26.83	8.66 26.69	8.64 26.60	8.62 26.50	8.60 26.41	8.58 26.35	8.57 26.27	8.56 26.23	8.54 26.18	8.54 26.14	8.53 26.12
4	7.71 21.20	6.94 18.00	6.59 16.69	6.39 15.98	6.26 15.52	6.16 15.21	6.09 14.98	6.04 14.80	6.00 14.66	5.96 14.54	5.93 14.45	5.91 14.37	5.87 14.24	5.84 14.15	5.80 14.02	5.77 13.93	5.74 13.83	5.71 13.74	5.70 13.69	5.68 13.61	5.66 13.57	5.65 13.52	5.64 13.48	5.63 13.46
5	6.61 16.26	5.79 13.27	5.41 12.06	5.19 11.39	5.05 10.97	4.95 10.67	4.88 10.45	4.82 10.27	4.78 10.15	4.74 10.05	4.70 9.96	4.68 9.89	4.64 9.77	4.60 9.68	4.56 9.55	4.53 9.47	4.50 9.38	4.46 9.29	4.44 9.24	4.42 9.17	4.40 9.13	4.38 9.07	4.37 9.04	4.36 9.02
6	5.99 13.74	5.14 10.92	4.76 9.78	4.53 9.15	4.39 8.75	4.28 8.47	4.21 8.26	4.15 8.10	4.10 7.98	4.06 7.87	4.03 7.79	4.00 7.72	3.96 7.60	3.92 7.52	3.87 7.39	3.84 7.31	3.81 7.23	3.77 7.14	3.75 7.09	3.72 7.02	3.71 6.99	3.69 6.94	3.68 6.90	3.67 6.88
7	5.59 12.25	4.74 9.55	4.35 8.45	4.12 7.85	3.97 7.46	3.87 7.19	3.79 7.00	3.73 6.84	3.68 6.71	3.63 6.62	3.60 6.54	3.57 6.47	3.52 6.35	3.49 6.27	3.44 6.15	3.41 6.07	3.38 5.98	3.34 5.90	3.32 5.85	3.29 5.78	3.28 5.75	3.25 5.70	3.24 5.67	3.23 5.65
8	5.32 11.26	4.46 8.65	4.07 7.59	3.84 7.01	3.69 6.63	3.58 6.37	3.50 6.19	3.44 6.03	3.39 5.91	3.34 5.82	3.31 5.74	3.28 5.67	3.23 5.56	3.20 5.48	3.15 5.36	3.12 5.28	3.08 5.20	3.05 5.11	3.03 5.06	3.00 5.00	2.98 4.96	2.96 4.91	2.94 4.88	2.93 4.86
9	5.12 10.56	4.26 8.02	3.86 6.99	3.63 6.42	3.48 6.06	3.37 5.80	3.29 5.62	3.23 5.47	3.18 5.35	3.13 5.26	3.10 5.18	3.07 5.11	3.02 5.00	2.98 4.92	2.93 4.80	2.90 4.73	2.86 4.64	2.82 4.56	2.80 4.51	2.77 4.45	2.76 4.41	2.73 4.36	2.72 4.33	2.71 4.31
10	4.96 10.04	4.10 7.56	3.71 6.55	3.48 5.99	3.33 5.64	3.22 5.39	3.14 5.21	3.07 5.06	3.02 4.95	2.97 4.85	2.94 4.78	2.91 4.71	2.86 4.60	2.82 4.52	2.77 4.41	2.74 4.33	2.70 4.25	2.67 4.17	2.64 4.12	2.61 4.05	2.59 4.01	2.56 3.96	2.55 3.93	2.54 3.91
11	4.84 9.65	3.98 7.20	3.59 6.22	3.36 5.67	3.20 5.32	3.09 5.07	3.01 4.88	2.95 4.74	2.90 4.63	2.86 4.54	2.82 4.46	2.79 4.40	2.74 4.29	2.70 4.21	2.65 4.10	2.61 4.02	2.57 3.94	2.53 3.86	2.50 3.80	2.47 3.74	2.45 3.70	2.42 3.66	2.41 3.62	2.40 3.60
12	4.75 9.33	3.88 6.93	3.49 5.95	3.26 5.41	3.11 5.06	3.00 4.82	2.92 4.65	2.85 4.50	2.80 4.39	2.76 4.30	2.72 4.22	2.69 4.16	2.64 4.05	2.60 3.98	2.54 3.86	2.50 3.78	2.46 3.70	2.42 3.61	2.40 3.56	2.36 3.49	2.35 3.46	2.32 3.41	2.31 3.38	2.30 3.36
13	4.67 9.07	3.80 6.70	3.41 5.74	3.18 5.20	3.02 4.86	2.92 4.62	2.84 4.44	2.77 4.30	2.72 4.19	2.67 4.10	2.63 4.02	2.60 3.96	2.55 3.85	2.51 3.78	2.46 3.67	2.42 3.59	2.38 3.51	2.34 3.42	2.32 3.37	2.28 3.30	2.26 3.27	2.24 3.21	2.22 3.18	2.21 3.16
14	4.60 8.86	3.74 6.51	3.34 5.56	3.11 5.03	2.96 4.69	2.85 4.46	2.77 4.28	2.70 4.14	2.65 4.03	2.60 3.94	2.56 3.86	2.53 3.80	2.48 3.70	2.44 3.62	2.39 3.51	2.35 3.43	2.31 3.34	2.27 3.26	2.24 3.21	2.21 3.14	2.19 3.11	2.16 3.06	2.14 3.02	2.13 3.00
15	4.54 8.68	3.68 6.36	3.29 5.42	3.06 4.89	2.90 4.56	2.79 4.32	2.70 4.14	2.64 4.00	2.59 3.89	2.55 3.80	2.51 3.73	2.48 3.67	2.43 3.56	2.39 3.48	2.33 3.36	2.29 3.29	2.25 3.20	2.21 3.12	2.18 3.07	2.15 3.00	2.12 2.97	2.10 2.92	2.08 2.89	2.07 2.87
16	4.49 8.53	3.63 6.23	3.24 5.29	3.01 4.77	2.85 4.44	2.74 4.20	2.66 4.03	2.59 3.89	2.54 3.78	2.49 3.69	2.45 3.61	2.42 3.55	2.37 3.45	2.33 3.37	2.28 3.25	2.24 3.18	2.20 3.10	2.16 3.01	2.13 2.96	2.09 2.89	2.07 2.86	2.04 2.80	2.02 2.77	2.01 2.75

(Cont.)

Table A.6 (Continued)

n_1 degrees of freedom (for greater mean square)

n_2	1	2	3	4	5	6	7	8	9	10	11	12	14	16	20	24	30	40	50	75	100	200	500	∞
17	4.45 / 8.40	3.59 / 6.11	3.20 / 5.18	2.96 / 4.67	2.81 / 4.34	2.70 / 4.10	2.62 / 3.93	2.55 / 3.79	2.50 / 3.68	2.45 / 3.59	2.41 / 3.52	2.38 / 3.45	2.33 / 3.35	2.29 / 3.27	2.23 / 3.16	2.19 / 3.08	2.15 / 3.00	2.11 / 2.92	2.08 / 2.86	2.04 / 2.79	2.02 / 2.76	1.99 / 2.70	1.97 / 2.67	1.96 / 2.65
18	4.41 / 8.28	3.55 / 6.01	3.16 / 5.09	2.93 / 4.58	2.77 / 4.25	2.66 / 4.01	2.58 / 3.85	2.51 / 3.71	2.46 / 3.60	2.41 / 3.51	2.37 / 3.44	2.34 / 3.37	2.29 / 3.27	2.25 / 3.19	2.19 / 3.07	2.15 / 3.00	2.11 / 2.91	2.07 / 2.83	2.04 / 2.78	2.00 / 2.71	1.98 / 2.68	1.95 / 2.62	1.93 / 2.59	1.92 / 2.57
19	4.38 / 8.18	3.52 / 5.93	3.13 / 5.01	2.90 / 4.50	2.74 / 4.17	2.63 / 3.94	2.55 / 3.77	2.48 / 3.63	2.43 / 3.52	2.38 / 3.43	2.34 / 3.36	2.31 / 3.30	2.26 / 3.19	2.21 / 3.12	2.15 / 3.00	2.11 / 2.92	2.07 / 2.84	2.02 / 2.76	2.00 / 2.70	1.96 / 2.63	1.94 / 2.60	1.91 / 2.54	1.90 / 2.51	1.88 / 2.49
20	4.35 / 8.10	3.49 / 5.85	3.10 / 4.94	2.87 / 4.43	2.71 / 4.10	2.60 / 3.87	2.52 / 3.71	2.45 / 3.56	2.40 / 3.45	2.35 / 3.37	2.31 / 3.30	2.28 / 3.23	2.23 / 3.13	2.18 / 3.05	2.12 / 2.94	2.08 / 2.86	2.04 / 2.77	1.99 / 2.69	1.96 / 2.63	1.92 / 2.56	1.90 / 2.53	1.87 / 2.47	1.85 / 2.44	1.84 / 2.42
21	4.32 / 8.02	3.47 / 5.78	3.07 / 4.87	2.84 / 4.37	2.68 / 4.04	2.57 / 3.81	2.49 / 3.65	2.42 / 3.51	2.37 / 3.40	2.32 / 3.31	2.28 / 3.24	2.25 / 3.17	2.20 / 3.07	2.15 / 2.99	2.09 / 2.88	2.05 / 2.80	2.00 / 2.72	1.96 / 2.63	1.93 / 2.58	1.89 / 2.51	1.87 / 2.47	1.84 / 2.42	1.82 / 2.38	1.81 / 2.36
22	4.30 / 7.94	3.44 / 5.72	3.05 / 4.82	2.82 / 4.31	2.66 / 3.99	2.55 / 3.76	2.47 / 3.59	2.40 / 3.45	2.35 / 3.35	2.30 / 3.26	2.26 / 3.18	2.23 / 3.12	2.18 / 3.02	2.13 / 2.94	2.07 / 2.83	2.03 / 2.75	1.98 / 2.67	1.93 / 2.58	1.91 / 2.53	1.87 / 2.46	1.84 / 2.42	1.81 / 2.37	1.80 / 2.33	1.78 / 2.31
23	4.28 / 7.88	3.42 / 5.66	3.03 / 4.76	2.80 / 4.26	2.64 / 3.94	2.53 / 3.71	2.45 / 3.54	2.38 / 3.41	2.32 / 3.30	2.28 / 3.21	2.24 / 3.14	2.20 / 3.07	2.14 / 2.97	2.10 / 2.89	2.04 / 2.78	2.00 / 2.70	1.96 / 2.62	1.91 / 2.53	1.88 / 2.48	1.84 / 2.41	1.82 / 2.37	1.79 / 2.32	1.77 / 2.28	1.76 / 2.26
24	4.26 / 7.82	3.40 / 5.61	3.01 / 4.72	2.78 / 4.22	2.62 / 3.90	2.51 / 3.67	2.43 / 3.50	2.36 / 3.36	2.30 / 3.25	2.26 / 3.17	2.22 / 3.09	2.18 / 3.03	2.13 / 2.93	2.09 / 2.85	2.02 / 2.74	1.98 / 2.66	1.94 / 2.58	1.89 / 2.49	1.86 / 2.44	1.82 / 2.36	1.80 / 2.33	1.76 / 2.27	1.74 / 2.23	1.73 / 2.21
25	4.24 / 7.77	3.38 / 5.57	2.99 / 4.68	2.76 / 4.18	2.60 / 3.86	2.49 / 3.63	2.41 / 3.46	2.34 / 3.32	2.28 / 3.21	2.24 / 3.13	2.20 / 3.05	2.16 / 2.99	2.11 / 2.89	2.06 / 2.81	2.00 / 2.70	1.96 / 2.62	1.92 / 2.54	1.87 / 2.45	1.84 / 2.40	1.80 / 2.32	1.77 / 2.29	1.74 / 2.23	1.72 / 2.19	1.71 / 2.17
26	4.22 / 7.72	3.37 / 5.53	2.98 / 4.64	2.74 / 4.14	2.59 / 3.82	2.47 / 3.59	2.39 / 3.42	2.32 / 3.29	2.27 / 3.17	2.22 / 3.09	2.18 / 3.02	2.15 / 2.96	2.10 / 2.86	2.05 / 2.77	1.99 / 2.66	1.95 / 2.58	1.90 / 2.50	1.85 / 2.41	1.82 / 2.36	1.78 / 2.28	1.76 / 2.25	1.72 / 2.19	1.70 / 2.15	1.69 / 2.13
27	4.21 / 7.68	3.35 / 5.49	2.96 / 4.60	2.73 / 4.11	2.57 / 3.79	2.46 / 3.56	2.37 / 3.39	2.30 / 3.26	2.25 / 3.14	2.20 / 3.06	2.16 / 2.98	2.13 / 2.93	2.08 / 2.83	2.03 / 2.74	1.97 / 2.63	1.93 / 2.55	1.88 / 2.47	1.84 / 2.38	1.80 / 2.33	1.76 / 2.25	1.74 / 2.21	1.71 / 2.16	1.68 / 2.12	1.67 / 2.10
28	4.20 / 7.64	3.34 / 5.45	2.95 / 4.57	2.71 / 4.07	2.56 / 3.76	2.44 / 3.53	2.36 / 3.36	2.29 / 3.23	2.24 / 3.11	2.19 / 3.03	2.15 / 2.95	2.12 / 2.90	2.06 / 2.80	2.02 / 2.71	1.96 / 2.60	1.91 / 2.52	1.87 / 2.44	1.81 / 2.35	1.78 / 2.30	1.75 / 2.22	1.72 / 2.18	1.69 / 2.13	1.67 / 2.09	1.65 / 2.06
29	4.18 / 7.60	3.33 / 5.42	2.93 / 4.54	2.70 / 4.04	2.54 / 3.73	2.43 / 3.50	2.35 / 3.33	2.28 / 3.20	2.22 / 3.08	2.18 / 3.00	2.14 / 2.92	2.10 / 2.87	2.05 / 2.77	2.00 / 2.68	1.94 / 2.57	1.90 / 2.49	1.85 / 2.41	1.80 / 2.32	1.77 / 2.27	1.73 / 2.19	1.71 / 2.15	1.68 / 2.10	1.65 / 2.06	1.64 / 2.03
30	4.17 / 7.56	3.32 / 5.39	2.92 / 4.51	2.69 / 4.02	2.53 / 3.70	2.42 / 3.47	2.34 / 3.30	2.27 / 3.17	2.21 / 3.06	2.16 / 2.98	2.12 / 2.90	2.09 / 2.84	2.04 / 2.74	1.99 / 2.66	1.93 / 2.55	1.89 / 2.47	1.84 / 2.38	1.79 / 2.29	1.76 / 2.24	1.72 / 2.16	1.69 / 2.13	1.66 / 2.07	1.64 / 2.03	1.62 / 2.01
32	4.15 / 7.50	3.30 / 5.34	2.90 / 4.46	2.67 / 3.97	2.51 / 3.66	2.40 / 3.42	2.32 / 3.25	2.25 / 3.12	2.19 / 3.01	2.14 / 2.94	2.10 / 2.86	2.07 / 2.80	2.02 / 2.70	1.97 / 2.62	1.91 / 2.51	1.86 / 2.42	1.82 / 2.34	1.76 / 2.25	1.74 / 2.20	1.69 / 2.12	1.67 / 2.08	1.64 / 2.02	1.61 / 1.98	1.59 / 1.96
34	4.13 / 7.44	3.28 / 5.29	2.88 / 4.42	2.65 / 3.93	2.49 / 3.61	2.38 / 3.38	2.30 / 3.21	2.23 / 3.08	2.17 / 2.97	2.12 / 2.89	2.08 / 2.82	2.05 / 2.76	2.00 / 2.66	1.95 / 2.58	1.89 / 2.47	1.84 / 2.38	1.80 / 2.30	1.74 / 2.21	1.71 / 2.15	1.67 / 2.08	1.64 / 2.04	1.61 / 1.98	1.59 / 1.94	1.57 / 1.91
36	4.11 / 7.39	3.26 / 5.25	2.86 / 4.38	2.63 / 3.89	2.48 / 3.58	2.36 / 3.35	2.28 / 3.18	2.21 / 3.04	2.15 / 2.94	2.10 / 2.86	2.06 / 2.78	2.03 / 2.72	1.98 / 2.62	1.93 / 2.54	1.87 / 2.43	1.82 / 2.35	1.78 / 2.26	1.72 / 2.17	1.69 / 2.12	1.65 / 2.04	1.62 / 2.00	1.59 / 1.94	1.56 / 1.90	1.55 / 1.87

df																								
38	4.10 / 7.35	3.25 / 5.21	2.85 / 4.34	2.62 / 3.86	2.46 / 3.54	2.35 / 3.32	2.26 / 3.15	2.19 / 3.02	2.14 / 2.91	2.09 / 2.82	2.05 / 2.75	2.02 / 2.69	1.96 / 2.59	1.92 / 2.51	1.85 / 2.40	1.80 / 2.32	1.76 / 2.22	1.71 / 2.14	1.67 / 2.08	1.63 / 2.00	1.60 / 1.97	1.57 / 1.90	1.54 / 1.86	1.53 / 1.84
40	4.08 / 7.31	3.23 / 5.18	2.84 / 4.31	2.61 / 3.83	2.45 / 3.51	2.34 / 3.29	2.25 / 3.12	2.18 / 2.99	2.12 / 2.88	2.07 / 2.80	2.04 / 2.73	2.00 / 2.66	1.95 / 2.56	1.90 / 2.49	1.84 / 2.37	1.79 / 2.29	1.74 / 2.20	1.69 / 2.11	1.66 / 2.05	1.61 / 1.97	1.59 / 1.94	1.55 / 1.88	1.53 / 1.84	1.51 / 1.81
42	4.07 / 7.27	3.22 / 5.15	2.83 / 4.29	2.59 / 3.80	2.44 / 3.49	2.32 / 3.26	2.24 / 3.10	2.17 / 2.96	2.11 / 2.86	2.06 / 2.77	2.02 / 2.70	1.99 / 2.64	1.94 / 2.54	1.89 / 2.46	1.82 / 2.35	1.78 / 2.26	1.73 / 2.17	1.68 / 2.08	1.64 / 2.02	1.60 / 1.94	1.57 / 1.91	1.54 / 1.85	1.51 / 1.80	1.49 / 1.78
44	4.06 / 7.24	3.21 / 5.12	2.82 / 4.26	2.58 / 3.78	2.43 / 3.46	2.31 / 3.24	2.23 / 3.07	2.16 / 2.94	2.10 / 2.84	2.05 / 2.75	2.01 / 2.68	1.98 / 2.62	1.92 / 2.52	1.88 / 2.44	1.81 / 2.32	1.76 / 2.24	1.72 / 2.15	1.66 / 2.06	1.63 / 2.00	1.58 / 1.92	1.56 / 1.88	1.52 / 1.82	1.50 / 1.78	1.48 / 1.75
46	4.05 / 7.21	3.20 / 5.10	2.81 / 4.24	2.57 / 3.76	2.42 / 3.44	2.30 / 3.22	2.22 / 3.05	2.14 / 2.92	2.09 / 2.82	2.04 / 2.73	2.00 / 2.66	1.97 / 2.60	1.91 / 2.50	1.87 / 2.42	1.80 / 2.30	1.75 / 2.22	1.71 / 2.13	1.65 / 2.04	1.62 / 1.98	1.57 / 1.90	1.54 / 1.86	1.51 / 1.80	1.48 / 1.76	1.46 / 1.72
48	4.04 / 7.19	3.19 / 5.08	2.80 / 4.22	2.56 / 3.74	2.41 / 3.42	2.30 / 3.20	2.21 / 3.04	2.14 / 2.90	2.08 / 2.80	2.03 / 2.71	1.99 / 2.64	1.96 / 2.58	1.90 / 2.48	1.86 / 2.40	1.79 / 2.28	1.74 / 2.20	1.70 / 2.11	1.64 / 2.02	1.61 / 1.96	1.56 / 1.88	1.53 / 1.84	1.50 / 1.78	1.47 / 1.73	1.45 / 1.70
50	4.03 / 7.17	3.18 / 5.06	2.79 / 4.20	2.56 / 3.72	2.40 / 3.41	2.29 / 3.18	2.20 / 3.02	2.13 / 2.88	2.07 / 2.78	2.02 / 2.70	1.98 / 2.62	1.95 / 2.56	1.90 / 2.46	1.85 / 2.39	1.78 / 2.26	1.74 / 2.18	1.69 / 2.10	1.63 / 2.00	1.60 / 1.94	1.55 / 1.86	1.52 / 1.82	1.48 / 1.76	1.46 / 1.71	1.44 / 1.68
55	4.02 / 7.12	3.17 / 5.01	2.78 / 4.16	2.54 / 3.68	2.38 / 3.37	2.27 / 3.15	2.18 / 2.98	2.11 / 2.85	2.05 / 2.75	2.00 / 2.66	1.97 / 2.59	1.93 / 2.53	1.88 / 2.43	1.83 / 2.35	1.76 / 2.23	1.72 / 2.15	1.67 / 2.06	1.61 / 1.96	1.58 / 1.90	1.52 / 1.82	1.50 / 1.78	1.46 / 1.71	1.43 / 1.66	1.41 / 1.64
60	4.00 / 7.08	3.15 / 4.98	2.76 / 4.13	2.52 / 3.65	2.37 / 3.34	2.25 / 3.12	2.17 / 2.95	2.10 / 2.82	2.04 / 2.72	1.99 / 2.63	1.95 / 2.56	1.92 / 2.50	1.86 / 2.40	1.81 / 2.32	1.75 / 2.20	1.70 / 2.12	1.65 / 2.03	1.59 / 1.93	1.56 / 1.87	1.50 / 1.79	1.48 / 1.74	1.44 / 1.68	1.41 / 1.63	1.39 / 1.60
65	3.99 / 7.04	3.14 / 4.95	2.75 / 4.10	2.51 / 3.62	2.36 / 3.31	2.24 / 3.09	2.15 / 2.93	2.08 / 2.79	2.02 / 2.70	1.98 / 2.61	1.94 / 2.54	1.90 / 2.47	1.85 / 2.37	1.80 / 2.30	1.73 / 2.18	1.68 / 2.09	1.63 / 2.00	1.57 / 1.90	1.54 / 1.84	1.49 / 1.76	1.46 / 1.71	1.42 / 1.64	1.39 / 1.60	1.37 / 1.56
70	3.98 / 7.01	3.13 / 4.92	2.74 / 4.08	2.50 / 3.60	2.35 / 3.29	2.23 / 3.07	2.14 / 2.91	2.07 / 2.77	2.01 / 2.67	1.97 / 2.59	1.93 / 2.51	1.89 / 2.45	1.84 / 2.35	1.79 / 2.28	1.72 / 2.15	1.67 / 2.07	1.62 / 1.98	1.56 / 1.88	1.53 / 1.82	1.47 / 1.74	1.45 / 1.69	1.40 / 1.62	1.37 / 1.56	1.35 / 1.53
80	3.96 / 6.96	3.11 / 4.88	2.72 / 4.04	2.48 / 3.56	2.33 / 3.25	2.21 / 3.04	2.12 / 2.87	2.05 / 2.74	1.99 / 2.64	1.95 / 2.55	1.91 / 2.48	1.88 / 2.41	1.82 / 2.32	1.77 / 2.24	1.70 / 2.11	1.65 / 2.03	1.60 / 1.94	1.54 / 1.84	1.51 / 1.78	1.45 / 1.70	1.42 / 1.65	1.38 / 1.57	1.35 / 1.52	1.32 / 1.49
100	3.94 / 6.90	3.09 / 4.82	2.70 / 3.98	2.46 / 3.51	2.30 / 3.20	2.19 / 2.99	2.10 / 2.82	2.03 / 2.69	1.97 / 2.59	1.92 / 2.51	1.88 / 2.43	1.85 / 2.36	1.79 / 2.26	1.75 / 2.19	1.68 / 2.06	1.63 / 1.98	1.57 / 1.89	1.51 / 1.79	1.48 / 1.73	1.42 / 1.64	1.39 / 1.59	1.34 / 1.51	1.30 / 1.46	1.28 / 1.43
125	3.92 / 6.84	3.07 / 4.78	2.68 / 3.94	2.44 / 3.47	2.29 / 3.17	2.17 / 2.95	2.08 / 2.79	2.01 / 2.65	1.95 / 2.56	1.90 / 2.47	1.86 / 2.40	1.83 / 2.33	1.77 / 2.23	1.72 / 2.15	1.65 / 2.03	1.60 / 1.94	1.55 / 1.85	1.49 / 1.75	1.45 / 1.68	1.39 / 1.59	1.36 / 1.54	1.31 / 1.46	1.27 / 1.40	1.25 / 1.37
150	3.91 / 6.81	3.06 / 4.75	2.67 / 3.91	2.43 / 3.44	2.27 / 3.14	2.16 / 2.92	2.07 / 2.76	2.00 / 2.62	1.94 / 2.53	1.89 / 2.44	1.85 / 2.37	1.82 / 2.30	1.76 / 2.20	1.71 / 2.12	1.64 / 2.00	1.59 / 1.91	1.54 / 1.83	1.47 / 1.72	1.44 / 1.66	1.37 / 1.56	1.34 / 1.51	1.29 / 1.43	1.25 / 1.37	1.22 / 1.33
200	3.89 / 6.76	3.04 / 4.71	2.65 / 3.88	2.41 / 3.41	2.26 / 3.11	2.14 / 2.90	2.05 / 2.73	1.98 / 2.60	1.92 / 2.50	1.87 / 2.41	1.83 / 2.34	1.80 / 2.28	1.74 / 2.17	1.69 / 2.09	1.62 / 1.97	1.57 / 1.88	1.52 / 1.79	1.45 / 1.69	1.42 / 1.62	1.35 / 1.53	1.32 / 1.48	1.26 / 1.39	1.22 / 1.33	1.19 / 1.28
400	3.86 / 6.70	3.02 / 4.66	2.62 / 3.83	2.39 / 3.36	2.23 / 3.06	2.12 / 2.85	2.03 / 2.69	1.96 / 2.55	1.90 / 2.46	1.85 / 2.37	1.81 / 2.29	1.78 / 2.23	1.72 / 2.12	1.67 / 2.04	1.60 / 1.92	1.54 / 1.84	1.49 / 1.74	1.42 / 1.64	1.38 / 1.57	1.32 / 1.47	1.28 / 1.42	1.22 / 1.32	1.16 / 1.24	1.13 / 1.19
1000	3.85 / 6.66	3.00 / 4.62	2.61 / 3.80	2.38 / 3.34	2.22 / 3.04	2.10 / 2.82	2.02 / 2.66	1.95 / 2.53	1.89 / 2.43	1.84 / 2.34	1.80 / 2.26	1.76 / 2.20	1.70 / 2.09	1.65 / 2.01	1.58 / 1.89	1.53 / 1.81	1.47 / 1.71	1.41 / 1.61	1.36 / 1.54	1.30 / 1.44	1.26 / 1.38	1.19 / 1.28	1.13 / 1.19	1.08 / 1.11
∞	3.84 / 6.64	2.99 / 4.60	2.60 / 3.78	2.37 / 3.32	2.21 / 3.02	2.09 / 2.80	2.01 / 2.64	1.94 / 2.51	1.88 / 2.41	1.83 / 2.32	1.79 / 2.24	1.75 / 2.18	1.69 / 2.07	1.64 / 1.99	1.57 / 1.87	1.52 / 1.79	1.46 / 1.69	1.40 / 1.59	1.35 / 1.52	1.28 / 1.41	1.24 / 1.36	1.17 / 1.25	1.11 / 1.15	1.00 / 1.00

Note. Reprinted by permission from *Statistical Methods* Seventh Edition © 1980 by The Iowa State University Press, 2121 South State Avenue, Ames, Iowa 50010. Values in regular type: .05 level; values in bold type: .01 level.

Table A.7 Critical Values of the Studentized Range Statistic

df for S_w^2	$1 - \alpha$	k = number of means or steps between ordered means								
		2	3	4	5	6	7	8	9	10
1	.95	18.0	27.0	32.8	37.1	40.4	43.1	45.4	47.4	49.1
	.99	90.0	135	164	186	202	216	227	237	246
2	.95	6.09	8.3	9.8	10.9	11.7	12.4	13.0	13.5	14.0
	.99	14.0	19.0	22.3	24.7	26.6	28.2	29.5	30.7	31.7
3	.95	4.50	5.91	6.82	7.50	8.04	8.48	8.85	9.18	9.46
	.99	8.26	10.6	12.2	13.3	14.2	15.0	15.6	16.2	16.7
4	.95	3.93	5.04	5.76	6.29	6.71	7.05	7.35	7.60	7.83
	.99	6.51	8.12	9.17	9.96	10.6	11.1	11.5	11.9	12.3
5	.95	3.64	4.60	5.22	5.67	6.03	6.33	6.58	6.80	6.99
	.99	5.70	6.97	7.80	8.42	8.91	9.32	9.67	9.97	10.2
6	.95	3.46	4.34	4.90	5.31	5.63	5.89	6.12	6.32	6.49
	.99	5.24	6.33	7.03	7.56	7.97	8.32	8.61	8.87	9.10
7	.95	3.34	4.16	4.69	5.06	5.36	5.61	5.82	6.00	6.16
	.99	4.95	5.92	6.54	7.01	7.37	7.68	7.94	8.17	8.37
8	.95	3.26	4.04	4.53	4.89	5.17	5.40	5.60	5.77	5.92
	.99	4.74	5.63	6.20	6.63	6.96	7.24	7.47	7.68	7.87
9	.95	3.20	3.95	4.42	4.76	5.02	5.24	5.43	5.60	5.74
	.99	4.60	5.43	5.96	6.35	6.66	6.91	7.13	7.32	7.49
10	.95	3.15	3.88	4.33	4.65	4.91	5.12	5.30	5.46	5.60
	.99	4.48	5.27	5.77	6.14	6.43	6.67	6.87	7.05	7.21
11	.95	3.11	3.82	4.26	4.57	4.82	5.03	5.20	5.35	5.49
	.99	4.39	5.14	5.62	5.97	6.25	6.48	6.67	6.84	6.99
12	.95	3.08	3.77	4.20	4.51	4.75	4.95	5.12	5.27	5.40
	.99	4.32	5.04	5.50	5.84	6.10	6.32	6.51	6.67	6.81
13	.95	3.06	3.73	4.15	4.45	4.69	4.88	5.05	5.19	5.32
	.99	4.26	4.96	5.40	5.73	5.98	6.19	6.37	6.53	6.67
14	.95	3.03	3.70	4.11	4.41	4.64	4.83	4.99	5.13	5.25
	.99	4.21	4.89	5.32	5.63	5.88	6.08	6.26	6.41	6.54
16	.95	3.00	3.65	4.05	4.33	4.56	4.74	4.90	5.03	5.15
	.99	4.13	4.78	5.19	5.49	5.72	5.92	6.08	6.22	6.35
18	.95	2.97	3.61	4.00	4.28	4.49	4.67	4.82	4.96	5.07
	.99	4.07	4.70	5.09	5.38	5.60	5.79	5.94	6.08	6.20
20	.95	2.95	3.58	3.96	4.23	4.45	4.62	4.77	4.90	5.01
	.99	4.02	4.64	5.02	5.29	5.51	5.69	5.84	5.97	6.09
24	.95	2.92	3.53	3.90	4.17	4.37	4.54	4.68	4.81	4.92
	.99	3.96	4.54	4.91	5.17	5.37	5.54	5.69	5.81	5.92
30	.95	2.89	3.49	3.84	4.10	4.30	4.46	4.60	4.72	4.83
	.99	3.89	4.45	4.80	5.05	5.24	5.40	5.54	5.56	5.76

40	.95	2.86	3.44	3.79	4.04	4.23	4.39	4.52	4.63	4.74
	.99	3.82	4.37	4.70	4.93	5.11	5.27	5.39	5.50	5.60
60	.95	2.83	3.40	3.74	3.98	4.16	4.31	4.44	4.55	4.65
	.99	3.76	4.28	4.60	4.82	4.99	5.13	5.25	5.36	5.45
120	.95	2.80	3.36	3.69	3.92	4.10	4.24	4.36	4.48	4.56
	.99	3.70	4.20	4.50	4.71	4.87	5.01	5.12	5.21	5.30
∞	.95	2.77	3.31	3.63	3.86	4.03	4.17	4.29	4.39	4.47
	.99	3.64	4.12	4.40	4.60	4.76	4.88	4.99	5.08	5.16

*This table is abridged from Table II.2 in *The probability integrals of the range and of the Studentized range*, prepared by H. Leon Harter, Donald S. Clemm, and Eugene H. Guthrie. These tables are published in WADC tech. Rep. 58—484, vol. 2, 1959, Wright Air Development Center, and are reproduced with the kind permission of the authors.

Table A.8 Critical Values of Chi-Square

	Probability under H_0 that $\chi^2 \geq$ chi-square													
df	.99	.98	.95	.90	.80	.70	.50	.30	.20	.10	.05	.02	.01	.001
1	.00016	.00063	.0039	.016	.064	.15	.46	1.07	1.64	2.71	3.84	5.41	6.64	10.83
2	.02	.04	.10	.21	.45	.71	1.39	2.41	3.22	4.60	5.99	7.82	9.21	13.82
3	.12	.18	.35	.58	1.00	1.42	2.37	3.66	4.64	6.25	7.82	9.84	11.34	16.27
4	.30	.43	.71	1.06	1.65	2.20	3.36	4.88	5.99	7.78	9.49	11.67	13.28	18.46
5	.55	.75	1.14	1.61	2.34	3.00	4.35	6.06	7.29	9.24	11.07	13.39	15.09	20.52
6	.87	1.13	1.64	2.20	3.07	3.83	5.35	7.23	8.56	10.64	12.59	15.03	16.81	22.46
7	1.24	1.56	2.17	2.83	3.82	4.67	6.35	8.38	9.80	12.02	14.07	16.62	18.48	24.32
8	1.65	2.03	2.73	3.49	4.59	5.53	7.34	9.52	11.03	13.36	15.51	18.17	20.09	26.12
9	2.09	2.53	3.32	4.17	5.38	6.39	8.34	10.66	12.24	14.68	16.92	19.68	21.67	27.88
10	2.56	3.06	3.94	4.86	6.18	7.27	9.34	11.78	13.44	15.99	18.31	21.16	23.21	29.59
11	3.05	3.61	4.58	5.58	6.99	8.15	10.34	12.90	14.63	17.28	19.68	22.62	24.72	31.26
12	3.57	4.18	5.23	6.30	7.81	9.03	11.34	14.01	15.81	18.55	21.03	24.05	26.22	32.91
13	4.11	4.76	5.89	7.04	8.63	9.93	12.34	15.12	16.98	19.81	22.36	25.47	27.69	34.53
14	4.66	5.37	6.57	7.79	9.47	10.82	13.34	16.22	18.15	21.06	23.68	26.87	29.14	36.12
15	5.23	5.98	7.26	8.55	10.31	11.72	14.34	17.32	19.31	22.31	25.00	28.26	30.58	37.70
16	5.81	6.61	7.96	9.31	11.15	12.62	15.34	18.42	20.46	23.54	26.30	29.63	32.00	39.29
17	6.41	7.26	8.67	10.08	12.00	13.53	16.34	19.51	21.62	24.77	27.59	31.00	33.41	40.75
18	7.02	7.91	9.39	10.86	12.86	14.44	17.34	20.60	22.76	25.99	28.87	32.35	34.80	42.31
19	7.63	8.57	10.12	11.65	13.72	15.35	18.34	21.69	23.90	27.20	30.14	33.69	36.19	43.82
20	8.26	9.24	10.85	12.44	14.58	16.27	19.34	22.78	25.04	28.41	31.41	35.02	37.57	45.32
21	8.90	9.92	11.59	13.24	15.44	17.18	20.34	23.86	26.17	29.62	32.67	36.34	38.93	46.80
22	9.54	10.60	12.34	14.04	16.31	18.10	21.34	24.94	27.30	30.81	33.92	37.66	40.29	48.27
23	10.20	11.29	13.09	14.85	17.19	19.02	22.34	26.02	28.43	32.01	35.17	38.97	41.64	49.73
24	10.86	11.99	13.85	15.66	18.06	19.94	23.34	27.10	29.55	33.20	36.42	40.27	42.98	51.18
25	11.52	12.70	14.61	16.47	18.94	20.87	24.34	28.17	30.68	34.38	37.65	41.57	44.31	52.62
26	12.20	13.41	15.38	17.29	19.82	21.79	25.34	29.25	31.80	35.56	38.88	42.86	45.64	54.05
27	12.88	14.12	16.15	18.11	20.70	22.72	26.34	30.32	32.91	36.74	40.11	44.14	46.96	55.48
28	13.56	14.85	16.93	18.94	21.59	23.65	27.34	31.39	34.03	37.92	41.34	45.42	48.28	56.89
29	14.26	15.57	17.71	19.77	22.48	24.58	28.34	32.46	35.14	39.09	42.56	46.69	49.59	58.30
30	14.95	16.31	18.49	20.60	23.36	25.51	29.34	33.53	36.25	40.26	43.77	47.96	50.89	59.70

*Table A.8 is abridged from Table IV of Fisher & Yates: *Statistical Tables for Biological, Agricultural and Medical Research*, published by Longman Group Ltd. London (previously published by Oliver and Boyd, Ltd., Edinburgh), and by permission of the authors and the publishers.

Table A.9 Critical Values of T in the Wilcoxon Matched-Pairs Signed-Ranks Test

	Level of significance for one-tailed test		
	.025	.01	.005
	Level of significance for two-tailed test		
N	.05	.02	.01
6	1	—	—
7	2	0	—
8	4	2	0
9	6	3	2
10	8	5	3
11	11	7	5
12	14	10	7
13	17	13	10
14	21	16	13
15	25	20	16
16	30	24	19
17	35	28	23
18	40	33	28
19	46	38	32
20	52	43	37
21	59	49	43
22	66	56	49
23	73	62	55
24	81	69	61
25	90	77	68

Material from *Some Rapid Approximate Statistical Procedures*, Copyright © 1949, 1964, Lederle Laboratories Division of American Cyanamid Company, All Rights Reserved and Reprinted With Permission.

Table A.10 Values of Spearman r_s for the .05 and .01 Levels of Significance

N	.05	.01	N	.05	.01
6	.886	—	19	.462	.608
7	.786	—	20	.450	.591
8	.738	.881	21	.438	.576
9	.683	.833	22	.428	.562
10	.648	.818	23	.418	.549
11	.623	.794	24	.409	.537
12	.591	.780	25	.400	.526
13	.566	.745	26	.392	.515
14	.545	.716	27	.385	.505
15	.525	.689	28	.377	.496
16	.507	.666	29	.370	.487
17	.490	.645	30	.364	.478
18	.476	.625			

From E.G. Olds, Distribution of sums of squares of rank differences for small numbers of individuals, *Annals of Mathematical Statistics 9*: 133-48 (1938), and E.G. Olds, The 5% significance levels for sums of squares of rank differences and a correction, *Annals of Mathematical Statistics 20*: 117-18 (1949). Copyright 1938 and Copyright 1949 by the Institute of Mathematical Statistics, San Francisco, Calif. Reprinted by permission of the publisher.

□

SPSSx Computer Programs and Examples for Mainframe and Microcomputers

---

Statistical Analysis Using the Computer

Sample Computer Programs to Calculate

- Mean and Standard Deviation
- Correlation
- *t* Test Between a Sample and a Population Mean
- Dependent *t* Test
- Comparison Between *t* and *r*
- Comparison Between *t* and *F*
- Simple ANOVA
- Factorial ANOVA
- Repeated Measures ANOVA
- Reliability From ANOVA

STATISTICAL ANALYSIS USING THE COMPUTER

Katherine T. Thomas

The statistical package SPSS (SPSSx) has been adapted for use with personal computers (SPSSPC+). This means that the same procedures, or commands, will yield the same result using either the mainframe or the microcomputer (PC). Of course, your computer or system must have purchased the right to use SPSS (SPSSx or SPSSPC+). The SPSS is available at most colleges and universities, which means that, after following the procedure at your institution of obtaining computer access, you can begin to solve the problems in this book using the computer.

The type of operating system and the techniques for access vary at each university; this is true for both the mainframe and the PC. There are some commonalities. The mainframe requires an operating system that will tell the computer what to do with your SPSSx programs (run, print, save, etc.). The information necessary to use your system should be available through your computer center. The SPSSPC+ can be used from a disk-operating system (DOS) or from the SPSSPC+ prompt. Again, you may have a system that provides a menu (list or directory) of programs on your PC as well as automatic routing to the program selected. If you have questions, ask someone who uses the same system, but when all else fails read your manual.

There are advantages and disadvantages for both the mainframe and the PC when using SPSS. The mainframe has two advantages. First, the capacity is greater; thus, when you have large data sets, the system can handle the work load. Second, the mainframe allows you to correct errors or to alter information throughout your program. This advantage is tied closely to the major dis-

advantage, which is that the jobs (programs) on the mainframe are run as "batch jobs." This means that your program is not run until you have completely finished the entire program. In fact, your job is grouped with many other jobs to be run, and this is a more efficient way to operate. This means that if you make an error (e.g., you type "lits" instead of "list") early in the program, you will not know about the error until the program has been run and you get an error message from the computer.

The PC will run SPSS jobs in two ways: as a batch, where you type the entire job and then run it (as with the mainframe), or interactively with the PC. This is one of the advantages of the PC: As soon as you make an error, the computer lets you know so that you can correct the error before going on. The PC is also better than the mainframe because you do not have to wait for the computer to run several jobs, which, during busy times, may mean long delays in processing. The PC works for you and on your time schedule but does have a disadvantage when working interactively in that you cannot correct errors on previous lines once you have pressed the enter (return) key.

To begin on the mainframe you will need to know the operating system, several of which work with SPSSx. Some of these require job control language (JCL), which comprises the first two lines and the last line in the sample programs (these always begin with / /). These are not necessary on the PC. On the mainframe, commands (statements that tell the computer what to do) always begin in the first column; subcommands (statements that specify or modify commands) must begin in any column (from numbers 2 to 80) so that the computer knows a new command is being presented when information appears in the first column. The only exception to this is that data can appear in the first column. On the PC, commands and subcommands can begin in any column, and commands with subcommands are separated with a period, which tells the PC to expect a new command.

Once you have a prompt, or cursor (the flashing line or box on the screen), you have gained access to the system. On the mainframe you will need to write your program into a file, which is a name for a program that is stored or being used. The screen will usually look like a matrix, with column numbers across the top and line numbers down the side. Remember that the first column is reserved for commands. Once you have typed your program, you will need to save the program. Then you will probably want to run the program and perhaps print it. The actual program is presented in the samples; all you need to do is type the statements (commands and data) into your file. You will need to learn how to access, save, run, and print on the basis of the system used at your institution.

On the PC you will use DOS and get into review; or, after SPSSPC+: prompt, type your commands and data. Again you will need to learn these steps (access, print, etc.) on your individual systems. It is important that you save your program! You usually have a choice of saving either to the hard drive or to a diskette on the PC.

All the sample programs contain the data. The actual measurements taken on the subjects will appear after the command "begin data" and end before the statement "end data." Another way to manage large data sets is to put the data in a separate file (program) and refer to this file in your program (command file). This approach is better if you have large data sets with many observations or are reading the data from an electronic scanner or some other piece of equipment. However, this process is too complex to be covered in this book. Once you are familiar and comfortable with the simple programs in

this book, you can experiment with the more complex computer techniques.

The program shown in Figure B.1 was written to run on the mainframe. You will notice the first two lines are JCL and begin with //. Each command begins in the first column and all subcommands in the second column. Type the data after "begin data" and stop before "end data." You will need to verify (check for accuracy) your data. This can be done on the screen after the data are typed or on the output when you use "list" as a command. If your results are different than expected, the first thing to check is the data. The computer does not know that "76" was supposed to be "67."

Figure B.2 is the data from Table 5.3 (Calculation of Mean and Standard Deviation). The terminal screen shows the columns across the top and the line numbers down the side (e.g., 0001).

The output (the answer the computer printed on the screen or on paper) is presented in Figure B.3.

Figure B.4 is the input (program) for Table 5.3 using the PC. Notice the use of periods and that the calculation is done immediately after the command. The command "finish." is not part of the SPSSPC+ program, so you must save your program (usually by using the F10 key). In SPSSPC+, "finish." will exit you from the SPSS and back to your DOS or other menu.

The remaining computer programs are presented in forms for the mainframe only. To use those programs on the PC, simply

1. delete the JCL,
2. place a period at the end of each command (this will be at the end of the last line in a series of lines that are typed in the second column), and
3. save your file before typing "finish." or the file will not be saved.

```
// JOB
// EXEC SPSSX
DATA LIST /
 CASEID 1-2
 VARX 4-5
SET WIDTH=80
VARIABLE LABELS
 CASEID 'SUBJECT IDENTIFICATION NUMBER'
 VARX 'DEPENDENT VARIABLE X'
TITLE 'CALCULATION OF MEAN AND STANDARD DEVIATION'
SUBTITLE 'TABLE 5.3'
BEGIN DATA
01 02
02 03
03 04
04 05
05 06

END DATA
LIST
DESCRIPTIVES VARX
FINISH
//
```

Figure B.1 The program to calculate the mean and standard deviation using SPSSx on the mainframe computer. See page 94.

COMMAND?

```
ID=    LINES 22              CHGS 0
DSN=WYL.AG.JRT.LIB(TBL53)              PO U  7476/7476
       ----+----1----+----2----+----3----+----4----+----5----+----6----+----7---
*****  **************************** TOP OF DATA ********************

001.0  // JOB
002.0  // EXEC SPSSX
003.0  DATA LIST /
004.0      CASEID 1-2
005.0      VARX 4-5
005.1  SET WIDTH=80
006.0  VARIABLE LABELS
007.0      CASEID  'SUBJECT IDENTIFICATION NUMBER'
008.0      VARX    'DEPENDENT VARIABLE X'
009.0  TITLE 'CALCULATION OF MEAN AND STANDARD DEVIATION'
010.0  SUBTITLE 'TABLE 5.3'
011.0  BEGIN DATA
012.0  01    02
013.0  02    03
014.0  03    04
015.0  04    05
016.0  05    06
```

Esc-chr: ^K help: ^K? port:2 speed: 2400 parity: none echo:rem vt102 . . . .

Figure B.2 The terminal screen will look similar to this as you type in the SPSSx program to calculate the mean and standard deviation. The line numbers are the numbers on the left side, and the column numbers run across the top with the asterisks between them and the lines. See page 94.

```
CASEID        VARX

   1            2
   2            3
   3            4
   4            5
   5            6
```

NUMBER OF CASES READ =   5   NUMBER OF CASES LISTED =   5

NUMBER OF VALID OBSERVATIONS (LISTWISE) =   5.00

VARIABLE   VARX   DEPENDENT VARIABLE X

MEAN   4.000   STD DEV   1.581
MINIMUM   2   MAXIMUM   6

VALID OBSERVATIONS -   5   MISSING OBSERVATIONS -   0

Figure B.3 The output on the screen or printout will look similar to this for the SPSSx program to calculate the mean and standard deviation when using the mainframe.


```
SPSS/PC: data list/
         : caseid 1-2
         : varx 4-5

SPSS/PC: begin data.
01  02
02  03
03  04
04  05
05  06
end data.
```
            5 cases are written to the uncompressed active file.

```
CASEID                        VARX
   1                            2
   2                            3
   3                            4
   4                            5
   5                            6
```

Number of cases read =   5   Number of cases listed =   5

Number of Valid Observations (Listwise) =   5.00

Variable	Mean	Std Dev	Minimum	Maximum	N	Label
VARX	4.00	1.58	2	6	5	

Figure B.4 Your terminal screen and printout will look similar to this when you calculate the mean and standard deviation on your PC using SPSS/PC.

Following are program statements and output from the examples in the book where you were referred to Appendix B. The order of examples follows:

- Chapter 5—means and standard deviations
- Chapter 6—Pearson r (and regression)

- Chapter 7—t tests (independent, dependent, t, and r)
    - Simple ANOVA (also ANOVA and t)
    - Factorial ANOVA
    - Repeated measures ANOVA
- Chapter 16—Repeated measures ANOVA for reliability estimation

```
// JOB
// EXEC SPSSX
DATA LIST /
 CASEID 1-2 GROUP 4 JOG 6-9(2)
SET WIDTH=80
VARIABLE LABELS
 CASEID 'SUBJECT IDENTIFICATION NUMBER'
 GROUP 'GROUP MEMBERSHIP'
 JOG 'JOGGING ERROR IN METERS'
TITLE 'RESEARCH METHODS PROBLEMS'
VALUE LABELS
 GROUP 0 'EXPERIMENTAL' 1 'CONTROL'
BEGIN DATA
01 0 2.55
02 0 3.62
03 0 3.42
04 0 2.86
05 0 2.00
06 0 1.08
07 0 1.16
08 1 7.86
09 1 6.80
10 1 5.68
11 1 3.97
12 1 7.23
13 1 5.48
14 1 6.03
END DATA
BREAKDOWN TABLES=JOG BY GROUP
FINISH
//
```

Figure B.5 Input (program) for calculating the mean and standard deviation problem. See page 104.

Criterion Variable Broken Down by		JOG GROUP	JOGGING ERROR IN METERS GROUP MEMBERSHIP		
Variable	Value	Label	Mean	Std Dev	Cases
For Entire Population			4.2671	2.2495	14
GROUP	0	EXPERIMENTAL	2.3843	1.0166	7
GROUP	1	CONTROL	6.1500	1.2877	7

Total Cases = 14

Figure B.6 Output from calculating the mean and standard deviation problem.

```
// JOB
// EXEC SPSSX
DATA LIST /
  CASEID 1-2 BODYWT 4-6 PULLUP 8-9
SET WIDTH=80
VARIABLE LABELS
  CASEID 'SUBJECT IDENTIFICATION NUMBER'
  BODYWT 'BODY WEIGHT IN POUNDS'
  PULLUP 'NUMBER OF PULL-UPS'
TITLE 'CALCULATING CORRELATION'
BEGIN DATA
01 104 04
02 086 02
03 092 06
04 112 01
05 096 04
06 098 13
07 110 00
08 086 09
09 105 01
10 091 10
END DATA
CORRELATION VARIABLES=BODYWT PULLUP
  /STATISTICS=DESCRIPTIVES
FINISH
//
```

Figure B.7 Input (program) for calculating the correlation. See page 112.

VARIABLE	CASES	MEAN	STD DEV
BODYWT	10	98.0000	9.4399
PULLUP	10	5.0000	4.3970

	BODYWT	PULLUP
BODYWT	1.000 (10) P= .	-.5381 (10) P= .054
PULLUP	-.5381 (10) P= .054	1.000 (10) P= .

(COEFFICIENT / (CASES) / 1-TAILED SIG)

" . " IS PRINTED IF A COEFFICIENT CANNOT BE COMPUTED

Figure B.8 Output from calculating the correlation.

```
// JOB
// EXEC SPSSX
DATA LIST /
 X 1-3 Y 5-7
SET WIDTH=80
VARIABLE LABELS
 X 'BODY WEIGHT' Y 'STRENGTH'
BEGIN DATA
112 215
098 210
104 190
105 180
110 170
092 175
086 150
091 130
086 125
096 125
END DATA
TITLE 'SAMPLE PROGRAM-- CORRELATION'
PEARSON CORR X Y
REGRESSION VARIABLES = X Y
 /DEPENDENT = Y
 /METHOD = ENTER
FINISH
//
```

Figure B.9 Input to calculate the second correlation problem. Data are from Figure 6.2, p. 109.

— — — — — — — — — — — PEARSON CORRELATION COEFFICIENTS   — — — — — —

```
                X       Y

X           1.0000    .6813
            (  10)    (  10)
            P= .      P= .015


Y            .6813    1.0000
            (  10)    (  10)
            P= .015  P= .
```

(COEFFICIENT / (CASES) / 1-TAILED SIG)

"." IS PRINTED IF A COEFFICIENT CANNOT BE COMPUTED

* * * * * * * MULTIPLE REGRESSION * * * * * *

Listwise Deletion of Missing Data

Equation Number 1   Dependent Variable..   Y   STRENGTH

Beginning Block Number 1. Method: Enter

Variable(s) Entered on Step Number
   1..   X   BODY WEIGHT

Multiple R   .68130
R Square   .46417
Adjusted R Square   .39719
Standard Error   26.02218

Analysis of Variance

	DF	Sum of Squares	Mean Square
Regression	1	4692.76808	4692.76808
Residual	8	5417.23192	677.15399

F=   6.93013   Signif F=   .0301

— — — — — — — — — — — Variables in the Equation   — — — — — — — — — —

Variable	B	SE B	Beta	T	Sig T
X	2.418953	.918875	.681301	2.633	.0301
(Constant)	-70.057357	90.424978		-.775	.4608

End Block Number   1   All requested variables entered.

Figure B.10 Output from the second correlation problem (problem from p. 119 with data from 6.2, p. 109).

```
// JOB
// EXEC SPSSX,PRTCLAS=R
DATA LIST /
 CASEID 1-2 TRI 4-5 SUP 7-8
SET WIDTH=80
VARIABLE LABELS
 CASEID 'SUBJECT IDENTIFICATION NUMBER'
 TRI 'TRICEPS SKINFOLD X VARIABLE'
 SUP 'SUPRAILIAC SKINFOLD Y VARIABLE'
BEGIN DATA
01 16 09
02 17 12
03 17 10
04 15 08
05 14 08
06 11 06
07 11 05
08 12 05
09 13 06
10 14 05
11 04 01
12 07 04
13 07 01
14 10 03
END DATA
TITLE 'RESEARCH METHODS PROBLEM TWO'
LIST
CORRELATION VARIABLES=TRI SUP
 /STATISTICS=DESCRIPTIVES
PLOT HSIZE=50 / VSIZE=50 /
 FORMAT=REGRESSION /
 PLOT=TRI WITH SUP
SUBTITLE 'TESTING HYPOTHESIS WITH REGRESSION'
REGRESSION VARIABLES = TRI SUP
 /DEPENDENT = TRI

 /METHOD = ENTER
FINISH
//
```

Figure B.11 Input to calculate the correlation problem. See page 127.

CASEID	TRI	SUP
1	16	9
2	17	12
3	17	10
4	15	8
5	14	8
6	11	6
7	11	5
8	12	5
9	13	6
10	14	5
11	4	1
12	7	4
13	7	1
14	10	3

VARIABLE	CASES	MEAN	STD DEV
TRI	14	12.0000	3.9614
SUP	14	5.9286	3.2217

	TRI	SUP
TRI	1.0000 (14) P= .	.9162 (14) P = .000
SUP	.9162 (14) P= .000	1.0000 (14) P= .

(Cont.)

Figure B.12 Output from calculating the correlation problem (p. 127).

Frequencies and symbols used (not applicable for control or overlay plots)

1 - 1	11 - B	21 - L	31 - V
2 - 2	12 - C	22 - M	32 - W
3 - 3	13 - D	23 - N	33 - X
4 - 4	14 - E	24 - O	34 - Y
5 - 5	15 - F	25 - P	35 - Z
6 - 6	16 - G	26 - Q	36 - *
7 - 7	17 - H	27 - R	
8 - 8	18 - I	28 - S	
9 - 9	19 - J	29 - T	
10 - A	20 - K	30 - U	

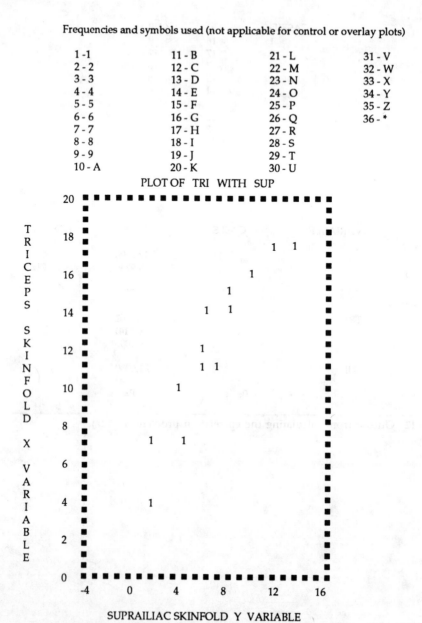

PLOT OF TRI WITH SUP

TRICEPS SKINFOLD X VARIABLE

SUPRAILIAC SKINFOLD Y VARIABLE

14 cases plotted. Regression statistics of TRI on SUP:
Correlation .91617 R Squared .83937 S.E. of Est 1.65249 Sig. .0000
Intercept(S.E.) 5.32133 (.95204) Slope(S.E.) 1.12652 (.14226)

(Cont.)

Figure B.12 (Continued)

Listwise Deletion of Missing Data

Equation Number 1　　　　Dependent Variable ..　　TRI　　TRICEPS SKINFOLD X VARIABLE

Beginning Block Number 1. Method: Enter

Variable(s) Entered on Step Number
　　　1 ..　SUP　　SUPRAILIAC SKINFOLD Y VARIABLE

Multiple R	.91617
R Square	.83937
Adjusted R Square	.82598
Standard Error	1.65249

Analysis of Variance

	DF	Sum of Squares	Mean Square
Regression	1	171.23134	171.23134
Residual	12	32.76866	2.73072

F=　62.70553　　Signif F = .0000

— — — — — — — — — — Variables in the Equation　　— — — — — — — — — — —

Variable	B	SE B	Beta	T	Sig T
SUP	1.126522	.142261	.916171	7.919	.0000
(Constant)	5.321334	.952043		5.589	.0001

End Block Number 1　　　All requested variables entered.

Figure B.12　(Continued)

```
// JOB
// EXEC SPSSX
SET WIDTH=80
DATA LIST /
 M1 1-2 M2 4-5 SM 7-8 SR 10-11
BEGIN DATA
81 76 09 32
END DATA
COMPUTE S1=SQRT(SR)
COMPUTE T=(M1-M2)/(9/S1)
LIST
FINISH
//
```

Figure B.13　Input for t test between sample and population means. See page 131 (Table 7.1).

M1	M2	SM	SR	S1	T
81	76	9	32	5.66	3.14

NUMBER OF CASES READ = 1   NUMBER OF CASES LISTED = 1

Figure B.14 Output from *t* test between population and sample means.

```
// JOB
// EXEC SPSSX
DATA LIST /
  SUBJECT 1-2 PRE 4-5 POST 7-8
SET WIDTH=80
VARIABLE LABELS
  SUBJECT 'SUBJECT IDENTIFICATION NUMBER'
  PRE 'PRETEST SCORE JUMP AND REACH'
  POST 'POSTTEST SCORE JUMP AND REACH'
TITLE 'A DEPENDENT T-TEST'
BEGIN DATA
01 12 16
02 15 21
03 13 15
04 20 22
05 21 21
06 19 23
07 14 16
08 17 18
09 16 22
10 18 23
END DATA
T-TEST PAIRS = PRE POST
CONDESCRIPTIVES VARIABLES = PRE POST
FINISH
//
```

Figure B.15 Input to calculate the dependent *t* test. See page 136 (Table 7.3).

— — — — — — — — — — — — — T - TEST — — — — — — — — — — —

VARIABLE	NUMBER OF CASES	MEAN	STANDARD DEVIATION	STANDARD ERROR
PRE	PRETEST SCORE JUMP AND REACH			
	10	16.5000	3.028	0.957
	10	19.7000	3.129	0.989
POST	POSTTEST SCORE JUMP AND REACH			

(DIFFERENCE) MEAN	STANDARD DEVIATION	STANDARD ERROR	* CORR.	2-TAIL PROB.	* T VALUE	DEGREES OF FREEDOM	2-TAIL PROB.
-3.2000	2.098	0.663	* 0.768	0.009	* -4.82	9	0.001

NUMBER OF VALID OBSERVATIONS (LISTWISE) = 10.00

VARIABLE	PRE	PRETEST SCORE JUMP AND REACH	
MEAN	16.500	STD DEV	3.028
MINIMUM	12	MAXIMUM	21
VALID OBSERVATIONS -	10	MISSING OBSERVATIONS -	0

— —

VARIABLE	POST	POSTTEST SCORE JUMP AND REACH	
MEAN	19.700	STD DEV	3.129
MINIMUM	15	MAXIMUM	23
VALID OBSERVATIONS -	10	MISSING OBSERVATIONS -	0

Figure B.16 Output from dependent *t* test.

```
// JOB
// EXEC SPSSX
DATA LIST /
 SUBJECT 1 (A) DUMMY 3 DEPVAR 5-6
SET WIDTH=80
TITLE 'COMPARISON OF R AND T'
VARIABLE LABELS
 DUMMY 'DUMMY CODE -- GROUP MEMBERSHIP'
 DEPVAR 'DEPENDENT VARIABLE'
BEGIN DATA
A 1 01
B 1 02
C 1 03
D 1 04
E 1 05
F 0 06
G 0 07
H 0 08
I 0 09
J 0 10
END DATA
PEARSON CORRELATION VARIABLES = DUMMY DEPVAR
T-TEST GROUPS= DUMMY (0,1) / VARIABLES = DEPVAR
FINISH
//
```

Figure B.17 Input to compare *t* and *r*. See page 140 (Table 7.4).

— — — — — — PEARSON   CORRELATION   COEFFICIENTS — — — — — — — — —

	DUMMY	DEPVAR
DUMMY	1.0000 (10) P= .	-.8704 (10) P= .001
DEPVAR	-.8704 (10) P= .001	1.0000 (10) P= .

(COEFFICIENT / (CASES) / 1-TAILED SIG)

" . " IS PRINTED IF A COEFFICIENT CANNOT BE COMPUTED

— — — — — — — — — — — T - TEST — — — — — — — — — — — — — —

GROUP 1 - DUMMY   EQ   0
GROUP 2 - DUMMY   EQ   1

VARIABLE	NUMBER OF CASES	MEAN	STANDARD DEVIATION	STANDARD ERROR
DEPVAR	DEPENDENT VARIABLE			
GROUP 1	5	8.0000	1.581	0.707
GROUP 2	5	3.0000	1.581	0.707

		* POOLED VARIANCE ESTIMATE *				SEPARATE VARIANCE ESTIMATE		
F VALUE	2-TAIL PROB.	T VALUE	DEGREES OF FREEDOM	2-TAIL PROB.		T VALUE	DEGREES OF FREEDOM	2-TAIL PROB.
1.00	1.000	5.00	8	0.001		5.00	8.00	0.001

Figure B.18 Output from comparing t and r.

```
          // JOB
          // EXEC SPSSX
          DATA LIST /
           GROUP 1 DV 3
          SET WIDTH=80
          BEGIN DATA
          1 2
          1 4
          1 3
          1 3
          1 2
          1 1
          1 1
          2 8
          2 7
          2 5
          2 4
          2 7
          2 5
          2 6
          END DATA
          TITLE 'COMPARISON OF F AND T'
          ONEWAY DV BY GROUP (1,2)
          T-TEST GROUPS=GROUP(1,2) / VARIABLES = DV
          FINISH
          //
```

Figure B.19 Input comparison of t and F. See page 146 (Table 7.8).

— — — — — — — — — — — — — — T - TEST — — — — — — — — — — — — — — —

GROUP 1 - GROUP   EQ   1
GROUP 2 - GROUP   EQ   2

VARIABLE	NUMBER OF CASES	MEAN	STANDARD DEVIATION	STANDARD ERROR
DV				
GROUP 1	7	2.2857	1.113	0.421
GROUP 2	7	6.0000	1.414	0.535

		*	POOLED VARIANCE ESTIMATE		*	SEPARATE VARIANCE ESTIMATE		
F VALUE	2-TAIL PROB	* T VALUE	DEGREES OF FREEDOM	2-TAIL PROB.	*	T VALUE	DEGREES OF FREEDOM	2-TAIL PROB.
1.62	0.575	-5.46	12	0.000		-5.46	11.37	0.000

— — — — — — — — — — — — ONE WAY — — — — — — — — — — — — —

     VARIABLE   DV
By   VARIABLE   GROUP

ANALYSIS OF VARIANCE

SOURCE	D.F.	SUM OF SQUARES	MEAN SQUARES	F RATIO	F PROB.
BETWEEN GROUPS	1	48.2857	48.2857	29.8235	.0001
WITHIN GROUPS	12	19.4286	1.6190		
TOTAL	13	67.7143			

Figure B.20 Output from comparing t and F.

```
// JOB
// EXEC SPSSX
DATA LIST /
 GROUP 1 DV 3-4
VARIABLE LABELS
 GROUP 'GROUP MEMBERSHIP'
 DV 'DEPENDENT VARIABLE'
TITLE 'SIMPLE ANOVA'
BEGIN DATA
1 12
1 10
1 11
1 07
1 10
2 09
2 07
2 06
2 09
2 04
3 06
3 07
3 02
3 03
3 02
END DATA
ONEWAY DV BY GROUP(1,3)     / RANGES = SNK
STATISTICS 1
FINISH
//
```

Figure B.21 Input to calculate simple ANOVA. See page 143 (Table 7.6).

— — — — — — — — — — — — — — ONEWAY — — — — — — — — — — — — — —

	VARIABLE	DV	DEPENDENT VARIABLE
By	VARIABLE	GROUP	GROUP MEMBERSHIP

ANALYSIS OF VARIANCE

SOURCE	D.F.	SUM OF SQUARES	MEAN SQUARES	F RATIO	F PROB.
BETWEEN GROUPS	2	90.0000	45.0000	10.0000	.0028
WITHIN GROUPS	12	54.0000	4.50000		
TOTAL	14	144.0000			

GROUP	COUNT	MEAN	STANDARD DEVIATION	STANDARD ERROR	95 PCT CONF INT FOR MEAN		
GRP 1	5	10.0000	1.8708	.8367	7.6771	TO	12.3229
GRP 2	5	7.0000	2.1213	.9487	4.3661	TO	9.6339
GRP 3	5	4.0000	2.3452	1.0488	1.0881	TO	6.9119
TOTAL	15	7.0000	3.2071	.8281	5.2239	TO	8.7761

GROUP	MINIMUM	MAXIMUM
GRP 1	7.0000	12.0000
GRP 2	4.0000	9.0000
GRP 3	2.0000	7.0000
TOTAL	2.0000	12.0000

(Cont.)

Figure B.22 Output from calculating simple ANOVA.

———————————— ONEWAY ——————————————

	VARIABLE	DV	DEPENDENT VARIABLE
By	VARIABLE	GROUP	GROUP MEMBERSHIP

MULTIPLE RANGE TEST

STUDENT-NEWMAN-KEULS PROCEDURE
RANGES FOR THE 0.050 LEVEL -

        3.08   3.77

THE RANGES ABOVE ARE TABLE RANGES.
THE VALUE ACTUALLY COMPARED WITH MEAN (J) -MEAN(I) IS...
   1.5000 * RANGE * DSQRT(1/N(I) * 1/N(J))

   (*) DENOTES PAIRS OF GROUPS SIGNIFICANTLY DIFFERENT AT THE 0.050 LEVEL

```
                              G  G  G
                              r  r  r
                              p  p  p

MEAN            GROUP         3  2  1

4.0000          GRP 3
7.0000          GRP 2         *
10.0000         GRP 1         *  *
```

HOMOGENEOUS SUBSETS   (SUBSETS OF GROUPS, WHOSE HIGHEST AND LOWEST MEANS DO
                                NOT DIFFER BY MORE THAN THE SHORTEST SIGNIFICANT
                                RANGE FOR A SUBSET OF THAT SIZE)

SUBSET 1

GROUP	Grp 3
MEAN	4.0000

SUBSET 2

GROUP	Grp 2
MEAN	7.0000

SUBSET 3

GROUP	Grp 1
MEAN	10.0000

Figure B.22 (Continued)

```
// JOB
// EXEC SPSSX
DATA LIST /
 SUBJECT 1-2
 DAYS 4
 INT 6
 DV 8-11
SET WIDTH=80
VARIABLE LABELS
 DAYS 'DAYS PER WEEK OF EXERCISE'
 INT 'INTENSITY OF EXERCISE'
 DV 'MEASUREMENT'
VALUE LABELS
 DAYS 2 'TWO DAYS PER WEEK' 3 'THREE DAYS PER WEEK' /
 INT 1 '40% INTENSITY' 2 '60% INTENSITY' 3 '80% INTENSITY'
TITLE 'AN EXAMPLE OF A TWO-WAY FACTORIAL ANOVA'
BEGIN DATA
01 2 1 2940
02 2 1 3070
03 2 1 3100
04 2 1 2925
05 2 1 3050
06 2 2 3150
07 2 2 3020
08 2 2 2990
09 2 2 3050
10 2 2 2980
11 2 3 3170
12 2 3 3120
13 2 3 3050
14 2 3 3110
15 2 3 3105
16 3 1 2980
17 3 1 3160
18 3 1 3025
19 3 1 3045
20 3 1 2990
21 3 2 3720
22 3 2 3630
23 3 2 3570
24 3 2 3690
25 3 2 3710
26 3 3 3920
27 3 3 4040
28 3 3 4110
29 3 3 4005
30 3 3 3990
END DATA
ANOVA VARIABLES = DV BY DAYS(2,3) INT(1,3)
 /STATISTICS=ALL
FINISH
//
```

Figure B.23 Input to calculate factorial ANOVA. See page 150 (Table 7.11).

**** CELL MEANS ****

DV	MEASUREMENT
BY DAYS	DAYS PER WEEK OF EXERCISE
INT	INTENSITY OF EXERCISE

TOTAL POPULATION
3313.83
(30)

DAYS

2	3
3055.33	3572.33
(15)	(15)

INT

1	2	3
3028.50	3351.00	3562.00
(10)	(10)	(10)

		INT		
		1	2	3
DAYS				
	2	3017.00	3038.00	3111.00
		(5)	(5)	(5)
	3	3040.00	3664.00	4013.00
		(5)	(5)	(5)

**** ANALYSIS OF VARIANCE ****

DV	MEASUREMENT
by DAYS	DAYS PER WEEK OF EXERCISE
INT	INTENSITY OF EXERCISE

SOURCE OF VARIATION	SUM OF SQUARES	DF	MEAN SQUARE	F	SIG OF F
Main Effects	3448499.167	3	1149499.722	257.279	.000
DAYS	2004667.500	1	2004667.500	448.681	.000
INT	1443831.667	2	721915.833	161.578	.000
2-Way Interactions	1010355.000	2	505177.500	113.068	.000
DAYS INT	1010355.000	2	505177.500	113.068	.000
Explained	4458854.167	5	891770.833	199.594	.000
Residual	107230.000	24	4467.917		
Total	4566084.167	29	157451.178		

(Cont.)

Figure B.24 Output from calculating factorial ANOVA.

**** MULTIPLE CLASSIFICATION ANALYSIS ****

	by	DV	MEASUREMENT
		DAYS	DAYS PER WEEK OF EXERCISE
		INT	INTENSITY OF EXERCISE

Grand Mean = 3313.83

Variable + Category	N	Unadjusted Dev'n	Eta	Adjusted for Independents Dev'n	Beta
DAYS					
2 TWO DAYS PER WEEK	15	-258.50		-258.50	
3 THREE DAYS PER WEEK	15	258.50		258.50	
			.66		.66
INT					
1 40% INTENSITY	10	-285.33		-285.33	
2 60% INTENSITY	10	37.17		37.17	
3 80% INTENSITY	10	248.17		248.17	
			.56		.56
Mutitple R Squared					.755
Multiple R					.869

Figure B.24 (Continued)

```
// JOB
// EXEC SPSSX
DATA LIST /
  SUBJECT 1 TRIAL1 3-4 TRIAL2 6-7 TRIAL3 9-10
SET WIDTH=80
TITLE 'ANOVA WITH REPEATED MEASURES ON TRIALS'
BEGIN DATA
1 12 09 06
2 10 07 07
3 11 06 02
4 07 09 03
5 10 04 02
END DATA
MANOVA TRIAL1 TRIAL2 TRIAL3
  /WSFACTORS=TRIALS(3)
  /PRINT=CELLINFO(MEANS)
FINISH
  /WSFACTORS=TRIALS(3)
  /PRINT=CELLINFO(MEANS)
FINISH
//
```

Figure B.25 Input for ANOVA with repeated measures on trials. See page 157 (Table 7.15).

**** ANALYSIS OF VARIANCE ****

5 cases accepted.
0 cases rejected because of out-of -range factor values.
0 cases rejected because of missing data.
1 non-empty cell.
1 design will be processed.

Cell Means and Standard Deviations
Variable .. TRIAL1

	Mean	Std. Dev.	N
For entire sample	10.000	1.871	5

Variable .. TRIAL2

	Mean	Std. Dev.	N
For entire sample	7.000	2.121	5

Variable .. TRIAL3

	Mean	Std. Dev.	N
For entire sample	4.000	2.345	5

**** ANALYSIS OF VARIANCE -- DESIGN 1 ****

Tests of Between-Subjects Effects.

Tests of Significance for T1 using UNIQUE sums of squares

Source of Variation	SS	DF	MS	F	Sig of F
WITHIN CELLS	26.00	4	6.50		
CONSTANT	735.00	1	735.00	113.08	.000

****ANALYSIS OF VARIANCE -- DESIGN 1 ****

Tests involving 'TRIALS' Within-Subject Effect.

Mauchly sphericity test, W=	.85714
Chi-square approx. =	.46245 with 2 D.F.
Significance =	.794
Greenhouse-GeisserEpsilon =	.87500
Huynh-Feldt Epsilon =	1.00000
Lower-bound Epsilon =	.50000

AVERAGED Tests of Significance that follow multivariate tests are equivalent to univariate or split-plot or mixed-model approach to repeated measures. Epsilons may be used to adjust d.f. for the AVERAGED results.

(Cont.)

Figure B.26 Output from calculating ANOVA with repeated measures on trials.

**** ANALYSIS OF VARIANCE -- DESIGN 1 ****

EFFECT .. TRIALS
Multivariate Tests of Significance (S = 1, M = 0, N = 1/2)

Test Name	Value	Exact F Hypoth.	DF	Error DF	Sig. of F
Pillais	.88933	12.05357	2.00	3.00	.037
Hotellings	8.03571	12.05357	2.00	3.00	.037
Wilks	.11067	12.05357	2.00	3.00	.037
Roys	.88933				

Note .. F statistics are exact.

- -

**** ANALYSIS OF VARIANCE -- DESIGN 1 ****

Tests involving 'TRIALS' Within-Subject Effect.

AVERAGED Tests of Significance for TRIAL using UNIQUE sums of squares

Source of Variation	SS	DF	MS	F	Sig of F
WITHIN CELLS	28.00	8	3.50		
TRIALS	90.00	2	45.00	12.86	.003

5160 BITES OF WORKSPACE NEEDED FOR MANOVA EXECUTION.

Figure B.26 (Continued)

```
// JOB
// EXEC SPSSX
DATA LIST / STUDENT 9(A) TRIAL1 3 TRIAL2 5 TRIAL3 7
SET WIDTH=80
VARIABLE LABELS
 STUDENT 'STUDENT IDENTIFICATION NUMBER'
 TRIAL1 'TRIAL ONE'
 TRIAL2 'TRIAL TWO'
 TRIAL3 'TRIAL THREE'
TITLE 'SUMMARY OF ANOVA FOR RELIABILITY ESTIMATION'
BEGIN DATA
A 3 3 4
B 4 6 6
C 2 3 4
D 1 3 4
E 2 4 2
END DATA
LIST
MANOVA TRIAL1 TRIAL2 TRIAL3
  /WSFACTORS=TRIALS(3)
  /PRINT=CELLINFO(MEANS)
FINISH
//
```

Figure B.27 Input for reliability from ANOVA with repeated measures on trials. See page 351 (Table 16.1).

**** ANALYSIS OF VARIANCE ****

5 cases accepted.
0 cases rejected because of out-of-range factor values.
0 cases rejected because of missing data.
1 non-empty cell.

1 design will be processed.

Cell Means and Standard Deviations
Variable .. TRIAL1   TRIAL ONE

	Mean	Std. Dev.	N
For entire sample	2.400	1.140	5

Variable .. TRIAL2   TRIAL TWO

	Mean	Std. Dev.	N
For entire sample	3.800	1.304	5

Variable .. TRIAL3   TRIAL THREE

	Mean	Std. Dev.	N
For entire sample	4.000	1.414	5

**** ANALYSIS OF VARIANCE -- DESIGN 1 ****

Tests of Between-Subject Effects.
Tests of Significance for T1 using UNIQUE sums of squares

Source of Variation	SS	DF	MS	F	Sig of F
WITHIN CELLS	14.93	4	3.73		
CONSTANT	173.40	1	173.40	46.45	.002

**** ANALYSIS OF VARIANCE -- DESIGN 1 ****

Tests involving 'TRIALS' Within-Subject Effect.

Mauchly sphericity test, W=	.83102
Chi-square approx. =	.55529 with 2 D.F.
Significance =	.758

Greenhouse-Geisser Epsilon =	.85545
Huynh-Feldt Epsilon =	1.00000
Lower-bound Epsilon =	.50000

AVERAGED Tests of Significance that follow multivariate tests are equivalent to univariate or split-plot or mixed-model approach to repeated measures. Epsilons may be used to adjust d.f. for the AVERAGED results.

(Cont.)

Figure B.28 Output from calculating ANOVA for reliability with repeated measures on trials.

**** ANALYSIS OF VARIANCE -- DESIGN 1 ****

Tests involving 'TRIALS' Within-Subject Effect.

AVERAGED Tests of Significance for TRIAL using UNIQUE sums of squares

Source of Variation	SS	DF	MS	F	Sig of F
WITHIN CELLS	5.07	8	.63		
TRIALS	7.60	2	3.80	6.00	.026

5160 BYTES OF WORKSPACE NEEDED FOR MANOVA EXECUTION.

**** ANALYSIS OF VARIANCE -- DESIGN 1 ****

EFFECT . . TRIALS
Multivariate Tests of Significance (S = 1 , M = 0, N = 1/2)

Test Name	Value	Exact F	Hypoth. DF	Error DF	Sig. of F
Pillais	.82222	6.93750	2.00	3.00	.075
Hotellings	4.62500	6.93750	2.00	3.00	.075
Wilks	.17778	6.93750	2.00	3.00	.075
Roys	.82222				

Note . . F statistics are exact.

Figure B.28 (Continued)

Appendix C

□

Descriptions of Statistical Packages
for Mainframe Computers

Statistical Analysis System (SAS)

Statistical Package for the Social Sciences (SPSS)

Biomedical Computer Programs, P-Series (BMDP)

SAS (STATISTICAL ANALYSIS SYSTEM)

SAS INSTITUTE (1982).
SAS USERS GUIDE: STATISTICS.
CARY, NC: SAS INSTITUTE.

SAS is an acronym for Statistical Analysis System, which has developed into an all-purpose data analysis system that provides tools for information storage and retrieval, data modification and programming, report writing, statistical analysis, and file handling. However, in this book we are mainly concerned with the statistical analysis part of the system.

The SAS statistical manual is divided into sections: Regression, Analysis of Variance, Categorical Data Analysis, Multivariate Methods, Discriminant Analysis, Clustering, Scoring, and MATRIX. Within each major section, an introductory chapter describes the procedures. Then, each procedure is a separate chapter. Each chapter is divided into abstract, introduction, specifications, details, examples, and references.

The section on regression serves as a good example. The first chapter is "Introduction to SAS Regression Procedures." This is followed by separate chapters:

NLIN—builds nonlinear regression models

REG—performs general purpose regression with many diagnostics and input/output capabilities

RSQUARE—builds models and shows fitness measures for all possible models

RSREG—builds quadradic response–surface regression models

STEPWISE—implements several stepping methods for selecting models

SAS runs interactively (communicates back and forth with a terminal) or in batch (all programming and data read in without stopping). The data can be input from cards, disks, or tape and organized into an SAS data set. Of course, all options may not be available at all computer centers.

SPSS (STATISTICAL PACKAGE FOR THE SOCIAL SCIENCES)

SPSS INC. (1983).
SPSS USER'S GUIDE
CHICAGO: SPSS INC.

SPSS is an acronym for Statistical Package for the Social Sciences. Although older editions were not as flexible as SAS, the latest edition is quite flexible and usable. SPSS has features that allow data verification and updating, development of tables and reports, and graphics, as well as comprehensive statistical procedures.

The SPSS manual is divided by sections according to statistical procedures. Suggested statistical guides and bibliographies are also included to aid the user in appropriate application. The statistical sections include the following:

Frequency Distributions and Descriptive Statistics

Relationships Between Two or More Variables (CROSSTABS)

Correlation Coefficients and Scatterplots

Multiple Regression Analysis

Factor Analysis

Discriminant Analysis

Survival Analysis

Analysis of Additive Scales

Nonparametric Statistics

Log-Linear Models

Box-Jenkins Analysis of Time Series Data

Again to use regression as an example, SPSS allows six equation-building methods, including the following:

FORWARD—forward entry of variables with an entry criterion

BACKWARD—backward elimination of variables with a removal criterion

STEPWISE—stepwise selection with both entry and removal criteria

ENTER—an option to control the order of entering variables

REMOVE—an option to force the order of variables removed

TEST—a means of testing specific subsets of variables for the maximum R^2

SPSS may be used interactively or through the batch mode if your computer center is set up for both.

BIMED (BIOMEDICAL COMPUTER PROGRAMS, P-SERIES) (BMDP)

DIXON, W.J., & BROWN, M.B. (1981). *BMDP STATISTICAL SOFTWARE 1981 MANUAL.* BERKELEY, CA: UNIVERSITY OF CALIFORNIA PRESS.

BMDP (or BIMED) is an acronym for Biomedical Computer Programs, P-Series. BIMED is one of the oldest (begun in 1961) and probably the most widely used mainframe statistical package. While the programs have their own internal control language (which is very consistent across programs), BMDP also allows user-specified FORTRAN (a widely used computer language) statements.

The BMDP manual has seven introductory chapters to teach the use of the system. These are followed by the statistical section (each containing chapters for the various techniques):

Data Description

Data Into Groups

Plots and Histograms

Frequency Tables

Missing Values

Regression

Nonlinear Regression (maximum likelihood estimation)

Analysis of Variance and Covariance

Nonparametric Analysis

Survival Analysis

Time Series

Again using the regression section as an example, BMDP has five techniques for developing regression equations:

P1R—multiple linear regression using all the predictor variables

P2R—stepwise regression using either forward or backward stepping with specified criteria

P4R—regression on the principal components derived from the set of predictor variables

P5R—used when the criterion variable has a nonlinear relationship to the predictors

P9R—regression using all possible subsets of predictor variables

Although BMDP is not as flexible for data management as SAS, the newer version is much improved. BMDP may be used interactively or in batch, depending on the capabilities of your computer center.

Appendix D

□

Sample Consent Forms

Application for the Conduct of Research Involving Human Subjects

Informed-Consent Form for Adults

Informed-Consent Form for Minors

Samples of Child Assent Forms

Animal Protocol Review

Sample Form D.1

Application for the Conduct of Research Involving Human Subjects
Arizona State University
University Human Subjects Research Review Committee

The Arizona State University Human Subjects Research Review Committee reviews all requests to conduct research involving human subjects. In completing the following application, be advised that the persons reviewing it may be entirely unfamiliar with the field of study involved. Present the request in typewritten form and in nontechnical terms understandable to the committee. It is the investigator's responsibility to give information about research procedure that is most likely to entail risk *but not to express judgment about the risk*. Please submit a copy of your complete proposal, an informed-consent/assent form as subjects will view it, and a curriculum vita or biographical sketch.

Principal investigator/director:	Department/center:	Date of request:

Type of review: New ☐   Renewal ☐   Continuation ☐

Exempt ☐   Identify by numbers that apply (see page 2) _____

Expedite ☐   Identify by numbers that apply (see page 4) _____

If Renewal or Continuation, are there any substantive changes?   Yes ☐ No ☐

Project title:

Agency submitted to:	Submission date:	Location of project:

1. General purpose of the research:

2. Data obtained by: Mail ☐   Telephone ☐   Interview ☐   Observation ☐   Experiment ☐   Secondary Source ☐   Other (explain) _____

3. Project description: The committee must have sufficient information, nontechnical and detailed, about what will happen with/to subjects to evaluate/estimate the risks. Assurance from the investigator, no matter how strong, will not substitute for a description of the transaction between investigator and subject. *If a questionnaire is used, attach a copy.*

When visual or auditory stimuli, chemical substances, or other measures might affect the health of subjects, a statement from a qualified person or other appropriate documentation will aid in evaluating the nature of any risk created. In questionable cases, the committee will require such documentation.

---

4. Subject selection: Will subjects be less than 18 years of age?   Yes ☐ No ☐
   How many subjects will participate? _____ Male ☐ Female ☐ Age __ to __
   Will subjects be students at Arizona State University?   Yes ☐ No ☐
   Source:_____

---

5. How will subjects be selected, enlisted, or recruited?

---

6. How will subjects be informed of procedures, intent of the study, and potential risks to them?

---

7. What steps will be taken to allow subjects to withdraw at any time without prejudice?

---

8. How will subjects' privacy be maintained and confidentiality guaranteed?

Attachments: Please indicate those items we can expect to find as attachments.

Complete proposal   ☐   Informed-consent form (as subjects will view it)   ☐
Questionnaire   ☐   Assent form (as child will view it)   ☐
Other instrumentation   ☐   Curriculum vita or biographical sketch   ☐
Other documentation _____

In making this application, I certify that I have read and understand the *Policies and Procedures for Projects that Involve Human Subjects*, and that I intend to comply with the letter and spirit of the university policy. Significant changes in the protocol will be submitted to the committee for written approval prior to these changes being put into practice. Informed-consent/assent records of the subjects will be kept for at least (3) years after the completion of the research.

Signatures: *Principal investigator (faculty)*	*Department chair*	Date

(Cont.)

Sample Form D.1 (Continued)

This application has been reviewed by the Arizona State University IRB:

Full Board Review ☐   Exempt ☐   Expedite ☐   Categories: _____

           Approved ☐   Deferred ☐   Disapproved ☐

Project requires review more often than annual ☐   every _____ months.

Renewal or continuation ☐   Approved with no substantive changes ☐

        Disapproved ☐   Approved with changes attached ☐

                       Third-party verification sought ☐

Comments, modifications/conditions for approval, or reason for disapproval:

Signature:

Chair of the University Committee   Date

Sample Form D.2

Informed-Consent Form for Adults

Read and address each numbered element of this model form in developing an informed-consent form for the proposed human research study. The items numbered and in quotations are to be included in the consent form. PLEASE NUMBER THE CONSENT FORM FOR SUBMISSION TO THE COMMITTEE. You may request the numbering be waived during data collection. The consent form must be written in lay language and must be typewritten. The language may be further simplified to meet the needs of a specific population. Add additional statements when appropriate.

1. *"Investigator's name,* who is *title/position,* has requested my participation in a research study at this institution. The title of the research is *title of research."* [Place title of project at top of all pages of consent form.]
2. "I have been informed that the purpose of the research is to . . ." [Describe the justification for the research. If appropriate, indicate the number of subjects involved and why the subject is included.]
3. "My participation will involve . . ." [Describe the subject's participation and identify those aspects of participation that are experimental. Indicate the expected duration of the subject's participation.]
4. "I understand there are foreseeable risks or discomforts to me if I agree to participate in the study. The possible risks are . . ." "Possible discomforts include . . ." [Any foreseeable risks or discomforts are to be explained/described.]

    OR

"There are no foreseeable risks or discomforts."

5. "I understand that there are alternative procedures available. Alternative procedures include . . ." [Describe any alternative procedures to be included in language the subject can understand.]

OR

"There are no feasible alternative procedures available for this study."

6. "I understand that the possible benefits of my participation in the research are . . ." [Describe the benefits of participation, or lack of benefits, to the individual subject as well as to society.]

7. "I understand that the results of the research study may be published but that my name or identity will not be revealed. In order to maintain confidentiality of my records, *name of investigator* will . . ." [Indicate specifically how the investigator will keep the names of the subjects confidential, the use of subject codes, how this information will be secured, and who will have access to the confidential information. "Confidentiality will be maintained" is not acceptable.]

8. "I understand that in case of injury I can expect to receive the following treatment or care which will be provided at my expense:" [If *more* than minimal risk of foreseeable injury is anticipated, describe the facilities, medical treatment, or services that will be made available in the event of injury or illness to a subject. Description may include on- and off-campus services.]

OR

"I have been advised that the research in which I will be participating does not involve more than minimal risk." [If the research will *not* involve more than minimal risk, briefly explain how or why the investigator determined that the subject would be exposed to no more than minimal risk.]

9. "I have been informed that I will be compensated for my participation as follows:" [If compensation is to be provided to subject, include amount of compensation, method of payment, and schedule for payment including whether payment will be made in increments or in one lump sum.]

OR

"I have been informed that I will not be compensated for my participation."

10. "I have been informed that any questions I have concerning the research study or my participation in it, before or after my consent, will be answered by *name of individual, address, and telephone number.*" [This refers to the principal investigator. In the event the investigator is a student, the name of the doctoral or thesis advisor (responsible faculty member) must be included.]

11. "I understand that in case of injury, if I have questions about my rights as a subject/participant in this research, or if I feel I have been placed at risk, I can contact the Chair of the Human Subjects Research Review Committee." [This information must be included in all consent forms.]

12. "I have read the above information. The nature, demands, risks, and benefits of the project have been explained to me. I knowingly assume the risks involved, and understand that

(Cont.)

Sample Form D.2 (Continued)

I may withdraw my consent and discontinue participation at any time without penalty or loss of benefit to myself. In signing this consent form, I am not waiving any legal claims, rights, or remedies. A copy of this consent form will be given to me.''

Subject's signature _____ Date _____

Other signature (if appropriate) _____ Date _____

13. "I certify that I have explained to the above individual the nature and purpose, the potential benefits, and possible risks associated with participation in this research study, have answered any questions that have been raised, and have witnessed the above signature.''
14. "These elements of informed consent conform to the Assurance given by Arizona State University to the Department of Health and Human Services to protect the rights of human subjects.''
15. "I have provided the subject/participant a copy of this signed consent document.''

Signature of investigator _____ Date _____

Sample Form D.3

Informed-Consent Form for Minors

The elements of the informed-consent form for adults are used with the following variations:

1. "*Investigator's name*, who is *title/position* at Arizona State University, has requested my minor child's (ward's) participation in a research study at this institution. The title of the research is *title of research*.''
2. [same as adult]
3. "My child's (ward's) participation will involve . . .''
4. [same as adult]
5. [same as adult]
6. "I understand that the possible benefits of my child's (ward's) participation in the research are . . .''
7. "I understand that the results of the research study may be published but that my child's (ward's) name or identity will not be revealed. In order to maintain confidentiality of my child's (ward's) records, *name of investigator* will . . .''
8. "I understand that in case of injury I can expect the following treatment or care to be provided at my expense . . .''

   OR

   "I have been advised that the research in which my child (ward) will be participating does not involve more than minimal risk.''
9. "I have been informed that compensation for participation is as follows: . . .''

   OR

   "I have been informed that I will not be compensated for my child's (ward's) participation.''

10. [same as adult]
11. [same as adult]
12. [same as adult]

Subject's signature _____ Date _____
(father, mother, legal guardian, or legally authorized official)

Other signature _____ Date _____

13. [same as adult]
14. [same as adult]
15. [same as adult]

Sample Form D.4

Child Assent Form

Language must be simplified as appropriate for the age-group used as subjects, such as:

    I, _____, understand that my parents (mom and dad) have

given permission (said it's okay) for me to take part in a project about _____

_____

done by _____.

    I am taking part because I want to, and I have been told that I can stop at any time I
want to and I won't get in trouble (nothing bad will happen to me if I want to stop).

                                                Signature

OR

(Cont.)

Sample Form D.4 (Continued)

I, _____, understand that my parents have given permission for

me to participate in a study concerning _____

_____

under the direction of _____.
My involvement in this project is voluntary, and I have been told that I may withdraw
from participation in this study at any time without penalty and loss of benefit to myself.

_____
Signature

Sample Form D.5

Date filed: _____   Project no.: _____

Animal Protocol Review
Arizona State University Animal Care and Use Committee

Please read "Instructions for Completing Animal Protocol Review."

  I. A. A single member of the university faculty and/or principal investigator is considered
the responsible individual.

      Name: _____ Campus phone: _____

    B. University position and department: _____

    C. Project/program title:_____

      _____

    D. __ Nonfunded research __ Teaching __ Grant/contract

    E. Protocol type: New __ Renewal __ Revision __ Previous no.__

    F. Research (see 1, 2, 3, and 4 below): __

      Teaching (see 5 and 6 below): __

      1. Granting agency: _____ Deadline: _____

      2. Coinvestigator(s): _____

3. Graduate student: _____ Phone: _____

4. Thesis/research degree program: _____

_____

5. Course title, schedule: _____

6. Teaching assistant/laboratory instructor(s): _____

_____

II. A. List species: _____

   B. Where will you prefer animals be housed? _____

   C. Does project require a waiver of provision(s) of PHS policy?

      No ___ Yes ___ (If yes, attach a Request of Waiver statement justifying the need for the waiver.)

      Review date(s): _____ Approval date: _____

      Signature, Chair: _____

III. A. *Abstract of planned use of animals.* Write a brief yet complete description of the planned use of animals. (Use additional pages if necessary.) Use language understandable to a layperson. One complete copy of a grant proposal or graduate student research proposal must be attached to the original.

    B. *Rationale for involving animals and the appropriateness of the species and number used* (include potential contribution the species may generate and state briefly why living vertebrates are required rather than some alternate model).

IV.   Animals to be used:

   A. Species (give both scientific and common names for unusual species): Is this a threatened or endangered species? Yes ___ No ___

   B. Estimated number: Per year _____ Entire study _____ Are these estimated number of animals maximum for the entire study?
                          Yes ___ No ___

   C. Sex and age (or weight range): _____

   D. Source (e.g., purchased, institutional bred, transferred from another study, donated, captured from wild):

_____

(Cont.)

Sample Form D.5 (Continued)

    E. Will animals stay in investigator's lab at any time? Yes __ No __

    If so, how long? _____

    If greater than 24 hours, state justification: _____

_____

    All facilities or laboratories that house animals for longer than 24 hours must be inspected and approved according to DHEW policy.

V.   Major categories of use:
Please check those applicable and attach appropriate sections concerning methodology from your grant proposal or a brief description of the methodology to be used in nonfunded project or course.

Yes No

__ __ a. Harvest tissue, blood, etc.

__ __ b. Immunization for antibody production; describe antigen adjuvant used, route of immunization, method of obtaining blood.

__ __ c. Physiologic measurements; if surgery is necessary, see "n."

__ __ d. Dietary manipulations (e.g., caloric restrictions, specific constituent restriction).

__ __ e. Pharmacologic/toxicologic material used, route of administration, etc.

__ __ f. Immunologic studies.

__ __ g. Behavioral studies.

__ __ h. Irradiation; include Radioisotope Approval Form.

__ __ i. Biohazardous materials (carcinogens, chemicals, etc.); include Biohazard Approval Form.

__ __ j. Infectious agents; include Biohazard Approval Form.

__ __ k. *Trauma, injury, burning, freezing, electric shock.

__ __ l. *Environmental stress (e.g., temperature, long-term restraint, forced exercise, nutritional distress).

__ __ m. Other: _____

__ __ n. Surgery: If "Yes," complete Item VI below.

        *Submit necessary justifications(s).

VI.   Surgical procedures:

A. Survival* _____ Nonsurvival _____
*All survival surgery will be performed under aseptic conditions.

B. Where is surgery to be performed? _____

C. Person performing surgery; person's qualifications: _____
_____

D. Anesthetic regimen:

Drug: _____ Dose:_____

Route: _____ Duration: _____

Monitoring procedures:

Who will administer/monitor anesthesia, and what are their qualifications?
_____

If anesthetics are not used, justify: _____
_____

E. Postoperative pain or distress:

Is postoperative pain or distress anticipated? Yes __ No __

Will analgesics/tranquilizers be used? Yes __ No __

Drug: _____ Dose: _____

Route: _____ Duration: _____

If pain/distress are anticipated but analgesics/tranquilizers will not be used, attach Justification of Pain or Distress statement.
_____
_____

F. Postoperative care:

Intensive care required? __ Yes __ No

What time period? _____

Who will provide care? _____

Postoperative routine:

Who will provide? _____

What monitoring will be performed? _____

What drugs administered? _____

Antibiotics (type/dosage/frequency)? _____
_____

(Cont.)

Sample Form D.5 (Continued)

Special care to be provided: _____

_____

Person(s) to contact in case of emergency:

_____

Phone: Office _____ Home _____

What postoperative complications may be expected? _____

_____

Method of treatment: _____

_____

G. Multiple surgical procedures: Will individual animals be subjected to more than one surgical procedure? __ Yes __ No
If yes, provide justification.

H. Have all personnel on this protocol been certified in the federal mandated training requirement? __ Yes __ No

VII.   Euthanasia
A. What is (are) method(s) of euthanasia?

Chemical/gas: Agent _____ Dose _____
               Agent _____ Dose _____

Physical: __ Cervical dislocation (mice, immature rats)

           __ Decapitation (rodents)

           __ Captive bolt

           __ Exsanguination under anesthesia

           __ Other* _____

           __ *Scientific justification (references if possible):

                _____

                _____

B. Name any qualifications of person(s) performing euthanasia:

_____

_____

_____

VIII. Assurance:

The information contained herein is accurate to the best of my knowledge. Procedures involving animals will be carried out humanely, and all procedures will be performed by or under the direction of trained or experienced persons. Any revisions to animal care and use in this project will be promptly forwarded to the Animal Care and Use Committee for review. *Revised protocols will not be used until committee clearance is received. The use of alternatives to animal models has been considered and found to be unacceptable at this time.*

_____ _____
Signature (individual listed on I.A. and graduate student, Date
if applicable)

IX. Additional approval:

The department chair and the college dean must sign the protocol after approval by the Animal Care and Use Committee.

_____ _____
Chair   Date

_____ _____
Dean   Date

Glossary

abscissa—The horizontal, or *x-*, axis of a graph.

absolute error (AE)—Amount of error, disregarding plus and minus signs and divided by number of scores.

absolute strength—The measure of a person's strength with no consideration given to body size or maximum strength.

Academic Learning Time in Physical Education (ALT-PE)—Observational recording instrument developed by Siedentop and graduate students (1979, 1982) that entails time sampling in which a child is observed for a specified period of time and the child's activities during that time period are coded.

acknowledgments—Section of a scholarly paper that credits individuals important to the development of the work.

adaptive testing—Practice of selecting test items that will best fit the ability level of each individual; also called *tailored testing*.

agility—The accuracy and speed of changing direction while moving.

agon—One of four classification categories of games that describes games in which competition is dominant.

alea—One of four classification categories of games that describes games in which the player has no control over the outcome and in which fate or luck is dominant.

alpha—A level of probability (of chance occurrence) set by the experimenter prior to the study; sometimes referred to as level of significance.

alternate-forms method—Method of establishing reliability involving the construction of two tests, both that supposedly sample the same material; also called *parallel-form method* or the *equivalence method*.

alternative format for thesis and dissertation writing—Attempt to move away from the traditional format of thesis and dissertation writing to facilitate the publication of them.

analysis of covariance (ANCOVA)—A combination of regression and ANOVA that statistically adjusts the dependent variable for some distractor variable called the *covariate*.

analysis of variance (ANOVA)—Test that allows the evaluation of the null hypothesis between two or more group means.

analytical research—Type of research that involves in-depth study and evaluation of available information in an attempt to explain complex phenomena; can be categorized in the following way: historical, philosophic, review, and meta-analysis.

analytic history—type of historical research that focuses on how something occurred and why someone did something.

analytic narrative—A short, interpretive description of an event or situation used in qualitative research.

annotated bibliography—List of resources that provides a brief description of the nature and scope of each article or book.

anticipation timer—Motor behavior task using a trackway with lights mounted at close intervals that turn on and off consecutively, simulating movement. The subject attempts to press a hand-held button when the last light turns on and off.

antiquarianism—Collecting of old things; appropriate for historical research.

applied research—Type of research that has direct value to practitioners but in which the researcher has limited control over the research setting.

approach—See *paradigm*.

Attitude Toward Physical Activity (ATPA) Inventory—Kenyon's (1968) well-constructed attitude inventory based on the premise that attitude toward activity is relatively stable, and that positive attitudes are manifested by active participation or by watching others perform.

Avis effect—A threat to internal validity wherein subjects in the control group may try harder just because they are in the control group.

backward selection—Procedure used in multiple regression and discriminant analysis in which all the variables are entered, then those that contribute least to predicting the criterion, or group membership, are sequentially removed.

basic research—Type of research that may have limited direct application but in which the researcher has careful control of the conditions.

beta—The magnitude of committing a Type II error; it also refers to the coefficient representing the slope of the line in regression.

biomechanics—The application of the physical laws of motion to the study of biological systems.

blind setup—Method of controlling a threat to internal validity in which the subject does not know if he or she is receiving the experimental or control treatment.

body composition measurement—Assessment of the ratio of lean body weight (composed of muscle, bone, and other tissues) to internal and subcutaneous fat weight.

broadness—A method of testing the validity of necessary and sufficient conditions in philosophic research in which the conditions must be narrow enough not to include illegitimate activities.

canonical correlation—A correlational technique that can determine the relationship when there are two or more criterion variables and two or more predictor variables.

case study—Form of descriptive research in which a single case is studied in depth to reach a greater understanding about other similar cases.

categorical response—Type of closed question that offers the subject only two responses, such as "yes" or "no."

categorical variable—A kind of independent variable that cannot be manipulated because it is categorized by age, race, sex, and so on; also called *moderator variable*.

Cattell 16 Personality Factor (PF) Questionnaire—Instrument that has frequently been used in research studies to assess personality traits.

central tendency (measure of)—A single score that best represents all of the scores.

central tendency error—Inclination of the rater to give an inordinate number of ratings in the middle of the scale, avoiding the extremes of the scale.

Cheffers' Adaptation of the Flanders' Interaction Analysis System (CAFIAS)—Observational recording instrument developed by Cheffers (1972) that provides a device for coding behavior through a double category system so that any behavior can be categorized as verbal, nonverbal, or both.

chi-square—Technique that provides a statistical test as to the significance of the discrepancy between the observed and the expected results.

chronicle—A listing of the happenings in time; used in historical research.

classical test theory (CTT)—A measurement theory built on the concept of observed scores being composed of a true score and an error score.

closed loop theory—Theory of motor skill learning advanced by Adams (1971) in which information received as feedback from a movement is compared to some internal reference of correctness.

closed question—Category of question found in questionnaires or interviews that requires a specific response and that often takes the form of rankings, scaled items, and categorical responses.

Coaches Behavioral Assessment Scale (CBAS)—Recording instrument developed by Smith, Smoll, and Hunt (1977) to record the reactive and spontaneous behaviors of the coach to actions of players during games.

coefficient alpha—See *Cronbach alpha coefficient*.

coefficient of correlation—A quantitative value of the relationship between two or more variables that can range from 0.00 to 1.00 in either a positive or negative direction; also called *correlation*.

coefficient of determination—The squared correlation coefficient; used in interpreting meaningfulness of correlations.

cohorts—Problem in cross-sectional design that questions whether all the age groups are really from the same population.

compound symmetry—Antiquated assumption that all variables within a group must have equal variances, all correlations among variables must be equal, and the covariance matrices of all groups must be equal.

concurrent validity—Type of criterion validity in which a measuring instrument is correlated with some criterion that is administered at about the same time, or concurrently.

confirmatory factor analysis—A type of factor analysis that tests hypotheses about the structuring of variables with regard to the expected number of significant factors.

constant error (CE)—Algebraic sum of plus and minus error divided by number of scores.

construct validity—Degree to which a test measures a hypothetical construct; usually established by relating the test results to some behavior.

content validity—Condition that is claimed (usually in educational settings) when a test adequately samples what was covered in the course.

context—In historical research, the total network of facts and meanings in the background of a subject.

contingency coefficient—Method of computing the relationship between dichotomous variables such as gender and race.

contingency table—A two-way classification of categories of occurrences and two or more groups that is used for computing the significance of the differences between observed and expected scores.

continual recording technique—See *narrative technique*.

control variable—A factor that could possibly influence the results and that is kept out of the study.

convergence—Consistency of results across two or more methodological techniques.

convergent validity—Correlations between measures of the same construct.

correlation—See *coefficient of correlation*.

correlation research—Research that explores relationships among variables; sometimes involves prediction of a criterion variable.

covariate—A distractor variable that is statistically controlled in ANCOVA and MANCOVA.

cover letter—The letter attached to a survey that explains the purposes and importance of the survey.

Cowell Social Adjustment Index—An early social behavior rating scale developed by Cowell (1958) that involves teacher ratings of the degree to which students display certain behavior traits.

criterion-based sampling—See *purposive sampling*.

criterion validity—The degree to which scores on a test are related to some recognized standard, or criterion.

critical theory—A value-based form of qualitative research that helps individuals make constructive choices.

Cronbach alpha coefficient—A technique used in estimating reliability of multiple trial tests; also called *coefficient alpha.*

cross-sectional study—Method of research in which samples of subjects from different age groups are selected in order to assess the effects of maturation.

cross-validation—Technique to assess the accuracy of a prediction formula in which the formula is applied to a sample not used when the formula was developed.

decision accuracy—Approach used to validate criterion-referenced tests that assesses the accuracy of classifications of individuals to mastery and nonmastery categories.

deductive reasoning—Logical process in which the researcher moves from a theoretical explanation of events down to specific hypotheses about events.

delimitation—A limitation, imposed by the researcher, in the scope of the study; a choice the researcher makes to effect a workable research problem.

Delphi survey method—Survey technique that uses a series of questionnaires in such a way that the respondents (usually experts) reach a consensus about the subject.

dependent *t* test—A test of the significance of differences between means of two sets of scores that are related, such as when the same subjects are measured on two occasions.

dependent variable—The effect of the independent variable; also called the *yield.*

descriptive history—A method of constructing a "map" of past experience that locates in time and place a person, a trend, an event, or an organization by providing answers to particular questions.

descriptive research—Type of research concerned with status, including techniques such as surveys, case studies, and developmental research.

developmental research—Study of changes in behavior across the life span.

discriminant validity—Evidence of validity demonstrated by weak correlations between measures of different constructs; also called *divergent validity.*

discussion—Chapter or section of a research report that explains what the results mean.

distribution-free statistics—See *nonparametric statistical test.*

divergent validity—See *discriminant validity.*

documentary analysis—Type of descriptive research directed primarily at establishing the status of certain practices; areas of interest; and the prevalence of certain errors, usage of terms, and space counts.

domain-referenced validity—The degree to which a test measures essential components or objectives of a domain.

double-blind setup—Method of controlling a threat to internal validity in which neither the subject nor the experimenter knows which treatment the subject is receiving.

D study—An approach employed in generalizability theory in which the researcher calculates generalizability coefficients for the various facets in the study.

dual publication—Occurrence of having the same scientific paper published in more than one journal or other publication; generally unethical.

duration method—Method of recording in observational research in which the researcher uses a stopwatch or other timing device to record how much time a subject spends engaged in a particular behavior.

dynamic balance—The ability to maintain equilibrium while moving.

ecological validity—The extent to which research emulates the real world.

effect size—A standardized value, the difference between the means divided by the standard deviation.

eigenvalues—The squared and summed correlations of each variable, or test, for a factor; the y-axis on a scree curve.

electrogoniometer—Instrument used to measure flexibility.

electromyography (EMG)—Technique that uses skin or muscle electrodes to pick up electrical activity caused by muscle contraction during movement.

empirical—Describes data or a study that is based on objective observations.

endogenous variable—A characteristic in path analysis whose variance is explained by exogenous variables, other variables within the model, or both.

equally likely events—A concept of probability in which the chances of one event occurring are the same as the chances of another event occurring.

equivalence method—See *alternate-form method*.

error score—In classical test theory, the part of an observed score that is attributed to measurement error.

error variance—The portion of the scores that is attributed to subject variability.

expectancy—A threat to internal validity in which the researcher anticipates certain behavior or results to occur.

experimental research—Type of research that involves the manipulation of treatments in an attempt to establish cause-effect relationships.

experimental variable—See *independent variable*.

exploratory factor analysis—Factor analysis performed for the purpose of identifying basic constructs, or factors, that underlie a set of measures.

exogenous variable—A characteristic in path analysis whose variance is explained by factors outside the model.

external criticism—Phase of historical research process that establishes the authenticity of the source.

external reliability—The content of the data in qualitative research that determines the degree to which a study can be repeated.

external validity—The generalizability of the results of a study.

extraneous variable—A factor that could affect the relationship between the independent and dependent variables, but that is not included or controlled.

extrapolations approach—See *implications approach*.

face validity—See *logical validity*.

factor analysis—A statistical technique used to reduce a set of data by grouping similar variables into basic components (factors).

factorial ANOVA—Analysis of variance in which there is more than one independent variable.

family resemblance theory—Theory in philosophic research in which, in an attempt to unify components of a concept, the researcher recognizes that though the components lack specific shared characteristics, they share a system of overlapping features.

fieldwork—A methodology common in qualitative research in which data are gathered in natural settings.

Fisher Z transformation—Method of approximating normality of a sampling distribution of linear relationship by transforming coefficients of correlation to Z-values.

flexibility—The range of movement about a joint.

force transducer—Device in biomechanical research that measures the forces exerted during motor performance, including the reactions between a runner's or jumper's feet and the ground as well as the forces exerted against equipment.

forward selection—Procedure used in multiple regression and discriminant analysis that enters the variables for prediction, or discrimination among groups, in order of their importance.

free editing—See *rule of omission*.

frequency counting method—See *tallying method*.

gain score—The result of subtracting each subject's pretest value from the posttest value.

Geisser/Greenhouse correction—A conservative approach to the adjustment of the epsilon estimate in repeated measures ANOVA that calculates adjusted degrees of freedom to find an *F* ratio to determine significance.

generalizability theory (G-theory)—An extension of intraclass reliability that enables the researcher to identify sources of error in estimating reliability of scores on a test.

goniometer—Instrument used to measure the range of motion in a joint.

goodness of fit—Approach to philosophic inquiry in which the researcher, following exposure to a paradigm, attempts to determine whether some activity or object can be shown to properly fit as an instance of that paradigm (also a χ^2 estimate used in confirmatory factory analysis).

grounded theory—A theory based on and evolving from data.

G study—An approach employed in generalizability theory that uses repeated measures ANOVA to help identify the relative importance of different sources of variance that contribute to measurement error.

halo effect—A threat to internal validity wherein raters allow previous impressions or knowledge about a certain individual to influence ratings on all of that individual's behaviors.

hardware—The mechanical units of a computer, such as the monitor, keyboard, disk drive, and printer.

high-speed cinematography—Most widely used measure in biomechanics in which a camera or cameras allow motion to be studied.

historical research—Type of research that deals with events that have already occurred.

hydrostatic weighing—Technique that measures body composition in which body density is computed by the ratio of an individual's weight in air and the loss of weight underwater.

hypothesis—The anticipated outcome of a study or experiment.

ilinx—One of four classification categories of games that describes games that are based on the pursuit of vertigo and that consist of an attempt to momentarily destroy the stability of perception.

implications approach—Method of philosophic research in which the researcher, following exposure to a paradigm, attempts to determine what a given phenomenon would or should be like if it were to conform to that paradigm; also called *extrapolations approach*.

independent *t* test—The most frequently used test to determine if two sample means differ reliably from each other.

independent variable—The part of the experiment that the researcher is manipulating; also called the *experimental* or *treatment variable*.

index of discrimination—The degree to which a test item discriminates between persons who did well on the entire test and those who did poorly; also called *item discrimination*.

inductive reasoning—Logical process in which the researcher moves from specific observations through testing hypotheses to developing a general theory.

inference—Generalization of results to some larger group.

interclass correlation—See *Pearson r*.

internal consistency—An estimate of the reliability of a set of scores that represents the consistency of repeated measures given on the same day; also called *same-day test-retest method*.

internal criticism—Phase of historical research process that establishes the credibility of a genuine artifact or document.

internal reliability—The extent of agreement among different observers concerning the description of events.

internal validity—The extent to which the results of a study can be attributed to the treatments used in the study.

interobserver agreement (IOA)—Common way of estimating reliability among coders by using a formula that divides the number of commonly coded behaviors by the sum of the commonly coded behaviors and behaviors coded differently.

intertester (interrater) reliability—The degree to which different testers can obtain the same scores on the same subjects; also called *objectivity*.

interval method—Method of recording in observational research, used when it is difficult to count individual occurrences, in which the researcher records whether the behavior in question occurs in a certain interval of time.

interval scale—Scale of measurement that provides not only the order between scores, but also the magnitude of the distance between them.

interview—Survey technique similar to the questionnaire except that subjects are questioned and respond verbally rather than in writing.

intraclass correlation—A correlation coefficient, computed by analysis of variance, that is used in estimating test reliability.

item analysis—Process in analyzing knowledge tests in which items are evaluated as to their suitability with regard to difficulty and discrimination.

item banking—The creation of large pools of test items that can be used for constructing tests that have certain characteristics with regard to the precision of estimating latent ability.

item characteristic curve (ICC)—Nonlinear regression for any item that increases from left to right, indicating an increase in the probability of a correct response with increased ability, or latent trait.

item difficulty—Analysis of the difficulty of each test item in a knowledge test determined by dividing the number of persons who correctly answered the item by the total number of people who responded to the item.

item discrimination—See *index of discrimination*.

item response theory (IRT)—A theory that focuses on the characteristics of the test item and the examinee's response to the item as a means of determining the examinee's ability; also called *latent trait theory*.

job analysis—Type of case study that determines the nature of a particular job and the types of training, preparation, skills, and attitudes necessary for success in the job.

kinesiology—The study of human movement dealing with the interrelationships of anatomy, neuromuscular physiology, and mechanics.

kinesthetic measurement—Measurement of one's ability to perceive body position and changes in force and degree of movement of the body and body parts.

known group difference method—Method used in establishing construct validity in which the test scores of groups that should differ on a trait or ability are compared.

Kuder-Richardson (K-R) method of rational equivalence—Formulas developed for estimating reliability of a test from a single test administration.

kurtosis—Description of the shape of the curve of the distribution of data, for example, whether the curve is more peaked or flatter than the normal curve.

Lakie Attitude Toward Athletic Competition Scale—Pencil-and-paper test of sportsmanship developed by Lakie (1964) in which the respondent is asked to indicate whether the course of action described is appropriate.

language analysis—Method of philosophic inquiry aimed at detecting contradictory or confusing ways in which terms are used.

latent trait theory—See *item response theory*.

law—Generalization about natural phenomena that describes what some "thing" is, often expressed mathematically.

leniency—Tendency for observers to be overly generous in rating.

Likert scale—Type of closed question that requires the subject to respond by choosing one of five scaled items with the assumption that there are equal intervals between items.

limitation—A possible shortcoming or influence that either cannot be controlled or is the result of the delimitations imposed by the investigator.

linear slide—A motor task in which a blindfolded subject attempts to move a near-frictionless handle down a trackway to some specified location or a certain distance.

linear structural relations (LISREL)—A statistical approach used to establish relationships and examine the structural equations model.

logical validity—Condition that is claimed when the measure obviously involves the performance being measured; also known as *face validity*.

logit—Probability of membership in a particular category occurring as a function of membership in other categories in multivariate contingency tables.

loglinear model—A system that analyzes multivariate contingency tables by transforming relative frequencies into logarithms.

longitudinal study—Research in which the same subjects are studied over a period of years.

main effects—Tests of each independent variable when all other independent variables are held constant.

mainframe—A large computer.

MAXICON principle—A method of controlling any explanation for the results except the hypothesis the researcher intends to evaluate. This is done by maximizing true variance, minimizing error variance, and controlling extraneous variance.

maximum R^2 method—A multiple regression method in which the so-called best of all possible one-variable models is selected, as is the best two-variable model, the best three-variable model, and so on until a predetermined criterion that ends the calculations is reached.

mean—A statistical measure of central tendency that is the average score of the group.

median—A statistical measure of central tendency describing the middle score in a group.

meta-analysis—A technique of literature review that contains a definitive methodology and the quantification of the results of various studies to a standard metric that allows the use of statistical techniques as a means of analysis.

microcomputer—A small desktop computer.

microform—A general term that encompasses microfilm, microfiche, and any form of data storage where the pages of a book, journal, or newspaper are photographed and reduced in size.

mimicry—One of four classification categories of games that describes games in which players make believe or try to make others believe that they are someone other than themselves.

mode—A statistical measure of central tendency that is the most frequently occurring score of the group.

moderator variable—See *categorical variable*.

motor time (MT)—The peripheral component of reaction time comprised of the interval between the first muscle action potential and the initiation of the movement.

multiple regression—Model used for predicting a criterion from two or more independent, or predictor, variables.

multivariate analysis of covariance (MANCOVA)—An extension of MANOVA in which there are two or more independent variables, two or more dependent variables, and one or more covariates.

multivariate analysis of variance (MANOVA)—Analysis of variance wherein a combination of dependent variables is made that will maximally separate the levels of the independent variables.

muscular endurance—The ability to persevere in working against a submaximal resistance.

narrative technique—Method of recording in qualitative research in which the researcher records in a series of sentences the occurrences as they happen; also called *continual recording technique*.

narrative vignette—Component of qualitative research reports that gives detailed descriptions of an event, including what people say, do, think, and feel in that setting.

narrowness—A method of testing the validity of necessary and sufficient conditions in philosophic research in which the conditions must be broad enough that legitimate activities are not ruled out.

negative case selection—Procedure used in theorizing in which the researcher looks for exceptions to the hypothesized construct that require either a reformulation of the hypothesis, a redefinition of the phenomenon, or a qualification of the circumstances.

negative correlation—When a small amount of the first variable is associated with a large amount of the second variable, and a large amount of the first variable is associated with a small amount of the second variable.

nominal measure—Method of classifying data into categories, such as gender, age, grade level, or treatment groups.

nominal scale—Scale of measurement in which the scores are classified by name.

nonparametric statistical test—Any of a number of statistical techniques used when the data do not meet the assumptions required to perform parametric tests.

normal curve—Distribution of data in which the mean, median, and mode are at the same point (center of the distribution) and $\pm 1\ s$ from the mean includes 68% of the scores, $\pm 2\ s$ from the mean includes 95% of the scores, and $\pm 3\ s$ includes 99% of the scores.

normal science—An objective manner of study grounded in the natural sciences that is systematic, logical, empirical, reductive, and replicable.

normative survey—Survey method that involves establishing norms for abilities, performances, beliefs, and attitudes.

null hypothesis—Hypothesis that is primarily used in the statistical test for the reliability of the results that says that there are no differences among treatments (or no relationship among variables).

objectivity—See *intertester reliability*.

oblique rotation—A method in factor analysis in which the factors are redefined (and allowed to correlate) in order to make sharper distinctions in the meanings of the factors.

observed score—In classical test theory, an obtained score which is comprised of a person's true score and error score.

observer bias error—Inclination of a rater to be influenced by his or her own characteristics and prejudices.

observer expectation error—Inclination of a rater to see evidence of certain behaviors and interpret observations in the expected direction.

Omega squared (ω^2)—A method of interpreting the meaningfulness of the strength of the relationship between the independent and dependent variables; the proportion of total variance that is due to the treatments.

one-tailed *t* test—Test that assumes that the difference between the two means lies in one direction only.

open-ended question—Category of question in questionnaires and interviews that allows the respondent considerable latitude to express feelings and to expand on ideas.

operational definition—Observable phenomenon that enables the researcher to empirically test whether or not the predicted outcomes can be supported.

oral presentation—Method of presenting a paper in which the author speaks before a group of colleagues at a conference following this format: introduction, statement of the problem, method, results, discussion, questions.

ordinal scale—Scale of measurement in which scores are classified by ranks.

ordinate—The vertical, or *y*-, axis of a graph.

original position—Philosophic concept that describes the hypothetical situation in which all people seek fulfillment of their personal interests and desires.

orthogonal rotation—Technique in factor analysis designed to maximize the loadings of the tests, or variables, and minimize the relation among factors; also called *varimax rotation*.

outlier—Unrepresentative score; a score that lies outside of the normal scores.

overlap—The use of two variables that measure the same thing, so that the inclusion of both is no more beneficial than the use of only one.

paradigm—A scientific model and the approaches used to test that model; also called *perspective*, *tradition*, and *approach* in historical research.

paradigm crisis phenomenon—Theory advanced by Kuhn (1970) that espouses that normal science does not really evolve in systematic steps the way scientific writers describe it.

parallel-form method—See *alternate-form method*.

parameter invariance—A postulate in item response theory that the item difficulty remains constant regardless of different populations of examinees and that examinees' abilities should not change when a different set of test items is administered.

parametric statistical test—Test based on data assumptions of normal distribution and equal variance.

path analysis—Technique used to explain how certain characteristics relate to each other, with the hope of implying cause, by using correlations among all the variables to estimate the linkages among measures.

Pearson product moment coefficient of correlation—See *Pearson r*.

Pearson *r*—The most commonly used method of computing correlation between two variables; also called *interclass* or *Pearson product moment coefficient of correlation*.

perspective—See *paradigm*.

phenomenology—Method of philosophic research that designates those inquiries that focus on attempts to describe consciousness of experience.

philosophical research—Type of research characterized by critical inquiry in which the researcher establishes hypotheses, examines and analyzes existing facts, and synthesizes the evidence into a workable theoretical model.

Physical Estimation and Attraction Scale (PEAS)—Sonstroem's (1978) attitude inventory based on the theory that attitude toward activity is modifiable by participation in physical activity.

pilot study—A preliminary study done to validate the research methodology.

placebo—Method of controlling a threat to internal validity in which a control group receives a "false" treatment while the experimental group receives the real treatment.

plagiarism—Using ideas, concepts, writings, and drawings of others as your own; cheating.

planned comparison—Comparison among groups that are planned prior to the experiment, rather than as a follow-up of a test like ANOVA.

population—The larger group from which a sample is taken.

population specificity—Phenomenon whereby a regression equation that was developed with a particular sample loses considerable accuracy when applied to others.

positive correlation—When a small amount of one variable is associated with a small amount of another variable, and a large amount of one variable is associated with a large amount of the other.

poster session—Method of presenting research at a conference in which the author places summaries of his or her research on the wall or on a poster stand and answers questions from passers-by.

post hoc comparison—Comparison made after obtaining significant differences in the ANOVA.

power (statistical)—The degree to which the chances of rejecting a false null hypothesis are increased.

power (work)—The change in work divided by the change in time, or the time rate of change of work; the product of force times distance divided by time.

prediction equation—A formula to predict some criterion (e.g., some measure of performance) based on the relationship between the predictor variable(s) and the criterion; also called *regression equation*.

predictive validity—Degree to which scores of predictor variables can accurately predict criterion scores.

preexperimental design—Three types of research designs that control very few of the sources of invalidity and that do not have random assignments of subjects to groups: one-shot study, one-group pretest-posttest design, and static group comparison.

premotor time (PMT)—The central component of reaction time comprised of the time interval between stimulus presentation until the first action potential in the muscle is manifested.

primary source—Firsthand source of data in historical research in which there is only one person between the event and the researcher.

probability—The odds that a certain event will occur.

proportion of agreement index—Test of reliability in criterion-referenced measurements proposed by Hambleton and Novick (1973) to assess the consistency of correct decisions.

proximity error—Occurs when a rater considers behaviors to be more nearly the same when they are listed close together on a scale than when they are separated by some distance.

pursuit rotor—Motor behavior task in which the subject attempts to keep a hand-held stylus on a small circle located on a rotating disk.

qualitative research—Research method that involves intensive, long-time observation in a natural setting; precise and detailed recording of what happens in the setting; interpretation and analysis of the data using description, narratives, quotes, and charts and tables. Can also be called *ethnographic, naturalistic, interpretive, grounded, phenomenological, subjective,* and *participant observational.*

quasi-experimental design—Research designs in which the experimenter tries to fit the design to more "real-world" settings while still controlling as many of the threats to internal validity as possible.

questionnaire—type of paper-and-pencil survey used in descriptive research in which information is obtained by asking subjects to respond to questions rather than by observing their behavior.

random numbers table—A table in which numbers are arranged in two-digit (or greater) sets so that any combination of rows or columns is unrelated.

ranking—Type of closed question that forces the subject to place responses in a rank order according to some criterion.

Rating of Perceived Exertion (RPE)—Self-rating scale developed by Borg (1962) to measure an individual's perceived efforts during exercise.

rating scale—A measure of behavior that involves a subjective evaluation based on a checklist of criteria.

ratio scale—Scale of measurement that has all of the properties of nominal, ordinal, and interval measures, plus a true zero value that represents a complete absence of the characteristic.

reader—Machine that enlarges microforms to make the information readable.

reaction time—Time elapsed from the presentation of a stimulus until the initiation of a response.

reductionism—A characteristic of normal science that assumes that complex behavior can be reduced, analyzed, and explained as parts that can then be put back together to understand the whole.

regression equation—See *prediction equation.*

relative frequency—A concept of probability concerning the comparative likelihood of two or more events occurring.

relative strength—The measure of the ability to exert maximum force in relation to a person's size.

reliability—The consistency and dependability of a measure.

repeated measures ANOVA—Analysis of scores on the same individuals on successive occasions such as a series of test trials; also called *split-plot ANOVA* or *subject × trials ANOVA.*

research hypothesis—Hypothesis deduced from theory or induced from empirical studies that is based upon logical reasoning and is predictive of the outcome of the study.

research proposal—A formal preparation that includes the introduction, review of literature, and proposed method for conducting the study.

residual score—The difference between the predicted and actual scores that represents the error of prediction.

results—Chapter or section of a research report that describes what the researcher found.

review—A research paper that is a critical evaluation of research on a particular topic.

robust—Characteristic of a statistical test when it is relatively accurate even with fairly severe violations of the assumptions.

round—Stage of the Delphi survey method in which respondents are asked their opinions and evaluations on various issues, goals, and so on.

rule of context—A rule of internal criticism in historical research that maintains that a word must be understood in relation to the words that precede and follow it and not in the historian's own contemporary usage.

rule of omission—A rule of internal criticism in historical research that maintains that most historical sources are not accounts of complete scenes. Also called *free editing*.

rule of perspective—A rule of internal criticism in historical research that requires the researcher to determine who left the record, relationship of a source to an event or group, and how the source collected the information.

same-day test-retest method—See *internal consistency*.

sample—A group of subjects selected from a larger population.

scaled item—Type of closed question that requires subjects to indicate the strength of their agreement or disagreement with some statement or the relative frequency of some behavior.

schema theory—Theory of motor skill learning advanced by Schmidt (1975) as an extension of Adams's closed loop theory. The theory proposed to unify two more general explanations under one theoretical explanation.

science—A process of careful and systematic inquiry.

scientific method of problem solving—Method of solving problems in which the following steps are used: developing a problem, defining and delimiting the problem, forming a hypothesis, gathering data, analyzing data, and interpreting the results.

scree curve—A method used in factor analysis to determine the number of important factors.

secondary source—Source of data in historical research in which there is more than one person between the event and the researcher.

semantic differential scale—Scale used to measure affective behavior in which the respondent is asked to make judgments about certain concepts by choosing one of seven intervals between bipolar adjectives.

semipartial correlation—A technique in which one variable is partialed out from just one of two variables in a correlation.

shrinkage—Tendency for the validity to decrease when the prediction formula is used with a new sample.

significance—The reliability of or confidence in a statistic as to its likelihood of occurring again if the study were repeated.

simple structure—Research design in which the investigator wants each item to correlate highly on the one factor that item was designed to measure and load to a low degree on the other factors.

sit-and-reach—One of the oldest tests for measuring flexibility; from a sitting position the subject reaches as far forward (toward toes) as possible.

skewness—Description of the direction of the hump of the curve of distribution of data and the nature of the tails of the curve.

software—The programs of instructions used to make computers function in the desired manner.

Spearman-Brown prophecy formula—Equation developed to estimate the reliability for the entire test when the split-half technique is used to test reliability.

speculation—The basic component of the inductive process and the key to developing theories; requires the researcher to go beyond the data and predict what will happen in the future.

sphericity—An assumption with regard to repeated measures to the effect that they are uncorrelated and have equal variance.

split-half technique—Method of testing reliability in which the test is divided in two and the two halves are correlated, usually by making the odd numbers one part and the even numbers the other part.

split-plot ANOVA—See *repeated measures ANOVA*.

Sport Competition Anxiety Test (SCAT)—Martens's (1977) sport-specific trait anxiety inventory that predicts trait anxiety in a sport context compared with general trait anxiety scales.

spurious correlation—Relationship in which the correlation between two variables is due primarily to the common influence of another variable.

stability—A coefficient of reliability measured by the test-retest method on different days; also called *test-retest method*.

stabilometer—Device for measuring balance consisting of a platform on which the subject attempts to stand, keeping the sides from tilting and touching the floor.

standard deviation—An estimate of the variability of the scores of a group around the mean.

standard error of estimate—See *standard error of prediction*.

standard error of prediction—The computation of the standard deviation of all of the residual scores of a population; the amount of error expected in a prediction; also called *standard error of estimate*.

stanine—Type of standard score, derived from the words "standard" and "nine" because there are nine standard score units that have a mean of 5 and standard deviation of 2.

state anxiety—An immediate emotional state of apprehension and tension in response to a specific situation.

static balance—The ability to hold a stationary position.

stepdown *F* technique—A procedure used as a follow-up in multivariate analysis to determine the actual differences among groups.

step test—Test used to measure cardiorespiratory fitness involving the measurement of pulse rate after stepping up and down on a bench.

stepwise regression method—Regression and discriminant analysis procedure similar to forward selection except at each step all of the dependent variables are evaluated to see if each still contributes to prediction or group separation. If one dependent variable does not it is stepped out (removed) from the linear combination. It is also used in multiple regression for predicting the criterion.

stratified random sampling—Method of stratifying a population on some characteristic prior to random selection of the sample.

subjective (personalistic) probability—Concept in probability regarding the subjective chances of occurrence of an event.

subject × trials ANOVA—See *repeated measures ANOVA*.

sum of squares—A measure of variability of scores; the sum of the squared deviations from the mean of scores.

survey—Technique of descriptive research that seeks to determine present practices or opinions of a specified population; can take the form of a questionnaire, interview, or normative survey.

T scale—Type of standard score that sets the mean at 50 and standard deviation at 10 to remove the decimal found in z-scores and to make all scores positive.

tailored testing—See *adaptive testing*.

tallying method—Method of recording in observational research in which the researcher records occurrence of a clearly defined behavior within a certain time frame; also called *frequency counting method*.

tapping board—Motor behavior task in which a subject attempts to tap a metal stylus as quickly as possible back and forth between two circles mounted a certain distance apart.

taxonomy—A classification system.

tenacity—An unscientific method of problem solving in which people cling to certain beliefs regardless of the lack of supporting evidence.

test-retest method—Method of determining reliability in which a test is given one day and then administered exactly as before a day or so later; also called *stability*.

theorizing—Cognitive process of discovering abstract categories and the relationships among those categories.

theory—Explanation of some aspect of practice that permits the researcher to draw inferences about future happenings.

Thurstone-type scale—Scale used to measure affective behavior in which the respondent expresses agreement or disagreement with each item, which has been rated by a panel of judges and scaled with a numerical value to reflect the most positive attitude.

tradition—See *paradigm*.

trait anxiety—General tendency to be anxious.

transferability—In qualitative research, the term analogous to external validity in experimental research.

treatment variable—See *independent variable*.

triangulation—Term borrowed from the field of surveying that refers to the use of more than one source of data to substantiate a researcher's conclusion.

true experimental design—Any design used in experimental research in which groups are randomly formed and that controls most sources of invalidity.

true score—In classical test theory, the part of the observed score that represents the individual's real score and does not contain measurement error.

true variance—The portion of the differences in scores that is (theoretically) real.

truth table—A graphic representation of correct and incorrect decisions regarding Type I and Type II errors.

truth value—In qualitative research, the term analogous to internal validity in experimental research.

t test—A statistical technique to assess differences between two groups.

two-tailed t test—Test that assumes that the difference between the two means could favor either group.

Type I error—A rejection of the null hypothesis when the null hypothesis is true.

Type II error—Acceptance of the null hypothesis when the null hypothesis is false.

Type III error—Solving the wrong problem.

Type IV error—Solving a problem that is not worth solving.

univariate technique—Statistical technique applied in the analysis of only one dependent variable.

user generalizability—Concept in which the user (reader) evaluates the findings of the carefully described and interpreted study and asks what things apply to his or her situation.

validity—Degree to which a test or instrument measures what it purports to measure; can be categorized as *logical*, *content*, *criterion*, and *construct*.

variability—The degree of difference between each individual score and the central tendency score.

variability of practice—Tenet of motor skill learning advanced by Schmidt in which the practice of a variety of movement experiences facilitates transfer to a new movement when compared to practicing a single movement.

variable error (VE)—The standard deviation of the average constant error (CE) score.

variance—The square of the standard deviation.

varimax rotation—See *orthogonal rotation*.

veil of ignorance—Philosophic concept that describes the hypothetical situation in which all people have a limited knowledge of class position, status, economic worth, natural abilities, and assets.

Wherry-Doolittle method—A multiple correlation technique used in test selection.

Yates' correction for continuity—Method of correcting a 2×2 contingency table by subtracting 0.5 from the difference between the observed and expected frequencies for each cell before it is squared.

yield—See *dependent variable*.

z score—The basic standard score that converts raw scores to a mean of 0 with a standard deviation of 1.0.

References

Abe, S. (1986). Zen and sport. *Journal of the Philosophy of Sport*, **13**, 45-48.

Adams, J.A. (1971). A closed-loop theory of motor learning. *Journal of Motor Behavior*, **3**, 111-150.

Agar, M.H. (1986). *Speaking of ethnography*. Beverly Hills, CA: Sage.

Alderman, R.B. (1974). *Psychological behavior in sport*. Philadelphia: W.B. Saunders.

Alston, W.P. (1967). Language, philosophy of. In P. Edwards (Ed.), *The encyclopedia of philosophy* (Vol. 4, pp. 386-390). New York: Macmillan.

American Alliance for Health, Physical Education, Recreation and Dance. (1980). *AAHPERD health related physical fitness test manual*. Reston, VA: Author.

American Alliance for Health, Physical Education, Recreation and Dance. (1989). *AAHPERD physical best: The AAHPERD guide to physical fitness education and assessment*. Reston, VA: Author.

American Association for Health, Physical Education and Recreation. (1958). *AAHPER youth fitness test manual*. Washington, DC: Author.

American Psychological Association. (1959). *Graduate education in psychology*. Washington, DC: Author.

American Psychological Association. (1981). Ethical principles of psychologists (revised). *American Psychologist*, **36**, 633-638.

American Psychological Association. (1983). *Publication manual of the American Psychological Association* (3rd ed.). Washington, DC: Author.

Anshel, M.H., & Marisi, D.Q. (1978). Effects of music and rhythm on physical performance. *Research Quarterly*, **49**, 109-115.

Arlin, M. (1977). One-study publishing typifies educational inquiry. *Educational Researcher*, **6**(9), 11-15.

Arnold, P.J. (1986). Kinaesthetic feelings, physical skills and the anti-private language argument. *Journal of the Philosophy of Sport*, **13**, 29-34.

Arnold, P.J. (1988). Education, movement, and the rationality of practical knowledge. *Quest*, **40**, 115-125.

Bain, L.L. (1988). Beginning the journey: Agenda for 2001. *Quest*, **40**, 96-106.

Bain, L.L. (1989). Interpretive and critical research in sport and physical education. *Research Quarterly for Exercise and Sport*, **60**, 21-24.

Barnett, V., & Lewis, T. (1978). *Outliers in statistical data*. New York: Wiley.

Bartling, J. (1989). Forty years in the gym. *Quest*, **41**, 156-157.

Bartz, A.E. (1976). *Basic statistical concepts in education and the behavioral sciences*. Minneapolis: Burgess.

Baumgartner, T.A. (1989). Norm-referenced measurement: Reliability. In M.J. Safrit & T.M. Wood (Eds.), *Measurement concepts in physical education and exercise science* (pp. 45-72). Champaign, IL: Human Kinetics.

Baumgartner, T.A., & Jackson, A.S. (1987). *Measurement for evaluation in physical education* (3rd ed.). Dubuque, IA: Wm. C. Brown.

Behnke, A.R., & Wilmore, J.H. (1974). *Evaluation and regulation of body build and composition*. Englewood Cliffs, NJ: Prentice-Hall.

Berelson, B. (1960). *Graduate education in the United States*. New York: McGraw-Hill.

Blattner, S.E., & Noble, L. (1979). Relative effects of isokinetic and plyometric training on vertical jumping performance. *Research Quarterly*, **50**, 583-588.

Bogdan, R.C., & Biklen, S.K. (1982). *Qualitative research for education: An introduction to theory and methods*. Newton, MA: Allyn & Bacon.

Borg, G.A. (1962). *Physical performance and perceived exertion*. Lund, Sweden: Gleerup.

➤ Borg, W.R., & Gall, M.D. (1983). *Educational research: An introduction* (4th ed.). New York: Longman

Boroviak, P.C. (1989). A golfer's dream. *Quest*, **41**, 104-105.

Boyer, C.J. (1973). *The doctoral dissertation as an informational source: A study of scientific information flow*. Metuchen, NJ: Scarecrow Press.

Bressman, S.S., & Pieter, W. (1985). Philosophic processes and the study of human movement. *Quest*, **37**, 1-15.

Brown, J.A.C. (1954). *The social psychology of industry*. Middlesex, England: Penguin.

Burdett, R.G. (1983). Status of biomechanical research in sport and physical education. *Research Consortium Newsletter* (AAH-PERD), **7**(1), 2, 4.

Burgess, R.G. (Ed.). (1982). *Field research: A source book and field manual*. London: Allen & Unwin.

Byrd, P.J., & Thomas, T.R. (1983). Hydrostatic weighing during different stages of the menstrual cycle. *Research Quarterly for Exercise and Sport*, **54**, 296-298.

Caillois, R. (1979). The classification of games. In E.W. Gerber & W.J. Morgan (Eds.), *Sport and the body: A philosophical symposium* (2nd ed., pp. 30-37). Philadelphia: Lea & Febiger.

Campbell, D.T., & Stanley, J.C. (1963). *Experimental and quasi-experimental designs for research*. Chicago: Rand McNally.

Carlberg, C.C., Johnson, D.W., Johnson, R., Maruyama, G., Kavale, K., Kulik, C., Kulik, J.A., Lysakowski, R.S., Pflaum, S.W., & Walberg, H. (1984). Meta-analysis in education: A reply to Slavin. *Educational Researcher*, **13**(4), 16-23.

Carron, A.V., Widmeyer, W.N., & Brawley, L.R. (1985). The development of an instrument to assess cohesion in sport teams: The Group Environment Questionnaire. *Journal of Sport Psychology*, **7**, 244-266.

Cheffers, J.T.F. (1973). The validation of an instrument design to expand the Flanders' system of interaction analysis to describe nonverbal interaction, different varieties of teacher behavior and pupil responses (Doctoral dissertation, Temple University, 1972). *Dissertation Abstracts Intenational*, **34**, 1674a.

Chein, I. (1981). Appendix: An introduction to sampling. In L.H. Kidder (Ed.), *Selltiz, Wrightsman & Cook's research methods in social relations* (4th ed.). New York: Holt, Rinehart & Winston.

Chelladurai, P. (1976). Manifestations of agility. *Journal of the Canadian AHPERD*, **42**, 36-41.

Christina, R.W., Fischman, M.G., Vercruyssen, M.J.P., & Anson, J.G. (1982). Simple reaction time as a function of response complexity: Memory drum theory revisited. *Journal of Motor Behavior*, **14**, 301-321.

Chronicle of Higher Education. (1983, September 14). APA Statement on authorship of research papers. *Chronicle of Higher Education*, **27**, 7.

Clarke, H.H. (Ed.). (1968, December). *Physical Fitness Newsletter*, **14**(4).

Clarke, H.H., & Clarke, D.H. (1970). *Research processes in physical education, recreation, and health*. Englewood Cliffs, NJ: Prentice-Hall.

Colvin, C. (1977). Basic locomotor skills: A language analysis. *Illinois Journal of Health, Physical Education and Recreation*, **2**(1), 9-13.

Colvin, C. (1978). *A slide by many other names*. Unpublished manuscript, 1978. (Available from C. Colvin, Western Illinois University, Macomb, IL 61455)

Conover, W.J. (1971). Practical nonparametric statistics. New York: Wiley.

Cook, T.D., & Campbell, D.T. (1979). *Quasi-experimentation: Design and analysis issues for field settings*. Chicago: Rand McNally.

Costill, D.L. (1985). Practical problems in exercise physiology research. *Research Quarterly for Exercise and Sport*, **56**, 378-384.

Cowell, C.C. (1958). Validating an index of social adjustment for high school use. *Research Quarterly*, **29**, 7-18.

Cox, R.H., & Serfass, R.C. (1981). *AAHPERD Research Consortium Papers* (pp. 5-60). Reston, VA: American Alliance for Health, Physical Education, Recreation and Dance.

Crews, D.J., & Landers, D.M. (1987). A meta-analytic review of aerobic fitness and reactivity to psychosocial stressors. *Medicine and Science in Sports and Exercise*, **19** (No. 5, Suppl. 5), 114-120.

Cronbach, L. (1951). Coefficient alpha and the internal structure of tests. *Psychometrika*, **16**, 297-334.

Davidson, M.L. (1972). Univariate versus multivariate tests in repeated-measures experiments. *Psychological Bulletin*, **77**, 446-452.

Day, R.D. (1983). *How to write and publish a scientific paper* (2nd ed.). Philadelphia: ISI Press.

Day, R.D. (1988). *How to write and publish a scientific paper* (3rd ed.). Phoenix: Oryx Press.

Decker, J.A. (1980). *Recreation and community education directors' perceptions of recreation services for the mentally retarded in Minnesota communities*. Unpublished doctoral dissertation, University of Minnesota, Minneapolis.

Delattre, E.J. (1975). Some reflections on success and failure in competitive athletics. *Journal of the Philosophy of Sport*, **2**, 133-139.

Dillman, D.A. (1978). *Mail and telephone survey: The total design method*. New York: Wiley.

Dixon, W.J., & Brown, M.B. (1981). *BMDP statistical software, 1981 manual*. Berkeley, CA: University of California Press.

Duncan, M.C. (1983). The symbolic dimensions of spectator sport. *Quest*, **35**, 29-36.

Edwards, A.L. (1957). *Techniques of attitude and scale construction*. New York: Appleton-Century-Crofts.

Erickson, F. (1986). Qualitative methods in research on teaching. In M.C. Wittrock (Ed.), *Handbook of research on teaching* (3rd ed.) (pp. 119-161). New York: Macmillan.

Esslinger, A.A. (1938). A philosophical study of principles for selecting activities in physical education (Doctoral dissertation, State University of Iowa). *Health, Physical Education and Recreation Microform Publications*, **1**, October 1949-March 1965, PE14.

Feltz, D.L., & Landers, D.M. (1983). The effects of mental practice on motor skill learning and performance: A meta-analysis. *Journal of Sport Psychology*, **5**, 25-57.

Fielding, N.G., & Fielding, J.L. (1986). *Linking data*. Beverly Hills, CA: Sage.

Firestone, W.A. (1987). Meaning in method: The rhetoric of quantitative and qualitative research. *Educational Researcher*, **16**(7), 16-21.

Fitts, W.H. (1965). *Manual: Tennessee self-concept scale*. Nashville: Counselor Recordings and Tests.

Flanders, N.A. (1970). *Analyzing teaching behavior*. Reading, MA: Addison-Wesley.

Fogelin, R.J. (1972). Sport: The diversity of the concept. In E.W. Gerber (Ed.), *Sport and the body: A philosophical symposium* (pp. 58-62). Philadelphia: Lea & Febiger.

Fox, L. (1975). A linguistic analysis of the concept of ''health'' in sport. *Journal of the Philosophy of Sport*, **2**, 31-35.

Fraleigh, W.P. (1970, December). *Theory and design of philosophic research in physical edu-*

cation. Paper presented at the meeting of the National College Physical Education Association for Men, Portland, OR.

Franks, B.D., & Huck, S.W. (1986). Why does everyone use the .05 significance level? *Research Quarterly for Exercise and Sport, 57*, 245-249.

French, K.E. (1985). *The relation of knowledge development to children's basketball performance*. Unpublished doctoral dissertation, Louisiana State University.

French, K.E., & Thomas, J.R. (1984). *Age differences in the motor performance of males and females*. Unpublished manuscript.

French, K.E., & Thomas, J.R. (1987). The relation of knowledge development to children's basketball performance. *Journal of Sport Psychology, 9*, 15-32.

Geisser, S., & Greenhouse, S.W. (1958). An extension of Box's results on the use of the *F* distribution in multivariate analysis. *Annals of Mathematical Statistics, 29*, 885-891.

Gerber, E.W. (1972). Identity, relation and sport. In E.W. Gerber & W.J. Morgan (Eds.), *Sport and the body: A philosophical symposium* (2nd ed., pp. 108-112). Philadelphia: Lea & Febiger.

Gerber, E.W. (1972). *Sport and the body: A philosophical symposium*. Philadelphia: Lea & Febiger.

Gerber, E.W., & Morgan, W.J. (Eds.). (1979). *Sport and the body: A philosophical symposium* (2nd ed.). Philadelphia: Lea & Febiger.

Gessaroli, M.E., & Schutz, R.W. (1983). Variable error: Variance-covariance heterogeneity, block size and Type I error rates. *Journal of Motor Behavior, 15*, 74-95.

Gill, D.L., & Deeter, T.E. (1988). Development of the Sport Orientation Questionnaire. *Research Quarterly for Exercise and Sport, 59*, 191-202.

Glaser, B.G., & Strauss, A.L. (1967). *The discovery of grounded theory*. Chicago: Aldine.

Glass, G.V. (1976). Primary, secondary, and meta-analysis. *Educational Researcher, 5*, 3-8.

Glass, G.V. (1977). Integrating findings: The meta-analysis of research. *Review of Research in Education, 5*, 351-379.

Glass, G.V., McGaw, B., & Smith, M. (1981). *Meta-analysis in social research*. Beverly Hills, CA: Sage.

Glass, G.V., & Smith, M.L. (1979). Meta-analysis of research on the relationship of class-size and achievement. *Evaluation and Policy Analysis, 1*, 2-16.

Glassow, R.B., Halverson, L.E., & Rarick, G.L. (1965). *Improvement of motor development and physical fitness in elementary school children* (Cooperative Research Project No. 696). Unpublished manuscript, University of Wisconsin, Madison.

Goc Karp, G. (1989). Participant observation. In P.W. Darst, D.B. Zakrajsek, & V.H. Mancini (Eds.), *Analyzing physical education and sport instruction* (2nd ed.) (pp. 411-422). Champaign, IL: Human Kinetics.

Goetz, J.P., & LeCompte, M.D. (1984). *Ethnography and qualitative design in educational research*. Orlando, FL: Academic Press.

Goldberger, M., & Moyer, S. (1982). A schema for classifying educational objectives in the psychomotor domain. *Quest, 34*, 134-142.

Grabe, S.A., & Widule, C.J. (1988). Comparative biomechanics of the jerk in Olympic weightlifting. *Research Quarterly for Exercise and Sport, 59*, 1-8.

Graves, R.M., & Kahn, R.L. (1979). *Surveys by telephone: A national comparison with personal interviews*. New York: Academic Press.

Greenockle, K.M., Lee, A.M., & Lomax, R. (1990). The relation between selected student characteristics and activity patterns in required high school physical education class. *Research Quarterly for Exercise and Sport, 61*, 59-69.

Griffin, P.S. (1985). Teacher perceptions of and reactions to equity problems in a middle school physical education program. *Research Quarterly for Exercise and Sport*, **56**, 103-110.

Griffin, P., & Templin, T.J. (1989). An overview of qualitative research. In P.W. Darst, D.B. Zakrajsek, & V.H. Mancini (Eds.), *Analyzing physical education and sport instruction* (2nd ed.) (pp. 399-410). Champaign, IL: Human Kinetics.

Guba, E.G., & Lincoln, Y.S. (1981). *Effective evaluation*. San Francisco: Jossey-Bass.

Haag, E.E. (1979). Literature searching in physical education. *Journal of Physical Education and Recreation*, **50**(1), 54-58.

Hackensmith, C.W. (1966). *History of physical education*. New York: Harper & Row.

Halverson, L.E., Roberton, M.A., & Langendorfer, S. (1982). Development of the overarm throw: Movement and ball velocity changes by seventh grade. *Research Quarterly*, **53**, 198-205.

Halverson, L.E., Roberton, M.A., Safrit, M.J., & Roberts, T.W. (1977). Effect of guided practice on overhand throw ball velocities of kindergarten children. *Research Quarterly*, **48**, 311-318.

Hambleton, R.K., & Novick, M.R. (1973). Toward an integration of theory and method for criterion-referenced tests. *Journal of Educational Measurement*, **10**, 159-170.

Hammersley, M., & Atkinson, P. (1983). *Ethnography: Principles in practice*. London: Tavistock.

Hardy, C.J. (1983). *The mediational role of social influence in the perception of exertion*. Unpublished doctoral dissertation, Louisiana State University.

Harris, C. (1963). *Problems in measuring change*. Madison: University of Wisconsin Press.

Harris, R.J. (1985). *A primer of multivariate statistics* (2nd ed.). Orlando, FL: Academic Press.

Hedges, L., & Olkin, I. (1980). Vote counting methods in research synthesis. *Psychological Bulletin*, **88**, 359-369.

Hedges, L., & Olkin, I. (1983). Regression models in research synthesis. *American Statistician*, **37**, 137-140.

Hedges, L.V. (1981). Distribution theory for Glass's estimator of effect size and related estimators. *Journal of Educational Statistics*, **6**, 107-128.

Hedges, L.V. (1982a). Fitting categorical models to effect sizes from a series of experiments. *Journal of Educational Statistics*, **7**, 119-137.

Hedges, L.V. (1982b). Estimation of effect size from a series of independent experiments. *Psychological Bulletin*, **92**, 490-499.

Hedges, L.V. (1984). Estimation of effect size under nonrandom sampling: The effects of censoring studies yielding statistically insignificant mean differences. *Journal of Educational Statistics*, **9**, 61-85.

Hedges, L.V., & Olkin, I. (1985). *Statistical methods for meta-analysis*. New York: Academic Press.

Heinert, L.D., Serfass, R.C., & Stull, G.A. (1988). Effect of stride length variation on oxygen uptake during level and positive grade treadmill running. *Research Quarterly for Exercise and Sport*, **59**, 127-130.

Helmstadter, G.C. (1970). *Research concepts in human behavior*. New York: Appleton-Century-Crofts.

Henry, F.M. (1964). Physical education: An academic discipline. *Journal of Health, Physical Education and Recreation*, **35**, 32-33, 69.

Henry, F.M. (1964). Physical education—An academic discipline. *Proceedings of the 67th Annual Meeting of the National College Physical Education Association for Men* (pp. 6-9). Washington, DC: AAHPERD.

Henry, F.M. (1974). Variable and constant performance errors within a group of individuals. *Journal of Motor Behavior*, **6**, 149-154.

Henry, F.M., & Rogers, D.E. (1960). Increased response latency for complicated movements and a "memory drum" theory of neuromotor reaction. *Research Quarterly*, **31**, 448-458.

Herkowitz, J. (1984). Developmentally engineered equipment and playgrounds. In J.R. Thomas (Ed.), *Motor development during childhood and adolescence*. Minneapolis: Burgess.

Hoch, D. (1985). What is sport law? Some introductory remarks and suggested parameters for a growing phenomenon. *Quest*, **37**, 60-70.

Hoenes, R.L., & Chissom, B.S. (1975). *A student guide for educational research* (2nd ed.). Statesboro, GA: Vog Press.

Hutslar, J. (1981). This thing we do: A model for sport and dance. *Quest*, **33**, 87-95.

Hyde, J.S. (1981). How large are cognitive gender differences? A meta-analysis using ω^2 and *d*. *American Psychologist*, **36**, 892-901.

Hyland, D.A. (1974). Modes of inquiry in sport, athletics and play. *Journal of the Philosophy of Sport*, **1**, 123-128.

Jacks, P., Chubin, D.E., Porter, A.L., & Connally, T. (1983). The ABCs of ABDs: An interview study of incomplete doctorates. *Improving College and University Teaching*, **31**, 74-81.

Jackson, A.W. (1978). *The twelve minute swim as a test for aerobic endurance in swimming*. Unpublished doctoral dissertation, University of Houston.

Jacob, E. (1987). Qualitative research traditions: A review. *Review of Educational Research*, **57**(1), 1-50.

Jacob, E. (1988). Clarifying qualitative research: A focus on tradition. *Educational Researcher*, **17**, 16-19, 22-24.

Jeu, B. (1972). What is sport? *Diogenes*, **80**, 150-163.

Johnson, B.L., & Nelson, J.K. (1986). *Practical measurements for evaluation in physical education* (4th ed.). Minneapolis: Burgess.

Johnson, R.L. (1979). *The effects of various levels of fatigue on the speed and accuracy of visual recognition*. Unpublished doctoral dissertation, Louisiana State University.

Jones, E. R. (1988, Winter). Philosophical tension in a scientific discipline: So what else is new? *NASPSPA Newsletter*, **14**(1), 10-16.

Kavale, K., & Mattson, P.D. (1983). "One jumped off the balance beam": Meta-analysis of perceptual-motor training. *Journal of Learning Disabilities*, **16**, 165-173.

Keenan, F.W. (1973). The athletic contest as a "tragic" form of art. In R.G. Osterhoudt (Ed.), *The philosophy of sport* (pp. 309-326). Springfield, IL: Charles C Thomas.

Keenan, F.W. (1975). Justice and sport. *Journal of the Philosophy of Sport*, **2**, 111-123.

Kendall, M.G. (1959). Hiawatha designs an experiment. *American Statistician*, **13**, 23-24.

Kennedy, J.J. (1983). *Analyzing qualitative data: Introductory loglinear analysis for behavioral research*. New York: Praeger.

Kennedy, M.M. (1979). Generalizing from single case studies. *Evaluation Quarterly*, **3**, 661-679.

Kenyon, G.S. (1968). Six scales for assessing attitude toward physical activity. *Research Quarterly*, **39**, 566-574.

Kirk, J., & Miller, M.L. (1986). *Reliability and validity in qualitative research*. Newbury Park, CA: Sage.

Kirk, R.E. (1968). *Experimental design: Procedures for the behavioral sciences*. Pacific Grove, CA: Brooks/Cole.

Kirk, R.E. (1982). *Experimental design: Procedures for the behavioral sciences* (2nd ed.). Belmont, CA: Brooks/Cole.

Kleinman, S. (1970). Kleinman's reply to Harper's reaction paper. *Proceedings of the Annual Meeting of the National College*

Physical Education Association for Men (pp. 73-75). Washington, DC: AAHPERD.

Kleinman, S. (1977). Kinesis and the concept of self in sport. In D.J. Allen & B.S. Fahey (Eds.), *Being human in sport* (pp. 147-155). Philadelphia: Lea & Febiger.

Kleinman, S. (1979). The significance of human movement: A phenomenological approach. In E.W. Gerber & W.J. Morgan (Eds.), *Sport and the body: A philosophical symposium* (2nd ed., pp. 177-180). Philadelphia: Lea & Febiger.

Kraus, H., & Hirschland, R.P. (1954). Minimum muscular fitness tests in school children. *Research Quarterly*, **25**, 177-188.

Kretchmar, R.S. (1971). A phenomenological analysis of the Other in sport (Doctoral dissertation, University of Southern California, 1971). *Dissertation Abstracts International*, **31**, 6113-6114. (University Microfilms No. 71-12, 397)

Kretchmar, R.S. (1974). Modes of philosophic inquiry and sport. *Journal of the Philosophy of Sport*, **1**, 129-131.

Kroll, W.P. (1971). *Perspectives in physical education*. New York: Academic Press.

Kuhn, T.S. (1970). *The structure of scientific revolutions* (2nd ed.). Chicago: University of Chicago Press.

Laabs, G.J. (1980). On perceptual processing in motor memory. In C.H. Nadeau et al. (Eds.), *Psychology of motor behavior and sport—1979* (pp. 431-444). Champaign, IL: Human Kinetics.

Lakie, W.L. (1964). Expressed attitudes of various groups of athletes toward athletic competition. *Research Quarterly*, **35**, 497-503.

Lane, K.R. (1983). *Comparison of skinfold profiles of black and white boys and girls ages 11-13*. Unpublished master's thesis, Louisiana State University, Baton Rouge.

Layne, C.S., & Abraham, L.D. (1987). Patterns of lower limb muscle activity in young boys during a one foot static balance task. *Research Quarterly for Exercise and Sport*, **58**, 36-40.

Lee, M. (1983). *A history of physical education and sports in the U.S.A.* New York: Wiley.

Lee, T.D. (1982). *On the locus of contextual interference in motor skill acquisition*. Unpublished doctoral dissertation, Louisiana State University.

Lee, T.D., & Magill, R.A. (1983). The locus of contextual interference in motor-skill acquisition. *Journal of Experimental Psychology: Learning, Memory and Cognition*, **9**, 730-746.

Lenk, H. (1976). Toward a social philosophy of achievement and athletics. *Man and the World: An International Philosophical Review*, **9**, 45-59.

Leonard, F.G., & Affleck, G.B. (1947). *A guide to the history of physical education* (3rd ed.). Philadelphia: Lea & Febiger.

Lewis, D., McAllister, D.E., & Adams, J.A. (1951). Facilitation and interference in performance on the modified Mashburn apparatus: I, After-effects of varying the amount of original learning. *Journal of Experimental Psychology*, **41**, 247-260.

Lincoln, Y.S., & Guba, E.G. (1985). *Naturalistic inquiry*. Newbury Park, CA: Sage.

Linn, R.L. (1986). Quantitative methods in research on teaching. In M.C. Wittrock (Ed.), *Handbook of research on teaching* (3rd ed.) (pp. 92-118). New York: Macmillan.

Locke, L.F. (1987). The question of quality in qualitative research. In J.K. Nelson (Ed.), *Proceedings of the Fifth Measurement and Evaluation Symposium* (pp. 31-36). Baton Rouge: Louisiana State University Press.

Locke, L.F. (1989). Qualitative research as a form of scientific inquiry in sport and physical education. *Research Quarterly for Exercise and Sport*, **60**, 1-20.

Locke, L.F., Spirduso, W.W., & Silverman, S.J. (1987). *Proposals that work: A guide for planning dissertations and grant proposals* (2nd ed.). Newbury Park, CA: Sage.

Looney, M.A. (1989). Criterion-referenced measurement: Reliability. In M.J. Safrit & T.M. Wood (Eds.), *Measurement concepts in physical education and exercise science* (pp. 137-152). Champaign, IL: Human Kinetics.

Lord, F.M. (1969). Statistical adjustments when comparing preexisting groups. *Psychological Bulletin*, **72**, 336-337.

Loy, J.W. (1968). The nature of sport: A definitional effort. *Quest*, **10**, 1-15.

Mabley, J. (1963, January 22). Mabley's report. *Chicago American*, p. 62.

Malcolm, N. (1967). Wittgenstein, Ludwig Josef Johann. In P. Edwards (Ed.), *The encyclopedia of philosophy* (Vol. 8, pp. 327-340). New York: Macmillan.

Manser, A. (1967). Games and family resemblances. *Philosophy*, **17**, 210-255.

Maples, M.G. (1977). *Second grade children's performance on the overhand throw in relation to maternal and self preference for play activities*. Unpublished master's thesis, Purdue University, West Lafayette, IN.

Margaria, R., Aghems, P., & Rovelli, E. (1966). Measurement of muscular power (anaerobic) in man. *Journal of Applied Physiology*, **21**, 1662-1664.

Martens, R. (1973, June). People errors in people experiments. *Quest*, **20**, 16-20.

Martens, R. (1977). *Sport Competition Anxiety Test*. Champaign, IL: Human Kinetics.

Martens, R. (1979). About smocks and jocks. *Journal of Sport Psychology*, **1**, 94-99.

Martens, R. (1987). Science, knowledge, and sport psychology. *The Sport Psychologist*, **1**, 29-55.

Matthews, P.R. (1979). The frequency with which the mentally retarded participate in recreation activities. *Research Quarterly*, **50**, 71-79.

McBride, F. (1975). Toward a non-definition of sport. *Journal of the Philosophy of Sport*, **2**, 4-11.

McBride, F. (1979). A critique of Mr. Suits' definition of game playing. *Journal of the Philosophy of Sport*, **6**, 59-65.

McCloy, C.H. (1960, October). A half century of physical education. *Physical Educator*, p. 91.

McPherson, S.L., & Thomas, J.R. (1989). Relation of knowledge and performance in boys' tennis: Age and expertise. *Journal of Experimental Child Psychology*, **48**, 190-211.

McPhie, W.E. (1960). Factors affecting the value of dissertations. *Social Education*, **24**, 375-377, 385.

Meier, K.V. (1988). Triad and trickery. Playing with sport and games. *Journal of the Philosophy of Sport*, **15**, 11-30.

Merriam, S.B. (1988). *Case study research in education*. San Francisco: Jossey-Bass.

Miles, M.B., & Huberman, A.M. (1984). *Qualitative data analysis: A sourcebook of new methods*. Newbury Park, CA: Sage.

Mood, D.P. (1989). Measurement methodology for knowledge tests. In M.J. Safrit & T.M. Wood (Eds.), *Measurement concepts in physical education and exercise science* (pp. 251-270). Champaign, IL: Human Kinetics.

Moore, R. (1989). The gallant ghost of handball. *Quest*, **41**, 150-151.

Morehouse, C.A., & Stull, G.A. (1975). *Statistical principles and procedures with applications for physical education*. Philadelphia: Lea & Febiger.

Morgan, W.J. (1976). An analysis of the Sartean ethic of ambiguity. *Journal of the Philosophy of Sport*, **3**, 82-96.

Morgan, W.J. (1977). Some Aristotelian notes on the attempt to define sport. *Journal of the Philosophy of Sport*, **4**, 15-35.

Morgenstern, N.L. (1983). Cogito ergo sum: Murphy's refutation of Descartes. In G.H. Scherr (Ed.), *The best of The Journal of Irreproducible Results* (p. 112). New York: Workman.

Morland, R.B. (1958). A philosophical interpretation of the educational views held by leaders in American physical education (Doctoral dissertation, New York University). *Health, Physical Education and Recreation Microform Publications*, **1**, October 1949-March 1965, PE394.

Morrow, J.R., Jr. (1989). Generalizability theory. In M.J. Safrit & T.M. Wood (Eds.), *Measurement concepts in physical education and exercise science* (pp. 73-96). Champaign, IL: Human Kinetics.

Morrow, J.R., & Frankiewicz, R.G. (1979). Strategies for the analysis of repeated and multiple measure designs. *Research Quarterly*, **50**, 297-304.

The National Children and Youth Fitness Study. (1985). *Journal of Physical Education, Recreation & Dance*, **56**(1), 44-90.

The National Children and Youth Fitness Study II. (1987). *Journal of Physical Education, Recreation & Dance*, **56**(9), 147-167.

Nelson, J.K. (1978). Motivating effects of the use of norms and goals with endurance tests. *Research Quarterly*, **49**, 317-321.

Nelson, J.K. (1988, March). Some thoughts on research, measurement and other obscure topics. LAHPERD Scholar Lecture presented at the LAHPERD Convention, New Orleans.

Nelson, J.K. (1989). Measurement methodology for affective tests. In M.J. Safrit & T.M. Wood (Eds.), *Measurement concepts in physical education and exercise science* (pp. 229-248). Champaign, IL: Human Kinetics.

Nelson, K.R. (1988). *Thinking processes, management routines and student perceptions of expert and novice physical education teachers*. Unpublished doctoral dissertation, Louisiana State University.

Newell, K.M., & Hancock, P.A. (1984). Forgotten moments: A note on skewness and kurtosis as influential factors in inferences extrapolated from response distributions. *Journal of Motor Behavior*, **16**, 320-335.

Nunnaly, J.C. (1978). *Psychometric theory* (2nd ed.). New York: McGraw-Hill.

Osbourne, R. (1979). *Competition and the ultimate athletic experience: A phenomenological approach*. Unpublished master's thesis, Western Illinois University, Macomb, IL.

Osterhoudt, R.G. (1972). A taxonomy for research concerning the philosophy of physical education and sport. *Proceedings, The First Canadian Symposium on the Philosophy of Sport and Physical Activity* (pp. 49-57). Ottawa: CAHPER.

Osterhoudt, R.G. (1974). Modes of inquiry concerning sport: Some reflections on method. *Journal of the Philosophy of Sport*, **1**, 137-141.

Osterhoudt, R.G. (1977). The term "sport": Some thoughts on a proper name. *International Journal of Physical Education*, **14**(1), 11-16.

Osterhoudt, R.G. (1978). *An introduction to the philosophy of physical education and sport*. Champaign, IL: Stipes Publishing.

Park, R.J. (1980). The *Research Quarterly* and its antecedents. *Research Quarterly for Exercise and Sport*, **51**, 1-22.

Pate, R.R. (1988). The evolving definition of fitness. *Quest*, **40**, 174-179.

Patterson, P. (1989). The use of validity generalization in exercise science. In M.J. Safrit & T.M. Wood (Eds.), *Measurement concepts in physical education and exercise science* (pp. 97-115). Champaign, IL: Human Kinetics.

Pearson, K. (1968). *Inquiry into inquiry*. Unpublished manuscript. (Available from K. Pearson, Western Illinois University, Macomb, IL 61455)

Pearson, K. (1972). A proposed model for philosophical conceptual analysis within the discipline and/or the profession of sport and physical activity. *Proceedings, The First Canadian Symposium on the Phi-*

losophy of Sport and Physical Activity (pp. 1-15). Ottawa: CAHPER.

Pearson, K. (1974). Some comments on philosophic inquiry into sport as meaningful human experience. *Journal of the Philosophy of Sport*, **1**, 132-136.

Pearson, K. (1978). Two approaches to doing philosophy of sport and physical education. In R.S. Kretchmar (Ed.), *A self-study guide for the philosophy of sport and physical education* (pp. 10-18). (Available from R.S. Kretchmar, Penn State University, State College, PA)

Pearson, K. (1979). Deception, sportsmanship and ethics. In E.W. Gerber & W.J. Morgan (Eds.), *Sport and the body: A philosophical symposium* (2nd ed., pp. 272-273). Philadelphia: Lea & Febiger.

Pedhazur, E.J. (1982). *Multiple regression in behavioral research: Explanation and prediction* (2nd ed.). New York: Holt, Rinehart and Winston.

Polanyi, M. (1958). *Person knowledge: Towards a post-critical philosophy*. Chicago: University of Chicago Press.

Popp, J.C. (1959). *Comparison of sophomore high school boys who have high and low physical fitness indices through case study procedures*. Unpublished master's thesis, University of Oregon, Eugene.

Porter, A.L., Chubin, D.E., Rossini, F.A., Boeckmann, M.E., & Connally, T. (1982, September-October). The role of the dissertation in scientific careers. *American Scientist*, pp. 475-481.

Porter, A.L., & Wolfle, D. (1975). Utility of the doctoral dissertation. *American Psychologist*, **30**, 1054-1061.

Progen, J.L. (1981). *An exploration of the flow experience among selected college athletes*. Unpublished doctoral dissertation, University of North Carolina at Greensboro.

Punch, M. (1986). *The politics and ethics of fieldwork*. Beverly Hills, CA: Sage.

"QUIRK theory" or the universal perversity of matter. (1968, December). *Illinois Technograph*, p. 59.

Ratcliffe, J.W. (1983). Notions of validity in qualitative research methodology. *Knowledge: Creation, Diffusion, Utilization*, **5**(2), 147-167.

Ravizza, K. (1977). Potential of the sport experience. In D.J. Allen & B.S. Fahey (Eds.), *Being human in sport* (pp. 61-72). Philadelphia: Lea & Febiger.

Ravizza, K., & Daruty, K. (1984). Paternalism and sovereignty in athletes. *Journal of the Philosophy of Sport*, **11**, 71-82.

Realist, B.A. [G. Benford]. (1982, March). How to write a scientific paper. *Omni*, p. 130.

Reeve, T.G., & Mainor, R., Jr. (1983). Effects of movement context on the encoding of kinesthetic spatial information. *Research Quarterly for Exercise and Sport*, **54**, 352-363.

Reid, L.A. (1970). Sport, the aesthetic and art. *British Journal of Educational Studies*, **18**, 249-258.

Roberton, M.A., Halverson, L.E., Langendorfer, S., & Williams, K. (1979). Longitudinal changes in children's overarm throw ball velocities. *Research Quarterly*, **50**, 256-264.

Roberts, T.J. (1986). Sport, art and particularity: The best equivocation. *Journal of the Philosophy of Sport*, **13**, 49-63.

Rosenthal, R. (1966). *Experimenter effects in behavioral research*. New York: Appleton-Century-Crofts.

Rosnow, R.L., & Rosenthal, R. (1989). Statistical procedures and the justification of knowledge in psychological science. *American Psychologist*, **44**, 1276-1284.

Rudy, W. (1962). Higher education in the United States, 1862-1962. In W.W. Brickman & S. Lehrer (Eds.), *A century of higher education: Classical citadel to collegiate* colossus (pp. 20-21). New York: Society for the Advancement of Education.

Rugg, H. (1941). *That men may understand.* New York: Doubleday Doran.

Ryan, E.D. (1970). The cathartic effect of vigorous motor activity on aggressive behavior. *Research Quarterly,* **41,** 542-551.

Safrit, M.J. (Ed.). (1976). *Reliability theory.* Washington, DC: American Alliance for Health, Physical Education and Recreation.

Safrit, M.J. (Ed.). (1980). *Research Quarterly for Exercise and Sport,* **51**(1).

Safrit, M.J. (1981). *Evaluation in physical education* (2nd ed.). Englewood Cliffs, NJ: Prentice-Hall.

Safrit, M.J. (1986). *Introduction to measurement in physical education and exercise science.* St. Louis: Times Mirror/Mosby.

Safrit, M.J. (1989). Criterion-referenced measurement: Validity. In M.J. Safrit & T.M. Wood (Eds.), *Measurement concepts in physical education and exercise science* (pp. 119-135). Champaign, IL: Human Kinetics.

Safrit, M.J., Cohen, A.S., & Costa, M.G. (1989). Item response theory and the measurement of motor behavior. *Research Quarterly for Exercise and Sport,* **60,** 325-335.

Safrit, M.J., Spray, A.J., & Diewert, G. (1980). Methodological issues in short-term motor memory research. *Journal of Motor Behavior,* **12,** 13-28.

Safrit, M.J., & Wood, T.M. (1983). The health-related fitness test opinionnaire: A pilot survey. *Research Quarterly for Exercise and Sport,* **54,** 204-207.

Sage, G.H. (1989). A commentary on qualitative research as a form of inquiry in sport and physical education. *Research Quarterly for Exercise and Sport,* **60,** 25-29.

SAS Institute. (1985). *SAS user's guide: Statistics, 1985 edition.* Cary, NC: Author.

Schein, E.H. (1987). *The clinical perspective in fieldwork.* Newbury Park, CA: Sage.

Scherr, G.H. (1983). Irreproducible science. In G.H. Scherr (Ed.), *The best of The Journal of Irreproducible Results* (p. 152). New York: Workman.

Schmidt, F.L., Hunter, J.E., & Urry, V.W. (1976). Statistical power in criterion-related validation studies. *Journal of Applied Psychology,* **61,** 473-485.

Schmidt, R.A. (1975). A schema theory of discrete motor skill learning. *Psychological Review,* **82,** 225-260.

Schmidt, R.A. (1988). *Motor control and learning.* Champaign, IL: Human Kinetics.

Schmitt, R. (1967). Phenomenology. In P. Edwards (Ed.), *The encyclopedia of philosophy* (Vol. 6, pp. 135-151). New York: Macmillan.

Schutz, R. (1979). Absolute, constant, and variable error: Problems and solutions. In D. Mood (Ed.), *Proceedings of the Colorado Measurement Symposium.* Boulder: University of Colorado Press.

Schutz, R.W. (1989). Qualitative research: Comments and controversies. *Research Quarterly for Exercise and Sport,* **60,** 30-35.

Schutz, R.W., & Gessaroli, M.E. (1987). The analysis of repeated measures designs involving multiple dependent variables. *Research Quarterly for Exercise and Sport,* **58,** 132-149.

Schutz, R.W., & Roy, E.A. (1973). Absolute error: The devil in disguise. *Journal of Motor Behavior,* **5,** 141-153.

Scott, M.G. (1955). Tests of kinesthesis. *Research Quarterly,* **26,** 234-241.

Segal, K.R., Gutin, B., Presta, E., Wang, J., & Van Itallie, T.B. (1985). Estimation of human body composition by electrical impedance methods: A comparative study. *Journal of Applied Physiology,* **58,** 1565-1571.

Sidaway, B. (1988). Fractioned reaction time in lower leg responses: A note on response programming time. *Research Quarterly for Exercise and Sport*, **59**, 248-251.

Siedentop, D. (1980). Two cheers for Rainer. *Journal of Sport Psychology*, **2**, 2-4.

Siedentop, D. (1989). Do the lockers really smell? *Research Quarterly for Exercise and Sport*, **60**, 36-41.

Siedentop, D., Birdwell, D., & Metzler, M. (1979, March). *A process approach to measuring teaching effectiveness in physical education*. Paper presented at the American Alliance for Health, Physical Education, Recreation and Dance national convention. New Orleans, LA.

Siedentop, D., Trousignant, M., & Parker, M. (1982). *Academic learning time—Physical education: 1982 coding manual*. Columbus: Ohio State University, School of Health, Physical Education, and Recreation.

Siegel, S. (1956). *Nonparametric statistics for the behavioral sciences*. New York: McGraw-Hill.

Sigerseth, P.O. (1970). Flexibility. In H.J. Montoye (Ed.), *An introduction to measurement in physical education* (pp. 88-131). Indianapolis: Phi Epsilon Kappa Fraternity.

Simon, R.L. (1984). Good competition and drug-enhanced performance. *Journal of the Philosophy of Sport*, **11**, 6-13.

Slavin, R.E. (1984a). Meta-analysis in education: How it has been used. *Educational Researcher*, **13**(4), 6-15.

Slavin, R.E. (1984b). A rejoinder to Carlberg et al. *Educational Researcher*, **13**(4), 24-27.

Smith, M.L. (1980). Sex bias in counseling and psychotherapy. *Psychological Bulletin*, **87**, 392-407.

Smith, R.E., Smoll, F.L., & Hunt, E. (1977). A system for the behavioral assessment of athletic coaches. *Research Quarterly*, **48**, 401-407.

Sonstroem, R.J. (1978). Physical estimation and attraction scales: Rationale and research. *Medicine and Science in Sports*, **10**, 97-102.

Sparling, P.B. (1980). A meta-analysis of studies comparing maximal oxygen uptake in men and women. *Research Quarterly for Exercise and Sport*, **51**, 542-552.

Spencer-Kraus, P. (1969). *The application of "linguistic phenomenology" to the philosophy of physical education and sport*. Unpublished master's thesis, University of Illinois, Urbana-Champaign.

Spielberger, C.D. (1966). Theory and research on anxiety. In C.D. Spielberger (Ed.), *Anxiety and behavior* (pp. 3-20). New York: Academic Press.

Spirduso, W.W. (1983). Exercise and the aging brain. *Research Quarterly for Exercise and Sport*, **54**, 208-218.

Spray, J.A. (1987). Recent developments in measurement and possible applications to the measurement of psychomotor behavior. *Research Quarterly for Exercise and Sport*, **58**, 203-209.

Spray, J.A. (1989). New approaches to solving measurement problems. In M.J. Safrit & T.M. Wood (Eds.), *Measurement concepts in physical education and exercise science* (pp. 229-248). Champaign, IL: Human Kinetics.

SPSS Inc. (1983). *SPSS user's guide*. Chicago: Author.

Stamm, C.L., & Safrit, M.J. (1975). Comparison of significance tests for repeated measures ANOVA design. *Research Quarterly*, **46**, 403-409.

Stoll, S.K. (1982). The use of phenomenology to investigate and describe sport in the historical genre: An alternative approach to sport history. *Quest*, **34**, 12-22.

Studer, G. (1977). Moment-to-moment experiences of self. In D.J. Allen & B.S. Fahey (Eds.), *Being human in sport* (pp. 157-162). Philadelphia: Lea & Febiger.

Suits, B. (1978). *The grasshopper: Games, life and utopia*. Toronto: University of Toronto Press.

Suits, B. (1979). What is a game? In E.W. Gerber & W.J. Morgan (Eds.), *Sport and the body: A philosophical symposium* (2nd ed., pp. 11-17). Philadelphia: Lea & Febiger.

Suits, B. (1988). Tricky triad, games, play and sport. *Journal of the Philosophy of Sport, 15,* 1-9.

Tangen, J.O. (1985). Defining sport: A pragmatic-contextual approach. *International Journal of Physical Education, 2,* 17-25.

Taylor, S.J., & Bogdan, R. (1984). *Introduction to qualitative research methods* (2nd ed.). New York: Wiley.

Tew, J. (1988). *Construction of a sport specific mental imagery assessment instrument using item response and classical test theory methodology.* Unpublished doctoral dissertation, Louisiana State University.

Tew, J., & Wood, M. (1980). *Proposed model for predicting probable success in football players.* Paper presented at The Second Measurement and Evaluation Symposium, Houston, TX: Rice University Press.

Thomas, J.R. (1977). A note concerning analysis of error scores from motor-memory research. *Journal of Motor Behavior, 9,* 251-253.

Thomas, J.R. (1980). Half a cheer for Rainer and Daryl. *Journal of Sport Psychology, 2,* 266-267.

Thomas, J.R. (Ed.). (1983). Publication guidelines. *Research Quarterly for Exercise and Sport, 54,* 219-221.

Thomas, J.R. (Ed.). (1984). *Motor development during childhood and adolescence.* Minneapolis: Burgess.

Thomas, J.R. (1986). Editor's viewpoint: Research notes. *Research Quarterly for Exercise and Sport, 57,* iv-v.

Thomas, J.R., & French, K.E. (1985). Gender differences across age in motor performance: A meta-analysis. *Psychological Bulletin, 98,* 260-282.

Thomas, J.R., & French, K.E. (1986). The use of meta-analysis in exercise and sport: A tutorial. *Research Quarterly for Exercise and Sport, 57,* 196-204.

Thomas, J.R., French, K.E., & Humphries, C.A. (1986). Knowledge development and sport skill performance: Directions for motor behavior research. *Journal of Sport Psychology, 8,* 259-272.

Thomas, J.R., & Nelson, J.K. (1985). *Introduction to research in health, physical education, recreation, and dance.* Champaign, IL: Human Kinetics.

Thomas, J.R., & Thomas, K.T. (1983). Strange kids and strange numbers: Assessing children's motor development. *Journal of Physical Education, Recreation and Dance, 54*(8), 19-20.

Thomas, J.R., Thomas, K.T., Lee, A.M., Testerman, E., & Ashy, M. (1983). Age differences in use of strategy for recall of movement in a large scale environment. *Research Quarterly for Exercise and Sport, 54,* 264-272.

Tolson, H. (1980). An adjustment to statistical significance: ω^2. *Research Quarterly for Exercise and Sport, 51,* 580-584.

Tran, Z.V., Weltman, A., Glass, G.V., & Mood, D.P. (1983). The effects of exercise on blood lipids and lipoproteins: A meta-analysis. *Medicine and Science in Sports and Exercise, 15,* 393-402.

Tuckman, B.W. (1978). *Conducting educational research* (2nd ed.). New York: Harcourt Brace Jovanovich.

Van Dalen, D.B., & Bennett, B.L. (1971). *A history of physical education* (2nd ed.). Englewood Cliffs. NJ: Prentice-Hall.

Vealey, R.S. (1986). The conceptualization of sport-confidence and competitive orientation: Preliminary investigation and instrument development. *Journal of Sport Psychology, 8,* 221-246.

Verducci, F.M. (1980). *Measurement concepts in physical education.* St. Louis: C.V. Mosby.

Webb, E.J., Campbell, D.T., Schwartz, R.D., & Sechrest, L. (1966). *Unobtrusive measures: Nonreactive research in the social sciences*. Chicago: Rand McNally.

Weiss, M.R., Bredemeier, B.J., & Shewchuk, R.M. (1985). An intrinsic/extrinsic motivation scale for the youth sport setting: A confirmatory factor analysis. *Journal of Sport Psychology*, **7**, 75-91.

Welter, K.A. (1978). *Complete moments in sport: A phenomenological approach*. Unpublished master's thesis, Western Illinois University, Macomb, IL.

Werner, P., & Rink, J. (1989). Case studies of teacher effectiveness in physical education. *Journal of Teaching in Physical Education*, **8**, 280-297.

Wertz, S.K. (1981). The varieties of cheating. *Journal of the Philosophy of Sport*, **8**, 19-40.

Wiebe, V.R. (1954). A study of tests of kinesthesis. *Research Quarterly*, **25**, 222-227.

Winer, B.J. (1971). *Statistical principles in experimental design*. New York: McGraw-Hill.

Wittgenstein, L. (1958). Language games. In *Philosophical investigations* (2nd ed.) (G.E.M. Anscombe, Trans.). Oxford: Basil Blackwell. (Original work published 1953)

Wood, T.M., & Safrit, M.J. (1987). A comparison of three multivariate models for estimating test battery reliability. *Research Quarterly for Exercise and Sport*, **58**, 150-159.

Yin, R.K. (1984). *Case study research: Design and methods*. Newbury Park, CA: Sage.

Yoon, S.H. (1988). *Relative isometric and dynamic endurance curves for different muscle groups of the upper extremities*. Unpublished doctoral dissertation, Louisiana State University.

Zeigler, E.F. (1964). *Philosophical foundations for physical, health and recreation education*. Englewood Cliffs, NJ: Prentice-Hall.

Zeigler, E.F. (1970, December). *A reaction to Fraleigh's assessment of philosophic research in physical education*. Paper presented at the meeting of the National College Physical Education Association for Men, Portland, OR.

Zeigler, E.F. (1973a, October). *An analysis of the claim that "physical education has become a 'family resemblance' term."* Paper presented at the First Canadian Congress for the Multi-disciplinary Study of Sport and Physical Activity, Montreal.

Zeigler, E.F. (1973b). The pragmatic (experimentalistic) ethic as it relates to sport and physical education. In R.G. Osterhoudt (Ed.), *The philosophy of sport* (pp. 229-274). Springfield, IL: Charles C Thomas.

Zeigler, E.F. (1979). A brief analysis of the ordinary language employed in the professional preparation of sport coaches and teachers. In E.F. Zeigler (Ed.), *Issues in North American Sport and Physical Education* (pp. 184-192). Washington, DC: AAHPERD.

Zeigler, E.F. (1983). Relating a proposed taxonomy of sport and developmental physical activity to a planned inventory of scientific feelings. *Quest*, **35**, 54-65.

Zeigler, E.F., & McCristal, K. (1967). A history of the Big Ten Body of Knowledge Project. *Quest*, **9**, 79-84.

Author Index

Subject Index